JEWISH FOLKWAYS IN GERMANIC LANDS

A *Kloyz:* The Study of a Jewish Scholar in the Middle Ages *(Courtesy, Hebrew Union College—Jewish Institute of Religion Library, Cincinnati)*. From *Menorah,* VI (No. 6-7, 1928, Vienna-Frankfort), 361.

JEWISH FOLKWAYS IN GERMANIC LANDS (1648–1806)

STUDIES IN ASPECTS OF DAILY LIFE

Herman Pollack

THE M. I. T. PRESS
Massachusetts Institute of Technology
Cambridge, Massachusetts, and London, England

Set in Monophoto Times Roman.
Printed by Publication Press, Inc.
Bound in the United States of America by The Colonial Press Inc.

[redacted]

ISBN 0 262 16025 0 (hardcover)

Library of Congress catalog card number: 69-11311

Dedicated to the memory of my beloved
Mother and Father, Tillie (תישע בת ר׳ אהרון)
and Jacob Morris (יעקב משה ב״ר אברהם) Pollack
who nurtured me and were my first teachers

PREFACE

The ancient sages taught that no one is so self-sufficient that he is not dependent on others; it may be for his food, clothing, shelter, or for cultural and spiritual resources that become part of his life. Thus, I feel a deep sense of gratitude to those individuals who encouraged me as I proceeded, step by step, in preparing this book. First of all, I wish to express my indebtedness to my esteemed teacher, Professor Salo W. Baron, for his counsel and personal interest in this project from the very outset. I derived much from Professor Baron's scholarly insight and vast erudition, more than I can possibly express in words. Any attempt on my part to strive to reach out toward his high standard of performance proved to be both a suspensive and exhilarating experience. I convey my deepest appreciation to Professor Harry A. Wolfson, who graciously made himself available whenever I wished to consult him or have him help me unravel a difficulty. His suggestions and insights proved to be invaluable and have become an integral part of this study. To my teacher of earlier student days, Professor Jacob R. Marcus, a debt of gratitude is owed for introducing me to *Simḥat ha-Nefesh*, a treasure-trove of cultural history and lore, and arousing my interest in Jewish folkways in Central and South Central Europe at the end of the Middle Ages. I benefited from the aid given to me by Professors Fritz Stern and W. T. H. Jackson.

Regretfully, several individuals whom I had consulted have since passed away. The comments and criticism of Professor Uriel Weinreich were beneficial. Helpful suggestions were received from Professor Isaac Mendelsohn. Bibliographical leads were generously offered by Drs. Joshua Bloch, Isaac Rivkind, A. A. Roback, and Jacob Shatzky. I hope that in some small way my efforts will honor their memory.

I appreciate the bibliographical assistance that I received from Abraham Berger, former Chief, Jewish Division, New York Public Library. Thanks are conveyed to Herbert C. Zafren, Librarian, Hebrew Union College-Jewish Institute of Religion, Cincinnati; to Ezekiel Lifschutz, Archivist, YIVO Institute for Jewish Research, and N. C. Sainsbury, Keeper of Oriental Books, Bodleian Library and the Curators of the Bodleian Library, Oxford, for granting me permission to use the manuscripts listed in the Bibliography and cited in the notes. Through the kindness of Martin S. Morton I secured the print for Fig. 4.

Likewise, I am indebted for the many courtesies that were extended to me by the staffs of the Columbia University Library, the New York Public Library, the Widener and the Houghton Libraries of Harvard University, the Harvard Divinity School Library, the Boston Public Library, the Hebrew Union College-Jewish Institute of Religion Libraries in Cincinnati and New York, the Jewish Theological Seminary Library, the library of the YIVO Institute for Jewish Research, and the library of the Hebrew Teachers College of Boston. The staff of the Widener Library of Harvard University made it possible for me to work consistently in the stacks. The private collection of the late Lee M. Friedman was used with profit. The late Menashe Vaxer enabled me to obtain some of the primary sources.

The translation of primary sources are by the author except where indicated. Biblical selections in English are based on the Jewish Publication Society translation. The English translation of passages of the Talmud, Midrash, and the *Zohar* follows in the main the Soncino editions in translation.

The transliteration of Hebrew has been suggested by the orthography adopted by the *Jewish Encyclopedia* (cf. any vol., p. vii) and the Library of Congress. The transliteration of Yiddish is in accordance with the transcription prepared by YIVO. In transliterating a text the "scientific" and the "idiomatic" forms of pronunciation were followed. The "idiomatic" expression accords with the Lithuanian use of Yiddish. The transliteration of a title as designated by an author is used even if it varies slightly from that of established procedure. The letter R. stands for the word Rabbi and b. for ben. The abbreviations used in the references will be found on p. 339. The spelling of titles in the Bibliography corresponds to the authors' usage.

The endpaper map represents the *gas* in Frankfort, as published in 1711, shortly after the great conflagration. It is reproduced by permission of the YIVO Institute for Jewish Research.

The publication of this book was aided by a grant of the Alexander Kohut Memorial Foundation and the American Academy for Jewish Research. Two decennial leaves, in 1956 and 1966, from the B'nai B'rith Hillel Foundations, afforded me the opportunity to complete the initial research for this study and prepare the copy for publication.

I am most thankful to the staff of the M.I.T. Press for their deep interest and painstaking efforts in making this book a reality. I especially appreciate the cooperation received from Joseph Stein, the editor.

To my wife, Sophie, I am grateful, in particular, for her devotion and tireless effort in typing and preparing the manuscript for publication. She cheerfully carried through this task along with many other demands made on her.

Much do I owe to my parents of blessed memory (*zikhronam li-berakhah*) who taught me in my childhood never to abandon the search for knowledge because of difficulties or hardships.

The acknowledgment, however, does not impose on any of the above individuals responsibility for shortcomings that an incisive reader may detect.

Cambridge, Massachusetts
January 1970

Herman Pollack

CONTENTS

CONTENTS

INTRODUCTION[1]

This study aims to portray major aspects of folk life in German-Jewish communities from 1648 to 1806, a period significant in the general history of the entire region. Folkways mirror the social life of anonymous individuals, as well as provide a diary of communal activity. Through an examination of popular practices we hope to find some clues that will enable us to reconstruct daily life within the community, often referred to as "inner life." "Inner life" differs from what is understood by "external" history, which considers political and legal relations between the larger community and the Jewish community or communities. Nor do folkways, or folk life, refer to an entity or unit as such; the term is descriptive of what is considered a phase, or phases, of "culture" or "social life." Obviously, "folkways," in its broad meaning, can encompass all of the social and cultural experiences of individuals and a community. Therefore, the meaning of "folkways" may be made more explicit by enumerating the phases of "culture" that we shall consider, that is, (1) topography and surroundings, the interior of the home; (2) the life-cycle of the individual—birth, marriage, and burial; (3) education and development of the individual; (4) physical existence, including dress, foods, and folk medicine; (5) customs relating to the synagogue, Sabbath, and festivals.

These categories are frequently in use in historical and cultural studies.[2] It was found, however, that though such subdivisions are suitable for grouping the data available, nevertheless, in describing social life, there will be overlapping in view of the relationships existing between one phase of culture and another. These different facets of Jewish folkways will not only be suggestive of the interconnections between the individual and the community but of an overall cultural pattern that embraced both the group and the individual.

The customs, or *minhagim*, current among the Jewish people may be divided into three general classifications: ritual *minhagim*, such as those associated with birth, marriage, and burial; dietary *minhagim*, related to foods and table usage; and extralegal *minhagim*, practices relied upon to overpower demons or evil forces.[3]

Wherever possible, the origin and background, as well as reason or reasons, for a custom will be considered. Some customs were local in character, while others were widely diffused and observed in different lands. Unless facts are available, the geographic spread of a practice will not be traced, and, at best, only the distribution over an area will be presented. Where parallel, or related, practices occurred outside of Germany, they will be cited for purpose of comparison. It is not within the scope of this study to decide whether customs which appear to be alike in communities remote from one another resulted from "diffusion" or from "local innovation." Thus, similar customs observed outside of the Holy Roman Empire will be presented as "facts," and no attempt will be made to review any intervening historical events that might explain how a specific practice had developed.

The sources are primarily chapbooks and pocketbooks—the informal literature of the time. Only occasional reference will be made to folk tales, folk songs, and proverbs; a special study would be required to deal more fully with these items.

The data obtained will not provide consistently adequate information concerning all phases of folkways. While some sections may be lacking in descriptive detail due to sketchy accounts in the sources, the available information should, nevertheless, provide insight into many aspects of social conduct.

Furthermore, no attempt will be made to judge folk practices in the light of contemporary knowledge. Popular views and customs of the past will be regarded as realities and events, or as Collingwood admonished: "If the reason why it is hard for a man to cross the mountains is because he is frightened of the devils in them, it is folly for the historian, preaching at him across a gulf of centuries, to say 'This is sheer superstition. . . .'"[4] While a psychological analysis of communal customs falls outside the scope of this work, psychological factors will be considered, but only if they can be derived from a source.

The geographical boundary of Germany during the period under consideration comprised the area generally known as the Holy Roman Empire, which included the Germanic lands of Austria, Bohemia, and Moravia. Bohemia and Moravia were of course influenced by Slavic culture, but we shall not deal with the Slavic elements in these countries. Bohemia and Moravia will be viewed in terms of their relation to German cultural life, for in the 17th and 18th centuries they were part of Germany. This geographical area can be regarded as a cultural unit, with Yiddish as the vernacular.[5]

The political geography of the German empire after the Treaty of Westphalia, in 1648, namely, a "loose confederation of some three hundred principalities and free cities," affected the social position of the Jews. As in the earlier Middle Ages, the local Jewish community was granted autonomy by the German political ruler in establishing and administering its religious and social institutions.[6] With the exception of Moravia and Hesse, no regional organization existed to unite on a territorial basis local Jewish communities of Germany so that they might deal more effectively with problems of mutual concern.[7]

The end of the Thirty Years' War marked the rebirth of Jewish communities in Germany.[8] In their effort to rebuild a war-torn country, German rulers afforded new political and social opportunities to communities that had been previously weakened or destroyed by the pogroms of the 14th and 15th centuries.[9] State officials, desirous of aiding the development of Germany, authorized the establishment of new Jewish communities.[10]

Another factor that influenced the development of Jewish communal life after 1648 was the migration and settlement of East European Jews in Germany as a result of the Chmielnicki pogrom. When the Jews of the Ukraine and Poland fled to Germany during the Cossack massacres, the cultural heritage that they brought with them influenced Jewish social life wherever they settled. The scholars, rabbis, and writers who came from Eastern Europe made a cultural impact on German Jewry at a time when communal life was being revived. As a result, East European lore spread in Germany and became part of the popular beliefs and customs of Jewish daily life.[11]

The growth of German-Jewish communities was not accompanied by any substantial change in the political and social status of the Jews, for they continued to live under the disabilities and insecurities that were characteristic of the Middle Ages. They had to wear a distinctive garb and paid heavy taxes to the emperor as well as to feudal and local authorities for the right of individual residence and communal autonomy. They also faced expulsion, as in Vienna, in 1670, and in Prague, in 1670 and 1744.[12] The political status of the Jews in Germany was not determined by a body of legal and political principles that recognized and applied universal rights, but by a policy of toleration dependent upon an emperor's will. Hence, in his study of customs Yuspa Shammash (Shammes) of Worms (d. 1678) concludes with a prayer, offered at the time of the coronation of Leopold I, in 1658, in which the hope is expressed that the new ruler will deal justly with the members of the Jewish community.[13]

In the 17th century the Jews of Germany were culturally "children of the Middle Ages," as Isaac Holzer has stated,[14] and their outlook was reflected in the folkways of the time, in every conceivable phase of the social life of both the individual and the group. An examination of popular *minhagim* will also show the influence exerted by the lore of the Cabala, as well as by a variety of practices then current in the general German environment.[15] This will be seen, in particular, in such areas as the "crises of life" and folk medicine.

After 1648, *musar* (*muser*), Jewish religio-ethical literature, became more and more didactic. The writers of *musar* were not only mentors in daily living, but outspoken critics desiring to correct communal weaknesses and abuses. Thus, the popular literature did not conceal incidents that did not present an ideal picture of Jewish cultural behavior. Such realistic accounts, in which folk life was often critically pictured, should prove to be revealing for the structure and outlook of Jewish social life in Germanic lands prior to the era of Jewish Emancipation.

JEWISH FOLKWAYS IN GERMANIC LANDS

CHAPTER I

Neighborhood and Home

1. Physical Surroundings

The topography of Jewish neighborhoods was not uniform. Fire, expulsion, and war disrupted physical continuity.[1] When a community was left in ruins by war,[2] and had to be rebuilt, its topography did not necessarily resemble that of the preceding period.[3] The tie with the past was not a physical one; continuity was maintained by religio-legal tradition and folk customs.[4]

The neighborhood where Jews lived was known as *di gas*, "the Jewish street," and here families lived in congested conditions, in tall, dingy buildings on narrow and crooked streets.[5] The map on the endpapers is an illustration of the physical lay-out of a German-Jewish community.[6] The location and setting of the *gas* (Ger.: *gasse*) implied that the Jewish community in Germany was inferior in social status; thus, the Portuguese Jews of Hamburg lived close to the "debris mound," *dreckwall,* the city refuse dump, which served also to divide the old section of Hamburg from the new;[7] the Frankfort Jews had their homes "near the moat" of the city which was used for "garbage disposal,"[8] and in Prossnitz, they lived on two streets adjoining the town wall.[9]

The physical appearance of the houses, run-down and dilapidated, blended with the drab outer surroundings of the neighborhood quarters, where there was no sign of trees or grass and the air was foul. A few of the dwellings were of brick, but most were of wood and therefore easily inflammable. The buildings in the *gas*, three and four stories high and joined together, would shut out the light, leaving the street dismal and dark.[10] In their physical appearance, the neighborhoods of the general community and "the Jewish quarter" were in fact more alike than different, judging from the description in a traveler's account of a 16th-century German town:

> As evening approaches, our traveler strolls forth into the streets and narrow lanes of the town lined with overhanging gables that almost meet overhead and shut out the light of the afternoon sun, so that twilight seems already to have fallen.[11]

However, the entire Jewish population did not necessarily reside in *gasen*; while in some communities they lived in segregated areas, in others no residential restrictions were imposed. More specifically, as Ya'ir Ḥayyim Bacharach of Worms (d. 1702) states, whenever Jews reside on "specified streets," as for example, in Worms, Frankfort, Hanau of the Rhineland, they are shut in at night behind a gate and are forbidden to leave their quarters without official approval. But in Coblenz, Trier, Mannheim, on the other hand, where the Jews do not live on "particular streets," they are not confined within a gate, and can go out whenever they wish.[12] From Meir Eisenstadt (d. 1744) we have another first-hand description of a *gas*, that of Sedlowitz, Moravia, adjacent to the town market-place and closed in by a gate.

> Sedlowitz has a gate for the Jews which leads to the market-place of the Christians. The gate is closed according to legal requirements. After both sides of the gate are opened, many persons can pass. . . .[13]

Thus a distinction has to be made between a Jewish neighborhood voluntarily established by a group of people who wish to live in accordance with their religious and social convictions and an area in which Jews were set apart from the rest of the community by the decision of governmental authority.[14] While the existence of the *gas* meant a position of social inferiority, with it went political and legal autonomy enabling the Jews residing there to set up their own communal institutions, as well as evolve unique forms of cultural expression.[15]

Bacharach poignantly tells of the hardships endured by a scholar, his wife and child who had to live in one room; their crowded living quarters gave them no privacy.[16] The difficult conditions in which this family lived were not unusual, but were even intensified by the experience of Glikl and her mother when each gave birth in the same house just eight days apart. They were confined together in a small room, Glikl tells in her diary, and although they enjoyed each other's company, it did not relieve their discomfort.[17] The housing congestion that must have existed becomes even more apparent from the following figures: In the Frankfort *gas*, which was one of the most important centers of German-Jewish life in the 17th century, 3000 people lived in 200 dwellings, and, according to an inventory of 1703, on the average three families lived in three rooms.[18] There were 596 Jewish persons occupying thirty-nine houses in Hotzenplotz, Moravia, at the end of the 18th century; sixteen or more persons would reside in one house. But in the same period, the general community with a population of 1977 individuals had 305 dwellings, averaging about six persons to a house.[19] Likewise, the housing proved to be inadequate for the growing Jewish population in Neu-Raussnitz.[20]

These figures not only tell us a good deal about the surroundings in which the Jews of Germany lived but also allude to economic hardships and political disabilities, to a life that was more precarious than secure. Yet within such surroundings a rather complex social life developed, which we hope to explore in part in this study of Jewish folkways.

2. The Interior of the House

We have only limited information about the interior of the home, its layout or arrangement; some details can be found in a record of the District Court of Vienna, belonging to the latter part of the 16th century, and in a census survey conducted in Neu-Raussnitz in the first decade of the 18th century. Usually the house has a yard and stable, and in most cases there are also a garden and well. The first floor (*bei der Erden*) consists of a storeroom, two bedrooms, a living room; the rooms of the next story include an anteroom (*vorheusel*), living room, bedroom; the third story has an anteroom, a living room, kitchen, and bedroom.[21]

An official inventory of Frankfort household possessions, made in order to determine tax assessments, offers information on several Jewish homes at the end of the 17th century. Since the tax survey lists the possessions of families in poor, moderate, and wealthy circumstances, it is possible for us to reconstruct in part the physical contents of a home.[22] In the home of the poorer household, identified as Seligmann zur goldnen Crone (Krone), "Seligmann at the Sign of the Golden Crown," the furniture is made of fir timber, a less expensive material, and is painted in green, a popular color of the time. The wood of nut and oak trees was used for more expensive furniture. With the exception of the one room set aside for utility storage, there is a bed in each room. The beds are made with posts, over which a canopy hangs; and when the canopy becomes worn, blue and white sheets are used instead. Even in the living room a folding bed is placed.[23] Again, we sense the congestion in the house as all available space is converted into sleeping quarters; for lack of storage facilities, the poorer home becomes cluttered.[24]

In addition to the beds, the rooms contained an extension table, a wardrobe, two goblets, two candlesticks, three brass lamps, four candle sconces, a black-framed mirror, three deer-heads mounted on the wall; various utensils of brass, copper, and tin; trunks with bedding; linen, including hand towels and napkins; clothing, and a collection of ninety-eight Hebrew books.[25] That Seligmann had this number of books suggests that a library was considered essential in the home, no less so in the case of a person of limited means. It is even more apparent that books were part of the furnishings, for in preparing a room to stage a *Purim* play in the home, books had to be moved aside with the table and bench.[26]

When Rabbi Elias Levin of Landsberg died in 1802, a list of his household possessions was prepared for sale for the benefit of his widow. The inventory shows that he lived in a home of better circumstances, although in some respects his furnishings were similar to that of Seligmann zur goldnen Krone. Among the items are bedding, hand towels and tablecloths, dishes, and utensils, such as six English tin plates, a tin pan, two silver spoons, a silver teaspoon, two copper pots. The furniture includes three tables, two reading chairs, five footstools, three spindles, four bedsteads, and four lamps. The books in his library are not listed; the ceremonial objects—Sabbath candlesticks, a *habdalah*, or incense box, and a *Ḥanukkah* candelabrum—suggest some of the religious observances closely identified with home life.[27]

The home of Elkan Moses zum Vogelgesang, "Elkan Moses at the Sign of the Singing Bird," in 1690, must have provided more comfort, for among his possessions are an armchair, two easy chairs, and a hanging candelabrum. Other items, as hand towels and three pitchers designed with flowers, would imply that this was a more elaborate and costly household that only wealthier individuals could have maintained. He had thirteen books, a number that might compare favorably with the size of libraries in some homes today.[28]

Meyer zur gelben Rose, "Meyer at the Sign of the Yellow Rose," had the most elaborate home, like that of the nobility, for according to the inventory of 1679, he owns an assortment of jewelry—diamonds, rubies, and pearls, rings of turquoise, onyx, and carnelian—two large mirrors, and a variety of dishes. His utensils are embellished with gold and silver; forks, knives, goblets are gilded; hand towels are embroidered with silver thread; a salt box and lamp are of silver, and women's belts are also gilded or made of silver. His home is decorated with curtains. Among his household belongings are a kitchen cupboard, a vault, tobacco, and morocco leather. His cultural possessions are a Scroll of Esther in a silver case, twenty-six Hebrew books, and a manuscript.[29] That Seligmann had more books in his home than Elkan and Meyer may signify that the person of economic means did not always encourage and support intellectual pursuits in the Jewish society.[30]

The inventory has further detail on the furnishings in the homes of Seligmann and Elkan Moses of Frankfort. The dishes, usually of pewter and round or square in shape, are soup bowls, plates, and butter containers, and the household utensils are flasks, pots, copper pails, kettles, a sieve, and mortar stone. There is also a flower box in the home to provide a touch of nature.[31]

Since the Jews of Frankfort were not allowed to operate shops or stores, they worked as peddlers, and whenever permission was obtained from the authorities they advertised their wares by posting announcements outside the house. The merchandise would be kept in the storeroom, and it was not unusual for a sample of goods to be displayed outdoors to catch the eye of a passer-by.[32] Wine and grain were stored in the home and used in lieu of currency to pay debts and make loans.[33] The retail goods were linen, lace, ticking, yarn, cotton, leather, sewing needles, soft soap, mastic (*mastix*, gum-like resin to repair and hold objects together), incense, glue (*leim*, an adhesive substance used as glue), wine board (*weinspan*), reams of white writing paper, and packs of cards.[34]

Inasmuch as "108 cards" are listed in the inventory, the question arises whether gambling was a popular form of diversion and whether it was tolerated by communal authorities. Later, this will be discussed in fuller detail,[35] but for the present it should be pointed out that while gambling was discouraged and opposed by communal legislation and rabbinic opinion, as well as in folk literature, games of chance were permitted on the festivals, *Ḥanukkah* and *Purim*, and on a happy event, as the birth of a child. The usual legal and moral attitude toward gambling is expressed in the witticism: "It [card-playing] is forbidden; [but] one may play by day without money, and by night in the dark."[36] By relaxing their opposition to gambling on special occasions, communal leaders were realistic enough to recognize that people needed diversion from their daily routine and strain, otherwise they might be inclined to flout the law.[37]

3. Private Library Collections

The extensive library built in the home—evident, for example, from an inventory of the personal possessions of Marx Lion Gomperz and Samuel b. Emanuel Oppenheimer—can be singled out as another cultural feature of 18th-century German-Jewish life. The inventory includes a list of books in their respective collections.[38] The titles are mainly works of the scholarly Talmudic tradition, past and current, as well as the more popular books of the time, and there appears to be greater interest in Biblical commentaries, in legal (halakhic) studies and codes, and less concern for philosophical and ethical subjects.[39] There must have been an interest in keeping abreast of the prolific output of *responsa,* containing the published opinions of rabbinic authorities on problems of immediate concern submitted to them. The *responsa* cover all ranges of social life, religious observance, economic questions, family difficulties, health conditions, social welfare, interpersonal conflicts, and non-Jewish relations.[40] Cabalistic and mystical literature also had an appeal in a period beset with fear and bewilderment. In all walks of life people were heartened by the outlook of Lurianic Cabala in its emphasis on man having the capacity for self-improvement and goodness and his being able to offset misfortune and overpower evil through personal conduct.[41]

The library of Samuel Oppenheimer contained books of an academic character. The sixty-four titles included a Hebrew Concordance; the Venice edition of the Bible (1524); the Mishnah; Talmudic tractates; the Code of Maimonides (*Yad ha-Ḥazaḳah*); the *Shulḥan 'Arukh* (Code of Law arranged by Joseph Karo); *novellae* on the *Shulḥan 'Arukh*, by Joshua Falk b. Alex ha-

Kohen;[42] *Sefer ha-Manhig*, by Abraham b. Nathan (Ibn ha-Yarḥi);[43] the Indices to the Talmud, by Joshua Boaz; commentaries on the *Zohar*, by Mordecai b. Judah ('Aryeh Leyb) Ashkenazi and Zebi Hirsh Chotsch. Manuscripts on Cabala and Arabic philosophy were also to be found in the library.[44]

The fifty-six titles in the library of Gomperz comprised a concordance; the Biblical commentaries of Naḥmanides, Samuel de Uceda, and Solomon Lentshits;[45] the *Meginne 'Ereẓ*, the *'Oraḥ Ḥayyim* of the *Shulḥan 'Arukh; novellae* on the Talmud, by Solomon ibn Adret (Rashba), Solomon Luria (Maharshal), and Samuel Edels (Maharsha); codes and commentaries, *halakhot* on the *Shulḥan 'Arukh,* by Isaac Jacob Alfasi (Rif), Phineas b. Simon Auerbach, Yeḳutiel b. Abigdor; *responsa,* by Ẓebi (Hirsh) Horowitz, Samuel b. David ha-Levi Meseritz;[46] homilies, by Naphtali Hirz b. Simeon Günzburg, Judah Rosanes, Bezalel b. Solomon of Kobrin; discourses on Cabala, by Aaron Selig of Żółkiew and Sabbatai (Sheftel) Horowitz.[47] Of the popular religio-ethical works the library included *Ḥobot ha-Lebabot,* by Baḥya ibn Paḳuda; *Leb Tob,* by Isaac b. Eliakim of Posen;[48] *Yesh Noḥalin,* by Abraham Sheftel Horowitz; *Shelah*, by Isaiah Horowitz.[49]

The outstanding private library among the Jews of Germanic lands in the 18th century was that of David Oppenheim of Prague, "the first great collector of a Hebrew library."[50] The collection comprised 7000 printed volumes and 1000 manuscripts, and it was the catalogue of this library that proved to be so helpful to Johann Christoph Wolf when he prepared his noteworthy *Bibliotheca Hebraea.*[51] After Oppenheim came to Prague, he found censorship so rigorously enforced that he decided to transfer his library to Hanover where his father-in-law resided.[52] Moses Mendelssohn considered the library of such importance that he endeavored to raise funds, between 50-60,000 *taler*, for its purchase; however, he did not succeed in the undertaking. Later, in 1829, the collection was acquired for the Bodleian Library at Oxford, where it is now housed.[53]

4. The "Shield" on the House

Little, if anything at all, is said in the book of customs about the outside appearance of the house, for its chief concern is with man's conduct, how he should behave at home and engage in his dealings with others. Among the few passages that we have pertaining to the exterior of the home is Kosman's description of the practice in the Frankfort *gas* of mounting a sign on the outside of the house to show the name of the family. In referring to "Hahn," his grandfather's name, Kosman explains that it was designated by the "red rooster sketched on the house."[54] As yet regular surnames were not adopted by the Jews of Germany,[55] but names derived from animals, plants, minerals, weapons and other objects were indicated on the "shields" by the figures of, for instance, a "Bear," "White Horse," "Black Shield," "Red Shield," "Drum," or "Ring."[56] In 1753, the 204 houses in the Jewish neighborhood of Frankfort had "shields" to represent the names of "Green Forest," "Bell," "Gold Crown," "Gold Ostrich," "Gold Mirror."[57] Of the forty-three houses in the *gas* of Worms, at the beginning of the 16th century, twenty-four had "shields" with the figures of a "Star," "Moon," "Rose," "Green Tree," "Horn of an Oak," "Horn of a Stag," "Hare," "Deer Wolf," "Sickle," "Kettle," and "Wheel."[58] The "shields" on the homes of the Jews of Vienna showed a "Bell," "Green Tree," "Red Deer," "Black Ox," "Gold Bear," "Gold Crown," "Green Lid," and "Blue Hat."[59] The similarity of names on the "shields" in Frankfort, Worms, and Vienna again would show how the Jews of Germanic lands shared a social pattern in common.

In Worms, the governmental legislation, *Stättigkeit*, of November 28, 1641, required "a large shield to be hung outside of the house" so that the Jewish residents could be recognized.[60] In addition to the "yellow badge" worn on the arm, the sign now served to identify a Jewish person.[61] No doubt the use of the "shield" to single out a Jewish family adumbrated the abandonment of the "badge" in the 18th century.[62] During the Middle Ages, first in Islamic and then Christian lands, the Jew was required to wear the "yellow badge" to differentiate him from the rest of the populace. Since the Jew did not wear the "badge" with consistency in the 17th century, authorities no longer could rely on the "badge" as the "mark" in identifying a Jew. Thereupon, he was ordered to mount the "sign" on his house in addition to wearing the "badge" on his arm, and by governmental legislation the meaning of the "marker" on the home was transformed from a mere sign to a symbol of social inferiority.[63]

There is no evidence of the "shield" in Silesia in the 18th century, but a Hebrew inscription in Biblical style appears on the houses. Such an inscription, written with a moral emphasis, reads:

> Who builds his house on justice and righteousness, establishes his acts on truth and right, his dwelling-place will be firm, his edifice will exist forever, and his honor will never be shaken.[64]

5. Outside of the "Gas"

That the home would also be used for storing wares and selling goods is indicative of an economic change taking place after the Thirty Years' War. With the incipient development of the capitalist economy, fewer Jews are now in money-lending, and more are becoming peddlers, tradesmen, and merchants.[65] In fact, by the end of the 16th century Christians are going to the *gasen* of Strasbourg and Frankfort to purchase merchandise, while at the city gate of Strasbourg Jews have established a market for horse-trading.[66] In the literature of the period sufficient mention has been made of the peddler to enable us to piece together a picture of him traveling from town to town, always in danger of being attacked by thieves and brigands lying in ambush. It was not unusual for a person away from home to be robbed and killed and the Jewish community had to send its official representatives to identify and claim

Fig. 1. A Jewish Peddler of Nuremberg Selling Wares, 18th Century (*Courtesy, Widener Library, Harvard University*). From *Jüdisches Lexikon, IV*[1] (1930), 538; originally, an 18th century engraving. Also, in George Liebe, *Judentum*, p. 115, plate # 94.

the body for burial.[67] The tradesman went from door to door just as Glikl's husband did when his first business venture was "to buy up gold."[68] Officials gave the Jews authorization to sell their goods in cities on market days and in the environing small towns on both market and non-market days.[69] And as the Jew attended a fair to dispose of his goods, he not only had reason to go outside the *gas* but opportunity to build new relationships with the non-Jewish society.[70]

The informal association that must have existed between Christian and Jew at the fair and during the sale of goods in the *gas* weakened "the wall of legal restriction" that isolated the Jew socially and gave him a position of inferiority.[71] Examples can be cited at random of Jews and Christians meeting together in the 17th and 18th centuries, even though law and custom over the centuries had frowned upon such contact. Non-Jewish persons were employed as servants in Jewish homes, or else ran errands and did the chores on the Sabbath.[72] On their holidays Christians would stroll in the *gas*[73]—perhaps out of the desire to see how people lived in this section of the town. Goethe, in his autobiography, tells of what prompted him to visit the Jewish quarter of Frankfort. His reasons were twofold; he enjoyed gazing at the beautiful Jewish girls, and he wanted to learn about the religious and social observances of the Jews. In his own words:

> Furthermore, the girls were pretty, and were quite pleased if a Christian lad showed himself friendly and attentive to them on the Sabbath in the Fischerfeld. . . . I was extremely curious to get to know about their ceremonies. I did not rest till I had often visited their synagogue, attended a circumcision and a wedding, and had formed a picture to myself of the feast of Tabernacles. Everywhere I was well received, excellently entertained.[74]

Jewish students could be found eating in Christian coffee houses,[75] and the inn became a meeting-place for Christians and

Jews wishing to transact business affairs. In her account of life in Hamburg, Glikl tells about the tavern *Schiffergesellschaft*, "Seamen's Rendezvous" ("Seamen's Society"), where "Jewish as well as non-Jewish merchants who have business to transact or accounts to handle, go . . . and drink ale from silver cups."[76] Jewish women were able to arrange to milk the cows belonging to Christians and then sell the milk in the *gas*.

> The women who were poor would arise early each morning and go outside of the 'Jewish Street' with large pails to milk cows in the yards [lit., homes] of Christians. The women milked the cows before they were taken to pasture and then sold the milk in the 'Jewish Street.'[77]

Jewish orchestras entertained in Christian homes,[78] and Christian musicians were hired to play at Jewish gatherings.[79] On occasion, nobility and other prominent non-Jews would attend Jewish family celebrations. Among the guests who were present at the wedding of Ẓipporah, the daughter of Glikl of Hameln, were Prince Moritz of the Duchy of Nassau and Prince Frederick, who later became Prince Elector of Brandenburg and then Frederick I of Prussia.[80] Michael Henrichs (Hinrichsen) of Glückstadt, a tobacco merchant of Portuguese descent, invited Christians of social prestige to the circumcision celebration for his son.[81] Jews are now teaching Torah to non-Jews, commented Isaiah Horowitz, who considered such conduct to be a violation of approved procedure.[82]

There were also occasions when Jews and Christians gave help and assistance to one another when they faced a difficulty or an emergency. At the time when Germany was invaded by the French army, during the Thirty Years' War, Christians befriended Jews, and Christians were able to conceal their personal possessions in Jewish homes to prevent confiscation by soldiers.[83] When Jews became homeless in Prague after the destruction of the *gas* in 1689, and in Frankfort after the fire of 1711, they were befriended and sheltered by Christians.[84]

It is apparent from a *responsum* of Bacharach, who cites the instance of a Jew and non-Jew owning a tavern together,[85] that Jews and Christians had now become partners in business. And through Ezekiel Landau we learn of a Jewish man who established a shop to make cloth. The features of this enterprise are indicative of the new trends in Jewish social and economic life; first, the shop is in a non-Jewish neighborhood; second, non-Jewish workers are employed; third, the Jewish owner has provided the tools and equipment required for the job; and finally, though the building with the shop is his, he does not live in it.[86] We also hear of Jewish merchants (*ha-soḥarim ha-gedolim*) who are importing "powdered sugar" for domestic sale.[87]

The growing toleration between Christian and Jew in the 17th and 18th centuries finds expression in Jacob Emden's statement that Christians cannot be considered idol worshipers; that they live by a system of beliefs and laws that is humane, embracing the seven Noachian principles of kindness and regard for others, and that it is incumbent upon every Jew to befriend the Christian in his need and sorrow as the sages of the Talmud taught (Git. 61a).[88] Messianic hopes then current no doubt have impetus to the vision of a world in which all groups will live harmoniously in an atmosphere of mutual respect and regard for one another. While there were persons who felt confident that a new era was about to emerge, one should bear in mind that the biases characteristic of the Middle Ages still prevailed.

Since the Jew spent only a small part of his life outside of the *gas*, usually as "a stranger" in the general society, our attention shall be focused on those customs that relate to his development as an individual. We shall now consider those aspects of Jewish social life that had direct bearing on his daily conduct from the moment of his birth.

CHAPTER II

Birth, Marriage, and Burial[1]

The customs relating to the life cycle embrace more than their obvious connection with either birth, marriage, or burial.[2] Their development and observance are associated with diverse phases of daily life, their scope thus entailing much more than what is ordinarily meant by the "crises of life."[3] The popular observances dealing with birth, marriage, and death have a varied background, for some customs are based on a religious tradition with roots in the ancient past, while other practices, local in character, are indigenous to a particular area or associated with a crucial historical event. A single community, thereby, could have "numerous customs peculiar to itself."[4]

By examining birth, marriage, and burial practices we can distinguish the ways in which relationships are established between an individual and the community. On certain occasions, such as birth and marriage festivities, or bereavement, the entire community is involved, and whoever joins with others in attending such gatherings will perform a meritorious act. There are practices, however, that only require the participation of the individual and not of the total community. A survey of customs pertaining to the life-cycle will show further how religious and social life became intertwined.[5] And in other instances, these practices reflect the influence of the German cultural environment on the daily life of the Jew. Obviously, social isolation did not make the Jewish community impervious to influences from the outside world. The Jews, sharing the fears and anxieties that were part of the folk life of Germany, held popular views that bore a similarity to the attitudes widespread in the general community.[6]

Demonology is an integral part of birth, marriage, and burial customs, as well as other facets of social life.[6] In Jewish lore the demon is regarded as much of a "fact" and as "real" as any physical object.[7] It is recognized that demons have their rightful place of residence, though not in areas where humans have settled. They can claim as their living quarters uninhabited regions, such as forests and deserts.[8] Evidently, demons cannot be annihilated, but they can be tolerated or controlled, with folk practices serving to restrain and check the array of "evil spirits" that maneuver to disrupt the moral life of individuals or the entire society.[9]

1. Birth

Birth customs are concerned with safeguarding the mother before childbirth, relieving her of pain during delivery, protecting the child after birth, performing the rite of circumcision, and giving the child its name. Uneasiness is expressed for the mother's safety prior to delivery, and as in the case of the bride, the groom, or the mourner, Hahn admonishes that she should not be left alone.[10] These persons are constantly threatened by evil spirits, and they therefore need special kinds of protection. Hence, when an expectant mother is by herself in the house, she is not considered safe unless she carries a knife, so as to repel any demon that attempts to attack her.[11] Since ancient times iron was relied upon as a weapon and safeguard against the machinations of evil spirits. Rabbinic authorities of the Talmudic period expressed no objection to using an iron object, since the intention was to prevent demons from inflicting harm. Otherwise, as they explained, an iron instrument could not be tolerated, as it might be associated with the customs of the Amorites, which are considered idolatrous. "When one places a firerod or a piece of iron under his head, he is following the practices of the Amorites. On the other hand, if [he does this] to protect himself it is permissible."[12]

To ease child delivery, any one of a number of folk practices known in various parts of Germany, as well as in Eastern Europe, could be followed.[13] Some of the procedures recommended for mothers during childbirth went back to the 12th and 13th centuries, if not earlier.[14] These "first aids" were also among the remedies included in folk-medicine handbooks.[15] In Frankfort, according to Schudt, during the festival of *Sukkot,* on *Hosha'ana' Rabbah,* women would bite off the petiole of an *'etrog,* citron, at the time of delivery so as to reduce birth pangs.[16] And in his section on folk medicine, David Tevle Ashkenazi of Moravia (d. 1734) describes methods that were to be followed to relieve women of pain during childbirth. For instance, the shore plant (*wallkraut*) might be mixed with white bread in a flax cloth, then dipped in wine and placed on the woman's abdomen. The core of a fungus could also be eaten to ease the pain of the mother. A flax cloth dipped in a mixture of boiled vinegar and red wine should be pressed against the nostrils of the woman to give her relief. An unwed girl, or else a married woman who until then had not attended a childbirth, would be asked to close her eyes, encircle the mother three times, each time touching her abdomen. The skin of a snake was then placed on her heart or abdomen[17] in order to make her more comfortable as she gave birth.[18]

Following the pattern of practical Cabala, *Sefer Zekhirah* advised that Psalm 20 should be recited to reduce the pain of childbirth. Since the Psalm has nine verses, corresponding to the nine months of pregnancy, it could be effective in bringing relief to the woman in delivery.[19] Furthermore, the Psalm has seventy words, symbolic of the seventy pangs experienced during childbirth.[20] While Zechariah Plungian (ca. 1725), the author of *Sefer Zekhirah,* lived in Eastern Europe, in Zamość, it can be assumed, however, that the customs that he describes, explains, or interprets were not unknown in German-Jewish localities. Through the works of Isaiah Horowitz (d. 1628) and Zebi Hirsh Kaidanover (d. 1712, Frankfort), practical Cabala had an influence on Jewish popular beliefs and practices in Germany. As early as the 13th century the lore of Cabala had become interwoven with the folkways of German Jewry through the mystical writings of Judah he-Ḥasid of Regensburg (d. 1217) and Eleazar b. Judah of Worms (d. 1238).[21]

Furthermore, we are told by Yuspa Shammes (Shammash), in his book of customs, of the device that had been employed in the community of Worms to safeguard both women and children following birth. After the child was born, a circle was drawn on the floor and within the circle the names of Lilith, Adam, Eva, Sannuj, Samsannug, Samiglof, among others, were written.[22] The circle was "regarded as a great protection against Satan and all misfortunes."[23] Both the mother and the child, it was feared, would be in constant jeopardy due to the devious ways in which evil spirits might be plotting against them.[24]

In outlining the ritual for observance in the local community, the book of *Minhagim* of Fürth, 18th century, portrays some of the customs that were part of the preparations for a circumcision ceremony. Women friends of the mother who had given birth would meet in her home and hold the ceremony of *yidish-kerts*, the "circumcision candle." During the three days that preceded and the three days that followed the *berit milah*, it was the custom to light candles. The women, while in the home, made twelve wax candles to symbolize the tribes of Israel;[25] however, there was no uniformity of procedure in the lighting of the candles. In some instances, for example, a large-sized candle was lit and then twelve small candles;[26] or on the three days before the circumcision, a total of twelve candles would be burned—four candles for each day.[27]

The *yidish-kerts* ceremony was likewise observed in Worms, according to Yuspa Shammes (Shammash),[28] but apparently in southern Germany[29] it was of a sectional character, being limited to the area between the Rhine Valley and the Fürth region. Culturally, this must have been a self-contained region, as there seems to be no indication that the *yidish-kerts* was practiced in other parts of Germany.

There is evidence that the *yidish-kerts* was known in communities along the Rhine during the earlier Middle Ages. Eleazar b. Judah relates how women friends of the mother, who had just given birth, would gather in her home and light an oil lamp. The women brought with them the oil that was needed.[30] When twins were to be circumcized in Mayence, the Maharil (Jacob Levi Molin, d. 1427, Worms) gave instructions to double the number of candles for the ceremony. Usually, twelve small candles and a large one were used whenever there was a circumcision.[31] The *yidish-kerts* is thus an example of a custom that has had a long history within the same cultural area. Not only the laity, but scholars as well, adhered to the practice of the "circumcision candle" with scrupulous care.

There is no one explanation that can be considered the most plausible in accounting for the possible origin and meaning of the *yidish-kerts*. One account states that it was an old practice among German Jewry to burn candles in a home in preparation for the *berit milah*; the lighted candles would serve as "an invitation" to passers-by to attend the circumcision.[32] The *yidish-kerts* could also have been related to an older practice known as *vakhnakht*, "watch night," "wakeful night." Held on the night before circumcision, the "watch" was intended to guard and protect the child against evil spirits. Before the circumcision the infant was considered to be in grave danger.[33] In a *responsum* of Ya'ir Ḥayyim Bacharach the dramatic incident is portrayed of a male infant who had been bewitched, sank into a stupor, and then died on the *vakhnakht*.[34] An eye-witness description of a *vakhnakht* held in a home in Vienna, at the beginning of the 15th century, summarized the features of this folk observance: On the night preceding the circumcision "friends gather in the home of the mother . . . , and they 'watch' ['sit up': *vakhen*] the entire night, so that Satan should not come and kill the child, and Lilith, the mother of Satan, should not strangle him."[35]

The *vakhnakht* was known in Jewish communities other than Germany. In Rome, for example, "the night" was devoted to study, and in North Africa a festive meal was served.[36] Erich Brauer has compared the Kurdistan "Night of *Sheshah,*" the evening before circumcision, with the *vakhnakht* in European-Jewish communities. The "watch night" was also established in Kurdistan for the protection of the mother and child. During "the night" the men of Kurdistan would read from the *Zohar*, and carry the Chair of Elijah from the synagogue for the circumcision.[37]

The women who gathered in the home of the confined mother also assisted her with household tasks for three to four days prior to the circumcision ceremony, and they would present her attendant with a gift of money.[38] According to the communal legislation of Hamburg and Altona of 1726, women in the community were expected to visit the mother who had given birth and bring her refreshments, "pastry, cakes, and brandy."[39]

When a male child was born, special festivities were held during the week preceding the circumcision.[40] On *Shabbat Zakhor*, the Sabbath before the circumcision ritual, a *se'udat miẓvah*, "a meal fulfilling a religious duty," was scheduled.[41] The "redemption meal," *yeshua' ha-ben,* for the first-born male in Talmudic times was the precedent for the *se'udah,* meal, on *Shabbat Zakhor,*[42] and Israel Isserlein (d. 1460, Neustadt) cites the *ri'shonim*, rabbinic authorities of the earlier Middle Ages, as having innovated the *se'udah* "on the Sabbath eve that follows the birth of a male child." This particular time was chosen, he explains, because on "the Sabbath eve everyone is found at home."[43] In the *Shabbat Zakhor* we have another instance of a custom that started around the beginning of the early Middle Ages and continued afterwards as a component of Jewish religious and cultural life.

In addition to the *Shabbat Zakhor*, the father arranged other meals during that week so as to honor the birth of a son. Thus the *Maḥẓor Vitry* (ca. 11th and 12th centuries) refers to the established practice of the father planning two meals before and after the circumcision.[44] From Bacharach we hear of the *minhag,* custom, of holding festive meals on the three days and nights before circum-

Fig. 2. The Celebration during the *Vakhnakht*, 18th Century (*Courtesy, Widener Library, Harvard University*). From George Liebe, *Judentum*, p. 108, plate # 88; originally, an engraving in Schudt, *Jüdische Merckwürdigkeiten*, by Peter Fehr, 1717.

cision,[45] and the final meal must have been part of the *vakhnakht* ceremonies. Ezekiel Landau favors having an address delivered on the evening preceding the circumcision, thereby enhancing the significance of the occasion. The celebrations throughout the week of the circumcision were familiar not only in European Jewish communities. The rabbinic background for these observances, which was no doubt widespread, accounts for a father in Kurdistan arranging meals for seven successive days to celebrate the birth of his son.[46]

Yuspa Shammash also pictures in his *Minhagim* the communal pattern for the observance of the *berit milah*. The most distinguished women escorted the child to the door of the women's synagogue, and the wife of the *sandeḳ*, godfather, carried the child into the synagogue. When the morning service terminated, she handed the child to her husband as he stood at the threshold of the door leading from the men's to the women's synagogue, which was in a separate room adjoining the men's synagogue. While the *mohel* was reciting the opening prayers, the *sandeḳ* would place the child in the right seat of the Chair of Elijah, then he took the left seat (the chair having two seats) and held the child on his knees through the circumcision ritual. After the ceremony, the women returned the child to his home. At noon the father arranged a meal, to which he invited the number of persons authorized by communal legislation. During the meal a learned discourse was delivered.[47] Later, in describing anti-luxury, or sumptuary, legislation, we shall hear how communities controlled the cost of the circumcision celebration, the number of guests who might attend, the amount of food that could be served, as well as the giving of gifts.[48]

The Chair of Elijah, used in the circumcision ceremony, bears its name in honor of the prophet, for, according to rabbinic lore, Elijah, who attends every circumcision, is given this recognition for his zealous adherence to the rite of circumcision when its observance was neglected during the reign of Ahab and Jezebel (I Kings 19:10).[49] The Chair of Elijah is brought to the synagogue

Fig.3. Circumcision Bench in the Synagogue of Zülz, Upper Silesia, 1782 *(Courtesy, Hebrew Union College-Jewish Institute of Religion Library, Cincinnati)*. From *Menorah, VI (no.* 5, 1928, *Vienna-Frankfort),* 259. Photo appears in E. Hintze, *Katalog . . . Judentum . . . Schlesiens,* plate xix, no. 469.

so that the circumcision can be held in "a holy place." Since the circumcision is considered a sacrifice, the synagogue becomes a more appropriate place for the ceremony than any home. The synagogue also provides more pleasant and aesthetic surroundings,[50] for, as already indicated, most houses were not kept clean due to poverty, congested living quarters, and lack of hygienic facilities.[51]

Since the most respected member of the community is to be the *kvater*, Elḥanan Kirchan reports that in a number of places it has become the custom to offer this honor to the rabbi. He also points out that it is the *kvater* who sits on the Chair of Elijah to hold the child during the *milah*, circumcision.[52] Thus, according to Kirchan, the *kvater* performs the role of the *sandeḳ*, whereas in the book of customs of Yuspa Shammash, the *sandeḳ* is the godfather.[53] When the *kvater* and *sandeḳ* are differentiated as to their function, *kvater* refers to the man who brings in the child for the circumcision. The child is handed to the *kvater* by the *kvaterin* after she carries him to the women's synagogue; but the *sandeḳ* is the one who holds the child on his lap for the circumcision.[54] While the *kvaterin* usually carries the child to the synagogue, custom does not prohibit a man from also performing this task.[55] Variations in the duties of the "godfather" may be illustrated further by citing, for comparative purpose, a custom observed in Rome, where the two godfathers would attend the circumcision, with one holding the child on his right knee and the other on the left.[56]

In his collection of ethical sermons Ephraim Solomon Lentshits of Prague (d. 1618) cites the custom of "hiding [i.e., burying] the foreskin in the earth" after the circumcision ceremony. He explains that the practice was introduced by the sages to symbolize the process in nature whereby "everything runs its course, returns to its source of being [origin] just as "clay which comes from dust . . . returns to dust."[57] Another reason for this practice is derived from a Midrashic homily on Numbers 23:10, "Who hath counted the dust of Jacob? Who, that is to say, can count the precepts that they perform in connection with the dust?" The "precepts connected with the dust" pertain to Balaam who became overawed when he saw how many foreskins of circumcized Israelites had covered the desert. This incident was the basis for the sages decreeing that "the foreskin should be covered with dust."[58] Mordecai Jaffe gives as an explanation the one that is based on Proverbs 25:21, "If thine enemy be hungry, give him food to eat." In this instance, "the enemy" is the serpent, and, according to a cabalistic view, the foreskin will supply food to the serpent who lives off the dust. By burying the foreskin in the ground, the serpent is appeased so that he will do no harm.[59]

The wine for the ceremony and the *yidish-vindl*, the "circumcision band," are provided by the *sandeḳ*. Following the circumcision, the embroidered band is presented to the synagogue as the child's gift, to be used as a *mappah* to tie the Torah. In three days, when the child is feeling better and is well enough to be bathed, a minor celebration is arranged for more intimate friends.[60]

The *Minhagim* book of Fürth also deals with some of the practices that regulate the kinds of clothing to be worn for the circumcision ceremony. If the circumcision is held in the evening, the godfather, *sandeḳ*, and the father will wear Sabbath garments. The godmother, *sandeḳet*, wears her Sabbath garment even if the *yidish-kerts* celebration should fall during the solemn "nine days" before *Tish'ah be-'Ab* commemorating the destruction of the Temple of Jerusalem. However, the other women, unlike the grandmother, abstain from using the white apron worn on the Sabbath, but are dressed instead in the more somber garments designated for the season of the Ninth of *'Ab*.[61]

It is the opinion of Joseph Kosman of Frankfort (d. 1752) that a child can be given the name of living grandparents if it does not offend the parents. Whether a child is named after the living or the dead will depend upon the feelings of the family. Kosman relates the incident of a man having an only child, a daughter, who gave birth to a son during his lifetime. The father thereupon instructed her to give the child his name. According to Kosman, no violation had been committed, since the grandfather did not consider the practice of naming children after the dead to have any special significance.[62] Kosman had apparently recognized that among European Jews there are differences in the way the custom was kept.[63] The Sephardic Jews in Holland were not reluctant to give their children the names of living grandparents;[64] on the other hand, among Ashkenazic Jews in Central and Eastern Europe it was the prevailing practice not to name a child after a living person,

Fig. 4. A Circumcision *Vindl* Becomes a Band to Tie the Torah *(Courtesy, Yeshiva Rabbi Samson Raphael Hirsch, New York City)*. From Moritz Oppenheim, a scene from *Jewish Family Life*.

parent or relative.[65] The incident, as told by Kosman, may have been one of the unusual examples in Ashkenazic Jewry of a child receiving the name of a living relative.

Among their accounts of local customs, Joseph Hahn, Samuel Meseritz of Kleinsteinach, Bavaria (d. 1681), and Joseph Steinhardt of Fürth (d. 1776) speak of the *Holekreisch (Holle Kreis, Holla-Kreisch)* ceremony held in German-Jewish homes to give the child a "second" name. The child's Hebrew name is first designated at the circumcision ceremony; then it is pronounced in the synagogue during the Torah reading at the point when the father is called upon to recite the benedictions. The *Holekreisch* takes place during the first month of the child's birth, on the afternoon of the Sabbath when the mother first feels strong enough to attend services following her confinement.[66] Children of the community gather around the infant, raise the cradle three times and exclaim, "*Holekreisch, Holekreisch*, what shall be the name of the child?" A Yiddish name is usually given. On occasion the cantor, *ḥazzan,* will lift the cradle, read passages from the Bible, and then he will call out *Holekreisch* and the name of the child.[67] As examples of names given during the *Holekreisch*, Hahn and Meseritz mention Selikman (Seligman, Seligmann), Zalman, and Zanvil.[68] Zalman is a name adopted for Shneur and Zanvil for Shemu'el (Samuel). After the ceremony, in honor of the joyous occasion, "rolls, cookies, and brandy" are served to the guests.[69] The *Holekreisch* may be cited as another example of a custom confined geographically to southern Germany, which, roughly speaking, was between the Rhine, the Main, and the Danube.[70]

Hahn and Meseritz state that they found an explanation for the *Holekreisch* in a *responsum* of Moses Minz, of Bamberg, who lived in the 15th century. The word *Holekreisch* is translated to mean "calling out the non-Hebrew name of the child," derived from two words, "common" (in Hebrew, *ḥol*) and "scream, cry out" (in German, *kreischen*).[71] *Holekreisch* was later traced to *kreis,* referring to the circle formed around the cradle to protect the mother and infant against demons.[72] A third definition associates *Holekreisch* with Frau Holle, the ancient goddess of mythology who brought children to the earth. German-Austrian folk ditties speak of the children who were found in the well of Frau Holle and each time that a child was drawn from the water, the question would be put, "What shall it be called?"[73] More recently, *Holekreisch* has been associated with "lifting the cradle," derived from two French words, *haler*, "to heave," "lift up" and *crèche*, "cradle."[74] There is certainly sufficient evidence of the influence of French culture on German social life to render this explanation plausible.[75]

The *Holekreisch* is considered by Hahn and Meseritz as a *minhag,* "custom," since it is not based on rabbinic law, *halakhah.*[76] While the original meaning of *Holekreisch* has not been confirmed, the practice no doubt stemmed from German folk influence and was adapted to Jewish social life.[77] Meseritz also observed that the *Holekreisch* was being abandoned in larger communities.[78] That it has continued in the smaller towns would again signify that German folk customs had a greater influence on the outlying rural areas than in the cities and large centers. From the opinions of Meseritz and Hahn we might infer that if the practice had been founded on a *din,* law, it would not be regarded as a *minhag,* or custom. The *minhag* originates from the feelings of the folk and has its roots in popular attitudes and desires, while the law has its foundation in rational procedures and logical principles. Hence, a practice based on a *din* has more consistency and stability than a *minhag,* which is more easily subject to impulse.

For the *Pidyon ha-Ben,* the ceremony to redeem the first-born male child, Kirchan points out that it is the practice in the Frankfort area to give the *kohen,* the priest, two Rhenish florins and four Polish gold coins. The worth of the coins is determined by weight, not by currency valuation. The unit of weight is a *lot* ($\frac{1}{2}$ oz.) and the combined coins weigh five *lots* ($2\frac{1}{2}$ ozs.), which correspond to the five shekels of silver specified for the redemption of the first-born in the Bible (Num. 18:16). If desired, an additional gift can be given to the priest, Kirchan states.[79]

The different birth customs described in the informal sources are not, as already stated, isolated facts, but phases of folk life that evolved from various strands, such as tradition, local innovation, and the influence of the general cultural environment.

2. Marriage

Jewish folkways prevalent in the 17th and 18th centuries can also be discerned from the pattern of courtship, marriage, and family life as treated in popular literature.[80] To begin with, there is the description by Glikl of Hameln of how parents planned matches for their children. She tells that while her husband was in Amsterdam, he arranged for their daughter to become engaged to Moses Krumbach of Metz. The final plans for the marriage were completed in Kleve by Elias Gomperz, the father of Glikl's son-in-law, Kossman. Elias Gomperz was given authorization by Abraham Krumbach, the father of Moses, to serve as his proxy in signing the betrothal agreement. Apparently, neither Glikl's daughter nor Moses Krumbach had any voice in deciding upon their marriage, and in accordance with the usual practice, the agreement specified that if either party violated the betrothal contract a fine, *ḳnas,* would be paid.[81] The imposition of a fine no doubt helped make the betrothal a stable rather than a casual relationship. The custom also prevailed among German Jewry to hold the *ḳnas-mol* (*ḳnas*-meal, "penalty meal") after the betrothal arrangement had been completed. Symbolically, the festive occasion affirmed that both parties would abide by the betrothal contract or else pay a fine. The celebration was held in the home of the groom, and the expenses entailed had to be covered by him.[82] Milk and honey were served as a separate dish at the betrothal meal,[83] and a plate would be broken "as a reminder of the destruction of the Temple of Jerusalem," with the guests taking

Fig. 5. Jewish Wedding Ceremony in Germany *(Courtesy, Widener Library, Harvard University)*. From Bernard Picart. *Ceremonies and Religious Customs . . . 1733-37*, I, 239.

home the pieces.[84] Following the *ḳnas-mol* (*ḳnas-mahl*) the mother and the bride refrained from visiting the home of the groom, obviously to discourage and prevent intimate association between the bride and groom once their betrothal had become official.[85]

Nevertheless, law—even through the threat of excommunication—and custom were not so binding that individuals did not attempt to cancel engagement contracts. Human situations might arise that precipitated the dissolution of betrothal agreements. Thus it was that a young man sought to break his engagement without incurring a fine because he found out that the woman was not a virgin.[86] After having a disagreement, one engaged couple asked for the termination of their betrothal.[87] On other occasions, the man wanted to break the engagement when he discovered that the woman had a long nose, a protruding lower lip, or other physical defects.[88]

Marriages were also arranged by the *shadkhan,* the matchmaker or marriage-broker, regarded as a professional with his own specialized skills. The social value of the *shadkhan* was not only based on his role as a middle-man who brought together those families interested in arranging a desirable match for their sons and daughters, but also in his negotiating an agreement acceptable to both parties that would later be included in the official marriage contract. The place of the *shadkhan* in the life of the community can be inferred from the kind of local legislation that was enacted, specifying the remuneration that he should receive for the services that he rendered.[89] The *Taḳḳanot* of Bamberg, 1678, states that after the *shadkhan* arranges a match between individuals who are unknown to each other, both parties, the bride and the groom, have to pay a fee.[90] The Minute Book of Bamberg, 1698, specifies that the *shadkhan* should receive from each party two percent of the first 100 *reichstaler* of the dowry, the amount given for *nadan*, that is, two *reichstaler* from both the family of the groom and of the bride. If the groom should be a widower, he is not obliged to pay the *shadkhan*; the bride's family, however, is required to pay the two percent fee.[91] The *shadkhan* is not to be compensated if the marriage does not take place after he has introduced the couple to each other.[92] In Hesse the remuneration for the *shadkhan* was also on a percentage basis, determined by the size of the dowry. For every 100 *reichstaler* in the dowry, the *shadkhan* received one half of a *reichstaler*, but no payment was made to him on a percentage basis for that part of the dowry exceeding the amount of 600 *reichstaler*.[93]

The communal legislation of Hamburg and Altona, 1726,

assisted needy young women to obtain a marriage dowry by scheduling public collections. It is there specified that a public collection is permissible to secure funds for either the "redemption of captives" or "the dowry of a bride."[94] Rendering financial aid to a prospective bride was thus placed in the same category as "the commandment of redeeming captives" which receives precedence over all forms of benevolence.[95] The regulation says further that the young woman is required to work in the community for three years as a domestic, and if she should prove to be satisfactory, she will receive the sum of twenty *mark* for her services. Having shown herself to be a worthy person, the community then provides an additional ten *reichstaler*, the value of thirty *mark*, to aid her in arranging the betrothal.[96]

The Hamburg and Altona communities also adopted a legislative regulation to enable an indigent father to secure a dowry for his daughter. If his relatives should refuse to assist him after he appealed to them, then two of the wealthiest are to be summoned to a meeting with the rabbi and *parnasim*, local communal leaders, whose majority decision will determine how much help is to be forthcoming from the relatives. Ordinarily the rabbi was instrumental in calling the meeting, but in those areas where there was no rabbi the meeting would be arranged by the leading communal figure and attended by two local leaders and two relatives of the poverty-stricken parent. The judgment of the group was considered as binding as a rabbinical decision.[97] That legal authority could be exercised by a group of laymen also shows the way in which a balance was maintained between social control and individual freedom. As in the case of religious matters, which were transacted without a hierarchy, communal affairs likewise were not administered only by an official ecclesiastical body.

A celebration known as *spinholts* was held on the Sabbath preceding the wedding.[98] The *spinholts* was of ancient origin, dating back to Talmudic times. In a literal sense *spinholts* means "spinning, or twirling, the spindle," and refers to the young woman who would spin yarn in her home to announce her approaching marriage. Since the act of spinning was a "symbol of skill," any woman who could spin with dexterity was regarded as a superior person.[99] It is doubtful whether the individuals who participated in the *spinholts* were aware of its origin; there was no obvious relationship between the meaning that *spinholts* might have first implied and the manner in which it was observed by German Jewry in the 17th and 18th centuries. As in the case of other customs, no connection seems to have existed between historical background on the one hand and function on the other.[100]

The *spinholts* required precise planning by the family, in accordance with communal practice. No individual could arbitrarily set a date for the festivity, as he was expected to abide by the usual time-schedule assigned for the *spinholts*. In the Frankfort community, the persons to be invited had to be checked with the sexton, *shammash*, and once the list was prepared no changes could be made.[101] Yuspa Shammash tells how the entire Jewish community of Worms would be called by the sexton to participate in the festivity of the *spinholts*. On the evening of the *spinholts* Sabbath the bride and groom were entertained in their respective homes. As the men sat at the table, "spread with fruit, sweets, and drinks," the women "stood behind them." Yuspa Shammash relates with rather graphic detail:

> Those who came sat around the tables for a short time, drinking 'a toast' and exchanging festive greetings with the groom. They remained until others arrived and then proceeded home. The second group was followed by a third group, until everyone [in the community] came. Finally, the young people came and took seats.[102]

When the festivities resumed on the Sabbath afternoon, the women entertained the bride in her home with love and wedding songs, as she sat on a stool wearing the gown, *rokel* (Yid.). Afterwards they formed a procession, led by jesters and musicians, and accompanied the bride to the *tants-hoyz* (Yid.), dance hall.[103] When the *spinholts* was held in Frankfort, unmarried girls sang and danced before the bride.[104] The bridegroom, in like manner, was entertained in the hall with song, dance, and wine, of which the older men partook. The merrymaking continued until the hour for the *minḥah*, afternoon, services, and the bride and groom would then be escorted home separately by a joyous procession.[105] That the *spinholts* was a special event in the life of the community is also evident from the practice of the groom and his parents to wear, for the occasion, their regular Sabbath apparel on *Shabbat Ḥazon*, the Sabbath that falls during the mourning period in the month of *'Ab* to commemorate the fall of Jerusalem. If *spinholts* was not observed, then the groom's father and mother would follow the usual procedure of not wearing Sabbath garments on *Shabbat Ḥazon*. But the groom, on the other hand, was permitted to dress himself in Sabbath clothing on *Shabbat Ḥazon* even if there was no *spinholts* celebration.[106]

Previously, we mentioned that in *responsa* literature—consisting of questions submitted to legal authorities for their considered opinion—different aspects of folk life are dealt with and examined. Since a *responsum* deals with an immediate problem concerning an individual or a community as a whole, the discussion offers a realistic picture of the opinions and observances current in German-Jewish life two and three centuries ago. Thus, in a *responsum*, Joel Sirkes (d. 1640, Cracow) speaks of the custom of honoring the bride with gifts in addition to her dowry. When Sirkes is asked regarding the disposition of such presents when a woman who had been married less than a year has passed away, he replies that the husband is not required to return them. And he thereupon cites the custom among the Jews of Germany of the husband returning special gifts given to his wife by relatives and friends at the time of her marriage. However, the practice was only regional; as Sirkes explains, in Eastern Europe or in other areas outside of Germany the husband was not expected to return gifts that supplemented the dowry.[107]

Marriage

The communal legislation of the province of Hesse, 1690, also directs our attention to the custom of presenting a special gift to the bride. On the day of the wedding the groom bought a new pair of shoes for the bride. Though he was expected, in accordance with the usual practice, to provide new shoes for several female relatives, the local regulation states that if he does not do so, he is not to be fined "as if he had broken his marriage contract."[108] This custom may have been influenced by the general folk attitude that the bride must wear something new at her wedding ceremony.[109] A similar custom was in vogue among the Jews of Germany during the 12th and 13th centuries: On the Thursday preceding the wedding ceremony the groom presented the bride with a belt, through the rabbi or the communal administrator and leader. By the 17th century, the practice of *aynvorf* was known; friends gave the bride a special supplementary gift, which was not part of the dowry.[110] During the time of Joseph Kosman, at the end of the 17th and the beginning of the 18th centuries, *siblonot* did not only refer to the special gift that the groom would give to the bride, but also to the gifts that both the bride and groom exchanged through the *'ab bet din,* the head of the the court, on the night preceding their marriage. The exchange of gifts would call for a celebration; a festive meal was served, and in honor of the event a procession with torchlights was staged, to the accompaniment of musical instruments.[111] Among her gifts, the bride received "a gold belt, cloak, and crown," and the groom, "a ring and shoes."[112]

When a young man living in the vicinity of Bamberg was betrothed, he would make a contribution to the school in proportion to the size of the dowry. Three *batzen* (coins) were specified as the amount for "the first one-hundred" of the dowry, and for each additional hundred, the gift of one *batzen* was designated. Whether the groom lived in a large or small community, the contribution was made, yet it would only be expected if the betrothed had some background in Jewish law.[113] Seven households that joined together to engage a teacher was considered to be the minimum size of a community eligible for the special educational gift. In Worms, on the first Sabbath after the *ḳnas-mol,* the groom served brandy to the students of the Talmudic Academy, and he offered more lavish refreshments if the betrothal occurred during *Ḥamishah 'Asar bi-Shebat,* Jewish Arbor Day, or *Lag ba-'Omer,* the Scholars' Holiday on the thirty-third day after the second night of Passover.[114] The custom was widespread that during the marriage feast the groom gave handsel money, *henzlgeld,* as his first payment to the local chest for the support of communal institutions and needs.[115] A communal legislation of Gaya, Moravia, 1650, authorized students to receive gifts of money from the groom on the day of his marriage, but the practice was abolished in 1754.[116]

Further, there were those practices related exclusively to the wedding ceremony, such as the father giving his son a myrtle plant.[117] Abraham Levesohn, in his work on the background and sources of Jewish customs, mentions that he saw the daughter of Akiba Eger wearing a "veil of twisted threads" at her wedding ceremony.[118] The word for "veil," *henuma',* referred originally in Talmudic times, to the couch on which the bride was carried during the wedding procession, and, later, to the wreath, or crown, of myrtle branches worn by the bride.[119] After the Talmudic period, the bride continued to wear the myrtle crown at her wedding.[120] The varied uses of the word *henuma'* are additional evidence that a term pertaining to a social custom was not necessarily arrived at through an awareness of the need for change or the application of logic. With considerable insight Yuspa Shammash comments that a custom has to be understood and described in terms of its origin and its relation to the life of individuals and their group. He therefore refrains from presenting customs that are based on opinion or conjecture, but instead has secured his information through direct observation or else from individuals whose opinions are widely respected and regarded as valid.[121]

The accounts of communal customs of Frankfort and Worms

tell how the head of the groom would be covered with the mourner's hood before the wedding ceremony. In Frankfort this practice would be observed on the day of marriage, and the explanation is given that through this association with death the groom is made aware of man's destiny, and he is thus restrained from feeling arrogant because he has become the focus of public attention.[122] On *spinholts* Sabbath, in Worms, the groom wore his silk mantle to the synagogue and brought the mourner's hood, or cowl, with him. When he was honored by being called to the Torah,[123] the hood was placed on his head and then removed when he returned to his seat.[124] According to the Maharil, who lived in the 15th century, this use of the hood by the groom was a characteristic "custom of the Rhine area."[125] The Maharil thereby furnishes us with evidence that the mourner's hood was related to the marriage ceremony during the Middle Ages.

We have already indicated in describing the observance of *spinholts* and *siblonot* that marriage was an occasion of festivity. The merriment at a wedding was provided by the *klezmer*, musicians, and by song and dance.[126] As a result of the suffering and despair, and the general cultural decline of the period after the Thirty Years' War, the entertainer at weddings (*marshelik*, *badḥan*) emphasized comic themes rather than the *muser-lider*, songs of ethical content complaining about "the evils of the world."[127] The popularity of music at the Jewish wedding is implied in a question submitted to Bacharach, namely, whether it would be in keeping with the station of a scholar if he should play an instrument during the wedding procession or feast. Bacharach replies that he saw no objection to this, as no commandment would be violated, and he therefore concludes his opinion: "If one makes it a practice to act frivolously, he does so because of the necessity of elevating [the community]. . . ."[128] The *responsum* of Bacharach acknowledges the extent to which music had become a part of the marriage celebration.

As she describes the festivity that took place during the

marriage of Ẓipporah, her eldest child, Glikl of Hameln mentions that the ceremonies concluded with the "Dance of the Dead," also called the "Dance of Death."[129] According to Grimm, this humorous allegorical dance possibly originated in France, prior to the 15th century, where it was called *la danse macabre.*[130] The "Dance of the Dead" had developed out of a choral dance of the 14th century that was staged during the Black Death to check the scourge of the plague. The dance symbolized man's courage to live and his victory over evil spirits, disease, and death.[131] An eye-witness account of the 15th century describes how the *todtentanz* was staged at a wedding celebration in Tangermünde, about 150 miles northeast of the town of Hameln. Lots were cast to select the man who would portray Death. The dance began with joyous music, with the couples dancing excitedly. The music then stopped, and the dancer, representing Death, made his appearance. While he was accompanied by the plaintive melody of a dirge, he fell to the ground, as though he were dead. The mournful music continued, young women appeared, encircled the "dead" man and kissed him. When the last woman had kissed him, he "came back to life", quickly arose, and the dance of merriment resumed.[132] A gay mood then prevailed.

After the dance became known in Germany, it was introduced at Jewish festivities.[133] Shlomo Rubin relates that he had attended services on *Shemini 'Aẓeret,* the eighth day of the festival of *Sukkot*, when he was in the city of Ostrog, Volhynia, Russia-Poland, in 1863. While the cantor was chanting "the priestly benediction" (Num. 6:24-27) during the *musaf* service, Rubin heard "a strange melody," which, as he describes, "had cut through the insides and blasted the ear. The priests responded after him [the cantor] in a tone of lamentation, which sounded like owls hooting . . . in desert country."[134] When Rubin made inquiry about the weird, "screaming" music, the cantor told him that it was the melody of "the Dance of Death, which was familiar in the city," but no one was able to explain the source of the tune.[135]

Marriage

In communal records and minute books, in the homily and *musar*, conduct at marriage festivities was sharply criticized. The regulation of the town of Runkel, in Hesse-Cassel, in the 18th century, states that "the observation has been made that during wedding celebrations men, both young and old, danced with strange women, and young men and women slept in the same room overnight."[136] And in the course of a sermon for the Ten Days of Repentance, Ezekiel Landau enumerates the "evils" that he had seen in the Prague community, and thereupon condemns the behavior of individuals at weddings. He refers specifically to young men and women dancing together. Behavior of this kind, he warns, will arouse "the desire to sin" and can only lead to disastrous consequences.[137] The rabbis frowned upon such sociability, but they would allow both sexes to dance together only if they were related; a father and daughter, a husband and wife, a brother and sister, could dance with each other.[138]

Conduct at weddings was not always orderly. Steps were taken by the Bamberg community to prevent the outbreak of quarrels and disturbances caused by excessive drinking.[139] The Bamberg communal Minute Book of 1698 speaks of "a great evil . . . of drunkenness" at weddings that "disrupted the joy of the occasion."[140] A procedure was introduced to help establish decorum; the best man would serve "candy at the beginning of the meal between the meat and fish dishes, while the guests were still sober."[141] No doubt the candy was intended to divert the guests from excessive drinking. In his didactic songs, Kirchan criticizes the rowdy conduct at weddings. "While it is an honor to make the bride and groom happy," Kirchan states, "it does not require us to sing and be noisy as though dogs were barking. Nor is it necessary to indulge oneself with overeating and over-drinking."[142] He comments further: "The behavior at weddings does not deserve mention. Words of learning are seldom heard. . . . Whenever a scholar speaks, whether in a profound or popular vein, devilish conduct takes place. . . . Frequently, . . . the voices of women and girls sound like a horn. They never permit a discourse [sermon] to continue, and force the speaker to stop before he finishes his subject. . . . As soon as the discourse ends, boisterous singing and romping resumes. . . . They clap their hands, stomp their feet, and jump on the table."[143] While Kirchan may have been exaggerating in some of his details, his account of wedding festivities was no doubt based on his own observations, in the same way as he described the characteristics of German-Jewish folk life, in small towns particularly, from first-hand experience.[144]

3. Death and Burial

Since popular attitudes concerning death and burial are also expressed through custom and communal legislation, the burial practices of German Jewry can be considered another aspect of their folk life.[145] Schudt, who caustically calls Jewish customs "oddities," has emphasized that the burial of the dead was the concern of the entire Jewish community. Immediate burial was always possible, he proceeds to explain, since the funeral service did not demand elaborate, costly preparation. Such simple demands enabled all persons to be present at a funeral.

> . . . Expensive mourning clothes, elegant coffins, lengthy eulogies for the dead, were not required. Those attending wore their every-day clothes. In addition, the men had a black cloth or hood [i.e., the mourner's cowl] on their heads. The women wore a black cloth on their heads and engaged in loud crying.[146]

It has already been mentioned that the burial customs of an earlier period had an influence on the social pattern of the community. Such observances did not terminate when the inner life of the community was disrupted by a pogrom or expulsion. Inasmuch as burial customs could be carried out by each person and his family, they did not depend solely on communal organization for their continuity. This is illustrated by the practice prevalent among German Jews in the 18th century that whenever there was a death in a home they would pour out all water that remained in vessels. The custom was an old one; it was based on the belief that "the Angel of Death" might have "cleaned his knife" and "left a drop of blood of the deceased in the water," and whoever drank the water would die.[147] Or, when a death occurred in the Frankfort community, a hand towel (*handzwehle*, *handtuch*) was hung on the door of the house of the deceased.[148] Everyone was thus silently informed of the death. Since ancient times a death has been announced not verbally but by means of a gesture or sign.[149]

In his Ethical Will, Naphtali Cohen leaves instructions to his family concerning the arrangements for his burial, and from his specifications of the manner in which they should proceed, the social characteristics of the funeral service can be derived in outline. At his deathbed, so he admonishes, the Holy Society is to summon a *minyan*, the required number of ten men for a congregational service.[150] Cohen recommends excommunication for any individual who will deliberately absent himself and fail to cooperate in forming the *minyan*. The *ḥerem*, or excommunication, was a form of punishment that could be employed if people did not abide by the norms of communal life, and that such a penalty is designated so pointedly would imply that negligence in attending services was not uncommon.[151] Inasmuch as Jewish social life was not a voluntary form of association, its cohesiveness was strengthened through such controls.

The community is responsible for the dead even as it is for the living; hence, the members of the Holy Society have the obligation to prepare the deceased for burial. They remove the body from the bed, place it on the floor, wash and clean it, make the coffin, sew the burial shrouds, accompany the departed to the cemetery, lower and cover the coffin in the grave.[152] After the bereaved family returns home from the cemetery, they are served the "meal of comfort," *se'udat habra'ah*, which is prepared by relatives or friends.[153] It has been a long-established practice that the mourner does not prepare the first meal when he comes home from the burial service.[154] The "consolation meal" is another example of an observance that had no geographical limits, for in addition to Germanic lands, the meal would be provided to mourners in various European and Oriental communities.[155]

The autobiography of Hahn describes the social circumstances that influenced the establishment of a Holy Society in Frankfort, called *Gomle Ḥasadim Ṭobim,* "Men Who Do Kind Deeds." He had taken the initiative of organizing the group because "many of the dead had not been buried" and "the religious duty of burying the dead had been neglected." It was not always possible to find someone to assist with the burial arrangements, especially before the Sabbath or a holiday, since a significant number of persons would be absent from their homes to attend the regional fair.[156] And those who were involved in making preparations for the funeral did not always know what Jewish tradition requires of them. Therefore, in the spirit of *musar*, which stressed the importance of ethical behavior and was critical of individual and social conduct, Hahn complains of the prevailing low cultural level.[157] He explains the need for a Holy Society, so that a group of responsible and competent men will be on hand at all times to arrange and carry through burial rites.[158]

Inasmuch as some form of study is usually engaged in when a death occurs, Naphtali Cohen makes the request that after he has passed away, ten or more men should form a circle around his body, as it is stretched out on the ground, and engage in studying verses of the Mishnah and in reciting Psalms, the first letters of which when read in sequence will spell his name.[159] Ezekiel Katzenellenbogen of Altona (d.1749) expresses the wish that at his deathbed learned men should surround him, study the Mishnah and recite Psalms.[160] Cohen also asks that during the mourning periods of *shib'ah* comprising seven days, and *sheloshim*, thirty days, he should be honored by having a group of scholars study Mishnah after services on weekdays, the Sabbath, and holidays. The entire Book of Psalms was to be completed within the week of *shib'ah,* and after the thirty-day mourning period, Cohen requests that the Mishnah and *Zohar* be studied each day and covered in their entirety. When the month of mourning has passed, the men who continue to study are to be compensated for their service.[161] Through their study his restless, wandering soul will find peace.[162] The belief was current that upon death the soul departs from the body and roams about, and the living have an obligation to aid it to secure anchorage. The proper form of burial, the practice of charity, prayer and study, are considered effective in enabling the soul to obtain rest. The soul, however, will haunt the living if they fail to provide suitable burial grounds or neglect to remember the deceased.[163] In recalling how the grave of her sister had been robbed, Glikl relates that the apparition of the dead woman appeared in a dream to inform the living that the shrouds were removed and that new ones should be made. The soul of her sister could not rest peacefully in the grave until shrouds again covered the body.[164]

Some burial customs were of local origin and setting, and since they varied, each practice will be cited or described separately so as to present different types of folk observance. In Frankfort, the body would be removed from the home just three hours before the funeral in order "to be certain that the deceased had no life."[165] Not everyone was buried in a coffin, and, according to a Frankfort tradition, a coffin was only required for a priest or a woman who died in childbirth. Hahn had heard that in Poland, on the other hand, the priest would be buried without even having as much as a board placed under his back.[166] "When my body will be lowered in the grave," Sheftel (Sabbatai) Horowitz states, "let seven upright men, who have studied with me, recite seven times verse seventeen of chapter ninety in the Psalms."[167] Naphtali Cohen and Ezekiel Katzenellenbogen, in their Ethical

Wills, had asked that holes be bored in their coffins so as to make it possible for "the flesh to decompose quickly."[168] Also, in the Worms community, Hahn relates, "When the women come to the cemetery to attend a burial service," it is the custom for "the men to turn their faces toward the side of the wall."[169]

Cohen requests further that during the year of mourning lighted candles should be placed on the seat that he occupied in the synagogue; and if necessary, a fee should be paid for the use of the seat. He suggests that the candles be placed near the *ner tamid*, the "perpetual light" of the ark, if the seat cannot be available. For the first thirty days of mourning the candles are to be lit in the home and in the synagogue, and thereafter only in the synagogue during the *yortsayt*, the annual observance of his passing.[170] There are those, Kosman states, who are of the opinion that after *shib'ah*, the seven days of mourning, a candle should continue to burn in the synagogue, and he explains that he has not been able to find the basis for such an observance in any of the sources, such as *Yosif 'Omeẓ*.[171] It was a regulation in Fürth that the *ḳaddish* prayer is to be recited by the mourner in the synagogue that he regularly attends. If a stranger found himself in the community, he would be assigned to a synagogue where he could say the *ḳaddish*. Each mourner recited the *ḳaddish* separately, and the order was determined by casting lots.[172]

Before passing away, a man of Amsterdam expressed the wish that ten men should gather daily in his home for study during the year of mourning. Since he had no sons, he left instructions for his daughter to recite the *ḳaddish* daily in his memory after the *minyan* completed the study session. This incident had been "widely publicized," Bacharach comments, as it is unusual that a daughter, and not a son, should say the *ḳaddish*.[173] The authorities and communal leaders claimed that there is no reason to declare her act invalid, for, as they stated: "A woman can also devote herself to *ḳiddush ha-Shem,* the sanctification of God's name, [and] a daughter can also be a source of comfort to the deceased because she was his offspring." It was made clear, nevertheless, that the community would designate a *minyan* of ten men to recite regularly the *ḳaddish* prayer in place of the male child as required by tradition.[174] When this innovation was brought to the attention of Bacharach for his opinion, he maintained that "it is necessary to be cautious [in introducing] such a procedure, as it can weaken the vitality of Jewish customs which are also part of the Torah." Bacharach states further that changes of this kind in religious practice might serve as a precedent whereby each person will consider himself an authority in determining what are valid methods of observance, and feel qualified "to build his own *bimah*, pulpit." The *minhagim*, customs of Israel, are derived from the Torah, Bacharach emphasizes, and, therefore, should be interpreted within the frame of reference of law, *halakhah*, not outside of it, according to Yeb. 36b.[175] While the basis for the pattern of the social life of the community was the Torah, nevertheless, not all customs were derived logically and rationally from halakhic principles. Some practices had developed irrationally; they were founded on human need, motivated by fear and insecurity, or influenced by the non-Jewish general environment.[176] In other words, along with the religious tradition, cultural factors had an influence on both the development and the forms of expression of German-Jewish folk life.

The book of *Minhagim* of Fürth had also prescribed the type of clothing the mourner should wear. The mourning attire, as it was explained, did not modify in any significant way the garments that were regularly worn. Such communal practice no doubt took into consideration that economic hardships would be imposed if the mourner's garments should be different from the clothes used daily. The local regulation states further that a widow in mourning should wear a black garment for thirty days and a white garment thereafter.[177] When mourning for her father or mother, she could wear her week-day clothes, except on *Rosh ha-Shanah* and *Yom Kippur* when she wore a *kitl,* smock, over her mourning garments.

Immediately after *haliẓah,* the ceremony by which she overtly rejected marriage to the brother of her deceased husband if there are no children, or after marriage during the year of mourning, she no longer wore the clothes of a widow.[178] When a man mourned for a parent, he wore the collar (*kragn,* Yid.; *kragen,* Ger.) around the neck on the Sabbath and festivals, but he dressed in everyday apparel on the intervening days of festivals. On *Rosh ha-Shanah* and *Yom Kippur* he wore a *kitl,* frock, the week-day cloak, and a hat.

The deeds of martyrs, scholars, and leaders were recalled at memorial services, and in the commemoration of the deceased, local customs arose. Conscious of its history, the German-Jewish community established a link between the past and present by

Fig. 6. Jewish Cemetery in Fürth, 18th Century *(Courtesy, Widener Library, Harvard University).* From Liebe, *Judentum,* p. 103, plate # 83; originally, an engraving in the Germanische Museum, Nuremberg, 18th century.

means of customs that honored the self-sacrifice and idealism of the departed.[180] After the First Crusade, in 1096, it became the practice to schedule services on the Sabbath preceding *Shabu'ot* and the Ninth of *'Ab. Yizkor,* the memorial service, was held before *Shabu'ot* so as to remember the season of the year when the persecution of the Crusades had begun, during which time mainly the communities on the Rhine, Worms, Cologne, and Mayence, were affected.[181] Thereafter, in the Middle Ages, when there was a communal catastrophe, martyrs would be commemorated in the local *memor*-book.[182] Local customs varied in honoring the deeds of martyrs; in the *memor*-books of Rhenish communities, for instance, all of the martyrs were mentioned as a single group, that is, as "the souls of the martyrs," whereas in other areas the "names of individual martyrs" would be specified.[183] Later, the names of persons who distinguished themselves for their devoted labors in the interest of the community were added to the memorial list of martyrs.[184] The *memor*-book reflected the period of stability and growth of German-Jewish communities following the Thirty Years' War.[185] The men and women honored were not only martyrs, but scholars, teachers, lovers of learning, authors, judges, and those who had contributed to the well-being of the community through acts of benevolence, such as, "aiding the poor," "befriending the stranger," and "caring for the sick". Thereby, individuals of a community were remembered for their virtues of kindness and humility.[186] The lay communal leader (*kotsn*, Yid.; *ḳaẓin*, Heb.: "a prominent man") was among those honored in the *memor*-book of the 17th and 18th centuries, and as a benefactor and "man of affairs" he wielded influence, enjoyed prestige and status like his counterpart in the larger community.[187]

The belief that the dead can intervene in behalf of the living also had an influence on the customs of German Jewry. Before *Rosh ha-Shanah* and *Yom Kippur* the graves of dear ones were visited in the cemetery,[188] and implicit in the practice is the appeal to the dead to induce a favorable heavenly decree for the new year.

Prayers were directed to the departed to act as other-worldly mediators by interceding in behalf of surviving relatives.[189] As an example, Isaiah Horowitz, the cabalistic and legal authority, gives a description of the folk practice of "encircling the grounds of the cemetery" on *Rosh ha-Shanah* and *Yom Kippur*.[190] In Eastern Europe before the holiday of *Rosh ha-Shanah*, three women would "measure the field [i.e., the grounds]" of the cemetery at the time when graves were visited. The act of "measuring the field" would symbolize the "transfer" of ownership of the cemetery grounds to living relatives who thereupon acquired the authority to instruct or direct the dead to aid them. After the specific graves were "measured," the deceased could be approached with appeals from the living.[191]

On Monday of the week of *sidrah Shemot*, when the Book of Exodus was begun as the portion of the Torah reading, the Holy Society of *Gemilut Ḥasadim* in Frankfort would visit the cemetery. Declared a *ta'anit ẓibbur*, the day was spent in fasting and in reciting penitential prayers. At the cemetery (*bet 'olamin,* "eternal house"), the preacher, *maggid*, of the *Ḥebra'*, or the head of the court, *bet din,* "would ask forgiveness from the dead [lit., 'those who dwell in the dust,' *shokhebe 'afar: sic;* cf. Is. 26:19] on behalf of all families [of the members] of the Society."[119]

In time of illness graves would also be visited. Isaiah Horowitz cites the instance of a woman walking around the cemetery grounds when her son became ill.[193] In the cemetery *teḥinot*, supplicatory prayers, would be recited and charity would be given for the poor, this being regarded as an efficacious act for both the living and the dead. The reciting of *teḥinot* and the giving of charity when one goes to a cemetery received enthusiastic encouragement from the Maharshal (Solomon Luria; d. 1573, Lublin), reputed Talmudic authority.[194] During a crisis such as the Frankfort fire of 1711, and the expulsion from Prague on March 31,1743, the Jewish residents fled to the cemetery, imploring the deceased to protect them.[195] Or even when one was perplexed and needed advice, he went to his parents' grave to seek their counsel.[196]

The validity of the custom of visiting graves had already been questioned by R. Meir of Rothenburg (d. 1293) when he urged that "the people pray directly to God as did Abraham." Only "a dog lies on a grave," he stated, and instead of praying to the dead, he wanted "each person to give as much *ẓedaḳah*, charity, as he can afford," for it is "through a practice such as *ẓedaḳah* that he will be saved when he cries out."[197] Apparently, the folk practice was not shaken by the critical viewpoint of this renowned scholar, but continued through the centuries.

In the main we shall observe that scholars and rabbis did not always challenge popular views and customs, and while intellectually opposed to the use of "magic," it would seem that they did not object to those practices considered effective in aiding man to overcome difficulties or problems that continually threatened his well-being.[198] In this context a custom is mainly a "technique" to control that part of the natural world menacing the security and happiness of the individual, his family, and the community.[199]

We attempted to show that local customs associated with the "crises of life" have their own background and motivation. The practices are culturally distinctive either as an informal development or the innovation of a communal decree. While they are part of communal life, there is no implication that a relationship always exists between the different practices. Moreover, a custom could have had an influence on a specific region but not necessarily on other areas. Since social life has its more subtle, as well as its obvious manifestations, more than an observing eye is needed to understand and explain the conflicting relationships between the values and ideals of a group and the daily practices of individuals.

CHAPTER III

Education: Individual and Communal

In the education of an individual an old precedent was followed: On the one hand, each parent was responsible for the child's schooling, and, on the other, the *kehillah*, community, established schools for all children and provided assistance whenever a family was too poor to engage a teacher and cover the cost of educating a child.[1] The importance placed on maintaining a school shows that education was basic to Jewish society at the close of the Middle Ages, preceding Emancipation, just as it had been through the centuries since Talmudic times. The concern for education stemmed from an ancient tradition that consistently stressed that communal life is never complete without a school.

In their portrayal of education, the authors consulted dealt with a diversified range of topics, such as, folk customs and regional practices, maintenance of schools, financial aid for needy students, teaching methods and content of curricula. And they showed sensitivity to the trends of the time; for as cultural life began to decline in the 17th and 18th centuries, individual teachers and leaders expressed concern over the lack of awareness of the new life conditions that were weakening the effectiveness and influence of education.[2]

1. Rearing a Child

Though the parents and the school are jointly regarded as being responsible for the education and development of the child, his first teacher and guide before he begins school is his parent.[3]

Sabbatai Horowitz, in his ethical writing, not only restates the ancient rabbinic dictum regarding each parent's responsibility for teaching his son and grandson, but expresses his own gratitude for the parental influence of his mother who, at personal sacrifice, consistently encouraged her household to be devoted to study.

> It is proper that I praise my mother, my teacher, my first instructor. . . . Truly she ate the bitter with the sweet [lit., the profane with the clean], for her hand always aided my father, my master, in that she distributed liberally the money that she acquired from her father, so that the material needs of the students of the Torah would be supplied.[4]

In its advice to women on how they should conduct themselves, the *Brandshpigl* says that the mother has as one of her duties to foster the love of learning in her child. She should "prevail upon her children to study Torah from the time they are young" and encourage their education by "taking them to the rabbi" who will be their teacher. As she rears and "watches over her children," she influences them by "speaking kind words and arousing in their hearts the desire for learning. . . ."[5] The mother, in addition, should urge her husband to study by placing a book on the table when he finishes the Friday evening meal.[6] Hahn also advises that the mother accompany her children to school so that her husband does not have to be disturbed and can remain at home and read.[7] At times the mother became the breadwinner of the family in order to enable her husband to devote all of his time to study.[8]

Devoting a chapter to the education and training of children in his book on customs in Frankfort, Hahn describes the role of the parent as teacher:

> A positive commandment is fulfilled when a father teaches Torah to his son or grandson, or engages a teacher. Do not consider as trivial what the sages of blessed memory would

say, 'When one teaches his son Torah, it is as if he has received the Torah from Mt. Sinai.'[9]

To the child, the father can be both parent and teacher, as Jacob Emden acknowledges in his autobiographical comment.

> . . . When I was a child [I was] carried in the arms of my father, my master [teacher] of blessed memory. . . . With fulness of speech, he would say, 'May you merit, my son, to become learned in the Torah, to write books and words of wisdom.'[10]

Hahn proceeds to outline what the parent should first teach his child. "As soon as the child begins to speak," so he states, "teach him, 'Moses commanded us a law, an inheritance of the congregation of Jacob (Deut. 33:4),' and the first verse in the recitation of the *Shema*' (Deut. 6:4)." He advises further, "Let the children say the *Shema*' as they dry their hands, and later he [the father] can teach them some of the verses (Deut. 6:5 ff.) by heart."[11] When the child becomes three years of age, the parent is expected to teach him how to read the Hebrew alphabet.[12] To teach the child how to read, Hahn favors, first of all, that the parent acquaint the child with the Hebrew letters, or consonants. When the child knows the alphabet thoroughly, he can then be taught the vowels, but he does not begin to "combine the consonants [i.e., read unvocalized text] until he reads fluently the letters with vowels." And Hahn has observed that there are "many splendid wholesome individuals with understanding [i.e., they have a good education] who do not know how to pronounce words accurately," and this he attributes to a bad method of teaching, namely, that "in their youth they did not develop the practice of reading with precision."[13]

The father is also responsible for teaching his son how to recite the benedictions before and after the meal, and to make the task easier, the suggestion is given that the "grace after the meal" be divided into four or five sections, the child learning a portion at a time until he can recite the entire prayer.[14] As part of his education, the child should also be involved in various communal functions, since he can learn by doing as he joins his father when he attends a wedding ceremony, visits the sick, or accompanies the dead to the grave.[15] A boy and girl are to be trained to fast when they become, respectively, twelve and eleven years of age. The boy commences by observing the fast on *Yom Kippur*, the Day of Atonement, while the girl first fasts on *Ta'anit 'Ester,* the Fast of Esther, the day preceding *Purim.*[16]

With considerable insight an appeal is made to parents to understand the temperament and ability of their children and to refrain from making unreasonable demands on them. Parents are warned not to dominate the child by the use of fear or physical punishment.

> 'Train a child in the way he should go, And even when he is old, he will not depart from it (Prov. 22:6).' ... Therefore do not allow excessive fear to be imposed, especially in the case of small children who are very tender-hearted. One should be aware, if the demand [lit., yoke] is severe, the child will become distraught [lit., run in all directions], and there is the possibility that [out of anguish] he may commit suicide. ... The parent should have an understanding of the disposition of his children, and in resorting to verbal or physical punishment, he should deal with them according to the level of their development. ... [17]

Instead of being harsh and strict with his child, let the parent be cheerful, patient, and understanding.

> If you see that your son is stupid, do not ask, 'Of what value is the instruction?' Instead say, 'If I teach him, there is still hope for him through study and ethical instruction.' If he is not able to understand very much of the Torah, let him

> at least study how to read the Torah and recite the liturgy [lit., pray]. At any rate, he [the parent] should strive to teach him [the child] the Scriptures, Mishnah, Talmud. Perhaps he will understand, but you must not despair over his studies until you have done everything that you possibly can in his behalf.[18]

Sabbatai Horowitz likewise advises parents that "they further the education of the child according to his ability."[19] In contrast, the Worms book of customs declares that a child is to be punished whenever he is indolent or fails to understand what is taught, and it lists different methods of punishment used, such as making the child wear a dunce cap, smearing his face with black paint, standing him against the wall, or giving him a physical beating.[20]

The child begins school at the age of five, with the exception of Berlin and Hungary where he starts at three years.[21] The day on which he first attends school—after *Pesaḥ* or *Sukkot* when each semester opens—is a special event. As on any festive occasion, the child is washed and then dressed in clean clothes,[22] and, in accordance with an old custom,[23] the parent escorts him to school on that morning.[24] Upon the child's arrival at school, the teacher places him on his lap, and for the first lesson he recites the Hebrew alphabet in regular and then reversed order—from *alef* to *tav* and from *tav* to *alef*.[25] After he pronounces the letters of the alphabet, the teacher recites to him, "Moses commanded us a law . . . ," and then the first verse of the Book of Leviticus. When both verses have been repeated, the teacher smears honey on the letters of the page, to be licked by the child. Then the father takes the child home.[26] On the way to and from school, the parent covers the child with his garment to protect him from "seeing anything unclean."[27]

After the first lesson, the child might receive a cookie and a hard boiled egg, on which words from Isaiah (50:4-5), Ezekiel (3:3)[28] or the Psalms (chap. 119) are written.[29] But before he eats, the inscription on the food is read to him, each word being considered part of a formula to safeguard the child entering school.[30]

On the day their child starts school, parents are advised to pray and fast, and in the evening they should arrange a festive meal to which they invite the poor. They are also encouraged to give charity according to their ability; for the charitable act will be efficacious in protecting the child against calamity and in assuring his well-being.[31]

At the age of five the child begins to read the Book of Leviticus as his first Hebrew text.[32] This is the same book from which his elders read to him during his circumcision ceremony and afterwards placed under his head, hoping thereby that he would be influenced to devote his life to study.[33] And even before he was born, his mother expressed the wish that he be a learned man. She prayed regularly from *'Emeḳ Berakhah*, a popular guide for daily ritual observance, that each of her sons should become a scholar.[34]

The homilies of the Midrash offer two explanations why a boy starts to study Leviticus rather than Genesis, the first book of the Bible. Leviticus, to begin with, is devoted to the subject of sacrifices, and inasmuch as "young children are pure and the sacrifices are pure," it follows that "the pure should engage in study about the pure."[35] Further importance is ascribed to the Book of Leviticus as "the body of the Torah," containing the principal laws that should be known and observed.[36]

That the child has to be encouraged to go to school is recognized; hence there are incentives to interest children of different ages in study: "Little children should be persuaded by giving them what they like, saying to them: Here are honey, roasted grain, and nuts for yourself, if you will go to school and study." When the child becomes older, and requires a new incentive, "the father should say that he will buy him nice clothes" if he studies diligently. Later, the child will be urged to study so that he may become, first, a "worthy pupil," then a "senior student," *baḥur;* a "wise man," *ḥakham;* or the head of the court, the leader in the community, and, finally, attain that understanding when one studies "for its own sake," with no thought of receiving a reward.[37]

2. The Daily School Schedule

Though most of our information about the schedule of the school is in the diary of Yuspa Shammash, most probably the daily class procedure was similar in other communities. During the winter months, the child rises one or two hours before daybreak and then proceeds to school, held in the teacher's home. He is in class until it is time for the morning prayers, and after services, when there is a recess, he goes home for a snack. At the "fifth hour," or eleven o'clock, the pupil has another recess, lasting an hour, during which time he returns home for his noonday meal. A short afternoon break takes place at three o'clock, the "ninth hour," so that again he can go home to eat and refresh himself. Following the recess, he remains in school until evening, attends services, and returns home. In the summer months he awakens in the early morning and after the morning prayers goes to school. On Saturday afternoons the pupils attend a class in the teacher's home to study the *sidrah,* the Torah portion of the week.[38] Every parent is urged to "study with his children, before and after the [evening] meal until they retire."[39] Once a pupil was enrolled in the elementary school the parents' responsibility for his education did not cease. Incidentally, we do not hear of parents shunning the intellectual discipline required of the child in school, as well as at home, because it is too rigorous and demanding. Rather, the children were expected to busy themselves in study, as they thereby fulfilled "a religious duty." To have the youth or adults engage in study was considered normal behavior, not anything unusual or out of the ordinary.

Since the child attended class from morning until evening,

the *ḥeder*, or elementary school,[40] had considerable influence on his most formative years from the age of five to thirteen. Based on a teaching in the Mishnah ('Abot 5:24), a schedule was proposed whereby the pupil would study the Bible at five years of age, the Mishnah at ten, and the Gemara when he reached fifteen. The Maharal (R. Judah Löw of Prague, d. 1609) and his associates considered this to be an ideal way of educating an individual.[41] A similar plan of study was favored by later scholars and teachers, like Lentshits, Bacharach, and Isaiah Horowitz, who stressed the importance of the three stages or levels of study in educating a child.[42] Some teachers would cover the entire Bible—the Pentateuch, Prophets, and Hagiographa—with their students before commencing to teach the Mishnah; and until they had gone through the Mishnah together, they would not proceed with the study of the Talmud.[43] The three steps in the education of a young person was applied as a study program for adults, with one third of each year devoted to the study of the Bible, another third to the Mishnah, and the remainder of the time to the Talmud.[44] By dividing the year into three parts for the purpose of study, the ancient rabbinic teaching, that each day be given over to the Bible, Mishnah, and Talmud could be realized. Talmudic sages proposed that every man "divide his years into thirds" in order to "read the Scriptures," "study the Mishnah," and "discuss the Talmud"; however, since no man knows what his life-span will be, "time" has been reduced to specific "days."[45]

3. A Young Person's Education

Great concern was expressed that there should be no illiteracy anywhere, and through the desire to carry out the Talmudic policy of compulsory education (B. Bat. 21a) all children were required to attend school at least until the age of thirteen.[46] In some cases the child was expected to go to school until fourteen years of age, as in Hesse, and even until fifteen, as in Pressburg.[47] Since education was not regarded as a privilege for the few, the community almost instinctively felt its responsibility in making it possible for every child to secure an education. When a father could not fulfill the obligation of supporting his son while he attended school, he would receive financial aid from the communal fund.[48] Or, when a child became an orphan, he did not have to stop his studies, since the community aided him to continue school until the age of thirteen when he reached his majority.[49] In time of any emergency or need, provisions were made in each locality to enable poor children to go to school.[50]

The father was also encouraged, and financially assisted if need be, to send his son to a larger town to study at a *yeshibah*, Talmudic Academy. If the boy should not be adept in his studies, he was not to be withdrawn from school before he became thirteen that he might learn a trade or engage in a business enterprise. And if his education was meager, he could later become an informed and intelligent person by acquiring a knowledge of the fundamental "laws and customs of Judaism," under the guidance of teachers, from anyone of the popular guide books that were available in the vernacular.[51]

The educational idea, however, was not always realized;[52] for example, in Hungary, because of greater poverty, fewer students could continue to go to school,[53] whereas in Frankfort, where economic conditions were more favorable, a larger percentage of young people were able to study even after they were married:

> In particular, here [in Frankfort] wealthy individuals marry off their sons when they are about fourteen or fifteen years of age. It is fitting that the father engage a teacher for his son even after marriage. . . . They [the sons] are supported financially for several years by their parents and in-laws. . . .[54]

Since the groom was relieved of the responsibility of earning a livelihood after his marriage, he was free to devote his time mainly to study.

Among the customs relating to festivals and special events, we have already discerned the close ties that existed between the community and the school;[55] and this is made further evident in that when holidays and festivities occurred the schools were dismissed to allow the children to participate in the same social life as the adults. There were occasions, however, as on *Purim,* when students held their own celebrations.[56] That a class was discharged so that students could attend wedding and circumcision festivities,[57] signifies that the school felt itself to belong also to the world outside of the classroom.

4. THE "BAR MIẒVAH"

When a boy becomes thirteen years of age, he reaches his religious and legal majority, and is inducted into the adult community through the ceremony of *Bar Miẓvah,* meaning "Son of Commandment" or "Son of Duty."[58] The *Bar Miẓvah* marks his "coming of age,"[59] when he is treated as an adult.[60] The period between childhood and manhood had not been prolonged in the medieval Jewish community, nor was a distinction made between younger and older persons. After the age of thirteen all males had the same responsibilities and enjoyed equal privileges in society.[61]

We have no single authentic explanation for the custom of *Bar Miẓvah,* since there is no agreement among authorities as to its possible origin and development. The *Bar Miẓvah,* Löw estimates, was instituted in the Middle Ages, during the 14th century.[62] An opposite view comes from Kaufmann Kohler, who claims that the *Bar Miẓvah* is of Mishnaic background, originating around the 2d century C.E.[63] But in the opinion of Solomon Schechter the *Bar Miẓvah* is not an ancient custom; importance was ascribed to the thirteenth year as it is the time of puberty.[64] For Isaac Rivkind, the *Bar Miẓvah* is a synagogue ceremony in recognition of the boy who has reached the age of thirteen. The ritual has two features, namely, the boy is called to the Torah, and the father recites the prayer thanking God for releasing him of all responsibility for the conduct of his son. The earliest evidence for the *Bar Miẓvah* observance, according to Rivkind, is during the 8th century in the Geonic period.[65] Of these explanations, Rivkind's seems the most plausible in that he considers the *Bar Miẓvah* in the specific cultural terms of a religious observance.[66] His date for the origin of *Bar Miẓvah* is based on the oldest known source that refers to this ritual.

On the first Saturday after the boy's thirteenth birthday the *Bar Miẓvah* ceremony is scheduled, thereby fulfilling the requirement that he be "thirteen years and one day old." If a boy became thirteen on a Sabbath, the regulation specifies that the *Bar Miẓvah* be not held on that very day.[67] It so happened, as Yuspa Shammash tells of himself, that his thirteenth birthday, which was on the 13th of Adar (1), 5377 A.M. (Anno Mundi; 1617 C.E.), fell on a Sabbath. He took it for granted, however, that for his *Bar Miẓvah* the Torah portion would be *Teẓaveh* (Ex. 27:20 - 30:10), which was read in synagogues on that Sabbath. After he had studied this Torah section, rabbinical authorities informed him that he had to read from *Ki Tissa* (Ex. 30:11 - 34:35), the *sidrah* of the following week, for he would then be past thirteen.[68]

The *Bar Miẓvah* boy participates in the Saturday morning service in the synagogue, renders as much of the liturgy as he is capable, and "if his voice is pleasant and he is qualified, he conducts the entire service." Unless he is able, he is not expected to conduct any part of the service; only one requirement is made of him, namely, that he read out of the Torah.[69] In the Hamburg-Altona communal regulation of 1726, it states that the boy had to receive authorization from the cantor to read from the Torah, and that approval would be granted only after the cantor had tested him and found that he could chant according to the cantillation marks of the text. When the cantor taught the boy how to read from the Torah, he received five marks as remuneration for the instruction.[70]

The *Bar Miẓvah* boy is "the Levi," that is, "the second one" called upon to read from the Torah, and for "the honor," he "pledges to donate a liter of wax oil for the [synagogue] light."[71] When the boy finishes reading from the Torah, "the father walks up to the *almemer* (*almemor,* 'reading desk'), places his hands on his son's head and says the customary benediction, expressing thanks to God for enabling his son to attain the age of religious majority."[72]

On that Saturday afternoon the festivity continues with the *Bar Miẓvah* meal,[73] considered to be on a par with the marriage feast. Parents were asked to celebrate the *Bar Miẓvah* just as they would their child's wedding.[74] One hour before *minḥah*, the afternoon service, the guests for the meal are personally invited by the *Bar Miẓvah* youth, "dressed in the new garments" worn at the morning services. At the meal he delivers an appropriate discourse, *derashah*, and he concludes the celebration by reciting "grace after the meal" with the group.[75]

Some of the features of the *Bar Miẓvah* celebration can also be gleaned from one of Bachrach's *responsa* in which he tells of being invited to a *Bar Miẓvah* ceremony in Wandsbek by "a man of learning who studied, taught, and ministered to many scholars." The *Bar Miẓvah* was held for an only son during the Sabbath of *Be-Shallaḥ*. Bacharach could not attend, but he sent a gift. In his acknowledgment to Bacharach, the father pictures the *Bar Miẓvah* as a distinctive occasion, made so by the personalities in attendance and by the address of his son.

> The leaders of the community were there. . . . [They] attended the celebration, not one of them remaining at home. . . . He [the son] was well-groomed for the Torah, and delivered a very enjoyable sermon during the meal.[76]

Replying to the father, Bacharach alludes to the type of education the young man probably received in preparation for the *Bar Miẓvah:* "Since you inform me that he [the son] delivered such a fine discourse, I surmise that he had studied . . . *'agadah* [the *exempla* and lore of rabbinic tradition], such as, *Midrash Rabbah* [homilies on the Bible], the beauty of *'En Ya'aḳob* [tales of the Babylonian Talmud, compiled by Jacob ibn Ḥabib, d. 1516], which are indeed popular among youth like an appetizer before the meal. . . ."[77] It can be assumed that by the time a boy became thirteen he had read rather widely in popular rabbinic texts, and had become acquainted with the aphorisms, tales, and lore regularly used in daily speech and correspondence. He spoke in the idiom of the adult, and by knowing the adult's language, he felt more at ease in being an adult and moving into the adult world.

5. Attending School Away from Home

When a community was small, with limited cultural opportunities, the student attended a school in another town. He either lived with a relative, or arrangements were made for him to room and board in the home of the rabbi or teacher.[78] The local community determined the amount of remuneration that was due a teacher for providing food and lodging to a student.[79] In their dealings, teachers were not always scrupulous, and there were times when they resorted to devious methods to obtain an additional fee from parents, or they neglected the child who required care and supervision away from his own home.[80] Commenting on his own experience as a child, the anonymous autobiographer of the 17th century bewails that he was sent to live with a teacher in Prague. He says that "in his [i.e., the father's] endeavor to save money he placed me for a small sum in charge of a teacher, who took little care of me, while I needed great attention if I were to be taught with any success."[81] The food proved to be harmful, as he had ulcers, and when he became ill he had to shift for himself. He recalls with regret that "nobody looked out for me to give me medical treatment."[82]

School Away from Home

After completing the *ḥeder*, the student continued his education by attending a *yeshibah.*[83] If there was no *yeshibah* in his locality, he went to a nearby community with better educational facilities. Arrangements were then made to provide him with maintenance;[84] and it was not unusual, so we hear, that needy students used schoolrooms as lodging quarters.[85] After he had attended the *yeshibah*, the individual continued his education, studying by himself or with a group.[86] Thus the elementary as well as the advanced school assumed considerable responsibility for the rearing of the student from childhood through young adulthood.

While the education of the male child was of primary concern, there is evidence that girls were students in elementary schools and that they had educational opportunities. The communal legislation of Nikolsburg of 1691 and the Minute Book of Runkel of November 19, 1733, refer to girls attending *ḥeder*;[87] and in her recollections of childhood, Glikl of Hameln relates that her "father gave his children, girls and boys, a secular as well as a religious education." Her account confirms that girls were provided with an elementary Hebrew education, as she attended *ḥeder* when she was a child.[88] Through the "ethical chapbook," *muser-bikhel,* in Yiddish, women acquainted themselves with a wide range of sources covering law, liturgy, ritual, and *exempla.*[89] What Solomon Schechter describes as the educational background of Glikl can no doubt be applicable to other women of her time and serve as the "norm" for the cultured Jewess of Germany in the 17th and 18th centuries: "We may also assume that she knew sufficient Hebrew to read her daily prayers and to understand various familiar phrases and terms, which became almost a part of the language of the Judengasse."[90] The quotations that Glikl cites from the Bible, *Pirḳe 'Abot* (Ethics of the Fathers), Talmud; her reference to the ethical writings of Abraham and Isaiah Horowitz; her acquaintance with folk tales of the Middle Ages, also are indicative of what the German-Jewish woman must have absorbed culturally from her environment.[91] And from Glikl's account of the passing of her husband, it would seem that religio-ethical writings were known to the Jewish woman. On his deathbed, Glikl's husband asked her to bring him a copy of the *Shelah* (*The Two Tablets of the Covenant*, by Isaiah Horowitz) that he might read it.[92] These incidents show that scholars and teachers of the period were concerned that Jewish women should receive an adequate education so as to enable them to carry out their personal and communal responsibilities.[93]

6. Some Customs Relating to Education

The school functioned as a communal institution,[94] not as an adjunct to a religious organization, since the responsibility for the school was assumed by the community as a whole rather than by a local synagogue, as is characteristic of American Jewish life today. The relationship between the school and the community was formalized through the *taḳḳanah*, the local or regional legislative regulation. However, the contact between the individual and the educational institution was not only maintained by legislation but by a body of customs, which were the same in most communities and in some cases were of a localized character.[95] We might make some common-sense generalizations about school practices without searching for the details of daily procedures and events; but it is doubtful whether we can have the same understanding and appreciation of the educational institution—its long tradition of love of learning—without examining, even if only at random, customs dealing with the school.

The *melamed*, the teacher, would instruct from eight to ten children at one time, which was considered a suitable number for the size of a class, according to the *Taḳḳanot* of Nikolsburg of 1676.[96] In the classroom four groups were scheduled, and, on the average, thirty minutes were devoted to the study of the

Hebrew alphabet or the Siddur, Prayer Book; forty-five minutes to the Ḥumash, Pentateuch; one hour to Gemara, Talmud, and one hour and fifteen minutes to Gemara and Tosafot, commentaries on the Talmud. The advanced classes, small and intimate, with a maximum of eight pupils at a session, concentrated on the Talmud, Rashi, and Tosafot.[97] Stress was placed on Talmudic studies,[98] the basic source of law and lore that governs individual relationships and determines communal policy.

During a regular day, the school was in session at least ten hours. The communal legislation of Hamburg-Altona, in 1726, on the other hand, did not expect the *melamed* to teach more than eight hours a day during the winter season and ten hours daily in the summer.[99] In accordance with traditional practice, the family paid the *melamed*,[100] but, significantly, the amount of his remuneration was not decided by the family but by communal legislation.[101] If the family should be negligent in paying the teacher's fee, he was not obliged to keep the child in class longer than eight days.[102]

The parents of Nikolsburg would send their children of pre-school age—from three to five years—to the *ḥeder* just to sit and listen to the discussion taking place in the class. A maximum of eight such "auditors" could be permitted in the classroom at one time.[103] Gemara students were dismissed from *ḥeder* as soon as their class finished, since they were not permitted to be in the schoolroom with the primary classes studying the alphabet, Prayer Book, and Pentateuch. Yet the students of Ḥumash could sit in the *ḥeder* when Gemara was studied, thus acting in accordance with the Talmudic maxim, "Sanctity should be elevated step by step and not be lowered (Shab. 21b)." Fifteen students at the most were allowed in the schoolroom at one time.[104]

The Moravian *Va'ad*, or Council, representing the entire province and exercising super-communal authority,[105] made the provision that each locality with thirty householders has the obligation of establishing a *yeshibah*. And where there were less than thirty householders, a community could not be excused from assuming educational responsibilities; it was never considered too small to engage and maintain a teacher. It was stressed by the Council of Moravia that support for the school must come from the entire community, not only from parents with children. Hence the *Taḳḳanah* of Gaya, Moravia, in 1650, states explicitly that the community, not the parent, is responsible for paying the teacher;[106] for it must have been too precarious to entrust the welfare of the school, teacher, and children to the philanthropic impulse and good-will of individuals. The legislation of Moravia also stipulates that the community provide funds for the teacher's fees when parents are indigent and unable to pay toward their child's education.[107]

When a community was too small to employ a *melamed,* the sexton served as teacher.[108] Even the smallest community has a school, Bacharach states in a *responsum*, and cites the instance of a village with "thirteen householders" that established "a fine schoolroom attached to the synagogue."[109]

Communal legislation required further that the *yeshibah* should enroll no less than sixty young men over thirteen years of age.[110] Various localities were responsible not only for the maintenance of *yeshibot* but also for providing support for students who were attending school during the winter season until the first of *'Adar,* around March, and in the summer until the first of '*Elul*, around August.[111] Between semesters the *yeshibah* students were placed with families in surrounding towns in order to relieve the local community that regularly maintained the school.[112] Due to the unfavorable economic conditions after the Thirty Years' War, with most people poor and heavily burdened with exorbitant taxes, communities were finding it increasingly difficult to maintain *yeshibot* and support needy students.[113]

7. Setting a Time to Study

The customs outlined in the handbook also aim at encouraging each person to develop the habit of daily study. The *musar*-book, in recommending a pattern of conduct for self-improvement, emphasizes study as an ideal for both personal and communal life.[114] Among its other concerns the popular handbook seeks to further education—and to such a degree that there will no longer be illiteracy. With this in mind, the author of the ethical chapbook suggests what should be read, yet takes into account individual differences in knowledge and cultural background. The adult is therefore urged not to feel self-conscious if he can only study on an elementary level. Characteristically, an anonymous book of customs[115] emphasizes that one should not hesitate to ask the local rabbi to translate a text if its meaning is not understood.

The importance of "a set time for study" *(ḳebi'at 'ittim la-Torah)* is also stressed. Each person is asked, as part of his daily routine, to engage in study in the morning before going to work and at night before retiring; and if he fails to adhere to the schedule, then he has to give a contribution to charity. Those involved in communal affairs are likewise expected to set aside time for study. Even during the season of the fair daily study is not to be neglected. The session of study could be omitted only if a person performs an act of kindness, such as "redeeming a captive" or "attending a funeral."[116] Granted that an individual has to make a living, Jonah Landsofer contends, he still has the responsibility of arranging his schedule so that some time is devoted to study each day.

> However, they must not exempt themselves completely from the study of Torah [because they are busy earning a livelihood]. They can try to study at night, on the Sabbath, holidays, and days when they are free [i.e., not working]. Do not behave like those heads of families who, when they

> are not at work, busy themselves in superficial things, in different kinds of sport and enjoyment.[117]

After the day's work, men turned to study by attending the *Ḥebra'*, the Talmudic Society, and when the discourse on the Talmud was finished, they read from popular books on religious and ethical themes.[118] That the admonition to study daily was taken seriously, especially in larger communities, is borne out in Joseph Kosman's narrative:

> I have to praise the larger communities where there are 'Holy Societies' that enable even the ill-lettered to abide by a daily set time for study. Moreover, the Sephardim have Houses of Study (*bate midrashim*) where some study Bible, others Codes (*posḳim*), and each person can find delight [in what he does].[119]

Advice is given to study for thirty minutes during the middle of the night, in the morning prior to and after attending services in the synagogue,[120] but the time considered most favorable for study is at night, before the dawn.[121] Or, as Isaiah Horowitz writes: "We have found that the night is a more suitable time for [the study of] Torah than the day, since the person is [then] relieved of his affairs [i.e., worldly occupation]. . . ."[122] When nights are long, Landau says, "it is not befitting to spend the entire night sleeping"; hence a specific time for study should be set during the night "whether one is a scholar or a person of humble status."[123] Before one becomes involved in daily routine, Moses Ḥasid wants him to study,[124] and similarly Hahn recommends that a short period be set aside for study after morning services.[125] But in addition to the routine of studying twice daily, it was also customary to study before and after meals:

> And it seems to me that whoever studies regularly in his home should not be concerned about having his meal on schedule. Let him study up to the time that he eats.[126]

Other practices pertaining to study also interested Hahn, and he relates how in former times individuals would stand when they read, but they became too exhausted and thereafter were seated when they studied.[127] He also describes the custom of removing books from the table before it was set, "so that the table might resemble the altar [of the Temple of Jerusalem]."[128]

The authors who were writing as "mentors of the folk" also suggest the subject-matter for individual study. While emphasizing Talmudic subjects, Lentshits specifies the Bible, Mishnah, Talmud, and Codes as the essential fields to be covered.[129] And in their list of texts for personal study, Horowitz, Bacharach, Moses Ḥasid, include medieval codes, and Landsofer adds legal authorities of a later period.[130] They recognize that not everyone will attain the same level of Talmudic scholarship, as "the pursuit of knowledge" is tedious and demanding. Even the study of the Bible, Landsofer claims, will prove to be difficult in that passages in the Minor Prophets remain obscure due to "hidden meaning."[131]

Men who were living in small towns and rural areas, or were working as peddlars and tradesmen, had little opportunity or time for study, and therefore had to rely on Hebrew texts with accompanying Yiddish translations as their main source of knowledge.[132] For the average person the translation of Hebrew books made Jewish law, liturgy, and customs more comprehensible. Such translations were used for both worship and study so that the Hebrew could be better understood.[133] Landsofer, during this period, became interested in preparing for the benefit of the unlettered person a popular Yiddish translation of the "613" (*taryag*) basic laws.[134] If a person is not a scholar, Landsofer proposes that he study in summary form the "613" commandments, attend lectures on the Bible, Mishnah, Midrash, *Shulḥan 'Arukh*, and if he is not able to read Hebrew texts, he "should not hesitate to study . . . in Yiddish the sermon of the *maggid* [the popular, itinerant preacher], the Bible, *Leb Tob*. . . ."[135]

The *Leb Tob,* written in Poland, was widely read by men in Germanic communities as a popularized *Shulḥan 'Arukh,*[136] again showing how the Jews of Central and Eastern Europe shared a common culture.

Moses Ḥasid also encourages tradesmen to read translations of Hebrew sources and refers to the *Brandshpigl* as a work in Yiddish that is popular.[137] The daughters and daughters-in-law of Sabbatai Horowitz are admonished by him to read regularly the *Ḥumash,* the Five Books of Moses, in the Yiddish translation.[138] Likewise, Ezekiel Landau stresses that each individual should study whatever he can in accordance with his ability:

> Let everyone study a new subject for which he is qualified. The average person will study the Midrash [and] ethical works. The person who has no educational background will study in the vernacular books that are commentaries on the Torah; [he will] even regard them as new interpretations. . . .[139]

Though Landau favors the vernacular when Hebrew is not known, he is concerned that the emphasis given to translations to assist the folk with limited education may result in the neglect of the study of the Hebrew language. He therefore speaks of "the shortcoming in using the vernacular (*leshon targum*) and not the holy tongue (*leshon ha-ḳodesh,* Hebrew)."[140] The use of the vernacular, however, for the study and discussion of religious topics receives general approval and encouragement. When Bacharach is asked whether a subject that deals with the Torah can be published in a language other than Hebrew, his reply may be considered as an expression of opinion prevalent at the time. He explains that it is content, not language, that determines whether a work is "profane" or objectionable. Since language is a means of expression, any work, such as a song, may be translated "as long as it consists of words of wisdom, ethics, and reverence." However, if the song is "in the language of lust, frivolity, and nonsense, then it is forbidden to be sung even if it is in Hebrew. Deduce from this that everything depends upon the content of words."[141] In short, a twofold cultural process was unfolding; on the one hand, Hebrew texts were rendered into Yiddish for the edification of the public, and on the other, secular works, whether Euclid's *Elements of Geometry* or the medical treatise by Ibn Sina (Avicenna), known as the *Qānūn (Canon),* were translated into Hebrew for scholarly study.[142]

When he was consulted as to what a post-*Bar Mizvah* youth should study, Bacharach stated that he could not arbitrarily favor some studies and reject others, since all subjects are of importance and can contribute to "the attainment of wisdom" as a "primary goal."[143] To engage in study is not regarded beyond the reach of any adult. No person is so unimportant or lowly as not to merit an education, for the acquisition of knowledge is not dependent upon birth or social position but upon interest and ability.[144] The Minute Book of the community of Runkel therefore declares that all children should be provided with the same educational opportunities. Even though a child might later become a water-carrier, he is not to receive inferior training.[145]

8. The Group at Study

In addition to studying by himself, the individual is encouraged to study with a group. The group or social character of Jewish education is conveyed by Bacharach in the advice that he gives to the father who consulted him about continuing his son's education.

> Even if the father engages a teacher for him [the son] alone, is it not more essential that the study be [conducted] in intimacy with other students. . .? This can only be carried through when five or six heads of families will come together and [arrange to] employ a teacher for their sons.[146]

Landsofer similarly suggests that even "if one can satisfy [his educational interest] without [the aid of] a teacher," he should arrange to meet with "a friend or a student" in order to benefit from "the oral type of study, which reviews each word at least twenty times."[147] Group study is considered essential for the small community that is not able to maintain a *yeshibah.* A *Taḳḳanah* of Moravia, at the end of the 16th century, describes how, by legislative means, group study was enforced in the small community:

> When a small community, having one or more individuals who are scholars of the Torah with rabbinical ordination, engages a teacher or a rabbi, but has no *yeshibah,* the household heads are morally obligated to designate a set time for study in the *bet ha-midrash.* . . . The leader of the community is responsible to supervise this [undertaking] with special care, and whenever he deems it fit, he should impose a heavy fine [for violating the regulation], so that the Torah will not be forgotten by Israel.[148]

Sabbatai Horowitz relates the experience that he had with group study when he was head of the *metibta'*, the academy, and the *bet din*, the court, in Frankfort (ca. 1632-50). At noon each day three groups—a large group, a smaller group with specialized interest, and a group of the faculty of the academy—met for study. Each group was led by a scholar who conducted the study and discussion on the level of the participants' knowledge. At every session, the *Ḳaddish de-Rabbanan*, the memorial prayer for scholars, was recited, after which a coin was placed in the charity box.[149] It was the wish of Sabbatai Horowitz that the Frankfort method of group study should serve as a model for other "towns, communities, and regions, small and large."[150]

Another example of group study has been described by Ezekiel Katzenellenbogen of Altona (d. 1749) in his Ethical Will:

> In particular, the scholars of the *kloyz*, with whom I had spent some years, were pleasant company. I studied Mishnah with them each day. They were about ten in number, although the regulation of the *kloyz* specified that a member of the group must not leave the building.[151]

Talmudic scholars were able to study continuously in the *kloyz* (see frontispiece) or *bet ha-midrash*; here they resided and were provided with the necessities of life that they required, so they would not have to be distracted by the exigency of earning a livelihood. According to Deutsch, it became the practice among wealthy individuals in Germanic lands in the 17th and 18th centuries to provide funds to support the *kloyzn,* and such "study-houses" were set up in various communities, among them Altona, Halberstadt, Mannheim, and Prague.[152]

Jacob Emden, in his autobiography, speaks of the *kloyz* in Altona that was established for his father (ca. 1690), who held a rabbinical position in the community. His account gives some details about the origin and purpose of the *kloyz*; it serves as a *yeshibah* and *bet ha-midrash*, having as its aim "to spread the true meaning of Torah for its own sake." Those who study in the *kloyz* also live there. The *kloyz* was made possible by contributions from wealthy persons in the three adjoining communities of Altona, Hamburg, and Wandsbek. For almost twenty years, Emden states, his father served as the leader of the *kloyz*.[153]

9. Evaluating the School

The educational institution was subjected to critical examination in the legal, communal, and popular sources of the 17th and 18th centuries that we have been considering. German-Jewish cultural life was stirred by the influences of Humanism and the Renaissance, the Protestant Reformation and Pietism;[154] by the emphasis these movements gave to scientific inquiry, the use of sources in the original, the study of the Bible in Hebrew with the aid of grammar and commentary; and by the importance that they ascribed to insight and feeling, that is, to inner experience, as a source of knowledge. Moreover, individual scholars and teachers would visit Italy and Holland in their travels, and when they saw that in these Jewish communities methods of education were more advanced, they were prompted to re-examine the curricula of their own schools in Germany.[155] Also, there was a continuing expression of interest in the problems and future goals of education, especially under the impetus of the Maharal of Prague.[156] The critics of communal life boldly attacked the shortcomings of education, and even more so the dangerous decline of educational standards.[157]

In Landsofer's report on cultural life in the community—particularly with regard to the deterioration of the standards of local leadership—we detect a concern that teachers have become too preoccupied with material gain. Ill-prepared and inexperienced students are not hesitating to accept communal posts for the benefit of the remuneration. No less disturbing to Landsofer is the students' loss of interest in their studies, their obvious preference for staying at home and not attending school.

> Scholars have begun to derive benefit from teaching the Torah, and due to this, its role [lit., life] has been reduced to that of the axe. . . . Immature youngsters and inexperienced pupils assume communal posts for the benefit of material gain. If one seeks remuneration, he merely has to sermonize on some nonsensical topic and leap in front of [i.e., entertain] the [communal] leader in a manner that pleases his light-mindedness. . . . The pupils abandon school to be at home, little disturbed that they have submitted to this foolish behavior. . . . Such a state of affairs does not concern our contemporaries, for they are not ashamed that youngsters do not study sufficiently and lack adequate training in ethics,

> because they are preoccupied with the vanities of youth. Furthermore, they have no knowledge of the nature of the Hebrew language, and do not have the understanding to know when a judicial decision is the result of distortion. . . . The people walk in darkness, and a child [i.e., an immature person] is their leader.[158]

And during this period there were also complaints that teachers are devoid of spiritual concerns, showing indifference toward their work, which they should regard as a noble calling.[159]

When Ezekiel Landau was chagrined because the people "show contempt for scholars and pious persons,"[160] this attitude could have been an expression of their own loss of faith and respect for educators and leaders who had selfish interests. Such a surmise seems plausible if we take into account Sabbatai Horowitz's scathing tone: ". . . There are some communities in a state of decline due to [the influence of] wealth, for they favor the selection of a rabbi because he is rich, ignoring rabbis of fine qualities and merit who are poor. . . ."[161] Apparently, it was not uncommon that bribery was resorted to in order to secure rabbinical titles.[162] It was not surprising, then, that the people had so little regard for teachers and communal leaders, knowing that these posts did not always go to the most deserving.

Since the schools did not receive adequate financial support because of prevailing economic difficulties, the position of the teacher became more and more precarious.[163] Evidently, teachers must have been facing hardships, for charity collections had to be made in their behalf.[164] With parents engaging and paying the teachers who instructed their children, the teachers became more and more dependent on them for their livelihood. A teacher therefore would not hesitate to use devious methods to gain the good will of parents as well as their children. To secure the commendation of parents, Lentshits remarks, teachers resort to flattery, even exaggerating the talents of their pupils,[165] and through such compromises, lose both their sense of independence and their effectiveness in their work.

Critics of the teaching methods in school held the opinion that the study of the Bible and Hebrew grammar is being neglected;[166] in fact, after the period of the Maharal, educational reformers are encouraging the study of the *sidrah,* the weekly Torah portion, so as to acquaint students with the Bible.[167] That the curriculum should place more stress on the study of the Bible, Hebrew grammar and syntax, is strongly advocated in the educational changes that Isaiah and Sabbatai Horowitz propose.[168] The Bible and Hebrew syntax are considered so important by Lentshits that he wants these subjects to be the very first that students will study in school.[169] In addition, Hahn objects to those teachers who have made it a practice not to read the Biblical text. "In our day," he states, "there are many rabbis who have not read the Bible during their lifetime."[170]

They also found fault with the mechanical manner of teaching. The criticism is made that children who study Gemara at the age of eight or nine have no comprehension of the subject-matter but repeat the translation by rote; yet the teacher defends his method of instruction, claiming that the pupil shows remarkable ability and is destined to be a scholar.[171] When he was a child, the anonymous autobiographer relates, he was taught Gemara *Soṭah* by his father, but, at the time, he lacked the maturity to understand what was discussed.

> My father thought that he himself would teach us, and my brother who was thirteen or fourteen years old actually learned haggadic literature from him, such as Rashi and Midrashim, as well as the laws of *Sheḥitah*; but I needed a special teacher. My father started to teach me Gemara *Sotah* once or twice, though I had never before studied Talmud or even Mishnah. Thus a long time passed by without my learning anything, until I became a thorn in my own eyes and even more so in the eyes of my father. . . .[172]

Isaiah Horowitz opposes *ḥilluḳ*, a pilpulistic way of teaching to sharpen the mind, and even regards those who support this method of education as extremists, "deserving excommunication." To engage in *pilpul* in the manner then prevailing, he contends, is a waste of time and a departure from the truth.[173] Sabbatai Horowitz is concerned that the subject matter taught in schools becomes distorted because of the way in which *ḥilluḳ* is used.[174] Lentshits relates how, in his opposing the *ḥilluḳ* method of teaching, he met with failure and disappointment, in that the scholars of his time favored this approach because of its popularity, and by adhering to it, they enhanced their own prestige among persons of influence and power. In the opinion of Lentshits, *pilpul* has been undermining the standards for study, and as a result students are made to feel that their educational pursuits have little value.

> I have had many controversies with scholars and leaders in the land that they abandon the teaching method of 'dialectics' (lit., the 'sharpness' and 'peppery debate': *ha-ḥiddud ve-ha-pilpul*). . . . I was not able to prevail over them, the reason being that they are in pursuit of the advantages of honor and position. . . . And they think that perhaps it is the *pilpul* that makes one stronger than the mighty. . . . Whoever practices this 'dialectical method' in studying the Torah, truthfully, never achieves what he claims, for we can see with our own eyes that there are those places, Palestine and other countries, where this false method of *pilpul* is not practiced. Young men [students] in particular see eye to eye how this 'sharpness' ['dialectics'] causes tremendous distortion. . . .[175]

Similarly, the pilpulistic method of study in vogue is discouraged by Hahn, Bacharach, and Landsofer.[176] And Eibeschütz, deploring the cultural regression that was then taking place, also attacks *pilpul* as educationally harmful: ". . . As I see the decline of [our] generation in all parts of Europe, there is no Talmudic Academy where knowledge is pursued for its own sake. As they [try to] deepen the law, the authorities falsify the Torah, not because of our many transgressions, but on account of the useless *pilpul* that has no regard for the truth."[177]

At the end of the 15th century scholars encouraged the use of *pilpul* so as to emulate the *ri'shonim,* the eminent Talmudic sages of France, namely, Rashi and his disciples. Since they did not succeed in imitating the French school, the pilpulistic approach proved to be a hindrance to education. In place of the simple, direct statements or interpretations characteristic of Rashi and his followers, fanciful and verbose formulations resulted from the *pilpul.* The conclusions arrived at were removed from reality—so unlike the *posḳim*, the legal authorities of the early Middle Ages, who applied halakhic principles empirically to problems that arose from experience.[178] In a pilpulistic discussion, a question need not be considered in terms of its validity, but simply because it is raised. Ehrentreu shows that a halakhic discussion has merit when, for instance, it deals with a difficulty that arises because the elements in a given situation seem on the surface to be similar, yet are different; or else there are elements that seem different, but are really similar. In each case, the similarity or difference has to be established through rational analysis and the application of logical principles or categories. The *pilpul* has been compared to "windjamming" because its discussion seems to be aimless, lacking the direction that results from a methodology or a systematic approach.[179] As scholarship declined after the Black Death, the *musar* writers of the 15th and 16th centuries tried to discourage *pilpul* because they saw in it an obstacle, not an aid, in furthering cultural life.[180] During the next two centuries, *pilpul* was also looked upon with disfavor by the *musar* teachers who espoused simplicity and eschewed pretense and ostentation.

Though a common cultural and religious heritage is the basis for organized living in the Jewish community, this does not imply that in personal beliefs and methods of observance differences never arose, or that divergent and conflicting cultural trends did not develop. While we have evidence of an interest in secular and scientific studies in such places as Prague and Worms,[181] there also are instances of secular studies being opposed. Finding support for his position in the opinions of Solomon ben Adret, Isaiah Horowitz considers scientific studies to be antithetical to the Torah, that the two areas, secular knowledge and Judaism, cannot be harmonized, and therefore admonishes: "Stay away from the study of philosophy; any of its ancient or later interpretations are forbidden. . . . For the wisdom of the Torah and that of philosophy are different in their approaches. . . ."[182]

In 1737, fourteen years after his turbulent controversy with Eibeschütz, Jacob Emden advises a medical student to desist from his secular studies, as it can only bring confusion. The student is criticized by Emden for allowing himself to become isolated from Jewish communal life, "the holy congregations of Israel":

> My son, who has given you the authority to rely on their interpretations and to study their laws, to go after vanity and confusion, to waste the time that should be set aside for reflection. It is an activity that is not essential for the individual, [one] in which our ancestors and sages did not involve themselves. . . . Do not attempt to acquire the knowledge of philosophers and thereby waste your time.[183]

Maimonides, so Emden explains, "has the distinction" of "having deepened his thought" through the use of philosophy and secular knowledge. The *Moreh (Guide of the Perplexed)*, however, was intended to meet "the need of his generation, for the generations that came after him had immediately rejected that book and there was no desire to go in his way." The later sages did not study the *Moreh*, Emden adds, as they were not in accord with Maimonides's philosophic position. In brief, Emden contends, "no man is entitled to have two tables,"[184] the one Jewish and the other secular. Like Isaiah Horowitz,[185] Emden contends that the Torah and secular learning cannot be unified into a single system without impairing Jewish tradition. And in Emden's opinion a study of the ethical views of philosophers will not offer anything not already stated in the teachings of the Bible and rabbinic literature. Though he does not deny that ethical teachings are universal and can be shared by all men, Emden emphasizes nevertheless that philosophers are not saying anything unique so far as Judaism is concerned. Their ideas are not original, and, as he puts it, "were taken [lit., stolen] from the prophets and sages, and placed in their vessels. They [just] dressed their system in different attire."[186]

The pursuit of secular knowledge will only have unfortunate consequences, Emden adds; thus "whoever brings into his house books other than the Bible introduces confusion. . . ."[187] From his own experience he found that secular studies caused him "considerable pain, anguish, and intense suffering." He considered hiring a teacher to instruct him in languages, and he also thought of studying secular subjects in secret, but such plans made him ashamed. Still he felt a need for secular information which he could not obtain "from our sacred books" (*sifrenu ha-ḳedoshim*). He wanted to learn about "the affairs of the world and nations, the ethics and beliefs of religions, their history and philosophy," as this kind of knowledge would "enable him to converse and mingle with people."[188] In so many words, Emden was saying that the Jew of the 18th century could not live a culturally isolated life in the *gas*; social changes were making it necessary for him to become acquainted with a new secular society so that he could live and participate in it. In Emden's time there were those who considered secular learning as an economic necessity—essential for an individual in order to earn a living.[189]

Secular subjects also had an influence on the education of women, apparent from Glikl's account that her stepsister spoke French "as easily as one drinks water" and knew how to play the clavichord.[190] The playing of musical instruments by young women did not have Hahn's approval, and his criticism shows that a musical education was limited to the more affluent families:

> In my opinion we should strongly oppose the wealthy merchants when they engage [teachers] for their daughters, to be instructed in playing musical instruments, for this is only done for reasons of self-gratification and haughtiness.[191]

Kaidanover and Hahn were also critical of the Frankfort Jews who study the German, French, and Polish languages. It has become the fashion, Kaidanover decries, for parents to teach their children French and other languages instead of Hebrew.[192] Similarly, Eibeschütz preaches in Metz against those who discard the study of the Torah for "the French language, writing, arithmetic, and dancing of both sexes together. . . ."[193] That "philanthropic-minded members of the community study German and Polish," disturbs Hahn; first, he is disappointed that they do not "show any sense of shame" for their conduct, and, then, he despairs that he is so helpless in remedying the cultural conditions that prevail. Resigning himself to the powerful forces altering the traditional pattern of German-Jewish life, Hahn says woefully:

> I am not able to affect a change, [or] influence individuals of such prestige. There will be no change in the educational practices of the region.[194]

Among the opponents of secular studies were rabbis who had engaged in secular learning, but their concern did not stem from the fear of an intellectual conflict arising from involvement in a secular field. The reservations that they had regarding secular influences were voiced by Eibeschütz: Once a person becomes absorbed in a secular subject, he may be inclined to neglect the study of the Torah and thus weaken his ties with Jewish tradition.[195] Secularism was opposed not so much on intellectual grounds as for reasons of group survival and group continuity.[196]

10. A Model School

When Sabbatai Horowitz visited Amsterdam in his travels, he was impressed by its systematic method of education. He wrote that each school has its own building and that the curriculum follows an orderly procedure, with the student first mastering the Bible, later studying the Mishnah, and then devoting himself to the Talmud and commentaries when he is old enough to understand the subject. When the Amsterdam student begins the study of the Talmud, he has had two advantages, namely, that he has received a thorough elementary education and has attained a maturity that enables him to have greater power of comprehension. To Sabbatai Horowitz the Spanish-Portuguese school in Amsterdam is a model to be emulated by Jewish communities everywhere.[197] Interest in the Amsterdam school-system continued with Sabbatai Bass (Meshorer), the "bass singer" in the *Alt-Neu* Synagogue of Prague (d. 1718). As he traveled in Poland, Germany, and Holland between 1674-79, he became acquainted with the Amsterdam school, and would have liked its method of education to serve as a standard for the schools of German Jewry.[198] He remarks that his own enthusiasm for the Amsterdam schools had been substantiated by Sabbatai Horowitz's observations.

In his account of the Amsterdam school, Bass tells in detail about the building, classrooms, curriculum, library, program of home study, and remuneration of teachers. The school has a separate building of six rooms which adjoins the synagogue structure, the *bet ha-miḳdash* and *bet ha-keneset.* When the total enrollment is just over one hundred students, they still assign a teacher to each room.[199] In describing the curriculum of the six classes, several features are of special interest to Bass, obviously because of the contrast with educational methods and policies in the German-Jewish community. As an example, when a passage is studied in the Bible, in the Amsterdam school, first it is read in Hebrew and then interpreted in Spanish by each student of the class. Classes are generally conducted in Hebrew, and considerable stress is placed on the study of Hebrew grammar. Students deliver lectures on *halakhah* until they are proficient enough "to be included in the category of a 'senior student' (*baḥur*)." All classes begin promptly at eight o'clock in the morning. A well-equipped library is accessible to students during class hours, but the books are not circulated for home use.[200] When the child returns home from school, his studies continue. The parents also engage a teacher to tutor him in writing Hebrew and Spanish poetry.[201] Bass reports another advantage to the Amsterdam system: Each teacher is remunerated by the community on the basis of "merit, need, and scholarship" from the funds of the Talmud Torah Holy Society. Such a procedure proves to be beneficial to all concerned—to the school, the teacher, and the student.

> There is no need for the teacher to curry the favor of anyone, for he teaches all pupils equally, the rich and poor, whoever has a mind that grasps [lit., has an understanding heart].[202]

As with the birth, marriage, and burial practices, the customs dealing with education are derived from three main sources, religious tradition, communal legislation, and local innovation and observances. A mutuality exists between the individual and the community inasmuch as the community is obliged to enable every child to secure an education. The education of the child is not limited to the classroom, since both the family and the school are responsible for his intellectual growth.[203] The adult is constantly encouraged to continue to study, by himself and in a group; and such devotion to learning is a religious obligation that is incumbent on all members of the community, not only the scholars and those steeped in classical texts. The influences of German Enlightenment, *Haskalah,* are apparent in the larger centers, in Frankfort, Hamburg, Prague, and then Berlin, where music, French, Polish, German, and secular subjects are included in the education of children. Yet there are those teachers and leaders who do not view with optimism the turn taken by Jewish cultural life. They see in the new developments, even though they are in the direction of Enlightenment, more of a threat to the community than a promise.

CHAPTER IV

Clothing: Daily and Festive Dress

1. Dress by Governmental Order

The clothing of the Jews was not only determined by general style and custom and by the influence of neighboring groups, but also by the legislation decreed by state authorities specifying a distinctive garb.[1] Since, historically, the dress of the Jew is not too different from that of the total society, the so-called Jewish garb had to be a creation of law and social practice. In the Middle Ages there were three forms of dress to identify the Jew, the "yellow badge," the "pointed" or "three-cornered" hat, and the "coat";[2] and when the "Jewish dress" was abolished by decree of Emperor Joseph II, in May 1722, the Jew was then distinguished by the beard as part of his traditional attire. The beard, at the time, was not in vogue in Germany, nor was it required by governmental regulation;[3] in fact, by the 13th century the beard, which had already disappeared in the German community in general, was only worn by "old people, pilgrims, and Jews."[4] But, in the 17th century, individual Jews, not wishing to be considered different from other human beings, started to shave their beards and ear-locks. So that they would "not be taken for Jews," they decided to change their appearance.[5]

Let us turn to a specific case to show how civil policy affected dress. To prevent Jews from crossing the Moravian boundary and leaving the country, the authorities ordered them to wear an "external sign" so they could be easily singled out and detected. For men, the "mark" was a kerchief around the neck in addition to the beard; and for women, a veil on the head. Berush Eskeles (d. 1753), the Chief Rabbi of Moravia, presented a refutation to this ruling by pointing out that "in matters of dress the custom of the land is followed,"[6] and he indicated thereby that the dress of the Jews is never unique or different unless it is required by the ruling of the state or unless brought by them from one country to another.

2. Anti-Luxury Laws: Sumptuary Regulation in Dress

Dress was not only determined by government order but by Jewish communal anti-luxury, or sumptuary, legislation which regulated the apparel to be worn. Sumptuary decrees were first introduced in the general German community in the 14th century to curb French cultural influences,[7] but in the case of the Jewish society, anti-luxury legislation was intended to restrain ostentatious behavior on the part of the Jew, make him less conspicuous in the eyes of the non-Jew, and maintain a high level of ethical conduct as a means of warding off disease and calamity.[8] Where there was moral turpitude, the people could expect to suffer;[9] therefore the *musar*-sermon emphasized that Israel's redemption from *galut*, exile, could be hastened through ethical behavior.[10] To be sure, instances may be cited of Jewish women wearing fashionable clothing and being more concerned about their dress than about their community's welfare in time of emergency,[11] but Schudt, who harbored no special sympathy for the Jews, acknowledges that the kind of clothing they usually wore was evidence of their poverty.[12]

The sumptuary laws concerning dress—as adopted by the Jewish communities of Frankfort, Nuremberg, Fürth, Hamburg as well as in Prussia and Moravia during the latter part of the 17th and the early 18th centuries—have a marked similarity. Even though the regulations were related to different geographical regions, they may be considered part of a single pattern of control.[13] Thus the various *taḳḳanot*, communal legislations, specify that women's new garments should not be made of velvet, damask, or satin, obviously because such apparel is luxurious and ostentatious. Clothes trimmed or embroidered in gold and silver can only be worn as special holiday raiment on the Sabbath and festivals. A shining veil[14] can be worn by women only when they attend the synagogue, participate in a circumcision ceremony as godmother, or serve as bridesmaid at a wedding. Silk hose are permitted as part of Sabbath dress, but the prohibition specifies that a gold or silver watch[15] attached to the stocking should not be worn.

The stress placed on simplicity of dress, even for the Sabbath, was dramatically expressed by Meir Eisenstadt, when he was asked if it is appropriate to wear white garments on the Sabbath. To wear white would be pretentious, he replied with ironical humor, as though the person were considering himself equal in stature to the pious men of the past who, on the Sabbath, would dress in white. To wear white is also ostentatious, as though one were "a groom among mourners (Shab. 114a)," implying superiority to everyone else.[16]

In order to maintain standards of simplicity in dress, no silk garments are to be used on weekdays, but it is permissible to wear clothes made of materials previously worn. Women's attire might be made of men's old garments and, in such instances, expensive furs of marten or sable are allowed. Women could wear a dress with one ruffle, a sleeveless mantle, a hoop petticoat, or a coiffure not too extreme. Gaudy garments were forbidden; and since bright colors were associated with the upper classes, this meant that sumptuary laws were designed to abolish the use of dress to designate social status. Embroidered or trimmed shawls, slippers, and shoes were prohibited—the regulation specifying that shoes are to be made of simple leather. It was forbidden to wear sleeping-coats of silk; shagreen[17] must not be used as a coat lining. Men might not wear blond wigs[18] nor use gold or silver buttons. Ornate and expensive jewelry was forbidden but used jewelry, or necklaces simply made, were acceptable. Jewelry could not be purchased from a non-Jewish person, apparently to avoid any possibility of arousing feelings of jealousy or creating the impression that Germanic Jews enjoyed a luxurious life. Sumptuary laws were also concerned with the dress of youth, forbidding the wearing of wigs, rings, or expensive jewelry.[19]

Those who formulated anti-luxury legislation did not confine themselves to regulating the kind of dress to be worn in public or to specifying the maximum outlay that could be permitted for a family celebration. They also sought to influence the behavior of the people, and by means of the communal enactment, *taḳḳanah*, correct the abuses singled out so unsparingly by the *musar* writer and teacher. The conduct of women is criticized, in the main, because they lack modesty in public. They walk the streets unchaperoned, do not hesitate to expose their bodies, and wear apparel that attracts men.[20] Household duties are neglected because so much of their time is spent away from home to find amusement at public festivities, where they drink recklessly and take part in gambling games. The boisterous and careless manner in which they conduct themselves at such gatherings is shockingly unbecoming.[21] To eliminate such conduct, the *Taḳḳanah* of Nuremberg and Fürth, in 1728, instructs a woman not to go to the synagogue without a companion or chaperon; but if she does, she is to be considered "an impudent hussy." When it becomes dark, arrangements are to be made for someone to accompany her home, so that she does not walk alone. For diversion, women may congregate with other persons in a neighbor's garden. Men are forbidden to visit public meeting places; both men and women are urged to retire on time, and students are instructed not to go anywhere during the week.[22]

3. Types of Clothing

Men's attire is usually the cloak or coat, mantle or cape, and hat.[23] Since the Jews *qua* Jews are not recognizable, the cape and hat also serve as the official garb of the Jew.[24] The Frankfort *Stättigkeit* of 1616 restates earlier legislation giving the Jews permission to wear a hat, black or gray, on the streets.[25] The "flat cap" (*barrette, barett*), used as a substitute for the hat, is forbidden.[26] Later, throughout the 18th century, the "*barrette* was the characteristic headgear of the Jews."[27]

The mantle, which has no sleeves, is thrown over the shoulders as a cape, and is worn over the coat.[28] During the 17th century it was shortened to the knee; previously it had dragged to the ground when worn.[29] The observation is made by Schudt that the hat, mantle, and other garments are of dark colors. According to Ezekiel Landau of Prague (d. 1793), red, which has become the conventional color of the hat, stands out in sharp contrast to the regular somber attire.[30] Jackets are made in various styles: black cloth with velvet sleeves, golden lace, and red-flowered silk with silver lace.[31] Men wear a linen kerchief which hangs loosely from their necks[32] or is suspended from the mantle.[33] A round white linen collar, of Spanish influence, is included as part of the attire of elders as well as other persons.[34] For their main apparel, the Jewish men of Moravia, for instance, wear breeches, long stockings, long coats, and shoes with silver buckles.[35] Men also use woolen shirts to which *ẓiẓit*, fringes, are attached.[36] Describing the dress of Abraham Metz of Altona, who was murdered and whose body was claimed for burial by the Jews of the community, Glikl tells that he wore "a shirt with a red lining, several silver buttons, and the *arbe-kanfos* [*ẓiẓit*]."[37] When Ezekiel Landau was consulted with regard to the identification of a man who had been killed while traveling from Braila (Brajlov), Rumania, to Little Poland, the widow of the deceased enumerated the clothing that her husband wore. In ascertaining whether or not a particular garment could be considered valid evidence (*siman ṭob*) as a means of identification, Landau records some of the garments men wore at the time. One of the identification marks is the undergarment with "fringes."[38] Men's collars vary in style and are of leather,

Fig. 7. Dress for Various Occasions, Nuremberg, 18th Century *(Courtesy, Widener Library, Harvard University)*. Top row, left to right: Attire of a Jewish Scholar in the *Gas*. A Man Dressed for the Synagogue. A Woman Dressed for the Synagogue. Bottom row: Attire of a Man in the *Gas*. A Jewish Woman in Her House Dress. A Man Carrying Wine for the Sabbath. From Liebe, *Judentum*, p. 101, plate # 81.

with and without points, and taffeta with golden points; women's collars are made of linen, trimmed with gold and lace and a thin plate of tin covered with silk.[39]

In the illustrations in Hottenroth[40] there are other examples of the dress worn by the Jews of Fürth in the 18th century. These pictures confirm and supplement what is known about the dress practices of Jews in Germany. Men's clothing comprises the *barett*, the flat cloth cap; the cloak, mantle, collar, neckpiece, vest, cuffs, shoes, gloves, and scarves.[41] Women's garments, most frequently cited, are the hood, mantle or cloak, apron, as well as collars.[42] The woman's headdress (*goldene Haube*, "golden hood"), in Moravia, covers the head so thoroughly that no part of the hair is seen.[43] During the winter season night caps are worn to keep warm.[44] A raincoat is referred to in Glikl's diary.[45] Women also wear a veil as a headgear,[46] and in mentioning the *shlayer*, or veil, Glikl is reminded of the fight that broke out in the women's synagogue on *Simḥat Torah*, in the course of which they pulled at each other's head veil.[47] Outdoors the unmarried girl could have her head uncovered as she did in her home.[48]

4. Some Customs in Dress

No unusual attire is required to participate in synagogue services; to observe the Sabbath and festivals; to attend a marriage celebration, the naming of a child, or funeral services.[49] For joyous and festive events a finer garment is used, but the style of the dress is no different from that worn during the week; obviously there is no sacred or secular clothing.

On the Sabbath men wear a special mantle to the synagogue, and women the cape with a hood. Even the humblest and poorest are dressed in the Sabbath mantle.[50] That the mantle was considered stylish probably explains why it became part of the Sabbath attire.[51] In Fürth, Frankfort, and environs the *shubitse*, "the long overcoat with wide sleeves," is used on festive occasions in

Fig. 8. Man and Woman of Nuremberg Going to the Synagogue, 18th Century Attire *(Courtesy, Widener Library, Harvard University)*. From *Jüdisches Lexikon,* IV^1 (1930), 539; originally an etching by Tyroff, Nuremberg, 1766.

place of the *mantl.*[52] Neither the mantle nor the cape had any religious significance as dress, but they became special garments when they were set aside for holidays. As Kosman states, the difference between the Sabbath and daily mantle is in its use.[53] The regular hat is replaced on the Sabbath by a flat hat (beret).[54] A white necktie is worn each Sabbath, but a black one on *Shabbat Ḥazon* preceding the Ninth of *'Ab*, when the destruction of the Temple of Jerusalem is commemorated.[55] The color of white has been associated with Sabbath joy, and black with mourning.

As the elderly men walk leisurely to the synagogue, they are attired in silk coats, expensive black mantles, wigs, and slippers.[56] In place of leather slippers, felt slippers are worn to the synagogue on *Yom Kippur* and the Ninth of *'Ab*. The *kohanim* wear felt slippers when they *dukhen*, chant the priestly benediction (Num. 7:23–27) in the synagogue on festivals.[57] Women attending the synagogue on the Sabbath are dressed in a veil of starched white linen, with corners trimmed in blue and white. Their hood has two points resembling horns, and, as is the custom, widows wear a white bonnet to the synagogue. Both men and women have round, starched collars attached to their mantles to make the Sabbath day distinctive.[58] For the woman, the Sabbath is made even more festive by wearing on her dress a brooch with an ornamental silver clasp,[59] while the man wears silver buttons on his Sabbath garments.[60] The Sabbath attire is usually more expensive than the clothing worn daily; however, nothing has been said or done to indicate that the Sabbath garment is invested with a hidden symbolic meaning or spiritual quality.

Any important or unusual happening could be honored by putting on the best garments that one had. So it was when the Jews of Hamburg—both Ashkenazim and Sephardim, those of Germanic and of Spanish cultural backgrounds—gathered in the Sephardic synagogue to hear the letters read that were received from Sabbatai (Shabbetai) Ẓebi, the Messianic leader in Smyrna. It was a day of rejoicing and therefore "the Sephardic youth came dressed in their best finery and decked in broad green silk ribbons, the gear [insignia] of Sabbatai Zevi."[61]

Some dress practices are introduced to aid the observance of the Sabbath and festivals, as in Frankfort and Worms, where a "closed sleeve" is sewed on to the mantle for the right hand. The sleeve, worn on the Sabbath and holidays, prevents one from grasping and carrying objects on the street.[62] That dress derives significance from definition and use is also illustrated by the custom of wearing special clothing at weddings. The attire is different only because the clothes ordinarily worn are not used on this occasion. Hence, the bride wears a special collar with silver points, and her face is covered with a veil during the bridal procession preceding the wedding ceremony.[63] Originally, the cowl, or hood, was worn to protect the head from inclement weather, but later it became mourning attire.[64] When the leaders gather for special events in the communal center, *bet ha-ḳahal*, they wear Sabbath garments, either the coat and cap, or the mantle and hat. Likewise, when an individual appears before the *bet din*, the communal court, he is expected to be dressed in Sabbath clothing.[65] Apparently, the garments are worn to honor the occasion and distinguish it from an ordinary event. The scholar, a revered person in the Jewish community, could be recognized by his dress. If he had the title *ḥaber* (*ḥover*, Ashken. pronun.: "scholar") he would wear a small collar, while the *morenu* ("our teacher") wore a large-sized collar.[66] No matter how impoverished a scholar might have been, he could still be identified by his clothing.[67] It has already been suggested that in the German-Jewish society dress was not a sign of superior or inferior social rank,[68] for the sumptuary laws did not allow wealthier individuals to wear more expensive clothing to the hurt or embarrassment of poorer persons. No one could assume importance because of elegant attire. In the instance of the scholar, however, he already had a position of honor based on merit and was distinguished from others by his dress, though the difference was only that of "a collar."

In advising on the appropriate dress to wear at a table during the recitation of grace, David Oppenheim specifies "the cloak [lit., top garment], hat or cap."[69] The cap no doubt served as a *yarmulke*, which was worn at home for prayer or under the hat, so as not to be bareheaded when doffing the hat to an official as a gesture of respect in accordance with "the custom of the land."[70] The *yarmulke* was known as *kapl* (Yid.) and *miẓnefet* (Heb.) and belongs to the category of "cap" with *barrette*, *gugel*, and *cucullus.*[71] Among Hottenroth's illustrations of clothing used by the Jews of Fürth in the 18th century is a portrait of a man at prayer, wearing a cap that serves as a *yarmulke.*[72] When Oppenheim uses the terms *koba*' and *miẓnefet*, he is probably referring to two different kinds of headgear. The *koba*' is the hat with a large brim and the *miẓnefet* (*kapl*), as mentioned, is a cap, having no brim. Since the *miẓnefet* was used as the "Jewish prayer cap," David Oppenheim very likely refers to the *miẓnefet* as the *yarmulke* of his time. No doubt, in the German-Jewish community of the 17th and 18th centuries, it was the custom to wear a cap in place of a regular hat while one recited prayer.

The influence that German fashions had on the attire of Jews shows that there was no "Jewish garb" as such, and what is known as "Jewish dress" was legislated by the state officialdom in order to affect social differentiation and ostracism of the Jews. Within the Jewish community sumptuary laws, economic privation, and religio-ethical ideas minimized the importance of ornamental clothing. Communal legislation was used as a check on any individual unduly preoccupied in making his wardrobe serve as personal adornment. The impact of ascetic teachings on medieval Jewish folk life, mainly through the channels of Cabala, also discouraged preoccupation with dress or food.

CHAPTER V

Diet and Table Customs

Foods, like other aspects of culture, were not confined to specific locales but spread from one area to another. Hence the same kinds of foods were usually prepared in the homes of Ashkenazic Jews, whether they lived in Central or Eastern Europe.[1] In most of the available sources, such as the book of customs and the popular daily guide, little is said of the route that had been taken in carrying food and table customs from one geographical region to another during the travels and wanderings of the Jews.[2] The foods are simply listed, and their ingredients specified, in order to confirm that ritual requirements have been met or that the proper benediction will be recited before eating.[3] Or else there is comment and discussion on the meaning of special foods assigned for festivals and important events.

The main diet of the Jewish family shows marked similarity to that of the German peasant who, as it was said, "ate his fill . . . in fish, in bread, in fruit. . . ."[4] That such foods were more easily accessible both in the general and Jewish communities in part accounts for their becoming synonymous with daily social life. The names of German foods, adapted to the vernacular of Yiddish, again reflect the cultural influence of the general environment on German-Jewish folkways. Some of the foods and table customs had their origin in an earlier age; however, the menu and food customs of Ashkenazic Jews of the 17th and 18th centuries continued to modern times as part of the family and communal life of European as well as American Jewry.[5]

1. Types of Food and Drink

Whether in Frankfort in the West or Prague in the East a full, hearty meal included fish and meat, supplemented by *tsimes* and pastry.[6] *Tsimes*, made of "raw turnips, carrots, cabbage, roots, greens," or "carrots, flour, sugar and cinnamon," is a dish acquired from the general, non-Jewish world, as were spiced vegetables and stewed fruit.[7] Jewish folk tradition interpreted "yellow" and "gold" of the carrot as "a sign of good fortune," because it resembles the "color of a coin." And an ethical meaning was ascribed to the carrot (*möhren, rüben,* Ger. pl.) by associating it with "increase," (*mehrn,* Yid.; *ribbuy,* Heb.), that is, an increase of "good deeds" as well as "material things."[8]

Mainly, the fresh-water fish pike, tench, and trout were eaten,[9] and though *gefilte fish* is not mentioned in the sources consulted, it is more than likely that this dish was known in German-Jewish communities. Inasmuch as the preparation of *gefüllter Hecht* is described in Hohberg's German cookbook, it is reasonable to suppose that this was also a favorite food among Jews.[10] As for dairy, or *milkhike*, foods, they consisted of eggs, cheese, milk, and butter[11]—with other standard foods being noodles, dumplings, and groats mush made of oats, corn, or barley—probably *kashe*—pea, groat, and dumpling soup, and stew.[12] *Kashe*, gruel, not originally a Jewish dish, was introduced into Germany from Eastern Europe.[13]

In noodles and noodle soup we have further examples of dishes popular in the general community becoming a component of the diet of German Jews. *Lokshn* was brought to Germany from across many lands, according to Grunwald; first from Persia, then to Slavic countries, and later to German-speaking regions.[14] Because the noodles are rolled and cut as "thin as paper," the name *vermicelli* was adapted to Yiddish.[15] The aphorisms and witticisms associated with *lokshn* indicate the extent to which this food of non-Jewish origin became deeply rooted in the folk life of European Jewry.[16] Raw and cooked vegetables also included green cabbage, peppers, stalks, carrots, turnips, cucumbers, compote, peas, beans, mushrooms, pumpkins, young onions, and onion buds.[17] Sourkraut was made of raw or cooked cabbage, while fruits and vegetables, such as cabbage, beets, and radishes, were pickled and preserved.[18]

The guide book of David Oppenheim, in enumerating the breads that were baked in the community, refers to the regular bread *(leḥem gamur),* made of risen dough *(baẓeḳ),* over which the *moẓi*, the benediction before eating, was recited. As the dough for white bread was used to bake "a satiating roll" (*gezatene zeml*), the *moẓi* could also be said over it. Another bread was made of prepared dough (*'isah*), which is "mixed with honey, fat, milk, and spices." Similar to coffee cake, this bread was eaten during or between meals. There was, in addition, a bread prepared from dough kneaded with milk and baked without water, which could not be used for the *moẓi*.[19] Dark bread and corn bread were also baked; and in listing the bread prepared from grain which belongs to the "seven species" (*shib'ah minim,* Deut. 8:8), Isaiah Horowitz mentions "bread made of spelt, called dark bread, and bread made of grain, called corn."[20] Rye bread was commonly used in the general German community, and especially among the peasants.[21] Bread was also made of rice, millet, buckwheat, and peas, and since this was not the "regular bread," it was not used at the beginning of the meal for the *moẓi*. In the Polish communities, Kirchan explains, bread is prepared from such grain.[22]

The pastry of *shmalts-kukhn* was made by mixing oil in dough, and *pasteten* were baked with a filling of meat, fish, cheese, or fruit.[23] The *pastete* is another example of a German dish that became part of Jewish culinary tradition. Other pastries were sweet bread (a biscuit made of almonds and sugar), almond tarts, and macaroons.[24] David Oppenheim—while describing the kinds of pastries made of dough—tells of the way the Jews of Prague would prepare waffles with a waffle iron: "In Prague waffle cakes are made of 'prepared dough,' and are baked between two irons."[25] And in Isaiah Horowitz's *musar*-treatise, there is a descriptive passage about the waffle iron of Prague:

> The 'prepared dough' is poured into the mould of the lower iron. . . . Then the upper and lower irons are squeezed like tongs and the waffle is immediately baked. . . . The engraved figure on the iron appears on the waffle.[26]

The waffle iron is another instance of an appliance or implement used in the general community and adopted by the Jews of Germanic regions.

Cooked fruits, a variety of raw and dried fruits, herbs, nuts, and seeds, were also part of the diet.[27] David Oppenheim enumerates apples, grapes, cherries, lemons, prunes, nuts, plum jam, dried peas, sunflower seeds, while Isaiah Horowitz, Ezekiel Landau, and Samuel ha-Levi of Meseritz mention the jams made of cherries and elderberries.[28] During the rite of circumcision, the *mohel* would dip an elderberry in the wine "to deepen its color and make it more appetizing." Elderberry jam was also used for medicinal purposes.[29] In addition, Hahn refers to herbs, dried fruits such as raisins, and an assortment of seeds; Kirchan lists apples, red grapes, large and small raisins, dates, olives, and caraway seeds among others; and Glikl of Hameln recalls that when her father-in-law moved to Hildesheim, he sent them "casks . . . with all kinds of foods, peas, beans, dried meat, and shop foods consisting of dried fruits, sliced stewed fruit. . . ."[30]

"Sweets" were prepared from nuts, fruit peels, honey, and spices. For example, Meir Eisenstadt (d. 1774; Eisenstadt, Hungary) speaks of candied orange peel, a delicacy made of "orange peels spiced with honey"; Samuel ha-Levi of Meseritz cites the preparation of "glazed nuts," and in the folk books containing the food customs of Prague and Frankfort there is mention of "almonds in cinnamon," "lemon, elderberry, and ginger spiced with honey," "preserved nutmeg, ginger, pepper, and lemon."[31]

And from Kirchan we hear that ginger, pepper, and cloves were the more commonly known spices.[32]

Beer, one of the popular drinks, was regularly served as a refreshment.[33] Wine and beer were used with other drinks and foods; olive oil or wine was mixed with beer, bread was dipped in wine, and nutmeg or bread crumbs would be placed in beer to add to its taste.[34] As for other drinks, they included whiskey, brandy, mead, prune juice, and vinegar diluted in water.[35]

2. Foods for Sabbath, Festivals, and Special Occasions

The custom of eating certain foods at stated times is an old one,[36] the Sabbath and festivals being among the occasions when special foods are prepared.[37] To be more specific, one of the table songs of *Simḥat ha-Nefesh*, while instructing and entertaining the folk, speaks of foods as an essential part of Sabbath festivity. "We shall usher in the holy Sabbath with joy, dressed like a man of riches. We shall not shun good food and good drink. . . . Nice *khales* (*ḥallot*) ought to be made. . . . One should not lack good fruit [and] good chickens. . . ."[38] The Friday evening meal generally would comprise fish, meat, soup, preserves *(ayngemakhts)*, and fruit.[39]

In western Hungary, the Friday noon-day meal which was eaten in the kitchen, not at the regular table, consisted of the sampling of foods prepared for the Sabbath. The Sabbath menu usually included a vegetable mixture, salad (*grintsayg*, Yid.; *grünzeug*, Ger.), grieves (a residuum of chicken fat: *griven*, Yid.), liver (*leber*), grits, and apple fritter (*epl-krepl*). On Sabbath *Be-Shallaḥ* it was the practice to eat a wheat or corn dish in addition to the regular *tsholnt* food.[40] Grits soup was served as a reminder of the Torah portion (Ex. 13:17 ff.), which relates how the Israelites crossed the Red Sea. Folk tradition pictures the Red Sea as having been split in two, like grits in soup.[41]

Since each locality had developed its own tradition in baking, it is not surprising that different kinds of *ḥallot* were prepared for the Sabbath and festivals.[42] In Prague and Hamburg the Sabbath bread—shaped as a hill—was known as *barkhes* and *berkhes*.[43] Through the Middle Ages in European Ashkenazic communities the Sabbath bread was also prepared as "cakes" (*pastida*), so we learn from Hahn and also from Kosman, who confirms the continuity of this custom by citing from the Maharil's collection of *Minhagim* and Moses Isserles's gloss on the code of law of the *Ṭur*. "Meat cakes" were eaten on the *Shabbat*, symbolizing the food of manna in the desert. By questioning whether *pastida* was still baked in Eastern Europe for the Sabbath, Kosman might have seen or else heard that the regular *khaleh* was used instead.[44]

Variations in local practice are also shown by the number of breads baked for the Sabbath. Kirchan, for instance, states that it was the custom to use three loaves of Sabbath bread, but according to Yeḥiel Epstein, four loaves were baked.[45] And as precedent, David Oppenheim mentions individual sages who had said that four loaves of bread should be placed on the table during a feast.[46] Since the Sabbath is a festive occasion, four loaves would be required.

Between *Rosh ha-Shanah* and *Hosha'ana' Rabbah* round *ḥallot* would be baked in German communities, the round shape representing one's hope that happiness will be continuous and uninterrupted throughout the year.[47] A festive meal was arranged in the town of Mattersdorf (western Hungary) on the afternoon preceding *Rosh ha-Shanah* eve, during which a round *barkhes* bread with carrots or cabbage was served.[48] Everywhere on *Rosh ha-Shanah* evening an apple dipped in honey was eaten at the beginning of the meal as a symbol of the "good fortune" and "sweet life" sought for the future. The apple alludes to the *sedeh tappuḥim*, "the Field of Apples" or "the Garden of Eden" in cabalistic literature. In rural areas,[49] in the 17th century, fresh foods and the head of a lamb were served on *Rosh ha-Shanah* for the evening meal.

Isaiah Horowitz gives the explanation that R. Meir of Rothenburg ate the head of a ram to recall "the sacrifice of Isaac" (Gen. 22:13). Carrots and fish, foods symbolizing "increase" or "fertility,"[50] were also served for *Rosh ha-Shanah*, the wish being thereby expressed that during the year "good deeds would multiply."[51]

The special foods for the festival of *Purim* were *kreplekh*, glazed nuts, and fruits.[52] Sometimes, as in Hamburg, words found on an amulet would be written on *Purim-kreplekh* and cookies, for such foods, as we have already seen, were regarded as efficacious in shielding one against misfortune.[53] In Mattersdorf, milk dishes were prepared for *Simḥat Torah* as well as *Shabu'ot*.[54] Cakes of meat or cheese, shaped as a ladder with seven rungs, were baked for the festival of *Shabu'ot*, to represent "the seven heavens which were torn open by God when the Torah was transmitted."[55] *Megileh-kroyt*, made of sourkraut, raisins, and sugar, was served on the eve of *Purim*, as well as on *Simḥat Torah* and at weddings. For the mid-day meal on *Purim*, sweet-seasoned beans were eaten. The *Purim-barkhes* bread, baked with special care by housewives, was decorated with "rosettes and coronets (little crowns)," and was called *gele barkhes* because of its yellow color.[56] On the Sabbaths between *Pesaḥ* and *Shabu'ot*, in the Mattersdorf community, *shlisl-matsos* were eaten. The *maẓẓot*, baked as round flat cakes, were pierced with a hollow key.[57] On the evening of *Tish'ah be-'Ab*, before the fast began, lentil soup and lentil dishes were served. Meat was not eaten on the eve of *Rosh Ḥodesh*, the new month, and on Mondays and Thursdays. A fuller meal—which included rice and *farfl*, baked crumbs of flour—was served at noon on the day of *Rosh Ḥodesh*.[58] Originally a German food, *farfl* became popular among the Jews of Central and Eastern Europe.[59]

The accounts of communal life in Nuremberg and Fürth tell of the banquets held to celebrate the joyous events of marriage, birth of a first-born son, circumcision, or moving into a new home. Some details are given for *Shabbat Zakhor*, the celebration held on the Sabbath preceding circumcision. On this occasion, four meals were prepared in accordance with the economic circumstances of the family, with the most expensive meal consisting of three hens—called turkey-cocks—and pike or trout. For the third grouping, two hens, sardines, and salmon were served.[60] In Hungary, peas (*sochorerbsen, zakhorerbsen*) fish oil (*sochorfisolen, zakhorfisolen*), pastry, and wine were served for *Shabbat Zakhor*.[61] A source dealing with Prague refers to the extensive baking that was prepared for the circumcision meal, but the only food mentioned is *reschige Ruten,* crisp rods wrapped in dough.[62] At some family celebrations in Mattersdorf, baked *flekn,* "speckles" of dough, would be distributed among the poor.[63]

The *se'udat miẓvah*, "a meal devoted to fulfilling a religious duty," was arranged for the festivals of *Ḥanukkah* and *Purim*; *Shabbat Zakhor*, the Sabbath preceding circumcision, and circumcision; *Pidyon ha-Ben*, the redemption of the first born, and marriage.[64] Such a meal would also be arranged to pay tribute to a visiting scholar, honor a person who had reached the age of seventy, or celebrate the occasion when a group of men, such as the *Ḥebrah* ("association, society"), had finished studying a book.[65] The communal character of "the festive meal," or *se'udah*, is given emphasis by Bacharach in that it involves more than one's immediate household.[66] The precedent for the *se'udat miẓvah*, Bacharach states, dates back to the Talmudic period, when a "redemption feast" was held for a first-born male child.[67] Through the years the *se'udat miẓvah* was observed, and by the 17th and 18th centuries festive meals would be arranged in honor of all special occasions. Hahn explains how the *se'udat miẓvah* was given impetus in the 15th century by R. Moses Minz who encouraged the holding of a festive meal whenever the study of a Talmudic tractate was completed. Then the *se'udah* became popular among the Jews of Germany, with Hahn later giving his support to holding such a meal, especially in those places where there was no *bet din*, court, to enjoin adherence to it.[68] Thus, a single scholar was the innovator of a *minhag*, or practice, that had a marked influence on Ashkenazic Jewish folk life.

The nature of local customs was also dealt with by Hahn as he questioned the validity of arranging a meal to felicitate the *Ḥatan Mosheh* (*Khosen Mosheh*), the person called upon to finish the scriptural cycle of reading during *Simḥat Torah.*

> The practice expounded by rabbinic authority to arrange a meal [in honor] of the *Ḥatan Mosheh* . . . should be given careful examination since the meal is not tendered to a scholar. I have never heard of arranging a meal for this purpose. However, nothing is conclusively proven by my claiming that I never heard of such a custom.[69]

In other words, Hahn points out that no scholar can question the authentic character of a local practice solely on grounds of personal observation and experience. Obviously, customs not known even to a man of learning might have existed in various places, and a custom might be so specific to its area that to people not living in the locality it would appear odd and meaningless.

Meals for special events were also scheduled by the *Ḥebra'* [*Ḥebrah*] *Ḳaddishah*, "Holy Society." When the society was established in Vienna in 1763, the five elected officers arranged a banquet at their own expense for the entire membership, but it was understood that a procedure so unusual as this one could not be repeated.[70] The leader of the *Ḥebra' Ḳaddishah* of Pressburg was authorized by the community to spend a maximum of 50 *gulden* to hold a meal (*brudermahl*) for the members of the society. But if he were to spend more than this amount, he could not expect to be reimbursed and would be obliged to pay personally for the additional expenditure.[71] On *Shabbat Parah* (Torah portion, Exod. 30-34), the *Ḥebrah shel ha-Ḳabranim* of Frankfort, "the Society of Gravediggers," would organize a banquet, a *se'udat miẓvah*, and in honor of the occasion hold a discussion on "the topic of ritual purification." The members of the society made it a practice to say to each other before separating: "Let us purify the unclean and thereby attain the highest state of sanctity."[72]

3. TABLE CUSTOMS

The sources on table customs provide information more suitable for descriptive than systematic discussion, as does the material already examined in our attempt to reconstruct some aspects of folk life. Not only were foods interpreted symbolically through association with religious holidays or social events, but they were also invested with meanings that grew out of popular belief, practice, and explanation. In addition to those food customs widely shared in all parts of the German-Jewish community, there were also practices of a local character in a given region having its own unique food tradition.[73]

Immediately after the table is covered with a cloth, salt is to be placed upon it; the grounds for this custom have been traced by Hahn to rabbinic tradition,[74] which recounts the instance of the ancient Israelites, who, while sitting at table, "postponed the washing of their hands and the recitation of the benediction before eating." When Satan brought charges against them for such negligent behavior, it was of no avail, for they "were protected by the covenant of salt" (Gen. 19:17-26).[75] By the use of cabalistic reasoning, Zechariah Plungian explains that salt is a "source of protection" when it is on the table, as it can "drive away the demon." And salt has such power, he continues, because its "numerical value is 78, equivalent to the numerical value of the word 'existence' (*havayah*), which is twenty-six multiplied by three." "Therefore," he concludes, during the meal "one should dip [food] three times in salt."[76]

Hahn also states that the knife and bread on the table have to be removed or covered prior to reciting the benediction after the meal. He finds this a valid custom, but he considers removing salt from the table when the meal is concluded "a foolish practice."[77] On the Sabbath, in the Frankfort community, all tables were covered with cloths, even those not in use. Likewise, the tables in the *sukkah*, booth, were covered to honor the Sabbath.[78] During a feast an empty space is left at the table, and the place is not set, David Oppenheim explains, in order to recall the destruction of the Temple of Jerusalem.[79] On days of mourning and sad occasions, peas and simple foods were eaten just as on the *vakhnakht* and *Shabbat Zakhor*.[80]

Dried fruit and bread were eaten either as part of the regular meal or else as a separate course between fish and meat, and since fish and meat were considered separate courses, the "washing of the hands" was required before eating each dish.[81] According to Kosman, this was done after eating the fish, before the meat, not only to be rid of "an offensive odor" but to "prevent a skin disease."[82] At a large banquet, Hahn tells, after the main meal was formerly concluded, by reciting the "grace" (*Birkhat ha-Mazon*), "a lesser meal of cheese" later followed.[83] In Frankfort, the length of time that elapsed between the eating of the meat and the cheese dishes was probably an hour; for Moses Isserles (d. 1572, Cracow), who lived 60 years before Hahn, related that "in these lands [Germanic and Slavic], the custom is widespread that after eating meat one waits an hour and then eats cheese . . ." (gloss on *Y.D.* 89: 1). Isserles's own inclination was to wait six hours after eating the meat. Some of the local differences in observing dietary regulations will be given further consideration.

The custom of eating sugar bread, cookies (*kikhelekh*), and cakes (*lekekh*) with the meal is also described by Kirchan. The pastry was used for *ḳinnuaḥ*, "wiping the mouth," so that the particles of food left from the first course could be removed before starting the next one.[84] In Prague, there was a similar practice of eating *shmalts-kukhn*, cookies made with fat, during the meal.[85] Between the fish and meat courses dried fruits were also used to "wipe the mouth."[86]

In the customs relating to food and dietary regulations, we note some of the differences in daily observance that existed among rabbinic authorities. First of all, Hahn would require five hours—

not the prescribed six—to pass before eating dairy foods after a meat dish:

> We are lenient in decreasing the waiting time an hour. [After eating] we do not have to wipe the mouth so as to remove particles of meat or rinse the hands. Meat needs to be removed only when we feel it in our teeth.[87]

Yet he does acknowledge that most "contemporaries, teachers, and colleagues are of the opinion that it is necessary to wait six hours after eating meat before having milk foods."[88] An opposing view is expressed by Zechariah Plungian, who derives his opinion from the *Shulḥan 'Arukh*, which "specifies a six-hour interval between eating meat and milk foods."[89] The opinion of Shabbetai Kohen (Shak) also supports the position taken by Plungian: If one tastes any kind of meat, even if it is not swallowed, he must wait six hours before drinking milk.[90] In practical Cabala, Plungian finds an allusion to the consequences that will befall any individual who fails to observe this dietary ruling: "A defiled [lit., ritually unclean] spirit will reside in him for forty days. If he begets a son during this forty-day period, he [the son] will be endowed with the soul of an evil [demonic] power."[91] Thus customs were invested with meaning and rationale derived from cabalistic and ethical writings; and woven into the texts of the folk book were the popular beliefs and practices associated with demonology, evil spirits, and transmigration of the soul.[92]

The religious and legal interpretations made by individual scholars had an influence on the way in which food customs were observed. Although it was the opinion of Elḥanan Kirchan that only cooked grain should be eaten, and not raw, a contrasting practice prevailed of eating any kind of grain to conclude the meal.[93] Upholding the view of Isaiah Horowitz, David Oppenheim permitted "whole grain" to be eaten before the meal, but only "dried or crushed grain" as part of the meal.[94]

In setting forth some of the folk practices connected with the

Sabbath and education, we have noted that study and song were considered essential to the meal.[95] Hence, Jonah Landsofer advised his children, "Do not sit down to eat your meal unless you have studied during the day." If they were to devote only one hour to study before the meal, they would fulfill his wish.[96] Meir Poppers, who was from Prague, wanted a passage read daily from the *Zohar*, before the morning and evening meals, so as to encourage the individual to acknowledge his shortcomings.[97]

Table songs for the Sabbath and festivals were included in the popularized *Shulḥan 'Arukh* and in the book of customs, the *minhogim-bukh*. Some songs were of local origin, as the ones Hahn had composed to be sung at the table to "create a festive mood" among "his large circle of pupils and friends."[98] In the second volume of *Simḥat ha-Nefesh*, Kirchan uses the table song to spread cheer in a time of anguish, to criticize social behavior, to offer instruction in ethics, religious observance and law, and raise the cultural level of the people. The songs were written in rhyme and accompanied by musical notes "composed by a musician so that the exact tune could be reproduced."[99] The music is also suitable for dancing. The reader is advised by Kirchan, "If the music is not understood, let him contact any of the easily accessible musicians to play the tune for him." And "those who learn the tune should teach it to others in order that the music be spread."[100] The music employed by Kirchan in his *musar*-book is another instance of the culture of the general society influencing the folk life in the *gas*.

4. Some Communal Problems in the Regulation of Food and Table Tradition[101]

As critics of social life, the authors of ethical folk books wanted to make the people aware of their failure to fulfill food and table regulations. They therefore singled out instances of negligence in matters of dietary ritual. While these writers no doubt exaggerated the extent of the negligence or violation, their statements were justified in the main by the facts of daily life. They not only spoke out with the authority that comes with knowledge, but they were also fully aware of events taking place in the home and on the street. The cases of non-observance which they cited may be attributed to the same human factors that accounted for absences from synagogue.[102] While synagogue attendance was made obligatory by communal regulation in order to assure the required quorum for worship, local authorities did not legislate the observance of religious practice incumbent on individuals in their homes.

The observation is made by Hahn that "individuals fail to wash their hands [i.e., before they eat]," and "they proceed with the meal before reciting the benediction."[103] No more specific reason is given for the neglect of this ritual, which is treated in the usual critical tone expressed in *musar*-writings with regard to "laxity in fulfilling religious duties and the preoccupation with superficial interests."[104]

When Meir Eisenstadt came to Prossnitz, Moravia, he noticed that when an animal was slaughtered not enough care was taken to check the gullet and confirm that it could be eaten in accordance with religio-legal dietary standards.[105] There are students in Prague, so Ezekiel Landau reports, who frequent coffee houses of non-Jews and readily drink from the dishes in these establishments, little concerned that they are rejecting the requirements of ritual adherence. "They are the children of the times," Landau despairs, "for they drink milk from [dishes] of non-Jews. They have knowledge, but no reverence. They are light-minded toward the observance of the law if they are [willing to be] guests when no other dishes are on hand. . . ."[106] Kirchan tells of a man who was not scrupulous about the food he ate and therefore violated dietary laws. "When I discovered this," Kirchan states, "the dishes had to be made ritually clean (*kosher*)."[107] This incident was probably not unusual, for the Polish Jews who settled in the Rhineland area became suspicious that the dishes used by the Jews of Germany did not meet the standards of ritual fitness. "Polish Jews should not eat from the dishes of the German Jews," Kirchan had advised, "because the Rhinelanders eat the scrapings of intestines and fats. The Polish Jews cite the opinion of 'Sifte Kohen' [Shak] when it is their intention to return home."[108] In other respects cleavages existed between the Jews of Central and Eastern Europe, which have continued through modern times.[109]

A sharp contrast is made between the larger and smaller communities in the ability of leaders to comply with ritual requirements in slaughtering and examining animals. Yeḥiel Epstein claims that the *shoḥaṭim u-bodḳim,* the slaughterers and examiners, in smaller communities are not competent, that they have no confidence in their own opinions, and that in their decisions they are swayed by fear of criticism. In larger communities, on the other hand, the "slaughterers and examiners" are considered qualified.[110] Kirchan, who also had firsthand knowledge of rural life, comments that the slaughterers, *shoḥaṭim*, in small towns are illiterate, "unable to read an *alef*." Their slaughtering knives are "rusty and blemished," and "seldom meet the standards required [for] ritual qualification."[111] Moses Ḥasid urges that scrupulous care be taken "to examine the knife" used in slaughtering and that the lungs and chest of the animal be checked for "adhesions."[112] A *Taḳḳanah* of the Budapest community took the precaution of allowing only those individuals who have a knowledge of the law to determine if food could be eaten whenever doubt arose as to its dietary fitness.[114] There was also a need for authoritative opinion to judge the ritual standard of foods eaten during the season of the fairs—when people were transients in outlying areas where there was no Jewish communal life.[115] In 1715, R. Simeon Frankel of Würzburg prepared a list of eighteen regulations specifying how wine should be made in the home in order to meet ritual requirements.[116] Obviously the leaders of the community were finding it necessary to provide basic information on the observance of dietary laws.

The *musar* writers who considered women careless or uninformed in fulfilling the standards required by the dietary laws usually wished to avoid generalizations. Their criticisms seem to be based on specific incidents, either personally observed or reported by others. Hence, Yeḥiel Epstein objected to women "placing slaughtered geese by the stove during cold weather . . . so as to facilitate the plucking of feathers." "And in some instances," he states, "the geese are placed on the stove," with the result that if the slaughtered fowl is sufficiently warmed "its fat melts and the blood is prevented from being drawn out through 'salting.'" He is also aware that in order to clean the fowls after they are plucked, women "will singe [them] over burning coals" instead of "scalding them in boiling water." Other women are careless in salting meat after it has been soaked. They do not "salt the meat on all sides," Epstein adds, but "some light-headed women use [only] a fist full of salt, insufficient to draw blood from the meat."[117] And Moses Ḥasid claims that "women are not conversant with the legal requirement of salting meat."[118]

Another difficulty lay in convincing people to take precautions against eating unsanitary or contaminated foods. Peas and grapes were among the vegetables and fruits grown in the yards for home use, but in Kirchan's opinion the peas were only suitable for cooking and were not sufficiently clean to be eaten raw.[119] Hahn cautions against buying wormy foods, explaining that "dried fruits . . . and seeds—purchased from storekeepers—are usually wormy and infested with mites."[120] Not only should dried fruits that became contaminated be avoided, but crushed cabbage as well.[121] Worms were found in the flour supplied by the store,[122] and a warning was also given not to eat wormy cherries, plums, and peas.[123] The community was likewise advised not to eat raw nuts when "covered by an outer green shell.[124] On the other hand, Kirchan expressed the more lenient opinion that contaminated foods might be eaten in case of scarcity.

> As to meat, fish, and bread that have become mouldy on the inside, these foods are suitable for eating because of need. . . . Fruit that has fermented due to the heat [lit., sun] may be eaten [also for the same reason].[125]

Precautions were taken to keep food out of the reach of rodents and domestic animals by having it "wrapped in bundles and suspended in the air."[126]

From the information on German-Jewish folkways, obtained from a survey of foods and table customs, a twofold process emerges. On the one hand, there is allegiance to the rabbinic dietary tradition, and on the other, foods of the general cultural environment are adopted and made part of the social regimen of the Jewish society. The continuity of table customs of an earlier period over the centuries was partly due no doubt to their relationship to holidays and festive events, and to the ethical interpretation given to such observances in popular literature. However, the over-all pattern of Jewish social life did not preclude the emergence of local customs that were unique to a given area.

Foods, such as *kugl, tsimes, farfl, kneydlekh, kikhelekh,* probably originated in Germany and were then carried to Eastern Europe, whereas *lokshn* and *kashe* are examples of foods in the German-Jewish community that came from Eastern Europe. There is no apparent conflict between the Jewish cultural and religious heritage and the influences that the German environment had on the preparation of foods. The integration of the tradition of the past with the culture of the present to become part of everyday life is no unique development in Jewish history.

Because of their sensitivity to cultural developments, the authors of the folk handbook and guide have again afforded us realistic glimpses of a significant aspect of social life.

CHAPTER VI

Folk Medicine: Popular Practices and Remedies[1]

Since the legal, folk, and communal literature of German Jewry in the 17th and 18th centuries showed a concern for matters of health, almost any person could learn about the more common ailments from the account of customs, the popular *Shulḥan 'Arukh*, or the handbook on medicine. Suggested "remedies and cures" (*segullot u-refu'ot*) would usually accompany the description of the symptoms of a disease. Medical information was interspersed with practices recommended for obtaining relief during illness, and in this body of folk medicine both knowledge and lore were combined.[2]

After the 16th century there was greater use of folk medicine books due, first of all, to the increased physical and mental suffering resulting from the Thirty Years' War; and, further, to the popular appeal of practical Cabala with its prescribed formulas to prevent demons from doing harm and spreading disease.[3] The characteristics of the folk-medicine handbook were described by David Tevle Ashkenazi (d. 1734) in his explanation for incorporating medical information in his Talmudic discourses: "By means of enigmatic words and practical Cabala, I have beheld wondrous things in addition to remedies and cures."[4] He states that he is eager to disseminate medical information in rural areas, in particular, where physicians are not always available and a home remedy is the only form of relief to which people can turn in time of illness.

> For I have seen many residents of forest regions and country towns who do not have access to experienced doctors.

> Furthermore, [though] remedies are used, [and] the *segullah* is applied effectively, still they are always in pain. Many die prematurely. We are not able to do anything extraordinary except through remedies and herbs. . . .[5]

Folk-medicine remedies must have helped the sick, for otherwise Jacob Coblenz would not have been able to boast of his accomplishments: "From others I have heard of prescribed remedies and cures that have been tried many times, and with the help of God many individuals were healed through me. Upon investigation . . . , I learned that most of the illnesses had been checked in seven, fourteen, or twenty-one days. . . ."[6] In submitting the remedies that he as well as others had found to be beneficial, Jacob Coblenz cites the legal latitude given to the doctor who, in order to save a person's life, does not have to hesitate to prescribe a remedy or perform any service so long as he is not engaging in "idolatry, incest, and bloodshed" (Ket. 19a). The preservation of a human being was given precedence over all other religio-legal and religio-ethical commandments.[7]

Remedies were also obtained from standard medical works translated into various languages,[8] for the information on medicine and health in a handbook, or in an ethical guide, was an adaptation of what originally appeared in the medieval *Canon* of Medicine.[9] In this way, the scientific and medical knowledge of the Middle Ages became accessible in Germany. Classical medical texts and sources were available through translations into Hebrew and Yiddish and through the inclusion of such knowledge in popular books intended for moral instruction and legal guidance.[10] The works of Ibn Sina, in Hebrew, were known to Bacharach and also to Jacob Emden and Ezekiel Landau.[11]

1. Disease and Popular Views

Disease was not only explained in terms of physical causes because ailments would often be attributed to evil spirits conspiring to do injury.[12] The educated man, therefore, was not only versed in "Talmud, Mishnah and Torah," but "he understood Kabbala and the mystery of creation," and "he could summon angels and conjure many demons," as well as "read the stars of heavens" and tell "what the leaves of the trees were saying. . . ."[13] The widespread notion that demons can cause disease was influenced in two ways, by ancient rabbinic lore transmitted through the ages, and by German folk practices and attitudes of the immediate surroundings.[14] Despite all of their intellectual discipline, the rabbis did not escape the impact of their environment and were therefore swayed by the views dominant among the people. And so they felt that demons were real and could affect human conduct; that the soul of the dead wanders from place to place searching for an abode where it can anchor itself, and that some persons have the power to perform miraculous deeds.[15] Though Jewish legal tradition is opposed in principle to magical practices, the use of an amulet or incantation to cure an illness was acceptable if, on the basis of trial, it proved to be beneficial.[16] Thus, the ambivalent position taken by the rabbis cannot be considered apart from the cultural currents of their time, for they were not governed solely by reason but by need and experience. They did not—and probably could not—follow consistently such advice as that given by Maimonides, "You must beware of sharing the error of those who write amulets (*kameoth*). . . . Rational persons ought not to listen to such men, nor in any way believe their assertions."[17] Yet, as we shall point out, they did make a distinction between a custom adhered to as an aid in overcoming human difficulties and a magical practice employed to alter the natural order of things.[18]

In view of the constant threat of demons, helpful "remedies" were prescribed in the same way that a cure would be recommended for physical disease. Since demons were considered potentially able to cause sickness and death, folk-medicine techniques were relied upon to protect one against such peril.[19] To curb evil spirits from doing harm, David Ashkenazi recommends: "Take the right eye of a rooster and bind it in the right hand," and if this is done, "no harm will befall you . . . either by a dog or demon. . . ."[20] The advice is also given to burn the head of a cat and hurl its ashes at demons whenever they become a menace, and by this procedure, one is assured that they will be routed: "It will appear to them [the demons] as if a multitude has assembled and they will flee."[21]

The folk-medicine book also advises how to cope with witchcraft, regarded as another force capable of undermining the health and well-being of the populace. It is not necessary to belabor the point that sorcery was known in the Jewish community as well as in the general community.[22] A query submitted to Samuel Meseritz implies that it was the practice "to consult sorcerers" in instances of illness and theft. Rabbinic authority saw no objection to seeking the opinion of a sorcerer or magician, "even if there is no serious illness," providing that the sorcerer did not resort to astrology or divination (Deut. 18:10–11; 2 Kings 17:17).[23] While tests were given to ascertain whether a person was a witch, and the recitation of "prayers" was suggested to overcome the malevolent powers of witchcraft,[24] we have not, however, found any evidence of witches being brought to trial in any of the German-Jewish communities.[25] Various procedures were prescribed in the folk-medicine handbook to nullify the effects of sorcery. The heart of a rabbit is tied to the side of a person who has been "bewitched." The skin of a donkey is burned seven times and then placed upon the troubled individual. A special bath is prepared from root plants. Or a "weasel is singed seven times over a flame."[26] To guard against witchcraft, sorcery, or the evil eye, amulets were worn that were made from any one of the following: the hair of a black donkey, the ashes of the buttocks of a rooster or chicken, unrefined silver of "white stones" found in the stomach of a chicken or rooster, a nut filled with salt and sealed with wax, or the head of a snake.[27] In Jewish lore the serpent is pictured as the beguiler of man; its poison is the source for the

Esaus and Hamans of history. The serpent is also associated with Sammael, the angel of death, "the chief of all demons."[28] Folk practices, however, sought to transform the role of the snake into something beneficial, namely, as an aid to the mother in reducing childbirth pangs or in preventing miscarriage.[29]

The placing of a new knife under the pillow guarantees one's safety against any evil force.[30] When a child is bewitched, three

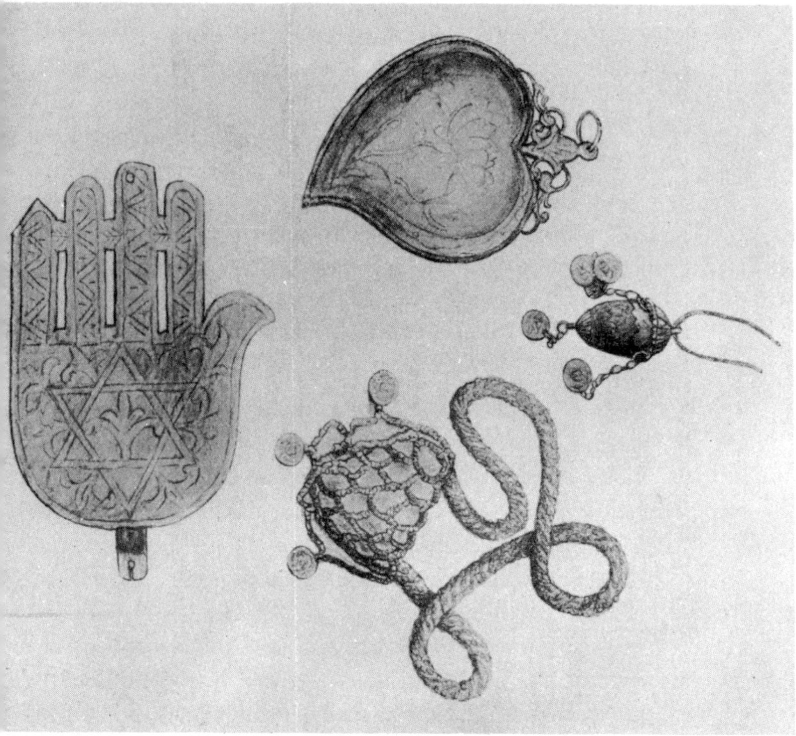

Fig. 9. Amulets to Counteract Evil Spirits *(Courtesy, Widener Library, Harvard University)*. From *Mitteilungen der Gesellschaft für jüdische Volkskunde, XXIX (N. S.,* 1926), plate # 2, beginning of the volume. Objects originally in the Jüdische Museum, Vienna.)

candles should be made, using the wax of a *habdalah* candle and a piece of the child's shirt for the wicks. The candles are to be placed beside three legs of the bed. This popular "remedy" must have consoled the child's family by the assurance: "As the candles burn, the child will utter a weird sound, but by the time the candles are consumed, he will be healed."[31]

Toward the end of his book David Ashkenazi relates that as he was once traveling "through villages and woods," several young men approached him in a courteous manner: "May we have a word with you? Give us some novel ideas or simple explanations that young persons should have when they attain the age of love-making and marriage. [Do this] with an inscription on parchment paper [i.e., an amulet]." Ashkenazi was apparently pleased to comply with their request, as he had with him inscriptions that could be used as amulets to forestall tragedy or circumvent any difficult situation that might arise.[32] In folk medicine the diverse uses of the amulet consist in controlling the weather, relieving a toothache, overcoming fear (*mora' shaḥorah*; *more shekhore*), checking fever, and easing childbirth.

A description of a 16th century German town relates how the itinerant student, traveling from one community to another, displayed "strange-looking phials, covered with cabalistic signs, a crystal globe and an astrolobe, followed by an imposing scroll of parchment inscribed with mysterious Hebraic-looking characters," and he "would probably drive a roaring trade amongst townsmen in love-philters, cures for the ague and the plague, and amulets against them, horoscopes, predictions of fate."[33] In other words, Jewish social practices were not only influenced by the general environment, but they also left their mark on the folkways of the Germanic community, especially through the lore of the Cabala.[34]

The incantation (*laḥash*) was another method prescribed to cure illness and restrain the evil eye from causing grief.[35] Incantations are similar in their forms of expression; there was no unique incantation, so to speak, that grew out of a local event, since the incantation was obviously concerned with ills that were universal and affected people everywhere. To give an example, Ashkenazi suggests that when someone is ill and wants relief, he should "take salt, go to a pit or stream, cast the salt toward the front, the back, [and] above the head—into the water—, and then recite: 'Just as the salt melted, may the sickness and the 'evil eye' that has possessed (. . . inserting name) disappear.'"[36] As an incantation, Jacob Coblenz offers the one that he heard R. Sender use "to check the flow of blood caused by a wound from a sword or spear." First, Coblenz explains, "Let him breathe" on the wound, "then say, '*laḥaneh, maḥaneh, raḥaneh,*' with a full pause at the *nun* [the *n*]." The incantation will bring good results, Coblenz continues, "if it is recited three times, in a whisper, with one breath." Not only does it stop the flow of blood, but it can prevent swelling, and it will also heal injuries.[37] Coblenz also knew of an incantation to cure fever, inflammation, and erysipelas, which were among the more prevalent ailments.[38] He testifies to the successful results obtained whenever the incantation was used, and in his account he also portrays the part that the handbook of remedies must have played in the life of the folk.

> Use this form of expression: 'Michael and Gabriel, march over the field and heal [lit., do right, plead with] the fever.' Then call, 'Fever, fever, I am on fire because of you, not in spite of you.' Say this three times, each time blowing on the feverish body with the mouth, and you will heal yourself quickly. I have tested this incantation among various persons, and it [also] proved effective with the help of God to prevent 'swelling', called *blozn*. I have also tried this incantation for many persons with the illness of *roytlof* (erysipelas) and derived satisfying results.[39]

However, Coblenz adds that there were individuals with inflammation who received no relief from the incantation, and he therefore advised them "to mix the yolk of an egg thoroughly with linseed oil," and apply the poultice "after the swelling came to a head [lit., had opened]."[40] During the crisis of the Frankfort fire, Schudt reports, an "incantation" was employed; the words of a "formula to quench fire" were written on a crust of bread and then hurled into the flames.[41]

The folk-medicine handbook does not limit itself solely to the subject of medicine but embraces a wide range of interests affecting a person's well-being. The formulas of folk remedies suggest, for example, how a thief is to be detected and a dead thief pacified; how the horoscope can determine the fortune of an individual, weather conditions, and the success of the season's crop; how one can become invisible, guard himself against attacks from dogs and scorpions, protect himself on a journey; in short, be safe at all times. Such diversified topics are the normal concern of folklore and folk medicine.[42] As an illustration, a thief could not molest the living after he died if the needle that sewed his shrouds were buried in the area where he usually walked. A thief could be detected if an egg held in the palm of a hand were placed on the heart of the suspect as he slept. Unwittingly, he would reveal everything that he had done.[43] It is possible to protect oneself against the attack of a dog or the bite of a scorpion, by carrying "the tooth of a dog or the tail of a scorpion."[44] This does not exhaust the number of objects that might be worn as a safeguard by any individual.[45]

How does the book of customs deal with the subject of magic? The "characteristics of *niḥush*, divination" (Levit. 19:26) are discussed by Hahn because in daily life one has to distinguish between a custom that, though superstitious, is still permissible, and a practice that is prohibited because it is magical. At the outset he states that he will confine himself to what the sages have indicated as magical, and for corroboration he cites from *Sefer ha-Yir'ah*, of Jonah Gerondi, that only those acts are magical which have been designated as such by Talmudic sages.[46] In the

Talmud itself, Hahn says later, in the course of his discussion, a distinction is made between miracles and magic.[47] The distinction evidently is that miracles are an expression of God's will, whereas magic is a human contrivance without any regard for the Divine will.

For a specific case of *niḥush*, he cites from *Sefer Ḥasidim* one example from among several, that is, being apprehensive of eating the head of a cow or the intestines of a cow when there is sickness. This, Hahn points out, is characterized by the sages as an imitation of the practices of the Amorites, which they evidently assumed to be magical. Hahn proceeds to say that "with regard to acts of divination now in practice there is no need to mention them except some which, though they have no natural explanation, are not prohibited in any authoritative work."[48]

Hahn then presents a series of examples of superstitious practices that have no natural explanation and seem to be magical but are not and are therefore not prohibited. First, there is the custom of waiting until *Rosh Ḥodesh* before beginning to study a new section of a book, on the assumption that such an act has special merit. Although one can find approval and justification for such conduct in the *Shulḥan 'Arukh*, Hahn states that this practice is of no significance to him. At first glance it may seem to be that of divination but, according to Talmudic teachers, it is not. Second, the custom of giving a child the name of a deceased, and not a living, relative, so as to prevent a mishap befalling him. This practice is not to be regarded as magical. To the non-Jew it is of no consequence if children are named for living parents, whereas for the Jew it is a matter of grave concern, as was already explained in note 65 of chapter 2. Third, the "lunar remedies" derived from the full moon. There are no objections, he says, to such practices; they are not considered magical. Fourth, certain practices to prevent injury by demons, of which he mentions, as examples, not to place under a drain whatever falls from a roof and not to drink water from a vessel until some of it is poured out.

The reason for such practices being allowed, Hahn adds, is that according to Talmudic lore demons do exist, are capable of doing harm, and consequently preventive measures should be taken.[49]

At the conclusion of his remarks, Hahn raises the following problem: In the Talmud there are "many instances of prohibitions because of the danger of evil spirits and demons and because of worry." However, the *poskim* do not mention them; the reason is: Men's beliefs about such matters have changed. What was once considered dangerous, later on was not so. And "to prove this, there are many things stated in the Talmud as consisting of great danger, but we have never heard or seen anyone injured by them." For this reason Hahn does not mention many prohibitions cited in the Talmud but only those in the later *poskim*. He does add some material from earlier *poskim*, because people accept their authority. Whoever wishes to abide by the Talmud in such matters, "blessings on him," he says, but he does not find it obligatory to follow the Talmud in these instances.[50]

The popular views of the folk also had an influence on prayer, especially when the welfare of the community was involved.[51] Special prayers were recited for the recovery of the sick,[52] and in the *Minhagim* of Fürth and the Vienna *Memor*-Book of 1669 prayers were included, based on the custom of *shinnui ha-shem*, of changing the sick person's name.[53] Since another name signifies a new person, by receiving a different name the sick man was enabled to start life anew.

> If death has been decreed for . . . let it not be fulfilled. Now he is a different person, like a new human being, a child just born.[54]

It should not be overlooked that individuals like Jonah Landsofer—no doubt influenced by the ideas of the scientific renaissance—expressed opposition to the popular use of prayer. Landsofer emphasized that one should not pray for a change in "the order of things" but for self-improvement; for "a prayer asking for help" can limit the free expression of one's will.[55]

Dreams are also dealt with in the handbook of "remedies and cures" and in the account of customs, the popularized *Shulḥan 'Arukh*, and *responsa*. Bacharach, Yeḥiel Epstein, Hahn, Kirchan, and Jacob Reischer discuss and summarize views on dreams as related to an older tradition. That is, dreams experienced during sleep are considered to be the result of daytime reverie;[56] a dream of evil or foreboding allusions is due to thoughts inwardly harbored.[57] When a dream implies that a disaster is impending, the individual must resort to fasting in order to prevent its occurrence. Since ancient Talmudic times fasting has been observed "to avert a bad dream" from being fulfilled.[58]

Kirchan sums up the procedure stated in the *Shulḥan 'Arukh* and *Shelah*: An individual who has had a bad dream on Friday night should not fast on Saturday, so that he does "not deflect from the joy of the Sabbath"; instead, he should select two other days for fasting during the week.[59] Hahn and Epstein present a more lenient viewpoint, namely that an individual can fast on the Sabbath if the dream causes undue grief and anxiety.[60]

In accordance with a Talmudic practice, the person experiencing a bad dream contacts three of his most intimate friends, and in their presence recites seven times, "I have beheld a good dream," and they answer him seven times, "You have beheld a good dream; [yes,] your dream has a good [omen]; may it be good; merciful God, make it good."[61] Epstein cites a prayer that he thinks should be recited on Friday night before retiring. The prayer expresses an attitude of indifference toward the evil forces that manipulate dreams: "If I should dream tonight, [let it be understood] that I shall not fast tomorrow." He implies that no dream can frighten him, and so he has no reason for fasting on the Sabbath.[62] Although he recognizes that the demons' world is real, he asserts nevertheless that he will not allow himself to be disturbed by any of their threats or intrusions into man's affairs. As Epstein explains,

"One does not fast so that the [evil] perpetrators of dreams will not have a sense of accomplishment."[63]

An incompleted dream, or a vague dream that could not be recollected, was also cause for concern. It was essential to know the content of the dream, first in order to determine whether the dream was good or bad, and then what precautionary measures would have to be taken to circumvent the occurrence of the ominous event. Ashkenazi therefore recommends, "If a dream is forgotten and the person wishes to recall it, let him reverse [his] undergarment . . . and go back to sleep. He will again have the [same] dream."[64] The folk-medicine handbook also provides a "prescription" to induce the type of dream that might be desired.[65]

2. Ailments and Remedies

The need for medical care increased in German-Jewish communities in the 17th century on account of the ailments carried by itinerant beggars and by refugees fleeing from Poland during the Chmielnicki pogroms.[66] More Jewish hospitals were established during this time, with houses being set aside especially to care for the sick.[67] At that time the doctor was spoken of more often, as is evident from Coblenz's advice to a man suffering from inflammation that he consult a competent physician associated with a hospital.[68] The hospital, previously known as *hekdesh*, was now called *bet ha-ḥoleh*.[69]

The popular cures in a medical handbook or guide for daily living, the reference to individual ailments in a *responsum*, or observations reported in an autobiography, are our main sources pertaining to diseases and remedies. Any information, no matter how sparse, on how a person treated himself during an illness throws further light on Jewish social life. Since hospitals and professional medical facilities were not always accessible, especially in small towns and rural areas, the remedies offered had to be simple so that they could be prepared at home. The medications of juices and salves were usually made of materials easily obtained.[70] In Jewish folk-medical practices we can also single out the influences of the general environment,[71] since popular notions and customs in Germanic life relating to disease and health became part of the body of folk remedies of Germanic Jewry.

Animals such as the hog, crow, rabbit, frog, horse, snake, ritually unclean according to *halakhah*, were used to supply the ingredients of folk remedies.[72] Urine and dung were considered to have drug components with healing power.[73] The *responsa* of Jacob Reischer and Elyakim Götz discuss the relation of folk medicine to *halakhah*, and specifically whether the use of ritually unclean animals and foods can be permitted for reasons of health. Reischer is asked for the reasons that "the dried and congealed blood of the male goat" can be given to a person who was not seriously ill but "collapses from an internal pain."[74] He explains that the basis for the practice is threefold: (1) the custom of a people has the weight of law; (2) the blood has no juice and is tasteless because it has congealed; for example, maw and tartar, ritually unclean, can be eaten when dried; (3) any internal ailment is considered serious, so much so that the Sabbath may be violated in order to prepare and administer a medical remedy.[75] By stating that he can find legal grounds to justify a custom of the people, Reischer again expresses the permissive attitude of individual rabbis, teachers, and scholars toward folk practices that were entrenched and became an integral part of social life.[76] Men of diverse walks of life, the scholar, rabbi, and physician, as well as a cross section of the population, shared in the performance of folk-medical practices.

We have already indicated that rabbis assumed a functional and pragmatic view of folk customs; if a practice aided people in time of difficulty or sickness, they were inclined to regard it as valid. They understood that a custom can have continuity and vitality of its own when it is adopted and adhered to by the group as a whole, and once it becomes part of the life of the people, it is not readily discarded because of the wishes of a few individuals of influence or knowledge.[77] Custom has been known to be more powerful than even rabbinic opinion.[78]

An individual who was not feeling well told Götz that some "authoritative persons" informed him that he could improve his health if he would place the bone of a dead person in his bath; but if this is not possible, then he should use burial shrouds instead. He asked Götz to advise him whether such a practice is permissible. In his reply Götz emphasizes that the Torah should not be violated for the "personal benefit" of an individual, that *halakhah* may be transgressed only when "there is a serious ailment," but that in this instance, where life is not in jeopardy, there is no justifiable reason for employing the bone of a corpse as a remedy.[79] Other rabbinic authorities, such as Menaḥem Mendel Krochmal[80] (d. 1661; Nikolsburg, Moravia) and Jacob Emden,[81] fully aware of the legal tradition that a dead body may not serve any utilitarian purpose, were willing to permit such use only when no other means of relief or cure was available. Emden required an authorization by a doctor, stating that the patient's life is in danger, before allowing any corpse to be touched. In other words, health measures are to be determined by medical knowledge, not by folk feeling and practice.

When a folk remedy was referred to as a *segullah*, it could serve either as "a medication" or as "a charm," but both functions were not carried through simultaneously.[82] For each one of the more common illnesses a medication was usually prescribed, and in the main the ailments dealt with in the Jewish folk-medicine handbook may be classified as follows: internal; speech, eye, ear, nose and throat; female disorders, pregnancy, and child delivery; wounds, fractures, amputation; care of the child, before and after birth; contagion and epidemics; skin; mental and psychological; miscellaneous, which include first aid, headache, toothache, loss of sleep. An illness was not always referred to by its name; thus in the eulogy for his father, Ẓebi Ashkenazi, Jacob Emden states that "pains and torments" afflicted him (his father) and made him "more dead than alive."[83] We do not imply that all ailments are listed in the handbook or guide on folk medicine. Paralysis, for example, is not mentioned, although the affliction is referred to in a *responsum*.[84]

There are remedies for bodily pains, loss of strength, and decline in health. For physical weakness, David Ashkenazi prescribes that the sick have the soles of their feet rubbed with hog fat and drink boiled water, or else gentian plant juice as a tonic.[85] The gentian was also taken as a home remedy for internal pains, heart, lung, or spleen.[86] Folk medicine sought to check fainting, dizzy spells, and listlessness. To overcome fainting, the text suggests to "grind the caraway that grows in the field, mix it with vinegar," and then inhale.[87] The root of the broom plant, or the sweet calamus, is considered effective in giving one strength. A swooning spell can be checked by dipping an apple in vinegar, putting it in each shoe, and then placing it on the head. Apparently the apple is the object to which the illness is directed or transferred. If someone becomes listless, he can prepare an "invigorating drink" by "putting the dung of a cat in a linen cloth and dissolving it in wine." If a person feels "troubled" or "depressed," he is also advised to try this drink.[88]

Fever is known by several terms, *ḳaddaḥat* or *fiver*,[89] *helish fayer* or *sarefet 'esh*,[90] and *brand*.[91] When Jacob Reischer is asked whether soil may be taken from a grave to cure a fever, he replies in the affirmative, since health is involved.[92] The remedies for fever follow the usual pattern of folk medicine, namely the preparation of an amulet pouch, the "ejection" of the disease into water,[93] the eating of food with an amulet inscription, the application of a rubbing liniment made with oil,[94] and the drinking of the juice of water cress.[95] When persons with a consumptive fever consult Coblenz about a remedy, he suggests that they wear an amulet pouch and also drink the juice of the "sheep's-rib" and the pea blossom.[96] And he also describes the "amulet for fever" that

Abraham Lissa of Frankfort (d. 1768) had given him. On three sides of an apple the words *biḳdesh*, *miḳdesh*, *niḳdesh* are written, with the fourth side left blank. The apple is then cut into four pieces; each day the sick person eats in one gulp a piece of the apple bearing the inscription, and on the fourth day he throws the blank piece behind him into the river.[97] Jacob Reischer, in another *responsum*, discusses the practice of wearing an "amulet of herbs" to check a "severe fever" (*ḳaddaḥat ḥam*). After the amulet is worn for "an unspecified period of time," it is "cast into a stream"; in case of grave illness it can be disposed of on the Sabbath. Inasmuch as "running a fever" was not uncommon, the expert opinion of a physician was required to ascertain when an individual with fever was seriously ill.[98] Otherwise, the Sabbath might be violated without justifiable grounds.

Jaundice is known as *gelsukht*, the "yellowish-looking" disease.[99] To check jaundice, the sick person is instructed to take the yellow agate stone with a liquid, morning and evening, for three days.[100] A plant remedy is also suggested; the roots of the carnation or the wild thyme, or the Easter Lucy and the nettle, are prepared with wine and taken before and after meals.[101] To cure jaundice, the physician Wallich of Frankfort prescribed four grains of tartar emetic, to be taken with water or wine.[102] As Wallich was a doctor, the drug cannot be considered a folk remedy. Only a limited number of drugs, it seems, were used in the preparation of folk medicines.[103]

Ulcers, swelling, chills, colic are among the more common ailments,[104] and in an anonymous autobiography of Prague there is an account of the effect of diet on ulcers: "I was full of ulcers, and the meals I ate were very unwholesome for me, for it is the custom in Prague to eat at the midday meal peas and millet with a little butter, which proved very injurious to me."[105] In the medical handbook home remedies are suggested to relieve stomach pains. For a swollen abdomen, the juice of the aloe root is mixed with honey and taken daily with a salted egg.[106] Another stomach remedy consists of heating nutmeg and flax from a growing or winding plant; the fluid resulting is poured on a new piece of canvas to form a poultice.[107] Stomach pains can also be checked by using an application of either warm wine or some pieces of wild chestnut mixed in two or three spoonfuls of wine or grain whiskey.[108] Other internal ailments, according to the folk-medicine manual, are inflammation, abscess, and erysipelas.[109] Meir Eisenstadt reports the case of a woman who suffered from an inflamed abscess.

> And she feels as if an abscess is under her heart, and as the pain spreads, a green secretion is discharged, which resembles the secretion from the abscess called 'swelling.'[110]

The treatment for swelling and inflammation does not differ from the standard remedy offered for most ailments, namely, the preparation of salves and medicines from plants and animal organs.[111] As a cure for a swollen body. Wallich offers the remedy that a Baron Hollander had used with success: A live frog is placed in a new clay pot, olive oil is poured over the frog, which is baked until a salve forms. The salve is then applied.[112] Again, the physician could offer no better remedy than that provided by the folk-medicine tradition.

The cause of heart disease, Ashkenazi explains, is a "gnawing worm."[113] However, the prescription for heart ailment did not differ basically from the treatment usually given for any pain.[114] The *responsa* of Meir Eisenstadt also speaks of women suffering from diuresis and "sand in the kidneys,"[115] and it would seem that diuresis was prevalent among Jews of Germany. Kidney, bladder, and stomach stones are other internal ailments discussed in the folk-medicine handbook.[116] And the treatment seems to be the typical folk remedy that was applied to a variety of diseases.[117] A similar treatment is thus prescribed for liver trouble: "If one spits blood because of a defective liver, let him take the liver of a crow, dry and crush it, mix it with wine, and drink it daily, morning and evening."[118]

Eye diseases are described as "the inflammation of the vessel" (conjunctivitis), "skin tissue [filament] on the eye," and "heat blisters" (sties).[119] Ear ailments are tinnitus, "a tinkling, ringing sound," and deafness.[120] Relief can be obtained for an "aching nose" by placing in the nostril the nail-wort plant.[121] The same treatment is offered for a sore throat, laryngitis, or a growth in the throat.[122] Speech defect is also given attention, and some remedies are prescribed for physical handicaps.[123] A *responsum* of Jacob Reischer mentions a case of leg amputation without giving the reason, and we can surmise how much the patient must have endured if he developed gangrene or an infection that could not be checked.[124]

In dealing with contagion, the folk-medicine handbook stresses, in particular, measles, smallpox, venereal disease, and the "plague."[125] That the treatment of venereal disease is incorporated in the handbook was due, no doubt, to the established procedure of including such information as part of the total body or canon of medicine. Arabic works on syphilis had spread over Western Europe in the 11th century and afterwards were included in the corpus of medical knowledge.[126] These medical data had practical value, since there is evidence of venereal disease among Jewish persons during the Middle Ages. While the integrity of family life is emphasized in Jewish tradition, these cases, though isolated, cannot be ignored; for it appears that the Jewish society did not escape divorce, adultery, and prostitution.[127] The remedies for venereal disease reflect, on the one hand, the type of treatment folk medicine usually prescribed, and on the other, the influence that German folk practices must have exerted on Jewish social life. For purposes of simplification, the treatment of venereal disease can be classified according to the materials used for general medication, namely, plants, animals, stones, drugs, and foods.[128]

Epidemics and plagues periodically threatened the Germanic communities, and whenever there were rumors of indications of an epidemic, fear gripped the people and their normal life was disrupted.[129] Bacharach describes the effect of the plague of 1636 in Worms, when the community was thrown into a state of confusion. The epidemic was so widespread, and so many people were confined to bed, that there was a shortage of attendants to nurse the sick. When the talented daughter of a wealthy and influential man became ill, the desperate father gave his consent to her marriage with a handsome butcher's assistant, provided that the young man would nurse and restore her to good health.[130] Understandably, emergency measures had to be taken during an epidemic, as in Prague in 1713, when the government decreed that "the dead cannot be buried in the usual cemeteries unless the bodies are covered with lime so as to hasten decomposition." In such circumstances, Reischer did not object to the use of lime,[131] although the tradition of burial—in anticipation of "the resurrection of the dead"—requires the body to be kept intact, without having its shape or form altered in any way.

During a plague, people abandoned their homes and fled for their lives as if escaping from an invading army. In her autobiography Glikl recalls how she and her children decided to leave the city of Hamburg when a plague was spreading. En route to her father-in-law, who lived in Hameln, they stopped at her brother-in-law's home in Hanover, to observe the festival of *Sukkot*. And while attending the festival services in the home of her brother-in-law, Glikl happened to notice that Ẓipporah, her daughter, had a boil under the arm.[132] Immediately, she thought of sending the child to the same barber who had treated her husband.

> My husband, too, was bothered with an abscess, which a barber [surgeon-barber] in Hannover had covered with a bit of plaster. So I said to my maid whom I had with me, 'Go to my husband—he is upstairs in the synagogue—and ask him who the barber was and where he lives. Then take the child to him and have him apply a plaster.'[133]

Whereupon panic seized the women in the synagogue; and in her graphic manner, Glikl sets forth their hysterical reaction:

> The women were gripped with fear, not merely because they were cowards in such matters, but coming from Hamburg we were held in suspicion. They quickly put their heads together, considering what to do.[134]

A Polish woman then intervened to allay the fear of the women: "Be not alarmed, 'tis nothing, I'll warrant. I have had to do with such things a score of times, and if you wish I'll go downstairs and have a look at the girl. . . ."[135] To the distraught Glikl, the woman identified herself as "a healer" who would be able "to doctor the child" and "soon have her cured."[136]

The dislocation of her family during a plague is also described by Glikl, who remembers vividly how her grandmother recounted the intense suffering that she and her two unmarried daughters had endured. As the sole survivors of the family—her husband and her other children had died of the disease—they became "destitute and in need" when they abandoned their home to escape the epidemic. They staggered from house to house begging for food, and whatever shelter they had at night they built of "boards, rubble, and stone." Thus they lived "until the wrath had passed" (Is. 26:20), and as soon as "the plague had somewhat subsided," the grandmother decided "to air out her house and live in it again." The house was "almost bare," with most of "her personal belongings removed." For during their absence their neighbors had become vandals and "had stripped the boards from the floor and wrecked what they could not take."[137]

The anonymous autobiographer, in his portrayal of Prague and its environs, tells how the Count of his village had set up a quarantine during the plague of 1680. The narrative also reveals the social position of the nobility, who were able to isolate and protect themselves when everyone else's life was in jeopardy.

> The plague was then raging all around our village, and the Count established a 'lazaretto,' i.e., a small wooden house of two rooms in the midst of a big forest about a mile away from

> his castle. If someone fell sick in one of the villages he was driven out of his house with all of his belongings, and had to go into that forest. The Count had set aside an open space some yards wide all around his castle, which only those living in the castle were permitted to approach. He only kept very few people in his castle, and enclosed himself in there, and never left it with his people. He admitted no outsider except my father. . . .[138]

The autobiographer's father had obtained a prescription from R. Samson of Kamenetz for treating the plague boils—the remedy consisting of a plaster made by mixing "the white of an egg with a little alum about the size of a nut."[139]

The folk-medicine handbook equipped the entire community to meet the contingencies of daily life by prescribing home remedies for every conceivable ailment, whether chronic or less acute. Be it a wound, an injury, or a skin disease—a blotch, boil, or itch—the individual knew in each instance of a remedy that could be prepared from medicinal herbs, foods, or minerals.[140] On occasion, however, it was advisable that the medication be prepared by an apothecary. Thus, when Coblenz submitted a prescription for a skin disease, consisting of quicksilver and the laurel plant, he emphasized that an expert apothecary would be needed to mix the ingredients.[141]

3. Women's and Children's Ailments

Folk medicine was also concerned with pregnancy, delivery, and the postnatal condition of the mother.[142] A woman who wished to become pregnant could choose any one of a number of popular "remedies." Since these "remedies" were of equal efficacy, and were interchangeable, the woman desiring pregnancy did not have to rely on only one procedure. She could wear a stone that had been placed in a raven's nest of eggs.[143] Or she could put a flint stone in a pot; and after she had prepared food in another pot, she would pour its contents into the pot with the stone and then drink wine—the amount of the size of a nut—from a flask made of the skin of a hare or tench.[144] Besides, she might take some Karlsbad mineral water or prepare a drink from the vervain herb.[145] The dung or the rennet (maw) of a hare was also considered efficacious.[146] If "a fish found inside of another fish" was baked in flour and water, and the juice thereof taken as a drink, pregnancy would result.[147] In folklore, as has been suggested,[148] animals such as the fish and rabbit symbolize fertility. To become pregnant, a woman ate or otherwise used their organs, so that their capacities for reproduction would be transferred to her.[149] Pregnancy also occurred if the woman wore a white zedoary flower.[150] Another aid to pregnancy was the heart-bone (*herts*[*harts*]-*beyndl*) plant wrapped in a cloth made of flax and worn around the neck as an amulet.[151] A woman could confirm that she was pregnant by eating some pepper kernels that look like a plant louse. If an attack of nausea followed, pregnancy was established.[152]

The folk-medicine handbook for women likewise considers emergencies that might arise during childbirth. If a woman hemorrhages, the flow of blood can be checked by preparing a drink with the shell of a freshly-hatched egg.[153] She will be able to prevent hemorrhaging during childbirth by wearing around her neck the ashes of a dry land frog calcined in a new dish.[154] The placenta can be removed by placing the root of the hellebore plant in the mother's nostril, or by serving her the liver of a pike with a drink—either wine or the juice of a primrose.[155] If a mother should die during an unsuccessful childbirth, several simple steps are suggested to deliver the child. The dung of a donkey might be bound to her stomach or birch fibers could be tied to her left foot. If nothing happens, then the feather of a stork should be tied to her left foot.[156] When a mother has difficulty during delivery, immediate birth can be expected if she will drink the milk of a dog with warm wine, or mix the dung of a donkey with any beverage. Childbirth is also made easier by placing the dung of a bear under the mother.[157] For prevention of miscarriage, the pregnant woman is advised to wear around her neck as a *segullah* the heart of a rabbit or a ruby stone.[158] She might, in addition, mix with wine a powder made by crushing the skin of a snake or else eat the powder with honey.[159]

A series of remedies are prescribed for the mother who recuperates too slowly after childbirth. She may apply a liniment composed of absinthe (wormwood) or a strong solution of alcohol quintessence and vinegar. If she has postnatal abdominal pains, and is not able to assume an erect posture, then the "five finger" herb has to be boiled with wine, and the "broth" therefrom taken "three times a day."[160] When a woman suffers from postnatal rectal hemorrhoids due to a difficult delivery, she is instructed to grind the cowparsnip plant, strain it through a sieve, and then add peppercorn with a seed coat and the milk of a deer. Hemorrhoids among males, it is explained, are caused by strain in carrying heavy objects.[161]

Women were also troubled by the uncertainty of the menstrual period, for not only were they handicapped in their regular ritual cleanliness, but their capacity for childbearing was also affected.[162] The folk-medicine handbook and some cases reported in *responsa* discuss the treatment of women's ailments, yet the prescriptions for female disease—more specifically for irregularity in menstruation—are no departure from the standardized remedies proposed, especially for becoming pregnant, childbearing, and delivery. The woman can take the skin of a snake, dry and crush it, mix the "powder" in honey, eat it, and then drink wine.[163] She may dip the feather of a chicken in her menstrual blood, burn the feather, and drink vermouth (wormwood) wine.[164] A female frog can be burned, the ashes then wrapped in a cloth and worn around the neck as a good-luck charm.[165] The bones of a pike, "found in another fish," can be crushed and the powder put into any liquid desired.[166] Or, while the woman is barefooted, the dung of a hog is placed in her right shoe.[167] The juice made by boiling the herbs "good nose" and "strong beak" may also be used as a beverage.[168] To maintain standards of feminine hygiene during irregular menstruation, the guide of Coblenz instructs women to make a drink by grinding and then boiling a combination of dough, lemon juice and peel, canary-sugar and gaping rose plants; and he attests that on various occasions the remedy proved to be successful.[169] In the event of a delay in menstruation, the woman is advised to prepare a drink of wine, the laurel plant, the "health root," and the elderberry.[170] When a woman has a breast pain, a poultice is prepared by mixing the dung of a pigeon in honey and wax. If her breast has sores, a poultice of honey, flour, licorice—or of bleached wheat flour and the yolk of an egg—is to be applied with a flax cloth. If a pregnant woman has pains in her breast, a poultice is prepared by mixing the yolk of a boiled egg and honey or by boiling in honey some powder made from flies.[171]

On the basis of popular practices, the folk-medicine handbook shows how the sex of an unborn child can be predicted. The procedures, however, are not consistent. If the pregnant woman mixes her milk in cold water and it coagulates immediately, she will give birth to a girl, but if the milk dissolves, the child will be a boy. In making the test, the mother can substitute a board or stone for the water. The handbook of David Ashkenazi, on the other hand, claims that if the milk congeals and floats on water, the child will be a boy, and if it dissolves, a girl.[172] When the pregnant woman's right side is larger than the left, it is an indication that she will have a son. The sex of an unborn child can also be predicted by the way in which the pregnant mother arises after being seated. If she supports herself with her right hand, the child will be a male, and if with the left hand, a female.[173] When a pregnant woman has a "beautiful rosy" complexion, it is a sign that a son will be born.[174] Pains during pregnancy can also foretell the sex of a child; if the mother has pain in her loin, she will give birth to a son, and if the pain is in her stomach, the child will be a girl.[175]

Special care for children is not emphasized in the folk-medicine handbook; the advice is evidently intended for all persons, whether young or old. There was little need or concern for specialized information corresponding to age groups, for childhood passed quickly and the span of "threescore years and ten" (Ps. 90:10) was an ideal beyond the reach of the average person. Furthermore, the emphasis on early marriage reduced the period of adolescence. When, at thirteen, the child reached his religious majority, he had already begun to assume the role of an adult. By the age of eighteen he usually shouldered the social and economic responsibilities of a fully matured man.[176] While the folk-medicine "remedies" do not devote special attention to the physical problems of adolescent youth, the few random references to child care and children's ailments do add some details on the characteristics of social life. Although these incidents are not always drawn from sources on German-Jewish folkways, they were not so unique that they could not have occurred in Germanic lands.

If, at birth, a child faces death, the beak of a rooster was placed in his rectum—"the child will then live, and the rooster will die, if it is God's will."[177] The rooster, apparently, serves as a "scapegoat," a substitute for the child's life.[178] Judging from an incident recorded in Aaron Kaidanover's *responsa*, infants were not always nursed by their own mother. The case is cited of a woman who did not nurse her child but engaged a wet nurse. She justified her conduct on the grounds that in her family no mother nursed her child and instead hired a wet nurse.[179] A head rash or boil was a common disease among children, and Tobias Cohn (d. 1729, Polish and Turkish physician) explains that while this condition was widespread in his region, it was also prevalent in Germany and Poland. He attributes the boil to "an ingrown hair" that became infected with "a white head [lit., point] on the top and a black spot underneath."[180] It is also related by Aaron Kaidanover how a father was disturbed because his son, who was approaching his religious majority—being under thirteen at the time—had not developed sexually for his age. In a community where early marriage was practiced, the elders would become perturbed when a young person was retarded in his sexual development.[181]

4. Psychological and Mental Illness

While major emphasis is placed on physical disease, psychological problems and mental illnesses are not dismissed. Thus the physician Abraham Wallich, in recognizing that mental ailments exist, asks that psychological difficulties should not be ignored but be treated with the same interest as any physical sickness.[182] In fact, mental illness had been on the increase ever since the 17th century, no doubt because of the turbulence and anxiety of the period.[183] It was not unusual that a well-known author would speak of the hardship he had endured,[184] nor was it uncommon that families became homeless and uprooted during a fire, military invasion, or expulsion.[185] The effect of psychological factors on one's physical well-being received due consideration from Jacob Reischer when his opinion was sought in the case of a young woman whose health was waning since she had become engaged. The suggestion was made that she might be ailing because of her distress over her betrothal to a young man in whom she had no interest. To help her regain her health, the engagement contract was seemingly dissolved. In a short time the young woman became well. With the father contending that her previous engagement was no longer binding, and the young man claiming otherwise, the judgment of Reischer was therefore sought by both parties. Reischer stated that the engagement was still valid, as there was no real intent at any time to terminate the original contract, the *ḳnas*. In other words, a pretended dissolution of the betrothal cannot be considered a breach of contract.[186] Although we are not told what happened after Reischer submitted his opinion, it may be surmised that the marriage was consummated as originally planned. It must be left to the imagination of the reader to decide whether the young woman had an unhappy married life, again became sick, and possibly died of a broken heart, or whether she resigned herself to the inevitable, made her adjustment, and later perhaps found happiness in her role as mother and home builder.

The state of depression, characteristic of melancholia, was personally experienced by Glikl and Jacob Emden. Glikl states frankly that after her husband had passed away, she became melancholic and suffered sleepless nights; it was then that she decided to write her memoirs, so that she might overcome the restlessness and despair that she felt when she had insomnia.[187] Jacob Emden acknowledges that he and his father both suffered from melancholia (*ḥoli ha-sheḥorah*). His father would "sink into a deep depression," as though "despairing because the doctors could offer him no relief." Similarly, Jacob Emden found no remedy for his dejected state of mind.

> I am not able to do anything with the melancholia that has overpowered me. . . . I have tasted death a hundred times, not once or twice. . . . Until now I have had no rest, joy, pleasure in the world. And who would think that I have not had one single day of peace. . . . I despise and hate life; I am constantly lamenting over the corruption of our time. Would that it were possible to correct what is wrong . . .![188]

The behavior of a mentally deranged man who lived in Nikolsburg, Moravia, is reported in a *responsum* of Joshua Höschel b. Joseph (d. 1648, Cracow). The details of his conduct are described in a complaint made by non-Jews of the vicinity.

> A Jewish man who is insane wanders around in their towns . . . , [and] asks for the direction to Poland and Little Poland. A number of times, he has gone the distance of almost a mile and then he returns. . . .[189]

A non-Jewish woman, the wife of a shepherd, states that the mentally ill man "had spent three nights with the flock," and by then "the town official had lost his patience." She also tells how she was "offered half a *reichstaler* [$1\frac{1}{2}$ *mark*] by a Jewish man" who was obliged to be away from his home for two or three days, and during his absence he wanted her to provide lodging for the "deranged person." Shortly afterwards the "insane man" disappeared, met with his death, and later his body was found and identified by individuals of the Jewish community. The town official considered the deceased as the bearer of "a dread disease"—obviously, because he was insane—and therefore ordered the area to be fumigated to prevent contagion from spreading.[190] As the details of the narrative imply, there was at the time a lack of medical and hospital facilities in small towns and rural areas to care for the sick. Mental illness was considered contagious and the mentally sick were feared and abhorred.[191]

The treatment of mental illness and psychological disturbance also depended upon folk practices, as in the instances of physical or somatic ailments. If a person was in a state of fear, he was advised to make an amulet of the head of a black rooster and white incense or of the horns of a deer.[192] Coblenz relates how he assisted a man of Frankfort in ridding himself of "lewd thoughts" by having him read daily from the Talmudic tractate of *Makkot* (*Punishments*), inasmuch as the numerical value, *gematreya*', of the word *makkot*, which is 466, equals that of *hirhurim*, "obscene imagination." Previously, the troubled man used various amulets, but none gave him relief. The "remedy," Coblenz states, had also aided other individuals who were in a similar state of mind.[193] When anyone suffers from a nervous condition, feeling as though "snakes and frogs [crawled] inside him," he should be given sugar, bread, and honey for two consecutive days, while on the third day he takes a powder made from the "bone of the skull of a man executed by governmental decree." First, the powder has to be mixed with sugar and afterwards with the "combination" used during the first two days.[194] But another way to be relieved of "disturbing internal sensations" is to drink a medication prepared from "the sweat of a white horse" and "the juice of roses."[195]

When a person has an epileptic attack, he is instructed to take a "sweat bath" before retiring at night and in the morning before he eats, and each time a "powder" made of "a live bird" is poured into the bath.[196] Among the cases submitted to Aaron Kaidanover for his legal opinion is the dramatic incident of a woman who left her husband because he had suffered from epileptic seizures since the beginning of their marriage. Declaring before the court that she found it impossible to live under the same roof with him, she asked to be granted a divorce; otherwise "she intends to be childless until she becomes gray [when she cannot bear a child].[197]

5. Miscellaneous Ailments and Remedies

Folk medicine also prescribes what to do for such diverse circumstances as stains on clothing, loss of hair, halitosis, insomnia, toothache, physical injury, and the bite of a mad dog. If one wishes to remove the odor of perfume, he washes himself with a preparation of burned cow's dung, the white of an egg, and lead.[198] A stain remover for clothing—to be applied with a sponge— can be made of alum, ox gall, and tartar.[199] In order to make hair grow, the bald spot is first shaved with a razor, after which milk or oil, with the blood of a bat or frog, is applied. If the hair still does not grow sufficiently, then the scalp has to be rubbed with the marrow and brain of a fox.[200] Halitosis can be checked by drinking wine with a spice mixture made of graptolite, hedge-hyssop, nutmeg, lyme grass, and mustard.[201] For insomnia, Coblenz proposes a remedy that was given to him by Abraham Lissa:[202]

> In the evening go to a hog sty, . . . take [some] of the straw under the head of a hog and place it under the head of the ill person, without his being aware that this is done . . . This has been tried any number of times when one could not sleep. . . .[203]

Quick relief from a toothache can be obtained by crushing a chestnut and placing it in the nostril of the person in pain; when sneezing begins, the discomfort is reduced. Experience has shown that this "remedy" is effective, so Coblenz confirms.[204]

A nosebleed can be stopped by resorting to the "transfer of disease" and "sympathetic magic." That is, the feather of a rooster or chicken, used respectively for male and female, is dipped in the blood, and when the feather dries, it is burned and the ashes are cast into a stream.[205] A woman of Offenbach, who suffered from nosebleeds, obtained immediate relief when Coblenz applied a folk remedy. By crushing the shell of a large walnut and inserting the "powder" in her nostril, he was able to stop the flow of blood. He also recommends the walnut-shell powder to check excessive bleeding during circumcision.[206] For a mad-dog bite, first aid can be given by applying bread to the wound, or a nettle plant mixed with salt.[207] It is claimed by Ashkenazi that "the bread can be effective in healing a person who has been bitten by a dog," and that "whoever tastes the bread will die."[208] And if there is an emergency need for counteracting a deadly poison, folk medicine advises that urine should be swallowed.[209]

Medical care was not limited exclusively to the home remedies in the folk-medicine handbook, but, as already mentioned,[210] competent physicians would be consulted, especially for more serious ailments.[211] Thus, during the illness of her husband, Glikl of Hameln sought the advice of a Dr. Lopez. A group of physicians and surgeons [i.e., chirurgeons] had previously examined him and concluded that "they could do nothing."[212] Later, Dr. Lopez called in another chirurgeon, who also considered the case hopeless and left immediately after he had made his diagnosis.[213] It must have been as a result of his own experience as well as that of others that Jacob Reischer urged that whenever a physician was called in for consultation he should do everything possible in behalf of the sick, even when there was only a small chance of recovery:

> When it appears [inevitable] that an individual will die, abandon [the] uncertainty [as to his recovery], [but] seize this as an opportunity to make him well. In any event, the doctor should not act superficially; rather he should always maintain suspended judgment [lit., wait] and consult [lit., to be on the alert or have his eyes opened] the most expert physicians in the city. . . .[214]

In a criticism of doctors, Aaron Kaidanover decries their professional attitude of "desiring to make a business of illness."[215] Seemingly, rabbis regarded the physicians in their communities as being too casual and impersonal in dealing with the sick, that they seemed to forget that negligence on their part in treating a disease was tantamount to "shedding human blood."[216] Already on the European continent the greed of the physician was a subject of literary satire:

> Be a physician, Faustus; heap up gold,
> And be eterniz'd for some wondrous cure:
> *Summum bonum medicinae sanitas,*
> The end of physic is our body's health.
> Why, Faustus, has thou not attain'd that end?
> Are not thy bills [i.e., prescriptions] hung
> up as monuments,
> Whereby whole cities have escap'd the plague,
> And thousand desperate maladies been cur'd?[217]

A sick person was not necessarily caught between the two extremes of the professional impersonality of the physician and the "magical" devices of folk medicine, as there are obvious instances of personal concern being shown for the sick and standards of public health being maintained. It is a communal practice—so we learn from a *responsum* of Jacob Reischer—to engage a sexton to devote his time to serving the needs of the sick. During the festival of *Sukkot*, the *shammash* is not required to eat in the

Sukkah or participate in any celebration in the community, so that he can be free to attend the sick at mealtime.[218] Apparently, no person in poor health was left to shift for himself and rely on his own resources; he must have felt reassured in knowing that he had the moral and economic support of the community during illness.[219]

To maintain health standards, rabbinic opinion gave support to physicians when they forbade the use of contaminated foods. Reischer was consulted at the time when a governmental regulation prohibited the eating of peas that were disease-carriers (that is, wormy), because health might be endangered. An appeal was made to Reischer declaring that "a large number of individuals depend on the peas for their main diet, and hence most of the community would find it a hardship to adhere to the legislation." Reischer realized that unless full cooperation was given to the physicians, they would be obstructed in implementing this health measure. He therefore gave the legislation his wholehearted support, emphasizing that a "rigorous position is taken because health might be jeopardized."[220] Reischer also deals with a regulation instituted by "governmental examiners" to prohibit the slaughter of cattle if they appear to be sick. It is maintained by Reischer that the use of the milk of such cattle be forbidden because of the grave danger of spreading disease.[221]

The popularity of mineral water as a remedy also proved to be an aid to public health. Hot mineral water was used both for bathing and drinking, and in Prague there were those who traveled to Eger, a distance of some eighty miles to the west, to drink the mineral water.[222]

Though the success of a folk remedy is frequently affirmed by the author of the popular handbook, Haggard maintains that the patients who were cured probably had mental ailments or else benefited from "the recuperative powers of the human body."[223] The German aphorism "Für den Tod ist kein Kraut gewachsen" alludes to the kind of protection and security that plant remedies must have provided in time of sickness. While the folk-medicine handbook makes no claim to offer a "cure for death," it still does provide an individual in time of emergency or distress with "prescriptions" for different ailments, including those of a serious nature.

As regards the influence that Germanic social life had on Jewish folkways, there are many examples of plants and remedies in general folklore and folk medicine being used freely in Jewish society, comparable to the large body of technological and material culture that may function separately and apart from tradition and belief. Hence, any Jewish person could have engaged in folk-medicine practices without finding himself in conflict with the basic teachings of his religious and cultural tradition, in the same way that the modern Jew uses electricity and rides in an automobile without having to ask whether his behavior is contrary to any fundamental concept or principle. In other words, precisely because the practices of folk medicine are regarded as "techniques," they entail no violation of *halakhah*, traditional Jewish law.

CHAPTER VII

Synagogue, Sabbath, and Festivals

When Isaiah Horowitz speaks of the differences in the customs of cities and rural areas with regard to the observance of *Rosh ha-Shanah*, he offers a clue to finding a variety of folk practices related to the synagogue, the Sabbath, and festivals in the popularized *Shulḥan 'Arukh* and the book of *Minhagim.*[1] This group of customs could also be divided, first, into folk traditions that are part of an old, continuing religious and cultural pattern, and, second, into regional practices. At times the local *minhagim* are based on crucial events, and as an example of this type of custom we cite the special fast days introduced in Frankfort to commemorate the tragedies that befell the community during the fires of 1711 and 1720.[2] The annual commemoration of such catastrophes was also known in other parts of Germany.[3] An examination of the origin, development, and meaning of various practices dealing with the synagogue and holidays should enable us, as we look into the past, to observe from a different vantage point some of the folk features characteristic of the daily life of the individual and the group.

1. Customs Relating to the Synagogue

We have already seen some of the specific ways in which the synagogue served as a focal point in the observance of the rituals associated with "the crises of life."[4] Each person's tie with the synagogue also resulted from local regulations and practices by making him feel responsible for the institutions of communal life.

As an example of the relationship between the individual and society, the *shammash* (sexton) would go from house to house before the break of dawn, knock on doors with his cane, and call people to the synagogue.[5] The service commenced as soon as the sexton informed the cantor that he had completed his round.[6] On Saturday, however, as Kosman relates, the sexton knocked on the door with his hand instead of using an object, which is prohibited on the Sabbath.[7] For the *minḥah*, afternoon, and *ma'arib*, evening services, the sexton called the people to the synagogue from the street, but in the morning he had to knock on doors in order to awaken them.[8]

The communal legislation of Bamberg and Düsseldorf placed on each individual the obligation of attending synagogue services,

Fig. 10 The Old and New Synagogues of Fürth, 1705 *(Courtesy, Widener Library, Harvard University)*. From Liebe, *Judentum*, p. 102, plate # 82; originally an 18th century engraving by J. A. Boener.

especially when he would be called upon to make up the *minyan* of ten worshipers.[9] No one was exempted from attending the synagogue in Bamberg unless he had to be away from home to earn his livelihood. If anyone refused to attend the synagogue, a fine of six *kreuzer*, farthings, was levied, which went to the Talmud Torah chest for communal public education.[10] The legislation of Düsseldorf fined the person who had abstained from attending the synagogue when the required number for a *minyan* was lacking.[11] In Runkel a fine of two *pfennige* was specified for the individual remaining at home instead of going to synagogue services.[12] Hence, it did not depend on the person's mood, wish, or choice whether or not he went to the synagogue. Such penalization for failing to attend services helped enforce and maintain religious observance without regard for the individual's preference.[13]

Judging from the local legislation enacted, synagogue attendance must have been a problem. There would have been no need for Moses Ḥasid to emphasize in his Ethical Will the importance of going to the synagogue if people had been attending with regularity.[14] And there must have been some basis for the complaint of Ezekiel Landau that "the *shammash* invites people to the synagogue, but no one responds." He was appalled that instead of attending the synagogue, people arranged *minyanim*, services, in their homes; nor could he understand why anyone would be content to hold a service "in the place where they engage in daily conversation and were involved in quarrels and lies, slander and jest." Landau regrets that he ever settled in Prague, where the *minyan* does not consist of adults but "young men (*baḥurim*) and lads (*na'arim*) who talk [to one another] during prayer."[15] Glikl of Hameln relates how arrangements were made to have "a quorum of public worship" available each day, by following the ancient Talmudic practice of engaging ten learned men whose sole responsibility was to study and attend services. The group, Glikl says, met each morning at nine o'clock to recite Psalms and study a portion of the Talmud.[16] A *minyan* was thus assured the mourner who had to say *ḳaddish*.[17]

Frank and realistic comments in folk and communal literature express concern for the maintenance of cleanliness and decorum in the synagogue. Zechariah Plungian, of Zamość, urges each person to examine himself carefully before leaving home for the synagogue, to be sure that his garments are clean, otherwise he might feel self-conscious about his appearance during services.[18] The advice that he gave the Jews of Poland must have been known to the regions of Germany, where his work also had appeal. The people are instructed, in the guide book and popular code of law, to take every precaution not to step in mud or filth as they walked to the synagogue, and thus avoid coming into the building with soiled shoes.[19] In order to assure clean and pleasant surroundings, the practice was introduced in the Middle Ages not to wear shoes inside the synagogue.[20] During the time of the Maharil, so Isaiah Horowitz recounts, it was customary to go all the way to the synagogue in stocking feet on the eve of *Yom Kippur*. The sexton would announce that everyone had to leave his shoes at home before going to the synagogue. An exception would be made, however, if a person found walking without shoes too strenuous, but as soon as he had arrived at the synagogue he was expected to give the shoes to one of his children to take home, or else leave them in an inconspicuous place.[21]

When it rained on the Ninth of *'Ab*, it was permissible to wear shoes to the synagogue rather than soil one's feet, but upon entering the building, the shoes had to be concealed.[22] Following the advice given by *Sefer Ḥasidim*, Hahn suggests that each person should own an extra pair of shoes to wear to the synagogue in place of the shoes that are used daily. He describes the practice then current in Germany to make a piece of iron available with which to scrape one's shoes before entering the synagogue.[23] And Joseph Kosman tells that he saw "pious men and individuals who are involved in communal affairs" keep "a [special] pair of shoes in the vestibule adjoining the synagogue"; thus they could be certain that the shoes worn in the synagogue would always be clean. This, however, was no practical solution, as most individuals were not able to afford the luxury of an extra pair of shoes, and therefore it became the practice, as Kosman relates, to clean one's shoes on "the iron [placed] at the entrance of the synagogue."[24]

In one of his barbed attacks on the low level of religious and cultural life in small towns, Kirchan decries the manner in which people act in the synagogues of the Frankfort area.[25] They "will go to all lengths to be called to the reading of the Torah [on the Sabbath] and each person is concerned with obtaining honor for himself." If anyone does not receive the recognition he desires, "quarrels break out because of jealousy and pride." "Most individuals attending the synagogue on the Sabbath," Kirchan continues, "also engage in discussing nonsensical matters and business affairs."[26] Evidently such conduct was not limited solely to the region of Frankfort; no less than nine times, during 1698-1776, townsfolk were admonished in the communal minutes of Dorn, Mülheim, Altenhofen—in the province of Düsseldorf—not to engage in idle talk in the synagogue on the Sabbath. An appeal, as recorded in these communal records, closely parallels the observation and criticism made by Kirchan: "It is obvious that there should be no quarrels and disputes in the synagogue."[27]

Disorderly conduct in the synagogue was not only common to rural areas. Ezekiel Landau admonishes against resorting to idle gossip in the synagogue, especially during the time when the cantor repeats the *'Amidah,* "Eighteen Benedictions." Their "vain talk" not only "desecrates the Holy Sanctuary," but "they confuse their neighbors so that they are not able to say 'Amen'." To Landau, the situation seems hopeless, since his own efforts did not result in making any significant changes. His homiletical diatribe is more than a complaint on the part of a rabbi against the laity:

During the *'Amidah* prayer I would look on all sides. Out of embarrassment they would refrain [from talking]. Now

> they do not even show any shame, and the habit [of talking] has become their characteristic [conduct in the synagogue].[28]

To maintain decorum in the synagogue, the Nuremberg and Fürth *Taḳḳanot* of 1728 prohibit the use of snuff.[29] The instruction is also given not to expectorate in the synagogue; the person heeding this counsel can be assured a *segullah*, "protection," against ill-fortune that always threatens. To avoid having to spit during services, the advice is given to "chew licorice root before going to the synagogue."[30]

Fathers who bring children of preschool age to the synagogue are criticized, for the children create a disturbance during the service when they cry for attention.

> The father becomes so concerned with supervising the child that he is not able to pray, even in a perfunctory manner. He is worried whether the child may soil himself. . . .[31]

Hahn recommends that steps be taken to end such distraction, either by imposing a fine on those parents who persist in bringing their youngsters to the synagogue, or by having the children accompany their mothers to the women's synagogue. "There is no objection if a young child attends the women's synagogue," he explains; and inasmuch as "their synagogue has no cantor, ark or scroll, less of an interruption will occur when a child soils himself." Children attending the men's synagogue should not require the attention or supervision of their parents, he contends; they should be sufficiently conversant with the order of services to know how "to respond with 'Amen'," and "how one should stand to show a reverent attitude."[32]

The lack of decorum in the synagogue is not only due to the noise and confusion caused by children. Orderly procedure is also disrupted by those who come late and then recite the prayers in haste so as to be able to join in the study session held after services.[33] Jonah Landsofer deplores that the impressiveness of the synagogue service has been undermined by the mechanical manner in which prayers are said.[34] Emphasis on orderly behavior in the synagogue does not imply that one has to ignore an elderly or sickly person who feels faint before the services finish. Coffee, tea, or chocolate should be provided in the synagogue; if anyone feels weak, he can refresh and strengthen himself.[35]

In Moravia, the seating arrangement in the synagogues would be posted on Mondays and Thursdays when the Torah was read, a procedure no doubt followed to avoid the confusion or friction that could easily arise if two persons were to claim the same seat.[36] A synagogue seat was considered the property of an individual and therefore could be "inherited, exchanged, sold, or presented as a gift." Estimated to have the value of 25 to 1000 *gulden*, a seat in the synagogue was often included in the dowry of a young woman during the 18th century. For instance, a groom named Michael Brass declared on December 22, 1783, his intention to sell half-interest in his synagogue seat so that he could pay a debt. According to the record of a transaction dated July 8, 1709, when Samuel Prager passed away his wife Zisel sold his seat to Samuel Dayyan.[37]

The synagogue was not always large enough to accommodate all the members of a community. The synagogue of Neu-Raussnitz, Moravia, which had seventy seats in the men's section and an equal number in the women's section, must have been overcrowded, since in 1790 the Jewish community comprised 900 persons.[38] On one occasion Menaḥem Mendel Krochmal was asked to help resolve a conflict that arose in an overcrowded synagogue. The difficulty had been reported as follows: Upon renovation the regular seating arrangement had been changed, with the result that when the synagogue was filled to capacity twelve men could not be seated. The suggestion was then made by a number of the congregants, including those left without seats, that chairs be placed in the space "between the *'aron ha-ḳodesh* (ark) and the *bimah* (reading table or desk)." As the Torah reading is considered the central part of the service, the seats in the synagogue were built around the reading table, thus enabling the entire congregation to surround the Torah when it is read. The nonseated congregants contended that use of this space would enable them to have individual reading stands, as well as leave a path for children to pass without causing any disturbance. But Krochmal counsels that benches be placed in the available space; his reason reflects the communal character of the synagogue. He contends that no individual should monopolize any space in the synagogue, as he is only entitled to the space that is needed for a seat. When the synagogue was erected, each person contributed according to his means, and those who gave larger contributions should not restrain the congregation from placing additional benches in the synagogue, even if they find the new seating arrangement is less comfortable. Only the *bet din*, the communal court, can decide whether everyone has ample space and is seated comfortably, not individuals exercising self-assumed authority.[39]

2. Customs of the Sabbath

We can discern how the daily life of the people influenced the origin and development of local customs that pertain to the Sabbath and festivals, and how a diversity of folkways became entwined in this body of practices. We might begin by citing the reason that Hahn gave for making a minor change in the wording of the *Lekhah Dodi*, the hymn "welcoming the Sabbath," by Solomon Alkabez, the cabalist of Safed (ca. 1569). Since the Jews of Germany could not follow the Palestinian tradition of ushering in the Sabbath outdoors, either in the field or the courtyard of the synagogue, Hahn therefore altered the third verse to read, "You have charmed me, Sabbath bride" in place of "Come, let us go to meet the Sabbath."[40]

Schudt, in his collection of "Jewish curiosities," states that the organ was played in the *Alt-Neu* Synagogue of Prague "to greet" the Sabbath:

> On Friday evening the Jews attending the synagogue in Prague would sing the hymn greeting the Sabbath [i.e., *Lekhah Dodi,* "Come my friend . . . ; let us welcome the presence of the Sabbath"] to the accompaniment of an organ played by a Jewish person. . . .[41]

And in a later comment, Schudt explains: "Many pious Jews who have resided for some time in Prague have assured me that there was an organ in the *Alt-Neu* Synagogue, used solely to accompany the hymn welcoming the Sabbath. Furthermore, in other localities all kinds of musical instruments have accompanied the singers. . . ."[42] Eliezer Lieberman, the son of Yuspa Shammash, confirms in a *responsum,* published together with a controversial debate concerning Jewish religious reforms in Hamburg, that an organ was played in the Prague synagogue: "When I visited Prague, I cannot enumerate how many times I was told by elderly men that they remember the organ in the synagogue, which was there by stipulation. It was played on Friday evening, *Rosh Ḥodesh*, and holidays. To this day the Sabbath is ushered in in the Old Synagogue with musical instruments, and the music is extended a half an hour after nightfall. The musicians are Jews."[43] After the Meisel Synagogue was erected in Prague, an organ was installed in 1598. This organ was also used to greet the Sabbath.[44] Samson Bacharach, the father of the noted scholar Ya'ir Ḥayyim, composed a hymn in 1629 to greet the Sabbath. The hymn was sung and played by his wife.[45] In his portrayal of local observances, Joseph Kosman attests that musical instruments served to welcome the Sabbath in a "joyous spirit."

> . . . Thus they receive the Sabbath with great joy—with beautiful songs, praises, and meditations. In a number of

communities they play instruments, the bass fiddle and violin. This is in accordance with what our teachers of blessed memory used to say: 'The Divine Presence rests [upon man] through joy. As it is said with reference to David [*sic* = Elisha]: 'And it came to pass, when the minstrel played, that the hand of the Lord came upon him' (Shab. 30b, cit.; 2 Kings 3:15).[46]

While rabbinic authorities were not opposed to having instrumental music played at weddings and celebrations by the *badḥan*, jester, and the *klezmer*, musician, they did not favor using instrumental music to accompany a religious song or hymn.[47] The traditional reasons for objecting to instrumental music during services are summarized by Hahn; first, in order to commemorate the destruction of the Temple of Jerusalem, music is not to be played during worship; second, any introduction of instrumental music in the synagogue would be an imitation of some of the features of non-Jewish religious life.[48] Hahn, however, does permit instrumental accompaniment to songs that are not part of "the established liturgy," as *'Adon 'Olam, Yigdal, Ẓur Mi-shel-lo;* but he would regard it as an act of frivolity, as well as blasphemy, if any prayer of the liturgy, for example, the *Ḳaddish, Ḳedushah, or Hashkibenu,* were to be recited with instrumental music.[49]

On the Sabbath eve, as Hahn describes, it is customary for the father to receive a kiss from his child after blessing it upon his return from the synagogue. The practice was influenced by the popular belief that the deeds of children could be effective in nullifying the "evil decrees Satan might devise against parents."[50] Friday evening became the occasion for the family's reunion, as it was not unusual for the father to be away at work during the week and return before the Sabbath to rejoin his household.[51] When he left home, it was mainly in order to peddle wares in neighboring communities, and while he was gone, his life was in constant jeopardy. Hence, the *Brandshpigl*, the popular guide for woman's conduct, instructs the wife, when her husband has to be absent from home, to pray for his welfare and for his safe return.

> And during the time that her husband is away, she should ask God to protect and guard him from every evil occurrence or mishap—from officials, evil spirits, wild animals, vicious persons; and that He enable him to earn his living with ease and spare him from having difficulty. . . . [Let her also pray:] May he derive his livelihood honestly and fairly, and whatever he earns, may it be obtained properly with 'the help of heaven.'[52]

In accordance with the instruction of the *Shulḥan 'Arukh*, the folk book also made generally known what each household was expected to carry out in making preparations for the Sabbath. It is incumbent on each person to perform whatever menial chores are necessary to usher in the Sabbath; and this responsibility cannot be delegated to others, not even to servants, Joseph Kosman emphasizes, basing his opinion on *Sefer Ḥasidim*.[53] The *Brandshpigl* calls upon the woman to have her "house . . . swept, cleaned, and made orderly before Friday evening."[54] Abraham Horowitz, in his Ethical Will, advises: For the Sabbath, be sure to wash the utensils and dishes as though they are to be used for a special event.[55] The wife is told, as in the *Brandshpigl*, to "wash her face, wear her clothes in an orderly manner," and it is likewise her responsibility to have her husband "wash himself," "comb his hair and beard," and wear clean clothes before he leaves for the Sabbath eve services in the synagogue.[56] And in honor of the Sabbath, they must also trim their nails.[57] Usually on Friday, prior to the Sabbath, the husband would go to the communal bath house. His wife accompanied him when she had her menstrual period. In the bath house she fulfilled her religious duty of lighting the Sabbath candles, while her husband was obliged to kindle the Sabbath lights in their home and place the candles on the table. This arrangement was followed when there was a fire hazard;

Fig. 11 Observance of the Sabbath in the Synagogue and Home *(Courtesy, Widener Library, Harvard University)*. From Johann Christoph Georg Bodenschatz, *Aufrichtig teutsch redender Hebräer* . . . , II (Frankfort-Leipzig, 1756), bet. 156-57, fig. 5.

but where there was no risk, the woman was advised to light the Sabbath candles in her home before going to the communal bath house. Then her husband would not be responsible for kindling the Sabbath lights.[58]

When the family gathered around the table for the Sabbath meal on Friday evening, the intent was "to honor the Sabbath" in "a joyous mood." And with this in mind, Abraham Horowitz urges the people to maintain a cheerful disposition after they come home from the synagogue, and Yeḥiel Mikhel Epstein states that every man should forget his cares on the Sabbath, otherwise it cannot be "a day of delight."[59] Bacharach, in his advice on Sabbath observance, expresses himself similarly: "The Sabbath cannot be sanctified unless there is a meal."[60] The poorest person was expected to have a Sabbath meal; it might have consisted of only a slight increase in the amount of food usually eaten during weekdays, or else it could have been cooked with special care.

> On the Sabbath let one derive delight from the odor of the food. There may be little to eat, but let it be tastefully prepared.[61]

From Talmudic times onward, fish became a popular Sabbath dish; by eating fish "the joy of the Sabbath" would be enhanced.[62] Since the Sabbath is regarded as a day on which one fulfills "the duty of procreation," and fish are associated with fertility, it is understandable that fish have figured so prominently in the lore of the Sabbath.[63] The purchase of fish has been regarded as an essential part of the preparation for the Sabbath, yet there were those who became displeased when "distinguished and honored persons" in a number of communities came to the market to buy fish. The question was therefore posed to Joseph Kosman whether these leaders acted in a manner befitting their status and whether legislation of some kind should not be introduced to curb such conduct in public. Kosman replied that he sees no reason for trying to stop noted personalities from making their own purchase of fish needed for the Sabbath, and for substantiation cites a *responsum* of Menaḥem Krochmal.[64]

Krochmal's *responsum* deals with the incident of non-Jewish vendors charging an exorbitant price for fish when they noticed how eager the Jews were to buy. The fish was being obtained for the Sabbath. As a result, the community—its name is not mentioned—decided not to purchase fish for a period of two months so as to force the price down. Krochmal was asked if this is a proper course of action inasmuch as "the expenditure for Sabbath and festivals is not fixed," as stated in Beẓah 16a. Should not one be willing to pay whatever is necessary in order to show proper regard for the Sabbath? Krochmal, in his reply, indicates that he approves of their decision. The honoring of the Sabbath does not depend on the serving of fish, but he feels nevertheless that the community has good reason for wanting to reduce the price. Unless the cost is reduced, a poor person will not be able to secure any fish for the Sabbath.[65] This obviously implies that steps had to be taken to set up and maintain a financial standard for Sabbath observance that would be within the reach of all individuals.[66] When the complaint was made to Joseph Kosman that prominent men were doing their own marketing for the Sabbath, it is likely that there was a fear, judging from the case that Krochmal discusses, that the cost of fish would rise. The prosperous appearance of these purchasers could give the impression that they were willing or able to pay whatever price might be demanded.

Hahn favors a lengthened service to usher in the Sabbath so as to enable people who are working late to attend the synagogue before the Friday evening meal.[67] When nights are long, it is suggested that the duration of the Sabbath meal be extended with song and study.[68] Throughout the Middle Ages, it was the custom in Germany to sing songs during the Sabbath meals.[69] Among the women, the Psalms, translated into Yiddish and adapted for folk use, became popular.[70] Ezekiel Landau, who wanted the Sabbath to be observed with study and song, criticizes the Jews of Prague for making it a habit to congregate in the market place and street after the Sabbath meal and engage in gossip and frivolous topics of conversation.[71] Joseph Kosman also regrets that a widespread indifference prevails to study on the Sabbath. Since there was no time for study during the week, because of the need to earn one's living, Saturday was the only day when one was free. But unfortunately, as Kosman points out, unlettered persons prefer sleeping; and even if books are available to them in the Yiddish vernacular, covering the Bible, Midrash, and Talmudic homilies, they still show no interest in study.[72] The concerns of Kosman suggest to us some of the cultural attitudes then shaping and molding folk life.[73]

The second Sabbath meal would be eaten after returning from the morning services in the synagogue, and, in Berliner's opinion, the scheduling of the second meal in the early afternoon must have been of non-Jewish influence.[74] However, the hour for the meal in the Jewish home could have been introduced independently of any external factors. Again, in dealing with folk life it is not possible to determine precisely what were the internal or external causes. During winter months, however, when days are shorter, an additional meal would be served on Friday night.[75]

The third meal was eaten on Saturday afternoon,[76] and the description of the *se'udah shelishit*, "third meal," provided by Rabbi Meir of Rothenburg, could be applicable to the later Middle Ages, as well as to the present day.

> . . . Such was the custom [proposed by] earlier righteous men *(ha-zaddiḳim ha-ri'shonim)*: On the Sabbath every person was to recite the morning prayer . . . , the afternoon prayer, and afterward hold 'the third meal' over wine [i.e., recite the benediction over the wine to honor the Sabbath], and he [then] would eat until the termination of the Sabbath.[77]

As we have stated, a mantle and cape would be set aside as the Sabbath dress so as to add distinction to the day.[78] Hahn, in a moment of reminiscing, describes the garments worn in the past by those attending synagogue:

> I remember the time when circumstances were better than now; most heads of families had a special cloak with folds that they wore to services. The wealthy father gave his son a cloak when he married. Likewise, the headgear (*mitron*), called *kape*, was worn in former times.[79]

In his own day, Hahn states further, most persons could not afford to wear a costly mantle to the synagogue. No doubt their Sabbath garment was similar in style and quality to what was worn on weekdays, but it became a Sabbath mantle when it was set aside for that purpose. As Hahn describes the practice of wearing on the Sabbath and holidays a "closed sleeve" attached to the right side of the mantle,[80] he is aware of a lack of sources and knowledge to provide an adequate explanation of the reasons underlying the observance of this custom as well as others.

> Based on the tradition that I received, I am writing to explain the reason for the custom of using 'a sleeve' specifically on the Sabbath and holidays. All the customs of our ancestors can be equated with Jewish law. What we do not know can be accounted for as being due to the limitation in our own knowledge or to the loss of earlier books during the persecutions that befell our leaders of blessed memory. . . .[81]

Communal legislation, for instance that of Nuremberg and Fürth in 1728, also specified what could be worn to the synagogue and on the Sabbath. Wigs (*perücken*) are permitted, but without powder, and the ordinance states further that the *ṭallit,* prayer shawl, worn in the synagogue had to be white. Scholars could wear their white capes only on the Sabbath. If students would persist in wearing capes, they did so at the risk of losing free board. Obviously, a student dressed in that manner was not considered in need. Red mantles and capes could not be worn to the synagogue; no doubt the intent was to curb ostentatious dress on everyone's part.[82]

Another development in Jewish folk life was the reading of the Prayer Book in the vernacular.[83] This included the *Siddur*, *Teḥinnah,* and *Maḥzor.* The wife of Samuel (Aaron Samuel) Kaidanover, the mother of Ẓebi Hirsh Kaidanover, so it is told, could not recite prayers in Hebrew. When she lit candles for the Sabbath, she would say the prayer in Yiddish.[84] Men and women in Frankfort and Prague who were not always able to pray in Hebrew also used Yiddish instead.[85] Joseph Kosman was of the opinion that the women of Frankfort who knew no Hebrew and men "whose minds were as feeble as women's" should pray in Yiddish. He preferred the prayer in the vernacular to having "the Hebrew language profaned because of the way it is used by the illiterate."[86]

There were other customs relating to the Sabbath that were closely associated with the folk life of German Jewry. On Friday, before the Sabbath began, the *gabba'i* (*gabbai*), the collector of taxes or public funds for communal charities, received tallow from each member of the congregation in order to supply the cantor with candlelight while he conducted services. The tallow was given as a communal tax.[87] During services on Saturday morning, when a person was called upon to recite the benedictions for the Torah reading or the chanting of the *maftir*, the section of the Prophets read after the Torah portion, he pledged a contribution that was added to the community chest for the aid of the needy or the education of poor children.[88] On Friday the poor gathered at the gates of the *gas* to obtain funds to provide for their Sabbath needs. With this practice as an example, it is possible to show how an ancient rabbinic tradition was the basis of the social pattern of Jewish communal life at the end of the Middle Ages.[89] And, likewise, no Sabbath meal could be considered complete unless a stranger was present, in accordance with the Talmudic teaching of inviting strangers to private homes as guests on the Sabbath.[90]

In Germany, in the 17th and 18th centuries, the Jewish transient population grew, consisting of the homeless, those uprooted during pogroms, the professional beggar, and the wandering troubadour, the *marshelik*.[91] It was not possible to care for such large numbers by relying solely on the benevolence of well-meaning individuals.[92] If it were left to the discretion of families to invite strangers to their homes, individual preferences might be shown, and as a result migrants would be stranded in the community. In Worms, Bamberg, Hesse, Runkel, Hildesheim, and Altona, for example, it was the procedure to assign a stranger in need of hospitality to specific homes. *Pletn*, "tickets," indicating where a Sabbath meal could be obtained, would be distributed among the transients. The family, chosen by lot, was obliged to extend hospitality to any one who presented such a "ticket." Measures of this kind were introduced to provide food and lodging for "many homeless migratory Jewish persons,"[93] since the existing communal buildings, the synagogue and the hospital, were not large enough to furnish shelter to all transients.

Let us not assume that the transient was always showered with benevolence; on the contrary, as Kirchan reports, the strangers who came to small towns sometimes received harsh treatment. "The care of a sick stranger is regarded as a chore, "Kirchan chides. "He is left to go his way in a wagon or cart, wandering from one town to another." Kirchan states further that such indifference often resulted in the stranger becoming a victim of brutality. At times a sick person, allowed to shift for himself, was found dead. The driver would pocket the money of the dead man and then discard the body in a field.[94] Apparently the observations of Kirchan were no exaggeration; his scathing denunciation of the mistreatment of the transient is echoed in an anonymous "Song of Complaint," published in the 18th century. The song condemns the abusive treatment traveling mendicants received in Frankfort; the homeless migrants, so the complaint asserts, were not welcomed with cordiality when they arrived:

> Listen, dear people, to what is happening at this time. . . . When we poor people, travelers, come marching to Frankfort, they do not let us pass through [their] doors. We are met by Jacob Fulvaser. . . . He asks: 'How long have you been here, and what is your name?' . . . He makes it appear that the funds for *pletn* are withdrawn [lit., taken away] and are not available. . . . They are in great fear—forbid it!—that as a result of their *ẓedaḳah* (charity), the wealth of the community will soon vanish. . . . They allow us poor strangers to stand in the same spot in the sun, and the result is that we almost melt and are scorched. . . .[95]

Risks were involved in befriending a stranger, as one of Bacharach's reports shows. The head of the house could expect to incur some loss whenever he extended his hospitality. On one occasion a tablecloth was burned because the guest had failed to put out the candle in the room before retiring for the night.[96] Evidently, the ethical teaching to show concern for the stranger was not easily implemented in the 18th century inasmuch as there were non-Jewish officials who regarded the Jewish migrant as a criminal element and the Jewish hostel as a rendezvous for gangs. Jewish beggars were accused of being members of "gangs of thieves and rogues" who wandered about Germany marauding and committing crimes.[97] When a series of house burglaries occurred in Ansbach, "Jewish beggars and gypsies" were recorded in official documents as the culprits. Church authorities of Ansbach in 1720 opposed the establishment of a hostel in the Jewish community because it would serve as a meeting place for "undesirable characters."[98] This hostility toward Jewish beggars was justified on the ground that their names had been included in the lists of known members of gangs. This may explain in part the indifference to the stranger that was voiced by Kirchan and in the "Song of Complaint." The Hebrew and Yiddish "slang" that became part of "the language of thieves" has been cited as additional proof that Jewish beggars associated with gangs in Germany.[99] There is evidence that this "social fact" was exploited by bias and used as a pretext to convict the innocent of crimes they had not committed.[100]

The writers of popular guides instructing the folk in their conduct also presented with candor the difficulties that arose in the observance of the Sabbath. Further facets of social life are disclosed in their account of problems pertaining to Sabbath religious practices. Elḥanan Kirchan and Yeḥiel Epstein are dissatisfied because residents of small towns show a lack of understanding of the distance that can be covered by foot on the Sabbath, according to religious law, since they do not hesitate to walk beyond the specified limit.[101] Kirchan tells how his father, in order to ensure accuracy, measured for the people the distance that they could go on the Sabbath, and how he also equated the *teḥum*, the "Sabbath limit" of 2000 ells (Ex. 16:29), with terms of standard measurement. Since an ell is estimated to be two feet, 4000 feet is the total distance allowed.

> The 2000 ells which a person may walk [during the Sabbath] must not be regarded as comparable to the ell used [in our time]. Our ell is not the ell that was established by Moses and used to measure the Tabernacle.[102]

To determine the distance of the *teḥum* on the Sabbath also became a matter of concern when someone traveled to another community during the season of the fair and temporarily stayed there. On one occasion Meir Eisenstadt was asked about the *teḥum* that a person should adhere to when going semiannually to Krems to sell goods. The question not only had a bearing on the relation of the Sabbath to the life of the people, but it also alluded to some of the informal social relationships that must have existed between the Christians and Jews of Germany.

> As to the large semiannual gathering of Jews in Krems,

> they sell their goods to non-Jews at doorways and in houses where they leave their wares. The Jews then become scattered throughout the city, here and there. . . . What should be the ruling as to [the distance] that can be walked in the city on the Sabbath?[103]

Kirchan also discusses the difficulty in using the '*erub*, the legal fiction of establishing another "residence" on the Sabbath and holidays by means of "eatables." Food, usually boiled meat and bread in a plate, can be deposited, before the Sabbath or festival, in a place that will serve symbolically as the location of one's home. The act of eating this food represents "a change of dwelling." On the Sabbath or holiday the individual then measures the distance that he is permitted to walk from the location of the new "home." The obstacles encountered in making an '*erub* are related by Kirchan on the basis of Samuel Kaidanover's experience. The incident pertains to the food for an '*erub* becoming "mildewed, decayed with holes, wormy [and] unfit to eat," with the result that Kaidanover "could not fulfill what is required [to 'transfer one's residence']."[104]

It would seem that Sabbath violations were not unusual, for there were instances, according to Kosman, Kirchan, and Landau, when some individuals, or even a significant part of the population, failed to abide by the tradition of the Sabbath. As an example, "in the summer time a section of the people allow fire to be made in the evening [i.e., on Friday] and prepare food that is raw. . . ."[105] On account of their lax attitude "they are [always] late in ushering in the Sabbath, but early in terminating it."[106] In addition, the *shoḥaṭim* and *bodḳim* who perform the ritual slaughter and examine animals for possible physical defects "are not scrupulous in observing [the Sabbath] commandments." When the Sabbath is approaching, "they [still] carry objects, [an act that is] not considered proper."[107] There are persons who allow their animals to work in the field on the Sabbath.[108] Servants and children pasture the animals, and often someone has to walk beyond the Sabbath limit to find the animals that have gone astray.[109] In a sermon devoted to Sabbath observance, Ezekiel Landau describes a "sickening evil" in Prague. "Transients purchase oats and fodder in the lodging house on the Sabbath," and thereby violate a basic law." Moreover, the transient "exchanges money on the Sabbath, [and] proceeds from market to market, securing a small or large amount until he has completed the purchase. . . ."[110]

Animals are not given the rest and care required by Sabbath law, Kirchan also notes. He refers to the practice in Poland as the proper way in which animals should be treated on the Sabbath: No feed-bag is placed on the horse's neck, and since the horse is not doing any work, there is no reason "to leave the halter or bridle on it."[111] A group of wagon-drivers who lived in the community of Nikolsburg, Moravia, and engaged in long-distance hauling, consulted Menaḥem Mendel Krochmal whether there was any basis in Jewish tradition for authorizing them to rent their horses and wagons to non-Jews who would work the animals on the Sabbath. Krochmal answered emphatically that he was not able to find anywhere in Jewish religio-legal and religio-ethical sources a justification for the proposed transaction.[112]

There is evidence that customs not sanctioned by *halakhah* also influenced Sabbath observance.[113] According to traditional law, a watch is not to be carried on the Sabbath.[114] A *responsum* of Meir Eisenstadt relates that in various communities it has become the practice to wear a watch on the Sabbath. The rabbinic regulation that objects should not be carried on the Sabbath in one's pockets was thereby dispensed with.

> This [i.e., wearing a watch] is only according to a custom. From the very outset there were individuals who did not accept this prohibition. I have seen in a number of commu-

> nities that even scholars delivering a discourse in public will take out a watch. . . .[115]

Referring to the Maharil as his authority, Eisenstadt was of the opinion that the practice is no violation of rabbinic law.[115a]

The reading on the Sabbath of the *nay-tsaytung*, a "news broadside" devoted to events of war, caused discussion as to whether this violated tradition. Jacob Reischer of Prague was asked if the sanctity of the Sabbath would be undermined by reading the news. The inquiring party was disturbed by the fact that even persons of good character had been reading the "broadside" on the Sabbath. In reply, Reischer said that he would not voice any objection to the reading of such news on the Sabbath; for self-protection and the protection of others it is essential to know what is happening in the land. He therefore felt that he had no reason to disapprove of what was read on the Sabbath so long as the content was not trivial.[116] On the other hand, a contrasting view was expressed by Jacob Emden, who opposed the reading of a broadside with war news on the Sabbath. In adopting a stricter position, Emden explained that he did not agree with those authorities who saw no objection to reading news on the Sabbath "in time of war and pillage, when there is great need to know which side is winning." Emden contended that the person who read the news did not confine himself only to military and political affairs, for at the same time he might be interested "in securing information about merchandise, property, garments for sale, and about business matters and the concerns of merchants." In conclusion, he states that "herein is sufficient grounds to prohibit such reading on the Sabbath."[117] In the same vein, he instructed a student not to read a medical book on the Sabbath, even if it is for the purpose of study.[118] He implied that the reading of secular literature would have the effect of weakening Sabbath observance. The difference between the views of Reischer and Emden may be accounted for in that the rabbis and Jewish scholars of Prague from the 16th century onward came under the intellectual influence of the Renaissance and the Enlightenment.[119] The questions raised with regard to reading broadside news on the Sabbath are additional evidence of the effect Germanic culture must have had on Jewish folk life, and the position taken by Reischer is indicative of a secular trend that had been developing in the German-Jewish community in the 18th century.[120] The differing opinions of Reischer and Emden foreshadow the conflict that was to take place between secular and traditional ideas in European Jewish life during the 19th century.

3. Some Festival Customs

If we consider the ways in which holidays were observed and celebrated, it will again be noted that the practices that became popular were not of local origin only. We shall also find instances of older customs undergoing modification due to changing circumstances in the social life of the community. And in some cases there will be enough evidence to suggest the reasons for a given practice to become an important part of folk life. The cycle of the Jewish calendar will be followed in dealing with customs associated with the holidays, and when a practice is related to more than one festival, this will be indicated in order to suggest interlocking cultural motifs.

As the people prepared for the High Holy Days during the month of *'Elul*, in the Frankfort community, an older person would conduct the services for *seliḥot*, "the recitation of liturgical poems of supplication." Even if the older man knew less than a younger person, he was still chosen to be the representative of the congregation. The book of *Minhagim* of Kosman advises, "If the older man does not know what the prayers mean, let him go to a scholar and receive instruction."[121] Why was an older person selected to lead the *seliḥot* ritual? The precedent for this is derived from the Mishnah,[122] which states that when a fast is declared during an emergency such as a famine, a *zaḳen*, an elder, prays in behalf of the community: As "they stand up for prayer, they place before the ark an old and experienced man, who has children and whose house is empty, so that his heart may be wholly devoted to his prayer." The word empty (*reḳan*) is interpreted to mean that "he has nothing in the house." Since he has accumulated no worldly goods, he is considered a highly ethical person; his livelihood depends solely upon whatever he is able "to harvest in the field."[123] During the penitential month of *'Elul*, when the mood is set for the holiday season of *Rosh ha-Shanah* and *Yom Kippur*, in Fürth the *shofar* would be blown at night as well as in the morning. This differs from the usual *minhag* of blowing the *shofar* only in the daytime and not at night.[124] We are told by Kirchan that during the night of *Rosh ha-Shanah* it is the custom to remain awake so as to engage in study,[125] as is done on the nights of *Hosha'ana' Rabbah* and *Shabu'ot*. And in his sharp criticism of the low cultural standards prevailing in rural areas, Kirchan pictures the absurd way in which *Rosh ha-Shanah* is observed:

> In small towns on the sacred day of *Rosh ha-Shanah*, the [actions of the] cantors [show that they] are illiterate and inexperienced, that they lack religious fervor and intellectual background. . . . Some individuals have made mouthpieces that they place on the front of the *shofar* in order to be heard more clearly. As they blow through the mouthpiece, it sounds like the trumpet used by nobility in the forest when they hunt hare [i.e., engage in a chase].[126]

On the eve of *Rosh ha-Shanah*, the Day of Judgment, the most pious persons of Frankfort would fast and abstain from food until the break of dawn, but the community as a whole did not fast. The average person fasted during the *'Aseret Yeme Teshubah*, the Ten Days of Repentance, between *Rosh ha-Shanah* and *Yom Kippur*.[127] This custom was based on the ancient Talmudic teaching that the "perfectly righteous" are judged on *Rosh ha-Shanah*, whereas in the case of "intermediate" persons, neither righteous nor wicked, judgment "is suspended from New Year till the Day of Atonement."[128] Thus, the customs observed between *Rosh ha-Shanah* and *Yom Kippur* express the concern of the "average individual" that he become worthy enough to be "inscribed in the Book of Life."[129]

We learn from Hahn that the people of Frankfort are finding it difficult to observe *tashlikh*, the *Rosh ha-Shanah* ceremony of casting one's sins into a running stream. He recounts that they do not have access to the river Main; the gate leading to the river is guarded by soldiers, with the result that not everyone is able to practice *tashlikh* and "the ceremony is being discarded." Those who adhere to the custom go to the dam and use the water that descends into a nearby ditch. Since the water is stagnant and refuse has been thrown into it, they are not abiding by the traditional requirement of going to a fresh, running stream.[130] With a touch of irony Hahn concludes his comments on *tashlikh* by mentioning his own failure to make the custom more effective:

> Thus I tried by my own devices to have access to the Main River. I discussed in confidence with the collector of the community charity fund my plan to gain the good will of the guards of the gates by means of wine of old vintage. By these efforts I had hoped to restore the custom to its former state of observance.[131]

Isaiah Horowitz cites the practice described by the Maharil that on *Yom Kippur* the synagogue is draped in colored cloth to honor the holiday, and the floor is covered with grass. The use of the grass is explained in two ways: first, it fulfills the Biblical injunction not to "bow down on any figured stone" (Levit. 26:1) and, second, it enables the worshipers to prostrate with ease on the floor.[132] Judging from the statement of Horowitz, we have no facts to show that the custom continued after the 15th century. Although the Maharil said nothing more specific about the "figures" on the floor, there is evidence that artistic symbols of nonhuman form appeared in synagogues of German-Jewish communities.[133]

On the Day of Atonement, the people would engage in study, and in many localities the Book of Psalms was recited on the night of *Yom Kippur*. If one became weary, only "the first four Psalms would be said before retiring."[134] Since the night is considered an ideal time to read and reflect,[135] it became customary to stay up all night on important holidays to take part in study.[136] Study is considered essential for the meaningful observance of festivals. In their guide books Isaiah Horowitz and Yeḥiel Epstein direct the people to another practice for the eve of the Day of Atonement. Upon retiring, so they advise, one should refrain from "wrapping himself in a covering that causes warmth," as this will "arouse the sexual desire"[137] on a night when the individual should engage in fasting and abstain from satisfying his physical appetites. Joseph Kosman enumerates the foods to be avoided before the eve of *Yom Kippur* in order to prevent a "seminal emission." Dairy foods or dishes made of milk are not to be eaten, since they can be the cause of a "mishap." It is the duty of each person to shun those foods that might cause a "nocturnal pollution" on the night of *Yom Kippur*.[138]

Ezekiel Landau, in presenting a realistic picture of the unesthetic, unsanitary physical surroundings that have to be faced when a *sukkah* is erected for *Sukkot*, the Feast of Booths, urges that precautions be taken to select a clean place where there is no refuse so that the *sukkah* can be built in hygienic surroundings. He also warns that "mosquitoes and flies will be plentiful in the booth," and advises everyone to be on the alert to protect himself against insects while sitting in the open.[139] As a health measure, we read of insect poison being used to rid homes of flies.[140]

A local custom may express symbolically the relationship that one festival has to another, such as the *minhag* of Frankfort in using the wax that remained from *Yom Kippur* candles to make candles for the eve of *Hosha'ana' Rabbah*, the seventh day of *Sukkot*, known as "the Great Deliverance."[141] Since the final decree in the Book of Life is extended from the Day of Atonement to the seventh day of *Sukkot*,[142] there is relevance in saving the *Yom Kippur* candle-wax for *Hoshana'ana' Rabbah*. The custom has acquired further significance through cabalistic interpretation, popular in its appeal to the folk: the candles for *Hosha 'ana' Rabbah* are to be made of five "capsules of wax" (*hamishah gib'olin*), as the number five corresponds to the Five Books of Moses, the Pentateuch. Each capsule of wax must have at least three leaves; the total of fifteen leaves represents the fifteen *Shir ha-Ma'alot* Psalms (120–134) and the fifteen letters in the Priestly Benediction (Num. 6:24-27).[143]

To study on *Hosha'ana' Rabbah* is regarded to be a decisive act, for it is also through study that people can expect to influence the "sealing of the decree" for the new year. On *Hosha'ana' Rabbah* they are up all night to read from the *Tiḳḳun*, a collection of passages selected mainly from the Bible, Mishnah, Talmud, and *Zohar*. The *Tiḳḳun* is widely used both on *Hosha 'ana' Rabbah* and *Shabu'ot*, the Feast of Weeks, or Pentecost. Kosman indicates that the *Tiḳḳun* was introduced to European countries from Palestine, where it originated in the Lurianic cabalistic, mystical school.[144] With regard to some of the regulations pertaining to *Ḥol ha-Mo'ed*, the period between the first two and last two days of *Sukkot* and *Pesaḥ*,[145] Ezekiel Landau adopts a lenient view. He contends that the *Shulḥan 'Arukh*[146] permits one to engage in any kind of work during the intervening days of the festival if he has no other way of earning his livelihood. Similarly, Landau saw no objection to an individual cutting his hair or trimming his beard during *Ḥol ha-Mo'ed* if he expects to be in the company of civil officials or nobility. The person, Landau states, may be embarrassed or subjected to ridicule if he is not neat in his appearance.[147] We can surmise that the association with a nobleman or official did not take the form of an informal social visit. For the Jew it

Fig. 12. The Procession on *Hosha'ana' Rabbah (Courtesy, Widener Library, Harvard University)*. From F. Thieberger, *Jüdisches Fest*, bet. pp. 320-22, plate # 18; originally an etching by Picart, 18th century.

meant his economic survival, as he was probably trying to interest his political superior in the wares he had for sale.

In his song for *Sukkot* and *Simḥat Torah*, Kirchan criticizes the practice of "making a fire, leaping over it, and shooting gunpowder" during the festival.[148] There is additional evidence that in the 18th century Ashkenazic Jews in Central and East European lands observed the custom of exploding gunpowder on *Simḥat Torah* as part of the holiday celebration.[149] In his *Minhagim* Yuspa Shammash (Shammes) also describes how the bonfire figured in the *Simḥat Torah* merriment. The two "bridegrooms," *Ḥatan Torah* and *Ḥatan Bereshit*, who respectively recited the benedictions for the concluding section of Deuteronomy and the beginning of Genesis, would invite their friends to the wedding hall behind the synagogue. The young man who assisted the sexton then announced in the street, "Lead 'the bride and groom' to the wedding hall in the rear." Fruit and wine were served to the guests, and the children were treated to delicacies. A large bonfire was built in the courtyard of the synagogue; the guests then assembled around the fire and engaged in spirited dancing. Yuspa Shammash's concluding description of the bonfire festivities conveys something of the hilarity that broke out on *Simḥat Torah*:

> At times the rabbi joined them in the joyous dancing around the fire in honor of the Torah. They would continue until *minḥah* [when afternoon prayers are recited]. They drank wine by the fire; the *ḥatanim* gave them wine. The sexton added wood to the fire, and the *ḥatanim* would "let go of themselves."[150]

Max Erik regards the *Johannes Feuer* to be the origin of the bonfire and gunpowder customs incorporated into the observance of *Simhat Torah.*[151] In the general community *Johannes Feuer* (also *Johannesfeuer* or *Johannisfeuer*) was observed at Easter, at which time gunpowder was exploded. The *Johannes Feuer* has been related to *Osterfeuer*, the Easter eve bonfire at the time of the vernal equinox. Wherever possible the fire was built on a hill, a high elevated spot, or else on the flat surface of a field. The fire was encircled to form a wheel, which symbolized the sun, and *Johannes Feuer* therefore became known as *Himmelsfeuer*. The act of jumping over the fire was part of a homeopathic rite to prevent fever and erysipelas;[152] for in German society the *Johannes Feuer* was not only a seasonal custom but was carried out whenever an epidemic or disease had become threatening. Straw effigies would be thrown into the fire as a safeguard against calamity—more specifically, "cattle disease, failure of crops, and damage by hail."[153]

Kirchan, however, does not state that his opposition to "jump-

Fig. 13. Celebration on *Simḥat Torah (Courtesy, Widener Library, Harvard University).* From Thieberger, *Jüdisches Fest,* bet. pp. 320-22, plate # 17; originally an engraving by Picart, 18th century.

ing over a fire and shooting gunpowder" on *Simḥat Torah* is due to the fact that the practice had been influenced by the *Johannes Feuer*. We might take it for granted that as the custom underwent redefinition and modification, its possible origin was forgotten or else was no longer so apparent as to be a matter of concern. Not all rabbinic authorities would concur with Kirchan's objection to the use of the bonfire and gunpowder on *Simḥat Torah*. In fact, fire was associated with *Purim*, the Feast of Lots, during the earlier Middle Ages. Rashi, the famous Talmudic authority and commentator of Troyes, France, in the 11th century, describes how children celebrated the festival of *Purim* by leaping over a fire made in a pit.[154] The children jumped over the fire as though engaging in a game of sport. It was also the practice on *Purim* to leap over fire with the effigy of Haman or dance around the fire before burning the effigy. Evidently by the 11th century the ceremony of dancing around a fire to destroy the "evil spirit" had become part of the *Purim* celebration.[155] And in later times those observing this custom seemed little concerned about the likely origin of their form of festivity. The folk combined the bonfire and gunpowder features of the *Johannes Feuer* with the observance of *Simḥat Torah* without questioning whether they might be undermining the original purpose of the holiday. We can consider the introduction of these elements into religious life as another instance where popular will overrode the opinion of authority.[156]

A festival was also an occasion when impoverished Jews living in the congested quarters of the *gas* would turn their thoughts to nature.[157] Such an occasion is described by Yeḥiel Epstein in his account of *Shabbat Shirah*, "the Sabbath of Song," that falls in the winter month of *Shebaṭ*, usually at the end of January or the beginning of February. The Torah portion read in the synagogue (*Be-Shallaḥ*, Ex. 13:17–17:16) suggests the name *Shabbat Shirah* given to this particular Sabbath, as it includes the song of the Israelites after they had crossed the Red Sea. When the Israelites escaped from the Egyptians, Epstein explains, "the birds also sang at the Red Sea"; hence on *Shabbat Shirah* the birds should be remembered and befriended by placing "cooked grains of wheat outside the windows."[158] The importance ascribed to *Shabbat Shirah* in connection with 18th-century festival observances may be noted further in a homily of Moses Sofer ("Ḥatam Sofer," b. 1763, Frankfort). At the outset he affirms that the basis for this custom *(minhag Yisra'el Torah hu)*, according to the opinion of various authorities, including Moses Isserles, is in the Scriptures (Ex. 16:32). The Biblical text, "that they may see the bread where-with I fed you," serves as a reminder that when the Israelites were provided manna in the desert, they were not self-sufficient and had to be fed like birds. Rabbinic sages, therefore, saw a comparison between the life of Israel and that of the bird that faces all kinds of uncertainties.[159] As the birds are fed on *Shabbat Shirah*, the people are to be reminded of their own precarious existence and of their survival made possible through God's providential care.[160]

Another meaning given to *Shabbat Shirah* is likewise derived from a homiletical interpretation of a verse in the Torah portion *Be-Shallaḥ* (Ex. 16:27).[161] When Moses said that there would be no manna in the field on the Sabbath, Dathan and Abiram sought to discredit him by spreading manna on the ground to make it appear that food would be supplied on the Sabbath. In the meantime, the birds ate all of the manna, and when Dathan and Abiram invited the people to see with their own eyes that manna was there, they found nothing, as the Bible states. The birds therefore deserve special consideration on *Shabbat Shirah* when the Torah reading recounts how manna served as the food of the Israelites.[162] In the lore associated with *Shabbat Shirah* we have another example of a custom having acquired its rationale through the interpretation of Biblical texts by scholars and teachers; and by means of such Midrashic, homiletic explanations the *minhag* of assigning a special Sabbath to birds gained wide attention.

In describing the attire in vogue in Germanic-Jewish life in the 17th and 18th centuries, we considered the type of dress worn on holidays,[163] as it was partly through the special garments set aside for a festival that the day could be distinguished from the rest of the year. Thus we find that on *Purim* as well as on *Ḥol ha-Mo'ed,* the Sabbath mantle and cape were worn to the synagogue to indicate that these were special occasions.[164]

During the festivals special contributions were made to aid communal needs and institutions, and even on the more solemn fast days it was the practice to give charity.[165] On *Sukkot* and *Pesaḥ* voluntary collections were scheduled for the support of schools,[166] while on *Simḥat Torah* a general contribution would be made for charity.[167] From Talmudic times on, *Purim* has been the occasion when money would be collected for charitable purposes.[168] Half a shekel was contributed on *Ta'anit 'Ester* (the Fast of Esther, which occurs on the 13th of *'Adar,* a day before *Purim*, and commemorates the fast of Queen Esther to avert the decree of Haman) for the *Ma'ot Purim,* the *Purim* charity fund;[169] in Frankfort 34 *pfennige* were given, for this amount corresponded to the numerical value of *dal*, the Hebrew word for "poor." Besides the half-shekel for *Purim* charity, four *pfennige* were contributed to the *Matnot 'Ebyonim*, the community chest for the poor.[170]

In former times,[171] one third of the *Ma'ot Purim* was given to the government. There was no separate *Matnot 'Ebyonim* fund, but the poor were assisted from the general chest collected on *Purim*. Hahn describes the method followed in Frankfort, prior to the Fettmilch Insurrection on August 23, 1614, of collecting funds on *Ta'anit 'Ester*. The charity administrators drew two circles, one for the half-shekel and the other for *Matnot 'Ebyonim*, and as contributions were made the administrators sat beside the circles to make sure that each fund would be kept separate.[172]

In addition to what was given to charity collectors for *Purim*, every person, even if poor, was expected to present two gifts as *Mishloaḥ Manot* (*Sholekh Mones*) to a neighbor. The *Mishloaḥ Manot*, or gifts, on *Purim* would consist either of two cooked foods, such as meat and fish, or one of these foods and drink.[173] Spices were also given as the second gift.[174]

Kirchan also criticizes the manner in which *Purim* is observed in small towns. The account of *Purim*, so he discovers, is read from a "paper scroll," not from a *Megillah*, the Book of Esther, on parchment; and in addition the benediction that precedes the reading is recited too hastily, as if it were for the regular Torah scroll.[175]

It is an old tradition to arrange a *se'udah*, meal, in honor of the *Purim* festival, and in his book of customs Kosman has recorded some of the details of the way in which the meal is held. Relatives, friends, and the poor are invited. Before the meal begins, they engage in study, and the association that *Purim* has with study and a feast is based on an interpretation the teachers of the Talmud made of a verse in the Book of Esther, "The Jews had light and gladness and joy and honour" (8:16). "Light," they say, means the Torah (Prov. 6:23), and "gladness" is related to a feast day (Deut. 16:14).[176] Kosman then presents the differences of opinion that arose over the hour when the *Purim* meal should take place. Israel Isserlein and later Isaiah Horowitz both contended that the meal should be served during the day and not in the evening.[177] On the other hand, there were communities that planned the meal in the evening, following *minḥah*, the afternoon services, at the usual time of the *shalosh se'udot*, the third meal on Saturday. Moses Isserles was one of the principal authorities referred to as being in favor of holding the *se'udah* celebration during the night time.[178]

Since Isserlein and Horowitz have elaborated their respective points of view in a *responsum* and a cabalistic ethical discourse, we are able to present their main arguments. Isserlein emphasizes that those who ate after *minḥah* might be inclined to dispense with the *ma'arib* services, and he is therefore concerned lest a religious duty be neglected if the *Purim* feast is held at night.[179] Horowitz also contends that a *se'udah* in the evening will interfere with the *ma'arib* services. He states further that the day time is more appropriate for *Purim* festivity, for it was during the day that Queen

Esther arranged the meal for King Ahasuerus that proved to be decisive in saving the Jews from Haman's plot (Esther 5:14; 7:1-2, 9-10). And it was also during the day that Haman was brought to justice (8:1).[180] For Kosman, however, the discussion concerning the proper time for the meal is not too significant.[181] Through his knowledge of the customs in each area, Kosman is fully aware of the differences with regard to the observance of this ritual; therefore he does not recommend any set time for the *Purim* feast. Instead, he would leave it to each locality to follow its own procedure and establish its own *minhag*.

There were times when the people could discard communal restraint and engage in gaiety to forget the monotony of their lives, in large measure caused by their physical environment and the hardships they had to endure to maintain their existence. We have already suggested how the celebrations for birth and marriage provided a festive outlet for the community as a whole. Holiday celebrations offered further opportunities for amusement, comedy, and hilarity. On *Ḥanukkah* and *Purim* the communal prohibition against gambling was lifted;[182] games of chance and lottery were permitted to add to the merrymaking. We hear from Bacharach that during a celebration on *Purim* a lottery was held and a gold-plated cup was raffled as the prize.[183] On *Purim* as well as on *Ḥanukkah*, popular gambling games were ticktack, heads or tails, chess,[184] and cards.[185] The game of ticktack is similar to that of backgammon, played on a board, with each player moving forward in accordance with the throw of dice. Of these games, ticktack was the most objectionable because it required dice, and from Talmudic times on the dice gambler has been considered a reprehensible person, never to be trusted, since he does not make "an honest living."[186]

While gambling games were tolerated as amusement only on stated occasions, there were nevertheless individual rabbis, teachers, and supporters of *musar*, ethical conduct, who did not relax their unreserved opposition to gambling at all times. Joseph

Fig. 14. Festivities on *Ḥanukkah* and *Purim* in the Synagogue and Home *(Courtesy, Widener Library, Harvard University)*. From Bodenschatz, *Aufrichtig teutsch redender Hebräer* . . . , II, bet. 250-51, fig. 10.

Kosman was among those who opposed gambling even as a diversion, and out of a desire to discourage participation in any game of chance, regardless of its nature, he declared that the money lost in gambling could be put to better use if, instead, special foods were purchased for the festival. Gambling is an evil influence, and is corrupting, he emphasizes; and like the pietist Judah he-Ḥasid, of the 13th century, he condemns all gambling games without exception. To gamble is compared "to stealing from a thief," and, as a result, one "has had a taste of thievery," as the Talmud states. The gambler is also likened to the robber, as the Talmudic teachers have put it, who "takes the law into his own hands" on pretext that "he is protecting his own interests."[187] We do not imply that the views of the pietists and moralists of Rhenish communities in the early and late Middle Ages hold good for rabbis in other regions during these periods. Studies of social life in Provence, Spain, and Italy show that scholars in these countries were less concerned about lapses in moral behavior than were the rabbinic authorities of Germany. In their greater tolerance toward the gambler, rabbis in southern Europe were no doubt influenced by their general social environment, where gambling was more prevalent and acceptable, in contrast to the more rigorous standards of moral conduct of the Rhineland.[188]

Communal leaders must have realized, however, that not everyone who played in a game intended to gamble but was only interested in finding some diversion from daily routine.[189] Otherwise, how might we explain that after the Frankfort fire in 1711—when this tragedy had been attributed to moral decline and a "mood of despair and contrition" had set in—that games of amusement could still continue? While all forms of entertainment were prohibited for a period of fourteen years, it was permissible for the sick and for mothers in confinement to pass the time in a game. Chess was allowed as a regular game, and parents could teach it to their children.[190] Although it was a time of sorrow, communal authorities must have understood that the people still had a need for some relaxation, and therefore did not forbid innocent games being played in the Frankfort *gas*.

Since the merriment on *Purim* was mainly derived from masquerade, drama, and parody, the festival has been likened to "the season of the Jewish carnival."[191] Masquerade is a feature of the *Purim* celebration since the beginning of the 16th century.[192] Though contrary to Biblical law (Deut. 22:5), it was not uncommon on *Purim* for a man to dress himself in a woman's costume, or a woman to disguise herself in a man's attire;[193] and rabbinic opinion did not concur as to the permissibility of this folk practice. Some said that there is no objection if men and women disguise their appearance through dress, providing this is limited to the *Purim* celebration. Others raised an objection to the masquerade attire because of the unfortunate consequences that occurred when men and women could not be told apart by their clothes. There was further disapproval on the grounds that the masquerade garments usually worn were *sha'aṭnez,* that is, woven from woolen and linen thread, in violation of the Biblical statute (Levit. 19:19; Deut. 22:11).[194]

In the 18th century, the *yeshibah baḥurim,* Talmudic students, who were studying in the Academy of R. David Oppenheim in Prague, organized themselves into a theatrical troupe to present *Purim* plays.[195] Such a group was not unique, as there were theatrical teams, made up of such diverse individuals as cantors, jesters, musicians, and students, who traveled from community to community to stage the *shpiln*, or drama, usually scheduled two weeks before and after the festival.[196] In addition to Prague, the main centers for the Jewish theater were in Metz, Frankfort, and Hamburg.[197]

As the Jewish theater developed in Europe after the 15th century into a vital cultural institution, the *shpiln* in the Yiddish vernacular became an essential part of the *Purim* celebration. The *Purim* plays were built around Biblical heroes, mainly Isaac, Joseph, David, Mordecai, and Esther, the most popular being

Fig. 15. The Presentation of a *Purim-shpil (Courtesy, Widener Library, Harvard University)*. From *Mitteilungen der Gesellschaft für jüdische Volkskunde*, XXXI-XXXII (N. S., 1929), 7; originally in Leusden, *Philologus Hebraicus*, 1657.

comic adaptations of the stories of Esther and Joseph, known by the titles of *Akhashveyros-shpil* and *Mekhires-Yosef* ("The Sale of Joseph").[198] The *Purim* play had wide appeal, for humorous songs, farcical speech, and lusty dialogue were incorporated in the framework of the Biblical story. People in the audience could easily identify themselves with any of the Biblical characters, who spoke in the popular idiom of the day. Like the *musar*-book, the drama of the 17th and 18th centuries also served as a medium to cheer people.[199] Within a period of twelve years (1708-20), in Germany, no less than eight *Purim-shpiln* dealing with Biblical themes were published, of which four were on the story of Mordecai and Esther, two on Joseph, and one on David and Goliath.[200]

According to the prologue of the *Akhashveyros-shpil* the play was staged in a home in improvised, makeshift surroundings. After the audience had gathered in the house, the performance would begin with the recitation of the prologue. King Ahasuerus was then introduced in a spirit of jest—similar to the manner in which the rabbi and communal leaders were "mocked," for on *Purim* even the sacred may be dealt with in a humorous, flippant vein:

> Here is something different. Stand by, stand by! Listen, counts, princes, here is something new, new, and even more: a king is coming, a lord. In the entire world you will not find anyone like him. [King Ahasuerus was then announced.][201]

The Prologue resumed—the guests were asked to clear the room for the actors about to enter: "Make room, make room, remove the furniture, the table [goes] on the bench, the books on the mattress, the chicken under the rooster, the wife under the husband, the maid under the servant. . . ."[202] Clearly, these were not the words of a *musar*-book, but the language of burlesque, the vulgarisms and obscenities of the street. The actors were not always gentlemen of learning and refinement but artisans and peddlers who did not hesitate to couch the *shpil* in the language most natural and familiar to them.[203] Nor did they resist the opportunity to irritate the "respected" members of the community with words such as: "Bless the 'gentlemen' [lit., 'lords,' 'noblemen': *hern*, Yid.] equally, be they rich or poor. . . ."[204] Thus the *shpil* was a medium of social and political satire, and the outbursts of laughter from the audience did not only arise from scenes of buffoonery.

In the *Akhashveyros-shpil* Haman was not only the wicked character of the story of Esther but also a symbol of the political rulers of the Middle Ages who resorted to devious means in order to exploit the Jewish community for personal gain. Haman was portrayed as trying to ingratiate himself with the king by offering to extract from the Jews the payment of a ransom for the life of Mordecai, as well as their own.[205] Hence, when Haman decides that "no one of 'the Jewish race' should remain [alive]—no man, woman, or child," he seems to be the mouthpiece for every official who advocated, at one time or another, the policy of exterminating the Jewish people.

Stately, dignified Mordecai was sometimes given a comic role in the *shpil*.[206] In the farcical spirit of the *Purim-ḳiddush*—a parody of the benediction recited over the wine on Sabbath and holidays—Mordecai expresses his desire to consort with a maiden or a young widow.[207] The bawdy language attributed to Mordecai shocked elders of the community, and the irreverent presentation of Mordecai as an obscene, lewd person must have precipitated their decision to have the text of the play burned.[208] When Jonathan Eibeschütz was rabbi of Metz, between 1741-50, he objected to the Jewish stage in his community, as it was his contention that whoever attended "a play, comedy, or opera staged in a theater would be in bad company," and under the influence of such surroundings the person will be more "inclined to commit a trespass."[209] While rabbis and communal leaders vigorously condemned the theater on the grounds of lowering moral standards, they did not, however, succeed in dissuading the people from watching *Purim* plays for their own pleasure.

The comic part played by Mordecai in the *Purim-shpil* is also evident from his parody on the *seliḥot*—the penitential prayers recited during the month of *'Elul* in preparation for *Rosh ha-Shanah* and on the *Yamim Nora'im,* the Days of Awe between *Rosh ha-Shanah* and *Yom Kippur*. Humor is expressed through a series of "curses," in colloquial language, directed at Haman:

> I wish to rattle off a few *seliḥot* (*ayn bisl selikhes klaprin* [*klapern*]) for you God, Who is long suffering. Haman should be declared guilty of treason. The worms should devour him. Haman should break his knee. His heart should burst asunder. He should suffer great pain; also, he should be diseased with blotches. Haman should kiss my. . . ." [In the text each curse is repeated.][210]

It seems that the curses were intended more to arouse laughter than to execrate the villain Haman, especially so in Yiddish, where the curse is a form of humor.

We shall not attempt to make a literary analysis of the *Akhash-veyros-shpil,* as our main concern is to single out some of the elements of the play that pertain to the folkways of the period. Similarly, what stand out in the *Mekhires-Yosef-shpil* are the popular views and practices that have a direct relationship to daily social life. First of all, *klag-lider*, dirges, are interspersed in the drama,[211] and through a song of lamentation Joseph tells of his misfortune when his brothers sold him as a slave. He prostrates himself on the grave of his mother Rachel and asks for her help: "I plead with you to awaken from your sleep, and take revenge on my murderous brothers. Dearest, beloved mother, who always favored me, my tongue has become too heavy for me to cry out nor [can I] weep any more on your grave."[212] The scene must have stirred the emotions of the audience by being reminded of their own experience when they visited the graves of relatives in time of difficulty.[213]

The comic character in the *Mekhires-Yosef* drama is "Piklhering" (Yid.), ("Pickelhäring," "Pickelhering," Ger.), dressed as a clown in "farcical, gay-colored clothes."[214] He introduces himself to the audience as "a babbler and liar."[215] "Piklhering," the *nar*, the fool, in the *Purim* play resembles the clown featured in the European theater since the 16th century.[216] The character Pickelhäring was probably first introduced into Germany in the 17th century by the comic actor Robert Reynolds of England, when he toured the country with a troupe.[217] Later, when Pickelhäring became known to the actors of the Jewish theater, he was made part of the *Purim-shpil* to add to the comedy of their performance. We mention the effect that the German stage must have had on the *Purim* play so as to illustrate another way in which the general environment influenced Jewish cultural life.[218]

The *tants*, dance, was also a form of amusement that contributed to the enjoyment of *Purim*. For comic effect, the "Dr. Faustus-Tanz (Tants)" was staged. The dance was a pantomime and "caricatured a doctor shaving his colleague as he kept time to gay music."[219] It was not uncommon for the doctor to be depicted as a charlatan, deceiving the public with the wonder drugs he peddles.[220]

The collection of customs and the *musar*-book emphasize that the festivity on *Purim* does not require excessive drinking or overindulgence. Let the people be merry, it is said, but they must also practice restraint.[221] And, as stated before, communal legislation was introduced in the 18th century to maintain orderly behavior during the festival.[222]

Yuspa Shammash describes how the youth of the Worms community would hold a special *Purim* celebration, called *Shabbat ha-Baḥurim*, "the Sabbath of the Youth," on the first Sabbath after the festival. The young men marched to the synagogue in a parade, wearing pointed hats and led by a member of their group who was dressed as a dunce and in jest played the part of the *knel-gabay*, the attendant supervising school children. They had special privileges on this day; they could sit on the pulpit in the seats usually occupied by the elders and enjoy unlimited latitude in conducting the services. On Friday evening, as the cantor commenced to chant the *Magen 'Abot* prayer, they descended from the pulpit and proceeded to the seat of the rabbi who then blessed them. Afterwards they went to the women's synagogue, in the adjoining room, where they were blessed by the rabbi's wife. For the festivity they wore the silk Sabbath mantle and hood. On Saturday morning, those adults who ordinarily expected to have an *'aliyah*, that is, be called upon to recite the benedictions before and after the reading of a Torah portion, could be ignored unless they agreed to give the students some wine.[223] Following the Sabbath morning services the students would go to private homes, where they were invited to a *Purim* meal. The leaders of the community gave a *tsetil* ("note") to the students, authorizing them to collect wine from individual households. While the notes lasted, the students drank wine. As part of the celebration they wore small lilac wreaths sewed to their caps.[224] In short, on *Shabbat ha-Baḥurim*, in the spirit of *Purim*, the young men were free to mock their elders and teachers, as well as cast aside orderly procedure in favor of confusion.[225]

There were also special customs that enabled the youth to participate in festival observances with adults.[226] On *Simḥat Torah* children carried flags in the synagogue, and those children who had not yet reached the age of *Bar Mizvah* were called to the Torah in a group and covered with a *ṭallit* as though they had attained their religious majority.[227] If the children were too young to attend *Simḥat Torah* in the synagogue, a celebration was arranged for them at home on *Shemini 'Aẓeret*, the eighth day of the *Sukkot* festival. The children were assembled, fruits and sweets were thrown to them, and they scampered to gather the delicacies.[228] Yuspa Shammash tells of a non-Jewish woman who celebrated *Simḥat Torah*. She owned a garden near the Jewish cemetery, and in her will specified that she was giving the garden to the Jews of Worms, with the understanding that on every *Simḥat Torah*, "until the coming of Messiah, the fruit thereof . . . must be thrown to the children behind the wedding hall."[229] It is reported by Yuspa Shammash that the garden was destroyed during the Thirty Years' War, but seven years later, in 1655, it was rebuilt.[230] We can assume that the adults then resumed serving fruit to the children on *Simḥat Torah*.

In the 18th century, the Passover folk song, *Ḥad Gadya'*, was dramatized as a game, with children enacting each scene.[231] To keep the children awake on Passover, they were given nuts and roasted grain.[232] During festivals in the German-Jewish community, two boys would stand at each side of the cantor as he chanted *Hallel* (Psalms 113-118). Each boy responded after the cantor by singing a verse.[233] In a *responsum* of Elyakim Götz, who lived in Posen in the 18th century, it is reported that on the days falling between the first two and last two days of the festivals of *Sukkot* and *Pesaḥ*, boys played music and danced. No objection was raised against young people enjoying themselves in this manner during holiday seasons, and in fact there were adults who played musical instruments at the time of festivals.[234] The precedent for this custom, as we may recall, was established in an earlier period.[235]

Isaiah Horowitz, commenting on the European and Palestinian custom of devoting the night of *Shabu'ot*, Pentecost, to study, attributes the popularity of this *minhag* to the wide distribution of printed sources that call upon everyone to study through the night of the festival.[236] The passage just cited from Horowitz is included verbatim by Yeḥiel Epstein in his supplement to the *Shelah*;[237] it is another instance of the cabalistic *musar-sefer* and the popularized *Shulḥan 'Arukh* influencing the conduct of the folk, for the average person relied upon a handbook, such as Epstein's, as his daily guide.

What was the reason for studying through the night of *Shabu'ot*? The explanation is based on a Midrashic interpretation of the verse in the Bible (Ex. 19:20), "And God descended on Mt. Sinai." When God was preparing to give the Torah to the children of Israel they were asleep and Moses had to awaken them so there would be no delay in their receiving the Torah.[238] Then it was decided that thereafter the people would not be found sleeping on *Shabu'ot*.[239] The custom is an old one, but we cannot be more specific about its origin. Its observance was stressed by the Cabalists in Palestine in the 16th century.[240] Horowitz indicates that in Palestine the practice of studying during *Shabu'ot* night was well known. That Jewish mystics had emphasized the importance of this custom is attested to in the *Zohar*, "The Book of Splendor," the classical cabalistic commentary on the Bible:

> We have learnt that the Torah which he ought to study on this night [*Shabu'ot*] is the Oral Law, and afterwards in daytime the Written Law can come and he can attach himself to it. . . . Therefore the pious ones of old used not to sleep on this night, but they used to study the Torah and say, Let us acquire a holy inheritance for ourselves and our sons in two worlds [i.e., in this world and the world to come].[241]

Since this passage is cited by Horowitz at the beginning of his discourse on *Shabu'ot*,[242] it would suggest that the Cabalists regarded the night of the festival to have special meaning. Without question, the symbolism of the Midrash must have appealed to the Cabalists of the Middle Ages who described the relation of God to Israel as that of a "betrothal."[243] The Midrash states that when Moses roused the children of Israel from their sleep, he said to them, "The groom [God] has already arrived and is looking for the bride [Israel] to lead her to the canopy."[244] This passage from the *Zohar*[245] continues with a figure of speech analogous to the Midrash: "Let us go and prepare the ornaments of the Bride [Israel], that tomorrow she may appear before the King [God] fitly adorned and bedecked. . . ."[246] The Cabalists must have considered *Shabu'ot* to have mystical significance because of the kinship established between God and Israel on that day.

In outlining what is to be studied on the night of *Shabu'ot*,

Isaiah Horowitz refers to selections from the Bible, the Pentateuch, Prophets, Hagiographa; the Mishnah; cabalistic writings, as *Sefer Yeẓirah* and the *Zohar;* and the *Sefer ha-Miẓvot,* "Book of Commandments," by Maimonides.[247] His list mentions the choice of material that served as the "model" for the *seder,* or arrangement, of the *Tiḳḳun Lel Shabuʿot,* a book of sources collected especially for reading on the night of Pentecost.[248] As there are similarities between the *Tiḳḳun Lel Hoshaʿanaʾ Rabbah* and the *Tiḳḳun Lel Shabuʾot,*[249] the selected passages for the night of each festival are often published in a single volume.

The book of *Minhagim* by Kosman describes how through the ages *Tishʾah be-ʾAb,* the ninth day in the month of *ʾAb,* has been observed with mourning and fasting to commemorate the fall of Jerusalem in 70 C.E.[250] In harmony with the mood of lamentation, a frugal meal of cold foods, hard-boiled eggs, and fruit is served before the fast begins in the evening.[251] Kosman suggests that berries be part of the meal preceding the fast (*seʿudah ha-mafseḳet*), as "they cause one to feel cool,"[252] and such food will not arouse sexual feelings.[253]

After the synagogue service was held on the Ninth of *ʾAb,* the congregants would proceed to the cemetery to appeal to the dead to "intercede" for them. The precedent for the practice dates back to Talmudic times when "a public fast" (*taʾanit ẓibbur*) was declared in time of drought. The living, out of their distress, called upon "the departed ones that they should pray for mercy in our behalf."[254] It is remarked by Rashi that "everywhere people go to cemeteries on *Tishʾah be-ʾAb.*"[255]

After presenting the background of this custom on *Tishʿah be-ʾAb,* Kosman then speaks of some of the difficulties that the people encountered in carrying out the observance:

> Do not proceed [to the cemetery] in a crowd, even if there are 'Burial Societies' (*Ḥaburot shel Ḳabranim*). There is a set fine for any person who fails to walk [on the street] as prescribed

Fig. 16. Mourning on *Tish'ah be-'Ab* (*Courtesy, Widener Library, Harvard University*). From Bodenschatz, *Aufrichtig teutsch redender Hebräer* . . . , II, bet. 94-95, fig. 2.

> [in the governmental ordinance]. You can go singly, but if you are with a crowd, it may give the appearance that you are taking a walk.[256]

His advice to avoid going in a group to the cemetery on the Ninth of *'Ab* must have taken into account the *Stättigkeit,* the official "residence agreement" granted to the Jews of Frankfort, specifying that "not more than two Jews can walk together at one time" on the streets of the city.[257] Evidently, Kosman was anxious that the *Stättigkeit* should not be violated in any degree, for otherwise the "right of residence" might be jeopardized. When Fritsch and Böhler, in 1705, attempted to arouse the hostility of the burghers against the Jews, as did Fettmilch in the previous century, they complained to the Frankfort Council that the Jews infringe upon the *Stättigkeit* by walking in the streets of Frankfort in "whole companies" (*in ganzen Kompagnien*) rather than "by twos."[258]

To reach the cemetery, the Jews of Frankfort had to go outside the city wall to *Fischerfeld*, "Fisher's Field," an area by the river Main where fishermen lived.[259] Frankfort was divided into three areas or "city fortifications"; since 1460 the Jews lived within the second one, also known as the *Wollgraben*, the "wall moat."[260] *Fischerfeld* was east of the first fortification,[261] adjoining the Main, and the Jews had to walk on the streets of Frankfort, where non-Jews lived, in order to reach the cemetery. Since the regulation in the *Stättigkeit* did not encourage Jews to leave their neighborhood, Kosman stresses the importance of adhering strictly to the legislation governing their residence in Frankfort.

As a sign of mourning, no shoes are to be worn on the Ninth of *'Ab.*[262] Kosman states that it may not always be possible to fulfill this requirement, for if the Jews were to walk on the streets of Frankfort without shoes, they could expect to encounter criticism from non-Jews. They are therefore cautioned by Kosman about their public behavior; he is concerned that they might offend or antagonize non-Jews "among whom they live."[263] In all likelihood, he continues, it would be impossible to walk to the cemetery barefooted because of the filth on the street. In these circumstances they had no recourse but to wear their shoes and then remove them after they arrived at the cemetery and when they returned home.[264] Hahn deplores the fact that on the Ninth of *'Ab* there are "many good people who wear shoes [on the outside]" because of the rainy season. They feel justified because two hundred years earlier, Isserlein, a noted authority, stated that if it rains on *Tish'ah be-'Ab,* one may wear shoes in order to be able to escape more easily should a robber appear.[265]

Conduct on the Ninth of *'Ab* is not always consonant with mourning; in small towns the people are not solemn but "boisterous and vulgar," so Kirchan reports.[266] However, such behavior did not only occur in the rural areas, for the Minute Book of *Tamuz* 22, 1655, of the Portuguese-Jewish congregation of Hamburg, refers to a disturbance breaking out in their synagogue on the Ninth of *'Ab*. As a sign of mourning, the congregation did not occupy their regular seats, and disorder resulted when David Bravo attacked Jacob de Simao Machoro for having occupied his seat.[267] A further objection is voiced by Hahn to those persons who do not hesitate to go for a walk on the Ninth of *'Ab*. Even if they are barefooted, Hahn maintains that they are not fulfilling the requirements of a day of mourning. They should be at home, "seated alone and in silence" (Lam. 3:28), or else engaged in reciting *ḳinot,* "lamentations." Hahn's objections continue: The Ninth of *'Ab* is not being observed in a serious mood because servants and children are permitted to play together just "at the time that the *ḳinot* are recited; [they behave] as though this were a festival celebration in the synagogue."[268] Scholars and communal leaders are too indifferent and unconcerned, Hahn feels; otherwise they would have taken the necessary steps "to fine and punish those who commit this offense" rather than "show [them] so much respect." He concludes, seemingly discouraged, that he cannot bring about a change: "It is known that this could be prohibited, but nothing is done."[269]

We have completed our survey of a group of practices relating to the synagogue, Sabbath, and festivals. We have noted that the *minhagim*, customs, of the 17th and 18th centuries were not merely routine or fixed procedures. The customs were complex; they varied in origin, background, and function, and were closely bound to different facets of daily life. When we were unable to find the reasons for a given practice, we tried to sense its significance or meaning by viewing it in the context of its cultural setting. Furthermore, we saw how these customs were an expression of the folk—in their serious and lighter vein, in their moments of idealism and courage, fear and frustration. By examining this body of customs we were able to come face to face with the tragedy and humor expressed in the Jewish community's major observances. Through our consideration of the folkways connected with the synagogue, Sabbath, and festivals we have attempted to glean some of the concrete manifestations of historical reality that otherwise might have eluded us.

. . . . .

A study of folk customs is one of the ways of seeing a society microscopically; that is, by examining smaller units the processes involving the larger or total body can be better understood. It is a misconception to assume that the more stable community existing at the end of the Middle Ages was static and had no dynamic character because the cultural pattern of daily life was set and clearly defined. We discover that wherever people live together and interact, human problems arise. Men suffer frustration and despair in times of famine, disease, and war. The person who is homeless and uprooted has to be reassured that he is not alone in the world. He seeks meaning, hope, and purpose in the face of the reality that is overwhelming him. Life was not simple and easy because one lived in a preindustrial, premechanized society.

More inquiry is required to distinguish between folk practice and magic. The popular customs that protect against demons are not necessarily magical, as is often implied. The distinction between a superstitious practice and magic has to be made in terms of the specific situation, not in broad generalities.

The factors influencing Jewish folkways were both internal and external. Superstitious customs did not only result from outside influence. Their rationale also arose out of internal psychological and cultural forces. Further study is needed to determine which customs developed internally, independent of the outside world, and which were borrowed from the general society and given Jewish form and content. A reciprocal process took place, in which the Jews were not only influenced by the prevailing culture, but also had an impact on the surrounding world through religio-ethical teachings and the lore of Cabala.

Notes

NOTES TO INTRODUCTION

[1] For purposes of convenience, terms such as "folk life," "social life," "cultural life" will be used interchangeably with "folkways."

[2] The work of Brauer, *Yehude Kurdistan* (Jews of Kurdistan) was helpful in suggesting "rubrics" for the classification of Jewish customs and beliefs. Likewise, R. Patai, "Jewish Folklore and Ethnology" (Hebrew), *Edoth*, I (no. 1, 1946), 1-12; A. Marmorstein, "The Place of Popular Traditions in the History of Religions," *Edoth*, I (no. 2, 1946), 75 ff., presented categories that can be useful in organizing specific cultural items of a society.

[3] See M. Steinschneider, "Der Aberglaube," *Sammlung gemeinverständl. wissen. Vorträge*, XV (1900), 370, that any phase of folklore, popular beliefs, or social practices express man's outlook on life.

[4] Collingwood, *The Idea of History* (Galaxy Book, 1956), p. 317.

[5] See the "Map of Yiddish Dialects" in *Algemayne Entsiklopedye*, II (1940), 65.

[6] Examples of such communal autonomy, involving administration of institutions, regulation of officials, and authority over individuals, can be found in a variety of sources, as: *Ẓemaḥ Ẓedeḳ*, no. 2, fol. 1b; *Shebut Ya'aḳob*, I, no. 11, fol. 3a; *Ḥavvot Ya'ir*, no. 213, fol. 202a; *Naḥalat Shib'ah*, II, no. 3, fol. 4a; *Ḥaḥam Ẓebi*, I, no. 14, fol. 20b; *Pene Yehoshua'*, II, no. 75a, fol. 55a; *Panim Me'irot*, II, no. 17, fol. 8a. Cf. "Communal Organization," "Communal Standards," in *RCC*, cits.

The role of communal autonomy is also indicated in Barbeck, *Gesch. der Juden in Nürnberg und Fürth*, p. 56 (*Taḳḳanah*, no. 4, 1719); S. Haenle, *Gesch. der Juden . . . Ansbach*, p. 38; Munk, "Constituten der hessischen Judenschaft (1690)," *Jubelschrift . . . Hildesheimer*, p. 73; Kaufmann, "Communauté de Metz," *REJ*, XIX (1889), 127 (Hebrew text); Fishman, *Jewish Education*, p. 16. Cf. also Löwenstein, *Gesch. der Juden in der Kurpfalz*, p. 77: In 1660 the Jewish community of Mannheim was granted, by the Elector Karl Ludwig, the legal right to appoint its rabbi, cantor, and teacher. For instances of such autonomy, see pp. 2–3, 32, 35–36, 65–66, 143–44.

[7] Cf. H. Schwenger, "Namensbeilegung der Juden in Kostel (1787)," *ZGJT* I[2] (1930), 116: "The Jewish community of Moravia was divided into three areas, with two deputies (*Landesälteste*) chosen in each area, subject to the confirmation of the sovereign power. In extraterritorial [i.e., extraregional] matters, the deputies represented the Moravian Jewish community, which was under the leadership of the *Landesrabbiner*." See Fishman, *Education*, p. 15; also p. 38, n. 133, based on Wolf, *Statuten Mähren*. (Ref. to Wolf, p. 6, #24, was checked, but could not be confirmed.) See Halpern, *Taḳḳanot Mähren*, Intro., p. 12, as to the cultural significance of the region of Moravia, especially in relation to the total Germanic Jewish community. Also, Dubnow, *Weltgeschichte* (Hebrew edit.), VII, 164: The important towns of Moravia included Holleschau, Kremsir, Nikolsburg, Trebitsch, Prossnitz.

[8] Halpern, *op. cit.*, Intro., p. 9.

[9] See Dubnow, *Weltgeschichte* (Hebrew edit.), VI, 127 ff.; VII, 163; VIII, 164, for the growth of Jewish communities in Frankfort, Prague, Kleve, Worms, Vienna, Eisenstadt, Strasbourg after 1648. For other significant Jewish communities, such as Altona, Wandsbek, Bamberg, Fürth, Hannover, Metz, see Brann, *Juden in Schlesien*, I, 176; Fishman, *Education*, p. 16; M. Weinberg, "Wesen des Memorbuches," *JJLG*, XVI (1924), 254, 263.

Other communities began to develop in the 17th century, as indicated in Baer, *Protokollbuch Kleve*, p. 13; Rosy Bodenheimer, "Juden in Oberhessen," *ZGJD*, III (1931), 265 f.; Eckstein, *Gesch. der Juden in Markgrafentum Bayreuth*, p. 65; Grunwald, *Gesch. der Wiener Juden*, p. 16; Samuel, *Gesch. der Juden in Essen*, pp. 39-40; Markgraf, *Gesch. der Juden in Leipzig*, pp. 4-5; Weihs, *Gesch. der Teplitzer Judengemeinde*, p. 9; H. Weynart, "Gesch. der Juden in Österreich," *Jahr. Gesch. Juden und Judenthums*, II, 382; Wolf, *op. cit.*, Pref., pp. iii-iv; Halpern, *Taḳḳanot Mähren*, Intro., pp. 1 ff.; p. 197, n. 2; Duckesz, *IWoH le-Moshab* (Communal History of Altona, Hamburg, Wandsbek), Intro., p. v; B. Brilling, "Prager 'Schammes' in Breslau," *ZGJT*, I[3] (1931), 140.

See B. Wachstein, "Pinkas Runkel," *ZGJD*, IV (1932), 129: The migration and new settlement started at the beginning of the 18th century. And, Arthur Cohen, "Münchener Judenschaft," *ZGJD*, II (1930), 262, 264: The Munich community developed after 1750; no ghetto existed there. See p. 2 for examples of Jewish neighborhoods without gates.

[10] See Duckesz, *IWoH le-Moshab*, Pref., p. vi; Spanish-Portuguese Jews first settled in Hamburg in 1648. That communities, such as Holitsch, Neu-Raussnitz, and Pressburg, developed after 1648, see B. Mandl, "Jüd. Gemeinde in Holitsch," *ZGJT*, I[3] (1931), 180; H. Flesch, "Juden in Mähren," *JJLG*, XVIII (1926), 26, 55; Max Schay, "'Chewra Kadischa' in Pressburg," *ZGJT*, III[2] (1933), 71. Cf. H. Schwenger, "Über die zweite Ansiedlung der Juden in Lundberg," *ZGJT*, 1[1] (1930), 37 f.: Lundberg was destroyed during the Thirty Years' War, but in 1667, the *shtadlan* Johann Pokornoy corresponded with Johanna Beatrix

(Joan Beatrice), the Fürstin (Princess) of Lichtenstein to gain permission for Jews to resettle there. Also, note the emergence of smaller communities in the 17th century, as described by Stahl, *Gesch. Nauheimer Juden,* p. 6.

[11] With regard to the influence that Polish Jewry had on German-Jewish social life after 1648, see Tsinberg, *Gesh. fun der lit.*, V, 148–49, 158, 164, 168–9. Also p. 70, n. 136; p. 150, n. 1 of the present volume.

[12] See pp. 9–10; 85–86, nn. 2, 6 with respect to the yellow badge and Jewish dress that were required by the law of the state. Cf. the regulation in *Ḥayye 'Adam* 56:15 (sec. "Hil. Shab."): ". . . and in the locality where it was decreed that each Jew must wear a 'yellow badge' (*ḥatikhat beged-gel*) . . . ." Cf. M. Bernstein, "Yiddish Glossary of *Ḥayye 'Adam,*" *Argentin. IWO Shrift.*, VI (Buenos Aires, 1955), 137, sec. 3, cit. See Dubnow, *Weltgeschichte* (Hebrew edit.), VII, 162-66, for a summary of the social status of Jews in German communities after 1648.

Concerning the legislation that affected the social position of the Jew, in that he was treated as an inferior and isolated from the general society, see the *Stättigkeiten* of Frankfort, during the 17th and 18th centuries, in *J.M.*, III (no. 6), p. 166, #29; Kracauer, *Frankfurt. Juden,* II, 119, n. 2; W. Basse, "Juden und die Spaziergänge . . . Frankfurt (1769)," *Zeit. deut. Kulturgesch.,* VI (1859), 564-65. The effect that the social and economic position of the Jew had on the cultural life of the community is suggested on p. 58, n. 53; p. 66, n. 13; p. 69, n. 132; p. 75.

[13] MS *Minhagim de-Ḳ. Ḳ. Worms* (Microfilm, OPP. 751, Oxford, Bodleian), fol. 106b or 107a (fol. not marked):

...ויי״ יגדיל חן עמנו בני ישראל בעיניו להטיב עמנו כאשר כבר יצא שמו שהוא בעל חסד וחסיד כן ירבה ויגדיל חסדו עמנו אמן:

"May God increase the favor that he [King Leopold] will express toward the children of Israel, doing good in our behalf, now even more so, since he is known as just and righteous. May his kindness toward us increase significantly." (It was during the reign of Leopold I that the Jews were expelled from Vienna.)

(Courtesy, Department of Oriental Books, Bodleian Library, Oxford.)

[14] Holzer, "Minhag Buch des Juspa Schammes," *ZGJD*, V (1935), 171-72.

[15] Regarding the influence of Western European culture on Jewish cultural life at the end of the 18th century, see Weihs, *Gesch. der Teplitzer Judengemeinde,* p. 9.

NOTES TO CHAPTER I

[1] See p. 47, n. 182; p. 48, n. 195; p. 131. For topographical sketches and descriptions of Jewish communal neighborhoods during the period, see Brann, *Gesch. Juden in Schlesien,* V, 219-23; Grunwald, "Mattersdorf," *JJV*, II (1925),

411-13; A. Kober, "Köln," *EJ*, X (1934), 223; Kracauer, *Judengasse in Frankfurt*, pp. 324-25; S. Krauss, "Wiener Synagogen in der Vergangenheit," *Menorah*, IV (Vienna-Frankfort, 1926), 15; Rotter-Schmieger, *Ghetto Wiener Leopoldstadt*, p. 45; Schwarz, *Wiener Ghetto*, p. 172. See also the sites of settlements in A. Pinthus, "Bauliche Entwicklung der Judengassen in deut. Städten," *ZGJD*, II (1930), 127-30; and note the pictures of the Jewish neighborhood in Altmann, *Juden Salzburg*, sketch no. 1; Flesch, "Pinax von Austerlitz," *JJV*, II (1925), bet. 610-11; Krauss in *Menorah*, IV (Vienna, 1926), 11; Marmorstein, "Beiträge zur Religionsgesch. und Volkskunde," *JJV*, II, bet. 352-53.

As to the factors disrupting the physical continuity of a community, cf. *Ḥavvot Ya'ir*, no. 165, fol. 163a; *J.M.*, II (Bk. 2), 70 ff.; III (No. 3), 63; Dubnow, *Weltgeschichte* (Hebrew edit.), VII, 160, 164; J. Freimann, "Juden in Prossnitz," *JJLG*, XV (1923), 26-27; Lieben, "Prager Brandkatastrophen" (1689 and 1754), *JJLG*, XIV (1928), 175 ff., 183 ff., 190–93; Kracauer, *Frankfurt. Juden*, II, 123; Rotter-Schmieger, *loc. cit.*, p. 59.

2 *'Ahabat Ẓiyon*, no. 1, fol. 2b, col. 2. Cf. also *Ḥavvot Ya'ir*, no. 126, fol. 119a; no. 134, fol. 125a; D. Kaufmann, "Jair Chayim Bacharach," *JQR*, III (O.S., 1891), 498, n. 3; 499, n. 1.

3 See topographic changes from the old to the new city: Kriegk, *Frankfurter Bürgerzwiste und Zustände im Mittelalter*, p. 273.

4 Suggested by Schwarz, *Wiener Ghetto*, p. 172.

5 See *di yidishe gas*: Erik, *Yid. lit.*, pp. 10, 385. Cf. *Shebut Ya'aḳob*, I, no. 47, fol. 11a: . . . *bi-reḥob ha-Yehudim*. . . .

Ḥavvot Ya'ir, no. 135, fol. 125a: . . . *dirat Yisra'elim . . . bi-reḥob meyuḥad*. . . . Also, *ibid.*: . . . *reḥobot ha-Yehudim*. . . .

See the physical characteristics of the Jewish neighborhood as described in H. Flesch, "Juden in Mähren," *JJLG*, XVIII (1926), 24; Freimann in *JJLG*, XV, 28; Kracauer, *op. cit.*, pp. 321, 324-25; Dubnow, *Weltgeschichte* (Hebrew edit.), VI, 127, #26; *idem*, *Weltgeschichte* (German edit.), VI, 235, #26; Shmueli, *Toledot 'Amenu*, I, 72. Cf. *J.M.*, I, 370, regarding "the narrow Jewish streets," *enge Gassen*, of Hamburg. Also in Mayer, *Wiener Juden*, p. 174, that "the street" of Pressburg was "narrow and congested."

6 The "Ground Plan of the Judengasse, 1711" (see endpapers) refers to the Frankfort community and was sketched shortly after the fire. Names of residents correspond with those found in communal listings of 1612 and 1753, in Kracauer, *Judengasse*, pp. 455 ff., 457 f., Appen. I, II. Residents of Worms had similar names: see *Levy in Worms*, p. 17.

7 *J.M.*, I, 372.

8 Cf. *Y.'O.*, #975; Abrahams, *Jewish Life*, p. 83; Oelsner, "Jewish Ghetto of the Past," *Yivo Annual Jewish Soc. Sc.*, I (1946), 25.

9 Freimann in *JJLG*, XV, 28.

[10] Kracauer, *op. cit.*, p. 321; Dubnow, *Weltgeschichte* (Hebrew edit.), VI, 127; Shmueli, *op. cit.*, pp. 71-72.

[11] Bax, *German Culture*, pp. 118-119.

[12] *Ḥavvot Ya'ir*, no. 135, fol. 125a:

... בעניין הקהילות שהם בעיירות המקופת חומה שיש להם רחוב מיוחד נסגרת בלילה ... כמו פה ק"ק וק"ק פראנקפורט הענא...ק"ק מיץ ובמקומות שאין להם רחוב כגון ק"ק טריר קובלנץ מנהיים היידלבורג....

Cf. D. Kaufmann, "Jair Chayim Bacharach," *JQR*, III (O.S.), 310, n. 1; also Abrahams, *op. cit.*, p. 78, n. 3.

See in *J.M.*, III (No. 7), 166-67, #26, 29, 30; 170, #46, the regulations of the Frankfort *Stättigkeit* (December 7, 1705), specifying when and how a Jew might leave the *gas*; likewise, Shmueli, pp. 73–74; also, p. 195, n. 257 of this volume.

[13] *Panim Me'irot*, I, no. 25, fol. 21b:

בשידלאווצי היה מבוי של יהודים פתוח לשוק של גוים ובכלות המבוי העמידו כמו שער כדינו עם צורת הפתח אך שהי' השער מופלג משני צדי המבוי ... ורבים היו יכולים לכנוס בפרצה מצד זה ומצד זה....

[14] See Abrahams, *Jewish Life*, pp. 78-80; Wirth, *Ghetto* (University of Chicago, Phoenix Book), p. 4.

[15] Cf. Dubnow, *Weltgeschichte* (Hebrew edit.) VI, 133: During the 17th century the Jews of Strasbourg were not considered settled residents, but a group of transients or strangers. Hence, Strasbourg had no *gas* comparable to the established communities of the period.

[16] *Ḥavvot Ya'ir*, no. 184, fol. 171b: ". . . He is compelled to live under crowded conditions. His books are in the one room where he and his family reside. . . ." Cf. "Conduct of life," *RCC*, cit.

[17] Kaufmann (ed.), *Glikl*, p. 71; Feilchenfeld (ed.), *Glückel*, p. 50. Trans. based on Lowenthal (ed.), *Glückel*, p. 36. Cf. Grunwald in *MGJV*, XVII (1906), 14, who cites p. 74 in *Glikl* instead of p. 71.

[18] Dubnow, *Weltgeschichte* (Hebrew edit.), VI, 127, #26; Schnapper-Arndt, "Jüd. Interieurs zu Ende des 17. Jahrhunderts" (Frankfort community), *ZGJD*, II (1888), 190. See the statistics in Kracauer, *Judengasse*, p. 321 (based on an official census report): In 1709, there were 3024 persons living in the Frankfort Jewish community. Also, *ibid.*, p. 395, n. 4; pp. 457-63, Appen. II, that in 1753, there were 204 houses in the *gas*. Abrahams, *Jewish Life*, p. 84, cites similar figures for an earlier period in Frankfort, when "4,000 persons lived in 190 houses, in a gloomy street twelve feet wide." Also, Barbeck, *Gesch. der Juden in Nürnberg und Fürth*, p. 87: At the end of the 18th century, the *gas* comprised 2400 individuals, and in 1807, the number was 2673.

[19] Richter-Schmidt, "Hotzenplotzer Judengemeinde," *MGJV*, XXXVII (1911), 33.

[20] H. Flesch, "Gesch. der Juden in Mähren," *JJLG*, XVIII (1926), 24.

[21] Schwarz, *Wiener Ghetto*, p. 111, Append., based on the *Hofquartierbuch*, 1566; Flesch in *JJLG*, XVIII, 58-59, 61, 63, nos. 4, 6, 10, a census survey authorized by Count Dominic Andreas von Kaunitz in Neu-Raussnitz, 1701. See Tietze, *Juden Wiens*, bet. pp. 96-97, for a portrait of houses during the second Jewish community of Vienna. See also portraits of the exterior of Jewish homes in Rotter-Schmieger, *Ghetto Wiener Leopoldstadt*, bet. pp. 100-101, 104-105, 108-109.

[22] Schnapper-Arndt in *ZGJD*, II (O. S.), 182 ff. See the account of this inventory in Kracauer, *Judengasse*, pp. 330-31; Freimann-Kracauer, *Frankfort*, pp. 151-54. Cf. I. Broyde, "Furniture," *JE*, V (1903), 531-33: In Biblical and post-Biblical times household furnishings consisted of a bed, chair, table, lamp, and chests. Note the similarity with the furniture in the home of Seligmann and in the *kloyz*, the study of a Jewish scholar, n. 152 to p. 73.

Of various works consulted on the interior of the German-Jewish home, the writer found relevant material in the study of Schnapper-Arndt, based on primary sources; in the works on the Frankfort Jewish community, by Kracauer and Freimann, and articles in *MGJV*. One is obliged to rely mainly on these sources for data on furniture and household furnishings; only on occasion are such items mentioned in the primary sources dealing with ethical, legal, or communal matters. For obvious reasons, household items gave no cause for serious discussion.

[23] Schnapper-Arndt, *op. cit.*, 186-87; Kracauer, *op. cit.*, p. 330. n. 1; Freimann-Kracauer, *op. cit.*, p. 151.

[24] See Freimann-Kracauer, pp. 151–52: "The house furnishings of the poorer Jews were most insufficient. Even their few possessions in the way of clothes and linens could not be kept in order for there was no room to set up wardrobes, but were often packed in chests or even in barrels."

[25] Schnapper-Arndt, *op. cit.*; Kracauer, *op. cit.*, p. 331. The titles of the books are not specified. For some examples of book lists and private library collections during this period, see pp. 7 f. herein. See Schnapper-Arndt, 190: An inventory in 1704 of a three room house—in which Moses zum Silbern [Silbernen] Leuchter, "Moses at the home of the Silver Lamp," resided—mentions among the household items six old shields on which names of residents were written and placed outside of this house, as mentioned on p. 9 and nn. 57-59. Three families lived in the house, in 1703.

For other examples of bedding and linen, see "a chest of linens": *Ḥavvot Ya'ir*, no. 169, fol. 159a. See also Kaufmann (ed.), *Glikl*, p. 36, n. 1; Feilchenfeld (ed.), *Glückel*, p. 30; Lowenthal (ed.), *Glückel*, p. 19: = prob. *bet-hemdir, bet-hemd* (Yid.), "bed clothes, linen." Cf. *bet-gevant* (Yid.), same meaning. And, the laundry list in B. Elsas, *MGJV*, XVI, 101, #2.

[26] *J.M.*, III, No. 9, 203. Cf. p. 186, n. 202 of this volume.

[27] B. Elsas, "Haushalt eines Rabbiners im 18. Jahrhundert," *MGJV*, XVI (1905), 98, 100-101. Note that chapter 7 deals with the relation of the holidays to social life in the community.

Notes to Chapter I

The interior of German and Jewish homes, e.g., the furniture and wall fixtures, were similar: see Schultz, *Deut. Leben,* II, 95-98, 109; also illustrated portraits, figs. 111-14, 118, 120-23, 139-40; Henne am Rhyn, *Kulturgesch. des deut. Volkes,* I, 264–65; II, 64. The differences, however, are to be found in the objects kept at home for religious and cultural purposes, such as ceremonials used on festivals and special occasions and books read daily and on the Sabbath.

[28] Schnapper-Arndt, *op. cit.,* 190, n. 1 to 187: *seidene und pluschene Handquehlen,* "linen and plush [? perhaps Turkish] hand towels." See Kracauer, *Judengasse,* p. 331; Freimann-Kracauer, *Frankfort,* p. 152. See also in Schnapper-Arndt, 193, a description of the home of Jacob David zum güldenen Rösslein; the furnishings were similar to that of Elkan Moses's house.

[29] Schnapper-Arndt, *op. cit.,* 191. The titles of the books are not given. See Kracauer, p. 331; also the description of the home of wealthy Aaron Baer in Freimann-Kracauer, *Frankfort,* p. 152-53.

For other examples of materials or goods, see Landau-Wachstein, *Jüd. Privatbriefe,* no. 3b, pp. 8, 14; no. 6a, pp. 11, 19; no. 10, pp. 16-17, 29, nn. 5, 8; no. 28, pp. 36, 62 (text and trans.): sheepskin fur, otter fur (purchased in Poland), damask, silk, velvet, cordovan (leather), fringe (trimming), velvet fringe, blankets. Also, Lewin in *JJGL,* XXX, 185, that individuals of Prague purchased buck-skin, elk-skin, neat's leather (leather of a heifer, neat), chamois leather, in Cracow, Poland. And, Schnapper-Arndt in *ZGJD,* II, 192: serge, fustian, frieze, buttons.

Cf. Freimann (ed.), "Document on Community Ills" (Hebrew), part of "Beiträge zur Geschichte der Juden in Prague in den Jahren 1742-1757," *Ḳobeẓ 'al Yad,* VIII (1898), 14; also n. 1: = *tishtsayg* (Yid.) = "tablecloth"; cf. *tishzeug* (Ger.), same meaning.

Cf. *Brandshpigl,* sec. 14, fol. 5a (no fol. mark): *bekhr* (Yid.) = "goblet, beaker"; cf. *becher* (Ger.), same meaning.

[30] See herein, p. 81, nn. 191, 192, concerning the attitude of social imitation expressed by wealthy persons who wanted to be like, as well as accepted by, the dominant community. As an example, see how Moses Levin of Bernburg made arrangements with officials to hold the festivities for the marriage of his daughter in the ball-room of the Town Hall: Shiper, *Yid. teater,* I, 156, n. 2; Liebe, *Judentum in deut. Vergangenheit,* p. 156.

[31] Schnapper-Arndt, 189: *Schachtel mit Safran Blumen,* "box with saffron flowers," i.e., flowers of saffron color.

Cf. *N.K.Y.,* fol. 27a, #4, a brass pitcher ornamented with the design of a rooster: . . . *me-ha-kiyor she-yesh bo tarnegol shel neḥoshet. . . .*

Cf. *B.D.,* fol. 24b: *teler* (Yid.) = "plate"; cf. *teller* (Ger.), same meaning. Cf. *teler* in *Derushe ha-Ẓelaḥ,* no. 4, fol. 9b, #24: ". . . a plate *(teler)* is placed in their hand on which the *shoḥet* (slaughterer) writes: [It is] *kosher. . . .*"

[32] Schnapper-Arndt, 182, 184. Cf. Kracauer, *Judengasse in Frankfurt,* p. 330; Freimann-Kracauer, *Frankfort,* p. 78.

[33] Schnapper-Arndt, 187.

[34] *Ibid.*, 190. Cf. *She'elat Ya'abeẓ*, I, no. 156, fol. 138b: *zeyf* (Yid.) = "soap"; cf. *seife* (Ger.), same meaning.

[35] See pp. 181, 183–84.

[36] Barbeck, *Juden in Nürnberg und Fürth*, p. 87.

[37] Public feeling could override the opinion of authority: see p. 177, n. 156; p. 187, also n. 208.

[38] Bernhard Wachstein, "Der Bücherbesitz von Samuel Oppenheimer dem Jüngeren und Marx Lion Gomperz," *MGJV*, XXX, 37 f. The list was deposited in the archives of the District Court of Vienna, 1746-47. See ref. to the library of Judaica in the home of Bendavid's father in Berlin: I. Barzilay, "Berlin Haskalah," in *Essays . . . in Honor of Salo W. Baron*, n. 23 to p. 189.

See Wachstein in *MGJV*, XXX, n. 1 to p. 36; Alexander Kisch, "Samuel Oppenheimer," *JE*, IX (1905), 419; Kaufmann, *Urkundliches . . . Leben Samson Wertheimers*, p. 51, for the genealogy of Samuel ben Emanuel Oppenheimer, who had the title of *Morenu*. Samuel Oppenheimer, his grandfather (d. 1703), was a court Jew and financier in Vienna. Marx Lion Gomperz was a descendant of the Amsterdam branch of the Gomperz living in Vienna; for his background, see Wachstein in *MGJV*, XXX, n. 2 to p. 36; David Baumgardt, "Gomperz," *JLex*, II (1928), 1206; Kaufmann-Freudenthal, *Familie Gomperz*, pp. 385-86. Like Samson Wertheimer and Samuel Oppenheimer, the Gomperz family was permitted to resettle in Vienna after the expulsion in 1670.

[39] The intellectual concerns of the 17th and 18th centuries are considered elsewhere; see pp. 73–81.

[40] See the description of *responsa* material p. 34; and Bibliography (pp. 341, 348 ff.), which includes examples of important *responsa* of the period. To illustrate the scope of subject-matter covered in *responsa* literature, see S. Wind, *R. Yeḥezḳ'el Landau*, pp. 56 ff; "The Responsum *Noda' bi-Yehudah* as a Source for Jewish History," *Ḥoreb*, X (1948), 57 ff.

[41] As to the cultural influence of Cabala in the 17th and 18th centuries, see Steinschneider, "Jüd. Lit.," *Allgemeine Encyclopädie der Wissenschaften und Künste*, XXVII (1850), sec. 20, 456; Eng. trans., *Jewish Lit.*, p. 230; Tsinberg, *Gesh. fun der lit.*, V. 144–46; Kaufmann in *JQR*, III (O.S.), 294, 306–307. See in this volume p. xvi; p. 17, n. 20; p. 20, n. 37; n. 76 to p. 105; p. 107, n. 91; p. 108, n. 97; chap. vi, *passim*. And also, pp. 348; 351–52, Bio-Bibliographical notes on Naphtali Cohen, Isaiah Horowitz, Ẓebi Hirsh Kaidanover, whose works contain cabalistic views.

For an example of the Messianic hopes that must have been widespread, cf. Kaufmann (ed.), *Glikl*, p. 27. Also, *S.H.*, II (Shatzky, ed.), fol. 22b (concl.): ". . . This is a bad time. May the Ineffable One, praised be He, give [us] better times, so that you will have happiness and joy."

[42] See p. 69, n. 129.

[43] See Bibliography p. 347.

[44] Wachstein in *MGJV,* XXX, 37–38, sec. A.

[45] See Bibliography, p. 354.

[46] *Ibid.,* p. 355.

[47] *Ibid.,* p. 351.

[48] *Ibid.*

[49] Wachstein in *MGJV,* XXX, pp. 38–39, Sec. B. See Bibliography below, p. 367.

[50] C. Duschinsky, "Rabbi David Oppenheimer," *JQR,* XX (1930), 217. For further accounts of the library, see S. H. Lieben, "David Oppenheim," *JJLG,* XIX (1928), 26 ff. (sec.: "IV. David Oppenheim als Mäcen und Bibliophile"); Alexander Marx, "Some Notes on the History of David Oppenheimer's Library," *Mélanges . . . Israel Lévi . . . , REJ,* LXXXII (1926), 451 ff., 457; *idem, Studies in Jewish History,* pp. 238 ff. See also Wolf, *Mähren Statuten,* pref. viii. See Bibliography, p. 354.

[51] Duschinsky in *JQR,* XX, 217. *Bibliotheca Hebraea,* in 4 vols., pub. in Hamburg, 1715-33.

[52] Duschinsky, 217-18; Lieben in *JJLG,* XIX, 28-29; Marx in Mélanges . . . Israel Lévi (*REJ,* LXXXII), 457-58.

[53] Duschinsky, 218; Lieben, 27-29; Marx, *op. cit.,* 459-60; Wolf, *op. cit.,* pref. vii. The sum paid for the library was 9000 *taler.*

[54] *N. K. Y.* Pref., fol. 2b (fol. not marked):

ומה שכיניתי לו בשם כנוי האן כי כן מרגלא בפומי דאינשי בק״ק פ״פ לכנות האיש על שם הבית, וביתו הי׳ תרנגול אדום חקוק עליו.

Cf. S. Mannheimer, "Joseph Yuspa Hahn," *JE* (1904), VI, 152, cit.

[55] Schnapper-Arndt, *op. cit.,* 182.

See in G. Wolf, *Die Juden,* p. 117; Heinrich Schwenger, "Namensbeilegung der Juden in Kostel" (1787), *ZGJT,* I², 117, the decree of 1784 and 1787 by Emperor Joseph II that the Jews should adopt surnames. Also, M. Grunwald, "Zur jüd. Kulturgeschichte im österreichischen Vormärz," *MGJV,* XLVI (1913), 23, #4 (July 13, 1787). In adopting names, the Jews were influenced by the cultural practices of Germany: Grunwald, "Altjüd. Gemeindeleben," *MGJV,* XLIII (1912), 75-76; Güdemann, *Gesch.,* III, 105-106. See John Meier, "Namen," in *idem* (ed.), *Deut. Volkskunde,* p. 132: By the 15th and 16th centuries the surname, derived from plants, geographical terms, became commonplace in Germanic lands. The Jews adopted names of dual form. For examples of Jewish surnames, see Hugo Gold, "Zur Gesch. der Juden in Pirnitz," *ZGJT,* I¹ (1930), 52-53; Max Schay, "'Chewra-Kadischa' in Pressburg," *ZGJT,* III² (1933), 82-83; Heinrich Schwenger, "Die Namensbeilegung der Juden in Kostel" (1787), *ZGJT,* I² (1930), 116, 119-22; B. Wachstein, *Grabschriften . . . Eisenstadt,* p. 123, n. 277; p. 125, n. 289; *idem,*

Handel und Industrie, p. 286, n. 34. Among the Jewish surnames there were: Austerlitz, Bauer, Bettelheim, Grünbaum, Heller, Lazarus, Lehmann, Lichtenstadt, Mattersdorf, Morgenstern, Pappenheim, Pressburg, Pulitzer, Schlesinger, Schneider, Schreiber, Schwarzenberg, Zoruf (= Goldschmidt).

[56] Dubnow, *Weltgeschichte,* (Hebrew edit.), VI, 127, #26; *idem, Weltgeschichte* (German edit.) VI, 235, #26; Freimann-Kracauer, *Frankfort,* p. 242; David Kaufmann, "Zu den jüd. Namen," *MGJV* (1898), I, 116. See the names of "Zum Bären," "Zum weissen Rössl," "Zum Schwarzschild," "Zum Rotschild," "Zur Wildente." *(Zum* = "at the home of. . . .")

Nicknames were also used. See the example in *Y. 'O.,* #368; Kaufmann, *MGJV,* I, 118: Rabbi Jacob Heilprin of Frankfort had the nickname of Dick, "fat, corpulent." Also, note the nicknames of Lang-Jacob (Lanky), Lang-Eisik, Lang-Leyb, Moses Lebereser (Moses the Liver-Eater) in Worms, in the 17th century.

[57] Kracauer, *Frankfurt Judengasse,* p. 395. With regard to the "shields" that were on Jewish homes in Frankfort, in 1612, cf. Pinthus in *ZGJD,* II, 289, #34, cit. Cf. the names on the houses in the Frankfort *gas,* according to the governmental legislation regulating the residence of Jews: *Stättigkeiten* of 1613 and 1705, in *J. M.,* III (No. 6), 151-54; (No. 7), 195-98.

[58] Levy, *Juden in Worms,* p. 17.

[59] Rotter-Schmieger, *Ghetto Wiener Leopoldstadt,* pp. 115-20.

[60] Wolf, *Juden in Worms,* p. 23; Levy, *op. cit .,* pp. 16-17.

[61] Freimann-Kracauer, *Frankfort,* p. 130; Levy, *op. cit.,* pp. 16-17.

[62] See Ida Posen, "Judentrachten," *Menorah,* VI (Vienna, 1928), 682; Philip Friedman, "Jewish Badge," *HJ,* XVII (1955), 41, also n. 1.

[63] See Wolf, *op. cit.,* 23; Levy, *op. cit.,* 16-17; Dubnow, *Weltgeschichte* (Hebrew edit.), VI, 127, #26; *idem, Weltgeschichte* (German edit.), VI, 235, #26. See Kracauer, *Juden in Frankfurt,* II, 119, that there were complaints that the Jew no longer wore "the yellow badge." The "hat" and "cloak," which the medieval Jew adopted from his non-Jewish neighbors, became the "distinctive Jewish garb" by legal decree: Posen in *Menorah,* VI, 682; *J. M.,* II (Bk. 6, chap. 14), 247, #11; Raphael Straus, "The 'Jewish Hat,'" *JSS,* IV (1942), 60, also n. 3.

It has been suggested by P. J. Diamont, "The Shield of David" (Hebrew), *Reshumot,* V (N. S., 1953), 94 ff., that the "shield" on the house probably originated from the shield that served as a coat of arms and insignia, in Frankfort, Worms, Vienna and Prague. Later, the shield was worn by all Jews, as in Frankfort after the Fettmilch Insurrection, in 1614, to signify their protection under the suzerainty of the king.

[64] Brann, *Juden in Schlesien,* V, 221.

[65] *Ẓemaḥ Ẓedeḳ,* no. 45, fol. 50b; *Ḥavvot Ya'ir,* no. 135, fol. 125a; J. Katz, *Ben Yehudim le-Goyim,* pp. 157-58; Eng. trans., *Exclusiveness and Tolerance,* p. 156; Minkoff, "Old-Yid. Lit.," *Jewish People: Past and Present,* III (1952). 160;

Kracauer, *Juden in Frankfurt,* II, 309 ff.; Erik, *Yid. lit.,* pp. 248-49, cit.; p. 294. Cf. Kracauer, "Frankfurter Juden im dreissigjährigen Kriege," *ZGJD,* III (O. S. 1889), 145; Esh, "Changes in the Book *Yosif 'Omeẓ*" (Hebrew), *'Kobeẓ' in Memory of Eliezer Shamir,* p. 61, n. 26; Shohet, *'Im Ḥillufe Teḳufot,* pp. 21–22, 49. See also p. 6; pp. 69, 155–56 of the present volume.

[66] Dubnow, *Weltgeschichte* (Hebrew edit.), VI, 128, 134.

[67] For example, cf. *Ẓemaḥ Ẓedeḳ,* no. 45, fol. 50a; *Pene Yehoshua',* II, no. 53, fol. 29b.

[68] Kaufmann (ed.), p. 69; Feilchenfeld, *Glückel,* p. 48; Lowenthal, *Glückel,* p. 34; Beth-Zion Abrahams, *Glückel,* p. 38.

[69] *Naḥalat Shib'ah,* II, no. 3, fol. 4b.

[70] For the participation of Jews in fairs, see *Y. 'O.,* p. 266 (1928 edit.); *Ḥavvot Ya'ir,* no. 201, fol. 192a; Halpern, *Taḳḳanot,* p. 88, #265 (market days in Linz and Krems, lower Austria); Kaufmann (ed.), Glikl, p. 219 (fairs of Leipzig and Frankfort on the Oder).

As to the effect that the new economic developments of the 17th century had on the social relations between Jew and non-Jew, see Jacob Katz, *Masoret u-Mashber,* chap. 23; Eng. trans., "Emergence of the Neutral Society," *Tradition and Crisis,* same chap.; *idem, Ben Yehudim le-Goyim,* chap. 13; Eng. trans., "The Development of Common Ground," *Exclusiveness and Tolerance,* also same chap.

[71] Regarding the social disabilities imposed on the members of the Jewish community by legislation, see above, pp. 4-5, n. 13. Cf. Dubnow, *Weltgeschichte* (Hebrew edit.), VI, 128; Kracauer, *Judengasse in Frankfurt,* p. 130; W. Basse, "Juden und die Spaziergänge in Frankfurt a. M. im Jahre 1769," *Zeit deut. Kulturgesch.,* IV (1859), 564-66.

[72] *Y. 'O.,* #608-609; *Ḥavvot Ya'ir,* no. 92, fol. 88b; *Sha'ar 'Efrayim,* no. 103, fol. 67b; *N. K. Y.,* sec. 300, fol. 38a, #8–9 ("Hil. Shab."); *Derushe ha-Ẓelaḥ,* no. 4, fol. 9b, #24.

[73] *Shebut Ya'aḳob,* I, no. 47, fol. 11a:

...עכו"ם ברחוב היהודים...ובפרטות ביום חגם שאז עוברין הרבה עכו"ם....

[74] J. W. Goethe, *Autobiograph. Schrift.: Aus Meinem Leben, Dichtung und Wahrheit,* VIII (2d edit., Stuttgart: J. G. Cotta; n. d., set pub. from 1950 on), 179. Trans., J. W. Goethe, *Autobiography: Poetry and Truth from My Own Life,* R. O. Moon, ed. (Washington, D.C., Public Affairs Press; 1949), p. 125. For the location of *Fischerfeld,* see p. 195 herein.

[75] See p. 109, n. 106.

[76] Kaufmann (ed.), *Glikl,* p. 244; cf. Feilchenfeld, Glückel, p. 235. Eng. cit. is based on Lowenthal (ed.), *Glückel,* p. 195.

[77] *Ḥavvot Ya'ir,* no. 188, fol. 199b:

...והולכו' חוץ לרחוב באמבטאות קטנות בל"א ציב"ר ...

Prob. *tsibr;* cf. *zuber, zober* (Ger.) = "tub."

Cf. Kaufmann, "Jair Chayim Bacharach," *JQR,* III (O. S., 1891), 499, n. 5.

78 Löw, *Lebensalter,* p. 311.

79 *N. K. Y.,* sec. 300, fol. 41a, #34 ("Hil. Shab.").

80 Kaufmann (ed.), *Glikl,* p. 146, n. 2; p. 148; Feilchenfeld (ed.), *Glückel,* p. 118, n. 8; pp. 119, 122; Lowenthal (ed.), *Glückel,* p. 285, n. 4; B. Z. Abrahams (ed.), *Glückel,* pp. 78–79, 80.

81 L. Donath, *Juden in Mecklenburg,* pp. 88-89. (Glückstadt: loc. in Holstein.)

82 Güdemann, *Quellen.,* p. 111; cit. from *Shelah.*

83 *Y. 'O.* (1637 edit.), Pt. 2, fol. 166b; (1928 edit.), p. 292 (sec. "Pereḳ ha-Biṭaḥon"). (Hereafter the 1928 edit. will be cited unless otherwise specified.) Cf. Brisch, *Juden in Cöln,* II, 115, n. 1.

84 Kracauer, *Juden in Frankfurt,* II, 122; Horovitz, *Frankfurt. Rabbin.,* II, 69-70; Dubnow, *Weltgeschichte* (Hebrew edit.), VII, 164. After the Frankfort fire Christian friends of Samuel Schotten enabled him to complete the printing of his book: Kaufmann, *Urkund. Samson Wertheimers,* p. 69. (R. Samuel Schotten of Frankfort was a contemporary and friend of Bacharach. Cf. Kaufmann in *JQR,* III [O. S., 1891], 502, n. 5, for fuller details.) Cf. S. Ochser, "Prague," *JE,* X (1905), 156: Until their homes were rebuilt in 1702, after the Prague *gas* was destroyed by fire, Jews found shelter among Christians.

85 *Ḥavvot Ya'ir,* no. 185, fol. 172b.

86 *Noda' bi-Yehudah* (Prague, 1811), II, no. 38, fol. 11a (sec. "'O. Ḥ."):

... על דבר היהודי שיש לו פאבריק של קארטון ....

fabrik (Yid.) = "factory"; cf. *fabrik* (Ger.), same meaning. Here the *fabrik* probably refers to a shop.

Prob. *korton;* cf. *kortn* (mod. Yid.) = "a kind of cloth"; cf. *cordon* (Ger.) = "comb wool."

Cf. Wind in *Horeb,* X, 58, nn. 4-5, for this and other examples of Jewish and non-Jewish economic relationships.

87 *Noda' bi-Yehudah* (Prague, 1811), II, no. 72, fol. 22a (sec. "'O. Ḥ.").

88 *She'elat Ya'abeẓ,* I, no. 41, fol. 71b. Emden expresses the same views elsewhere: cf. J. Katz, *Ben Yehudim le-Goyim,* pp. 166; 167, n. 33; Eng. trans., pp. 167; 168, n. 2; A. Schochat, "The Integration of German Jews within their non-Jewish Environment in the First-Half of the 18th Century" (Hebrew), *Zion,* XXI (N. S., 1956), 233-34, nn. 180-81. In this regard, note also in Katz and Schochat that other rabbinic authorities had views similar to Emden's. Cf. also Schochat (Shohet), *'Im Ḥillufe Teḳufot,* p. 68, nn. 152-54; p. 69, nn. 156-67.

NOTES TO CHAPTER II

[1] See chap. iii, pp. 50 ff., 59 ff., 62 ff., for the customs that deal with the rearing of a child, the *Bar Miẓvah* ceremony, and education.

[2] *Y. 'O.*, p. 351; Güdemann, *Gesch.*, I, 204, n. 4; J. Bergmann, "Schebua ha-Ben," *MGWJ*, LXXVI (1932), 467. See also Archer Taylor, "Germanic Folklore," in *Standard Dictionary of Folklore* (Funk and Wagnalls), I, 448; Viktor Geramb, "Die Knaffl-Handschrift, eine obersteirische Volkskunde aus dem Jahre 1813," *Quellen zur deutschen Volkskunde,* II, 55-68; Mogk, *Deut. Sitten und Bräuche* (ed. Fossler), pp. 3 f., 9 f., 21 f.

With regard to the bearing that birth, marriage, and death have had on folk beliefs, see *HDA*, IV (1931-32), 155, #3; 170-171; Sartori, *Sitte und Brauch,* I, 18 ff., 48 ff., 123 ff.

[3] See Frankfort (ed.), *Before Philosophy, the Intellectual Adventure of Ancient Man,* p. 32: "Time is experienced in the periodicity and rhythm of man's own life as well as in the life of nature. Each phase of man's life . . . is a time with peculiar qualities. The transition from one phase to another is a crisis in which man is assisted by the community's uniting in the rituals appropriate to birth, puberty, marriage, or death."

[4] David Kaufmann, "Jair Chayim Bacharach," *JQR*, III (April, 1891), 499. Note "the distinctive customs of Worms": Daniel (E.G.) Goldschmidt, "The Worms Maḥzor" (Hebrew), *Kirjath Sefer,* XXXIV (no. 3, June 1959), 388, n. 1; A. M. Habermann, "The Customs during the Month of *'Adar,* Derived from the 'Customs of Worms,' by Joseph Yuspa Shammes (Shammash)" (Hebrew), *Sinai Jubilee Volume* (Jerusalem, 1958), 482.

[5] That the religious and the social were closely interrelated in the Jewish community, see Güdemann, *Gesch.*, III, 103: Every phase of the individual's life "from his birth to his death was connected with some religious act," and participating with him in the various observances were "his family, his circle of friends, as well as the entire community." See also Marcus, *Communal Sick-Care in the German Ghetto,* p. 115, that no "distinction . . . [was] made between religious and social ideals," and what was considered "moral, religious, and decent was of one piece."

[6] See Bax, *German Culture,* pp. 100-6; Fritz Byloff "Berücksichtigung der Zauberei- und Hexenprozesse 1455 bis 1850," *Quellen zur deutschen Volkskunde,* III, no. 38, p. 27; no. 44–45, p. 32; Hermann Paul, "Das volkskundliche Material," *Grundriss der germanischen Philologie,* XII (1935), 281.

[7] See chap. vi, pp. 114, 115, 121–22; also, p. 16, n. 6.

[8] *Ḳ. H.*, 69:2–9. See Tsinberg, *Gesh. fun der lit.*, V, 190–93, n. 16; Trachtenberg, *Jewish Magic,* p. 53; David Kaufmann, "R. Naftali Cohen im Kampfe gegen Chajjun," *JJLG,* II (1899), 127, n. 3.

[9] See p. 105, n. 75; p. 116 f. Also, cf. in *Ḳ. H.*, 3:5–6, 4:3, 5:17, 87:13; *Y. 'O.*, #85–86, fol. 202b–205a (1723 edit.), pp. 348–52 (1928 edit.), the discussion on "law and magical practices"; *B. D.*, 33b, 40a; *Sefer Zekhirah*, 13b; Landau, *Derushe ha-Ẓelaḥ*, no. 3, fol. 6b, #5. See also M. Grunwald, "Various Charms and Magical Recipes" (Hebrew), *Edoth*, I (July 1945), 241-48, Hebrew texts of Ashkenazic European Jewish communities in the 16th-18th centuries; J. Wellesz, "Kabbalistische Rezepte, Wundermittel und Amulette," *MGJV* (1911-12), 127-130; Horowitz, *Frankfurt. Rabbin.*, III, 77; Erik, *Gesh. fun yid. lit.*, p. 303.

[10] *Y. 'O.*, fol. 204a-b (1723 edit.), p. 351 (1928 edit.); Güdemann, *Gesch.*, I, 204, n. 4. Hahn based his instruction on *Berakhot*, fol. 54a: A sick person, bridegroom, bride, mourner, and scholar were to be guarded against evil spirits.

[11] *Y. 'O.*, fol. 205a (1723 edit.), p. 351 (1928 edit.). Cf. the custom of protecting the mother in confinement by "placing iron weapons" under her pillow: Gaster, *Holy and Profane*, p. 62.

[12] *Tosef. Shab.* 6:7 (ed. Zuckermandel). That the customs of the Amorites are regarded as idolatrous, cf. *Shab.*, fol. 67a-b. See Grunwald, "Aus Hausapotheke und Hexenküche," *MGJV*, V (1900), 60-61, n. 201.

[13] See Elzet, "Some Customs of Israel" (Hebrew), *Reshumot*, I (1918), p. 362, #57; p. 363, #58; M. Grunwald, "Aus unseren Sammlungen 1," *MGJV*, I (1898), 90, sec. 7; 91, sec. 10.

[14] Güdemann, *Gesch.*, I, 214.

[15] Cf. *'Amtaḥat Binyamin* (Collect. Folk Remedies), fol. 16a ff.; 19a, #13-14; *Ta'ame ha-Minhagim*, II, fol. 42a-b, 61a. See pp. 133–35 herein, folk-medicine remedies prescribed to assist and confirm pregnancy, check hemorrhaging during childbirth, remove the placenta, and prevent miscarriage.

For related German practices to help child delivery, see Wuttke, *Deut. Volksaberglauben*, p. 355; Sartori, *Sitte und Brauch*, I, 22-28.

[16] *J. M.*, II (Bk. 6, chap. 26), 8.

[17] *Bet David*, fol. 23a-b. See Erich Brauer, "Birth Customs of the Jews of Kurdistan" (Hebrew), *Edoth*, I (1946), 66: Pregnant women wore the skin of a snake around the waist as an amulet.

[18] Löw, *Lebensalter*, p. 45; A. Marmorstein, "Beiträge zur Religionsgeschichte und Volkskunde," *JJV*, I (1923), 298.

See p. 117, n. 28; p. 135, n. 159. concerning the place of the snake in Jewish folklore and folk medicine.

[19] *Sefer Zekhirah*, fol. 12a.

[20] Levesohn, *Meḳore Minhagim*, p. 109.

[21] See G. Scholem, *Trends in Jewish Mysticism*, pp. 81 ff., regarding the effect that Jewish mysticism had on medieval Germany.

[22] Isaak Holzer, "Nach dem 'Minhagbuch des Juspa Schammes,'" *ZGJD*, V (1935), 171. See Eisenstein, "Yoledet" (Hebrew) in *'Oẓar Yisra'el*, V, 109:

The mother was protected by the circle and guardian angels. For a summary of the kinds of customs that were followed when a child was born, see Grunwald in *MGJV*, I, 83, sec. 3.

The study by Holzer is very useful because he dealt with the three recensions of the Yuspa Shammash *Minhagim* MS. However, he did not indicate when he was citing passages from the original MS; nor did he show which recension was used. Hence, it is not always possible to ascertain whether a source in italics is a direct translation or his paraphrase of the text. A description of the recensions of the Yuspa Shammash *Minhagim* MS is in A. Epstein, "Wormser Minhagbücher," *Gedenkbuch . . . an David Kaufmann*, pp. 308-9.

23 Arthur Goldmann, "The 'Vakhnakht' among the Jews of Vienna at the Beginning of the 15th Century," *Filolog. Shrift.*, I (Vilna, 1926) 93-94. In folklore the circle is considered to be efficacious in warding off evil spirits. See pp. 27–28, n. 72 in this volume.

24 See Trachtenberg, *Jewish Magic*, pp. 42, 106, 157, 170 ff., for ways of assuring safety to a mother and child after delivery.

25 *M. F.*, 25 *M. F.*, fol. 3a-b, #9:

שלשה ימים קודם המילה מכריז השמש ברחובות העיר (צור יודש קערץ) והנשים הקרובות מתאספין לבית היולדת ועושים [*sic*] **נר של שעוה שידליק** [*sic*] **עד יום השלישי למילה, וגם י״ב נרות מקולעים הנקראים (שבטים) ....**

Cf. *ibid.*, fol. 31a: . . . *'osim ha-yudish kerts . . . . yudish*="circumcision"; see E. Weill, "Le Yidisch Alsacien-Lorrain," *REJ*, LXXII (1921), 71: *jidsche (yidshe)*, "to perform the circumcision"; *jidschkerz (yidish-kerts)*, "the candle lit during the circumcision ceremony"; that is, the "circumcision candle." See also Chaim Gininger, "Sainéan's Accomplishments in Yiddish Linguistics," *The Field of Yiddish* (ed. Uriel Weinreich), p. 162: *yidishn*, "to circumcise." *kerts* (Yid.), "candle"; cf. *kerze* (Ger.), same meaning.

26 M. L. Bamberger, "Aus meiner Minhagimsammelmappe," *JJV* (1923), I, 327, #6.

27 Grunwald in *MGJV*, I, 84, sec. 3 (19).

See Brauer, "Circumcision and Childhood among the Jews of Kurdistan" (Hebrew), *Edoth*, I (no. 3, 1946), 132: The Kurdistan Jews, both men and women, would light candles in the home of the mother on the night preceding the circumcision.

28 Holzer in *ZGJD*, V, 172. See Schauss, *Lifetime of a Jew*, pp. 42-43, n. 58.

29 Bamberger in *JJV*, I, 327, #6.

30 *Sefer ha-Roḳeaḥ*, fol. 22b, #107. See Bamberger in *JJV*, I, 327, #6, n. 3.

31 *Sefer Maharil*, fol. 87a, "Hil. Milah" (Sabionetta, 1536); fol. 67a (Warsaw, 1874).

32 Bamberger in *JJV*, I, 327, #6.

33 Güdemann, *Gesch.*, III, 103-4; Grunwald in *MGJV*, I, 84, sec. 3 (11).

Cf. Wuttke, *Deut. Volksaberglaube,* p. 359: The German folk believed that "a child was in peril until given a name," and "it was therefore anxiously guarded" before baptism.

[34] *Ḥavvot Ya'ir,* no. 92, fol. 88b:

...ובליל שקודם המילה שקורין ווא״ך נכט כידוע ויהי בחצי הלילה נתכשף הילד שקורין בינו״מין וכאשר הקיצה אמך וכנערה משנתה ראתה כי מת הילד....

vakhnakht (Yid.) = "vigil night." See "vigil night" in Uriel Weinreich, "Mapping a Culture," *Columbia University Forum,* VI, (No. 3, 1963), 19, map 3: "Circumcision Observances." Prob. *binomin;* cf. *benommen* (Ger.) = "to be in a state of stupor; to be 'seized,' bewitched"; see Güdemann, *Gesch.,* III, 103-4, n. 2.

Cf. "watch night" in Perles, "Berner Handschrift des kleinen Aruch," *Jubelschrift . . . Graetz,* p. 23; the "Night of Watching," in Gaster, *Holy and Profane,* p. 62. See Fig. 2, p. 21.

[35] Goldmann in *Filolog. Shrift.,* I, 93-94.

[36] Bamberger in *JJV,* I, 323-24.

[37] Brauer in *Edoth,* I, 130-32; cf. *idem, Yehude Kurdistan,* pp. 136-37.

[38] Holzer in *ZGJD,* V, 172.

[39] M. Grunwald, "Die Statuten der 'Hamburg-Altonaer Gemeinde'" (1726), *MGJV,* XI (1903), 9, #121.

[40] Bergmann in *MGWJ,* LXXVI, 467-68.

[41] See pp. 102–3; the *se'udat miẓvah,* the festive banquet held on *Shabbat Zakhor,* is discussed in greater detail. As to the relationship of *Shabbat Zakhor,* to Jewish communal life, cf. *Y. 'O.,* #134, #1024; *N. K. Y.,* sec. 40, fol. 25a, #1; *Ḥavvot Ya'ir,* no. 70, fol. 74a. See also Halpern, *Taḳḳanot Mähren,* p. 199, n. 12; Barbeck, *Juden in Nürnberg und Fürth,* p. 84; Levesohn, *Meḳore Minhagim,* p. 92, #65.

[42] *B. Ḳam.,* fol. 80a: "Rab and Samuel and Rab Assi happened to come to the house [were guests] at a circumcision of a boy, or as some say, at the party for the redemption of a son [i.e., *Pidyon ha-Ben*]." (Trans. based on Son. edit., *Neziḳin,* I, *B. Ḳam.,* 456, also n. 5.) Cf. cits. in *Terumat ha-Deshen,* no. 269, fol. 36a; *N. K. Y.,* fol. 25a; Bamberger in *JJV,* I, 324, #3.

[43] *Terumat ha-Deshen, op. cit.*

[44] *Maḥzor Vitry,* #627.

[45] *Ḥavvot Ya'ir,* no. 70, fol. 74a. Cf. J. Glasberg, *Zikhron Berit la-Ri'shonim,* p. 65: The father would arrange a festive meal on the evening before the circumcision.

[46] Brauer in *Edoth,* I, 129. Cf. *idem, Yehude Kurdistan,* p. 135.

[47] Holzer in *ZGJD,* 172. Cf. *Y. D.,* 265:12, comment of Isserles; *Be'er ha-Golah,* n. 300; *Ket.,* fol. 8a, *Shab.,* 130a. Cf. *sandeḳ: M. F.,* fol. 3b, #9. The *se'udah,* on the day of the *berit milah,* is also an old custom. Cf. *Pirḳe Rabbi 'Eli'ezer,* chap. 29; *Sefer ha-Manhig,* fol. 99a-b; *Sefer Abduharam,* fol. 122b;

Mordecai Jaffe, *Lebush* (on *Y. D.*), III, fol. 145a, #12 ("Hil. Milah"). See also Brauer in *Edoth*, I, 134; *idem, Yehude Kurdistan*, p. 141, for the festive meal that followed the circumcision.

As to the festive character of the circumcision ceremony, see *Zikhron Berit la-Ri'shonim*, p. 62.

[48] See p. 82, also n. 8; pp. 87, 88, 94.

[49] *Pirḳe Rabbi 'Eli'ezer*, chap. 29. Cf. *Y. D.*, 265: 11. See the popular accounts of the origin of the Chair of Elijah in *Sefer ha-Manhig*, fol. 98a-b; *Sefer Abdu-haram*, fol. 122b; *Lebush* (on *Y. D.*), III, fol. 145a, #11; *Zikhron Berit la-Ri'shonim*, p. 60, cits.; Levesohn, *Meḳore Minhagim*, p. 93, #66, cit.; Bamberger in *JJV*, I, 172.

Note Chair of Elijah, Fig. 3, p. 23.

[50] *Zikhron Berit la-Ri'shonim*, p. 59; also, cf. cits.

[51] See above, p. 11, nn. 16-20; also, below, p. 304, n. 139.

[52] *S. H.*, I, 67a: *gefatr* = *kvater* (Yid.); cf. *gevatter* (Ger.), "assistant." *Gevatter* does not always mean "assistant," or even "godfather," but "gossip," "pal"—"companion," "intimate friend." Cf. Bamberger, *JJV*, I, p. 326, #5. The *gevatter*, who holds the child on his knee during the circumcision, is usually a scholar or relative. Cf. also *kvatershaft* in Landau and Wachstein, *Jüd. Privat-briefe*, no. 32, p. 41 (text), p. 70 (trans.). The rabbi is the *kvater*. Evidently, this is an older custom, as the Maharil states that he served as a *sandeḳ*: cf. *Maharil* (Sabionetta, 1556), fol. 87a ("Hil. Milah"). Judah A. Joffe, "Mutual Borrowings Between Yiddish and Slavic Languages," in *Harry A. Wolfson Jubilee Volume*, I, 423, shows the interrelationship of "the Greek sandek," "the Yiddish kvater," "the Middle High German gevater" to mean "the assistant at the circumcising of a child."

Cf. Levesohn, *Meḳore Minhagim*, p. 94, #67; *Sandeḳ* is related to *syndikos* (Gr.), "godfather"; cf. *beistand* (Ger.), "helper." Cf. *Mid. Tehillim* (ed. Buber) 35 :7; Bamberger in *JJV*, I, 326, n. 5, with regard to the *syndikos* who holds the child on his knees during the circumcision ceremony. Cf. Sheftel (Sabbatai) Horowitz, "Ethical Will" in *Ẓavva'ot . . . Dibre Ḳedoshim* (ed. Edelstein), fol. 3a, #8: *'inyan sandeḳ gadol ve-nora' hu.*

Cf. Wolf, *Mähren Statuten*, p. 78, #306, professional fees were not paid the *kvater*, or the *mohel* who circumcised the child, but voluntary contributions could be made for their services.

[53] Holzer in *ZGJD*, V, 172. Cf. the role of the *sandeḳ* in Isserles, gloss. 3, 10, 15 on *Y. D.*, 265: 1, 4, 11.

[54] Eisenstein, "Sandeḳ" (Hebrew), *'Oẓar Yisra'el*, VII (1912), 224; Schauss, *Lifetime of a Jew*, p. 38. Usually, the *kvaterin* is the wife of the *kvater*. However, it was not incumbent upon the man to ask his wife to assist him as the *kvaterin* in bringing the child to the synagogue. Cf. *Lebush* (on *Y. D.*), III, fol. 145a, #11.

[55] Grunwald, "Aus unseren Sammlungen 1," *MGJV,* I (1898), 84, #15.

[56] Bamberger in *JJV,* I, 327, #5. Cf. *Lebush* (on *Y. D.*), III, *op. cit.:* The *sandeḳ* may also be the one who carries the infant to the synagogue to be circumcised.

[57] Lentshits, *'Olelot 'Efrayim,* Pt. 3, fol. 91a, sec. 439. Cf. Hirschowitz, *'Oẓar Kol Minhage Yeshurun,* p. 100, sec. 417, #7.

[58] *Num. Rab.,* Par. 20, "Balaḳ". (Trans. based on Son. edit., *Mid. Rabbah,* II, 810.) Cf. cit. of the Midrash in Lentshits, *op. cit.* A similar Midrashic interpretation is in *Pirḳe Rabbi 'Eli'ezer,* chap. 29.

See the practice of burying the foreskin: *'O. Ḥ.* 255:10; *Sefer Maharil,* fol. 85b ("Hil. Milah"); *Sefer ha-Manhig,* fol. 99a; *Sefer Abduharam,* fol. 122b.

Cf. Brauer, *Yehude Kurdistan,* p. 140: The *mohel,* circumciser, places the foreskin in a dish of ashes and covers it with a bride's veil. See herein, p. 36, n. 119. Afterwards the mother ties the foreskin to the cradle. When it dries, the foreskin is worn as an "amulet" and as a "remedy," *segullah,* to aid barren women to become pregnant.

[59] *Lebush* (on *Y. D.*), III, fol. 145a, #10.

[60] Holzer in *ZGJD,* V, 172. Apparently, the first paragraph is a paraphrase, either in part or entirely, because it states that the "richly carved seats" of the Chair of Elijah used in the synagogue had been on exhibit in the Jewish Museum of Worms.

Cf. Wachstein, "Pinkas Runkel," *ZGJD,* IV (1932), 139, #36, the *kvater* serves food at the *berit milah.*

See Weill in *REJ,* LXXII, 71, sec. "J": *jidschwindel.* See the description of a *vindl* used as Torah band: Bamberger, *JJV,* I, 330-31, #11.

[61] *M. F.,* fol. 31a: *sharts* (Yid.), "apron"; cf. *schürze* (Ger.), same meaning. For *sharts,* see comment of Rashi on *ve-'efod* (Ex. 28:4). Cf. *sharts,* below, p. 91, n. 42 in this volume.

Cf. *Sefer ha-Roḳeaḥ,* fol. 22b, #108; *Y. D.* 266:2, that circumcision has precedence over the Sabbath and festivals.

[62] *N. K. Y.,* 22a. Cf. Bamberger in *JJV,* I, 328, n. 3.

[63] At the outset Kosman quotes from *Sefer Ḥasidim,* #460 (cf. Margulies edit., p. 315): "Among non-Jews sons are called by the names of their fathers, and no one regards this [practice] to be of any consequence. On the other hand, the Jews take precaution to avoid this. There are places where they do not use names of those who are living, but only after they are dead." Cf. Lauterbach, "The Name of Children," *CCARYB,* XLII (1932), 337, who quotes the above passage: *Sefer Ḥasidim* (ed. Wistinetzki), p. 114, #377. Cf. also cits. in Schauss, p. 310, n. 60; Freehof, *Reform Jewish Practices,* I, 112.

[64] Bamberger in *JJV,* I, 328; Lauterbach in *CCARYB,* XLII, 335; Zimmels, *Ashkenazim and Sephardim,* p. 165.

[65] Wolf, *Die Juden,* pp. 116-17; Lauterbach in *CCARYB,* XLII, 337-38.

Lauterbach explains that Ashkenazic Jewry was influenced by fear in naming their children after the dead. In case of mistaken identity, harm, sickness, or death could befall a young person if he should be confused with an older individual who bears the same name. Cf. *Sefer Ḥasidim* (ed. Wistinetzki), p. 114, #375. In his Ethical Will, *Ẓavva'ot* (ed. Edelstein), p. 8, #22, Sheftel (Sabbatai) Horowitz admonishes that an infant should not be placed in the bed of an adult. No doubt there was anxiety that the child might be prematurely exposed to dangers befalling an adult.

... הזהרו ... שלא לשכוב שום תינוק במטה שלכם קודם שהיו שתי שנים. ...

See Güdemann, *Gesch.*, I, 200, n. 4: According to German folklore, if the first-born child receives the name of his parents, he will die before them.

66 *Y. 'O.* (1928 edit.), Pt. 3, p. 362; *Naḥalat Shib'ah,* II, no. 17, fol. 11a; *Zikhron Yosef,* no. 5, fol. 6a-b (sec. "'O. Ḥ."). See also the *Holekreisch* in Bamberger in *JJV,* I, 329, n. 1; Löw, *Lebensalter,* p. 389, n. 9; S. Salfeld, "Welt und Haus," *JJGL,* XXIII (1920), 71-72; 84, n. 28; Th. H. Gaster, "Folkways," *JE,* VI (1904), 443; *idem, Holy and Profane,* pp. 36-37, n. 16; Schauss, *Lifetime of a Jew,* pp. 44-47. See below p. 151 in this volume.

67 Details of the *Holekreisch* ceremony are not given in *Y. 'O., Naḥalat Shib'ah,* and *Zikhron Yosef.* See the description of the *Holekreisch* in Assaf, *Meḳorot,* I, 123, #15; 124, #18; Grunwald in *MGJV,* I, 84, #22; A. Landau, "Fragekasten. Holekreisch," *MGJV,* IV (1899), 146, cit.; *idem,* "Holekreisch," *ZVV,* IX (1899), 72; Salfeld, *op. cit.,* 71-72.

68 *Naḥalat Shib'ah,* II, no. 17, fol. 11a; *Y. 'O.* (1928), Pt. 3, p. 362. According to Hahn, sometimes the Hebrew name would be derived from the father's side of the family and the Yiddish name from that of the mother.

69 *Naḥalat Shib'ah,* II, no. 17, fol. 11a. See also Landau in *MGJV,* IV, 146; Bamberger in *JJV,* I, 329: The children were given fruit and confection.

70 Cf. Löw, *Lebensalter,* p. 105; Perles in *Jubelschrift . . . Graetz,* p. 26; Landau in *ZVV,* IX, 72.

71 Cf. Löw, *Lebensalter,* p. 389, n. 98; Zunz, *Gottesdienst. Vorträge,* p. 454, n. d.; Perles in *op. cit.* The author did not locate any reference to *Holekreisch* when he checked *Maharam Minz,* (resp. no. 19).

72 Perles in *Jubelschrift . . . Graetz,* pp. 26-27; Gaster, *Holy and Profane,* p. 37, n. See Assaf, *Meḳorot,* I, p. 123, # 5: The woman attending the mother in confinement would encircle her with a drawn sword. With regard to the circle made around the mother after childbirth, see p. 18, nn. 22–23 herein.

73 Landau in *ZVV,* IX, 73. In one of the folk songs there is a version of "the cat in boots" who jumps into a well, finds a child, then asks what will be its name. See in Güdemann, *Gesch.,* III, 104, that *Holekreisch* is associated with "Hulda, Holda, Holle," i.e., Frau Holle. Cf. Grimm, *Deut. Myth.,* I, 221-23: Frau Holda (Hulda, Holle) is "the goddess who befriends man." She is known as the goddess of spinning and agriculture, and at all times resides in water, "in the sea and wells."

Cf. Gaster, *Holy and Profane*, p. 37: "Holle is the grisly witch who attacks children."

[74] This explanation has been suggested to the author by Theodor H. Gaster and Frederick Lowenthal, a physician in Boston who previously resided in Germany.

[75] See p. 81, n. 192.

[76] Above, n. 66, cit. from *Y. 'O.*

Naḥalat Shib'ah, II, no. 17, fol. 11a:

... הוא נבון דאין זה חיובא מן הדין רק מנהגא במקצת קהלות דהיינו במדינות אשכנזי עושין הולי קרייש לזכר.

Meseritz states that the *Holekreisch* is not observed in Poland, Moravia, or Austria.

[77] Cf. Güdemann, *Gesch.*, III, 104; Landau in *MGJV*, IV, 147; Perles, *op. cit.*, p. 27; Gaster, *Holy and Profane*, p. 27. Cf. *todtentanz*, herein, pp. 37–38; *Johannes Feuer*, pp. 174–75, 177.

[78] *Naḥalat Shib'ah*, II, no. 17, fol. 11a:

... כבר נשתקע המנהג מקרוב בקהלות גדולו׳ שלא לעשות הולי קרייש רק עושין לה מי שבירך בבית הכנסת....

[79] *S. H.*, I, 67b. Cf. *Y. D.*, 305:3, that the priest is given five *sel'aim*, or "the equivalent" thereof, for the redemption of the first-born. For differences in the valuation of German and Polish coins, cf. *Ḥavvot Ya'ir*, no. 1, fol. 3b-4a; *N. K. Y.*, sec. 80, fol. 31b, #3-4; fol. 32a, #4 ("Hil. Pidyon ha-Ben").

[80] See p. 130, n. 127, for some of the problems facing Jewish family life; and with regard to changes in marriage practices, see Jacob Katz, "Marriage . . . at the Close of the Middle Ages" (Hebrew), *Zion*, X (N.S., 1946), 24–25, 47–48, 51–52. Marriages were postponed for economic and cultural reasons, in order to attend school and study a profession. With the rise of individualism, matchmaking (herein, p. 3, n. 89) was on the decline, as each person wished to select his own mate. That in the second half of the 18th century the Jews of Central Europe were married at a later age, see also I. Halpern, "The 'Rush' into Early Marriages" (Hebrew), *Zion*, XVII (N. S., 1962), 56-57.

[81] Kaufmann (ed.), *Glikl*, p. 182; Feilchenfeld (ed.), *Glückel*, p. 157; Lowenthal (ed.), *Glückel*, p. 132. Cf. Abrahams, *Jewish Life*, p. 193, n. 4. That the *ḳnas* was binding, see also p. 138, n. 186 of this volume.

[82] Concerning the festive character of the *ḳnas-mol*, cf. *Ḥavvot Ya'ir*, no. 70, fol. 74a: "After writing the betrothal [engagement] agreement, a meal would be arranged, which is known as *ḳnas-mol*. . . ." See the *ḳnasmahl* celebration in Güdemann, *Gesch.*, III, 119, n. 2; Holzer in *ZGJD*, V, 175-76. Cf. Perles, "Jüd. Hochzeit," *MGWJ*, IX (1860), 342, cit.; *Mo'ed Ḳaṭan*, 18b, *se'udat 'erusin*, "a feast of betrothal." Also, Abrahams, *Jewish Life*, pp. 193-94; Schauss, *Lifetime of a Jew*, p. 165. See also in Liebe, *Judentum in der deut. Vergangenheit*, pp. 109-11, figs. 89-91, portraits of betrothal ceremonies.

[83] Grunwald in *MGJV*, I, 88, n. 1, sec. 4 (43); Güdemann, *Gesch.*, III, 119; *Sefer ha-Roḳeaḥ*, fol. 103b, #353. The custom of giving the bride and groom honey

and cheese to eat during the wedding ceremony is based on the verse (Song of Songs 4:11), "Honey and milk are under your tongue." That milk and honey are associated with the Messianic Era, cf. Perles in *MGWJ,* IX, 347, n. 7; *Pesiḳta Rabbati* (ed. M. Friedmann), chap. 37, fol. 163a: "Without any delay, the Holy One, Blessed be He, will prepare for the Messiah seven canopies made of precious stones and pearls. Within each canopy will flow four streams of wine, honey, milk, and pure balsam."

[84] Holzer in *ZGJD,* V, 175; Grunwald in *MGJV,* I, 85, sec. 4 (4).

As to the possible significance of breaking a dish at the *ḳnas-mol,* cf. Lauterbach, "Ceremony of Breaking a Glass at Weddings," *HUCA*, II (1925), 351 ff. Wuttke, *Deut. Volksaberglaube,* p. 196, #291, describes the German folk belief that the bride and groom would experience good fortune if many dishes were broken on their wedding day. A large number of such pieces was regarded as an omen of well-being for the couple.

[85] Holzer in *ZGJD,* V, 175. Cf. the communal legislation of Krems, 1694, in Halpern, *Taḳḳanot Mähren,* p. 154, #460 (18): The fathers of the bride and groom are forbidden to meet by themselves before the wedding. Cf. also Baron, *Community,* II, 315: "Some communities felt induced to supervise the behavior of betrothed couples before wedlock. . . ."

[86] *Ḥavvot Ya'ir,* no. 211, fol. 210b.

[87] *Shebut Ya'aḳob,* I, no. 105, fol. 27a.

[88] *Ḥavvot Ya'ir,* no. 220, fol. 207a; *Shebut Ya'aḳob,* I, no. 104, fol. 27a.

[89] See Abrahams, *Jewish Life,* p. 193, for a description of the social function of *shiddukhin.* Also, Jastrow, *Tal. Dict.,* II, 1525, *shiddukh, shiddukhin,* "negotiations preliminary to betrothal"; *shaddekh,* "to arrange a marriage by sending an agent to settle affairs," as in *Ḳid.,* 13a. Cf. also *Ḳid.,* 44b, *Shab.,* 150a; Perles in *MGWJ,* IX, 341, n. 6, as to the origin of the word *shiddukhin.* As an illustration of the twofold role of the *shadkhan,* cf. Halpern, *Taḳḳanot Mähren,* pp. 54-55, #170.

[90] Eckstein, *Juden . . . Bamberg,* pp. 69-70, #8.

[91] Kaufmann, "The Minute Book of the Congregation of Bamberg, 1698" (Hebrew), *Ḳobeẓ 'al Yad,* VII (1896-97), 5, #9.

[92] Kaufmann in *op. cit.,* VII, 4-5, #8. See Eckstein, *Juden . . . Bamberg,* pp. 72–73, #15: Communal legislation permitted a family to deduct from the amount of the dowry expenses incurred for the trousseau and wedding celebration. The value of the dowry not only included cash, but also all gifts given to the bride, gold and silver jewels, fineries, or a *ḳiddush* cup. A newly married couple was required to meet all outstanding bills before assuming any further obligations.

[93] Munk in *Jubelschrift . . . Hildesheimer,* p. 83 (Hebrew sec.). Cf. in Halpern, *Taḳḳanot Mähren,* p. 56, #173, the communal legislation of Gaya, Moravia, 1650, with regard to the remuneration received by the *shadkhan.* That the matchmaker received a fee for his special services, as did the rabbi or cantor of the community, cf. Wolf, *Statuten,* Pref., vi.

[94] Grunwald, "Statuten," *MGJV,* XI, 31, #77. Cf. in MS *Minhagim de-Ḳ.Ḳ.*

Worms, fol. 6 (one side), the practice of aiding the bride to obtain a dowry: ולסייעת נדוניית כלה. *(Courtesy, Department of Oriental Books, Bodleian Library, Oxford.)*

[95] Baron, *Community,* II, 333–34. Cf. *Y. D.,* 252:1; *M. T.,* "Hil. Matnot 'Aniyim," 8:10; Cronbach, "Jewish Philanthropic Institutions in the Middle Ages." in *idem, Religion and Its Social Setting,* pp. 138-39, n. 66.

[96] Grunwald in *MGJV,* XI, 31, #77. Cf. Halpern, *op. cit.,* p. 116, #348 (11): The communal legislation of Austerlitz, Moravia, requires that three gold coins be given the young woman for her bridal dowry.

[97] Eckstein, *Juden . . . Bamberg,* p. 70, #10. Cf. the communal legislation of Gaya, Moravia, in 1650, that specifies the responsibility of a wealthy relative in helping to provide one-third to the total amount of the bridal dowry: Halpern, p. 56, #174.

[98] *Y. 'O.,* #657; *N. K. Y.,* sec. 50, fol. 26b, #2; Holzer in *ZGJD,* V, 176-77; *Ḥavvot Ya'ir,* no. 66, fol. 74a; Kaufmann (ed.), *Glikl,* p. 64, n. 3; Feilchenfeld (ed.), *Glückel,* p. 42, n. 9; *M. F.,* fol. 31a.

See the description of *spinholts (spinnholz)* in Ocksman, "Customs of Frankfort" (Hebrew), *Reshumot,* III (1947), 101, 103; H. Ehrentreu, "Sprachliches und Sachliches aus dem Talmud," *JJLG,* IX (1911), 37, cits.; Perles in *MGWJ,* IX, 342, cits.; Press in *MGWJ,* LXXVI, 576; Güdemann, *Gesch.,* III, 69; 119, n. 2; Gaster, *Holy and Profane*, pp. 88–89.

Cf. *Sefer Maharil* (1556 edit.), fol. 82b, for a detailed account of the *spinholts* celebration in Germany in the 15th century. The *spinholts* was then held on the Friday preceding the wedding; at dawn the sexton called members of the community to the festivity. Cf. also *spinholts:* "Magen 'Abraham" on *'O. Ḥ.* 551:6 (sec. "Hil. Tish'ah be-'Ab) in *Meginne 'Ereẓ.*

[99] Feilchenfeld (ed.), *Glückel,* p. 42, n. 9; Ehrentreu in *JJLG,* IX, 37, cit.; *Giṭ.,* 89a, "spinning by lamplight" as a sign of betrothal. Cf. Berliner, *Deut. Juden im Mittelalter,* p. 45, cit.; *Yoma',* 66b: "There is no wisdom in woman except with the distaff, as it is said (Ex. 35 :25): 'All the women that were wise-hearted did spin with their hands.'" Cf. also Berliner, pp. 11, 45; Holzer in *ZGJD,* V, 176: When a daughter was born, the father would bless her, "May it be Thy will, Eternal God, that I rear my daughter to sew, spin, knit, and perform pious deeds." Prov. 31:19 regards spinning as one of the attainments of the 'woman of valour': "She lays her hands to the distaff, and her hands hold the spindle." That the spindle is a "symbol of womanhood" in German folklore, see Gaster, *Holy and Profane,* p. 82, n. 2.

[100] See "twirling the spindle" in Martha Bielenstein, "Bast und Rinde an der Kleidung," *ZVV,* III (1931), 155.

[101] *Y. 'O.,* #657. See Lewin, *Gesch. der badischen Juden,* p. 97, for communal authorization of marriage.

[102] MS *Minhagim de-Ḳ.Ḳ. Worms,* fol. 58a:
...וכל הבאים שמה יושבין סביבת שלחנת זמן מועט ושותין יין ושמחים עם החתן עד יבואו

אחדים ואז כת ראשונה הולכין לביתם והבאים יושבין בשלחן זמן מועט וגם המה הולכין...
[?]... עוד כת שלישי[ת]... ובסוף כולם הבחורי׳ באין ויושבין.....
(Courtesy, Department of Oriental Books, Bodleian Library, Oxford.)

[103] Holzer in *ZGJD,* V, 176-77. See Schauss, *Lifetime of a Jew,* pp. 166, 175.

That every large community in Germany had a *tants-hoyz,* where dances were held after weddings and on other festive occasions, cf. Shiper, *Yid. teater,* III, 69. Note the "dance house" in Güdemann, *Gesch.,* III, 138; Perles in *MGWJ,* IX, 350; Weissenberg in *MGJV,* XV, 72 f.

Cf. Baron, *Community,* II, 315: "The term communal 'dancing houses,' encountered in medieval German sources, is a misnomer; they were really wedding halls, where the dancing was almost never mixed except for an extremely chaste ritualistic dance with the bride." Cf. Perles in *MGWJ,* IX, 345; *Ket.,* 17a, for the custom of dancing with the bride during the wedding celebration. The father danced with the bride after the marriage meal: Weissenberg, *op. cit.,* 72.

The communal legislation of Karlsruhe forbade men and women to dance together: "Only women should dance with women and men with men": Y. Lifshitz, "The Struggle of R. Yedidiah Weil against Dance and Masquerade in Karlsruhe" (Yiddish) in *Arkhiv . . . gesh. fun der yid. teater* (ed. Jacob Shatzky), I, 453, #4. The basis for precedent was 2 Sam. 6:16, when David brought the tabernacle and danced alone while Michal looked out through the window; Ex. 15:20, at the time when Miriam and the women danced by themselves, and Judges 21:21, when the daughters of Shiloh danced together. Cf. L. Löwenstein, *Nathanael Weil,* in *idem, Gesch. . . . in der Kurpfalz,* II, 56, #d (Append. no. 9); Fecht, *Gesch. . . . Karlsruhe,* p. 248, #d.

[104] Ocksman in *Reshumot,* III, 101.

[105] Holzer, *op. cit.,* 177. See Abrahams, *Jewish Life,* p. 213: "In the middle ages the music [i.e., for the wedding] was provided, Saturdays excepted, by Jewish professionals."

Cf. in Schultz, *Deut. Leben,* I, 171, that a dance followed the wedding meal. Also, Sartori, *Sitte und Brauch,* I, 104, for the custom in Germany to hold dancing after the wedding; a joyous occasion implied a happy life for the couple. That events at the wedding affect their future, see Wuttke, *Deut. Volksaberglaube,* p. 196, #291. If the bride should tear her dress at the wedding ceremony, it was a sign that the marriage would be of short duration. During the banquet, if the bride gave a pin in her wearing-apparel to an unmarried woman, it meant that her wedding would soon ensue.

[106] *M. F.,* fol. 31a.

[107] *Bet Ḥadash,* no. 2, fol. 2a. Since Sirkes lived in Eastern Europe, his *responsum* is used for comparative purposes.

Cf. MS *Minhagim de-Ḳ.Ḳ. Worms,* fol. 51a: סבלונות; Landau Wachstein, *Jüd. Privatbriefe,* no. 37, pp. 46, 77 (text and trans.): *siblonot* = *brautgeschenke* = "betrothal gift." Cf. in *B. B.* 9:5; *Neziḳin,* IV (*Baba Bathra,* II, Son. edit.), 628, nn. 6–8, *siblonot* = *dona sponsalitia.* On the morning following the betrothal the groom would send gifts to the bride. The gifts could not be reclaimed if a divorce or death of the bride occurred before marriage.

[108] Munk in *Jubelschrift . . . Hildesheimer,* p. 83 (Hebrew sec.); p. 81, #28 (German sec.). Cf. Grunwald, "Statuten," *MGJV,* XI, 85, sec. 4 (5).

[109] The opinion of the writer. See the custom of the bride wearing new clothes at her wedding: Gaster, *Holy and Profane,* p. 102.

[110] Kaufmann (ed.), *Glikl,* p. 227:

. . . אך לכלה איין חשובי מתנה צו איין וואורף. . . .

aynvorf (aynwurf), Yid. = a wedding gift in addition to the dowry. Cf. *einwurf, darüberwurf* (Ger.). Cf. Ysaye-Landau, "Glossar" (Append. to "Memoiren der Glückel von Hameln"), *MGJV,* VII, 51, cit.; Güdemann, *Gesch.,* III, 119, n. 5.

[111] *N. K. Y.,* fol. 26b, #3, sec. 50 ("Hil. Nesu'in"):

והלילה שלפני החופה עושים סעודה ונקראת סבלונות, ונוהגין שהחתן והכלה אין אוכלין ואין שותין עד אחר ששלחו סבלונות זה לזו וזו לזה.

Ibid., fol. 27a, #4;

ונוהגין להכות בכלי זמר כשמביא הסבלונות ומדליקין מדורות והכל כדי לשמוח החתן והכלה.

[112] Salfeld in *JJGL,* XXIII, 73. The bride's mother would give the groom a belt embroidered with silver. For the kind of gifts that were exchanged, see Koppmann, *idem, Aus Hamburgs Vergangenheit,* II, 251; Abrahams, *Jewish Life,* p. 298, n. 5; B. Picart, *Ceremonies and Religious Customs,* I, 237; Gaster, *Holy and Profane,* p. 87.

Cf. Sartori, *Sitte und Brauch,* I, 98: Guests gave gifts to a newly married couple. Cf. Wuttke, *Deut. Volksaberglaube,* p. 90, #115; p. 196, #291, regarding the German folk belief that the gifts to the bride and groom will have a bearing on their future. If a present is received from a disagreeable person, the first child of the couple will be a boy. Knives, forks, and spoons are not desirable gifts; they can cause the marriage to be a failure.

[113] Eckstein, *Juden . . . Bamberg,* pp. 70–71, #11. See herein, pp. 65–66, that no community was considered to be too small in size to engage a teacher.

[114] Holzer in *ZGJD,* V, 176.

[115] Wachstein, "Wiener Chewra-Kadischa," *MGJV,* XXXIII (1910), 15, #14:

כבר נתפשט המנהג בכל תפוצות ישראל . . . שקורין בלע״ז הענזלין, זולי זעלבש הענזל געלד לקופה של חיוב. . . .

henzlgeld = prob. "handsel money," i.e., initiation fee, entrance money. Cf. *hänselgeld* (Ger.), same meaning. See *henzilgelt:* Halpern, *Taḳḳanot Mähren,* p. 101, #305; also n. 1.

[116] Halpern, *op. cit.,* p. 51, #155; also n. 1.

[117] A. Marmorstein, "Beiträge zur Religionsgeschichte und Volkskunde," *JJV,* II (1925), 358.

[118] Levesohn, *Meḳore Minhagim,* p. 99, sec. 70(1). Cf. *Sefer Maharil* (1556 edit.), fol. 82b, that "the bride wore a veil *(henuma')* on her face." (Akiba Eiger, b. 1761, Eisenstadt, Hungary; d. 1837, Posen; rabbi in Markisch Friedland, West Prussia, 1791-1815, and in Posen, 1815-37.)

[119] Levesohn, *op. cit.,* p. 99, sec. 70(1), cits. As to the custom of married women wearing veils, see Abrahams, *Jewish Life,* p. 304. Cf. Perles in *MGWJ,* IX, 346, cits.; Jastrow, *Tal. Dict.,* I, 348, cits.; Kohut (ed.), *Aruk ha-Shalem* (1882 edit.), III, 325; *Giṭ.,* 7a; *Soṭ.,* 49b; *Ket.,* 15b, 16b. Cf. *Nashim* VI (Son. edit.), 268, n. 48, comment on *Soṭ.,* 49b: Bridal crowns are designed with figures, as for example, the city of Jerusalem. Regarding the Talmudic background of *henuma',* "the crown of victory," see Baron, *Soc. and Relig. Hist.,* II (rev. edit.), 14, n. 14.

[120] Levesohn, *op. cit.,* p. 99, sec. 70(1).

Cf. Mogk, *Deut. Sitten und Bräuche* (ed. Fossler), p. 20: In German communities unmarried and married women would engage in "a tussling contest" after a wedding ceremony to remove the crown of the bride and replace it with the hood worn by married women.

[121] MS *Minhagim de-Ḳ.Ḳ. Worms,* fol. 7a:

הלא לא כתבתי משני דבר׳ קטנה או גדולה או על דעתי הקלושה השפלה רק כאשר ראיתי נוהגין ומה ששמעתי מאנשי סגולה, שהיו נוהגין כן והוא מנהג ישן נושן כי כן המנהג מתחלה.

(Courtesy, Department of Oriental Books, Bodleian Library, Oxford.)

Note variation in the wording of the passage in A. M. Habermann, "Customs Pertaining to the Month of *'Adar* in the 'Customs of Worms' by Joseph Yuspa Shammash" (Hebrew), *Sinai: Sefer Yobel* (Jerusalem, 1958), p. 483:

... כי לא כתבתי דבר קטנה או גדולה, ע״פ עצמי לפי דעתי הקלושה והשפלה, רק ראיתי ושמעתי מאנשי סגולה, היו נוהגים כן מנהג הוותיקים ישן נושן כי כן יסד המנהג מתחילה....

(Habermann used the MS that was in the possession of A. Epstein. Cf. Epstein, "Die Wormser Minhagbücher" in *Gedenkbuch . . . David Kaufmann,"* pp. 300 ff.; Assaf, *Meḳorot,* I, 117, pref., n.)

[122] Ocksman in *Reshumot,* III, 103. Cf. Perles in *MGWJ,* IX, 346, n. 41; *B. B.,* fol. 60b: Ashes are placed on the head of the groom. That the practice is a sign of "mourning for Jerusalem," cf. *Kol Bo* (1520 edit.), fol. 93b, #75; *Ṭa'ame ha-Minhagim,* I, #957, cit. Cf. Perles, *loc. cit.:* The custom was observed in Poland. Also, *Ṭa'ame ha-Minhagim, loc. cit.,* that the groom wore white garments and the *kitl,* robe, before the wedding ceremony in order to "remember the day of death."

[123] Bergmann in *MGWJ,* LXXVI, 469. From the 10th century on the groom was called to the Torah on the Sabbath preceding his marriage. A special Torah portion was selected for the groom; this procedure was abandoned in European-Jewish communities in the 17th century, but it continued in the Orient.

Regarding the silk mantle worn on the Sabbath, see p. 91, n. 50; and for the mourner's hood, pp. 94–95, n. 71.

[124] Holzer in *ZGJD,* V, 179, which is apparently a paraphrase of Yuspa

Shammash, *Minhagim . . . Worms*. Cf. *J. M.*, II (Bk. 6, chap. 37), 341, #1, concerning the cowl worn by the mourner. See Abrahams, *Jewish Life*, p. 203: "In Germany the bridegroom wore a cowl—a typical mourning garb."

Cf. *Sefer Maharil* (1556 edit.), fol. 82b: When the celebration on the Friday before the wedding terminates, the groom is escorted to the synagogue and the mourner's hood, *mitron*, is placed on him. (For *mitron*, cf. *mitra* [Lat.] "miter, head-covering.") Cf. Samuel Krauss, "Kleidung" (sec. "Im Mittelalter"), *EJ*, X (1934), 106, cit.; 107; Güdemann, *Gesch.*, III, 121, n. 5, that the hood is attached to the mantle, and during the wedding ceremony the groom wore the hood as if in mourning. Note the use of the mourning cowl in the general German community.

Cf. Kaufmann (ed.), *Glikl*, p. 99, n. 1: The hood (קורפוטז ; cf. *kapuze*, Ger.) is worn in the winter. See also, herein, p. 94, n. 64. Cf. also *kapuze* in Landau, *MGJV*, VII (1901), 31. Term in *Glikl* may be *korpots*; see Kluge-Götze, *Wörterbuch*, p. 350, under *kapuze*: earlier form = *ka(r)poets* (Dutch).

Cf. Wuttke, *Deut. Volksaberglaube*, p. 206, #312; pp. 206-7, #31; p. 346, #558; *HDA*, IV (1931-32), p. 153, #2: It was the belief of the German folk that a joyous occasion, such as a wedding, was threatened with tragedy. The apprehension of death was apparent at marriage festivities, for special precautions would be taken not to permit the joyous event from being disrupted either by arousing the anger of the "evil spirits" or by negligence in exercising control over them. See *HDA*, IV, 148, #1; 153, #2; 154, #2, for some general practices in warding off any threat of death during the marriage celebration. The bride and groom, for instance, visited the graves of their relatives before their wedding. See p. 188, n. 213. No marriage ceremony would be held while there was an opened grave in the cemetery. During the wedding every available chair was occupied, so that Death could not take a seat and bring harm to the couple.

125 *Sefer Maharil, op. cit.*

126 Freudenthal, "Wormser Gemeinde," *ZGJD*, V (1935), 107; Shiper, *Yid. teater*, I, 56–57, 157–58; III, 61. See herein, p. 108, n. 100. For examples of wedding songs, see Berliner, *Deut. Juden, im Mittelalter*, p. 53; S. Weissenberg, "Jüd. Hochzeit," *MGJV*, XV (1905), 65 f. Cf. *Sefer Maharil, op. cit.*: The community torch-light wedding procession on the Friday before the wedding included musicians. Cf. Salfeld in *JJGL*, XXIII, 76, for a summary account of the German-Jewish wedding ceremony in the 14th century, based on the Maharil, Berliner, Güdemann. Also, the description of a wedding procession, in 1729, which included the carrying of flags: R. Hallo, *Jüd. Volkskunst in Hessen*, p. 22.

The features of the marriage ceremony (for instance, the procession led by musicians; the bride with the *henuma'*, veil over her face; the groom wearing the mourner's hood; the *badḥan*, jester) are illustrated in portraits of German-Jewish life in the Middle Ages. See Fig. 5, p. 30; Liebe, *Judentum in deut. Vergangenheit*, p. 108, fig. 88; "Fries: Mittelalterliche Judenhochzeit," *Menorah*, VI (Vienna, 1928),

326; Rabinowitz (ed.), *Glikl,* bet. pp. 20-21, 60-61; Feilchenfeld (ed.), Glückel, bet. pp. 184-85, 192-93; Shiper, *op. cit.,* I, 200.

Cf. Mogk, *Deut. Sitten* (ed. Fossler), p. 19: The marriage in Germany was celebrated with "song, minstrel, and dance."

[127] Shiper, I, 157-58; also cf. 68-70, 73-74. For the possible origin and meaning of *marshelik, marshallik,* "jester," see Abrahams, *Jewish Life,* p. 214, n. 1.

[128] *Ḥavvot Ya'ir,* no. 205, fol. 194b-195b. Cf. Freudenthal in *ZGJD,* V, 107, cit.

[129] Kaufmann (ed.), *Glikl,* p. 147: . . . *ayn toytn-tants (toytntants). . . .* Cf. *toytn-tants* (Yid.), "dance of the dead." Cf. *todtentanz* (Ger.) in *ibid.,* n. 4. Cf. *meysim-tants* (mod. Yid.).

[130] Grimm, *Deut. Myth.,* III, 709. Cf. Feilchenfeld (ed.), *Glückel,* p. 121, n. 13; Rabinowitz (ed.), *Glikl,* p. 63, n. 1, that the dance was of Christian origin and first presented in churches. Cf. Hans Holbein, the younger (d. 1543), *Dance of Death,* esp. pl. 5, p. 5 ff., for the artist's interpretation of the *todtentanz.* See a portrait of the *danse macabre* in Vaillat, *Histoire de la danse,* bet. pp. 76–77; also in Koppman, *idem, Hamburgs Vergangenheit,* II, 241, 259, the description of the mourner's hood worn during a *todtentanz,* in Lübeck.

[131] Sachs, *Hist. of the Dance,* pp. 253-54; Gleichen-Russwurm, *Gotische Welt,* p. 237; Böhme, *Gesch. des Tanzes in Deutschland,* I, 322-24; Vaillat, *op. cit.,* pp. 80–81; Shiper, III, 16–17, 23.

[132] Gleichen-Russwurm, pp. 243-44. Cf. Böhme, I, 60, 322 ff.; Shiper, III, 73, n. 1; 74, n. 1.

[133] Feilchenfeld, *op. cit.;* Rabinowitz, *op. cit.* Cf. Lowenthal (ed.), *Glückel,* p. 99, n. 5: Masks were worn during the dance. The popularity of the dance is also suggested by M. Grunwald in *MGJV,* III (1898), 39.

[134] Rubin, "Dance of Death, *danse macabre*" (Hebrew), *Ha-Shaḥar,* VIII (1873), 3. The musical notes for the dance are in Böhme, II, 186, no. 305.

[135] Rubin, *op. cit.,* VIII, 3.

[136] Wachstein, "Pinkas Runkel," *ZGJD,* IV, 139, #35.

[137] *Derushe ha-Zelaḥ,* no. 23, fol. 35b, #19. Cf. B. Z. Katz, *Rabbanut, Ḥasidut, Haskalah,* I, 196, n. 142. See the admonition of Sheftel (Sabbatai) Horowitz in his Ethical Will, which opposed the dancing of opposite sexes: "If you dance face to face Satan dances between you." The traditional opposition to mixed dancing is in *Sefer Ḥasidim,* #168. The precaution taken by rabbinic authorities to prevent men and women from associating freely is affirmed in *'O. Ḥ.* 529:4. Cf. *Paḥad Yiẓḥak,* VI (1885), fol. 145a: "Riḳḳud."

[138] Shiper, III, 69; also note cits. See pp. 33–34, n. 103, with regard to the father dancing with his daughter.

[139] Eckstein, *Juden . . . Bamberg,* p. 71, #12. Cf. *Y. 'O.,* #368. Hahn criticizes the boisterous conduct that is engaged in at public drinking-places and at work,

and he may imply that German drinking-habits have been influencing Jewish social life. For further criticism of the people's behavior, both in eating and drinking, see Mordecai Kosover, "Jewish Foods" (Yiddish), *Yuda A. Yoffe-bukh,* p. 103, n. 331, based on *Ḳ. Shelah.* Cf. the account of drinking practices in Germany, in Haendcke, *Deut. Kultur,* pp. 254 f., 260. Cf. Baron, *Community,* II, 306, that ". . . boisterous family festivals in part compensated for general lack of amusements and the drabness of life."

[140] Kaufmann in *Ḳobeẓ 'al Yad,* VII, 7, #12.

[141] Kaufmann, *op. cit.;* Eckstein, *op. cit.*

[142] *S. H.,* II, 13b.

[143] *Ibid.,* 17b. Cf. Shatzky, Intro., *S. H.,* II, 36; Erik, *Gesh. fun yid. lit.,* p. 308.

[144] Cf. in Güdemann, *Gesch.,* III, 139, n. 4, the behavior of wealthy, influential German-Jewish men in the 18th century. During meals they would drink heartily from large glasses, toast each other, and then break the glasses after they had been emptied. Their conduct was criticized, and a general appeal was made against participating in such gatherings. (The source cited by Güdemann, namely, *Ḥavvot Ya'ir,* 47a, could not be confirmed by the writer.) And as it was suggested, evidently this pattern of conduct was not unique to the Jewish community: cf. Bax, *German Cultur,* p. 126; Schultz, *Deut. Leben,* I, 167-68. Cf. Elzet, "Customs in Jewish Life" (Hebrew), *Reshumot,* I, (1918), 354-55, #40, cit.; Güdemann, *Gesch.,* III, 122, for the German custom of breaking a glass after drinking. At the wedding ceremony, the breaking of a glass was a sign of virility. Cf. herein pp. 29–30, n. 84.

[145] Cf. Paul in *Grundriss der german. Philologie,* XII, 286-87; Taylor in *Stand. Dict. of Folklore* (Funk and Wagnalls), I, 448, for the relation of death and burial practices to Germanic folklore.

[146] *J. M.,* II (Bk. 6, chap. 37), 341, #1. It is an ancient Jewish regulation that "a dead body should not remain overnight without burial." Cf. *Sanhed.,* 46a-b, based on *Deut.,* 21:23; also the observance of immediate burial as stated in *S. H.,* I, 70b; *Ḥavvot Ya'ir,* no. 11, fol. 17a; *Ḥatam Sofer,* no. 338, fol. 136b (sec. "Y. D."). Cf. Zimmels, *Magicians, Theologians, and Doctors,* p. 57, n. 196. See also Gaster, *Holy and Profane,* pp. 142, 169, for popular ways of thinking associated with the immediate burial of the dead.

[147] Cf. Eisenmenger, *Entdecktes Judenthum,* I, 876; *idem,* The Traditions of the Jews (trans. Johann Stehelin), I, 227. Cf. "Ba'er Heṭeb," comment no. 2 on *lishpokh: Y. D.* 339:4. See also Grunwald in *MGJV,* I, 81, n. 7; Hirschowitz, *Minhage Yeshurun,* p. 311, sec. 73, #2. Cf. Wuttke, *Deut. Volksaberglaube,* p. 430: After the funeral, mirrors and pictures were covered with a white cloth, and "the water cask was overthrown," the reason being that "the soul of the dead person had bathed in it, and whoever drank from it would die the same year." See pp. 121–22 in this volume.

148 *J. M.*, II (Bk. 6, chap. 37), 351, #10.

149 Cf. "Be'er ha-Golah" comment no. 8 on *Y. D.* 339:4; *Pes.*, 3b, that whoever informs others of death by means of a verbal statement "causes evil tidings." Cf. also Eisenmenger, *op. cit.*, I, 879; *idem*, Eng. trans., I, 227.

150 N. Cohen, *Ẓavva'ah,* fol. 7b, #6. Cf. *ibid.*, fol. 7b, #1: The Society was known as *Ḥebra' Ḳaddisha'* (Holy Society, Brotherhood), *Ḳabranim* (Grave-diggers), and *Gomle Ḥasadim* (Men Who Do Kindness). See Abrahams, *Jewish Life,* p. 357, n. 3: "This title *Ḥebra' Ḳaddisha'* was also used in a generic sense, of any society formed for a religious purpose." The Holy Society performed various communal tasks, such as, caring for the sick, aiding the poor, dispensing bridal dowries, administering schools, preparing and conducting burial. Cf. MS (microfilm), *Ḥebrah Ḳaddisha' de-Biḳur Ḥolim . . . be-Ḳ. Ḳ. Altona,* fol. 1 (fols. not numbered), in which the *Ḥebrah Ḳaddisha'* of Altona (established in 1701 and reorganized on 7 *Tammuz,* 1823), defines as its aim:

. . . ואת הדרך אשר ילכו אצל משכן לנפטר, [אל] ב״ה [בית העולם] זו קבורה ללות את המת עד קברו ואת המעשה זו צדקה שיתנו לחולאים. . . .

(Courtesy, YIVO Institute for Jewish Research.)

See in Marcus, *Communal Sick-Care,* pp. 55 ff., 95ff., the historical background of the Holy Society and the social and cultural influences in its development. The activities of the Holy Society are described in detail in Güdemann, *Quellen.*, p. 301 (Supp. III, Frankfort communal record, 1662); Horovitz, *Frankfurt. Rabbin.*, II, 42; Cohn, *Das Eschweger Memorbuch,* p. 14; Eckstein, *Juden . . . Bamberg,* p. 97; *Festschrift . . . Chevra Kaddischa zur Königsberg (1704-1904)*, sec. on by-laws (Supp. II); Wachstein, "Wiener Chevra Kadischa," *MGJV,* XXXIII (1909), 99; Friedländer, *Tiferet Jisrael,* pp. 103, 105; L. Weisel, "Prager Juden," *BSV,* XVII (1926), 209; Mayer, *Wiener Juden,* p. 154; Schay, "'Chewra Kadischa' in Pressburg," *ZGJT,* III^2 (1933), 73, #1; *Taḳḳanot Ḥaberet Baḥurim de-Ḳ.Ḳ. Eisenstadt* (Constitution of the Society of Young Men of Eisenstadt, 1867), sec. 1, p. 1; sec. 6, p. 3.

(Note: There is no uniformity in spelling or transliterating the term *Ḥebrah Ḳaddisha'*. Hence, each time, the author has followed the usage occurring in a given text or source.)

For the tradition of visiting the sick and burying the dead, see *Y. 'O.* (1723 edit.), Pt. 2, fol. 187b (sec. "Biḳur Ḥolim"); *'Olelot 'Efrayim,* fol. 105–106a; Chajes, *'Aṭeret Ẓebi,* fol. 21b; *Pe'ah* 1:1.

See Mogk, *Deut. Sitten* (ed. Fossler), p. 25, as to the responsibility of the general German community for burial of the dead.

151 Cf. herein pp. 147–48; Abrahams, *Jewish Life,* pp. 66–67. The fine (above, p. 29), which is consistently mentioned in local legislation, also served to enforce communal regulations and practices.

MS *Ḥebrah Ḳaddisha'*, fol. 2, sec. 10: A member of the *Ḥebrah Ḳaddisha'* of Altona would be fined three shillings if he failed to visit the sick whenever the sexton called upon him:

ומי שמשיב לשמש שלא יוכל לבוא מחויב ליתן קנס שלשה שיל.

(Courtesy, YIVO Institute for Jewish Research.)

Cf. also Halpern, *Taḳḳanot Mähren,* p. 81, #244, concerning the authority that the Societies of Gravediggers *(Ḥaburot Ḳabranim)* had in enforcing their legislation.

[152] Cohen, *Ẓavva'ah,* fol. 7b, #21. Cf. MS *Pinḳas Ẓavva'ot* (Copies of Ethical Wills), Fürth, 1787-1819: Fürth VII), p. 4 (no folios, single pages): R. Leyb Bass, in his Ethical Will (1780), declares that his family "should not accompany his body to the grave" but "remain at home and recite the *ḳaddish* in the customary manner."

. . . ועל כל זרעי בכלל הריני גוזר בגזירת אב לבנים שלא להתלות אחר מטתי כלום אופן,
רק יהיו בביתי עד זמן סתימת הגולל לאמור קדיש כנהוג.

(Courtesy, Hebrew Union College-Jewish Institute of Religion Library Cincinnati.)

Cf. the custom of carrying the body to the grave in Kaufmann (ed.), *Glikl,* p. 259; Feilchenfeld (ed.), *Glückel,* p. 240; Lowenthal (ed.) *Glückel,* p. 210. Cf. *Ẓemaḥ Ẓedeḳ,* no. 42, fol. 40b: In 1646, Jews living in Nikolsburg accompanied the body of a deceased person to Vienna where the funeral was held. See p. 140, n. 190, of this volume with regard to communal concern for burying the dead.

[153] *Y. 'O.* (1723 edit.), fol. 191a. Cf. Press in *MGWJ,* LXXVI, 576. Cf. "mourner's meal" in Jastrow, *Tal. Dict.,* I, 192, under ברי (Hiphil), "to offer refreshment"; *Mo'ed Ḳaṭan* 3:7; fol. 24b.

[154] Cf. *Y. D.,* 378:1. See J. R. Marcus, "Triesch *Ḥebra Ḳaddisha,*" *HUCA,* XIX (1945), 197: It was the practice in the 18th century for the *shammash* to buy refreshments which were served to the mourner.

[155] Bergmann in *MGWJ,* LXXVI, 468.

[156] *Y. 'O.,* Intro., fol. 4a (1723 edit.); Intro., xii (1928 edit.). Cf. Horovitz, *Frankfurt. Rabbin.,* II, 12, n. 4; Gotthard Deutsch, "Ḥebra Ḳaddisha," *JE,* VI (1904), 299. Cf. *Ber.,* 18a: If one watches over a dead person, he is exempted from performing the precepts of the Torah, and if he does not accompany a burial, he is committing a blasphemy. Cf. also comment of "Bertinoro" on *Pe'ah* 1:1: "The practice of good deeds" was equated with "visiting the sick and burying the dead."

See herein p. 12, n. 70; Horovitz, III, 71, of instances when Jews participated in fairs. Cf. Abrahams, *Jewish Life,* p. 234, n. 2; *Ḥavvot Ya'ir,* fol. 230a: "When I [Bacharach] was 24 years of age, I delivered a sermon during the Frankfort fair before the multitude, and my words met with their satisfaction."

[157] As it will be noted, the outlook of *musar* was expressed in particular by Elḥanan Kirchan, Ẓebi Kaidanover, Yeḥiel Mikhel Epstein, as well as in communal legislation. Criticism of the decline of Jewish educational standards is dealt with on p. 50, n. 2; pp. 73–78, p. 82.

[158] *Y. 'O.* (1723 edit.), Intro., fol. 4a; Intro. (1928 edit.), p. xii.

[159] Cohen, *Ẓavva'ah,* fol. 8a. See below, n. 165. Cf. ref. to the Ethical Will of Eliezer b. Samuel ha-Levi of Mainz (d. 1337), in Eisenstein, *'Oẓar Yisra'el,* IX (1913), 17: The family was instructed to study a page of the Gemara when they recited the *ḳaddish* on the anniversary of his death. The *ḳaddish* alone was not to be said, he emphasized, but should be combined with the study of Talmud.

Cf. MS *Pinḳas Ẓavva'ot* (Copies of Wills, Fürth, 1787-1819: Fürth VII), p. 5, the Ethical Will of Frumet, the widow of Zechariah Frank (14th of *'Elul,* 1786):

בני התורני הר״ר זעקל סג״ל שי׳ זולי לתועלת נשמתי טוהן כמו מיר לבעלי המנוח זצ״ל גטוהן הבין דהיינו שיקח יו״ד לומדים כטוב בעינינו ללמוד עבורי בין מיתה לקבורה עד שיסתום הגולל ובני ר׳ זעקל שי׳ הנ״ל יאמר קדיש ויתן לכל א׳ וא׳ מלומדים הנ״ל טית פֿין ומעזבוני צו בצאהלין.

fin = prob. related to *pfennig,* "the one hundredth part of a mark." In Ethical Wills, communal minutes, and legislation, it was not unusual that Yiddish should be used simultaneously with Hebrew as in the above passage. *(Courtesy, Hebrew Union College-Jewish Institute of Religion Library, Cincinnati.)*

[160] Katzenellenbogen, *Ẓavva'ah,* fol. 4b.

[161] Cohen, *Ẓavva'ah,* fol. 9a, #23, #25. He mentions that, as compensation, a hundred books should be given from his library. Cf. Kaufmann (ed.), *Glikl,* p. 201:

. . . מיר האבין תכף מנין קבועה גיקראגין נון מלמדים דיא מיר דאז גנצי שנה בישטעלט האבין צו לערנין בביתי יום ולילה. . . .

Cf. MS *Pinḳas Ẓavva'ot* (Wills, Fürth, 1787-1819: Fürth VII), p. 2, #9:

תוך השלשים אחרי מותי זוללין עשרה אנשים לומדים בחדרי לערנין אונד מנוחה נכונה וקדיש זאגען, ומסוף שלשים עד תום י״ב חדשים ילמדו גימ״ל אנשים כנ״ל. . . .

MS *ibid.,* p. 5:

וכל רביעש שנה זולין גימל לומדים א׳ פרק משניות לערנין בבית בני ר׳ זעקל הנ״ל. ויאמרו מנוחה נכונה ויאמר בני הנ״ל קדיש עליו. וכל רביעת שנה זולי בני ר׳ זעקל הנ״ל ג׳ לומדים אחרים נעמין צו לערנין ויתן לכל אחד ואחד כנ״ל מעזבוני א׳ קויפענר ר״ט עד תמו י״א חדשים אחר העברי.

koypener (Yid.) = "copper"; cf. *kupfergeld* (Ger.) = "copper coin or money."

MS *ibid.*:

וביום יאהר צייט ראשון אהר העברי יקח בני ר׳ זעקל הנ״ל יו״ד לומדים וילכו על קברי ויאמרו מנוחה ויתן לכל א׳ חי׳ צ״ל.

(Courtesy, Hebrew Union College-Jewish Institute of Religion Library.)

Cf. *'Erub.,* 46a; *Ḥavvot Ya'ir,* no. 201, fol. 192b; *She'elat Ya'abeẓ* (Lemberg, 1884), II, no. 35, fol. 18b; Kaufmann (ed.), *Glikl,* pp. 200-201, 203, for instances of the seven and thirty days mourning periods.

[162] Cohen, *op. cit.,* fol. 9, #22, #26.

[163] Cohen, fol. 8b, #18; *M. F.,* 29a; *Ḳ. H.,* 6:2-5, 7-8; 87:5; Güdemann, *Gesch.,* I, 202; Eisenstein in *'Oẓar Yisra'el,* IX, 17.

Cf. *Ḥavvot Ya'ir,* no. 92, fol. 89a, in which Bacharach relates: " . . . I visited the graves of my parents; may they find rest in their graves." Cf. *Ma 'aseh ha-Ge'onim,* p. 48, #58, that the soul of the departed is in mourning during *shib'ah* and requires the consolation of the living to assuage its grief and restlessness.

164 Kaufmann (ed.), *Glikl,* pp. 34-35; Feilchenfeld (ed.), *Glückel,* pp. 21-22; Rabinowitz (ed.), *Glikl,* pp. 13-14; Lowenthal (ed.), *Glückel,* pp. 12-13; B. Z. Abrahams, *Glückel,* p. 20.

165 *Y. 'O.,* p. 327.

166 *Y. 'O.,* p. 328. Cf. Grunwald in *MGJV,* I, 95, n. 1.

Cf. Cohen, fol. 8b, #16–17: "I am to be placed in a coffin that I provided. . . . Inasmuch as I am a priest and a first born, I shall be buried in a perfect [i.e., solid] coffin." See Abrahams, *Jewish Life,* p. 145: Coffins for rabbis were made of the tables that they had used for study or for the meal when indigent strangers were invited to their homes. Likewise in Cohen, fol. 8b, #19, that each individual acquired burial ground on the cemetery. Cf. *Ḥavvot Ya'ir,* no. 11, fol. 17a: "It therefore became the practice for each person to acquire his burial-place in order to prevent any delay of burial." Also, Cohen, fol. 8b, #18: "At the time of the funeral, put my book, *Birkhat 'Adonai* [pub. as vol. I in *Semikhat Ḥakhamim* of which he was the author: Frankfort, 1704] on the coffin; let it remain there until the grave is reached. Do not place it in the grave." Cf. *Y. D.,* 353:2; 362:1.

167 "Ethical Will" in *Ẓavva'ot ve-gam Dibre Ḳedoshim,* p. 4, #3.

168 Cohen, fol. 8b, #17; Katzenellenbogen, *Ẓavva'ah,* fol. 5b.

169 *Y. 'O.,* p. 327. The reason for the practice is not stated. In the opinion of the writer the intent was to avoid placing the "evil eye" in an advantageous situation where a strange woman could tempt a man. A funeral is one of the occasions when demons will venture to undermine human stability.

170 Cohen, fol. 9a, #24. Cf. in *N. K. Y.,* fol. 10a, #6 (sec. "Hil. 'Abelut") the custom of burning a candle for the departed during the week of mourning.

Cf. Güdemann, *Gesch.,* III, 132; Abrahams, *Jewish Life,* p. 157, n. 2; *Ket.,* 103a: Before his death R. Judah ha-Nasi requested that the light that he had been using should "continue to burn in its regular place." Cf. in Landau and Wachstein, *Jüd. Privatbriefe,* no. 18b, pp. 26, 46, n. 5 (text and trans.) the custom of burning a *Yom Kippur* light *(Yom Kippur-likht)* and a *yortsayt* light *(yortsayt-likht)* on the Day of Atonement. The *Yom Kippur* light, symbolizing "the light of life," was burned for the living; the *yortsayt* light, representing "the light of the soul," was for the deceased (Prov. 20:27). Only a single *yortsayt* light was used on the anniversary of a death. For the observance of *yortsayt,* the anniversary of the passing of a parent, see above, n. 159; *N. K. Y.,* sec. 10, fol. 20a. Also, in Halpern, *Taḳḳanot Mähren,* p. 159, #471 (Lundenburg, 1697); *Ẓemaḥ Ẓedeḳ,* fol. 3b (Index to no. 25): *yortsayt.*

171 *N. K. Y.,* fol. 10a, #6.

There is evidence that after the week of mourning a candle would be lit in the synagogue in memory of the departed person. Cf. MS *Pinḳas Ẓavva'ot* (Wills, Fürth, 1787-1819: Fürth VII) p. 2, #9:

וגם אחרי מותי עד כלותי י״ב חדשים נר תמיד דרט ענין [*sic*] לוזן [*sic*]. . . .

Cf. also MS *ibid.*, p. 5:

נר של שעוה יודלק בשעת תפלת שחרית וערבית ומנחה בחול בבה״כ של ר׳ בערמן זצ״ל משך י״א חדשים. . . .

(Courtesy, H. U. C.-J. I. R. Library.)

[172] *M. F.*, fol. 14a, #83, #90; *Ẓemaḥ Ẓedeḳ*, no. 25, fol. 23b-24a: Lots would be cast to decide the order of reciting the *ḳaddish*. The mourner said *ḳaddish* alone, not jointly with other persons as is the custom today. Cf. *ḳaddish*, mourning customs in *Ḥavvot Ya'ir*, no. 201, fol. 192b.

[173] *Ḥavvot Ya'ir*, no. 222, fol. 208a:

. . . דבר זה נעשה באמשטערדם ומפורסם שם, שאחד נעדר בלי בן וצוה לפני פטירתו שילמדו עשרה כל יום תוך י״ב חודש בביתו בשכרם ואחר הלימוד תאמר הבת קדיש. . . .

In communities with a *Ḥebra' Tehillim* (Society to Recite Psalms), the *ḳaddish* would be said at the end of the study session. Cf. *Pene Yehoshua'*, I, no. 5, fol. 3a (see, "*'O. Ḥ.*").

[174] *Ḥavvot Ya'ir, op. cit.*

The attitude of the authorities in the Amsterdam Jewish community may have been influenced by the Enlightenment movement. Cf. Baron, *Soc. and Relig. Hist.*, II (1st ed.), 207-12, for a description of the Enlightenment in Holland during the 17th century.

[175] *Ḥavvot Ya'ir, op. cit.:*

. . . מ״מ יש לחוש שע״י כך יחלשו כח המנהגי׳ של בני ישראל שג״כ תורה הם ויהיה כל אחד בונה במה לעצמו ע״פ סברתו. . . . ומנהגין של ישראל תורה וצריך חיזוק כמבואר בגמ׳ יבמות דל״ו ע״ב. . . .

Cf. *Yebamoth*, I (*Nashim*, I, Son. edit.), 227, n. 8, on fol. 36a: "One has no right to give instructions which are contrary to the principles of the Torah. . . ."

[176] See pp. 15, 43, 123–24, 142, 175.

[177] *M. F.*, fol. 16a, #98. The garment referred to was probably *shtorts;* perhaps an "overgarment," "a cape."

Cf. *Ḳ. H.* 30:9, in which Kaidanover criticizes those who fail to show their parents proper respect when they pass away: ". . . No sooner do their parents die, they make new black garments of costly material, and engage in celebrating. . . ." See cit. in Schochat, "Integration of German Jews within their non-Jewish Environment . . . First-Half of the 18th Century" (Hebrew), *Zion*, XXI (N. S., 1956), 213, n. 37; *idem* (Shohet), *'Im Ḥillufe Teḳufot*, p. 53, n. 34.

[178] *M. F.*, fol. 16a, #98. Cf. *Y. D.*, 392:2; *'E. H.*, 13:1, that a mourner does not remarry until at least three months have elapsed.

[179] *M. F.*, fol. 15b-16a, #97.

For mourner's garments worn in Germany, see Wuttke, *Deut. Volksaberglaube,* pp. 300, 742; Sartori, *Sitte und Brauch,* I, 63, 129, the mourner's hat; 148, the mourner's cloak.

[180] Weinberg, "Memorbücher," *Menorah,* VI (1928, Vienna), 697 ff.; also p. 708, concerning the place of the *memorbuch* in Jewish cultural history. Cf. Berliner, *Deut. Juden im Mittelalter,* p. 109.

[181] *Maharil* (Warsaw, 1874), fol. 22a (sec., "Shabu'ot"), marginal comment; Weinberg in *Menorah,* VI, 697; Meisl, "Memorial Book of the Community of Halberstadt, 1695" (Hebrew), *Reshumot,* III (1947), 181, n. preceding text; Adolph Neubauer, "Le memorbuch de Mayence," *REJ,* IV (1882), 1 ff.; Weinberg, "Wesen des Memorbuches," *JJLG,* XVI (1924), 310-11. For the observance of this custom in Coblenz, Frankfort, Worms, Halberstadt, Cologne, etc., see Salfeld, *Martyrologium des Nürnberger Memorbuches,* pp. 1 ff.; Meisl *loc. cit.,* 181; Aaron Yellenik, "The Memorbuch of Worms, 1696" (Hebrew), *Ḳobeẓ 'al Yad,* III (1887), 8; Ocksman in *Reshumot,* III, 101.

[182] Cf. in Neubauer in *REJ,* IV, 18 ff., the list of martyrs of Nuremberg, 1298; also, Yellenik, *Ḳobeẓ 'al Yad,* III, 3, 5-7. Cf. Salfeld, *op. cit.,* pp. 73-77: The community of Worms commemorated the martyrs of the Black Death, Adar 2, 1349. Note further how martyrs were memorialized in the account of Moses (Moshe) Stern, "Vienna Memorbuch" (Hebrew), *Festschrift . . . Berliner's,* 119-20.

Weinberg in *Menorah,* VI, 701-702, explains that after the expulsion of the Jews of Vienna, in 1670, the *memor*-book of Vienna, written in 1633, was joined to the Fürth *memor*-book.

[183] Meisl, *op. cit.,* 181; Stern in *Festschrift . . . Berliner's,* pp. 125-26. Cf. Weinberg in *JJLG,* XVI, 306, 312, 315, after the Black Death, 1348-50, individual martyrs were remembered and the *memor*-book then included both martyrology and necrology. Martyrs of each age were added. Thus, the Fulda and Fürth *memor*-books included martyrs of the Chmielnicki pogroms in 1648.

[184] Weinberg in *JJLG,* XVI, 310-11.

[185] See Intro., p. xv.

[186] Meisl, *op. cit.,* 182, #3; 183, #3, #6; 185, #23-24. #29-30; 187, #42, #45; 190, #73; 191, #77; Horovitz, *Frankfurt. Rabbin.,* II, 103-4 (Supp. II); III, 90, n. 2 (Supp. II, 4); Marcus Brann, "Grabschriften," *MGWJ,* LXVI (1902), 560; Löwenstein, "Juden in Fürth," *JJLG,* VI (1908), 217-19 (Supp. II).

[187] Auerbach, *Israelit. Gemeinde Halberstadt,* pp. 21, 81; J. Cohn, *Eschweger Memorbuch,* pp. 12-13, n. 2; Kaufmann-Freudenthal, *Familie Gomperz,* p. 17, n. 1; p. 37, n. 1; p. 279, n. 1; Kaufmann (ed.), *Glikl,* p. 294, n. 1; *idem, Urkundliches aus dem Leben Samson Wertheimers,* p. 118; Meisl *op. cit.,* 187, #40, #42; 189-90, #68; 190, #73; 191, #75, cit.; Eckstein, *Juden Bayreuth,* pp. 66-67, 69; Stern in *Festschrift . . . Berliner's,* pp. 125-26.

Cf. Y. Sosis, "Counter-Social Legislation of the 16th and 17th centuries, based on *Responsa*" (Yiddish), *Zeitschrift*, I (Minsk, 1926), 222 ff., concerning the role of the influential lay-leader. Cf. in *Ya'arot Debash*, II, fol. 14a, a eulogy delivered for a *parnas*, communal leader. Cf. Jaroslav Rokycana, "Häuser des Jakob Bassevi von Treunberg," *ZGJT*, I^3 (1931), 254, for an example of the rise of the Jewish mercantilist. After 1623, Bassevi purchased his own homes in the *gas* of Prague. Previously, the homes were under the jurisdiction of the Prague *Altstadt*.

188 *M. F.*, fol. 4b, #20; 6a, #30; *N. K. Y.*, fol. 70, #4 (sec. "Rosh ha-Shanah"); *Ḳ. Shelah*, fol. 60b (sec. "Rosh ha-Shanah"). Cf. *Maharil* (Warsaw, 1874), fol. 37b, sec. "Rosh ha-Shanah": ". . . On the eve of *Rosh ha-Shanah* everyone goes to the cemetery and prostrates himself on the graves of *ẓaddiḳim*, righteous men. . . ."

Ḳ. Shelah, op. cit.: "Grass is plucked from the grave and stones were placed by the tombstone as a sign of respect, showing [thereby] that the grave has been visited."

N. K. Y., fol. 67a, #9 (sec. "Tish'ah be-'Ab"): Kosman states that the cemetery would be visited on *Tish'ah be-'Ab* after completing the service. No doubt this was a local custom of Frankfort.

189 Cf. Naphtali Cohen, *Ẓavva'ah*, fol. 9b, in which he assures his family: "If it is at all possible for us to do so, I shall pray in your behalf before the Throne of Glory." Also, Meisl, *op. cit.*, p. 190, #73, that the dead can be "a righteous defender"; Stern in *Festschrift . . . Berliner's*, p. 120, that the merit of martyrs will protect the poor and gain "mercy from God for the remnant of Israel. . . ." Cf. *Soṭah*, 34b; *Ta'anit*, 16a, 23b, for instances during the Talmudic period when graves were visited and the dead were appealed to by the living. See cits. in J. D. Eisenstein, "Views and Customs concerning Death," *JE*, IV (1903), 486. With regard to the custom of visiting the cemetery to "call upon" the deceased, see Baron, *Community*, II, 154.

190 *Shelah*, I, fol. 213b (sec. "Rosh ha-Shanah").

191 Cf. S. Weissenberg, "Das Feld- und das Kejwermessen," *MGJV*, XVII (1906), 39, 41-42.

192 *N. K. Y.*, fol. 49a, #1 (sec. "Ḥilluḳe ha-Parshiyot").

193 *Shelah, op. cit.* That it was a popular practice "to measure" the cemetery grounds during illness, see Grunwald, "Aus Hausapotheke und Hexenküche," *MGJV*, V (1900), 60, n. 201. See the general folk practice of visiting graves to heal the sick: Black, *Folk Medicine*, pp. 96-97.

Cf. the description of "measuring" and "encircling the ground with rope" in time of illness: *Sefer Ḥasidim* (ed. Margulies), #478; *Mas. Semaḥot* (ed. M. Higger), Intro., sec. 2, p. 77, cit.

194 *Shelah*, op. cit.:

... כמ״ש באגודה פרק ואלו מגלחין מעשה באשה אחת שחלה בנה והקיפה העזרה ....

The citation from *Sefer ha-'Aguddah*, by Alexander Suslin ha-Kohen (see Bibliography, p. 347), is not in *'Elu Megalleḥin* (relating to *Mo'ed Ḳaṭan*, chap. 3, fol. 14a ff.), but in *Semaḥot*, fol. 172a, col. 2, no. 3, which states:

מכאן נראה שנהגו להקיף בית הקברות:

Suslin derived his example from Tract. *Semaḥot*, chap. 6, fol. 46a. In the Talmudic passage (cf. *Mas. Semahot*, ed. M. Higger, p. 134; also n. 35) a daughter, not a son, is ill. The mother refuses to leave the cemetery until she is given the assurance that her daughter will be well. (Note: Since *'Elu Megalleḥin*, in *Sefer ha-'Aguddah*, precedes *Semaḥot* and heads the page, it is understandable how an error in the citation could have been made by Suslin.) For the background and historical precedents in "encircling the cemetery," see Higger (ed.), *op. cit.*, Intro., sec. 2, pp. 75-77.

Cf. *N. K. Y.*, sec. 300, fol. 40b, #32 ("Hil. Shabbat"), that charity would be given "in behalf of the deceased." Cf. *Sukkah*, 49b: The ". . . acts of loving kindness are for both the living and the dead." As another example that the act of giving charity is beneficial to the deceased, cf. MS *Pinḳas Ẓavva'ot* (Wills, Fürth, 1787-1819: Fürth VII), p. 2, #9:

. . . ובין מיתה לקבורה יחלקו ח"י גלט בין עניים לטובת נשמתי.

(Courtesy, H. U. C.–J. I. R. Library.)

The efficacy of charity is discussed further, p. 55, n. 31; p. 103, n. 63.

195 Kracauer, *Judengasse in Frankfurt*, p. 336; Ocksman in *Reshumot*, III, 100; Dubnow, *Weltgeschichte* (Hebrew edit.), VIII, 170; Hülsen, *Judenfriedhof in Frankfurt*, p. 10.

196 *Ḥavvot Ya'ir*, no. 92, fol. 89a. See p. 188, n. 212, the example from the *Mekhires-Yosef-shpil* of Joseph going to the grave of his mother Rachel to ask for her help in his plight when he was sold as a slave.

197 Meir ben Barukh, *Responsa* (Lwów, 1860), no. 164, fol. 13a. Cf. Berliner, *Deut. Juden im Mittelalter*, p. 119, n. 164; K. Kohler, "Cemetery," *JE*, III (1902), 640, cits. Similar criticism is expressed in *Shelah*, *op. cit*.

198 For instance, see pp. 34–35, n. 12. The attitude of Jewish law and rabbinic authority toward popular practices and "magic" is dealt with more fully in chap. VI, "Folk Medicine: Popular Practices and Remedies," esp. p. 125, n. 76; p. 127, n. 92.

199 Suggested by the general approach of Trachtenberg, *Jewish Magic*. A more detailed explanation of the social uses of "magic" is undertaken in our study, pp. 117–22; also nn. 48–50.

NOTES TO CHAPTER III

1 See Baron *Community*, II, 169; also above, pp. 57–58, 63, 66, 71. As to the relation of education to Jewish communal life, in addition to Baron,

op. cit., chap. 13, see Holzer in *ZGJD,* V (N. S., 1935), 173; Horovitz, *Frankfurt. Rabbin.*, III, 86-87; Jacob Katz, *Massoret u-Mashber*, pp. 213-14; Eng. trans., *Tradition and Crisis,* pp. 183-84.

[2] See in J. Katz, *op. cit.*, chap. 21; Eng. trans., *op. cit.; Shohet, 'Im Ḥillufe Teḳufot*, chap. 5, for the reasons institutions such as education were already weakening their ties with Jewish society before the advent of the modern era. See also in this volume pp. 73–81.

[3] Originally, the father was the sole teacher of the child, before schools were established in Talmudic times. Cf. *Ḳid.*, fol. 29b; also *Soṭ.*, 22a. See also *Ḳiddushin* (*Nashim,* VIII, Son. edit.), n. 8 to p. 140; Baron, *op. cit.*, II, 169-70.

[4] *Vave ha-'Amudim* (Append. to *Shelah,* II), Intro., fol. 2b. Also, chap. 5, fol. 9b.

As examples, in the Middle Ages, of the father being urged to teach his son and grandson, see *Maḥzor Vitry* (ed. Hurwitz, 1923), p. 628, #508, n. 1; "Hil. Tal. Torah," *M. T.* 1:2; *Y. D.* 245:1 (sec. "Hil. Tal. Torah"); *Kol Bo* (Venice, 1547), fol. 85a, #74. That the home in the Middle Ages was a center for educating the young, cf. Berliner, *Deut. Juden im Mittelalter,* p. 10. With regard to the role of the mother in encouraging the education of her children, see Alexander Marx, "Seventeenth Century Autobiography," *JQR,* VIII (N.S., 1917-18), 270; Regina Lilienthal, "Kind," *MGJV,* XXVI (N. S., 1908), 48.

[5] *Brandshpigl* (Frankfort, 1676), sec. 1; fol. 1a (no fol. mark). Cf. *ibid.*, sec. xv, fol. 1a (no fol. mark): . . . *un lernt di kindr (kinder)*. . . .

[6] *Ibid.*, sec. viii, fol. 1b (no fol. mark).

[7] *Y. 'O.*, Pt. 2, fol. 159b, sec. "Limmud Banim Ḳeṭanim" (1637 edit.); p. 283 (1928 edit.).

[8] *Brandshpigl,* sec. xv, fol. 1a (no fol. mark), beginning with: . . . *vi zi zikh zol far haltn (farhalten) im oyz (hoyz)*. . . . Also, Marx in *JQR,* VIII, 270.

[9] *Y. 'O.*, p. 283. Cf. *Ḳid.* 30a, based on Deut. 11:19. Cf. the parent as teacher: *Shelah,* I, fol. 181a (sec. "Shabu'ot"). See also the grandfather as a teacher at home in Stern, *JJLG,* XIX, 43.

For Hahn's views on education and child guidance, cf. *Y. 'O.*, Pt. 2, pp. 263-91. See the summary of Hahn's method of education in Güdemann, *Quellen.*, pp. 181 ff.; Horovitz, *Frankfurt. Rabbin.*, II, 14-15; Kracauer, *Juden in Frankfurt,* II, 277; Strassburger, *Gesch. der Erziehung,* pp. 107-8. For the family's part in educating a child, see J. Katz, *op. cit.*, pp. 214-15, n. 1; Eng. trans., pp. 184-85.

[10] *She'elat Ya'abeẓ* (Altona, 1739), I, Pref. (no pag.). In *Leḥem Shamayim* (Jerusalem, 1958), Pref. p. 6, Emden also recognizes the influence that his father had on him as teacher.

[11] *Y. 'O.*, p. 280. A similar method of instruction is outlined by Maimonides: *M. T.*, "Hil. Tal. Torah," 1:6. Cf. among others *Sukkah* 42a: When a minor "is able to speak, his father must teach him Torah [i.e., Deut. 33:4] and the reading of

the Shema'." Cf. also *Sifre,* fol. 37a, col. 145, Par. "'Eḳeb," on Deut. 11:19, '... As soon as the child begins to speak ..., his father should teach him Torah." Cf. *M. T.,* "Hil. Tal. Torah" (Mosad Harav Kook edit., 1957), II, 85, n. 4. That this practice was continued through the years, see Friedländer. *Tiferet Jisrael,* p. 14: In Moravia children were taught prayers as soon as they commenced to speak. Cf. the advice by Jonah Landsofer in his "Ethical Will," *Derekh Ṭobim,* fol. 8b-9a, #15, to teach children how to recite and read prayers: "And do not neglect to give whatever time is necessary, even if it amounts to a full year. . . ."

[12] *Y. 'O.,* p. 280 (sec. "Giddul Banim"). Cf. the gloss of Isserles on *Y. D.,* 255:8 (sec. "Hil. Tal. Torah"): "As soon as the child is three years of age, he is taught the letters of the Torah. . . ." Isserles's statement is based on Abravanel's commentary on *Pirḳe 'Abot.* Cf. Isaac Abravanel, *Naḥalat 'Abot* (Constantinople, 1505), fol. 52b (commenting on *'Abot* 5:21), that the child is taught the alphabet at three years of age. By comparing the child to a tree, he is, at three years of age, *'orlah* (Levit. 19:23-25); hence the fruits of his learning are not to be eaten until he is five, when he begins to read the texts of Scripture.

[13] *Y. 'O.,* p. 284.

[14] *Ibid.,* p. 283.

[15] *Ibid.,* p. 281. Children accompany their parents to the synagogue on the Sabbath, festivals, and participate in the observances; for *Simḥat Torah, Ḥanukkah,* and *Purim* the children have their own forms of group activity: Grunwald in *MGJV,* XI, 11-12, #28-29; Güdemann, *Gesch.,* III, 112; Assaf, I, 118; *idem,* "Erziehung: Im Mittelalter," *EJ,* VI (1930), 750-51; J. Katz, *op. cit.,* pp. 214-16; Eng. trans., pp. 184–86. See in this volume, pp. 59, 62; also, Löw, *Lebensalter,* pp. 129–30: The parent teaches the child to practice charity.

[16] *Y. 'O.,* p. 283. Hahn explains that this practice is due to the fact that the children of Frankfort are weak; in other communities the boy begins to fast at eleven years and the girl at ten. This is another example of a variation in a custom because of local factors. Hahn does not explain why Frankfort children are weaker. Cf. Landsofer, "Ethical Will," *Derekh Ṭobim,* fol. 11b, #23: Originally sages married at eight years of age, later at 15, and then at 18, as their physical strength declined, and they required a longer period of time to reach maturity. Cf. the *responsum* of Emden, *She'elat Ya'abeẓ* (Altona, 1739), I, no. 14, fol. 33b, that the age of a girl's marriage is determined by her physical development, not chronological age.

[17] *Y. 'O.,* p. 279.

[18] *Ibid.,* p. 280.

[19] *Vave ha-'Amudim,* chap. 5, fol. 9b. Similar counsel was given at an earlier period; cf. comment on *'Avot* 5:21 in *Pirḳe 'Avot* (misc. collection of commentaries from medieval sources; no author, Cracow, 1657); *Sefer Ḥasidim* (ed. Wistinetzki), p. 201, #801; Assaf, *Meḳorot,* I, 70, sec. 40, cit. See also Berliner, *Deut. Juden im*

Mittelalter, p. 9, that the child should be educated according to his abilities. (Henceforth Assaf, *Meḳorot* = Assaf.)

[20] MS *Worms Minhagim* in Assaf, I, 119, sec. 56, #6, also n. 4. Cf. *Shebut Ya'aḳob,* I, Pref., fol. 1a: While recognizing the validity in using "the rod and strap" by a member of the court to enforce law, "corporal punishment" in the home is described as an outmoded practice. Note the contrast in *Maḥzor Vitry,* p. 628, #508: "When the child is taught for the first time [in school], at the start he is pacified, and toward the end [of the session] the strap [is used] on his back." This practice is also mentioned by Maimonides, *M. T.,* "Hil. Tal. Torah," 2:2.

[21] Holzer in *ZGJD,* V, 173; Güdemann, *Gesch.,* I, 104; Assaf, I, 22, sec. 11, #1; IV, 7. See Moritz Stern, "Jugendunterricht in der Berliner jüd. Gemeinde . . . 18. Jahrhund.," *JJLG,* XIX (1928), 39. See also Assaf, *Meḳorot,* IV, Intro., 6, cit.: At the age of three the child is sent to a private teacher.

[22] Cf. *Maḥzor Vitry,* p. 628, #508; *Kol Bo,* fol. 85a, #74; Zunz, *Zur Gesch.,* p. 167; Bamberger in *JJV,* I, 331, n. 1; Friedländer, *Tiferet Jisrael,* pp. 14-15, cit.

[23] Cf. *Maḥzor Vitry,* p. 628, #508; *Kol Bo,* fol. 85a, #74.

[24] *Ḳ. H.* 72:7; *Y. 'O.,* p. 283; Holzer in *ZGJD,* V, 173. See *Y. 'O., loc. cit.:* The father has the responsibility of accompanying the child to school, and in doing so, he imitates King Hezekiah of Judea, who would carry his child on his shoulders, and also R. Ḥiyya bar Abba and Rab Ḥuna.

[25] *Ḳ. H.* 72:8. Cf. Trachtenberg, *Jewish Magic,* p. 82: The German cabalists of the early Middle Ages believed in releasing "mysterious powers" by "combining and recombining" the "letters of the Hebrew alphabet." The popular views of the 13th century must have had an influence on the outlook of Kaidanover and his contemporaries.

[26] *Ḳ. H.* 72:9. Cf. *Maḥzor Vitry,* p. 628, #508; *Kol Bo,* fol. 85a, #74. See Zunz, *op. cit.,* pp. 167-68, n. a. to p. 169; Bamberger in *JJV,* I, 331-32, nn. 1-2.

[27] *Ḳ. H.* 72:7. Cf. *Maḥzor Vitry,* p. 628, #508; *Kol Bo,* fol. 85a, #74. Also, Zunz, p. 168; Bamberger in *JJV,* I, 332, n. 2. See Schauss, *Lifetime of a Jew,* pp. 101-2, for the customs of the Middle Ages observed when a child first attended school.

[28] Zunz, p. 168; Bamberger in *JJV,* I, 332. Usually, the cake is a "honey cookie," called *honigkuchen* (Ger.); prob. *honig-kikhel* (Yid.).

[29] Berliner, *Deut. Juden im Mittelalter,* p. 142.

[30] Friedländer, *Tiferet Jisrael,* p. 15. See herein p. 102, n. 53. See Zunz, p. 169, n. a.; *'Aruk ha-Shalem,* VII (1891), 114: *kalir,* a cookie named for R. Eleazar Kalir, noted medieval *payṭan,* composer of liturgical poems, who had "regained his sight" by eating "a cookie on which was written the inscription of an amulet."

[31] *Ḳ. H.* 72:9. Through the centuries, the day on which a child started school was celebrated with a festive meal: *Maḥzor Vitry,* p. 628, #508; *Kol Bo,* fol. 85a, #74. Cf. the description of the meal in Zunz, p. 167, n. a.; Bamberger in *JJV,* I,

331, n. 1; Friedländer, *op. cit.*, pp. 14-15. Among the Jews of Moravia it was not the practice to hold a celebration when a child began school.

For the other occasions when festive meals were arranged, see pp. 20, 29, 36, 55, 61, 103, 178.

See p. 103, n. 63. regarding the custom of inviting the poor to a meal. The giving of charity to the poor is considered a "good omen" and one of the ways of warding off "evil spirits." See Trachtenberg, *Jewish Magic,* pp. 157 ff. Also, herein p. 48, n. 194.

32 *Y. 'O.*, p. 284. As Hahn states, the custom is based on a Midrash (no source cited). Cf. this practice in Bamberger, *JJV,* I, 331, n. 1; Assaf, I, 22.

33 Sabbatai Horowitz, "Ethical Will," in *Ẓavva'ot . . . Dibre Ḳedoshim,* fol. 5b, #27. Cf. this custom in *Maḥzor Vitry,* p. 618, #508; *Kol Bo,* fol. 85a, #74; *Sefer Ḥasidim* (Basel, 1591), #1140. See also Zunz, n. a. to p. 169.

34 Sabbatai Horowitz, *op. cit.,* fol. 4b, #22. See "Bibliography," below, p. 351; Abraham Sheftel Horowitz, the grandfather of Sabbatai (Sheftel) Horowitz, is the author of *'Emeḳ Berakhah.*

In the general community special power was attributed to the book; for instance, a book would be placed under the pillow of a child to prevent him from becoming bewitched: Seligmann, *Der böse Blick,* II, 302.

35 *Lev. R.* 7:3 (Sid. "Zav").

36 Cf. *Gen. R.* 3:5; *Song of Songs R.* 5:12; also Intro., p. 1, to *Sifra: Torat Kohanim* (Petrokov, 1911); Intro., pp. 1-2, to *Sifra de-Be Rab* (Breslau, 1915).

37 *Y. 'O.*, pp. 280-81.

For the meaning of *baḥur,* see Güdemann, *Quellen.*, p. 113; *idem, Gesch.*, III, 62 f.; Landau-Wachstein, *Jüd. Privatbriefe,* no. 18b, pp. 26, 46 (text and trans.): *baḥur* = *schüler* = student; Fishman, *Jewish Education,* p. 29, *baḥur* = "a fully-fledged student," who serves as a tutor to two "junior students," *na'arim*. Cf. Löw, *Lebensalter,* pp. 123-24, #8-9, for the etymology of *na'ar* and *baḥur;* in the 17th cent. the *baḥur,* the *yeshibah* student, had a respected position in the community. And also Halpern, *Taḳḳanot Mähren,* p. 2, #3, #4 (Gaya, 1650). (Loc. of Gaya [Kyjou, mod. sp.]: in southern Moravia. In 1688, Gaya had twelve houses of Jewish residents, and in 1727, under Charles VI, it became an independent municipality. See Moritz Bauer, "Gaya," *JE,* V [1903], 576.)

To "study Torah for its own sake" *(Torah li-shemah),* with "no selfish end," devoid of "ulterior motives," is an ideal since ancient times: cf. *Sanh.*, 99b, Pes., 50b, and others. See Jastrow, *Tal. Dict.* II, 1590: *shem*. Also *Sanhedrin,* II (*Neziḳin,* VI, Son. edit.), 675, n. 1.

38 *Minhagim of Worms,* Assaf, I, pp. 117-18, sec. 56, #1, with excerpts from MS *Yuspa Shammash,* based on two recensions, one of which Güdemann used. Cf. Güdemann, *Quellen.*, Pt. 2, p. 218, for excerpts from MS Yuspa Shammash; also Holzer in *ZGJD,* V (N. S.), 173. Also, Fishman, *Education,* p. 82, n. 57. (Hereafter cited only as Fishman.)

[39] Güdemann, *Quellen.*, p. 218 (text), p. 221 (trans.), from MS *Yuspa Shammash;* also Assaf, I, 117-18.

[40] Cf. Strassburger, *Gesch. der Erziehung,* p. 155: The elementary school was called *ḥeder* since the classes were usually held in "one room." Cf. the example of a *ḥeder* in Vienna, 1660: *J. M.*, I (Bk. 5, chap. 4), 350, #11. See herein, p. 57.

[41] Assaf, I, Intro., xix.

[42] Cf. *'Olelot 'Efrayim,* Pt. 3, sec. 486, fol. 99a, #3.

[43] *Ḥavvot Ya'ir,* fol. 116b.

[44] *Shelah,* I, 181a:

... לעולם ישלש אדם שנותיו שליש במקרא שליש במשנה שליש בתלמוד....

Cf. the stages in the education of a child in Sabbatai Horowitz, "Ethical Will," *op. cit.*, fol. 5b, #27.

[45] *Ḳid.*, 30a. According to Rashi (commenting on "days" in *ibid.*), the week is to be divided into three parts for each of the subjects. Maimonides states that each day should be divided into three separate parts to engage in such study: *M. T.*, "Hil. Tal. Torah," 1:11–12; also n. 9 to 1:11 (Mosad Harav Kook edit.).

[46] Halpern, *Taḳḳanot Mähren,* p. 6, #14 (Gaya, Moravia, 1650); p. 182, #524 (1) (Konitz, Moravia, 1713); Wolf, *Mähren Statuten,* Pref., p. vi; p. 4, #14; p. 127, #2, Assaf, I, 137, #14; IV, 7. See instances of "obligatory schooling" in the European Jewish community: Baron, *Community,* II, 175. Also, J. Katz, *Massoret u-Mashber,* p. 220; Eng. trans., p. 189, that the "minimum age for starting work ... generally ranged between thirteen and fifteen."

[47] Munk in *Jubelschrift ... Hildesheimer,* p. 81, the regulation of 1690 (Hebrew sec.). Cf. Assaf, IV, Intro., 7, legislation of the 18th century.

[48] Munk in *op. cit.*, p. 77, #14 (Ger. sec.).

[49] M. Grunwald, "Jüd. Waisenfürsorge," *MGJV,* LXVI (1922), 19, n. 79; Wolf, *Mähren Statuten,* p. 4, #15; Assaf, I, 137, sec. 60, #15. See in Grunwald, *op. cit.*, 20 ff., other instances of the community assuming responsibility for the orphan.

[50] Cf. Halpern, *Taḳḳanot Mähren,* p. 6, #15; p. 182, #524 (communal legislation of Gaya, 1650; Konitz, 1713).

Cf. Schultz, *Das häusliche Leben,* pp. 183 ff., 199 ff., 218: In the general German community, there was no comparable educational opportunity, or concern, for the populace. The children of nobility and burghers were "the educated classes." The average peasant was illiterate, and the extent of his education usually comprised the catechism and church songs taught by the clergy. Cf. Henne am Rhyn, *Kulturgeschichte,* II, 208: Following the Thirty Years' War, educational reforms were introduced in Germany; the *Volksschulen* replaced the Latin schools and the vernacular—usually German, sometimes French—became the language of instruction.

[51] Assaf, I, 137, #14; IV, Intro., 7; Wolf, *op. cit.*, p. 4, #14. In the period of the Maharal, the *Taḳḳanot* of Moravia states that if a student has shown little

promise, he should nevertheless study the Prayer Book, the Pentateuch, and Prophetic Portions *(Hafṭorot)*, as well as reading and writing in the Yiddish vernacular. Cf. Güdemann, *Quellen.*, Pref. p. xxii; and p. 69, this volume.

52 See p. 66, n. 113, as to the effect of economic difficulties on education.

53 Assaf, IV, Intro., 7; Munk in *op. cit.*, pp. 76-77, #14 (Ger. sec.).

54 *Y. 'O.*, p. 282:

...ובפרט פה עמנו שהעשירים משיאים בניהם כבני י״ד ט״ו שנה שראוי לאב לשכור לבנו מלמד גם אחר נשואיו ... שיש להם כמה שנים מזונות על שלחן אביהם וחמיהם....

Cf. J. Katz in *Zion*, X (N.S. 1946), 25, n. 28. Wealthy families could provide more easily for their children to continue to study after marriage. See chap. II, n. 80 to p. 29. The age of marriage is not the same for all periods. That after his marriage, the groom and his family are supported by his father-in-law, cf. *Naḥalat Shib'ah* (Amsterdam, 1667), I, no. 8, fol. 17a; no. 9, fol. 31b, #8-9; Dubnow, *Pinḳas ha-Medinah*, p. 40, #190; p. 75, #379; Kaufmann (ed.), *Glikl*, p. 68. See *kest:* B. Z. Abrahams (ed.), *Glückel*, p. 38, n. 1. See also Marx in *JQR*, VIII, 270; Landau-Wachstein, *Jüd. Privatbriefe*, no. 3a, pp. 4-5, 8-9 (text and trans.); Baron, *Community*, II, 175; J. Katz in *loc. cit.*, 25, nn. 27-28.

55 See pp. 60–61; also p. 53, n. 15. Cf. Assaf, I, 117–18, sec. 1; 121–22, sec. 6; Fishman, pp. 82–83.

56 See pp. 189–90.

57 Assaf, I, 118. Cf. H. Ehrentreu, "'Pilpul' in den alten Jeschiboth," *JJLG*, III (1905), 216, for the kinds of social relationship that the student could have with the adult community.

58 Cf. the account of *Bar Miẓvah* in Löw, *Lebensalter*, p. 210 f.; Abrahams, *Jewish Life*, p. 160.

59 Gaster, *Holy and Profane*, p. 67.

60 Güdemann, *Gesch.*, III, 111-12.

61 Rivkind, *Le-'Ot u-le-Zikkaron: Bar Mitzvah, A Study in Cultural History*, pp. 17, 19.

62 Löw, *Lebensalter*, p. 211.

63 Kohler, "Bar Miẓwah," *JE*, II (1902), 509. Cf. *'Abot* 5:21, that "the age of thirteen [is] for [the fulfilling of] the commandments." See a similar view in D. J. Bernstein, "Bar Mizwa," *EJ*, III (1929), 1035; Leopold Neuhaus, "Barmizva," in Thieberger (ed.), *Jüd, Fest*, pp. 426–27.

64 Solomon Schechter, *Studies in Judaism*, I, 307, 312. Cf. Rivkind, *op. cit.*, p. 16, n. 10. For the physical characteristics of puberty, see *Niddah* 6:11; fol. 52a.

65 Rivkind, p. 16, n. 12.

66 Cf. *'Eben ha-Shoham*, no. 26, fol. 13a: A father wishes to confirm the proper wording of the benediction that he is to recite during the *Bar Miẓvah* ceremony of his son *(. . . 'im yeborekh be-shem u-malkhut. . . .)*, and asks whether

it should be: "Praised be He who has released me from being responsible for this one." Cf. "Confirmation: Conduct of Life," *RCC,* cit. Cf. the gloss of Isserles on *'O. Ḥ.* 225:2: The father makes no mention of "the name of God or His kingdom" in the benediction. Isserles disagrees with the *Maharil* (Warsaw, 1874), fol. 63a, and Mordecai Jaffe, *Lebush,* I (on *'O. Ḥ.*), 214:1, who uphold a differing opinion.

[67] MS *Yuspa Shammash* in Assaf, I, 120, sec. 4. Also, *Y. 'O.*, p. 357: Cf. Grunwald in *MGJV,* XI, 48, #152; Rivkind, pp. 29-30.

[68] *Yuspa Shammash* in Assaf, I, 120, sec. 4.

[69] *Yuspa Shammash* in Assaf, I, 118, #1.

[70] Grunwald in *MGJV,* XI, 48, #152.

[71] *Yuspa Shammash* in Assaf, I, 120. Cf. cit. of *Worms Minhagim* in Holzer, *ZGJD,* V, 173: "For being called to the Torah, he should make a contribution of candle wax to the synagogue." Cf. chap. VII, p. 162, n. 87, concerning the communal tax that is levied on individuals to furnish tallow for the reading-light of the cantor. Cf. *Zikhron Yosef,* no. 5, fol. 6b (sec. "'O. Ḥ."), that it also was a custom for the husband to donate wax to the synagogue when his wife had a successful childbirth. The wax was given "as an exchange for her life."

[72] *Worms Minhagim* in Holzer, *ZGJD,* V (N. S.), 173.

[73] *Yuspa Shammash* in Assaf, I, 118, #1.

[74] *Ḳ. H.* 21:8. Cf. "Ba'er Heṭeb," n. 4 to *'O. Ḥ.* 225:2.

[75] *Yuspa Shammash* in Assaf, *op. cit.* For a summary of the main characteristics of the *Bar Miẓvah* Sabbath, cf. *Y. 'O.*, p. 357.

[76] *Ḥavvot Ya'ir* no. 123, fol. 115b-116a. See *Shabbat be-Shallaḥ,* chap. VII, p. 178. Cf. the *Bar Miẓvah* feast and sermon in Löw, *Lebensalter,* pp. 213–14, 216–17; Rivkind, *Le-'Ot u-le-Zikkaron,* pp. 40 ff., 47 ff. The address, delivered at the meal by the youth, probably became an established part of the *Bar Miẓvah* festivities between the 16th and 17th centuries: Löw, *op. cit.,* p. 216, n. 86; p. 222; Abrahams, *Jewish Life,* p. 148. See Rivkind, p. 40, that the first *Bar Miẓvah* sermon to be published was that of Lentshits, as in n. 144 to p. 71, chap. III.

[77] *Ḥavvot Ya'ir,* no. 123, fol. 116a. Cf. *Y. 'O.*, p. 271, who listed the important *sifre musar,* ethical writings, as: *Sha'are Teshubah* (by Jonah of Gerona [Gerondi] d. 1263); *'Orḥot Ẓaddiḳim* (anonymous, 15th cent., Germany; first pub. in Prague, 1581); *'En Ya'aḳob; Menorat ha-Ma'or* (by Isaac Aboab, ca. 1320), and Midrashim. (Note that the *Menorat ha-Ma'or* was translated into Yiddish by Moshe Frankfurt, 1722.)

[78] Kaufmann (ed.), *Glikl,* p. 231:

...בני ר׳ יוסף סג״ל איזט באותו פעם איין יונגיר מן י״ד שני׳ גיוועזין, גאר איין פיין קינד
אונ׳ גאר וואול גילערניט אלזו העט איך אים גערין הין וועק גשיקט צו לערנין ....

Cf. Feilchenfeld (ed.), *Glückel,* p. 206. "Mein Sohn Joseph war damals ein Junge von vierzehn Jahren; er war ein sehr feines Kind und hat sehr gut 'gelernt.' Darum hatte ich ihn gern zum 'Lernen' weggeschickt . . ."

For further examples of students attending school away from home, cf. Fishman, p. 21, n. 32; Assaf, I, 135, #4, #5; Landau-Wachstein, *Jüd. Privatbriefe,* no. 35, pp. 44, 74 (text and trans.). Marx in *JQR,* VIII, 278, 291 (text and trans.); J. Katz, *Massoret u-Mashber,* pp. 217-18; Eng. trans., p. 187; Halpern, *Bet Yisra'el be-Polin,* II, 270, sec. 40.

79 Suggested by Wolf, *Mähren Statuten,* p. 1, #2.

80 Kaufmann (ed.), *Glikl,* p. 231 f.; Feilchenfeld, 206 f.; Lowenthal, p. 180 f.; Ysaye, "Glückel von Hameln," *MGJV,* VII (1901), 15; Fishman, *op. cit.,* pp. 20-21, n. 31; Marx, *op. cit.*

81 Marx in *op. cit.,* 278-79, 291 (text and trans.).

82 *Ibid.,* 278, 291.

83 Cf. the description of the *yeshibah* in Strassburger, *Gesch. der Erziehung,* p. 155; J. Katz, *op. cit.,* pp. 223–25; Eng. trans., pp. 192–93. See herein p. 65.

84 Halpern, *Taḳḳanot Mähren,* p. 2, #5; p. 3, #6 (Gaya, 1650); Assaf, I, 134, #3; 136, #13; Güdemann, *Gesch.,* III, 102; Fishman, p. 33.

85 Strassburger, pp. 155-56.

86 See chap. III, p. 72.

87 Güdemann, *Quellen.,* p. 260, #19 (*Taḳḳanot* of Nikolsburg):

כמו כן מי שמחזיק בחדר שלו חמשה בתולות אינו רשאי ללמוד חומש עם נערים.

Cf. Fishman, pp. 118-19, n. 4. See Wachstein, "Pinkas Runkel," *ZGJD,* IV (1932), 136, #17, that the remuneration given to the teacher in an elementary school was for "both boys and girls." For other instances of the education of women in Germanic-Jewish communities, cf. also Fishman, pp. 118–21.

88 Kaufman (ed.), *Glikl,* p. 24:

. . . זייני קינדיר זוא וואול זין אלש טעכטיר לאזין לערנין במילי דשמיא ובמילי דעלמא. . . .

Cf. Feilchenfeld, p. 14; Eng. cit. from Lowenthal (ed.), *Glückel,* p. 6. Also, Fishman, p. 118, n. 3; Erik, *Yid. lit.,* p. 395. (Hereafter cited only as Erik.)

Kaufmann, p. 26:

. . . אונ׳ אליש איין קינד דאז אין חדר האט זיטצין מוזין. . . .

Cf. Feilchenfeld, p. 17: ". . . als ich noch im Cheder. . . ." And, Ysaye in *MGJV,* VII, 5. Cf. S. Adler, "Entwicklung des Schulwesens der Juden zu Frankfurt a. M.," *JJLG,* XVIII (1926), 167-68: Girls learned to read and write, and were taught at home or attended school. See also Kaufmann in *JQR,* III (O. S., 1891), 294, the example of an educated woman who knew Hebrew, Aramaic, the Bible, Midrash, *'agadah,* and liturgy.

89 *Sifte Yeshenim,* I, Intro., fol. 6a, #9. In explaining why he includes Yiddish books in his "Bibliographical Manual," Sabbatai Bass states that Yiddish serves as a common language. Translations into Yiddish made literature available to the public, especially to women and children. See examples of the literature read by women, in Tsinberg, *Gesh. fun der lit.,* VI, 162-63, 180-81, 197; Erik, pp. 36-37; Minkoff in *Jewish People,* III, 158, 160, 162; Lowenthal, *op. cit.,* Pref., pp. xxix-xxxi.

Concerning the spread of the "pocketbook" after 1600, see Erik, p. 214; Steinschneider, "Volkslitteratur der Juden," *Archiv für Litteraturgeschichte*, II (1871), 2-4, 14; *idem, Jewish Literature*, p. 224.

[90] Schechter, "Memoirs of a Jewess," in *idem, Studies in Judaism* (Second Series), p. 138. Cf. Fishman, p. 120. See also the educational background of Glikl in Erik, p. 36.

[91] Cf. Kaufmann (ed.), *Glikl*, pp. 9-13; p. 238, n. 1. Glikl was familiar with *musar* works and had a knowledge of medieval folk tales. See Adler in *JJLG*, XVIII, 167, that young women read, in Yiddish, popular literature. Cf. Erik, p. 51, 261, 353-55: Tales were usually taken from the *Mayse-Bukh*, a collection of folk tales, Talmudic, mystical, and of local color that were popular in the Middle Ages. Cf. Jakob Meitlis, *Ma'assebuch*, pp. 38-40, 44. In the 18th century the *Mayse-Bukh* was widely read and published in at least 12 editions with new material being added. For instance, in the Frankfort edit., 1703, there was incorporated a group of tales of cabalistic influence expressing the Messianic hopes of the Sabbatai Ẓebi movement.

[92] Kaufmann (ed.), *Glikl*, p. 199. Cf. Feilchenfeld, p. 177; Lowenthal, p. 151, n. 2.

[93] *Sifte Yeshenim*, fol. 6a, #9. See Berliner, *Deut. Juden im Mittelalter*, p. 12, for a summary of the education Jewish women received in Germany to prepare them for life. They were urged to read ethical works. That girls were made acquainted with the ritual and laws of Jewish tradition, see Adler in *JJLG*, XVIII, 167. As an example of the *musar*-book explaining to the woman her religious duties, cf. Brandshpigl, sec. 11; sec. 13, esp. fol. 2a (no fol. mark).

[94] Cf. Haarbleicher, *Gemeinde in Hamburg*, p. 37.

The administration of the school is outside the scope of this account; further detail can be found in Baron, *Community*, II, 170 ff., 185ff.; Fishman, pp. 15 ff.; J. Katz, *op. cit.*, pp. 219-20; Eng. trans., pp. 188-89.

[95] See localized cultural areas, chap. V, p. 105, n. 73.

[96] Güdemann, *Quellen.*, Pt. 2, p. 255, #1; Assaf, I, 138, #1, also n. 1. Cf. Wolf, *Mähren Statuten*, p. 1, #1: A communal regulation of Moravia specifies that the school should have at least twelve pupils, divided into two groups consisting of six older and six younger students. See the standard of Maimonides, *M. T.*, "Hil. Tal. Torah," 2:5, that at no time should a teacher teach more than twenty-five pupils.

Cf. also *J. M.*, I (Bk. 5, chap. 6), 366-67, #18. Schudt records a description given to him of the school *(bet ha-midrash, lehrschule)* of Nuremberg: "Above the door was a blue lion with his paw and head on a gilded globe," and "on both sides [of the lion] were Hebrew inscriptions." The *bet ha-midrash* "could also be used as a synagogue." This again illustrates the close relationship of the school to the religious and cultural life of the adult community.

[97] Assaf, I, 138-39, sec. 61, #1-2; Fishman, p. 155, n. 25. Cf. also Nikolsburg *Taḳḳanot* of 1676 in Güdemann, *Quellen.*, p. 256, #2.

[98] Cf. Güdemann, *op. cit.*, pp. 106-108, 124-25; Assaf, I, Pref. xxi; 65, #37, based on Isaiah Horowitz, Solomon Lentshits, and Joseph Hahn. As to the emphasis on Talmudic subjects in the school curriculum, see J. Katz, *op. cit.*, p. 222; Eng. trans., p. 191. With regard to the similarity between the classroom curriculum and the program suggested for individual study as, for example, in this volume, chap. III, pp. 57, 68, cf. *Shelah*, I, 181a; *Y. 'O.*, p. 269; *Ḥavvot Ya'ir*, no. 123, fol. 116b; Landsofer, *Ethical Will*, p. 9, #25-26. Cf. also select. from Landsofer, *Ethical Will*, in Assaf, I, 179, and the "advanced rabbinic curriculum" in Baron, *Community*, III, 168, n. 22.

[99] Grunwald in *MGJV*, XI, 48, #152; Assaf, I, 189, #91. Cf. Horovitz, *Frankfurt. Rabbin.*, II, 53: The *melamed* was expected to teach eight hours in the winter and nine hours in the summer (*Taḳḳanah* of Frankfort, 1684). Cf. also Wolf, *Mähren Statuten*, p. 1, #3; and herein, p. 66, n. 111.

[100] *Y. D.* 245:4; cf. J. Katz, *op. cit.*, p. 218, n. 9; Eng. trans., p. 187. See *rebbi-meyos, rebbi-lon = lehrgeld:* Kaufmann (ed.), *Glikl*, p. 231, nn. 1, 3; also, *rebbi-gelt*, "the fee paid a teacher for instruction": I. Rivkind, *Yid. gelt*, p. 241, sec. 566.

For other instances of parents engaging and remunerating teachers, see Munk in *Jubelschrift . . . Hildesheimer* (Hebrew sec.), p. 181. Three or four parents residing in the same locality *(yishub)* would jointly select a teacher.

[101] See, for instance, Grunwald in *MGJV*, XI, 48, #152; Assaf, I, 189, sec. 91. The *taḳḳanah* states that the *melamed* should receive a maximum fee of four *reichsthaler* for each pupil taught during a school term. Cf. Wolf, *Mähren Statuten*, p. 1, #1: For an older pupil, the teacher's fee is 12 *kreutzer*, and for a younger pupil, 7 *kreutzer*. (A *kreutzer = kreuzer* = 1/60 *gulden*; a *gulden* = about 42 cents.) Cf. also Horovitz, *Frankfurt. Rabbin.*, II, 53, n. 3: During a semester the *melamed* receives 36 *thaler (taler)* for teaching Talmud and 45 *thaler* for teaching Tosafot. (*Taler* = 3 marks, not coined today.) Likewise, Wachstein, "Pinkas Runkel," *ZGJD*, IV (1932), 136, #17: The teacher is to be remunerated according to the amount of time that he spends with a class. The compensation is less for an elementary class, which meets for a half an hour, but more for classes in Bible, Mishnah, and Gemara, which last an hour each.

[102] Grunwald in *MGJV*, XI, 48, #152; Assaf, I, 139, #5.

[103] Assaf, I, 146, #2, n. 3 (*Taḳḳanah* of 1756): *iber-zits ḳinder*. See *iberzetsn* (mod. Yid.), "to put in another seat." Cf. *einsitzen* (Ger.), "to set, place." Cf. *ibid.*, IV, Pref., 7.

[104] Assaf, I, 142, #14 (Nikolsburg *Taḳḳanah* of 1689).

[105] The inter-regional scope of the Moravian Council has already been suggested: Intro., p. xv. See also, Baron, *Community*, I, 338–39; J. Katz, *op. cit.*, p. 151, n. 2; Eng. trans., p. 123.

[106] Halpern, *Taḳḳanot Mähren,* p. 1, #1; p. 5, #12. Cf. Wolf, *Mähren Statuten,* Pref., p. vi; p. 1, #1. Cf. Assaf, I, 134, #1; 136, #12 (*Taḳḳanot* of Moravia, at the end of the 16th cent., which include MS material in Hebrew and Yiddish). For similar legislation in Hesse, cf. Munk in *Jubelschrift . . . Hildesheimer,* p. 81 (Hebrew sec.); Assaf, I, 150-51, #64; IV, Pref., 8-9, n. 6. Cf. Löwenstein, *Juden in der Kurpfalz,* p. 77: In Mannheim each family pays toward the over-all educational program. Cf. also in Halpern, p. 182, #524 (1), the communal legislation of Konitz (Moravia), 1713, that the five communities in the area have the responsibility to establish a *yeshibah.*

[107] Assaf, I, 136, #12 (date and place of the *taḳḳanot* not specified). Cf. Wachstein in *ZGJD,* IV, 136: Those without children were assessed to support educational institutions in the community. It was also recognized by Landsofer ("Ethical Will," *Derekh Ṭobim,* fol. 9b, #17) that there were parents who could not afford to pay the fee of a teacher.

That the community consistently felt that it had an obligation in assisting children of poor parents to secure an education, see Moses Isserles, gloss on *Ḥ. M.* 163:3: ". . . When residents of a city appoint a teacher and parents are not able to pay a fee for the instruction of their children, it is incumbent upon the *ḳahal* (community) to make such a payment [in their behalf]. . . ." Cf. J. Katz, *op. cit.,* p. 219, n. 10; Eng. trans., p. 188.

[108] Halpern, *Taḳḳanot Mähren,* pp. 5-6, #13 (Gaya, Moravia, 1650); Wolf, *Mähren Statuten,* p. 3, #13; Assaf, I, 136, #13. See in chap. II, p. 33; n. 154 to p. 42 for examples of the role of the *shammash* in the community.

[109] *Ḥavvot Ya'ir,* no. 186, fol. 173b.

[110] Assaf, I, 134, #1. See the *yeshibah* in J. Katz, *op. cit.,* p. 217; Eng. trans., p. 187; also in this volume, pp. 58, 66.

[111] As to the support given the *yeshibah* student by individual families and the community, cf. Halpern, *Taḳḳanot Mähren,* p. 3, #6; pp. 5-6, #13; Güdemann, *Gesch.,* III, 102; Fishman, p. 33; J. Katz, pp. 224-26; Eng. trans., pp. 193-94. See the school semesters, herein, p. 111, and in Katz, p. 227; Eng. trans., p. 195.

[112] Assaf, I, 134, #3 (*Taḳḳanot* of Moravia, 16th cent.). Cf. Halpern, pp. 5-6, #13; Assaf, *loc. cit.,* #4; Katz, p. 225; Eng. trans., p. 194: Communities without a *yeshibah* are asked to support those regions where *yeshibot* are maintained.

[113] Cf. Berman, *Toledot ha-Ḥinnukh,* p. 90; Fishman, p. 37, nn. 129, 130; p. 38: Communities economically hard-pressed had limited resources with which to support education. That cultural retrogression resulted from the economic stresses of the period, cf. Ezekiel Landau, *'Ahabat Ẓiyon,* no. 1, fol. 2b, col. 2; Jakob Meitlis, "'Libes Brif': Pre-Haskalah Reform Writing" (Yiddish), *Yivo Bleter,* II (1931), 309, 316 ff., 320 ff; Fishman, p. 136, n. 1; Shohet, *'Im Ḥillufe Teḳufot,* p. 90.

The economic difficulties of the time are dealt with in *Derushe ha-Ẓelaḥ,* no. 23, fol. 35b, #14; Horovitz, *Frankfurt. Rabbin.,* III, 65, n. 2; Wind, *Horeb,* X, 57; B. Z. Katz, *Rabbanut,* I, 77-78, among others.

As an example of the burdens of heavy taxation borne by the people, cf. *Me'il Ẓedaḳah,* Pref., fol. 2a (no fol. mark):

...והעמיד עלינו שרי מסים למען ענותינו קציני׳ שבנו והצליחו והגדילו וברוב עושרם מקבוצת
ממון שאינו שלהם יתהללו ויעשו להם חבור׳ כל איש שוגה ופתי:

". . . Tax collectors have been appointed over us, so that our communal leaders might oppress us; they [the leaders] have prospered greatly. By their immense wealth, an accumulation that is not rightly theirs, they honor themselves. They bring into their company any individual who errs and is foolish. . . ."

114 For instance, cf. Moses Isaac ha-Levi of Złótowó, Posen, "Ethical Will," in *Naḥalat 'Abot* (Frankfort, 1898), p. VIII.

115 *Sefer Minhagim* (Offenbach, ca. end. 18th cent.), fol. 2a. Cf. Landsofer, "Ethical Will," *Derekh Ṭobim,* fol. 9b, #17: "And do not be ashamed to ask him [i.e., a teacher or person who knows more] so as to understand the meaning of the words. . . ."

116 *Y. 'O.,* pp. 265-66. Note similar advice in *Shelah,* I, fol. 181a, 182a. According to ancient rabbinic teaching (as in *Ket.,* 17a; *Meg.,* 3b), study should only be interrupted to perform a charitable act or to bury the dead.

A characteristic appeal that everyone should study, regardless of occupation, is in *Vave ha-'Amudim,* chap. 5, fol. 9b:

על כן מהראוי לכל איש ישראל לעסוק בדברי תורה אפילו בעל משא ומתן יבחר לו שעה א׳
ידוע[ה] מידי יום ביומו. . . .

Cf. Rivkind, "Prague Ordinances" (Hebrew), *Reshumot,* IV (1925), 347, for the custom of setting aside a specific time for daily study. See *'Erub.,* 54b; *'Abot* 1:15 as examples of Talmudic emphasis to designate a "fixed time for study."

117 Landsofer, "Ethical Will", *Derekh Ṭobim,* fol. 12b, #24. Cf. Moses Ḥasid, "Ethical Will," *Derekh Ṭobim,* Pt. 2, fol. 28a, #3.

118 Kaufmann (ed.), *Glikl,* p. 235:

... אונ׳ האט איין אידריר זיין חברה דאז ער גיט לערנין אונ׳ גיט דען היים לביתו ....

Cf. Lowenthal (ed.), *Glückel,* p. 185: "Or they have every one his *chevra* (society) where they study Talmud and then betake themselves home." Furthermore, when Glikl's husband came home from work, he never failed to study: Kaufman, p. 69. Cf. Feilchenfeld, p. 48; Lowenthal, p. 34; B. Z. Abrahams, p. 38.

Seder Tefillah Derekh Yesharah, Pref., 2a (no fol. mark):

אך אין דיא (קהלות) גין דיא (בעלי בתים) אלי טאג לערנן צו מיין (חברה) איין שיעור צו הערן.
דא ווערן גלערנט (ספרים) דיא דא רידן פון (יראת שמים). . . .

Ḥavvot Ya'ir, no. 163, fol. 151a: The "Society of Clothiers" studied daily with a teacher to whom they would submit their problems for his authoritative opinion. Cf. Kaufmann in *JQR,* III (O. S.), 487, n. 1.

119 *N. K. Y.,* sec. 300, fol. 41b, #35 ("Hil. Shab.").

120 Moses Ḥasid, "Ethical Will," *Derekh Ṭobim,* Pt. 1, fol. 19a-b, #12.

121 *Shelah,* I, 182a, *Y. 'O.,* p. 267; *Derushe ha-Ẓelaḥ,* no. 4, fol. 9b, #21.

To study at night was also encouraged by Sabbatai Horowitz: see select. from *Vave ha-'Amudim* in Assaf, I, 69, #39.

That the night is the ideal time for study, according to rabbinic tradition, see *Ḥag.*, 12b; *'Abot de-Rabbi Natan,* chap. 29; *M. T.*, "Hil. Tal. Torah," 3:13; *Menorat ha-Ma'or* (ed. H. G. Enelow), III, Intro., 46, #3; 287-88 (text), "Pereḳ Tal. Torah." Also, *'A. Z.*, 3b.

122 *Shelah,* I, 182a.

123 *Derushe ha-Ẓelah,* fol. 9b.

124 Moses Ḥasid, *op. cit.*

125 *Y. 'O.*, p. 267.

126 *Ibid.*, p. 266. For the practice of study before and after meals, see chap. V, pp. 107–8; chap. VII, p. 159, n. 68.

127 *Ibid.*, p. 268.

128 *Ibid.*, p. 278. Cf. *Ba'er Heṭeb,* comment on *shulḥano:* n. 1, to *'O. Ḥ.*, 262:1: *dugmat shulḥan ha-miḳdash.*

129 *'Amude Shesh,* fol. 23b (sec. "Musar 'Amud ha-Torah"). Cf. Güdemann, *Gesch.*, III, 63; Kaufmann in *JQR,* III (O. S.), 302: Talmudic subjects are the main courses of study for the school and the individual. Cf. also Horovitz, *Frankfurt. Rabbin.*, III, 87-88, Append. II: In the communal *memorbuch,* the scholar Jacob Joshua Falk is described as versed in Bible, Mishnah, Talmud (Babylonian and Jerusalem), halakhic Midrashim, and commentaries. See herein, pp. 65, 69.

130 *Vave ha-'Amudim,* 9b; *Ḥavvot Ya'ir,* no. 123, fol. 116a-b; Moses Ḥasid, "Ethical Will," *Derekh Ṭobim,* Pt. 2, fol. 26a, #13; Landsofer, "Ethical Will," *Derekh Ṭobim,* fol. 5b-6a, #6; fol. 7b, #10; fol. 10a, #18.

Moses Ḥasid, *op. cit.*, Pt. 3, fol. 29a, #6, enumerates the following medieval works as well known and regularly used in his time: *Zohar; Shelah,* by Isaiah Horowitz; *Sefer ha-Miẓvot,* by Maimonides, published with the comments of Naḥmanides; *Megillat 'Ester*, a commentary on Maimonides, *Sefer ha-Miẓvot*, by Isaac Leon Sefardi. Cf. Güdemann, *Quellen.*, p. 138. See also in this volume pp. 82–83.

131 Landsofer, *op. cit.*, fol. 5b, #5.

132 See Erik, p. 294; Minkoff in *Jewish People,* III, 160, 162. See also B. Z. Katz, *Rabbanut,* I, 197: More and more persons were becoming preoccupied with earning a living and had less time for study.

133 Cf. *Y. 'O.*, p. 271, in which Hahn recommends that translations be used for study. Cf. Eliezer Lieberman, *'Or Nogah* (pub. with *Nogah ha-Ẓedeḳ*, 1818), I, 2, #1: ". . . those who have been accustomed to pray in Yiddish *(be-lashon 'Ashkenazi). . . .*" Also, *ibid.*, 4, #4. Regarding the liturgy translated into Yiddish, see Minkoff in *Jewish People*, III, 153–56; also herein, p. 162.

134 Landsofer, *op. cit.*, fol. 5a, #4.

[135] *Ibid.*, fol. 8a, #12. For examples of books published in Yiddish, see p. 58; p. 63, also n. 89.

[136] Cf. Erik, pp. 294-95; also Minkoff in *op. cit.*, 160, as to the popularity of *Leb Tob* among men.

[137] Moses Ḥasid, *op. cit.*, Pt. 2, fol. 28a.

The *Brandshpigl,* one of the popular *musar*-books in Germany in the 17th and 18th centuries, was widely read by women (Bibliography, p. 347) as an ethical guide for personal conduct. See, for instance, *Brandshpigl,* secs. ix, xii, as well as xv cited above, p. 51, nn. 5, 8, in which the woman is told of her obligations to her husband and family. She is to make home life pleasant and cheerful (below, p. 156, n. 54), and likewise have great concern for the education of her children.

[138] Sabbatai Horowitz, "Ethical Will," *Ẓavva'ot . . . Dibre Ḳedoshim,* fol. 4b, #22: "You, my daughters and daughters-in-law. . . . let it be your practice to read the Five Books of Moses *(Ḥumesh, Ḥumash)* in Yiddish *(be-lashon 'Ashkenazi)*. . . ." Cf. similar advice in *Vave ha-'Amudim,* as cit. in Assaf, I, 69, #39. Cf. Rivkind in *Minḥah li-Yehudah . . . Zlotnik* (Festschrift), p. 241: Women entertained the bride with Yiddish songs. See also herein, pp. 33–34.

[139] *Derushe ha-Ẓelaḥ,* no. 4, fol. 8b, #9. Cf. *ibid.*, no. 4, fol. 9b, #21: If a person has limited knowledge, he still can engage in study by reciting the Psalms. See Erik, p. 38, that the Psalms in the *gebet-bukh,* Prayer Book, are read both in the synagogue and home. In time of illness or distress the Psalms serve as a *segullah,* "a source of remedy and protection." To illustrate the use of the segullah, see p. 113; n. 42 to p. 120.

[140] *'Ahabat Ẓiyon,* no. 1, fol. 1a, col. 2. Cf. B. Z. Katz, *Rabbanut,* I, 198-99, also cits. Landau fears that reliance on translation would cause the Hebrew language to be neglected, and he therefore opposes Mendelssohn's translation of the Bible into German. Instead of learning to read the text in the original Hebrew, the student would be satisfied to rely on the translation in a secular language. To Landau, Hebrew is not just another language.

[141] *Ḥavvot Ya'ir,* no. 106, fol. 103b.

[142] *Ibid.*, fol. 104a. Even secular books should be respected, Bacharach says: "I have a book on Euclid and Ibn Sina on medicine published in Hebrew. While they have no spiritual content, and are of no intellectual use and benefit, still we should refrain from treating such books with contempt, by wiping oneself with them, throwing them to the ground, or letting them be destroyed." See Euclidean geometry in Hebrew, at the end of Landsofer, *Me'il Ẓedaḳah,* fol. 81a-82a; and also Hebrew books on algebra and astronomy, published in the 18th century: M. Eliav, *Ha-Ḥinnukh ha-Yehudi be-Germanniyah* (Jewish Education in Germany in the Period of Enlightenment and Emancipation), pp. 20-21. Concerning Hebrew as one of the languages in which philosophic and scientific books were written in the Middle Ages, see H. A. Wolfson, *Philosophy of Spinoza* (Meridian Books, 1958), pp. 10-11.

[143] *Ḥavvot Ya'ir,* no. 123, fol. 116a. Cf. select. in Güdemann, *Quellen.,* p. 143 f., sec. 36; Assaf, I, 125 f., sec. 58. Bacharach makes the observation (fol. 116b) that those studying the Mishnah in his time may find it difficult because originally it was studied orally when printed texts were not available: "In ancient times the mind was wide open like the door of a vestibule, whereas our minds have the opening of a needle-hole. This is due to the fact that in the past the words of the Mishnah were not recorded, and it was forbidden to do so under any circumstance as printing was not known."

Cf. *Mafteaḥ ha-Yam,* Intro., fol. 3b, in which Jacob Meir Coblenz of Offenbach (d. ca. mid. 18th cent.) describes how he memorized sections of the Mishnah by attending a study group and rehearsing to himself what he had acquired orally: "And I drew close to those persons who were studying Torah. I gleaned from them as they studied orally, my ears gaining bits of knowledge until I learned orally—in succession—four 'Orders' of the Mishnah. I repeated this day and night until I achieved fluency in the entire arrangement of the Mishnayot."

[144] Cf. Baron, *Community,* II, 169-70, esp. the educational reform of Joshua b. Gamala and the Code of Maimonides on education. See herein, p. 50, n. 3.

Merely from the content of the *Bar Miẓvah* homily of Ephraim Lentshits (*'Olelot 'Efrayim,* Pt. 3, sec. 486, fol. 99a) it is possible to sense the extent to which knowledge was regarded as essential for all persons.

[145] Wachstein in *ZGJD,* IV, 136.

[146] *Ḥavvot Ya'ir,* no. 123, fol. 116a.

. . . ואף אם ישכיר אביו לו לבדו מלמד הלא הצורך הגדול אל הלימוד דיבוק חברים. . . .
ואין תקנה לזה רק אם יתאספו חמשה או ששה ב״ב יחד וישכרו מלמד לבניהם. . . .

A similar thought is in *Shelah,* I, fol. 181a; Güdemann, *Quellen.,* Pref. xxv ff.; *idem, Gesch.,* III, 11, n. 5; Assaf, I, 156.

[147] Landsofer, "Ethical Will," *Derekh Ṭobim,* fol. 9b, #17. See herein, p. 54, n. 26.

[148] Assaf, I, 137, #16. Cf. Wolf, *Mähren Statuten,* p. 4, #16; p. 52, #191: Where communities had no schools, the rabbi or lay-scholars would serve as teachers. In accordance with rabbinic teaching, the scholar was morally responsible for sharing his knowledge with others.

[149] *Vave ha-'Amudim,* chap. v, fol. 9b: *'adarim* = large groups; *kittot* = smaller, specialized groups; *ḥaburot* = groups of scholars. Cf. Güdemann, *Quellen.,* p. 112; Assaf, I, 70, #40.

Cf. *Y. 'O.,* p. 268. It was customary for the *Ḥaburah,* the Society devoted to study, "to have in their possession a charity box, and before their study began, each member of the group placed a coin in it." See charity custom herein, p. 55, n. 31. Cf. Prov. 10:2. "Righteousness *(ẓedaḳah)* delivereth from death" as discussed in *B. Bat.,* 8b ff., and note the instances when the practice of charity saved one from calamity and death. See Cronbach, "Philanthropy in Rabbinics," in *idem, Religion and Its Social Setting,* pp. 101-102, nn. 7-8, 17-19; Baron and Blau,

Judaism, Post-Biblical and Talmudic Period, pp. 168 ff.; also n. 123. Cf. the practices of *ẓedaḳah* in Löw, *Lebensalter,* p. 129; Schauss, *Lifetime of a Jew,* pp. 258, 264. Cf. *Sefer Zekhirah,* fol. 8a: The giving of charity is a *segullah,* a protection against Satan's charges: "There is also protection through the giving of a coin for charity before the prayer of 'Eighteen Benedictions' is recited. This safeguards one from charges brought by any accuser (*mekaṭreg,* i. e. Satan), for the 'accuser' bypasses each place where charity is given. As it is said, 'As for me, I shall behold Thy face in righteousness' (Is. 17:15). This verse applies to the giving of charity to the poor." Cf. in *Y. 'O.,* #86, the prayer of Jonah Gerondi to cope with the accusations and intrigues of Satan.

[150] *Vave ha-'Amudim,* chap. v, fol. 9b.

[151] *Zavva'ot,* fol. 5a:
וביחוד הקלויזנר באלטונא אשר הייתי עמהם כמה שנים צוותן בסימא ולמדתי עמהם פרק משניות בכל יום. המה יהיו בין העשרה אף שלפי התקנה בקלויז שאין יוצאין חוצה מן הקלויז. . . .
kloyz (Yid.) = "house of worship or study"; *kloyzner* (Yid.) = "one who devotes himself to study in a house of worship or study." See the function of the *kloyz* in G. Deutsch, "Klaus," *JE,* VII (1904), 518-19.

[152] Deutsch, *op. cit.,* 518, also cits.; Moritz Rosenfeld, "Klaus," *JLex,* III (1929), 731. Cf. Auerbach, *Israelit. Gemeinde Halberstadt,* p. 61: In 1703, Bermann (Berent Lehmann) established a *kloyz* in Halberstadt where Jewish scholars could live and study daily. The *kloyz* was provided with a synagogue and library, and the community planted a garden to supply the resident scholars with vegetables. Cf. the two *kloyzn* in Mannheim: Löwenstein, *Juden in der Kurpfalz,* p. 215. That a *kloyz* was established in Mannheim in 1708 through the philanthropy of Lemle Moses Reinganum, cf. Isak Unna, "Klausstiftung in Mannheim," *JJLG,* XVII (1925), 134; Assaf, IV, 80 ff., sec. 76, cit. Also, J. Lewin in *JJGL,* XXX (1937), 181, for the *kloyz* in Prague. And, the *kloyz* in Fürth: M. Weinberg, "Untersuchungen . . . des Memorbuches," *JJLG,* XVI (1924), 266; *kloyzn* in Darmstadt, Hesse, and Frankfort: Kaufmann in *JQR,* III (O. S.), 502, n. 4. See the portrait of a *kloyz* in the frontispiece of this volume. Cf. also pp. 5–6, n. 29.

[153] *Megillat Sefer* (Kolomea, Galicia, 1886), fol. 24a:
...ושם באלטונא בנה לו ה׳ בית נאמן והקים לו בהמ״ד [בית המדרש] הגדול קלויז, שיסדו לו גבירי ועשירי הג״ק [שלש קהלות: אלטונא, המבורג, וואנזבעק]....
Cf. also *ibid.,* fol. 24b. The above passage is also in *Megillat Sefer* (ed. David Kahana: Warsaw, 1896), p. 11; cf. Deutsch in *J. E.,* IV, 518, cit.

[154] Cf. Randall, *Making of the Modern Mind,* pp. 304, 400-2; Fishman, p. 13, for cultural and educational trends in Germany after the Thirty Years' War. Cf. the impact of the Protestant Reformation on Jewish life: Güdemann, *Quellen.,* Pref., p. xxvi.

The program of educational reform, fostered by the Enlightenment movement during Mendelssohn (1729-86), falls outside the scope of this study.

However, it is recognized that the educational trends of the 17th and 18th centuries did affect the emergence of the era of Emancipation. See chap. V, pp. 78–81, p. 108, n. 109. Cf. Berman, *Toledot ha-Ḥinnukh*, pp. 105–10; Fishman, pp. 128–31; Baron. *Soc. and Relig. Hist.* (1st edit.), II, 212-18 (sec. "German Haskalah"); III, 140 ("Notes: Emancipation"). Cf. in Stern in *JJLG,* XIX, 45, the autobiographical account of Lazarus Bendavid (1762-1832): His parents engaged for him "a French-speaking teacher who knew philosophy and also taught him Latin in strictest confidence [i.e., with no one aware of this]." In the meantime, Bendavid read widely in non-Jewish sources on religion, philosophy, and medicine, an interest aroused by German *Haskalah*. See also Baron, *Community,* II, 360.

[155] Sabbatai Bass, *Sifte Yeshenim,* fol. 6a, #9; *Vave ha-'Amudim,* fol. 9b; Louis Ginzberg, "Shabbethai b. Joseph Bass," *JE,* II (1902), 583, cits.; Güdemann, "Education," *JE,* V (1903), 47; Güdemann, *Quellen.,* p. 112, n. 2; Assaf, I, Pref., xiv; Erik, p. 207.

[156] Cf. Assaf, I, Pref., x, xviii, xxiii; xxvi, n. 4; 63, regarding the effect of the Maharal on his contemporaries and future generation, such as Lentshits, Isaiah and Sabbatai Horowitz, Bacharach. The Maharal had regard for the educational reforms of Lentshits. Cf. in Kohut, *Gesch. deut. Juden,* p. 569; A. Neher, "The Humanism of the Maharal of Prague," *Judaism,* XIV (No. 3, 1965), 290-91, that the Maharal manifested an interest in secular learning. Cf. Berman, *op. cit.,* p. 105 f.; Fishman, pp. 13-14: Until the beginning of the 17th century, Prague was an intellectual center, with the Maharal influenced by his acquaintance with non-Jewish scholarship.

For examples of a secular cultural emphasis in the Prague Jewish community, cf. Landsofer, *Me'il Ẓedaḳah,* fol. 69a-b; Assaf, I, Pref., xxiii; Israel Bettan, "The Sermons of Ephraim Luntshitz," *HUCA,* VIII-IX (1931-32), 446; Bondy-Dworský, *Juden in Böhmen, Mähren, und Schlesien,* II, 1047, n. 1346; Dubnow, *Weltgeschichte* (Hebrew edit.), VI, 149-150, #31; *idem, Weltgeschichte* (Ger. edit.), VI, 275-76, #31; Graetz, *Gesch. der Juden,* IX, 475; Kaufmann in *JQR,* III (April 1891), 507, 516, 519; Shohet, *'Im Ḥillufe Teḳufot,* p. 198, n. 3.

[157] Cf. Assaf, I, Pref., xvi; I, 205, #1; III, Pref., iv-v; Erik, p. 213, for a critique of the Jewish educational system in Germany. See also above, refs. in n. 2.

[158] *Me'il Ẓedaḳah,* Pref., 2a (fol. not marked). Note the rowdy and unruly behavior of children on the street when they leave school: Lentshits, *'Amude Shesh,* chap. 24, fol. 23a (sec. "Musar 'Amud ha-Torah"); and cf. B.Z. Katz, *Rabbanut,* I, 80.

See a similar description of cultural decline in Landsofer, "Ethical Will," *Derekh Ṭobim,* fol. 6a; fol. 7a, #8; fol. 14a-b, #28; fol. 16a, #25. Cf. also *Vave ha-'Amudim,* chap. v, fol. 31b-32a; Güdemann, *Quellen.,* pp. 116-17, cit.

[159] *Ḥavvot Ya'ir,* no. 123, fol. 116a; Assaf, I, 126; Fishman, p. 19, n. 16.

[160] *Derushe ha-Ẓelaḥ,* no. 23, fol. 36a, #21.

[161] *Vave ha-'Amudim,* fol. 32a.

[162] Landsofer, *op. cit.,* fol. 14a-b, #28. That rabbinical posts were purchased in Germany during the 17th and 18th centuries, see J. Katz in *Zion,* X (N. S., 1946), 26, n. 33.

[163] See above, n. 52 for a summary of the economic conditions in the school.

[164] *Derushe ha-Ẓelaḥ,* no. 4, fol. 9a, #18. Further evidence of economic stress in the teacher's life is in Rivkind, *Yid. gelt,* p. 238, sec. 561 ("Rosh Ḥodesh Gelt").

[165] *'Amude Shesh,* fol. 23a:

והמלמד אינו מקפיד על התכלית האמיתי כל עיקר. ואדרבה הם מטעים גם את אבותם ע״י החנופה שבפניהם משבחים ואומרים הנער הזה גדול בתורה יהיה כדי שישכור אותו למלמד וכשהנער ראוי ללמוד הלכה הוא אומר לו שהוא ראוי ללמוד תוספות. . . . .

Cf. Bettan in *HUCA,* VIII-IX, 463-64, that teachers were preoccupied too much with their own welfare and concern. Cf. Berman, *Toledot ha-Ḥinnukh,* pp. 90-91; Fishman, p. 18, n. 7. On the other hand, cf. Stern in *JJLG,* XIX, 40-41: A teacher engaged by a private family was provided with lodging and maintenance and thus treated like a domestic servant. Cf. also Fishman, p. 20. Obviously, teachers must have had their grievances and must have felt that they were not shown the consideration to which they were entitled.

[166] As suggested by Assaf I, Pref., xvi.

[167] *Ibid.,* Pref., xvi-xvii.

[168] *Shelah,* I, fol. 181a:

...כשיתחיל ללמוד מקרא לא יזח עד גמר תורה ונביאים וכתובים היטב היטב...ולא יזח משום פסוקים עד שידע הנער פי׳ המלה עם הפעולה והחיבור. . . .

Cf. Güdemann, *Quellen.,* p. 106: *ha-pe'ullah* = "grammar"; *ha-ḥibbur* = "syntax." Cf. also the emphasis of *Shelah* on studying the Bible and Hebrew grammar: B. Z. Katz, *Rabbanut,* I, 52.

Sabbatai Horowitz, "Ethical Will," *Ẓavva'ot . . . Dibre Ḳedoshim,* fol. 5b, #27:

גם תלמדו עמהם דקדוק שידעו ויבינו נוכח נסתר יחיד ורבים לזכרים ולנקבות.

"Furthermore, you should study grammar with them, so they can know the present tense, the third person, the singular and plural of the masculine and feminine."

[169] *'Amude Shesh,* fol. 23a: "It is a good procedure to teach them first of all the Bible with syntax. . . ." Cf. Lentshits's view that the Bible should be studied before anything else: B. Z. Katz, *op. cit.,* I, 80.

[170] *Y. 'O.,* p. 270:

. . . שבדורותינו יש כמה רבנים אשר לא ראו המקרא מימיהם.

Regarding the neglect of Bible study in Jewish schools, see Assaf, I, Pref., xvi, n. 5; 80. #47; Baron, *Community,* II, 193-4; Berman, *Toledot ha-Ḥinnukh,* p. 91, cit.; Erik, pp. 208, 230-31; Fishman, p. 97, n. 81.

171 Assaf, I, Pref., xvii.

172 Marx in *JQR*, VIII, 270 (trans.); 279 (text).

173 *Shelah*, I, fol. 181a (sec. "Shabu'ot"):

והנה יש כת משוגעים האומרים החילוק מחדד. האומר כן ראוי לנזיפה. . . .

nezifah, a lower degree of excommunication. Here it probably means reprimand, Professor Baron suggests. Cf. Güdemann, *Quellen.*, pp. 107-108, cits. As to Horowitz's opposition to *ḥilluḳ*, cf. also H. Ehrentreu in *JJLG*, III (1905), 209, #10; 215, #18.

174 *Vave ha-'Amudim*, chap. 5, fol. 10a. Cf. in Strassburger, *Gesch. der Erziehung*, pp. 141, 159; Friedländer, *Tiferet Jisrael*, p. 85; Baron, *Community*, II, 195, the treatment of *pilpul*, "the dialectical method of talmudic instruction" in Europe. As to the effect that *ḥilluḳ* had on education in Germany during the 17th and 18th cents., cf. Fishman, pp. 104, 106, cits.; J. Katz, *op. cit.*, pp. 226-27; Eng. trans., pp. 194-95.

175 *'Amude Shesh*, fol. 23b:

. . . הבחורים נראה [*sic*] עין בעין איך חידוד זה גורם להם קלקול גדול. . . .

176 *Y. 'O.*, p. 272; *Ḥavvot Ya'ir*, no. 123, fol. 116a, 117a; Landsofer, "Ethical Will," *Derekh Ṭobim*, fol. 6a, #6; fol. 6b, #7.

As to Bacharach's opposition to *pilpul*, see *Ḥavvot Ya'ir*, no. 152, fol. 138b-139a; Kaufmann in *JQR*, III (O. S.), 293; Tsinberg, *Gesh. fun der lit.*, V, 166. Also note the opponents of *pilpul* in B. Z. Katz, *Rabbanut*, I, 82, 140.

177 *Ya'arot Debash*, I, 12a. Cf. the attitudes of Eibeschütz and Landau regarding "pilpulistic excesses": Baron, *Community*, II, 195.

178 Based on Shiper, *Yid. teater*, II, 61-62; J. Katz, *Massoret u-Mashber*, p. 226, n. 29; Eng. trans., pp. 194-95.

179 Ehrentreu in *JJLG*, III, 213-14, #14-15; 215, #17. His examples of a constructive kind of discussion are centered around *Shab.*, 115b; *Ḥul.*, 12a.

180 Shiper, *op. cit.*

181 See herein, p. 24, n. 57; p. 74, n. 156. Cf. the examples of Eibeschütz and Emden as rabbis in Germany who had secular knowledge: Barzilay, *Essays . . . in Honor of Salo W. Baron*, pp. 185-86, nn. 14-15. That Samuel Schotten of Frankfort, a friend of Bacharach, knew Latin and studied secular subjects, see Kaufmann in *JQR*, III (O. S.), 502-503.

182 *Shelah*, I, 183a:

. . . כי חכמת התורה וחכמת הפלסופי׳ אינן ע״ד [על דרך] אחד. . . .

Isaiah Horowitz cites Rashba's *Responsa*, no. 419; cf. Shlomo ben Adret, *She'elot u-Teshubot* (Vienna, 1812), fol. 53a ff., esp. 58b-60a. Cf. Güdemann, *Quellen.*, p. 109, cit.

Cf. *Ḥavvot Ya'ir*, no. 123, fol. 116b:

...כי טוב ויפה לנו ולבנינו להאמין האמונו׳ המוטלים עלינו בלי חקירה....

See in Tsinberg, *Gesch. fun der lit.*, V, 167; Shohet, *'Im Ḥillufe Ṭekufot*, p. 199, n. 6;

also, p. 198, n. 1, how Bacharach gave up the study of science because it led to scepticism. As to Bacharach's interest in secular knowledge, see also Kaufmann in *JQR*, III (O. S.), 293.

[183] *She'elat Ya'abeẓ* (Altona, 1739), I, no. 41, fol. 73b. Cf. B. Z. Katz, *Rabbanut*, I, pp. 157-58, cit.

[184] *She'elat Ya'abeẓ, op. cit*. Cf. Emden's attitude toward secular knowledge in Shohet, *op. cit.*, pp. 201-202.

[185] *Shelah*, I, fol. 183a:

... כי יהיה לבו תמיד על חכמ׳ הטבע ותעלה ברוחו להשוות שתי החכמות יחד ולהביא ראיה מזו לזו ויעות משפט כי שני הפכי׳ הם צרות זו לזו ולא ישכבו במקום א׳ ...

[186] *Migdal 'Oz*, fol. 107b, sec. "'Aliyat ha-Ḥokhmah";

... גנבו מדברי הנבואה ומחז״ל, וישימו בכליהם, וילבישו החכמה בגדים אחרים. ...

[187] *Ibid*. Emden quotes *Ḳohelet R*. 12:13, which admonishes that apocryphal books, like Ben Sira (Ecclesiasticus) and Ben Tagla (not extant), should not be read. See *Mid. R. Ecclesiastes* (Son. edit.), VIII, 315, n. 1.

[188] *Megillat Sefer* (Warsaw, 1896), pp. 96-97. Cf. the similarity of Emden's experience in obtaining secular knowledge with that of Bendavid, as above, p. 251, n. 154. There were individuals who were autodidactic in secular study: M. Eliav, *Ha-Ḥinnukh ha-Yehudi*, pp. 15, 20.

[189] Eliav, *op. cit.*, pp. 15-16.

[190] Kaufmann (ed.), *Glikl*, p. 34:

... ובמעשיה פראנצעזיש אליש איין וואשיר ביקענט. ...

Cf. Feilchenfeld, p. 21: "Französisch konnte sie wie Wasser. . . ." Also, *ibid.*, n. 12. Cf. also Rabinowitz (ed.), *Glikl*, p. 13; Lowenthal, p. 11. See Shohet (Schochat), *'Im Ḥillufe Teḳufot*, p. 60, n. 93.

Kaufmann, *op. cit.*:

בתו חורגה שטייט ביי דער קלאף צימיר אונ׳ שפילט דרויף. ...

Cf. folkloristic usage of *klaffzimmer* (Ger.), *clavier* (Fr.): *ibid.*, n. 4. Cf. Feilchenfeld, p. 22: "Seine Stieftochter steht bei dem Clavicymbel und spielt darauf. . . ." Cf. Lowenthal, p. 12: *klaffzimmer* = "clavichord." Clavichord = "a spinet or harpsichord"; "origin is obscure" (Eric Blom, ed., *Grove's Dictionary of Music and* Musicians [5th edit., New York, 1954], II, 336); the forerunner of the modern piano. See also Shiper, *Yid. teater*, I, 187: *klavir*.

See Fishman, p. 120, cit.; p. 114, n. 1; pp. 115-16, nn. 9-11, concerning secular influences on German-Jewish women (based on the Maharal and Emden). Also, Baron, *Community*, II, 179.

[191] *Y. 'O.*, #890:

... לכן מה מאד נחשב בעיני לאיסור גדול מה שהעשירים שוכרין לבנותיהם יודע נגן ללמדם כלי שיר כי אין זה אלא להתענג ולהתיהר בם. ...

Cf. Adler in *JJLG*, XVIII, 168, n. 3. That wealthy parents had greater contact with the general community, and were more inclined to teach their children secular subjects, see J. Katz, *op. cit.*, p. 216, n. 6; Eng. trans., p. 186. Also, above, n. 154 to p. 73. This is also borne out by Schochat's study of social imitation in the German-Jewish community; the Jews of the upper classes associated much more with the non-Jewish society and were more willing to imitate the prevailing culture. Cf. A. Schochat in *Zion,* XXI (N. S., 1956), 212; 217, n. 67; *idem, 'Im Ḥillufe Teḳufot,* p. 40, nn. 91, 93.

192 *Ḳ. H.,* 82:2: "At presenṭ the French language is all-important, but the Torah is incidental." Cf. Güdemann, *Quellen.,* p. 180; Kracauer, *Juden in Frankfurt,* II, 278-79; Tsinberg, *Gesh. fun der lit.,* V, pp. 194-95; Erik, p. 398; Shohet, *'Im Ḥillufe Teḳufot,* p. 61, n. 98. While Kaidanover no doubt exaggerates, the French language and culture did influence Germany and Poland. Cf. Schultz, *Das häusliche Leben,* p. 183, that French had the status of a classical or elite language. Children of the nobility in Germany had private tutors to teach them Latin and French. See in this volume, p. 28, n. 75; n. 1 to p. 85 for French cultural influences in Germany.

193 *Ya'arot Debash,* I, fol. 8a (sermon of 1743). Cf. Eliav, *Ha-Ḥinnukh ha-Yehudi,* p. 16, n. 3. Also, Assaf, I, 205, #1, n. 1; Fishman, p. 116, #1, n. 1.

194 *Y. 'O.,* #47.

195 *Ya'arot Debash,* I, 8a.

196 Based on Eliav, *op. cit.*, p. 16.

197 *Vave ha-'Amudim*, chap. 5, fol. 9b. Cf. Güdemann, *Quellen.*, pp. 112-14, cit. Cf. also Güdemann, "Education," *JE,* V (1903), 47; Sabbatai Horowitz wanted the Amsterdam school to serve as a "pattern to the congregations of Germany, Austria, and Poland." According to Güdemann, Spinoza attended the school.

198 Louis Ginzberg, "Shabbethai b. Joseph Bass," *JE,* II (1902) 583-84. Cf. I. Markon, "Sabbatai ben Josef Bass," *EJ,* III (1929), 1155; Heinrich Loewe, "Sabbataj ben Josef Bass," *JLex,* I (1927), 1154.

199 *Sifte Yeshenim,* I, fol. 8a:

והנה עד כה שמעתי קול איש קדוש קורא...כמוהר״ר שבתי שעפטל הורוויץ הלוי בספרו
...ושם פתח פיהו לדבר נפלאות בענין סדר הלימוד של ק״ק ספרדים....

Cf. Güdemann, *Quellen.*, pp. 112-13, n. 2, trans.

200 *Ibid.,* 8a. See *baḥur,* above, n. 37 to pp. 55–56.

201 *Ibid.,* 8b. Cf. Güdemann, *op. cit.,* p. 113, n. 2, trans.

202 *Ibid.,* 8b.

203 Cf. also Stern, *JJLG,* XIX, 39.

[1] Posen in *Menorah,* VI, 681; *J. M.*, Bk. 6, chap. 13, 242, #4; 247, #11. See Abrahams, *Jewish Life,* pp. 304-5, for the internal and external factors affecting dress.

Cf. Richter, *Kulturgeschichte,* II, 375, that the clothes worn in Strasbourg showed the influences of Italy, France, Hungary, and Bohemia. See also Samuel Steinherz, "Die Einwanderung der Juden in Böhmen," in *idem, Die Juden in Prag: Festgabe,* p. 47: The dress of the Jews of Prague was influenced by the Jews of Poland who migrated there. That customs were not confined to precise geographical limits, but spread from one area to another, see Pref., p. xvi, n. 11; p. 42; n. 39 to p. 100.

[2] Cf. *J. M.*, III, No. 6, 126-27, 155, the provisions in the *Stättigkeit* of Frankfort, 1613; Friedländer, *Tiferet Jisrael,* p. 47, n.; Stobbe, *Juden in Deutsch.*, p. 175; Hottenroth, *Deut. Volkstrachten,* III, 10, 133; Posen in *Menorah,* VI, 681-82; Straus in *JSS,* IV, 60, n. 3; 65, n. 21. Pictures of the "badge," "hat," and "mantle" are in *J. M.*, III, 127; No. 7, 155; Hottenroth, II, 7, fig. 2 (2-3); III, supp. plate 2; Posen, 681, 683. Cf. Stobbe, *loc. cit.*: In Nuremberg, the color of the hat was usually red, but the "Jewish hat" was "yellow," the same color as the "badge," no doubt to connote inferiority. (Henceforth Hottenroth, *Volkstrachten* = Hottenroth.)

For "mantle" = *mantl* (Yid.); *sarbal, gelimah* (Heb.), see below, pp. 89, 91; p. 93, n. 62, and cf. *Brüll, Trachten der Juden,* I, 28, 88–89; *N. K. Y.*, fol. 1a, #7; *Y. 'O.*, #3, #591, #594.

See "hat" above, p. 94, n. 69, cit. from *H. 'A.*; also *Sefer ha-Manhig,* fol. 39b, #14. See week-day "mantle" and "hat," above, p. 46, n. 179. Cf. ***hut; hut-shnir***, "hat-cord, hat-string": ***Pene Yehoshua',*** **II**, no. 58, fol. 40a.

[3] The Jews cannot be distinguished from their neighbors by their dress: cf. *J. M.*, II (Bk. 6, ch. 13), 240, #2; Kracauer, *Juden in Frankfort,* II, 119. See also Posen in *Menorah,* VI, 684; Friedländer, *op. cit.*, p. 47, that the clothes worn by Jews in Germany differed only slightly from those of the general society. As further evidence that the Jews tended to wear the same clothes as non-Jews, see Schochat in *Zion,* XXI (N. S.), 212-16; esp. 213, n. 37, cit. of *Ḳ. H.* 30:9; *idem* (Shohet), *'Im Ḥillufe Teḳufot,* pp. 54-55.

[4] Straus in *JSS,* IV, 68, n. 32. Cf. *J. M.*, IV (Bk. 6, chap. 14), 253, #13. That a missing Jewish person was identified by the beard that he wore, cf. *Ẓemaḥ Ẓedeḳ,* no. 45, fol. 50b; *Shebut Ya'aḳob,* II, no. 115, fol. 18b; *Pene Yeshoshua',* II, no. 53, fol. 29b; no. 58, fol. 40a. Cf. "Costumes," *RCC,* cit.

[5] Cf. *Ya'arot Debash,* I, 13b; Schochat, *Zion,* XXI (N. S.), 217, n. 60. For some other cases of Jews shaving their beards and earlocks, cf. *S. H.*, I, fol. 63a (sec. "Dine Pe'ot"); *Ḥavvot Ya'ir,* no. 139, fol. 127b; Schochat, 217, nn. 65, 68.

Further examples of this kind are in Schochat, 216-18, nn. Cf. *idem* (Shohet), *'Im Ḥillufe Teḳufot,* pp. 55-58, inc. nn.; esp. p. 56, n. 57.

6 Dubnow, *Weltgeschichte* (Hebrew edit.), VII, 166; (German edit.), VII, 280.

7 Cf. Richter, *Kulturgeschichte,* II, 372; Posen in *Menorah,* VI, 683; Weiss, *Kostümkunde,* II, 1035-36; Boehn, *Deutschland im XVIII. Jahrhundert,* II, 483-84, 502; Valentin, *German People,* pp. 231, 259.

Cf. Bax, *German Culture,* pp. 126-27: A Lindau (Bavaria) sumptuary law of 1497 states that "the common peasant man and the labourer . . . 'shall neither make nor wear cloth that costs more than half a gulden the ell, neither shall they wear gold, pearls, velvet, silk, nor embroidered clothes, nor shall they permit their wives or children to wear such.'" That the anti-luxury ruling in the German community of Bamberg was to control the dress and behavior at weddings, see Richter, II, 377.

Sumptuary legislation in the non-Jewish community did not apply to women's shoes, which were gaudy in appearance. Furthermore, brides wore expensive shoes during the wedding ceremony. The religious leaders in the general community were critical of this mode of dress. Cf. Koppmann, "Mannstracht der Hamburger," *idem* (ed.), *Aus Hamburgs Vergangenheit,* II, 251.

8 See Baron, *Community,* II, 301-2, for the historical background of anti-luxury legislation in German-Jewish life. Regarding Jewish communal regulations to control wedding celebrations and festive meals, in addition to dress, see herein, p. 33, n. 101; p. 39, nn. 139–41; pp. 161–62, n. 82. For some examples of communal anti-luxury ordinances, see Wachstein, "The Prague Anti-Luxury Ordinance of 1767" (Yiddish), *Yivo Bleter,* I (1931), 335 ff; Munk in *Jubelschrift . . . Hildesheimer,* p. 81, #30; p. 83; Halpern, *Taḳḳanot Mähren,* #306, #574 (6), #653 (7, 8); Kaufmann, "Minute-Books of the Province of Düsseldorf" (Hebrew), *'Oẓar ha-Safrut,* III (1889-90), 8-9, #3-4 (record of 1698); Grunwald in *MGJV,* XI, 9, #21; *idem,* "Luxusverbot der Dreigemeinden," *JJV,* I (1923), 227 ff.

See Kracauer, *Juden in Frankfurt,* II, 124, who points out that sumptuary regulations sought to curb pleasures as a reaction to the Frankfort fire of 1711. That these laws controlling entertainment and dress, were a restraint against normal enjoyments, see *ibid.;* Freimann-Kracauer, *Frankfort,* pp. 123-24. Such communal legislation was not observed, and therefore required constant reenactment: Kracauer, *Judengasse,* p. 426.

9 Cf. I. Rivkind, "A Codex of Prague Ordinances" 1613 (Hebrew), *Reshumot,* IV (1926), 345-46, 350: During a plague in Prague, self-examination was intensified and moral concern heightened.

10 *Derushe ha-Ẓelaḥ,* no. 4, fol. 9b, #21. The Messianic hopes of the time are suggested further in chap. iv, p. 93, n. 61.

11 Cf. Franz Kobler, *Letters of Jews through the Ages,* II, 473, sec. 11: Although war conditions prevailed in 1619, "many ladies of the upper class asked their relatives and friends for articles apparently not available in the capital [i.e., Vienna]."

For instance, Resel Landau of Prague (*ibid.*, 473) wrote to her daughter Hannah, of Vienna, in a critical tone for being so concerned with her dress when more essential items for living could not be obtained. Friedel, the daughter of Israel Hammerschlag of Prague wrote to Mirel, the daughter of Israel Auerbach of Vienna (*ibid.*, 474): ". . . I let you know that I discharged your commission well and ordered the coat to be made for you in the best and finest fashion possible in the world. . . . Therefore, do not omit to send me money in order . . . [to] buy a beautiful smooth otter fur in Poland. . . . I could obtain otter fur here, but they are dyed." See chap. I, n. 29 to p. 6 as to the purchase of otter fur in Poland.

[12] See cit. n. 146 to p. 40.

[13] Refs. to the different types of anti-luxury legislation are combined in n. 8.

[14] Halpern, *Taḳḳanot Mähren,* p. 100, #298, n. 1: *glintsir (glentser) shlayer.* See below, p. 91, n. 46.

[15] Barbeck, *Juden in Nürnberg und Fürth,* p. 86: *zwickelstrumpf.* (Henceforth cited only as Barbeck.)

[16] *Panim Me'irot,* II, no. 44, 72a-b. Cf. "Costumes," *RCC.* See n. 5 on *Shab.* 114a in *Shabbath* II (*Mo'ed,* II, Son. edit.), 559.

[17] Cf. *chagrin* (Fr.) = "leather."

[18] The use of the wig is another instance of non-Jewish attire influencing the dress of German Jews. See the import of men wearing wigs as another departure from adherence to tradition: Shochat, *Zion,* XXI (N.S.), 212.

[19] Halpern, *Taḳḳanot Mähren,* 99, #297; 100, #298 (Gaya, 1650); 160, #473 (6) (Lundenburg, 1697); 199-200, #575 (7) (Bodspitz, 1720); Wolf, *Mähren Statuten,* Pref., p. vii; p. 115, #6; p. 138, #7; A. L. Feinstein, "Clothing Regulations" (Prussia, 1628), sec. 1: "The Limit on a Permissible Act" (Hebrew), *Ha-'Asif,* VI (1893), 171; Barbeck (*Taḳḳanot* of 1728 paraphrased), pp. 85-86; *J. M.,* IV, Pt. 3, 77-106, "Neue Frankfurter Jüd. Kleider-Ordnung" in 1711; Kayserling, "Luxusverbote," *MGJV,* XIII (1904), 40 f.; Kracauer, *Judengasse in Frankfurt,* p. 337, n. 7; p. 425, nn. 9, 10; Kracauer, *Juden in Frankfurt,* II, 124, n. 2; Horovitz, *Frankfurt. Rabbin.,* II, 52; Posen in *Menorah,* VI, 683-84; Schnapper-Arndt in *ZGJD,* II, 188.

Jewelry was not popular in the general German community, we are told by Glikl: ". . . burghers and engaged couples among the non-Jews seldom or never wore jewels. Instead, it was the fashion to wear gold chains (*goldini ketin* [*goldene keytin*])": Kaufmann (ed.), *Glikl,* p. 69; Feilchenfeld p. 48; Lowenthal (ed.), pp. 33-34. (Trans. based on Lowenthal.)

[20] *Brandshpigl,* sec. 14, fol. 4b (no fol. mark): Women should not wear a sleeveless dress:

דאש איר ניקש אם לייב הרויש גיט, אונ׳ די אויבר העמדר ביט אופּין זיין אונטר דער אויקשל.

See *Ket.* 7:6; *M. Nashim* (ed. Blackman), III, 161, nn. 8, 9: The woman is not to go outside on the street "with her arms exposed," nor "converse with all men." Cf.

Notes to Chapter IV

Shohet, *'Im Ḥillufe Teḳufot,* p. 54: Communal legislation of Altona, Hamburg, and Wandsbek required women to have their arms covered.

Derushe ha-Ẓelaḥ, no. 23, fol. 36a, #21:

...והעינים בהסתכלות בנשים ובתכשיטיהן ובמלבושיהן....

Cf. *'O. Ḥ.* sec. 303, "Laws Pertaining to Women's Ornamentation."

Ḳ. H. 82:1: "... It is incumbent upon the women to be more modest than the men, and not follow their own inclinations with regard to dress. The downfall of most men results from gazing at women. This is proof enough that a man should not look at a woman, not even when she wears bright colors. They [the women] are adding to sin when they allow themselves to be exposed and naked from the neck to the breast. ..." Cf. Schochat in *Zion,* XXI (N. S.), 214, n. 40. See Erik, p. 256: *Musar* literature condemns Jewish young women for aping the dress of non-Jews.

21 *Brandshpigl,* sec. 5, fol. 2b (no fol. mark):

לויפֿט אל צייט אויש דעם הויש צום ויין צום ביר צום שפיל אין די הויזר דא קורצווייליבן דיא צייט....

Prob. *kurtsvaylnen,* related to *kurzweilen* (Ger.), "to amuse, divert."

S. H., II, fol. 17a; Erik, p. 308.

Cf. herein, p. 39, nn. 139–41, the communal legislation of Bamberg, in 1698, to curb rowdiness at weddings. This contradicts Kracauer's opinion (n. 8, above) that the people were unduly restrained by communal practice and legislation. Social life must be seen in terms of the background of that period and not on the basis of modern moral standards and attitudes. Cf. realistic portrayal of conduct of the time in Shohet, *'Im Ḥillufe Teḳufot,* pp. 162-64.

22 Barbeck, p. 86. See communal legislation forbidding women to enter alone the home of a non-Jew: Rivkind in *Reshumot,* IV, 348-49; also, Bernstein, *Takones bay yidn kegn lukses,* no. 31, p. 31, that the legislation of Altona, Hamburg, and Wandsbek, of 1715, forbids women to enter the homes of merchants unless chaperoned.

For a description of a neighbor's garden in the general German community where people met and socialized, cf. Schultz, *Deut. Leben,* I, 128.

23 *Y. 'O.,* #3. Cf. *seide mantil (mantl),* "silk mantle": *Minhagim ... Worms:* Assaf, *Meḳorot,* I, 126, #6; Epstein, "Wormser Minhagbücher," *Gedenkbuch ... David Kaufmann,* pp. 314-15. See cape, mantle in Schnapper-Arndt, *ZGJD,* II, 188; *bloyen mantl:* Shiper, *Yid. teater,* I, 182.

24 *J. M.,* II, 247, #14. Cf. *Shebut Ya'aḳob,* II, no. 115, fol. 18b: *(... ayn mutsin lebir* [*leber*]*-farb 'im kaftorim shel kemlhor. ...)* Cf. "Costumes," *RCC,* cit.

mutsin, probably a cape with a hood or cowl. Cf. *mits* (mod. Yid.), "cap"; same as *miẓnefet,* below, p. 94. Cf. *mütze* (Ger.), "cowl." See *müze:* Hottenroth, I, 28. *leber-farb* (Yid.) = "liver-colored or brown." Cf. *leberfarben* (Ger.), same meaning.

[25] Cf. *J. M.*, IV (Bk. 6, chap. 14), 247.

[26] *Ibid.*, 252; Posen in *Menorah,* VI, 682. See Straus in *JSS,* IV, 63, n. 18, that originally the *barrette* was worn as a hood. See the *gugel,* "cowl, hood": below, pp. 94–95, n. 71; Straus, 63, n. 18; 66; Grunwald, "Volkstracht . . . VI" ("Aus unseren Sammlungen"), *MGJV,* I (1898), 113, sec. 1, no. 1. (Note that the spelling of *barrette* varies and is cited each time according to the source.)

[27] Hottenroth, I, 131. See the illustrations of the *barrette* in Grunwald, *MGJV,* I, 114, #21, and in Hottenroth, I, 197, fig. 74 (3-6), a portrait of the clothes worn by Jews in Fürth, the latter part of the 18th century. See also in Hottenroth, III, 36, fig. 14 (3), and Supp., plate no. 23, the clothes of Frankfort Jews in the 17th century.

[28] *Mas'at Binyamin,* no. 80, fol. 46b. See in Posen, *Menorah,* VI, 684, a description of the way the mantle was worn.

[29] Posen in *Menorah,* VI, 681. Cf. Henne am Rhyn, *Kulturgeschichte,* I, 263, that it was the fashion in Germany to wear long garments during that period.

[30] *J. M.*, IV (Bk. 6, chap. 14), 247-48, #12.

Noda' bi-Yehudah, I, no. 36, fol. 25b (sec. "'E. H."):

. . . דרוב העולם הולכין בכובע פיקס עם בגד שחור:

piḳas (Heb.) = "red color." (Note: Unless specified the Berdiczew edit., 1812, is cited in all instances.) Cf. Hottenroth, I, 130: The Frankfort regulation of 1452 required Jews to wear garments of dark color. However, regional practices varied; in southern Germany the garments were of bright colors. See also Grunwald in *MGJV,* I, 113, #1 (1).

[31] See Schnapper-Arndt in *ZGJD,* II, 188. Cf. *Shebut Ya'aḳob,* II, no. 115, fol. 18b: *(. . . ve-gam ayn kamizol lebr* [*leber*]*-farb. . . .)* Cf. "Costumes," *RCC,* cit.

kamizol = prob. related to *kamisol* (Ger.), "jacket, waistcoat." See *kamezelke,* "waistcoat" (mod. Yid.): Harkavy, *Verterbukh* (New York, 1925), p. 441.

[32] *J. M.*, IV (Bk. 6, chap. 14), 247, #11, #12. The dragoons and grenadiers wore their handkerchiefs this way.

[33] See pp. 85–86, for the "kerchief around the neck."

[34] *J. M.*, pp. 247-48, #12. See Grunwald, "Trachten der Juden," *JL,* IV^2 (1930), 1015, the *Ḥebra' Ḳaddishah* in the Hamburg-Altona region wore mantles of Spanish style. Cf. the influence of Spanish fashions on men's clothes in the kaiser's court in Vienna: Boehn, *Deut. im XVIII. Jahrhundert,* II, 484.

Cf. Grunwald in *MGJV,* I, 113, #1 (1), *kniehosen,* "breeches"; Elsass in *MGJV,* XVI, 101: *hosen.* See also Spanish influence, below, n. 58 to p. 93.

[35] Friedländer, *Tiferet Jisrael,* pp. 47-48. Cf. in *Y. 'O.*, Pt. 2, fol. 187a; Pt. 2, p. 322; Grunwald in *MGJV,* I, 113, #1 (1); 114 #1 (24b), n. 13, the mantle, hat, and coat. See *kota* = prob. related to *cotte* (Fr.), "coat," and is the same garment as *rok* (Yid.), *rock* (Ger.). The *rok* is a topcoat or overcoat, without a lining: cf.

Mas'at Binyamin, no. 80, fol. 47a. Cf. *rekel* (*rokel,* Yid.): *Pene Yehoshua',* II, no. 68, fol. 40a. Cf. *Ẓemaḥ Ẓedeḳ,* no. 42, fol. 40b: *rok fun tukh* = "cloth coat." Cf. also Koppmann in *idem* (ed.), *Aus Hamburgs Vergangenheit,* II, 241, *rock . . . tuch.* Cf. *Ya'arot Debash,* I, fol. 13a, *rok;* Shiper, *Yid. teater,* I, 159, *a langn zaydenem rok.*

Cf. Posen in *Menorah,* VI, 682, in 1432: The Jews of Augsburg asked the authorities for the right to wear the long cloak, *rock.* For other examples of "the coat," cf. Schnapper-Arndt in *ZGJD,* II (O. S.), 188, *rock* with gold and silver points, made of camel's hair. See in *Shebut Ya'aḳob,* I, no. 171, fol. 47b, camel hair used as material for garments: ". . . a garment [made] of camel's hair *(ẓemer gemalim)* that is called *keml-hor* in Yiddish *(bi-leshon 'Ashkenaz). . . .*"
Cf. "Costumes," *RCC,* cit.

Cf. Hottenroth, I, 18-19, 33, 38, 87: The *rock* was known in the German community as a man's and woman's coat. In the 16th century, the *rock* was worn with headgear and then as a long coat; in the 18th century it was shortened to the knee and resembled a jacket. The use of the *rock* further indicates non-Jewish influence on the dress of the German Jews. For illustrations of the *rock,* cf. Hottenroth, I, 19, fig. 8 (2); 21, fig. (1, 3-5); 34, fig. 18; III, fig. 14 (3).

Landau (*responsum* cit. above, n. 30) supplies some details on men's dress. Chiffon was used for fine garments. Mention is also made of "a sleeve trimmed with dark red material":

אין די ארביל אן גיזעצט מיט גוואנט צבע גראנט. . . .

Prob. *gevant* (Yid.) = "garment"; cf. *gevand* (Ger.), same meaning. Prob. *granat* (Ger.) = "garnet (dark red)."

36 *Y. 'O.,* #227: *volen-hemd* (Yid.) = "woolen shirt." Cf. shirts in Schnapper-Arndt, *ZGJD,* II, 188. Cf. Emden, *She'elat Ya'abeẓ* (Lemberg, 1884), II, no. 32, fol. 18a: A woman sewed a cotton *'arba'-kanfot* to a woolen garment. Isaiah Horowitz and Ezekiel Landau warn the people not to use thread that is a mixture of linen and wool, *sha'aṭnez:* cf. *Shelah,* I, fol. 106a (sec. *"Sha'ar ha-'Otyot"*); *Derushe ha-Ẓelaḥ,* no. 4, fol. 9b. Horowitz lists as thread:

. . . חוטין הנקראי׳ שני״רליך או בער״טליך. . . .

Cf. *shnirlekh,* pl. dimin. of *shnur* (Yid.), "cord, string, lace." Cf. *schnur* (Ger.), same meaning.
bertlikh = possibly related to *bortn* (Yid.), "edge, shore." Cf. *borte* (Ger.), "trimming." Cf. also in Emden and Landau, *loc. cits.,* hemp (*ḳanbos,* Heb.) and flax threads.

37 Kaufmann (ed.), *Glikl,* p. 245: ". . . a red lined *(futir, futer)* shirt *(hemid, hemd)* with several silver buttons *(knepkhir, kneplekh),* and he had on his *arbe-kanfes. . . .*"

futer (Yid.) = "lined"; cf. *futter* (Ger.), same meaning. (Abraham Metz was married to Glikl's cousin, Sara, daughter of Elia Cohen: Kaufmann [ed.], *Glikl,* p. 234; Feilchenfeld [ed.], *Glückel,* p. 210, n. 38.) See n. 38 for *arbe-kanfes.*

Cf. *Brandshpigl,* sec. 14, fol. 4b (no fol. mark): *oyberhemder* (Yid.); cf. *oberhemd* (Ger.), "dress shirt." Cf. *Pene Yeshohua',* II, no. 58, fol. 40a: *hemd.*

[38] *Ẓemaḥ Ẓedeḳ,* no. 45, fol. 51a:

וגם האט ער נאך אן זיד גיהאט איין שטיק סרדקי״ל נעגיל ברוין מיט ציצית. . . .

Cf. "Costumes," *RCC.*

negil-broyn; cf. *nogl-broyn* (Yid.), "nail-brown color."

Cf. *Shebut Ya'aḳob,* II, no. 115, fol. 18b:

. . . גם קפתורים קטנים שהיה לו במלבוש קטן שקורין בל״א סרדקי״ל. . . . וגם שהי׳ לו טלית קטן שקורין צרדקי״ל. . . .

Cf. "Costumes, Germany, 17th-18th cent.," *RCC.* Cf. also *Noda' bi-Yehudah,* I, no. 36, fol. 25b: *layb-sardakl* (Yid.) = *arbe-kanfes,* "the undergarment with fringes." Cf. Landau-Wachstein, *Jüd. Privatbriefe,* p. 130 ("Gloss."): *serdekel.*

For other instances of a dead person being identified by the clothes he wore, see *Glikl,* p. 245; *Pene Yeshohua',* II, no. 53, no. 58, fol. 39b; and herein, p. 140, n. 190. See also in *Maharam Mintz,* no. 21, fol. 56a, concerning the identification of a deceased, in the 15th century.

[39] Cf. "collars with points" in *Ẓemaḥ Ẓedeḳ,* no. 45, fol. 50b:

. . . זיין קראגין האט שיפקין (פירוש דבריו שפיצליך). . . .

Cf. Koppmann in *idem* (ed.), *Aus Hamburgs Vergangenheit,* II, 238, a linen shirt with a plain collar.

Cf. Schnapper-Arndt in *ZGJD,* II, 188, 192, that the collars of men and women—for example, the bride—were embellished with gold and silver points. It seems that this was not considered ostentatious, otherwise the sumptuary laws would have prohibited such dress. See *kragen* in Grunwald, *MGJV,* I, p. 113, #1 (2). Also, for the collar worn in the 17th and 18th centuries, see Weiss, *Kostümkunde,* II, 1038, fig. 370.

[40] See nn. 27, 35 to p. 89; n. 66 to p. 94.

[41] Cf. portraits in Hottenroth, I, 197, fig. 74 (1, 3-6). For the "flat cap," see chap. IV, p. 89, n. 26; p. 92, n. 54; p. 94, nn. 65, 69; p. 95, n. 71.

Noda' bi-Yehudah, I, *op. cit.: brust-tukh* (Yid.) = "chest cloth." Cf. Schnapper-Arndt in *ZGJD,* II (O. S.), 192: *halstücher,* "scarfs." Cf. Grunwald in *MGJV,* I, 113, #1 (1). Also, Schnapper-Arndt, 188: brocade worn on the breast; red velvet breast-piece made with a gold trimming. See *brüstling* in Hottenroth, I, 36, fig. 8.

Cf. ". . . a shirt with a Polish collar. . . .": *Pene Yehoshua',* II, no. 58, fol. 40a; see n. 58 to p. 93.

Shelah, I, fol. 106a (sec. "Sha'ar ha-'Otyot"): *zoken* (*zokn,* Yid.), "stockings."

Kaufmann (ed.), *Glikl,* p. 27: may be *shtrimpf* (Yid.), prob. related to *strumpf* (Ger.), "stocking." Cf. Schnapper-Arndt, 192: *strümpfe.*

Y. 'O., #3: *hentshukh* (Yid.). Cf. Schnapper-Arndt, *loc. cit.:* (Ger.), gloves." See chap. VII, n. 81 to p. 161.

For shoe-styles in the German community, see Koppmann (ed.), *Aus Hamburgs Vergangenheit*, II, 250. Shoes were low with laces, also high and pointed.

42 Hottenroth, I, 137, 197; figs., 74 (2, 7); III, 36 (3). Cf. Kaufmann (ed.), *Glikl*, p. 168, n. 1: *robe*.

Cf. *Glikl*, p. 396: *sarbal*, "mantle," worn by Glikl. See trans. of *sarbal*, n. 49.

For "apron", see chap. II, p. 25, n. 61. Cf. *Ḥavvot Ya'ir*, no. 161, fol. 150b: ". . . what is called *fartukh* [*fartekh*] in Polish and *sharts* in Yiddish (*bi-leshon 'Ashkenaz*). . . ."
See Hottenroth, I, 43, that the "apron" was known in Germany by the 15th century. Cf. a green apron made of cloth with silver fringes: Schnapper-Arndt, 188.

Cf. woman's headgear (*haube*, "hood"): *J. M.*, IV, 101, #31; Schnapper-Arndt, 188. Also, portraits of the "hood" in Hottenroth, I, 72, fig. 37 (4); 132, fig. 57 (3); supp. plate no. 23.

For the woman's belt, see chap. II, p. 35; also, Grunwald in *JLex*, IV², 1022: *gürtel*.

43 Friedländer, *Tiferet Jisrael*, p. 48. See hood (*Stuart-Haube*) worn in Germany in the 17th and 18th centuries: Weiss, *Kostümkunde*, II, 1038, fig. 370.

44 *Ḥavvot Ya'ir*, no. 143, fol. 131a:

. . . שלובשים בחורף שתי מצנפת לילה על ראשם. . . .

Cf. "Clothing," *RCC: miẓnefet* = "night cap." See in Schnapper-Arndt, 108, "night caps with golden edges." See also *Shelah*, I, 106a:

. . . בגדי נשים הנקראות שוו״יף. . . .

Prob. *shveyf* (Yid.). Cf. *shvaaf* (Yid.), "tail." Cf. *schweif* (Ger.) = "border or edge of a garment": Kluge, *Wörterbuch*, p. 691.

45 Kaufmann (ed.), *Glikl*, p. 229, n. 1: *regin klayt* (*regen klayd*). See the illustration of a *regenkleid* in Hottenroth, III, 180, fig. 69 (1).

46 See above, p. 87, n. 14. Cf. *royten shlayer;* Shiper, *Yid. teater*, I, 182. See also Hottenroth, II, 72: *schleier* (Ger.), "veil," serving as a headdress.

47 Kaufmann (ed.), *Glikl*, p. 333: ". . . [They] tore each other's *shlayer* from [the] head. . . ." Cf. Feilchenfeld, pp. 304-5.

48 *Shebut Ya'akob*, I, no. 103, fol. 26b-27a. The *minhag*, or practice, is based on *'O. Ḥ.* 75:2.

49 See herein, pp. 25, 34, 37, 93. See also Joseph Jacobs in *JE*, IV (1903), 300, that there was no special dress for religious services. The description of clothes worn by royalty, officials, clergy, and commoners in Germany is not applicable to the dress in the Jewish community: Hoffstaetter-Peters, *Sachwörterbuch*, II, 1189-91.

50 *Y. 'O.*, #592: . . . *sarbal shel Shabbat*. . . .

N. K. Y., fol. 1a, #7:

ואותו שהולכין כל היום מלובש׳ בסרבל יש להם סרבלים אחרים מתוקנים באופן אחר כמו שו״ל

מאנט״ל בק״ק פ״פ וק״ק הסמוכות לשם, וכמו הלעטני״ק וה״שויבן אשר במדינת פולין פיה״ם ומערהרי״ן. . . .

sarbal (Heb.) = *shul-mantl* (Yid.). See *shul-mantl* in Bernstein, *Takones . . . kegn lukses*, p. 11, and the special cloak *(gebottmantel)* worn to the synagogue on the Sabbath and holidays: Schnapper-Arndt, 191.

letnik (Pol.) = "summer dress": cf. J. Stanisławski, *Eng.-Pol. and Pol.-Eng. Dict.* (Philadelphia, 1940), Pt. 2, p. 99, under *letni* = (adj.) pertaining to summer.

shoybn; cf. *schaube* (Ger.) = "long cloak or mantle."

פיה״ם (בהם) = Bohemia.

On the assumption that the terms *shul-mantl, letnik,* and *shoybn* are of different styles, then the text may be retained as printed and is to be translated as follows: "And those who go around the whole [Sabbath] day wearing a certain mantle have also other mantles, each tailored in a different style." But if the terms *shul-mantl, letnik,* and *shoybn* are all of the same style, then the term *'aḥer* in the text is to be emended to read *'eḥad,* and the latter part of the text is to be translated: ". . . have also other mantles, all tailored in the same style. . . ."

51 See Posen in *Menorah,* VI, 684.

52 Friedländer, *op. cit.*, p. 48. Cf. *Mas'at Binyamin*, no. 80, fol. 87a: The *rok*, coat, is often lined with fur and made into a *shubitse:*

. . . ולפעמים רגילין לתפור בו פליצה מעורות שועלים או שאר עורות חיות ובהמות וקורין אותו שויב. . . .

pelitsah (Yid.); cf. *pelts* (mod. Yid.) = "pelisse, a long cloak or coat made of fur, or lined or trimmed with fur." Cf. *pelz* (Ger.), "fur."

shube, shubitse (Yid.) = "fur coat." Cf. Elsass in *MGJV,* XVI, 101: *schubetze;* also, Grunwald in *MGJV,* I, 115, sec. l.

53 See above, n. 30.

54 *Pene Yehoshua',* I, no. 16, fol. 11a (sec. "*'O. Ḥ.*"):

. . . לצאת בשבת וכובע על ראשיהם שקורין בריט״ליך. . . .

Cf. "Costumes," *RCC,* cit.

breytlikh (bretlikh) = prob. Yid. dimin. related to *bret,* "board, plank."

J. M., (Bk. 6, chap. 14), 252, #13. The beret is called *Schabbes-Deckel* (i. e., *Shabes-Dekel*) due to its flat shape. Cf. Friedländer, *op. cit.*, p. 48: The *barett* is described as a *haubenbrettel,* a cap that is flat like a board. Cf. Grunwald, "Trachten der Juden," *JLex,* IV (1930), 1014: *barett* = *brettel* (Ger.); Halpern, *Taḳḳanot Mähren,* p. 183, #530 (7): *bretil* (Yid.) = "cap." Cf. also M. Bernstein, "Yiddish Glossary of *Ḥayye'Adam,*" *Argentin. IWO Shrift.*, VI (Buenos Aires, 1955), 137, sec. 2, cit.; *Ḥayye 'Adam,* 42:6 (sec. "Hil. Shab."): . . . *be-ro'sho be-Shabes (Shabbat) (braytul)*. . . . See also *barrette,* p. 94.

Schudt's description of Sabbath garments is confirmed by pictures of Jewish men and women of Nuremberg, in the 18th century, dressed for the synagogue (see Liebe, *Judentum in der deut. Vergangenheit,* pp. 96–97, figs. 78–79; figs.

7–8 in this chap.). Two of these pictures are in Posen, *Menorah,* VI, 683–84. Fig. 79 also appears in Erik, bet. pp. 401-2.

[55] M. Grunwald in *MGJV,* I, 113, #1 (4): *krawatten,* "neckties." Cf. *kravat* (Yid.).

[56] *J. M., op. cit.*

[57] *Panim Me'irot,* II, no. 28, fol. 13b.

[58] *Ḥavvot Ya'ir,* no. 143, fol. 131a: . . . *beys (bet) ha-ẓavva'r meḥubar ba-beged.*

Cf. "Costumes," *RCC,* cit.

Shabes-mantl with *kragen*: see n. 78 to p. 160, cit. from *M. F.*

J. M., II, 252, #13; also illustrations.

See Posen, *Menorah,* VI, 683: the ruffled collar, of Spanish influence, was introduced in Germany at the beginning of the 17th century. By the 18th century the collar was part of the conventional dress of German Jews.

See in Schnapper-Arndt, 188, the Sabbath mantle with gold trimming, gold clasps, and silver *crappen* (?).

[59] Schnapper-Arndt, 191; also, 188.

[60] *Shebut Ya'aḳob,* II, no. 115, fol. 18b. Cf. "Costumes," *RCC,* cit.

[61] Kaufmann (ed.), *Glikl,* p. 81; Feilchenfeld, pp. 61-62; Lowenthal, p. 46. (Trans. is from Lowenthal.) Cf. Grunwald, "Beiträge zur jüd. Kulturgesch.," *MGJV,* XVII (1906), 25, cit.; Ysaye in *MGJV,* VII (1901), 9.

[62] *Y. 'O.,* #591; see chap. VII, p. 161, n. 81.

[63] Schnapper-Arndt, 192. See "veil" of bride, herein, p. 36. See pictures of bridal procession in Liebe, *Judentum in der deut. Vergangenheit,* p. 108, fig. 88; Posen in *Menorah,* VI, 684. During the procession the bride's face is covered with a veil. (The portrait in Posen pertains to Fürth).

[64] Cf. Koppmann in *idem, Hamburgs Vergangenheit,* II, 237, the cowl or hood. Cf. Hottenroth, I, 49, the headgear for bad weather. Cf. Epstein in *Gedenkbuch . . . David Kaufmann,* pp. 314-15: When the *mitron,* cowl, is tied to the neck, it is a sign of mourning; when worn loosely, it is no longer a mourner's attire. How the cowl became a mourner's garment deserves further investigation.

[65] Cf. communal legislation of Konitz, 1713: Halpern, *Taḳḳanot Mähren,* p. 183, #530 (7), n. 9: *hil-rok;* cf. *hüllrock,* "coat" (cf. N. Prilucki, *Dos gevet,* p. 124); *bretil* is a pointed cap that does not reach the forehead. The "flat cap" is described above, p. 91, and elsewhere as cited, n. 54.

[66] Posen in *Menorah,* VI, 683. Cf. Hottenroth, I, 197, fig. 74 (4): A pictorial illustration of dress worn by rabbis of Germany in the 18th century shows a cap, large white collar, and long coat.

That high regard is shown the scholar *(ḥaber* and *morenu),* see Baron, *Community,* II, 206. In the Middle Ages, *morenu* was the title of rabbinical status and authority. The title of *ḥaber* was given to a student of the Torah. See Mordecai

Breuer, "The 'Ashkenazi Semikha'" (Hebrew), *Zion,* XXXIII (N. S., 1968), 16: *Morenu* as the title for those ordained as rabbis was in all probability introduced in the 14th century.

[67] Ginzberg, *Students, Scholars and Saints,* pp. 149-50.

[68] Above, p. 87; n. 49 to p. 91.

[69] *H. 'A.*, chap. iii, 3a (no fol. mark):

ישים בגד העליון וגם הכובע או המצנפת על ראשו בשעת בה"ם....

Cf. Bernstein in *Argentin. IWO Shrift.*, VI, 141, sec. 10, cit.; *Ḥayye 'Adam,* 37:1: ". . . [The] headgear of felt *(kob'im shel lebadin)* called *kapelushin* or [the] *yarmelke* [*yarmulke*]. . . ."

[70] Cf. Rivkind, "A *Responsum* of Leon da Modena on Uncovering the Head," *Louis Ginzberg Jubilee Volume* (Hebrew), pp. 403-4, n. 3, the *responsum of* Rabbi Shlomo Kluger; p. 404, n. 3, the *responsum* of Rabbi M. L. Winkler:

... לצאת בהמצנפת שקורין קאפיל תחת הכובע....

kapil; cf. *kapl* (Yid.) = "cap"; cf. Hottenroth, I, 28-29.

[71] See "cap," n. 123 to p. 37; p. 91, n. 41; p. 92, n. 54. Cf. W. G. Plaut, "Origin of the Word Yarmulke," *HUCA,* XXVI, (1955) 568-69: *gugel* = "cap," which was first attached to a cape. Also, Hottenroth, I, 28: *gugel* = *cuculus (cucullus),* Lat. And, Straus in *JSS,* IV, 62-64, nn. 18-19, *cucullus* was originally *cappa* (Lat.), "a wrap with a hood," as suggested above, n. 26 to p. 89. Cf. also Halpern, *Taḳḳanot Mähren,* p. 183, #530 (7), n. 9: *bretil* is related to *kippah* (Heb.), "a skull-cap, cap" = *yarmulke* (Yid.); N. Prilucki, *Dos gevet,* p. LXXXI, n. 21 ("Notes to Reg."), "beret" = *yarmulke.*

[72] See Hottenroth, I, 197, fig. 74 (1).

NOTES TO CHAPTER V

[1] Elzet (Zlotnik), *Yid. maykholim* (Jewish Foods), Pt. 1, pp. 7-8. (Hereafter cited as Elzet.)

[2] Cf. M. Kosover, "Jewish Foods," in *Yuda A. Yoffe-bukh,* p. 5. (Hereafter cited as Kosover.)

[3] *Ibid.*, pp. 5-6, 11-12.

[4] Bax, *German Culture,* p. 127. See ref. to the diet of the non-Jewish population in Elzet, p. 22. For cookery in Germany in the 17th century, cf. W. H. Hohberg, *Koch-Buch (Georgica Curiosa Aucta; Adelichen Land- und Feld-Lebens,* III*), passim.* (Hereafter cited as Hohberg.)

[5] See Wilhelm Goetz, "Speise und Trank . . . in deut. Landen," *Oeffent. Vorträge,* VI (1882), 9, that the main diet in Germany during the 18th century continued to the modern era.

[6] *Y. 'O.*, #135-136. Cf. Tsinberg, *Gesch. fun der lit.*, V, 87-88, for the foods in *Y. 'O.*

S. H., I, fol. 47a, the foods of "meat, fish, and bread."

Shelah, I, fol. 91a (sec. "Sha'ar ha-'Otyot"): ". . . meat and fish and greens . . . fruits, dates and grapes, etc. . . . and wafers. . . ."
Cf. gloss on *'O. Ḥ.* 158:1: פי׳סטורט״ר used by Isserles as a synonym for *laḥmaniyot,* "wafers."

J. M., III, No. 9, 203, from the "Akhashveyros (Aḥashverosh) Shpil":
מיר האבן הינן מעד אונ׳ וויין, מעד אונ׳ וויין אונ׳ הינר אונ׳ פֿיש, עש שטיט גאר וויניג אויף דעם טיש.
Cf. Hohberg, pp. 31-34, 41, meat and fish as main dishes in Germany. Cf. also Elzet, Pt. 1, p. 9, for a festive meal, *se'udah,* the foods included meat and fish. Cf. *Ḥavvot Ya'ir,* no. 198, fol. 189b, fowl meat is provided domestically: "There are many householders who raise roosters and chickens during the summer season. . . ." See also p. 111, home-grown vegetables.

S. H., I, 46b: In addition to the main courses for a full meal, the menu consisted of *shlotn* (Yid.); cf. *schlotten* (Ger.), "vegetable stalks"; *putir (puter) kukhin (kukhn),* "butter cookies"; *shmalts kukhin (kukhn)* = "cookies made of fats," and פאשטיד וועז שון מיט אופש געפילט איז (prob. *pashtid* [Yid.]; cf. *pastete* [Ger.], "pie"; see above, p. 98, n. 23). See in *Leḳet Yosher,* I, 47 (sec. *'O. H.*); also Kosover, p. 80. n. 216. Prob. *ops* or *obs* (Yid.), "fruit"; cf. *oybs* (mod. Yid.); *obst* (Ger.), same meaning. Cf. Grunwald, "Aus dem jüd. Kochbuch," *Menorah,* VI (Vienna, 1928), 518-19. Cf. *Ḳ. Shelah,* fol. 48a: *shlotn;* also, "cucumbers . . . were salted, the water drained, and then dipped in olive oil and vinegar." Cf. Grunwald, "Gemeinde Proklamationen," *MGJV,* XXXIX (1911), 123, #7 (legislation of Sivan 3, 5491 = 1730): *butterkuchen, putterkuchen;* A. Berliner, "Jüd. Speisetafel," *JJGL,* XIII (1910), 206: *pasteten* is included with a list of pastry.

Naḥalat Shib'ah, II, no. 71, fol. 37b: *pretsin* = prob. derived from *prezen* (Ger.), "pretzel." Cf. "Foods," *RCC,* cit. See *pretsn:* Kosover, p. 116f.

[7] *S. H.,* I, 47a. Cf. Elzet, Pt. 1, p. 29, *tsimes;* Grunwald in *Menorah,* VI, 518: "Zimmes (. . . Zumuss, Kompott oder gewürztes Gemüse) als: Pflaumenzimmes, Möhrenzimmes (Mohrrüben, Mehl, Zucker und Zimt)." See Franze Fuhse, *Sitten und Gebräuche der Deutschen beim Essen und Trinken,* pp. 20, 38: In the early Middle Ages the principal foods in Germany were meat, soup, fish, bread, vegetables *(gemüse),* and fruit for dessert. See also Hohberg, p. 6: *allerley muesse (= allerlei müse).* Cf. *zugemüse* = "vegetables eaten or served with meat." Cf. Güdemann, *Gesch.,* II, 212, *compot;* cf. *kompot* (Yid.), "stewed fruit."

[8] Elzet, "Jewish Customs," *Reshumot,* I (1918), 341, #7: *rendlekh = mehrin = ruvya' (robya').*
Cf. *H. 'A.,* fol. 2b (chap. xviii, fol. not marked): *ribin u-mehrin (mehrn); ribin* (Yid.), "turnips"; cf. *rüben* (Ger.), same meaning. *mehrn̄* (Yid.), "carrots"; cf. *möhren* (Ger.), same meaning. (Henceforth, all refs. and cits. in *H. 'A.* are from chap. xviii unless specified.) Cf. *Shelah,* I, fol. 214b (sec. "Rosh ha-Shanah"): . . . *ruvya' yirbu zekhiyosenu (zekhiyotenu). . . .*
Cf. *Ḥayye 'Adam* 139:6 (sec. "Hil. Rosh ha-Shanah"): ". . . all kinds of carrots

(*liftan, mehrin* [*mehrn*]), which can be interpreted to mean 'increase' (*she-hu leshon ribbuy*). . . ."

liftan (Heb.) = "carrot."

Cf. also Bernstein in *Argentin. IWO Shrift.*, VI, 134. Cf. Hohberg, p. 74: *möhren, gelbe rüben.* Cf. Elzet, Pt. 1, p. 32; *mehren-tsimes* is considered a *refu'ah,* with the healing power of a folk remedy, as in chap. VI, n. 29.

[9] *B. D.*, fol. 22a: *hekht* (Yid.); cf. *hecht* (Ger.), pike. *shlayen* (Yid.); cf. *schleien* (Ger.), tench, a fish related to the pike. Cf. Kaufmann (ed.), *Glikl,* p. 256, for "a variety of fish." Cf. Barbeck, *Juden in Nürnberg und Fürth*, p. 84 (based on the *Taḳḳanot* of 1728): *hecht; forellen* = trout. Cf. A. Wiener, *Jüd. Speisegesetze,* p. 312: *stör,* sturgeon; Berliner in *JJGL,* XXX, 208: *barbe=flussfisch,* barbel, a fresh-water fish; Grunwald in *Menorah,* VI, 520, pike; Elzet, Pt. 1, p. 30: *hekht.* See *hecht, forellen,* and *karpffen* (*karpfen,* carp) fish in Hohberg, pp. 12-13, 25-26; Thiemen, *Haus- Feld- Koch- und Wunder-Buch,* p. 819, #6-7; pp. 324-28, #31-57; pp. 828-29, #58-69. Grunwald in *Menorah,* VI, 520, pike.

[10] Cf. Hohberg, pp. 12-13.

[11] *Y. 'O.*, #112, 137; *S. H.*, I, 47a; *H. A.*, fol. 3a. Cf. Kaufmann (ed.), *Glikl*, p. 256: "milk dishes." Cf. also Elzet, Pt. 1, pp. 10-11; Pt. 2, p. 95: "milk dishes."

Cf. *Ẓemaḥ David,* fol. 85a, #398, for the basic foods in Bohemia in the 16th century, viz., eggs, meat, and bread.

[12] *H. 'A.*, 1b: *kreplikh* (*kreplekh,* Yid.) = "dumplings"; *lokshin* (*lokshn,* Yid.) = "noodles"; cf. also *kreplekh* in *ibid.*, chap. iii, 2b.

Y. 'O., #398: אכן קרעפליך מעשה קדירה פאציוש פפֿאנקוכ"ן. . . .

fankukhen (Yid.), "pancake"; cf. *pfannkuchen* (Ger.), same meaning, also "fritter." Cf. also *fankukhen* in *ibid.*, #391; *H. 'A.*, 1b. See *kreplekh* and *fankukhen* in Kosover, pp. 71f., 77f. Cf. Dornseiff, *Deut. Wortschatz,* p. 135, sec. 2, #27: *pfannkuchen,* a German food.

S. H., I, 46b: ... גריץ וואז מן קאכֿט גידכֿט פון האבר ווייץ גערשט....

H. 'A., 2b: *arbiz-zupa; S. H.*, II, 7a: *arbiz-zubin* = *arbiz-zup* (mod. Yid.) = "pea soup"; *erbsensuppe* (Ger.), same meaning: cf. Hohberg, p. 5, for *erbsensuppen.* Cf. *Y. 'O.*, #387-88: *zupa; maraḳ* (Heb.): ". . . Soup prepared without any ingredients *(shnitn)*. . . ." *shnit* (Yid.) = "cut, slice"; *schnitt* (Ger.), same meaning. Cf. also Kaufmann (ed.), *Glikl*, p. 296, n. 2: *suppe.*

S. H., I, 46b: ". . .grits as thin as soup *(zub)*. . . ."

גברנטי זוב = prob. related to *gebrannte suppe* (Ger.) = "stew";

קלימף = prob. *klimf,* may be related to *klumpf* (Ger.) = "ball"; *kneydlikh* (*kneydlekh*, Yid.); cf. *knödel* (Ger.), "dumpling." Cf. Thiemen, *Haus- und Koch-Buch,* p. 845, #91: *knödel.* Cf. Elzet, Pt. 1, p. 11, *kneydlekh* is another East European dish that probably originated in Germany.

[13] Grunwald in *Menorah,* VI, 518. Cf. *Ḥayye 'Adam,* 52:6 (sec. "Birkhat ha-Nehnin"): ". . . and thus *retsine kashe* from which soup *(zupa)* is made. . . ."

retsine: cf. *grits* (mod. Yid.) = "grits, groats"; *grütze* (Ger.), same meaning. Cf. Bernstein in *Argentin. IWO Shrift.*, VI, 140, sec. 7, cit. Cf. Elzet, Pt. 1, p. 11; Pt. 2, p. 91: *kashe;* cf. *kasha* (Rus.), "porridge, gruel." Cf. also Renner, *Origin of Food Habits,* p. 243, *kasha* as a Russian food.

[14] Grunwald in *Menorah,* VI, 518; Sidgwick, *Home Life in Germany,* p. 159.

[15] *Shelah,* I, fol. 90b (sec. "Sha'ar ha-'Otyot"):

...לאקש״ן שקורין בל״א ורימז״ליך....

Cf. gloss of Isserles, no. 4 on *'O. Ḥ.* 168:12: . . . .

... לאקשין שקורין ורומזלי״ך ....

See *frimzlikh* (Yid.) = *khremzlakh* (mod. Yid.) = "vermicelli." Probably related to *vermicelli* (Ital.); *vermicelle* (Fr.). Cf. Webster *Twentieth-Century Dictionary* (New York, 1939), p. 1862: "vermicelli," Ital., lit. = "little worms," from Lat. *vermiculus,* dim. of *vermis,* a "worm." A full treatment of the etymology of the word is in Kosover, pp. 63 ff. Cf. *Ḥayye 'Adam* 54:2 (sec. "Birkhat ha-Nehnin"):

... שחותך העיסה לפרודין קטנים כמו (לאקשין פארפיל....)

Also, Bernstein in *Argentin, IWO Shrift.*, VI, 141, sec. 9, cit. See p. 179.

[16] Grunwald in *Menorah,* VI, 519. Such aphorisms are: "Es mit lokshen far Shabes," to prepare for a rainy day. "A sakh zmires un wenig lokshen," there is much talk and little substance. "A langer loksh," referring to a person who is not very adept. See *lokshn* as a food of Eastern Europe in Elzet, Pt. 1, p. 13; Pt. 2, pp. 111-12. For examples of aphorisms, *sprikhverter,* referring to *lokshn* and other foods, *kugl, kashe,* and *kreplekh,* see Elzet, Pt. 1, pp. 31, 38; Pt. 2, pp. 91-93; 111-12; 121-22.

[17] *Y. 'O.*, #391, #662; *H. 'A.*, fol. 2b; *S. H.*, I, 46b-47a; *Shelah,* I, 94a: *veygen pfefer:* cf. *veykin fefer* (mod. Yid.), "soaked pepper"; cf. *weichen* (Ger.), same meaning. *yungi tsvifl* (Yid.); cf. *junge zwiebel* (Ger.), "young onions"; cf. *tsibele* (mod. Yid.), "onion." *yungi (yunge) kneplikh* (*kneplekh,* Yid.) = "young buds (onions)"; cf. *knepele* (mod. Yid.), "bud"; *knopf* (Ger.), "onion bud." Cf. F. A. Specht, *Gastmähler und Trinkgelage bei den Deutschen,* p. 12: *zwiebeln.*

[18] *S. H.*, I, 47a. Cf. Hohberg, p. 13: *sauerkraut,* pickled cabbage.

[19] *H. 'A.*, 1a-1b; *Shelah,* I, 90b. *H. A'.* 1b:

... גלוסקאות שקורים בל״א גיזאטניר זעמיל. ...

geluska' (Aram.) = "white bread". Cf. *Naḥalat Shib'ah,* II, no. 72, fol. 37b: "white bread made by a baker." Also, *geluska'ot*, comment on *'abal perusah shel ḥiṭin* in "Tosaf." to *Ber.* 39b.

[20] *Shelah,* I, fol. 89b:

... כוסמין (שקורין טינקיל) או שיפון שקורין (קארין)....

Prob. *tinkil* (Yid.) = "dark"; *karin* = prob. *karn* (Yid.) = "rye"; cf. *korn* (mod. Yid.); *kern* (Ger.) = "grain of corn."

For bread made of wheat and barley, which belongs to the "seven species," cf. *Shelah,* I, 89b. Cf. also *Ḥavvot Ya'ir,* no. 15, fol. 20a.

Cf. *Ḥayye 'Adam* 42:5 (sec. "Hil. Se'udah"):

... פת קיבר (שקורין גראבע ברויט). . . .

ḳibbar (Heb.) = "coarse bread."

Also, Bernstein in *Argentin. IWO Shrift.*, VI, 138, sec. 3, cit.

[21] Cf. Renner, *Origin of Food Habits*, p. 179. The rye bread of Prussia and Westphalia became known as *pumpernickel.*

[22] *S. H.*, I, 47b:

איבר רייז אונ׳ הירש טאטירקי גיקאכט אך איז (שכ̄יח) במדינות̄ פולן). . . . אך ווען מן מאכט ברויט אויז ארביזן אונ׳ דר גלייכ̄ן. . . .

Cf. *Ḥayye 'Adam* 42:2: ... קמח רעצקי שקורין (טארטקע). . . .

Cf. *retshke, retshene* = "buckwheat" (Yid.); *tatirki*, etc. = buckwheat grain. For *tatreke* bread, see Kosover, p. 136, n. 461. Cf. *Y. 'O.*, #400, bread made of rice and millet: *hirsh;* cf. *hirse* (Ger.), "millet."

[23] *Shelah,* I, fol. 90b:

עגות שקורין שמא״לץ קוכ״ן שעירב בלישתן שומן וטעם השומן ניכר בעיסה. . . .

H. 'A., 1b:

עוגות שקורין שמאליץ קוכין שעירב בלישתן שומן ולא יאכל אלא בתוך הסעודה:

Shelah, I, 91a:

... המוליית׳ שקורין פשטי״ידא הנאפ׳ בתנור בבשר או בדגי׳ או בגבינה. . . .

Y. 'O., #392:

פשטידא שמולייתא שבתוכה היא מבשר ודגים וגבינה ומיני קמחים ואף אם מעט ענבים קטנים שקורין וויינפרליך. . . .

vaynperlikh (Yid.), "currants." Cf. *weinbeere* (Ger.) = "grapes."

Cf. *Y. 'O.*, #394: ואם הפשטידא ממולאה בפירות כתפוחים. . . .

H. 'A., 1b: ... פשטיד׳א הנאפה בתנור בבשר או בדגים או בגבינה. . . .

See above, n. 6 to p. 97: *pastete.* Cf. *S. H.*, I, 46a: *pashtid.*

pashtida = prob. *pastete* (a German dish), "pasty," a small pie filled with meat, fish, fruits, or vegetables; cf. Adelung, *Wörterbuch*, III, 669; Grimm, *Wörterbuch*, VII, 1491-92. See examples of *pasteten* in Hohberg, pp. 31, 33; Thiemen, *Haus- und Koch-Buch*, p. 817, #42-43; pp. 866 ff. Cf. Halpern, *Taḳḳanot Mähren*, p. 199, n. 11 (communal legislation of Budapest, 1720), pastry of *fladin* (Yid.) = "cake filled with fruit"; cf. *flodn* (mod. Yid.) = "flat cake." Cf. *flodn* in Kosover, p. 97f.; pp. 99-100, nn.

[24] *H. 'A.*, 1b: cf. *martsipan* (mod. Yid.) = "marchpane" (sweet bread or biscuit made of almonds and sugar); cf. *marzipan* (Ger.), same meaning. See origin and definition of *martsipan* in Kosover, pp. 113-14.

[25] *H. 'A.*, 1b:

אותן עיסות שעושין בפראג שקורין וואפלטקי״ז ואופין אותן בין שני ברזלים. . . .

[26] *Shelah,* I, fol. 90b:

... בעיר פראג ... ושופך אותה [העיסה] בדפוס של ברזל וקורין אותו פורב״ן ויש למעלה עוד ברזל אחר כמוהו והעיסה נשפך בין שני הברזלי׳ וכשמהדק ברזל בברזל יחד כעין צבת

שקורין צוואנג . . . ואז נאפה מיד . . . ויעלו על אותן הרקיקין צורות ותמונות . . . כצלם ודמו׳ הברזל . . . ונקראים אותן הרקיקי׳ בלשון פיהם וואפלטקו״ס. . . .

Cf. "waffle iron" in "Ba'er Heṭeb," no. 34 on *'O. Ḥ.* 168:15.

Pastries classified with waffles are *nalisniki, nalisnekes* and *hoyzn-blozn:*

H. 'A., chap. iii, fol. 2b (fol. not marked): *nalisnekes.*

Shelah, I, fol. 90b:

...וקורי׳ אותן רקיקים בלשון רוס״יא נאליסנק״י ע״ש שאופין אותן על העלין....

nalisnikes = "pancakes"; cf. Kosover, p. 135, n. 457.

H. 'A., loc. cit.: hoyzn-blozn.

Shelah, I, 90b: *hoyzn-blozn.*

Cf. *hoyzn-blozn* in *Ḥayye 'Adam* 43:10 ("Hil. Se'udah"). Cf. "Ba'er Heṭeb," no. 19 on *'O. Ḥ.* 168:8 (based on "Ṭure Zahab"):

וואפלטק״ס והויז״ן בלאזי״ן שקורין פריטלי״ך. . . .

hoyzn-blozn = "fritters" (pancakes like *nalisnikes*): cf. Kosover, pp. 141-42, inc. n. 482, cit.: "Ṭure Zahab" to *'O. Ḥ.* 168:8.

27 For cooked fruits, see *S. H.*, I, 46b. Also, 47a: "When fruits are not ripe, we may not eat them, but they should be cooked in the same manner as a grass herb."

28 *H. 'A.*, fol. 1a, 2a-b, 3a-b: *kirshn, powidl.* Cf. Halpern, *Taḳḳanot Mähren,* p. 199, #573 (6); *Shebut Ya'aḳob,* III, no. 104, 17b; *Naḥalat Shib'ah,* II, no. 71, fol. 37b, for *powidl.*

Ẓemaḥ Ẓedeḳ, no. 52, fol. 60b:

. . . על הלוטוורג שעושין מן הפירות שקורין קירכ״ן, ויש קורין אותם פלוי״מן, ובמדינת הללו קורין אותו פאווי״דלי שעושין מן הפירות הנ״ל. . . .

Cf. "Foods," *RCC,* cit.

S. H., I, fol. 46b: *latwerge* made of fruit.

Cf. *Y. 'O.* #380: *spiling:* cf. *spilling* (Ger.), "small yellow plum." Cf. *latwerge* = *powidl,* "plum jam" = *pflaumenmus,* "jelly confection": Dornseiff, *Deut. Wörterbuch,* sec. 2, p. 135, #27.

Prob. *kirshn* (Yid.), "cherries"; cf. *karshen* (mod. Yid.), *kirschen* (Ger.). See *Leḳeṭ Yosher,* I, 40, n. 1 (sec. "'O. Ḥ."): *kirshn;* also "cherry preserves": Bernstein in *Argentin. IWO Shrift.*, VI, 137, sec. 3.

Shelah, I, fol. 93a:

לטוו״רגא הנקרא בלשון אשכנז פאוו״ידלא שעושין ממגדניות שקורין ווייק״סילין....

vayksilin = related to *vaynshl* (Yid.) "cherries"; cf. *weichsel* (Ger.) "cherry": Kluge-Götze, *Wörterbuch,* p. 863. Cf. *Shelah,* I, fol. 94b:

ועל הלונ״דרא...הפירי שבאותו האילן וקורין אותן שוו״רצי קיר״שן....

Also, *Naḥalat Shib'ah,* II, no. 72, fol. 38a:

הלטווערגה . . . של הולדר . . . כמו שאר פובידלא. . . .

Cf. "Foods," *RCC,* cit. Cf. *holunder* (Ger.) = "elder tree"; *holder* (Ger.) = *(holunder)* = "elder tree." Cf. *S. H.*, I, 47a:

...אין גמאכֿט....האלדר בליט....

Cf. *holder (holunder) blüte* (Ger.) = "elder-blossom."

Derushe ha-Ẓelaḥ, no. 23, fol. 36a, #21:

...מיני מרקחת...וויינקסלען....

("... a variety of jam [syrup] made of cherries. ...) Cf. "jam (syrup)": *Y. 'O.,* #419. For *vaynkeslen,* "cherries," see *vaynshl* above.

See apples, nuts, and lemons in *Shelah,* I, fol. 93a; lemons, oranges, and apples in Hohberg, p. 83.

29 *Naḥalat Shib'ah,* II, no. 72, fol. 38a. Cf. *Shelah,* I, fol. 94b. For other examples of foods being used as home remedies, see herein, p. 120, n. 40; p. 128, n. 106; pp. 135–36. Cf. Grimm, *Wörterbuch,* VI, 282, plum jam *(latwerge)* served as a medicine. See also above, n. 8 to p. 97.

30 *Y. 'O.,* #402: ...הייד״ל בער״ן גראשיל״ן שליא״ן....

Cf. *heidelbeere* (Ger.) = "bilberry plant"; *gräslein* (Ger.) = "little blade of grass"; *schlehe* (Ger.) = "sloe, wild plum." See chap. VI, n. 140 to p. 133: *schlehenblüte* (Ger.) = "sloe blossom."

Y. 'O., #145:

...שאר מיני פירות יבשין כגון קוועטשין רוזיינן ומיני זרעונים....

S. H., I, 46b: *kvetshin* (*kvetshen*) *floymn* (Yid.), "dried plums, prunes": *kvetshen* (Yid.) = "to squeeze"; cf. *kvetshen* (mod. Yid.); *quetschen, zwetschgen,* (Ger.) = "dried fruit." (*kvetshen* = *ẓimuḳim,* Heb.). For other examples of dried fruits (raisins, prunes, etc.), see *Pene Yehoshua',* II, no. 21, fol. 8a (sec. "Y. D."); *N. K. Y.,* fol. 9b, #2; *Shelah,* I, fol. 77b, 93a. And, in Schnapper-Arndt, *ZGJD,* II, 189, the inventory of "retail articles and foods" listed a cask of "small raisins" *(kleine Rosinen).*

S. H., I, 47a: prob. *vayn rutn* (Yid.) = "vine rods." *tatlin* (Yid.) = "dates"; cf. *datteln* (Ger.), same meaning. Prob. *oylber* (Yid.) = "olive"; cf. *aylbert, aylberl* (mod. Yid.); *ölbeere* (Ger.), same meaning. *kiml* (Yid.) = "caraway seed"; cf. *kümmel* (Ger.), same meaning. See the use of the caraway seed in folk medicine: herein, p. 127, n. 87. *anis* = prob. related to *anis* (Ger.) = "aniseed, anise" (a fragrant plant belonging to the carrot family).

Kaufmann (ed.), *Glikl,* p. 82.

31 *H. 'A.,* 2b: ...אגוזים המטוגנין בדבש שקורין בל״א נויהנ״ט....

Shelah, I, fol. 94b: אגוז המטוגן בדבש שקורין בל״א נו״יאט....

Y. 'O., #418: אגח המטוגן בדבש שקורין נויאט....

Naḥalat Shib'ah, II, no. 72, fol. 38a: "Large nuts spiced in their shells. ..." Cf. "Food," *RCC,* cit.

S. H., I, 46b: "... sugared almonds. ..."

Y. 'O., #416: "Almonds covered with sugar and cinnamon. ..." Also, *B. D.,* fol. 24b, for "glazed nuts."

S. H., I, 46b: *muskatnus*; cf. *muskatnuss* (Ger.) = "nutmeg."

Cf. *Y. 'O.*, #417: "*Ḳinnamon* which is called *tsimrind*. . . ." *ḳinnamon* (Heb.) = "cinnamon"; prob. *tsimrind* (Yid.); cf. *tsimring* (mod. Yid.) = "cinnamon"; cf. *zim(me)t* (Ger.), same meaning. Cf. *Shelah*, I, fol. 95a: prob. *kanila* (Yid.); cf. *kaneyl* (mod. Yid.), "cinnamon"; cf. *kaneel* (Ger.), same meaning. See also "nutmeg," p. 129, n. 107.

Y. 'O., #418: ". . . an *'etrog* spiced with honey. . . ."

S. H., I, 46b: ". . . sugared orange peels. . . ."

Panim Me'irot, I, no. 65, fol. 53a: ". . . orange peels spiced with honey. . . ." Cf. *Shelah*, I, fol. 94b: Preserves made of fruits with honey.

32 *Y. 'O.*, #419: ". . . various jams with spices . . . ." See above, n. 28.

S. H., I, 47a: *neglikh:* prob. related to *nägelchen* (Ger.), "clove." *zitfer:* prob. related to *zitwer* (Ger.) "zedoary plant." See p. 134, n. 150, *zitwer* in folk medicine. קרימום = ? Cf. Lewin in *JJGL*, XXX, 185-86, 208: Pepper and ginger were staple items, useful in cooking foods and preparing spices. Pepper was valued as a spice, and it was also made available in Europe by Jews who traveled and traded in the Orient.

33 *S. H.*, I, 47a. Cf. Elzet, Pt. 2, pp. 107-108, beer; also beer in J. Blau, *Böhmerwälder, Hausindustrie, und Volkkunst*, II (*BDBV*, XIV²), 202.

34 *S. H.*, I, 43a.

Ibid., 46b: ". . . olive oil (*boym-oyl*, Yid.) mixed with beer. . . ." Cf. Schnapper-Arndt in *ZGJD*, II, 189: *baumöl* (Ger.) = "olive oil." *Baumöl* is used in folk medicine.

Y. 'O., #389: . . . בפת השרוי ביין שקורין וויי"ן מער"ט. . . .

וויי"ן מער"ט = prob. *vayn mert* (Yid.). Professor Dov Sadan points out that *mert* is related to *mähren* (Ger.), from which *märte, mährte, märde, mehrde* are derived. See Grimm, *Wörterbuch* (Leipzig, 1885), VI, 1468: *mähren*, "to stir, dip; mainly to soak bread in liquor"; *mährte*, "mixture of food and drink; pastry, peelings dipped in a drink"; *mährde*, "the practice of dipping bread in wine or in a drink"; *märde*, "peelings dipped in a drink"; *märte, biermaerte, weinmaerte*, "peelings dipped in beer or wine. . . ." For similar definitions of *mähren, mahrte, brotmahrten, mährte, weinmährte*, see Adelung, *Wörterbuch* (Leipzig, 1798), III, 34, 35. See explanation of the word *mert* in Dov Sadan, *Yerid ha-Sha'ashu'im*, p. 201, in connection with the aphorism, "a poor man eats *morde* [i.e., his nose]." which refers to the evening meal, namely, "a poor man eats only in the evening," that is, once a day. Cf. also Sadan's cit. of *maẓot mert*, "pieces of *maẓot* dipped in wine," based on the Yiddish comment of Yeḥiel Mikhel Epstein, *Seder Tefillah Derekh Yesharah* (Frankfort-on-the-Oder), fol. 16b, sec. "Dine Berakhot"; our cit.: Epstein, *op. cit.* (Fürth, 1768), fol. 189a, sec. "Dine Birkhat ha-Mazon."

S. H., I, 46a: "When *penits* are soaked in beer or bread in wine. . . ." Cf. *Shelah*, I, fol. 92a (sec. "Sha'ar ha-'Otyot"): ". . . Concerning the pieces of bread that are called *penits* (בל"א פעניץ), they are dried over live coals and afterwards dipped in sugar. . . ." See similar description in "Ba'er Heṭeb," no. 26, on *'O. Ḥ.* 168:1, based on *Shelah,* no. cit. That the *penits* are pieces of bread that are warmed over coals and then dipped into beer (as described by Kirchan), cf. Kosover, p. 59, nn. 120–22.

S. H., I, 46b: "nutmeg in beer." *Ibid.,* 47b: "When warm beer is made, we can place a small amount of bread in it, so that the beer can be tasty. We can sip the beer with the crumbs in it. . . ." *krumfn* = prob. related to *krümchen* (Ger.), "crumbs."

[35] *S. H.,* I, 48a: "[They] eat preserves *(ayn-gimakht, ayngemakhts)* or cake *lekukhin, lekekhn),* and drink brandy *(brandi-vayn).* . . ." Cf. *branntwein* (Ger.) = "brandy." Cf. *Derushe ha-Ẓelaḥ,* no. 4, fol. 9b, #23: *shekhar* (Heb.) = "intoxicating drink"; *yayin saruf* (*saraf,* Heb.) = "whiskey, brandy." See in *Naḥalat Shib'ah,* II, no. 35, fol. 22b, the custom of reciting *ḳiddush* over brandy on Saturday morning. Also, "brandy" in Blau, *Böhmerwälder,* II (*BDBV,* XIV²), 205.

Shelah, I, fol. 93a: ". . . brandy or honey that is called *med.* . . ." Cf. *J. M.,* III, 203: ". . . brandy and wine. . . ."
med (Yid.), "mead, hydromel" (a fermented drink made of honey, water, and yeast).

S. H., I, 46b: ". . . the juice of dried plums (prunes). . . ."

H. 'A., fol. 3a: ". . . drinking vinegar mixed in water. . . ."

S. H., I, 47b: ". . . drinking vinegar. . . ." Also, "The juice of cooked prunes. . . ."

[36] See *Yalḳut Shim'oni* (Żólkiew, 1858), I, fol. 51a, sec. 248 on Ex. 16: "Be-Shallaḥ."

[37] See chap. VII, p. 158. Cf. Löw, *Flora der Juden,* III, 217; Foods are also associated with the performance of religious duties, for example, bringing to the sick an apple as a delicacy. See in Berliner in *JJGL,* XIII, 206-7; Abrahams, *Jewish Life,* pp. 166-67, the relation foods have to the Sabbath and festivals. For a description of the preparations made for the Sabbath meal and the foods that are served, see *S. H.,* I, fol. 49b; *Ẓemaḥ Ẓedeḳ,* no. 28, fol. 24b; Berliner in *op. cit.,* 202; S. Krauss, "Jüd. Volksküche," *MGJV,* LIII (1915), 1 ff.

[38] *S. H.,* II, fol. 2a (Sabbath Song, No. 1). Cf. *Brandshpigl,* sec. 8, fol. 3a (no fol. mark):. . . . *teyg di khaleh (ḥallah).* . . . The *ḥallah* is "usually a twisted white loaf": Elzet, Pt. 1, p. 27: Cf. Elzet in *Reshumot,* I, 339, n. 1: "*Ḥallot* in Lithuania were white bread, made of wheat flour without twists." See above, p. 98, n. 19. Cf. *Sha'ar 'Efrayim,* no. 1, fol. 4a: ". . . loaves *('ugot)* baked for the Sabbath *(le-ẓorekh Shabes* [*Shabbat*]. . . .")

[39] Grunwald in *Menorah,* VI, 519. The order of the foods is suggested above, p. 106, the fish course was followed by the meat. See also, pp. 96, 97. Cf. *Shelah,* I, fol. 133a (sec. "Shab."): ". . . And in every respect one should enjoy [on the Sabbath] good bread and fish, meat and wine. . . ." Since Talmudic times fish is eaten to enhance "the joy of the Sabbath": see Eisenstein, "Fish" (Hebrew),

'Oẓar Dinim u-Minhagim, p. 82, cit.; also, chap. VII, p. 158, nn. 62–63. Israel Isserlein tells that he remembers eating, on Friday evening and Saturday, herring and onions in place of fish: *Leḳeṭ Yosher*, I, 52 (see "'O. Ḥ.")

Cf. Elzet, Pt. 1, p. 8: It is a universal custom in European Jewish communities to serve similar foods on Friday evening. In addition to fish (Pt. 1, pp. 29, 32, 35, 38; Pt. 2, pp. 111-13, 117, 118), the Friday evening meal includes meat, *lokshn, farfl* (above, p. 102) *kugl, tsimes,* and fresh cake. Cf. Grunwald in *Menorah,* VI, 519, *kugl* as a Sabbath food. Cf. Freybe, *Deut. Volksaberglaube,* p. 178: *Kugel,* a food in the non-Jewish German community, is made of black and white bread or bread and cheese.

40 Grunwald in *JJV,* II, 442, #14, #16. Cf. *Sefer Maharil* (Warsaw, 1874), fol. 28b ("Hil. Shab."): ". . . pieces of goose's skin (*ḥittukhe 'or shel 'avavvza'*) that are known as *griven. . . .*"

At the second Sabbath meal, following services, a warm dish *(tsholent)* is served. The term *tsholent* is probably related to *chaleur,* "warmth," *chaud,* "warm" (Fr.), according to Berliner, *JJGL,* XIII, 205; Idelsohn, *Ceremonies of Judaism,* p. 9. (A similar suggestion is made by Grunwald in *Menorah,* VI, 520.) The *tsholent* dish might be beans, grits, stewed meat, or *kugl:* cf. Grunwald, *loc. cit.* See Elzet, Pt. 1, p. 39.

41 Samuel Black, "Aus dem ehemaligen Kurhessen," *Menorah,* IV (Vienna, 1926), 587.

42 Elzet in *Reshumot,* I, 339; Grunwald in *Menorah,* VI, 518. Cf. Elzet (*op. cit.*), 339, n. 1. Also, Elzet, Pt. 1, p. 27; "*Ḥallot* . . . baked of wheat flour, powdered sugar (*tsuker-mehl*), eggs, and oil."

43 *S. H.*, I, 50a: פֿרייטיג צו אובנט ליגט מן בערכֿס....

Cf. Grunwald in *MGJV,* V, 34, n. 50: *barkhes = Sabbatbroten; idem* in *Menorah,* VI, 519: *barkhes, berkhes* is derived from *berg,* "hill." Cf. Berliner in *JJLG,* XIII, 206, that *berkhes* is from *birkhat,* the first word of Prov. 10:22, "The blessing of the Lord, it maketh rich. . . ."

The term *barkhes* was used in eastern Germany, whereas in western Germany the Sabbath bread is *tadsher,* derived from the last word of Prov. 10:22 = *ta'ashir.* Cf. Krauss in MGJV, LIII, 3; Max Wiener, "Der Sabbat," *Jüd. Fest* (ed. Thieberger), p. 85, n. 2, *barkhes* is traced to *prezel, bretzel, bretzen* ("pretzel"), a twisted loaf baked for the Sabbath. In Schauss, *Jewish Festivals,* p. 31, *barkhes* is described as "oblong loaves of twisted Sabbath bread," and is traced to *Berchta,* the German goddess of vegetation, for whom German women "baked braided loaves." Cf. Berliner in *loc. cit., bretzel* (= *brett* = board, plank), a flat bread, resembling a board or plank. It was a custom, particularly in the 13th century, to distribute the *bretzel* among those who attended the circumcision festivity.

44 *Y. 'O.,* #613; *N. K. Y.,* sec. 300, fol. 37b, #4 ("Hil. Rosh Ḥodesh ve-Shab."): ...עושין מולייתא שקורין פשטידא....

See above, *pastete*, p. 97, n. 6. Cf. *Sefer Maharil* fol. 28a ("Hil. Shab."):

. . . טעמא דאוכלין מולייא בליל שבת זכר למן שהיה מונח על למעלה על למטה ה״נ הבשר מונח בין שני דפי עיסה.

Cf. "Darkhe Mosheh," no. 1 on *Ṭur 'O. Ḥ.*, sec. 402 ("Hil. Shab."), in which Isserles refers to the *Maharil,* as above.

[45] *S. H.*, I, fol. 50a; *Ḳ. Shelah,* fol. 43b.

[46] *H. 'A.*, chap. xxiii, fol. 3a.

[47] Grunwald in *Menorah,* VI, 518, 519: The *ḥallot* for the festivals are designed with symbols pressed into the dough, such as, "a ring or coin for *Rosh Hashanah,* a dove or ladder for *Yom Kippur*, a key for *Hoshana Rabba*." Cf. Elzet, Pt. 1, 341, #8-9, the tradition that *ḥallot* for *Hosh'ana' Rabbah* are to be round, made with a hand, so as to symbolize the "receiving of the decree for the new year," and for *Rosh ha–Shanah* and *Yom Kippur* in the shape of a ladder or with a key to represent "the opening of the gates." Cf. *Ta'ame ha-Minhagim,* I, #731: "For the eve of *Yom Kippur* round shaped *ḥallot* are made in the form of calves with wings . . ., the reason being that on this day the Jewish people are compared to angels."

[48] Grunwald in *JJV,* II, 451, #53. Note also Press in *MGWJ,* LXXVI, 576, the custom of serving mourners during the *se'udat habra'ah,* the consolation meal (chap. II, pp. 41–42), a round roll and an egg. Both foods represent the cycle of life.

[49] See p. 146, n. 1.

[50] Above, p. 97, n. 8; also, p. 158, n. 63.

[51] *Shelah,* I, fol. 214b (sec. "Rosh ha-Shanah"); *Ḳ. Shelah,* fol. 50b (sec. "Rosh ha-Shanah"); *Y. 'O.* #964; *N. K. Y.*, fol. 71a, #3 (sec. "Rosh ha-Shanah"). Cf. these customs in: *Sefer Maharil,* 38a (sec. "Rosh ha-Shanah"); *'O. Ḥ.* sec. 583; *Ḥayye 'Adam* 139:6 (sec. "Rosh ha-Shanah"); Bernstein in *Argentin. IWO Shrift.*, VI, 134; *Ta'ame ha–Minhagim,* III, fol. 91b (sec. "Rosh ha-Shanah"). See also K. Kohler, "Apple," *JE,* II (1902), 24, cit.

See Berliner in *JJGL,* XXX, 207-208, that the eating of honey on *Rosh ha–Shanah* was an ancient custom, dating back to Talmudic times. Cf. *Yoma',* fol. 83b: ". . . for honey and very sweet food enlighten the eyes of man."

Cf. the "Field of Apple-Trees; the Garden of Eden" in *Zohar* (Son. edit.), II, 401 (Gloss.); the "dew of heaven" fell on the "field of consecrated apples": *Zohar* ("Tol' doth"), fol. 143b. Cf. *Pes.*, fol. 54a: The Garden of Eden existed before the world was created. See Ginzberg, in *Legends of the Jews,* V, 97-98, n. 70, cit.; *Shabbath,* II (*Mo'ed,* II, Son. edit.), 418, n. 10, the comment on *Shab.*, 88a, "the Israelites were compared to an apple tree"; *tappuaḥ* was probably translated incorrectly as "apple" instead of "lemon."

Cf. Elzet, Pt. 1, p. 33, that *mehren-tsimes* is served on *Rosh ha–Shanah* and *Hosh'ana' Rabbah*.

[52] *H. 'A.*, 1b: ". . . *kreplikh* [*kreplekh*] that are made on *Purim*. . . ."

Shelah, I, 90b: "We have the custom of making *kreplekh* for *Purim*. The dough is kneaded with honey. . . ."

Cf. *Leḳet Yosher,* I, 34, #5; "Ba'er Heṭeb," no. 11 on *'O. Ḥ.* 168:11: *kreplekh* on *Purim.* Cf. in Elzet, *Reshumot,* I, 344, n. 5, the tradition of eating *kreplekh* on the eve of *Yom Kippur, Hosh'ana' Rabbah,* and *Purim.* For *Purim kreplekh,* cf. also Elzet, Pt. 2, p. 121; Black in *Menorah,* IV, 587.

Shelah, I, 91a: Fruits are served at the *Purim se'udah.*

S. H., I, 46a: אן פורים ליגט מן נאוויט אויף לעקוך....

Cf. also *Purim lekekh* in *Maharil* (Warsaw, 1874), fol. 61a ("Hil. Purim").

H. 'A., 2b: אותן נויה״בט שעשועים בפור׳ על לעק״ך....

Cf. "Ba'er Heṭeb," n. 20 to *'O. Ḥ.* 168:8: ...כגון מה שמטגנין בפורים נו״אט....

See herein, n. 28 to p. 54. Cf. Grunwald in *Menorah,* VI, 518: ". . . aus Nüssen und Honig, besonders am Purim." Cf. also in Güdemann, *Gesch.,* II, 212-13: In Italian communities nuts are dipped in honey on *Purim.* That the nut is a symbol of fertility, see the following: Grunwald in *MGJV,* V. 46, n. 111; *Ber.,* 50b; *'E. H.,* 63:2; Perles in *MGWJ,* IX, 347; Gaster, *Holy and Profane,* pp. 121–22; Schauss, *Lifetime of a Jew,* p. 217.

53 Shulman, *Sefat Yehudit-'Ashkenazit,* p. 79, n. 1. The formula is: *sliḳ, ḳlin, lisḳ, lsḳ, ḳsil, sḳil.* See amulets and inscriptions on food, chap. III, n. 30 to p. 55. For some examples of amulet inscriptions during this period, cf. *Sefer Zekhirah,* fol. 13b; *Semiḥat Hakhamim,* fol. 49b. See also Fig. 9, p. 117; p. 118, n. 32; p. 128, n. 97; p. 128, n. 98. Cf. *Y. 'O.,* #656: Hahn admonishes that food with an inscription should not be eaten unless the letters are clearly cut. See Elzet, Pt. 1, p. 16; In Bessarabia, the pregnant woman wore a butter-bun around the neck as a food amulet.

54 Grunwald in *JJV,* II, 442, #14. Cf. the custom of eating dairy foods on *Shabu'ot: S. H.,* I, 56a. See also Elzet, Pt. 1, p. 43, a dairy diet *(milkhige se'udah)* is served on *Shabu'ot.*

55 Ocksman in *Reshumot,* III (1943), 102. For a similar design on *Shabu'ot* flatcakes, see Berliner in *JJGL,* XIII, 207. Cf. the "seven firmaments": *Ḥag.,* 12b; *Sefer Zekhirah,* 10b.

56 Grunwald in *JJV,* II, 449, #38.

57 *Ibid.,* 450, #44. Cf. *shlisl* (Yid.) = "key." As to the significance of the "key," see above, n. 47.

58 Grunwald in *JJV,* II, 442, #14; "Am Erew Tischobeaw ass man zu Mittag Linsensuppe und ein Linsengericht, am Abend allgemein Lokschen." (*linsen,* Ger. = "lentils"; cf. *linzen,* Yid.) That lentils is a "food of mourners" and is therefore eaten on *Tish'ah be-'Ab,* see *Sefer ha-Manhig,* fol. 50b, #24; *'O. Ḥ.* 552:5.

59 See Elzet, Pt. 2, p. 112; *farfil, farfl* (Yid.). Also, Kosover, pp. 143-44: *farfl.* See above, p. 103: *flekn.* Cf. *farvel* (Ger.), "farinaceous food" (*mehlspeise*).

60 Barbeck, *Juden in Nürnberg und Fürth,* pp. 84-85. The foods served were regulated by the *Taḳḳanot* of 1728: "Die Vorzüge der letzteren Mahlzeitklasse waren 3 welsche Hühner, Hechte oder Forellen (beide zugleich nicht); die der

dritten Class [*sic*] 2 Hühner, Sardellen und Lachsfische. . . ." No further reference is made to the menus for *Shabbat Zakhor*. *Wälsch* = turkey-cock hen. Cf. *Ḥayye 'Adam*, 3:2: prob. *velishe hener*; cf. *wälsche Hühner*. Cf. in *Shelah*, I, fol. 136a, fish *(mine dagim)* as part of the menu for festive and special events. See above, p. 97, n. 9; p. 100, n. 39. Cf. Hohberg, p. 14: *sardellen*.

Cf. Abrahams, *Jewish Life*, p. 160; Joseph Meisl, "Communal Legislation of Halberstadt (1776)" (Hebrew), *Reshumot*, I (1945), 142 ff., for a description of the celebration on *Shabbat Zakhor*. Cf. *Derushe ha-Ẓelah*, nos. 10-11, fol. 19a-b, that the occasion of *Zekhor ha-Berit* also merits a special sermon, according to Ezekiel Landau. For festive meals held before circumcision and on the day of circumcision, cf. Isserles on *'O. Ḥ.*, 255:12; also, Press in *MGWJ*, LXXVI, 575. See n. 47 to p. 22, chap. II.

61 Grunwald in *Menorah*, VI, 520; cf. Black in *Menorah*, IV, 587. In northern Germany, the custom was widespread to eat peas on *Shabbat Zakhor*.

62 Landau-Wachstein, *Jüd. Privatbriefe*, no. 5, pp. 9 and 16 (text and trans.). Cf. Grunwald in *JJV*, II, 443, #23: Aṭ family festivities *reschige Ruten* are given to children as a delicacy. The recipe for *reschige Ruten* is thus described: ". . . Dough is wrapped around a wooden staff . . ., over which the yolk of an egg is spread, and [it] is then baked over coals." At the banquets of the *Ḥebra' Ḳaddishah* it was also the custom to eat *reschige Ruten*. Cf. *reshitke* baking: Kosover, p. 112; also pp. 110-11.

63 Grunwald in *JJV*, II, 443, #21, #23. The *flekn* are made of *ḥallah* dough set aside to prepare baked food for the poor. See chap. III, p. 55. Cf. Dornseiff, *Deut. Wortschatz*, p. 135, sec. 2, #27: *fleckerln* = *mehlprodukte*. See also *farfl*, above, p. 102, n. 59.

64 *Shelah*, I, fol. 263b (sec. "Ner Miẓvah"); *Y. 'O.*, #134; *Ḥavvot Ya'ir*, no. 70, fol. 73a-74a. For examples of meals scheduled during the "crises of life" and special events, see herein, n. 41 to p. 20; n. 82 to p. 29; p. 55, n. 31; p. 61, n. 73. Cf. in *S. H.*, II (ed. *Shatzky)*, fol. 13b ("Wedding Song"), the meal to celebrate a wedding; *N. K. Y.*, fol. 25a, #1 (sec. 40), the meal on the Saturday preceding a circumcision. Cf. also Elzet, Pt. 1, pp. 18, 46, the occasions for a *se'udat miẓvah* in Eastern Europe.

65 *Y. 'O.*, #134; #130.

Ḥavvot Ya'ir, fol. 74a. Cf. Assaf, *Meḳorot*, I, 120, #5, cit. from Worms *Minhagim*, that a *se'udah* would be arranged upon completing a tractate of the Talmud.

66 *Ḥavvot Ya'ir*, fol. 73b: ". . . the meal with a friend and one's household. . . ."

67 *Ibid.*, fol. 73a, based on *B. Ḳam.*, 80a. See n. 47 to p. 22.

68 *Y. 'O.*, Pt. 2, p. 273 (sec. "Ha-Limmud be-'Aẓmo"):

. . . ואנו בני אשכנז מקפידים מאד בכבוד הסיום כל הקהל כאחד ויפה הוא, ולכן נזדרזתי

בכל תוקף בעתים שלא היה פה אב״ד [אב בית דין] לקיים המנהג...
Cf. Horodetzky, *Le-Ḳorot ha-Rabbanut* (Some Aspects of the History of the Rabbinate), pp. 117-18: There were two types of customs, those that individual scholars initiated and those that arose out of the experience and need of the people. But, in addition, as we have already said, practices were introduced through communal legislation.

[69] *Y. 'O.*, #134.

[70] Wachstein, "Gründung der Wiener Chewra Kadischa" (1763), *MGJV*, XXXII (1909), 100.

[71] Max Schay, "'Chewra-Kadisha' in Pressburg," *ZGJT*, III^2 (1933), 73-74, #2. Cf. Elzet, Pt. 1, p. 16: After the *Ḥebrah Ḳaddisha'* buried the dead, the members of the society, in Eastern Europe, ate "a snack" to refresh themselves. (Translit. of *Ḥebrah Ḳaddisha'* corresponds to the spelling in Elzet.)

[72] Ocksman in *Reshumot*, III, 101.

[73] Cf. in Sartori, *Sitte und Brauch*, II, 28, food customs with local characteristics; and in Grunwald in *Menorah*, VI, 518 ff., local differences in preparing foods.

[74] "Tosaf." to *Ber.*, 40a, commenting on "Hebi' Meleḥ"; *Gen. R.* 51:7, Sid. "Vayera'." Cf. also *Ber.*, 2b: "From the time that the poor man comes [home] to eat his bread with salt till he rises from his meal."

[75] *Y. 'O.*, #88:
תיכף אחר כסוי שלחן במפה יהיה מלח עליו... השטן מקטרג עליהם וברית מלח מגין עליהם. על כן כל בעל הבית ראוי להשגיח על זה.
Cf. *Leḳeṭ Yosher*, I, 34 (sec. "'O. Ḥ."):
...מה שהביא מלח על השלחן כדי שלא יקטרג השטן מה שממתין בין נטילה לברכת המוציא....
Cf. *'O. Ḥ.* 167:6: "... And before one eats, he says, 'Bring the salt....'"
In the passage above, from *Y. 'O.*, Hahn refers to a Midrash relating to the incident of Lot's wife failing to carry out "the covenant of salt." Cf. *Gen. R.* 50:8 that when the angels visited Lot prior to the destruction of Sodom and Gomorrah (Gen. 19:1-3), she refused to show them hospitality. She gave the guests no salt by calling it an "evil practice." See also trans. *Mid. Rab., Gen.* (Son. edit.) I, 436, sec. 4.

[76] *Sefer Zekhirah*, 18b:
סגולה כה״ם [כתבו המקובלים] ליתן מלח על השלחן לגרש הקליפה כי מלח גמטרי׳ ג׳ הוייות ולכן תטבול ג״פ [שלש פעמים] במלח.
Cf. *Sefer Ta'ame ha-Minhagim*, I, sec. 182; also n. 2. See Elzet, Pt. 2, pp. 100-101, cit.: In European Jewish homes salt is served with each meal. Agadic, or folklore, interpretation associates salt with wisdom and health. See, for e.g., Grunwald in *MGJV*, V (1900), 32, n. 41; 40, n. 76a, that bread and salt protect women who give birth, and children. Also, *Shab.*, 129b; Grunwald, "Childbirth," *JE*, IV (1903), 29: Salt is sprinkled on a newborn child. With regard to the efficacy of salt in folk practice, see p. 116, n. 27; p. 119, n. 36; n. 120 to p. 130.

[77] *Y. 'O.*, #161:

מנהג העולם שמסירין או מכסין סכין ולחם שלם בשעת ברכת המזון ולישאר פתיתין על השלחן, יש להם על מה שיסמוכו. אבל הסרת המלח אין לו עיקר... שמנהג שטות הוא.

Cf. the incident of an individual who, during *Birkhat ha-Mazon,* stabbed himself with a knife that was on the table: Grunwald, "Aus unseren Sammlungen: IV Sitte und Brauch," *MGJV,* I (1898), 81. Cf. also Wuttke, *Deut. Volksaberglaube,* pp. 291-92, 451: A knife should not be left in the bread after it has been cut, as life is thereby endangered. If the knife remains on the table, it must be covered.

78 Ocksman in *Reshumot,* III, 101.

79 *H. 'A.,* fol. 1a-b.

80 See Berliner in *JJGL,* XXX, 208; Press in *MGWJ,* LXXVI, 575. See also Elzet in *Reshumut,* I, 243, #14. And, also, chap. II, pp. 19, 20.

81 *Y. 'O.,* #135. Cf. *'O. Ḥ.* 173:2. Cf. also *Y. 'O.,* #118.

82 *N. K. Y.,* fol. 28b, #3, sec. 60. See herein, p. 133. Also, *Leḳeṭ Yosher,* I, 35 (sec. *"'O. Ḥ."*): In Italian communities the hands are washed between fish and meat dishes, "perhaps because [they are greasy from] the fish that had been dipped in olive oil during baking."

83 *Y. 'O.,* #136:

לכן בסעודות גדולות שרגילים לאכול גבינה אחר בשר וקורין סעודה קטנה ההיא נוך (צעך)....

Prob. *nokh tsekh* (Yid.); cf. *nach zech* (Ger.) "after the banquet."

84 *S. H.,* I, 46b:

... מן עשט נאר צו קנוח אלז אייער קנאפף קוכ̄ן צוקר ברוט קיכ̄ליך לעקוכ̄ן....

Prob. *knop-kukhn* (Yid.) = "button cookies."

Cf. *Shelah,* I, fol. 180b (sec. "Shabu'ot"):

העולם נוהגין לאכול בחג השבועות מאכלי חלב, ואח"כ אוכלין בשר לקיים ושמחת בחגך ואין שמחה בלא בשר... אז צריך לדקדק... לעשות קינוח והדחה היטב....

Cf. *Ḥul.,* 105a, *ḳinnuaḥ,* "wiping the mouth with bread to remove particles of cheese before eating meat." For *kikhelekh* and *lekekh,* see Kaufmann (ed.), *Glikl,* p. 292, n. 5; Berliner in *JJLG,* XIII, 206. Also, *Ḥayye 'Adam* 43:9 ("Hil. Se'udah"); Bernstein in *Argentin. IWO Schrift.,* VI, 142, sec. 30, cit. And, Elzet, Pt. 1, p. 17; Kosover, p. 100 f., sec. 7. Cf. *küchlein, kuchen* in Hohberg, pp. 92-93.

85 *H. 'A.,* 1b. Cf. *Ḥayye 'Adam,* 43:9: *shmalts-kukhn.* See above, n. 6 to p. 97.

86 *Y. 'O.,* #112. See *kvetshin (kvetshen),* above, n. 30 to p. 99.

87 *Ibid.,* #136:

אכן אנו מקילין בשהיית שעה אחת ואפילו בלא קינוח והדחה רק אם ירגיש בשר בין שניו צריך להסירו.

Cf. Isserles on *Y. D.,* 89:1:

... י"א דאין צריכין להמתין שש שעות... והמנהג הפשוט במדינות אלו להמתין אחר אכילת הבשר שעה א' ואוכלין אח"כ גבינה....

88 *Y. 'O.,* #137. Cf. *N. K. Y.,* sec. 60, fol. 29a, #4 ("Hil. Se'udah"): Kosman would wait six hours; for his authority he cites *M. T.,* "Hil. Ma'akhalot 'Asurot," 9:28; *Hul.,* fol. 105a.

[89] *Sefer Zekhirah,* 16a, based on *Y. D.,* sec. 89, comment no. 2.

[90] "Sifte Kohen" on *Y. D.,* sec. 89, comment no. 2.

[91] *Sefer Zekhirah,* 16a. Plungian refers to *Zohar,* Par. "Mishpaṭim," Ex. 21.

[92] For examples of popular beliefs that were then current among Germanic Jews, see *Sefer Zekhirah,* fol. 7a-b, 11a-b, 12a; *B. D.,* 33b, 40a, 49b; *Ḳ. H.* 5:17; 6:9; 33:12, 14-15; *M. H.,* 13b; *Ẓemaḥ Ẓedeḳ,* no. 67, fol. 81a; *J. M.,* II, Pt. 4, 19. Also, "Gilgul (Transmigration)," *RCC,* cit. And, see in this volume p. 16; pp. 118–19; p. 120, n. 45; pp. 121–22, n. 49; p. 142.

The relationship of Cabala to the history of general thought is discussed by Lehmann, *Aberglaube,* pp. 162 ff. See chap, VI, n. 34 to p. 118.

[93] *S. H.,* I, 47b.

[94] *H. 'A.,* fol. 2a.

[95] *S. H.,* II (ed. Shatzky), 2a: . . . *un Toreh lernen* . . . . See chap. III, p. 68, n. 126; chap. VII, p. 159, n. 68. For the tradition of studying during mealtime, see *Pirḳe 'Abot* 3:3-4; *Y. D.* 246:4, 23; *Ta'ame ha-Minhagim,* I, fol. 23a, #183 (sec. "Birkhat ha-Mazon"), among others.

[96] Landsofer, "Ethical Will," *Derekh Ṭobim,* fol. 5a, #4.

[97] *Sefer Musar,* fol. 99a; also, p. 197.

[98] *Y. 'O.* (1928 edit.), "Toledot ha-Meḥaber" (Biog. Sketch), p. vi; #589. See *ibid.,* #601, table songs for the Sabbath, *Ḥanukkah,* and *Purim;* #368, the *musar*-song in Yiddish, by Jacob Heilprin (Halpern), criticizing the unbecoming conduct of youth. Also, Löwenstein, "Lieder," *Jubelschrift . . . Hildesheimer,* pp. 135-36, no. 24, a Sabbath Song by R. Semelin. For examples of festival songs, see W. Bacher, "Lied zu Simchath-Torah," *MGJV,* XXXII (1907), 37; S. Seligmann, "Purimlied," *MGJV,* XX (1909). 33 f.; Grunwald in *JJV,* II, 443-45, #24; 448, #35, songs for *Pesaḥ, Purim,* and other occasions.

The folk song is receiving the attention of the folklorist. Specialized studies are being made of the folk song; for instance, Y. L. Cahan, *Shtudies vegn yidisher folksshafung* (*Studies in Yiddish Folklore,* ed. Max Weinreich); *idem, Yidishe folkslider mit melodyes* (*Yiddish Folksongs with Melodies,* ed. Max Weinreich).

[99] *S. H.,* II (ed. Shatzky), fol. 1b (Intro. by Kirchan; no fol. mark):
דרום האב איך דיזי זמירות גמאכֿט. פֿיל דינים פֿון אלי טאג אונ׳ שבתות וימים טובים זיינין
דרינן גמעלט. אונ׳ וואול נאך גזאנג אין גריים גשטלט. אך גשטלט ... בייא איינים מוזיקאנד
דען רעכֿטן ניגון.

Cf. *ibid.,* fol. 2a ff., for the musical notes and words of the table songs. The cultural background and significance of these songs are dealt with by Shatzky in *S. H.,* II, Intro., 1 ff.; Erik, pp. 304-8. According to Erik (p. 305), Kirchan reworked earlier popular songs and poems. The purpose of Kirchan's folk book is to cheer, as well as instruct, the people.

[100] *S. H.,* II, 22b.

[101] The term "tradition" is used to include both custom and law.

[102] See pp. 147–48.

[103] *Y. 'O.*, #92. Cf. the description of religious trends in the German-Jewish community preceding Emancipation: Shohet, *'Im Ḥillufe Teḳufot,* chap. 7.

[104] The characteristics of *musar* literature are referred to on p. 67, nn. 114–15; p. 68, n. 117. For a fuller discussion of the role of *musar,* see Erik, pp. 308 ff.; Tsinberg, *Gesh. fun der lit.*, VI, 178 ff.; Minkoff in *Jewish People: Past and Present,* III (1952), 150 ff.; *S. H.*, II (ed. Shatzky), Intro., pp. 44-45; Steinschneider, *Jewish Lit.*, pp. 224-25; Güdemann, *Quellen.*, Intro., pp. xiii-xiv; Weinryb in *UJE,* VIII, 43-44.

[105] *Panim Me'irot,* I, no. 1, fol. 1a. The gullet had to be checked for perforations, *be-dine veshet*. (The laws of *veshet* are important in *sheḥiṭah,* ritual slaughter.)

[106] *Noda bi-Yehudah,* I, no. 36, fol. 32b (sec. "Y. D."). Cf. Wind in Ḥoreb, X, 74, n. 72, that Landau was opposed to such festivity together with non-Jews on the ground that dietary laws could be violated. See Jewish men "drinking ale from silver cups" in a Hamburg tavern: chap. I, p. 13, n. 76. Cf. Shohet, *op. cit.*, p. 141, that Jews frequented non-Jewish taverns. Also, pp. 139-40 for examples of violating ritual food laws through fraternization with non-Jews.

[107] *S. H.*, II (ed. Shatzky), fol. 17a:

אך האט זיך מיר צו גטראפֿין איין עם הארץ האט דעם חבֿר טריפֿה כשר גמאכֿט. . . . האבי
דר נאך ארפֿארין האט מוזין דיא כלים כשר מאכֿין:

Prob. *erforin (erforn)*; cf. *erfahren* (Ger.), "to discover."

[108] *S. H.*, I, 60a:

ווער זייט ממדינות פולין דיא דארפֿן ניט עשין אויז די כלים פֿון די אשכנזים די ריינישי פונצין
עשין אזו פסקנת דר שפתֿי כהן וועז זי ווידר האבן בדיעה אהיים צו גיין.

The meaning of *puntsin* is suggested by Epstein in *Ḳ. Shelah,* 13a:

. . . כגון שומן הכנתי שקורין מיק״ר או בני מעים שקורין פונצי״ן ודקין דער״ם. . . .

"I thus designated what is meant by 'fat' by using terms related to it, namely, 'intestines,' 'small intestines,' and the like."

puntsin = prob. related to *pansen* (Ger.) = *kaldaunen* (Ger.) = "intestines, tripe, scrapings of fat." *Pansen* is derived from *pantex, pantices* (Lat.) = "intestines"; *panses* (Fr.) = "paunch, belly"; cf. Muret, *Wörterbuch,* II^2 (1897), 1540. *derm* (Yid.), "intestines"; cf. *darm* = *bauchfett, gedärm* = "intestines": *Kluge-Götze, Wörterbuch,* p. 125. In culinary art, *darm* = "intestines": Muret, II^1, 808.

See Bibliography, p. 352 (under Karo), for the life and work of Shabbetai Kohen (Shak), "Sifte Kohen." Cf. "Sifte Kohen" on *Y. D.* 98:3; 100:3, pertaining to *ma'akhalim 'asurim,* foods that should not be eaten when one suspects that ritual requirements have not been met.

[109] Cf. Güdemann, *Gesch.*, III, 9: Müller, *Gesch. der mährischen Judenschaft,* p. 33; Fishman, *Education,* p. 58. Cf. Bato, *Juden in alten Wien,* p. 99: Jews of Vienna express hostility toward *fremde Juden.* Also, H. Flesch, "Juden in Mähren," *JJLG,* XVIII (1926), 24, that in Moravia it was felt that "outsiders" did not belong

in the community; hence housing and synagogue seats would be restricted to regular residents, to "proper" persons, and not to "strangers."

There were also barriers between Sephardic and Ashkenazic Jews. A *responsum* of Ephraim ha-Kohen (*Sha'ar 'Ephrayim,* no. 13, fol. 14a) deals with the question whether Sephardic and Ashkenazic Jews can pray together in one synagogue and effectively fulfill their religious duty. Cf. *J. M.*, I (Bk. 5, chap. 8), 372, #1; Dubnow, *Weltgeschichte* (Ger. edit.), VII, 311; 316-17, #37; *idem, Weltgeschichte* (Heb. edit.), VII, 184, 186-87, #37, that the Sephardic and Ashkenazic Jews of Hamburg had separate synagogues. For examples of differences between the Ashkenazim and the Sephardim, see Zimmels, *Ashkenazim and Sephardim,* chaps. 6, 8, and 9.

110 *Ḳ. Shelah,* fol. 13a. See the religious and cultural standards of small towns as portrayed by Erik, p. 308, based on *S. H.,* II; *S. H.,* II (ed. Shatzky), Intro., 16, 43-44; fol. 17a-20b.

111 *S. H.,* II, 17a. Cf. Jacob Emden's denunciation of the incompetence, "impudence and arrogance" of *shoḥaṭim: She'elat Ya'abeẓ,* I, no. 56, fol. 83a-b; B. Z. Katz, *Rabbanut,* I, 158, n. 55. Cf. also in *Shohet,* p. 147, n. 69, Jacob Emden's criticism of *shoḥaṭim.* For other examples of *shoḥaṭim* being reprimanded by *musar* writers for their indifference and carelessness in maintaining the standards incumbent upon them, see Shohet, *op. cit.,* nn. 65-68, 70.

112 *Ethical Will,* fol. 26a, #11.

113 Halpern, *Taḳḳanot Mähren,* p. 91, #278.

114 *Ibid.,* p. 176, #506 (b).

115 *Ibid.,* p. 176, #506 (b) (Yid. text). Cf. *Panim Me'irot,* III, no. 1, fol. 1a: The problem is posed of regulating proper religious behavior during the market season when Jews travel to neighboring towns to sell goods. See also, chap. VII, p. 167, n. 110, regarding the laxity of observance on the part of transients.

116 H. Bamberger, *Juden in Würzburg,* pp. 40-43 (Hebrew and Yiddish text).

117 *Ḳ. Shelah,* fol. 13a. Cf. comment on *limlog* in "Tosaf." on *Beẓah,* fol. 34a, to scald a fowl to complete the cleaning.

118 *Ethical Will,* fol. 26a, #11. Cf. the title page of Epstein, *Derekh ha-Yashar le-'Olam ha-Ba'* (Frankfort, 1685): "In regard to many matters, such as soaking and salting meat, women should be aware of the way in which they conduct themselves. Foods not fit to eat, according to law, should not be kept in the house."

119 *S. H.,* I, 47a.

120 *Y. 'O.,* #145:

לכן שאר מיני פירות יבשין . . . שקונים אותם אצל הסוחרים ורגילים להיות מתולעים שקורין מילב״ן. . . .

milbn (Yid.), "mites, small insects"; cf. *milben* (Ger.), same meaning. Cf. *milbn* in dried fruits as cited in *Pene Yeshohua',* II, no. 21, fol. 8a (sec. "Y. D."). Cf. also the problem of wormy foods in *Maharil,* fol. 75a (sec. "Din Tola'im").

[121] *Ḥavvot Ya'ir,* fol. 260b (Addenda; comment on fol. 119a):

דברים . . . שנהגו בק"ק כגון שנזהרין מחמאה של גוים וכרוב כבוש ופירות יבשים:

Cf. Kaufmann in *JQR,* III, 499, n. 5.

[122] *Ḥavvot Ya'ir,* no. 109, fol. 105b.

[123] *Y. 'O.,* #380: *spiling.* Cf. *spilling* (Ger.), "small yellow plum."

N. K. Y., fol. 66b, #1 (sec. "Ereb Tish'ah be-'Ab"). For other examples of wormy foods, cf. *Shelah,* I, fol. 77b (sec. "Sha'ar ha-'Otyot"); *N. K. Y.,* fol. 9b, #2; *Ẓemaḥ Ẓedeḳ,* no. 52, fol. 60b; *Pene Yeshoshua',* II, no. 21, fol. 8a (sec. "Y. D."); *Naḥalat Shib'ah,* II, no. 71, fol. 37b.

[124] *Y. 'O.* #663:

אסור לפרק האגוזים או לוזים מתוך קליפתן החיצונה הירוקה שקורין לייפלן.

luzim (Heb.) = "hazel-nuts." Cf. *Maharil* (Warsaw, 1874), fol. 28a: *luzim* = *hezilnis* (Yid.). *layfln;* cf. *ibid.,* 28a-b:

. . . מתוך קליפה חיצונה שלהן שקורין (לייפון). . . .

Prob. *layfln, layfun,* the "outer shell of the nut"; may be related, according to Professor Uriel Weinreich, to *laybl, layb.* Cf. *laybl* (mod. Yid.) = "waist, jacket"; *layb* (mod. Yid.) = "body."

[125] *S. H.,* I, 47a. See chap. VI, p. 144, n. 220, for another opposing view, as stated by Jacob Reischer, who objected to using contaminated foods even in time of economic plight.

[126] *Y. 'O.,* Pt. 2, p. 275 (sec. "Ha-Limmud be-'Aẓmo").

NOTES TO CHAPTER VI

[1] In *Bet David* and *Mafteaḥ ha-Yam,* there are more details about folk medicine than in the other primary sources that were checked. In Ephraim Reischer, *Sha'ar 'Efrayim* (Fürth, 1728), there is a section on *segullot u-refu'ot;* see the passage from Reischer, *Sha'ar 'Efrayim* in I. Goldhizer, "Muhammedanischer Aberglaube," *Festschrift . . . Berliner's,* p. 144. See also the bibliography of folk medicine in Grunwald, "Bibliomantie und Gesundbeten," *MGJV,* X (1902), 81. The copies of *Sha'ar 'Efrayim* that were available (Fürth, 1728; Dyhernfurth, 1739) do not include the two chapters or sections on folk medicine as indicated in the title page of the Fürth edit.

[2] That the Jewish folk-medicine book of the 17th and 18th centuries is a mixture of cabalistic thought, popular attitudes, and medical data, see Shatzky, "*Sefer ha-Ḥesheḳ,* a Lost Medical Book of the 18th Century" (Yiddish), *Yivo Bleter,* IV (1932), 224, 231. Folk medicine and medical knowledge are intertwined: cf. Jacob Meir Coblenz, *M. H.,* fol. 33a; *'Amtaḥat Binyamin* (Collect. Folk Remedies), title page.

. . . . וגם ידעו להזהר ברפואות הגוף הן דרך הטבעי ושלא דרך הטבעי. . . .

As an example of the way in which *musar,* ethics, is incorporated into a medical work, see *Dimyon ha-Refu'ot,* pp. 22-23, 27-28, 30, 36. See also below, n. 182 to p. 138.

[3] With regard to the wide distribution of folk-medicine books in the 17th and 18th centuries, see Grunwald, "Aus Hausapotheke und Hexenküche," *MGJV,* V (1900), 10-11; Bernstein, "Two *Retsepten-Bikher"* (Yiddish), *Davke,* XVII (Buenos Aires, 1953), 334. See also the handbooks of folk medicine in Abraham Berger, "Lit. of Jewish Folklore," *Journ. Jewish Bibliog.,* I (1938-39), 4-5. Note the spread of *kräuterbücher,* books of herb remedies, in Germany during the 16th and 17th centuries: Höfler, *Volksmedizin. Botanik,* p. 114. (Henceforth cited only as Höfler.)

[4] *B. D.,* Pref.

[5] *Ibid.*

As to the use of plants in German-Jewish medieval folk medicine, see S. Rubin, *Ha-Ẓemaḥim ve-'Ototam,* p. 12; Güdemann, *Gesch.,* I, 205; Grunwald in *MGJV,* V, 15-16, sec. 6, #e.

See also plant remedies, below, n. 123 to p. 130. That plants are prescribed or approved by physicians, see *Dimyon ha-Refu'ot,* p. 24; *M. H.,* fol. 34b. Concerning the ways in which plants are employed in German folk medicine to cure disease, see Höfler, pp. 6, 23-24; Black, *Folk-Medicine,* pp. 37 f., 130; Geramb and Mackensen (ed.), *Quellen zur deut. Volksgeschichte,* II, 32 ff.; Wuttke, *Deut. Volksaberglaube,* pp. 308 ff.; Fritz Byloff, "Volkskundliches aus Strafprozessen der Österreichischen Alpenländer," *Quellen zur deut. Volkskunde,* III, 29, n. 5.

[6] *M. H.,* 33a.

[7] *Ibid.:*

. . . ניתן רשות לרופא לרפאות ומצוה הוא ובכלל פיקוח נפש ואם מונע עצמו הרי זה שופך דמ׳. . . .

Cf. cit. in *Y. D.* 336:1; "Be'er ha-Golah," n. 1, cit., commenting on *Y. D. loc. cit.; B. Ḳam.* 85b, in which "authorization [is granted] to the medical man to heal," based on Ex. 21:19. See I. Jakobovits, *Jewish Med. Ethics,* p. 3, nn. 9-10; also pp. 4-5, for the permission given to the physician to cure the sick. Cf. *Shab.,* 30a, that the Sabbath may be set aside for a sick person whose life is in danger. Likewise, *M. T.,* "Hil. Shab.," 2:1, 9; *'O. Ḥ.* 328:2, 7-10, concerning the circumstances that permit the violation of the Sabbath during an illness. And, *Noda' bi-Yehudah* (Berdiczew, 1812), I, no. 49, fol. 42a, sec. "Y. D." with regard to the care that a doctor gives to the sick on the Sabbath. Cf. *Derushe ha-Ẓelaḥ,* no. 31, #1: In time of illness a doctor should be consulted.

[8] Suggested by Steinschneider, *Heb. Übersetz,* pp. 650 ff.

[9] Cf. Muntner (ed.), *R. Shabetai* [*Shabbetai*] *Donnolo (913-985), Medical Works, the Earliest Hebrew Book in Christian Europe* (Hebrew), Pt. 1, Intro., pp. 1-4; Ennemoser, *Hist. of Magic,* II, 94-95. As to the remedies of medieval medicine that could have been incorporated into the German-Jewish folk medicine

pocketbook, see Gruner (ed.), *The Canon of Medicine of Avicenna*, p. 249, # 434 ff.; Karl Opitz (ed.), "Avicenna, das Lehrgedicht über die Heilkunde (Canticum de Medicina)," *Quellen und Stadien zur Gesch. der Naturwissen. und der Medizin,* VII (1940), 173, sec. 3 ff.; 175, #320 ff., the symptoms of illness; 206, sec. 2 ff., the remedies; Muntner (ed.), *loc. cit.,* Pt. 1, pp. 14-15, #7 ff.

[10] See refs. to Aristotle, Galen, Hippocrates, Bartholinus, Blenquerius (?) (= בלאנקארטוס), in *Dimyon ha-Refu'ot,* pp. 22, 24, 26-27; also pp. 44-48, the Latin text and Hebrew version of a regulation for diet. (Wallich knew Latin, having studied medicine in Padua.) Cf. Menaḥem Mendel Lefin (Levin, 1741-1819) of Poland, *Refu'ot ha-'Am,* a Hebrew translation of the medical work of Samuel Tissot of Switzerland. The title page states that Tissot's book first appeared in French in 1791; translated into ten different languages, it was known throughout Europe. See Peter Wiernick, "Mendel Levin," *JE,* VIII (1904), 41.

[11] *Ḥavvot Ya'ir,* no. 106, fol. 104b. See herein, p. 71, n. 142.

She'elat Ya'abeẓ, no. 41, fol. 70a.

Cf. Wind in *Ḥoreb,* X, 76, n. 82; *idem, Rabbi Yeḥezke'l Landau,* p. 91, n. 84 (based on *Noda' bi-Yehuda*).

[12] As to the mischief that Satan and demons can perpetrate against human beings, cf. *Ḳ. Shelah,* fol. 57a; *Sefer Zekhirah,* fol. 9a; Sheftel (Sabbatai) Horowitz, "Ethical Will," *Ẓavva'ot ve-Gam Dibre Ḳedoshim,* fol. 2b, #2; Abrahams, "Jewish Ethical Wills," *JQR,* III (O. S., No. 11, April 1891), 479; Horovitz, *Frankfurt. Rabin.,* III, 77. See Güdemann, *Gesch.,* I, 203-4, 215, for examples of demons being a menace and causing disease. See also the danger of the evil eye in Regina Lilienthal, "Evil Eye" (Yiddish), *Yid. Filolog.,* I (Nos. 4-6, 1924), 245-48; Löw, "Die Finger," *Gedenkbuch . . . David Kaufmann,* pp. 75, 77; Shatzky in *Yivo Bleter,* IV, 235; Adolf Löwinger, "Der böse Blick," *Menorah,* IV (Vienna, 1926), 551 ff.; Zimmels, *Magicians, Theologians, and Doctors,* p. 89, nn. 120, 124. Cf. the injuries caused by demons: Grimm, *Deut. Myth.,* II, 920-21. (Hereafter Zimmels, *Magicians, Theologians, and Doctors* is Zimmels.)

[13] Kaufmann (ed.), *Glikl,* p. 131; Eng. trans. is based on Lowenthal, p. 89. See in Erik, pp. 303-304 (based on *Simḥat ha-Nefesh*), the instances of a child who "spoke about the great mysteries of the Torah without being conscious of what she said" and a girl who talked "as though she were under the influence of a demon."

[14] That demons were considered real in Talmudic times, cf. among others *Shab.,* 2b; *Giṭ.,* 68a; *Meg.,* 2b, also "Tosaf." commenting on *shem'a shed hu,* "because he might be a demon." Cf. also the fear of night: *Soṭ,* 21a. See other examples of demons in rabbinic literature in Ginzberg, *Legends,* V, 303, n. 259; 405, n. 72; VI, 299, n. 84.

Regarding the prevalent view in the general society that demons can cause disease, see Grimm, *Deut. Myth.,* II, 965; Hermann Paul, "Das volkskundliche Material," *Grundriss der german. Philologie,* XII (1938), 294. See the influence of German popular beliefs and practices on Jewish social life: Güdemann, *Gesch.*, I, 216, 220. Also, Grunwald, "Childbirth," *JE*, IV (1903), 31: "Most of the customs and superstitions are not of Jewish origin; but they have been borrowed from neighboring peoples." And, Jakobovits, *Med. Ethics*, p. 29, for non-Jewish influences on Jewish folk medicine.

[15] Cf. among others *Ḳ. H.*, 69:1-5; *Y. 'O.*, #85-86; *Derushe ha–Ẓelaḥ*, no. 2, fol. 6a, #3-4; no. 3, fol. 6b, #3, #5; no. 23, fol. 35b, #19.

Cf. *Brandshpigl*, sec. 3, fol. 1a (no fol. mark), that the glutton dies like an animal and is seized upon by evil spirits. Cf. the instance of a woman possessed by a *gilgul*, "a wandering soul": *Ẓemaḥ Ẓedeḳ*, no. 67, fol. 81a. Cf. also "Gilgul," *RCC* cit.

As to rabbis and scholars sharing the popular opinions of their times, see, for example, Güdemann, *Gesch.*, I, 199, 222; Erik, pp. 303-304; Baron, *Soc. and Relig. Hist.* (rev. edit.), II, 14-22; Trachtenberg, *Jewish Magic*, pp. 22-24; Ludwig Blau, "Magic," *JE*, VIII (1906), 255. See also Salo W. Baron, "Azariah de' Rossi," *Jewish Studies in Memory of Israel Abrahams*, p. 19, that Azariah accepts "the existence of demons."

[16] Cf. *San.*, 65b-66a (on Deut. 18-10); 67a-b (on Ex. 22:17), in which opposition is expressed to the use of magic, witchcraft, or sorcery for the purpose of employing demons. In contrast, cf. *Shab.*, 53a, 61a-b, 66b-67a: Amulets and magical incantations are approved if found helpful. Commenting on these disparate views, and what obviously seems to be a contradiction, I. Epstein (ed. Son. Tal.), *Shab.* (*Mo'ed*, I), 243, n. 1 (fol. 53a) says: "The Rabbis, though opposed to superstitious practices in general, were nevertheless children of their age and recognized their efficacy." See also n. 3 to *ibid.* The principle was thus established that what is used for remedial purposes is not considered magical. See *Shabbath*, I (*Mo'ed*, I, Son. edit.), 321, n. 1; also below, p. 127, n. 93.

[17] Maimonides, *Guide of the Perplexed* (ed. M. Friedländer), I, 230.

[18] See above, pp. 118–19, 125–26, 127–29, 139–41, 142; and also, p. 16, n. 12; p. 38.

[19] *'Amtaḥat Binyamin*, fol. 7a: Magic is resorted to only when the individual faced "danger and insecurity." That folk practices are intended to aid the individual in his difficulties, see, for instance, Lilienthal in *Yid. Filolog.*, I, 248 ff.; E. Sosnovik, "Jewish Popular Medicine in White Russia," *Yid. Filolog.*, I (1924), 164-65. See also above, p. 118, n. 32.

[20] *B. D.*, fol. 25a. See the example of a fowl used as an "amulet": Lilienthal, *op. cit.*, 257.

[21] *B. D.*, *op. cit.*

[22] Cf. *Ḥavvot Ya'ir*, no. 221, fol. 207b. See Zimmels, p. 35, n. 187; also Güdemann, *Gesch.*, I, 202; Löw, *Lebensalter*, p. 338.

[23] *Naḥalat Shib'ah*, II, no. 76, fol. 39b:

... שרבים מן ההמון נוהגים כשנעש׳ להם גניבה שואלין למכשפים וכן בחולי אפי׳ אין בו סכנה
רגיל ושכיח אצל רבים ששואלין למכשפים. . . .

Cf. "Folk Belief," *RCC*, cit. See Zimmels, p. 35, for examples of sorcerers administering "cures." See above, pp. 120–22, for possible reasons for this folk practice.

[24] Cf. *B. D.*, fol. 33b. Cf. *Sefer Zekhirah*, fol. 12a, in which Zechariah Plungian suggests a "prayer" to be recited as a safeguard against a witch. The first three words of the prayer have to begin with an *alef*, the three letters being an abbreviation for *'Eyeh 'Asher 'Eyeh* ("I AM THAT I AM," Ex. 3:14). The prayer was also said upon passing a woman.

[25] See Güdemann, *Gesch.*, I, 202, that witches were not tried in the Jewish community, because rabbinic tradition discourages capital punishment. Furthermore, since the women in question were considered "bewitched," they could not be held accountable for their actions.

As to the role of witches and their trials in Germany during the 16th to 18th centuries, see Bax, *German Culture*, pp. 105-106; Richter, *Kulturgeschichte*, II, sec. 4, 391 ff.; Ennemoser, *Hist. of Magic*, II, 123-24, 127; Black, *Folk-Medicine*, p. 20; A. Sach, *Deut. Leben in der Vergangenheit*, II, 471 ff.; Byloff in *Quellen zur deut. Volkskunde*, III, no. 34, 24 ff.

[26] *B. D.*, 33b: *fatligan* plant(?); may be related to *fettkraut, fette blume*. *gikondros* plant(?) = prob. *gungerose* = "rock-rose." Cf. Ashby-Richter-Bärner, *Eng.-Deut. Bot. Terminolog.*, p. 144: *fettkraut* = "butterwort"; Marzell, *Wörterbuch der deut. Pflanzennamen*, V (Leipzig, 1957), 123, *fette-blume*. Also, Pritzel, *Volksnamen der Pflanzen*, p. 29: *gungerose*.

[27] *B. D.*, fol. 33b, 40a. Examples of such amulets are to be found in Lilienthal, *Yid. Filog.*, I, 253 f. That a man uses a rooster and a woman, a chicken, cf. Isserles, gloss no. 1 on *'O. Ḥ.* 605:1.

See H. Flesch, "Sympathetische Mittel und Rezepte aus dem Buche *Mif'alot 'Eloḳim*," *MGJV*, XLII (1912), 46, #27: A bride can be protected against witchcraft by pouring some silver and salt into a nut, "which is sealed with wax and then worn around the neck." For the uses of salt in making an amulet or preparing a home remedy, see Lilienthal in *Yid. Filolog.*, I, 256; Flesch in *MGJV*, XLII, 45, #21. Also, above, p. 119, n. 36; n. 120 to p. 130. See Grunwald in *MGJV*, V, 32, #41; 34, #52: Salt can also be an aid in winning a court trial, as well as be a protection on a journey. For the significance of salt in Jewish lore, see I. Löw, "Das Salz," *Jewish Studies in Memory of George A. Kohut*, pp. 454-55. And also chap. V, p. 105.

[28] *Shelah*, I, fol. 49b (sec. "Ba-'Asarah Ma'amarot"); fol. 135b-136a (sec. "Shabbat"); *Shelah*, II, fol. 330a (sec. "Luḥot ha-Berit"). See p. 17, n. 18; p. 135, n. 159.

Regarding the snake in Jewish folklore, see Muntner (ed.), Moshe ben Maimon, *Poisons and their Antidotes* (Hebrew), II, 75-77; Grünbaum, *Jüdischdeut.*

Chrestomathie, p. 569 (based on *Mishle Shlomah: Yid. Tiryak*, fol. 9a, #20 : שלאנגן באלג; cf. *schlangenbalg* [Ger.], "snake skin"); I. Scheftelowitz. "Tierorakel im altjüd. Volksglauben," *ZVV*, XXIII (1913), 387-88. Note also the use of the snake skin as part of a folk medicine compound: Hovorka-Kronfeld, *Vergleich. Volksmedizin*, I, 381; II, 14, 137, 301, 322. (Henceforth cited only as Hovorka-Kronfeld.)

29 See p. 17, n. 18; p. 135, n. 159.

30 *B. D.*, fol. 40a. Cf. the related practice of protecting a woman in confinement by placing a knife under her pillow: p. 16, n. 11.

31 *B. D.*, fol. 33b-34a. See in Lilienthal, *Yid. Filolog.*, I, 257, that the shirt of a child was used for an amulet. Also, Grunwald in *MGJV*, V, 40, n. 76a: "In Poland, as a protection against the 'evil eye,' especially in the case of children, the *habdalah* candle was lit, placed in front of the opened mouth . . . , then put out, so that the smoke could enter." See herein, pp. 18–19, the *yidish-kerts*, "candle ceremony," that was held following the birth of a child. See also the *Kerze für Heilzauber*, the candle to counteract physical harm resulting from sorcery: *HDA*, V, 1066, #2; X, 182.

32 *B. D.*, fol. 49b: "Without having to look through [many] pages, I had on hand simple statements; page 20 related to circumcision; page 7, to marriage, and page 13, to boys who will have their *Bar Miẓvah*. As a supplement, I inscribed words of efficacy from *Minḥat Ya'aḳob:* 'May you have a table, a knife, and food in a measure of abundance without end.'" (*Minḥat Ya'aḳob:* a Prayer Book devoted to the order of the Sabbath service. Cf. Friedberg, *Bet 'Eḳed Sefarim*, p. 382, no. 1314.) See "the love potion" in Flesch, *MGJV*, XV, 41, #2.

That the amulet was written on parchment, cf. *'Amtaḥat Binyamin*, fol. 19a, #15; *Ṭa'ame ha-Minhagim*, II, fol. 43a. For examples of amulet inscriptions, cf. herein, n. 53 to p. 102; *J. M.*, II, Pt. 4, p. 19, an amulet of Frankfort shaped as a *Magen David*, the Star of David, with "the word" אגלא written in each of the six corners; *Sefer Zekhirah*, fol. 13b, the amulet of Joel Ba'al Shem of Ostrog (ca. 1648) on which he inscribed:

אדני שדי צמרבר אנקתם הסתם הספסים דיונסים יהוך:

See also the amulets in Flesch, *MGJV*, XLII, 47, #31, #33; Joel Heilprin (d. 1810, Poland), *Mif'alot 'Eloḳim*, fol. 41 ff. And Marx in *JQR*, VIII, 274. The amulet has prophylactic and therapeutic purposes: Jakobovits, *Med. Ethics*, pp. 35-36.

33 Bax, *German Culture*, p. 118.

34 See Throndike, *Hist. Magic and Exp. Sc.*, IV, 485, 487. Also, n. 92 to p. 107, chap. V.

35 See the examples of incantations to heal a wound, cure sickness, and counteract the evil eye, in J. Wellesz, "Volksmedizin. aus dem jüd. Mittelalter," *MGJV*, XXXV (1910), 117; S. Weissenberg, "Jüd. Beschwörungsformel gegen den bösen Blick," *MGJV*, XXXVI (1910), 166-67. Then cf. the incantations in Grimm, *Deut. Myth.*, III, 492 ff.

[36] *B. D.*, 30a. See above, p. 119, n. 27, for the use of salt in folk medidine.

[37] *M. H.*, fol. 33b. The incantation can also check nosebleed. See p. 142, n. 205.

[38] See p. 129, n. 109, for inflammation and erysipelas.

[39] *M. H.*, fol. 34a:

...אונד רופיטן בראנד בראנד, ברעני איבר דיר אונד ניכט אונדר דיך....

brand (Yid.) = "fever." See above, p. 119, n. 39, *blozn;* cf. *blozn zikh* (mod. Yid) = "to swell"; *blasen* (Ger.) = "inflammation." See *gegen blasen* in Grunwald, *MGJV,* V, 46, #115. Prob. *roytlof;* cf. *rotlauf* (Ger.) = "erysipelas": Höfler, p. 133; *idem, Volksmedizin. Botanik,* p. 30.

[40] *M. H.*, fol. 34a.

[41] *J. M.*, II (Bk. 6, chap. 6), 75, #5. The "inscription" included Num. 11:2. Cf. Grunwald in *MGJV,* V, 10, n. 5 (cit. *J. M., op. cit.*, 78).

[42] See Grunwald in *MGJV,* V, 13-17; 21, #4; 23, #8, #9; 24, #11; 34, #51-#54 (based on Naḥmanides and *Sefer Ḥasidim*); 35, #55. For the varied social and cultural items that the folk-medicine book deals with, cf. Heilprin, *Toledot 'Adam* (Folk-Medicine Handbook), Pt. 2, fol. 2a; Bernstein in *Davke,* XVII, 335 f. Cf. also the *segullah,* remedy, to earn a livelihood in *Ta'ame ha-Minhagim,* II, 41b.

[43] *B. D.*, fol. 25b. See methods to identify a thief in *Ta'ame ha-Minhagim,* II, 43a; Bernstein in *Davke,* XVII, 342, *tsu geneveh.*

The relationship between Jewish and non-Jewish folklore is also evident from the similarity of methods used to detect a murderer or find a thief. For instance, see Grunwald, *MGJV,* V, 20, #1; 29, #30a; 34, #48-49; 35-36, #56. Similarly, Heinrich Lewy, "Beiträge zur jüd. Volkskunde," *ZVV,* XXXVII (1927), 88. Also, Güdemann, *Gesch.*, I, 200, that if a murderer should approach his victim, the dead man's wounds would bleed. Cf. *HDA,* II (1929-30), 124, on "influencing" the thief to return what he stole. Also, Byloff in *Quellen zur deut. Volkskunde,* III, 27.

[44] *B. D.*, fol. 49b. In this regard, see Grunwald in *MGJV,* V, 13, sec. 3, #3.

[45] *B. D.*, fol. 39b. For safety on a journey, the traveler should wear in his garment a needle that had been used to sew a white shroud. That there is no definite color for burial shrouds, see *Shab.*, 114a. The shrouds are usually white: Schauss, *Lifetime of a Jew,* p. 232. Cf. *HDA,* V, 1066, that magical power could be attained by wearing some part of the clothing of the dead. See above, p. 126, n. 79, how the limbs of the dead were considered to have healing potency.

Cf. also *B. D.*, 28b: For protection against any injury by a tool or weapon, "carry the buttocks of a cat" or "wear a belt made of the skin of a dead snake found on the road" and then "rubbed in oil." That the same "remedy" could be used in more than one way, see above, p. 116, n. 27.

[46] *Y. 'O.* (1928 edit.), Pt. 3, p. 348, based on *Sefer ha-Yir'ah,* fol. 13b (pub. with *Ḳab ha-Yashar,* Lemberg, 1862).

47 *Ibid.*, pp. 348-49, based on *Ḥul*, 95b, and Rashi's comment on . . . *bayit, tinoḳ, ve-'ishah*. . . .

48 *Ibid.*, p. 348, based on *Sefer Ḥasidim*, #59. Among the examples of *niḥush* that Judah he-Ḥasid enumerates are: not to eat eggs upon the termination of the Sabbath; not to take fire out of a stove when someone is sick or a woman is about to give birth. See Amorite practices and divination, chap. II, p. 16, n. 12. Cf. *Shab.*, 67a, b; *Ḥul.*, 77a, b, for further instances of Amorite practices and divination. Cf. also Amorite customs in *Tosef. Shab.*, fol. 87a ff. (7:1-4); cit. n. 2 to #59, *Sefer Ḥasidim* (ed. R. Margulies). Note that rabbinic authorities do not provide a general definition of magic. Rather, they deal with sorcery on the basis of specific acts. Amorite practices are enumerated so that they can be differentiated from superstitious customs that are not magical. The meaning of magic—in the sense that Hahn speaks—is stated classically in *M. T.*, "Hil. 'Abodat Kokhabim," 11:6. See also Eisenstein, "Magic" (Hebrew), *'Oẓar Yisra'el*, V (1911), 298.

Y. 'O., p. 348:

ועניני ניחוש הרגילות עתה אין צריך לכתוב אותם רק מה שאין לו טעם בטבע ואינו מפורש בספר אסור.

Cf. *ibid.*, p. 350: Hahn again indicates that any practice that is founded on "a natural reason cannot be called divination. . . ." The contrast between "black" and "white" magic is thus stated by Bax, *German Culture*, p. 112: In the case of the former "operations are conducted through the direct agency of evil spirits," while that of the latter "sought to subject Nature to the human will by the discovery of her mystical and secret laws."

49 *Y. 'O.*, pp. 348-49. The *Rosh Ḥodesh* custom, as cited by Hahn, is to be found in *Sefer Ḥasidim*, #59, and in the gloss of Isserles on *Y. D.* 179:2.

See herein, pp. 25, 27, n. 65, for the reason a child is not named for a living relative. And as we already suggested (pp. 16, 18, 19), the fear of demons is reflected in popular customs associated with critical moments in life, such as birth or the naming of a child.

50 *Y. 'O.*, p. 349:

. . . וזה יוכיח שהרי כמה דברים אמרו בגמרא שיש בהם סכנה גדולה עד מאד ומעולם לא שמענו ולא ראינו מי שניזוק בהם, לכן לא אכתוב רק מה שכתבו הפוסקים האחרונים. . . .

51 Cf. the special prayers in time of drought: *M. F.*, fol. 17b-18a. Also, in *Ṭa'ame ha-Minhagim*, II, fol. 40a, a prayer for health; and in fol. 57a, the verse from Num. 24:2 and the prayer *Piṭṭum ha-Ḳeṭoret* recited to counteract the "evil eye." See in Bernstein, *Davke*, XVII, 339, 343, a prayer for traveling.

52 Cf. in *M. F.*, fol. 23a-27a; *Shelah*, I, fol. 146a (sec. "Pesaḥim"), prayers recited for the sick. Cf. in *Sefer Zekhirah*, fol. 11b, a prayer as a *segullah* for health; *'Amtaḥat Binyamin*, fol. 13a, a prayer during a plague. See in Marcus, *Communal Sick-Care*, pp. 215 f., "healing through prayer."

53 *M. F.*, 27b, 28b; Stern in *Festschrift . . . Berliner's, p.* 116.

54 Stern, *op. cit.* See this practice in Löw, *Lebensalter*, p. 107; Gaster, *Holy*

and Profane, p. 34. For instances when names were changed during illness, see Flesch, "Pinax von Austerlitz," *JJV,* II, 576, n. 1: "Ḥayyim," meaning life, was added to the regular name of Joseph. Also, J. R. Marcus, "Triesch *Ḥebra Ḳaddisha," HUCA,* XIX (1945-46), 169, n. 1, that "Moses" was appended to the name of David Bacharach of Triesch. And likewise, Schauss, *Lifetime of a Jew,* p. 75: "In the case of a severe illness a new special name was added to the old one. . . . The practice of changing the name of a person as a charm against demonic powers was widespread among all peoples, and in the Middle Ages it became popular among Jews also."

Cf. also *'Amtaḥat Binyamin,* fol. 33b: In time of illness "coins or nuts" were "counted up to 160." This number was chosen because the letters of the words *ẓelem* (image) and *'eẓ* (tree), respectively, have the value of 160.

55 *Me'il Ẓedaḳah,* no. 7, fol. 13a.

56 *S. H.,* I, fol. 49a: ". . . for most dreams *(rov ḥalomos)* result from thought *(gedankn, gedanken)*. . . ."
See *traumbücher:* Wuttke, *Deut. Volksaberglaube,* p. 213, #324. Concerning the psychological nature of dreams, see Trachtenberg, *Jewish Magic,* p. 233; Lehmann, *Aberglaube,* p. 528: "assoziationsträume"; Ennemoser, *Hist. of Magic,* I, 35, the dream as a result of "inner psychological impressions."

57 *Shebut Ya'aḳob,* II, no. 34, fol. 6a. Cf. "Dreams," *RCC,* cit. See Eisenstein, "Dreams" (Hebrew), *'Oẓar Yisra'el,* IV (1910), 283, that "the reflective processes do not completely cease during sleep." In medieval folklore the dream is regarded as an expression of the spiritual realm, occurring when the soul is not constrained by contact with physical reality: Trachtenberg, *op. cit.,* p. 231; Wuttke, *op. cit.,* pp. 209-10, #319; Paul in *Philolog.,* XII, 295.

58 *Ḳ. Shelah,* fol. 49b; *S. H.,* I, fol. 49a.

Cf. *Shab.,* 11a: "Fasting is good to avert a bad dream." Also, *Ta'anit,* 12b: "Fasting is as efficacious for a bad dream as fire is for tow. . . ." Cf. *Y. 'O.,* #944, that "one fasts to turn a dream to good." See the discussion of dreams in Zimmels, p. 51, cits.; L. Blau, *JE,* IV (1903), 656; Trachtenberg, pp. 244-45.

Cf. *Y. 'O.,* #944; *Ḳ. Shelah,* fol. 49b (based on *'O. Ḥ.* 288:5): Something specific is seen in "a bad dream," viz., a Torah burning, the concluding *Ne'ilah* service on the Day of Atonement, the beams of one's home, or the loss of teeth. Epstein also cites as examples seeing in the dream how someone or the person having the dream is called upon to recite the blessings over the Torah or how he marries a woman. For the symbolism and meaning of the dream in folklore, see Trachtenberg, p. 107; Lehmann, pp. 407 f., 412 f.; Wuttke, p. 77, #92; pp. 213-14, #325. See also the interpretation of dreams in Grunwald, *MGJV,* V, 21, #3.

59 *Y. 'O.,* #944; *Ḳ. Shelah,* fol. 49b.

Cf. *Shelah,* I, fol. 134b (sec. "Shab."): "Whenever I am asked . . . concerning dreams on the Sabbath, in most cases it is my practice to express the opinion that one should not observe at once the two fast days, but [instead] uphold the 'joy of the Sabbath' by assuming responsibility for two fast days during the week. Whoever fasts on the Sabbath fasts [an additional day] for having fasted on the Sabbath. Thus . . . the responsibility for the two days." Cf. *Ta'anit,* 12b: "What amends shall he make [for having fasted on the Sabbath]? He should observe an additional fast [i. e., observe a fast for his fast]." Cf. *'O. Ḥ.* 288:4: The second fast day "expiates one for suspending the Sabbath joy"; also *ibid.* 288:1, that the fast on the Sabbath began at noon. With regard to fasting on the Sabbath because of a dream, see Zimmels, p. 35, n. 187.

60 *Y. 'O.,* #943, #946: The fast is observed on the Sabbath, *Ḥanukkah, Purim, Rosh Ḥodesh,* the new moon, and the intervening period between the first two and last two days of the festivals of *Sukkot* and *Pesaḥ.* If the content of the dream is clear, then he has to fast on the Sabbath, otherwise on a weekday. Cf. the fast on *Rosh ha-Shanah* due to a dream: *Leḳeṭ Yosher,* I, 124 (sec. "'O. Ḥ.").

Ḳ. Shelah, fol. 49b: ". . . One does not fast unless he is in a state of anxiety and is troubled. Then the fast will be a source of enjoyment to him [as it will bring relief on the Sabbath]." That "evil dreams cause anxiety," see *Ber.,* 60b; also Blau in *JE,* IV, 656, cit.

61 *Ḳ. Shelah,* fol. 50a. Cf. *Ber.,* 55b: "If one has a dream which makes him sad, he should go and have it interpreted in the presence of three. . . . Say rather . . . , he should have a good turn given to it in the presence of three." Cf. *Y. 'O.,* #943, cit.; *S. H.,* I, fol. 49a. A fuller description of the ritual recited is in *Ḳ. Shelah,* 50a. Epstein states that he has presented excerpts from the work of Isaac Luria (the "'Ari") that are to be read to prevent a bad dream from taking effect. See Trachtenberg, p. 247, for a detailed account of this practice, observed during an earlier period by Jews of medieval Europe. This is another example of the continuity of a tradition that does not belong to any specific period of time and is not confined to a particular geographical area.

62 *Ḳ. Shelah,* fol. 49b:

שמעתי מחכם אחד שיאמר האדם קודם ששוכב אפי׳ בלשון אשכנז (דא בין איך אויף מיר מקבל אלז וואז מיך וועט היינ׳ טרוימין וויל איך מארגין ניט פאשטין)....

63 *Ibid.,* 49b-50a. On counteracting a dream about demons, see Grunwald, *MGJV,* V, 36, #58.

64 *B. D.,* fol. 28b.

65 See in Flesch, *MGJV,* XLII, 42, #9, a suggested formula to dream of paradise.

66 Kaufmann (ed.), *Glikl,* p. 36: . . . *an-shtekindige* [*anshtekendike*] *krenk.* . . . Cf. Feilchenfeld, pp. 30-31: *ansteckende Krankheiten.* Also, Rabinowitz (ed.), *Glikl,* p. 14; Lowenthal, p. 19, "contagious diseases"; Ysaye in *MGJV,* VII, 7. And, B. Z. Abrahams (ed.), *Glückel,* pp. 20-21.

Glikl relates: "At that time there was no Jewish hospital *(heḳdesh),* nor were there any houses available where the sick could be accommodated. Therefore, no less than ten sick persons were given lodging in the loft [i. e., garret, attic] of our house. My father provided for them. . . ." (Trans. based on above edits. of *Glikl.*)

[67] Zimmels, p. 111. See Schwarz, *Wiener Ghetto,* p. 46: A *heḳdesh* was established in Vienna in 1349, but this was not typical of all places. See also Haarbleicher, *Juden in Hamburg,* p. 46: The *Taḳḳanah* of 1782 stipulates that support should be given to the communal hospital of Altona through assessments.

[68] *M. H.,* fol. 34b:

...שישאל תחילה לרופא מומחה שה׳ בעת ההיא ויוצא ונכנס בבית החולה הנ״ל....

Cf. Feibelman (Feibelmann), the physician of Trier: *Shebut Ya'aḳob,* II, no. 115, fol. 18b. Also, the Jewish physicians in *J. M.,* II (Bk. 6, chap. 23), sec. 1, 282 ff. See E. Shmueli, *Toledot 'Amenu,* I, 76: "A doctor was engaged by the Jewish community of Vienna to care for the sick who were too poor to pay a fee. It was his duty to call on them, either in their homes or at the hospital." For other examples of Jewish physicians at this time, see also Eliav, *Ha-Ḥinnukh ha-Yehudi be-Germanniyah,* p. 20, n. 38.

[69] Cf. cit. in Eliezer ben Yehudah, *Millon* (Hebrew Thesaurus), III (1914), 1172: *heḳdesh,* "hospital." Cf. F. H. Wettstein, "Past History of the Jews of Cracow and Poland Based on Early Communal Minutes" (Hebrew), *'Oẓar ha-Safrut,* IV (1892), 588: According to a record of 1595, hospitals—designated as *bate ha-heḳdesh u-bate ha-ḥolim*—were supported by funds collected for communal institutions. Cf. *Pene Yehoshua',* I, no. 1, fol. 30b (sec. "'E. H."): *bet ha-heḳdesh;* Leopold Weisel in *BSV,* XVII (1926), 209: *heḳdesh = krankenhaus.* See Marcus, *Communal Sick-Care,* p. 169, that originally the *heḳdesh* was not a hospital in the modern sense, administering to the sick of a community, but a hostel "for the itinerant" both "sick and well." *Ibid.,* p. 167: The *kloyz* (chap. III, p. 73) also served as a "hospital" or shelter.

[70] Cf. *Dimyon ha-Refu'ot,* pp. 23, 28; *Ma'aseh Ṭobiyah,* II, fol. 103b, sec. 5-6: *Segullot* for various ailments are prepared from trees, plants, flowers, vines, seeds, roots, stones, oils, spices, and liquids. See below, n. 111 to p. 129, for the remedies made of plants. See Höfler, p. 28, that the plants used in home remedies grew near homes. Also, Renner, *Origin of Food Habits,* p. 203: "Kitchen herbs were grown much earlier and far more frequently used than vegetables. Good health has always been attributed to them."

[71] Cf. *M. H.,* fol. 33a: cit. *Yoma',* fol. 84a, that R. Yoḥanan and Abaye used remedies obtained from non-Jews. "R. Johanan suffered from scurvy. He went to a matron who prepared something for him. . . . Abaye said: I tried everything without achieving a cure for myself, until an Arab [i. e., a traveler, Arab caravan merchant] made a recommendation. . . ." Cf. *Y. D.* 155:1: Non-Jewish authorities are consulted and non-Jewish resources are used for medical purposes. An incan-

tation with idolatrous language is permitted so long as the sick person does not recollect the incident.

For examples of different groups having contact with one another in the field of medicine, see F. T. Haneman, "Medicine," *JE,* VIII (1904), 417; Steinschneider, *Heb. Übersetz.,* pp. 652 f.; Ludwig H. Friedländer, *Gesch. der Heilkunde,* pp. 180 f.; Neuburger, *Gesch. der Medizin,* II, Pt. 1, 187-89; Singer, *Short Hist. Med.,* p. 67; Sarton, *Intro. Hist. Sc.,* II, Pt. 2, 563 f.; 857-58.

72 It was already noted (p. 114, n. 7) that law is not absolute and rigid where human life is involved. Cf. in addition, *Yoma',* 84b.

73 As this is not a study in the history of science or medicine, no attempt is made to establish the validity of any of the remedies of folk medicine then current in Germanic-Jewish life.

74 *Shebut Ya'aḳob,* II, no. 70, fol. 11a:

על מה סמכו העולם לנהוג היתר לאכול ולשתות דם הנקרש ונתייבש מתייש שקורין באקס בליט שנתייבש בחמה אף בחולה שאין בו סכנה רק בנפילה בעלמא שכואב לו אחד מאברים הפנימים:

Prob. *boks blut* (Yid.), "blood of a male goat"; cf. *bocksblut* (Ger.), same meaning. Cf. "Medicine," *RCC,* cit. And Zimmels, p. 125, n. 8: "Blood of a he-goat, dried in the sun, was taken as a general medicine." See Wind in *Ḥoreb,* X, 76, n. 82, and *Rabbi Yeḥezḳe'l Landau,* p. 91, n. 84 (based on *Noda' bi-Yehudah): Ṭerefot,* foods prohibited as ritually unfit, may be used for medicinal purposes if no better remedies are known.

75 *Shebut Ya'aḳob, op. cit.* Cf. *'Erub.,* 14b: "'What is the law?'—'Go,' the other told him, 'and see what is the usage of the people.'" Cf. *Yer. Yebom.,* XII, 1, 12c: ". . . And the custom nullifies the law." Also expressed in *Yer. B. Meẓ,* VII, 1, 11a. Cf. *minhag* in Levy, *Wörterbuch*, III. 150.

Shebut Ya'aḳob, loc. cit.

. . . ומה"ט [ומן הטור] נוהגין היתר בהנקרש על דופני חביות שקורין וויי"ן שטיי"ן. . . . וכן במה שקורין בלא"ז שמשתמשין בו לקשור על כלי שתי' אף שהם מבהמ' טריפה או נבילה ג"כ מתירין מה"ט. . . .כיון שכואבים לו איברים הפנימים דהוי מכה של חלל. . . .

Prob. *vayn-shteyn;* cf. *weinstein* (Ger.) = "tartar, argot (a drug)." *dofanne ḥabuyot* (Heb.) = "paries of the abdomen that are covered." Prob. *bloz;* cf. *blase* (Ger.) = "vesicle." *ḥalal* (Heb.) = "internal (of the body)." The above opinions of Reischer are based on *Y. D.* 87:10; 123:16; *'O. Ḥ.* 328:3; *M. T.,* "Hil. Shab." 2:5.

See folk remedies that prescribe the use of the blood of an "unclean animal": below, p. 129, n. 118; n. 128 to p. 130; p. 134, n. 149; p. 141, n. 196. The unclean animal is burned or crushed, made into a powder, and then taken with a liquid. See also Jakobovits, *Med. Ethics,* p. 89, n. 144, concerning ritually unclean food that may be used for medicinal purposes "once it is transformed into a carbonised state by burning."

[76] For the attitude that was usually held by rabbis with regard to folk customs during the Talmudic and medieval periods, see Lauterbach, *Rabbinic Essays,* p. 342; Baron, *Community*, II, 154; *idem*, *Soc. and Relig. Hist.* (rev. edit.), II^{2}, 22, n. 26; 316; Grunwald in *MGJV*, I, 70, n. 7; Zimmels, pp. 121-22; Twersky, *Rabad of Posquières,* pp. 241-42.

[77] Suggested by Wind, *Rabbi Yeḥezḳe'l Landau,* p. 89, n. 76.

[78] See the examples of *Simḥat Torah* and *Purim* customs, p. 177, n. 156; p. 187, nn. 208–209.

[79] *'Eben ha-Shoham,* I, no. 30, fol. 14b:
נשאלתי על אחד שיש לו חולה שאין בו סכנה והגידו אנשים המומחים לדבר זה שיקח עצם ממת ויעשה לו מרחץ....
Cf. "Medicine," *RCC,* cit.

[80] *Ẓemaḥ Ẓedeḳ*, no. 13, fol. 13b.

[81] *She'elat Ya'abeẓ* (Altona, 1739), I, no. 41, fol. 70b.

Cf. "Pisḥe Teshubah," n. 1 on *Y. D.* 349:1, commenting on *ben 'obed kokhabim,* that the body of a deceased Jew cannot be used for *hana'ah,* "benefit" or "pleasure" (based on Deut. 21:23). And by rabbinical enactment, *mi-de-rabbanan* (*Giṭ* 61a), it is forbidden to use the corpse of a non-Jew for one's benefit. See below, p. 140, n. 194, for the circumstances that allow the bone of a deceased person to be used as a remedy.

[82] Rodkinson, *Hist. Amulets,* p. 93.

[83] *Yaẓẓib Pitgam* (Kolomea, 1886), fol. 11a.

[84] Cf. *Ḥatam Sofer,* no. 338, fol. 136b (sec. "Y. D."): . . . *beḥoli ha-shituḳ (shlag)*. . . .
shituḳ (Heb.) = "paralysis." *shlag* (Yid.) = "stroke"; cf. *schlag* (Ger.), "paralysis": Höfler, p. 573.

[85] *B. D.,* fol. 29a: *ḳaḥ shuman ḥazir;* fol. 25b: *pekh shisl-vasir* (*vaser:* Yid., "water") = "pan of water boiled over pitch." *lungi (lung) herts (harts)-vasir* = "lung of heart juice"; cf. *lungenblume* = *enzian* = "gentian." Cf. *HDA,* V, 1463, that the *lungenkraut* plant was used as a remedy. See *mashkeh refu'ah,* "health drink," in Muntner, *Donnolo,* Pt. 1, p. 1, n. 3. Cf. *Dimyon ha-Refu'ot,* p. 77, sec. 1, "hog fat" as a remedy; and *ibid.,* pp. 75 ff., for a list of plant juices prepared and sold by Frankfort apothecaries for medicinal purposes.

[86] *B. D.,* fol. 29a. The same folk remedy is designated for more than one disease; however, repetitions are not omitted in order to present the over-all pattern of folk medicine.

[87] *Ibid.,* fol. 30a: *kholoshes,* "weakness, fainting"; cf. *khaloshus* (mod. Yid.). See chap. V, p. 99, n. 30; *kiml* (Yid.) = "caraway." Cf. H. Marzell, "Pflanzen," *Deut. Volkskunde* (ed. John Meier), p. 62: The caraway is one of the "health plants" *(heilpflanzen)*.

B. D., fol. 36a: *shvindl* (Yid.), "dizziness." Cf. *schwinden* (Ger.) same meaning: Wuttke, *Deut. Volksaberglaube*, p. 301, #476. See above, n. 74 to p. 125: *nefilah*, "collapsing, falling." According to Landau, *Derushe ha-Ẓelaḥ*, no. 4, fol. 9a, #18, in Prague many were sick from weariness and faintness.

For the "magic of plants," see Gubernatis, *Mythologie des Plantes*, I, 231. Also, Höfler, p. 52, that plants are a protection against "thunder, fire, snakes, demons, wild animals, and magic."

88 *B. D.*, 30a: ...היידנש פרוסט ווארץ...
Cf. *heide* (Ger.) = "broom plant (woodlands)."

Ibid.: ". . . and there are those who call it *kalmusi*." Cf. *kalmus* (Ger.) = "sweet calamus or cane": *HDA*, X, 176; Meigen, *Deut. Pflanzennamen*, p. 111.

About the act of "transferring" disease, see Güdemann, *Gesch.*, I, 202; Wuttke, *op. cit.*, p. 315, #499.

B. D., 24b: ....חולה הנקרא בער מוטר
May be related to *bärmüde* (Ger.) = "weary and listless like a bear"; cf. *hundemüde* (Ger.) = "dog tired." Cf. *Toledot 'Adam*, Pt. 2, sec. 1, fol. 4a: בער מוטר.

89 *M. H.*, fol. 33a; *Shebut Ya'aḳob*, III, no. 94, fol. 16a; *Dimyon ha-Refu'ot*, pp. 34, 41, 42; *Ma'aseh Ṭobiyah*, Pt. 2, fol. 103a; *Toledot 'Adam*, fol. 10a, #100; *Refu'ot ha-'Am*, sec. 15, 18.

See examples of fever and remedies for fever, in Steinschneider, *Heb. Übersetz.*, Pt. 3, p. 655, #415, no. 13; *Ṭa'ame ha-Minhagim*, II, fol. 44b, 45a, 62b; Grunwald in *MGJV*, V, 50, #129; Shatzky in *Yivo Bleter*, III, 234-35, #5; Bernstein in *Davke*, XVII, 336. Cf. description of fever (Deut. 28:22) in Rashi's comment on *u-ba-ḳaddaḥat: fiverhits (fieberhitze), mal du feu*. See Biblical and Talmudic references to fever (e. g., Levit. 26:16) in Katzenelsohn, *Talmud ve-ha-Refu'ah*, p. 308; p. 309, n. 1. Cf. *fieber*, "fever" in Höfler, p. 29; Wuttke, p. 301, #476; p. 315, #498; Grimm, *Deut. Myth.*, II, 1106.

90 *B. D.*, fol. 29b, 37a. Cf. *hellfeuer* (Ger.) = "bright (burning) fever."

91 *M. H.*, 34a. See *brand*, above p. 119, n. 39. Cf. *brand* in Höfler, p. 135; Wuttke, p. 300, #476; Grimm, *Deut. Myth.*, II, 1106.

92 *Shebut Ya'aḳob*, III, n. 94, fol. 16a.
. . . מי שיש לו חולה קדחת ורוצים ליתן לרפואה עפר מקבורת מתים אם יש להתיר ליהנו׳ מעפר הקבר לרפואה זו. . . .
See p. 48, n. 193, for the custom of visiting a cemetery during illness.

93 *M. H.*, fol. 33a: For *ḳaddaḥat*, an amulet pouch was made of the following ingredients: seven pieces of bread of equal size, salt, the white of a hard-boiled egg, seven pieces of a swallow cut into equal size, leaves of the pointed plant (*ha-'eseb she-ḳorin shpitsi vayarikh*; cf. *spitze weihrauch; weihrauch* [Ger.] = "incense"). The pouch was worn on the back nine times and afterwards thrown into water. As to the efficacy of salt in Jewish lore, see p. 105. See in Karl Huss, *Schrift*

'Vom Aberglauben,' p. 17, the portrait of an amulet to counteract fever. For a related practice of throwing bread and salt into water to be rid of fever, see Wuttke, pp. 315-16.

Concerning the use of the egg as a remedy in Jewish folk medicine, see Grunwald in *MGJV,* V, 58, #181. Also, Zimmels, p. 85. And, below, p. 133, n. 139; p. 134, n. 153. In European communities a poultice made with an egg was applied to the circumcized child: *Zikhron Berit la-Ri'shonim,* p. 21, also n. 2, comment of "Be'er Ya'aḳob." In general folk medicine, eggs are prescribed with remedies (Radford, *Ency. of Superstitions,* p. iii), and egg shells serve to check fever (*HDA,* II [1929-30], 1450, #4).

94 *B. D.,* 29b: To check *helish fayer,* mix and boil together strong vinegar with the dung of sheep, or make a poultice of honey, the white of an egg, and oil, to be applied daily in a linen cloth for one hour until the fever is gone. See below, n. 125 to p. 130, "holy fire."

95 *Dimyon ha-Refu'ot,* p. 75, sec. 1, *brunin-kresin,* the "juice of the water cress," as a remedy for fever. Cf. *brunem-krese* (mod. Yid.); *brunnenkresse* (Ger.). See *kresse* in Höfler, p. 30.

96 *M. H.,* fol. 33a:

... לאיזה בני אדם שהי׳ להם חולי אויזצעהרונג . . . וזה החולי מקורו הוא קדחת וע״כ קורין אותו הרופאי׳ בלשונם שלייכנט פיבר. . . . וגם ישתו המים שמבושלים בתוכם ב׳ מיני העשבים שקורין שאף ריפה ועבריצה. . . .

See *oystserung* (Yid.) = "consumption"; cf. *auszehrung* (Ger.), same meaning. *shlaykhnt fivr*; cf. *schleichend* (Ger.) = "creeping fever, ephiosaur." *shaf-ripah*, may be related to *schafrippe* (Ger.) = "sheep's-rib [plant]." *abritsah* = perhaps *arbitsah* (?); cf. *arbes* (Yid.) = "pea"; *arwiz, erbsen, erbsenblüte* (Ger.), "pea blossom." See Höfler, p. 6: Through reification plants were identified with animals and human beings. Some plants, *blutwurz, blutkraut* (*ibid.,* p. 106) were regarded as "blood-builders." For examples of plants to which human characteristics are ascribed, see below, p. 136, n. 168.

97 *M. H.,* fol. 33a-b. Note also (fol. 33a) that three almonds might be used in place of the apple; on one *agen* is written; on the second, *magen*; and the third, *nagen;* for three successive days the feverish patient eats the almonds in alphabetical order. For similar remedies, see Bernstein in *Davke,* XVII, 340; cf. Schairer, *Relig. Volksleben,* p. 105. See again the examples of amulet inscriptions on foods, herein, n. 30 to p. 55; p. 102, n. 53. That the apple serves as a remedy in Jewish folk medicine, see below, n. 119 to p. 130; Bernstein in *Davke,* XVII, 353; Grunwald in *MGJV,* V, 69, # 244-45. See also above, p. 276, n. 51, concerning the significance of the apple in Jewish folklore. As to the use of the apple in ancient medicine, cf. Wittstein, *Handwörterbuch,* p. 37.

98 *Shebut Ya'aḳob,* II, no. 50, fol. 8a:

מי שחולה בחולי קדחת... ועשה לו א׳ רפואה... קמיע של עשבים....

His opinion is substantiated by *'O. Ḥ.* 328:7; *Shab.*, fol. 7b. Cf. "Sabbath," *RCC*, cit. See above, p. 114; below, p. 144.

99 *B. D.*, 28a: *gelsukht* (Yid.), "jaundice"; cf. *gelbsucht* (Ger.), same meaning. For instances of jaundice, see *Dimyon ha-Refu'ot*, p. 24; *Toledot 'Adam*, Pt. 2, fol. 4b, sec. 2. Also, *Ṭa'ame ha-Minhagim*, II, 45b; Grunwald in *MGJV*, V, 55, #164. That jaundice must have been a common ailment in the general German community, see Höfler, p. 29; Hovorka-Kronfeld, II, 57; Wuttke, p. 312; Grimm, *Deut. Myth.*, II, 970.

100 *B. D.*, 28a: *gelin-oygin(oygn)-shteyn*. Cf. below, n. 117 to p. 129. Cf. *augenstein* (Ger.) = "agate." Cf. remedy for jaundice in *Toledot 'Adam*, Pt. 2, fol. 4b, #3: *ayzn-kroyt;* cf. *eisenkraut* (Ger.) = "verwain." See Wittstein, *Handwörterbuch*, p. 188; *eisenkraut*, an ancient medicinal plant, has been used for fever, physical debilitation, headaches, as well as other ailments.

101 *B. D.*, 28a: *inkli vorts* (?) may be *nelke wurz* (Ger.) = "carnation root." See *nelke* plant in *HDA*, VI (1934-35), 1002 f; Meigen, *Deutsch. Pflanzennamen*, pp. 55, 114. *kvintl;* cf. *quendel* (Ger.), "wild thyme." See *quendel* in *HDA*, VII (1935-36), 417 f.; Meigen, pp. 80, 115. *Ostir-Lutsi vorts (vortsl); Osterluzi wurz* (Ger.) "Easter Lucy root." See *Osterluzi* plant in *HDA*, VI, 1340 f.; Meigen, pp. 84, 114. *nestil vorts(vortsl);* cf. *nesselwurz* (Ger.) = "nettle root." See below, n. 123 to p. 130. Cf. Höfler, p. 78: The "nettle plant" was used in remedies for intestinal worms, nosebleeds, and loss of hair.

102 *Dimyon ha-Refu'ot*, p. 25. See W. Bonser, "Gen. Med. Pract. in Anglo-Saxon Eng.," *Essays in Honour of Charles Singer*, I, 163: Popular medieval remedies "would have been more useful as emetics than as medicine."

103 See below, p. 133, n. 141.

104 *B. D.*, fol. 25a, 37b.

105 Marx in *JQR*, VIII, 279 (text), 291 (trans.).

106 *B. D.*, fol. 25a: . . . *alint vorts (vortsl) zaft*. . . .

Perhaps related to *aloe wurz* (Ger.) = "aloe root." *zaft* (Yid.) = "juice"; cf. *saft* (Ger.), same meaning. Fresh treacle is suggested to check swelling; it is also used as medication for veneral swelling; see below, n. 128, to p. 130.

107 *Ibid.* See *muskat* (Yid.), "nutmeg," chap. V, p. 99, n. 31; also in *Ḥayye 'Adam* 51:14; Bernstein in *Argentin. IWO Shrift.*, VI, 142, sec. 40.

108 *M. H.*, 34b:

רפואה בדוקה לחולי קוליג שקורין בל״א פערין מוטר, יקח ערמן יער הנקרא ווילדי קעסט ויסיר הקליפה ויקח ממנה שיעור ב׳ או ג׳ פולין....

Cf. *kolik* (Ger.) = "colic." Prob. *fahren müde* (Ger.) = "leading to listlessness"; see above, n. 88 to p. 127. See *wilde keste* (Ger.) = "wild chestnut."

109 *B. D.*, 39a; *Ma'aseh Ṭobiyah*, II, fol. 112b: *geshvilakhs* (Yid.) "swelling."

Cf. "hydropsia, swollen body" in *Dimyon ha-Refu'ot,* p. 26. See examples of inflammation and erysipelas, above, p. 119, n. 38. Cf. *ha-shoshannah,* "erysipelas": *Refu'ot ha-'Am,* chap. 19, #273.

[110] *Panim Me'irot,* II, no. 156, fol. 75a:

... ליחה ירוקה כליחה היוצא[ת] ממורסא שקורין בל"א גשוויר. ...

Cf. "Diseases," *RCC,* cit. See also in *Pene Yehoshua',* I, no. 1, fol. 11b, a woman having an abscess that discharges pus.

mursa' (Heb.) = "abscess," as in *Ket.,* fol. 6b; Masie, *Sefer ha–Munnaḥim,* p. 3, cit. *geshvir* (Yid.) = "abscess"; cf. *geschwür* (Ger.) same meaning: Hovorka-Kronfeld, II, 391. See remedy for an "abscess" *(geshvir)* in Bernstein, *Davke,* XVII, 355.

[111] *B. D.,* 39a: (1) a rubbing ointment prepared from garlic and oil boiled together (also used to counteract poison); (2) a medicine made by mixing white cabbage, milk, and unstrained fat; (3) salve from flour, olive oil, and wine; (4) an application from a pigeon cut into pieces and mixed with honey and wax; (5) blains (pustules), causing swollen feet, are rubbed with radish oil; (6) a plaster of salt, the dung of a dog, and vinegar, or an emulsion of linseed oil and the yolk of an egg. For examples of plant remedies, see above, n. 70 to p. 125; and for the use of garlic in folk medicine, see Grünbaum, *Chrestomathie,* p. 569 (based on *Yid. Theriak,* chap. I, fol. 9a, #20); Löw, *Flora der Juden,* IV, 103; Lilienthal in *Yid. Filolog.,* I, 257, n. 3. See garlic as a healthful plant: Marzell in *Deut. Volkskunde* (ed. Meier), p. 62; Höfler, p. 103. And in Seligmann, *Der böse Blick,* II, 71, garlic as a protection against witchcraft; also, as a "nightcap" for a mother who is confined; and pp. 70-71, for the practice in Bulgaria of pinning garlic on a child after baptism.

See Bonser, *Essays in Honour of Charles Singer,* I, 163. The generalization concerning medicine in England during the Middle Ages could apply to Jewish folk cures in Central Europe. "But by far the largest number of remedies prescribed were herb remedies. . . . The number of animal remedies employed was but few compared with the number of herbal remedies. . . . So that the various parts of the animal may be drunk or applied, the instructions are that they should be mixed with oil, wine, vinegar, or honey, so as to dissolve them or to make them into a salve. But the methods employed can hardly have disguised the ingredients, which, considering their extreme nastiness in many cases, must have been obnoxious to the patient." For examples of "nauseous drugs" in general folk medicine, see Jakobovits, *Med. Ethics,* pp. 41-42.

[112] *Dimyon ha-Refu'ot,* p. 26.

[113] *B. D.,* 36a. See in Hovorka-Kronfeld, I, 455, the *herzwurm* as the cause of heart ailment. Cf. *Ma'aseh Ṭobiyah,* II, fol. 114b, #4, #5: "coronary palpitation" and "weak heart."

[114] *B. D.,* 36a: "Squeeze the juice of an onion, mix it with salt, then grind and apply it to the heart."

115 *Panim Me'irot,* I, no. 12, fol. 12b:

... בחולי הארי״ן ווינ״ד שדרכו לבוא עם מי רגלים והיא מרגשת כאב. ...

"... Diuresis occurs when one feels pain in urinating. ..." See "diuresis" in Masie, *Sefer ha-Munnaḥim,* p. 231.

Ibid., II, no. 156, fol. 75a, query concerning a woman who has "sand in her kidneys": *(ḥoli she-ḳorin zand).* The woman, speaking in Yiddish, tells of her difficulty. Cf. *B. D.,* 30a: ailment of *zand.*

116 *Panim Me'irot,* I, fol. 13b: "kidney stone."

B. D., fol. 24a: *lendin-shteyn;* cf. *lendenstein* (Ger.) = "loin, kidney, lumbar stone." Cf. kidney ailment in *Pene Yehoshua',* II, no. 29, fol. 15a: "... She would see blood when she passed water. ..." Cf. kidney disease, nephritis (kidney stones and inflammation): *Dimyon ha-Refu'ot,* p. 29; Steinschneider, *Heb. Übersetz.,* Pt. 3, p. 664, #423, no. 2; Bernstein in *Davke,* XVII, 354. Cf. also in *B. D.,* 24a, a stone in the stomach and in the *membrum virile.*

117 *B. D.,* 24a. To dissolve a stone, three pieces of warm dove's dung and the mustard plant are bound to the stomach after urinating. Other plant and stone remedies used are: *shmaltsine*[*r*] *Haynrikh* (cf. *schmalzener Heinrich,* "greasy Henry"); Persian kernels, which are beaten into a powder. A bath is taken in water cress (above, p. 127, n. 95). Also used medicinally are: the *hertsin-tsung;* cf. *herzenzung, herzenszung* (Ger.) = "tongue of heart"; *zibn-boym-vasr (vaser);* cf. *siebenbaum wasser* (Ger.) = "savin" (brushy shrub or small tree). See Höfler, pp. 25-26: The plant *stolzer Heinrich* is the bearer of the soul of "proud Henry," illustrating again how plants are personified in German folklore. Cf. *stolzer Heinrich* in Seligmann, *Der böse Blick,* II, 86; *guter Heinrich* in Wittstein, *Handwörterbuch,* p. 241. *shaḥor-oyg-shteyn* = black agate stone (above, n. 100) is crushed and taken with a drink while one bathes.

B. D., fol. 24a-b, enumerates other "remedies" to remove internal stones, such as: (a) flaxseed is beaten, heated, and eaten with a roasted egg without salt; (b) drinking powders were made of the vine plant, flour, and crystal.

118 *Ibid.,* 35a. This is another example of "sympathetic magic." For instance, see Wuttke, pp. 301-302, that "like cures like," *similia similibus curantur.* To treat "a diseased [lit., decayed] liver," the vine shoot (*venrikh vortsl;* cf. *weinwurzel,* Ger.) is boiled in water and used as a drink.

119 *B. D.,* fol. 36a. *Ibid.,* fol. 40a: *oygin(oygn) mit hits blate*[*r*]*n;* cf. *blotern* (Yid.) = "blister"; *blattern* (Ger.), "pustule, pimple." See Bernstein in *Davke,* XVII, 352, #557: "pustules in the eyes."

Remedy for an eye inflammation; B. D., 36a: Apply the white of the bile of an ox to the eye thirty-four times.

Remedy to remove the skin from the eye; ibid., 36a: Apply twice daily an eyewash made from the acrea plant and camphor. Prob. *tuti;* cf. *tute* (Ger.) = "acrea plant": *Der Grosse Brockhaus,* XII (1930), 211.

Remedy for "heat blisters"; ibid., 40a: Prepare an eye poultice from the inside of an apple without peelings or seeds, by crushing it on a mortar, boiling it in goat's milk, mixing it with rose water (prob. *royzin-vasir;* cf. *rosenwasser,* Ger.), straining it through a cloth, and then mixing it with פרעפוריטי טוטציא (?) and the thyme plant (*kvint;* cf. *quendel,* Ger.). A mucous substance, formed when mixed with rose water, is applied to the eye. See above (p. 128, n. 97), the apple as a remedy. Cf. *royznvaser* in *Dimyon ha-Refu'ot,* p. 75, sec. 1. Cf. *B. D.,* 30b-31a: The woman who cannot make herself ritually clean uses *royznvaser.*

[120] *B. D.,* fol. 30a; fol. 24b. See the instance of defective hearing or partial deafness, in *Shebut Ya'aḳob,* II, no. 33, fol. 5b.

Remedy for tinnitus; B. D., 24b: Mix dog dung and honey in a cloth and apply to the pain; or pour oil into an apple, then heat and apply it to the ear.

Remedy for deafness; ibid., 30a: Put white salt into fresh earthen clay with holes; a clay pot is placed underneath; the fat substance found in the pot is applied twice daily to the ear. See "salt" chap. V, p. 105, n. 76.

[121] *Ibid.,* 30a: *negli;* cf. *nagelkraut* = "nail-wort." Cf. *Dimyon ha-Refu'ot,* p. 78, sec. 2: *neglkhr balsum* (*balzam,* mod. Yid.); cf. *nagelkraut balsam.* See the *nagelkraut* as a medicinal plant: Wittstein, *Handwörterbuch,* pp. 65, 296-97.

[122] *Ibid.,* fol. 25b. As a remedy for a sore in the throat, the lovage plant (prob. *lib-shtigl;* cf. *liebstöckel*) is recommended. The *liebstöckel* is one of the *heilkräuter,* "medicinal herbs": *HDA,* III, 1681 f.

Ibid., fol. 25b: A remedy for an ache in the neck, or a growth in the mouth, is prepared from oil, lion's dung, and boiled water.

[123] *B. D.,* fol. 30a: Remedies for speech defect: (a) ocher, yellow clay (prob. *okeres;* cf. *ocker,* Ger.) is placed under the nostril and the sageleaf plant (prob. *zalvi;* cf. *salvei, salbei*) under the tongue (see *HDA,* III, 1681: *salbei* as a *heilkraut; ibid.,* VII, 814, 819, 893 f., for the folklore relating to *ocker* and *salbei*); (b) a mouthwash is prepared by placing the sage plant in water.

B. D., 30a: As a remedy for a mute person, pepper grass seeds *(kresin zamin;* cf. *kressen sammen)* or the marrow of the nettle plant (prob. *nestlin;* cf. *nessel*) are prescribed. See nettle, above, p. 128, n. 101; Meigen, *Deutsch, Pflanzennamen,* p. 114.

Ibid.: For the lame, plant remedies can be prepared from: (a) the white onion plant *(tsibel*[*e*] *vays)* boiled in water (*HDA,* IX 968-69, for the medicinal uses of the onion); (b) a healing plant (*hayl-alir-*[*aleh*]*-bald kroyt;* cf. *heilkraut,* a medicinal herb offering immediate relief (*HDA,* III, 1681, for the *heilkräuter* by their names).

[124] *Shebut Ya'aḳob,* II, no. 101, fol. 29b.

For physical handicaps, such as a crushed limb (*B. D.,* 35a), the juice of the quince herb *(kvitin kroyt;* cf. *quitte kraut)* is recommended. See *HDA,* VII, 426; VIII, 206, for *quitte kraut.* The quince juice is to be taken with absinthe (prob. *virmit;* cf. *wermut,* "vermouth") for a liver cold and fever, and as a tonic or bodybuilder.

B. D., fol. 35b: Remedies for aches, pains, and physical handicaps: (a) massaging; (b) a massaging ointment is prepared from duck's oil mixed with the crushed entrails of a cat.

Cf. pain of the loin, hip (*lend,* Yid.), in *'Abodat ha-Gershuni,* no. 59, fol. 296; "aching loins": *B. D.,* 36b.

[125] *B. D.,* 32a: *pokn, blotern* (Yid.), "small pox." See above, n. 119: *blotern.*

Ibid., 25a: The kinds of venereal disease are: "pain in the *membrum virile";* "swelling of the organ"; "perforation of the organ." Cf. "French disease" and "venereal disease": *Ma'aseh Ṭobiyah,* II, fol. 120a, #11. The European origin of the disease was traced by Tobias Cohn to Columbus's first contact with the Americas; it then spread from Italy to France and other sectors of Europe: cf. *ibid.,* Pt. 2, fol. 112b, #11; also, Zimmels, pp. 96-97, nn. 17, 26; Singer, *Short Hist. Med.,* p. 98; *idem* (ed.), Sudhoff, *The Earliest Printed Literature on Syphilis* (1495-1498), *Intro.,* pp. ix ff.; *HDA,* III (1930-31), 734, "Geschlechtskrankheiten"; V, 1275, "Liebeskrankheit."

For smallpox remedies, cf. *B. D.,* 32a: (a) boil raisins, lentils, and peelings (husks); (b) massage with olive oil. To prevent blotches from reaching the eyes and nose, move a sapphire over the eye; then prepare an eyewash of rose water (above n. 119) mixed with two or three drops of a mother's milk; also massage the nose with the rose-water preparation.

Cf. *Dimyon ha-Refu'ot,* p. 34 (sec. "Epidemics"), for a description of typhus and measles: ". . . A continuous high fever [is] called in Yiddish typhus fever, and measles [is] known as 'holy fire' and marmor pimples." See *flekn fiver* (Yid.), "fever spots"; cf. *feuer-flecken, roten petechien* = "petechial (typhus) spots": Höfler, p. 154. *rublis;* cf. *rubeola* (Ger.) = "rubella, German measles." Prob. *redlin (roytlin);* cf. *röteln* (Ger.) = "epidemic roseola, German measles." May be *fayer-aleh;* cf. *höllenfeuer* (Ger.), "holy fire, plague of divine punishment": Höfler, p. 136. See also above, n. 90 to p. 127, "hell-fire." *marbili;* cf. *marbel, marmor* (Ger.) = "marmor, marblelike." Cf. *ibid.,* pp. 49-50, for typhus and description of measles. See the effect of smallpox in *Pene Yehoshua',* I, no. 13, fol. 45a (sec. "'E. H."): ". . . His face did not have its usual color but became flushed because of the pox fever. He had the pox on his face and nose."

[126] See *HDA,* III, 734; V, 1275; Singer, *op. cit.,* pp. 96, 98, that in the Middle Ages syphilis was included among contagious diseases and epidemics, and, therefore, was not differentiated from other infections.

[127] See in Zimmels, pp. 96-97, instances of venereal disease in the German-Jewish community. For examples of adultery, illegitimacy, prostitution, sex laxity, cf. *Ḥavvot Ya'ir,* no. 31, fol. 36b; *Noda' bi-Yehudah,* I, no. 92, fol. 98b (sec. "'E. H."); *Shebut Ya'aḳob,* III, no. 108, fol. 18a; no. 109, fol. 20b; "Marriage," *RCC,* cit.; *Ḥaḥam Ẓebi,* no. 44, fol. 45b; Baron, *Community,* II, 205, n. 27; 312-15; III, 205-6, n. 28; Marcus, *Communal Sick-Care,* pp. 46, 133; Shohet, *'Im Ḥillufe Teḳufot,* p. 166. That family stability is on the decline, evidenced by increasing

erotic attitudes and sex license, see also J. Katz, *Zion,* X (N. S., 1946), 46 ff. See also in Rivkind, "Codex of Prague" (Hebrew), *Reshumot,* IV (1925), 351, the order issued, in 1613, that prostitutes must be removed from the community and homes. And, *Pene Yehoshua',* I, no. 1, fol. 30b (sec. "'E.H."), the case of a woman who had engaged in adultery. While relevant for Eastern Europe, it may be assumed that such instances also occurred among Jews in Germany. See also Katzenelsohn, *Talmud ve-ha-Refu'ah,* p. 318, sec. 6; p. 376, sec. 7; p. 378, sec. 8, that venereal disease was regarded as "a fact" in ancient times.

[128] *Remedies (used externally) for venereal disease:*

Drug: B. D., 25b: saltpeter heated in olive oil.

Drug and Stone: Ibid., 25b: argol (above, n. 75; below, n. 199) and eye-stone (*krepzin oygin;* cf. *krebs auge,* Ger. = "crab's eye").

Plant: Ibid., 25a: theriak or treacle (above, n. 106).

Animal: Ibid., 25b: fat obtained by cutting and boiling the foot of a cow.

Plant and animal: Ibid., 25a: rock-moss. *(shteyn-kroyt ha-gadol;* cf. *steinkraut)* and the fat of a hog are boiled together and used as an application.

Plant and food: Ibid.: verdigris *(grin-shban;* cf. *grünspan),* fat, milk, and linseed oil. See *HDA,* V, 838: *grünspan,* used as a remedy in ancient times, more extensively after the 16th century. *B. D.,* 25a-b: alga (seawood) juice (prob. *mayim alzian;* cf. *alge wasser*) and achene fruit (may be *akhen-leb;* prob. related to *achäne,* Ger.).

Plant, animal, and food: Ibid., 25b: olive oil, the fat of a lamb's entrails, the blood of a white rooster, and red earth worms.

[129] See Zimmels, pp. 99-100; Marcus, *Communal Sick-Care,* pp. 17-18, 218 f. Note the moral attitude expressed in Prague during a plague: Rivkind, *Reshumot,* IV, 345-46. See also A. P. Bender, "Beliefs, Rites, and Customs," *JQR,* VI (O. S., 1894), 335: When a plague occurred, it meant that the Angel of Death was given "absolute power . . . to slay indiscriminately."

For some examples of cholera and plague, cf. *Ḥatam Sofer,* no. 338, fol. 136b (sec. "Y. D."); *Y. 'O.,* #500; *Ẓemaḥ Ẓedeḳ,* no. 40, fol. 39a ff.; *Shebut Ya'aḳob,* II, no. 97, fol. 15b. And as to the anxiety caused when "a disease had spread," cf. *'Abodat ha-Gershuni,* no. 10, fol. 5a. See cits. in Zimmels, p. 58, n. 205; p. 100, nn. 69, 74, 75.

[130] *Ḥavvot Ya'ir,* no. 60, fol. 62b:

מעשה שאירע בק״ק ווירמיישא ברעש הגדול שנת שצ״ו...שחלתה בת יחידה של אחד מן הגדולים ועשירים אשר בק״ק במגפה...לא היה בנמצא משרתת או משרת שישמשנה בחוליה....

Cf. Zimmels, n. 70 to p. 100.

[131] *Shebut Ya'aḳob, op. cit.* That the body is to remain intact after death, cf. *Y. D.* 362:1-2 (based on Deut. 21:23; *San.,* 46b). Also, see Eisenstein, "Burial" (Hebrew), *'Oẓar Yisra'el,* IX (1913), 93, cit.; Jakobovits, *Medical Care,* p. 146 (based on Ezekiel Landau).

[132] Kaufmann (ed.), *Glikl,* p. 85, n. 5. Cf. Feilchenfeld, p. 65. Cf. in *Dimyon ha-Refu'ot,* pp. 35-36, the symptoms of "the bubonic carbuncle." See the plague in Hamburg, in 1565: Thorndike, *Hist. Magic and Exp. Sc.,* VI, 210.

[133] Kaufmann, pp. 85-86. Cf. Feilchenfeld, p. 65. Eng. cit. based on Lowenthal, p. 49. Cf. also B. Z. Abrahams, p. 48.

Cf. Kaufmann, p. 196, n. 3. See "surgeon," below, p. 142, n. 212. Note description of the functions of the surgeon-barber: Marcus, *op. cit.,* p. 37 f., 45 f. Also, "Barber," *Ency. Britan.* (1910, 11th edit.), III, 386, that the barber served as a dentist and also performed "minor operations of blood-letting."

[134] Kaufmann, p. 86; Feilchenfeld, p. 66. Eng. cit. based on Lowenthal, pp. 49-50. Cf. Kaufmann, p. 325; Feilchenfeld, p. 299, for another instance of confusion breaking out in the women's synagogue during an epidemic. Geographical, cultural, and social cleavages are suggested in chap. V, p. 110, nn. 108–109.

[135] Kaufmann, p. 325; Feilchenfeld, p. 299; Lowenthal, p. 50; B. Z. Abrahams, pp. 48-49.

[136] Kaufmann, pp. 86-87; Feilchenfeld, p. 66, n. 10. Eng. cit. based on Lowenthal, pp. 49-50. See ref. to *Glikl* in Marcus, *Communal Sick-Care,* p. 211, n. 232.

[137] Kaufmann, p. 31; Feilchenfeld, pp. 25-26. Eng cit. based on Lowenthal, pp. 15-16. See Lewin in *JJGL,* XXX, 177, that as a result of a plague in 1588, the community of Cracow became poverty-stricken.

[138] Marx in *JQR,* VIII (O. S.), 280 (text); 293 (trans.). The *lazaretto* was a leper home in France in the 11th century: Zimmels, p. 166. See Marx in *op. cit.,* 270, n. 2, that a plague, in Prague, in 1681, took more than 83,000 lives.

[139] Marx in *op. cit.*, 281 (text); p. 295 (trans.). See above, p. 127, n. 93, for the uses of an egg in preparing folk remedies.

As a remedy for the plague, cf. *Dimyon ha-Refu'ot,* p. 37. Wallich prescribed *phenicin thorium* with a strong solution of vinegar. He also advised that camphor incense, myrrh, and aromatic bark be inhaled. The incense was placed on hot coals, and as it burned, the aroma permeated the house. See remedies for an epidemic in *Sefer Refu'ot,* fol. 4b; *Ṭa'ame ha-Minhagim,* II, 44a; Grunwald in *MGJV,* V, 51, #136. In time of a plague, Wallich (*Dimyon ha-Refu'ot,* p. 38) urges that the streets and markets should be cleaned, all debris and rubbish removed—further evidence of the lack of hygienic facilities. The inadequate sanitation facilitates have been suggested, herein, p. 1; pp. 149–50; p. 172, n. 139; in addition, see *Ma'aseh Ṭobiyah,* II, fol. 122b, #3; Sosnovik in *Yid. Filolog.,* I, 166, #32.

[140] For "pustule" (above, n. 119), "boil," "itch" *(kratsin),* cf. *B. D.,* fol. 32b, 36b, 49a; *M. H.,* 33b. Cf. "boil" in *Ḥavvot Ya'ir,* no. 221, fol. 208a. Also, *Pene Yehoshua',* II, no. 29, fol. 15a (sec. "Y. D."), regarding a woman who "felt a boil in her chest."

A. ***Remedies for boils: B. D.,*** fol. 24b: For a black boil: (a) wine and the crimson plant, i. e., a plant producing red juice: (*roytin;* cf. *röte, rubia:* Meigen, *Deutsch. Pflanzennamen,* pp. 69, 115); (b) wine and the lily root *(lilgin vortsil (vortsl);* cf. *lilien wurzel: HDA,* VII, 1548, #3); (c) boil aniseed. *B. D.,* fol. 49a, ointment for a boil: (a) ten kernels, the white of an egg, and verdigris (above, n. 128); (b) a frog that was caught, killed and then suspended in the air, would protect an individual from developing a boil; to cure a boil, a frog is dipped in water and then placed on the boil. Cf. *M. H.,* fol. 36b, for a similar remedy.

B. *Remedies for boils* (cont.): *B. D.,* fol. 34a: twice daily, the juices of the elder and sloe blossom plants are to be taken with water (*holder-bliht;* cf. *holder-blüte* = "elder blossom." *shleyi-bliht;* cf. *schlehenblüte* = "sloe blossom." See Höfler, p. 114: Sour dough is mixed with cress to heal a carbuncle.

141 *M. H.,* fol. 34a: *lorber* = "laurel plant"; cf. *lorbeer* (Ger.), same meaning. See *lorbeer,* below, p. 136, n. 170. For a list of drugs, which were prescribed in Frankfort during the 18th century and prepared by apothecaries, see *Dimyon ha-Refu'ot,* pp. 74 ff.

142 For physical ailments and medical problems that concerned women, see Lefin, *Refu'ot ha-'Am,* chap. 26; also #352, that the more sedentary existence of the woman made her weaker. See also female ailments in Muntner (ed.), *Donnolo,* p. 26; *'Emunat Shemu'el,* no. 1, fol. 1a f.; no. 57, fol. 42a. And, *Ḥatam Sofer,* no. 338, fol. 136b, women suffer from abdominal cramps that cause excrutiating pain.

143 *B. D.,* fol. 22b. See Wuttke, p. 96, #125; p. 116, #162; Hovorka-Kronfeld, p. 354, that the raven and raven's nest are associated with good fortune in German folklore; hence, a root found in a raven's nest, or the "raven's stone" *(rabenstein)* from the sea, would be worn.

144 *B. D.,* 22a. See below, p. 135, n. 158. That the skin of unclean animals may be used for utensils or shoes, see *Ḥul.,* fol. 122a; also, Eisenstein, "Skin, Skins" (Hebrew), *'Oẓar Yisra'el,* VIII (1912), 36, cit.

145 *B. D.,* fol. 22a: *ve-Karlovski trang* (*trank*); may be related to karlovarský, adj. of Karlovy Vary = Karlsbad: Cheshire, Jung, *et al., Czech-Eng. Dict.* (1933, Prague), I, 423. See below, n. 222 to p. 144 for the remedy of Karlsbad water.

146 *Ibid.,* 22b.

147 *Ibid.;* also, 22a. See Elzet in *Reshumot,* I, 363, #58, that a barren woman would swallow with water "a small egg found in a larger egg." The "fish within the fish," or "the egg within the egg," no doubt represents the fetus, and it is therefore eaten by the woman to bring about pregnancy.

148 See p. 158, n. 63.

149 For the significance ascribed to animals as an aid to pregnancy, see Rubin, *Segullot Ba'ale Ḥayyim ve-'Ototam* (Symbolic Meaning of Animals as Remedies), p. 25; Grunwald in *MGJV,* II, 56, #1 ("Fragekasten"); *HDA,* III, 1506-7, #3; I. Scheftolowitz in *ZVV,* XXIII, 390.

150 *B. D.,* 22b: *lovon tsitva;* prob. related to *zitwer* = zedoary plant. Cf.

Dimyon ha-Refu'ot, p. 79, sec. 2: "zedoary balsam."

[151] *B. D.,* 22b.

[152] *Ibid.,* 22a: *platloyz;* cf. *blattlaus* (Ger.), "plant louse." See *HDA,* I (1927), 1366: Remedies for an earache and toothache are prepared with "plant lice" *(blattläuse).*

[153] *Ibid.,* fol. 24a. The eggshell is ground. Cf. *ibid.,* 23b: To avoid a miscarriage, the shell of a hatched egg is put into a drink. See again above, n. 93 to p. 127, regarding the uses of the egg as a folk remedy. See also the practice of placing a fresh egg on a child's eyes and saying: "Your eyes should be as 'healthy' *(frish)* as the egg."

[154] *Ibid.,* 24a. Cf. *ibid.,* 23b, that a pregnant woman can prevent a miscarriage if she crushes a frog with her feet.

[155] *Ibid.,* fol. 22b: *nis-vorts (vortsl);* cf. *nieswurz* (Ger.), "hellebore root." This causes sneezing.

Ibid., 22b-23a: . . . *be-mashkeh ha-nikra' shlisl-blumin vasir (vaser)*. . . . Cf. *Dimyon ha-Refu'ot,* p. 77, sec. *shlisl-blumin;* cf. *schlüsselblume* (Ger.) = "primrose (cowslip) plant." See Grimm, *Deut. Myth.,* II, 812, that the *schlüsselblume* is associated with the "tragedy of the keys," that is, with the incident of the ancestral mother who used the keys entrusted to her to open what she thought was a treasure box. Cf. the tale of Pandora; there was no treasure in the box but all of the troubles that have plagued man since.

Regarding the significance of the placenta in Jewish folklore, see Güdemann, *Gesch.,* I, 204-205.

[156] *B. D.,* fol. 22b: *rutin faybish;* may be related to *rute fiber* (Ger.) = "birch-rod fiber."

[157] *Ibid.,* fol. 23a. See "stillbirth" in Zimmels, p. 71.

[158] *Ibid.,* fol. 23b. Again, note the use of the hare and the frog in folk medicine for female ailments (see above, n. 149; below, p. 135, n. 165). Cf. frogs in general folk medicine: Black, *Folk-Medicine,* p. 61. In general folklore, the ruby is a protection against evil spirits, witchcraft, and is a talisman for strength and health: *HDA,* VII, 841-42.

See Güdemann, *Gesch.,* I, 214, 216: As a safeguard during pregnancy, the woman would wear around her neck a stone, the size of an egg.

[159] *Ibid.,* 23b. See herein, p. 17, n. 17, for the use of the snakeskin in easing child-delivery and for the relation of the snake to birth. See also above, p. 116, n. 27, regarding the snake in folklore.

[160] *Ibid.,* fol. 38a: *virmit;* cf. *wermut* = "absinthe, wormwood": Meigen, *Deutsch. Pflanzennamen,* p. 119; *HDA,* IX, 497 f. *bren eslayn;* cf. *brand essenzlein* = "burning quintessence, an alcoholic extract."

Ibid., fol. 38a: *finf-fingr (finger) kroyt;* cf. *fünffingerkraut* = "five-finger herb." Cf. "postnatal pains" in *'Amtaḥat Binyamin,* fol. 19a, #15.

[161] *B. D.,* fol. 23a:

מכה הנקרא פיינן שבית אצל הנשים הבא מכח קישו[י] לידה וגם אותו מכה שבית אצל אנשים מכח משא כבידה....

Prob. *paynen;* cf. mod. Yid. = "pains"; cf. Ger. *pein.* Cf. *bärwurz,* "cow parsnip."

[162] Cf. *Panim Me'irot,* II, no. 156, fol. 75a, 85a, for examples of menstrual irregularity. Cf. the discussion of the time-cycle most suitable for pregnancy: *'Eben ha-Shoham,* I, no. 14, fol. 7b. Cf. "Disease," *RCC.* See in Güdemann, *Gesch.,* I, 216, the treatment of female ailments, and also in Bernstein, *Davke,* XVII, 352, 354.

[163] *B. D.,* fol. 23b. See parallel practice, above, n. 159.

[164] *Ibid.,* fol. 39b. See "sympathetic magic," above, p. 129, n. 118.

[165] *Ibid.,* fol. 39b.

[166] *Ibid.,* 23a.

[167] *Ibid.,* fol. 39b.

[168] *Ibid.,* 23b: *'eseb ha-niḳra' gutes neser;* cf. *gute nezer* (Yid.) = "good noses." *shtarken shnabl 'eseb;* cf. *starken schnabel* = "strong beak." See above, n. 96, p. 127, concerning the ascription of human qualities to plants.

[169] *M. H.,* 33b: *keneri-tsukr (tsuker)* = *kanarienzucker* = "canary-sugar." Cf. Wittstein, *Handwörterbuch,* 377: *kanariengras,* fodder for canary birds; used for medication. *klaf-rozen* = *klaffenrosen* = "gaping (yawning) rose."

[170] *B. D.,* fol. 23b. See "laurel," above, n. 141. Prob. *hayl-vorts (vortsl);* cf. *heilwurz,* "medicinal herb." See "health plants," above n. 140. *holdr-ber;* cf. *holderbeere,* "elderberry," chap. V, p. 99, n. 28.

[171] *Ibid.,* fol. 22a: *zis-holts;* cf. *süssholz* (Ger.) = "licorice". See "licorice" in Elzet, *Maykholim,* Pt. 2, pp. 73, 109; herein, p. 151, n. 30. Cf. Muntner, *Donnolo,* Pt. 1, p. 26; *Toledot 'Adam,* Pt. 2, sec. 7: breast ailment and treatment.

[172] *Ibid.,* fol. 22a-23b. A similar practice is described in Güdemann, *Gesch.,* I, 212: If the milk of a pregnant woman congeals on a stone, she will give birth to a male, but if it dissolves, she will have a girl. When her milk floats in water, (i.e., congeals), it means that a son will be born, and if it dissolves, a daughter.

[173] *Ibid.,* 23b. See Güdemann, *op. cit.:* If the pregnant woman's right breast is larger than the left, the child will be a male.

[174] *Ibid.,* 24a.

[175] *Ibid.* Cf. *Ibid.,* 23a: If a pregnant woman should eat beans, she will give birth to a child with boils. See popular views concerning prenatal influence in chap. III, n. 34 to p. 55. Cf. *Ḳ. H.* 33:8, that children conceived while parents are excommunicated will be "sinners and informers."

[176] Cf. *Pirḳe 'Abot* 5:24; David Philipson, "Old-Age," *JE,* I (1901), 230. For this period, the author has found no mention of the institution of the aged, the Old Folks' Home, *moshab zeḳenim.* The older person was an intrinsic part of the larger family unit then existing.

[177] *B. D.,* fol. 34b.

[178] See "the transference of disease" to animals, dogs, frogs, fish, and fowl, in Black, *Folk-Medicine,* pp. 35–36, 48. Also above, p. 127, inc. nn. 88, 93.

Cf. children's illness in *Toledot 'Adam,* Pt. 2, sec. 40; Lefin, *Refu'ot ha-'Am,* chap. 27.

[179] *'Emunat Shemu'el,* no. 2, fol. 3b. Cf. "Medicine," *RCC,* cit. See Marcus, *Communal Sick-Care,* p. 184, concerning the wet-nurse in Hamburg and Prague.

[180] *Ma'aseh Ṭobiyah,* Pt. 2, fol. 109a:

נגעי הראש או שחין רע מאד מצוי בקטני׳ וביותר בארצות האלו וגם בארץ אשכנז ופולוניאה אותותם הם אם נשרש איזה שער ונמצא בשרשו עוקץ לבן עם נקודה שחורה בתחתיתו.

Cf. the remedy for boils on children in *Ṭa'ame ha-Minhagim,* II, 49b.

[181] *'Emunat Shemu'el,* no. 12, fol. 14b.

[182] Cf. *Dimyon ha-Refu'ot,* title page: "There is a relationship between the remedies of the mind and that of the body." The thoughts of man affect his health: p. 18. And in this regard, see Marcus, p. 192; M. Seligsohn, "Wallich," *JE,* II (1905), 460. Note that Landau makes a distinction between the mind and body in matters of illness: *Derushe ha-Ẓelaḥ,* no. 31, #1, 2, 3.

[183] See Zimmels, p. 111: Mental ailments are listed as "melancholia, mania, megalomania, hysteria, and imbecility." Cf. "hypochondria," "melancholia" in *Ma'aseh Ṭobiyah,* Pt. 2, fol. 103a, #3; fol. 118a, #9; "melancholia" in Muntner (ed), *Donnolo,* Pt. 1, 122, n. 116. See also Grunwald in *MGJV,* V, 55, #163: "gegen melancholie."

[184] Kaufmann (ed.), *Glikl,* pp. 80-81; Feilchenfeld, pp. 60-61; Lowenthal, pp. 45-46; *Ḳ. H.,* Pref.; *'Eben ha-Shoham,* I, no. 13, fol. 6b; *Megillat Sefer,* fol. 22a-b.

[185] Cf. the sermon delivered by Eibeschütz when the Jews were expelled from Prague: *Ya'arot Debash,* I, 45b. For the hardships brought on by fire, war, and expulsion, cf. A. Marx, "Notes on . . . Bacharach," *Essays Presented to J. H. Hertz,* pp. 310-11; B. Rosenthal, "Briefe von Mannheimer Juden (1695-97)," *ZGJD,* VII (N. S., 1937), 99; Richter-Schmidt, "Hotzenplotzer Judengemeinde," *MGJV,* XXXVII (1911), 33. See the stresses of the period mentioned herein, p. 1, n. 1; n. 84 to p. 13; nn. 2–3 to p. 146.

[186] *Shebut Ya'aḳob,* I, no. 106, fol. 27b. Cf. "Folk-Medicine," *RCC,* cit. (*in re:* "A fictitious breach of engagement"). See *ḳnas,* betrothal contract, chap. II, pp. 29–31.

[187] Kaufmann (ed.), *Glikl,* p. 3. Cf. Feilchenfeld, p. 11; also cits. in Ysaye in *MGJV,* VII, 104; XII, 2; Landau in *MGJV,* VII, 26; Erik, *Yid. lit.,* pp. 395-96.

[188] *She'elat Ya'abeẓ,* I (Altona, 1739), Pref.; II (Lemberg, 1884), Pref. Cf. B. Z. Katz, *Rabbanut,* I, 152, n. 4.

[189] *Pene Yehoshua',* II, no. 58, fol. 39b.

[190] *Ibid.,* 40a.

[191] See Zimmels, p. 165: That mental institutions had been first established

in the 18th century is indicative of a lag in providing medical facilities for the mentally sick.

[192] *B. D.*, fol. 38a: *vayarikh;* cf. *weihrauch* = "incense." See Marx in *JQR*, VIII, 274: Memory can be improved by means of diet, eating one meal a day, at noon. Also, *Dimyon ha-Refu'ot*, fol. 2b: To "eliminate forgetfulness," saltpeter is to be used.

[193] *M. H.*, fol. 33b.

[194] *B. D.*, fol. 39a:

לנחש או צפרדע בגופו של אדם ... וביום הג׳ ישים בתוכו עצם מן מוח של איש שנהרג על ידי פסק דין של אומת, וכתוש אותו לעפר ושים בתוך שכר ויצאו ממנו:

See above, p. 126, for the folk tradition that the bones of a dead person have healing power. Apparently, there were instances when the bone of a corpse would be ground to dust and the powder formed would be used as a medicine: see, for example, Zimmels, p. 126; Bernstein in *Davke*, XVII, 352. According to general folklore, the dead can heal the sick; hence, a powder made of a dead man's skull and bones is regarded as an effective medication. Also, the "dead stroke"—that is, a sick person touched by a man about to be executed—offers a remedy: cf. Black, *Folk-Medicine*, pp. 95-97, 101.

[195] *B. D.*, 39b. See *HDA*, VI, 1644: In general folklore, the perspiration of a horse serves to check epilepsy and insanity, ease childbirth, and dispel vermin. Cf. Hovorka-Kronfeld, II, 723, that the juice of the rose plant is considered effective as an eyewash and a skin remedy.

[196] *B. D.*, fol. 38a, sec. 50. Cf. the disease of epilepsy in *Ma'aseh Ṭobiyah*, Pt. 1, fol. 108a-b; Lewin in *JJLG*, XVI, 65; also in Steinschneider, *Heb. Übersetz.*, Pt. 3, sec. 415, p. 653, #7; Bernstein in *Davke*, XVII, 353. For other epilepsy treatments, cf. *B. D.*, fol. 38b-39a. In Jewish and general folklore popular remedies for epilepsy include plants, amulets, skin of a wolf, among others: Löwinger in *Menorah*, IV, 559; Höfler, p. 24; Grimm, *Deut. Myth.*, II, 978; Black, *op. cit.*, p. 153.

The term *nikhpeh*, an "epileptic," means "to be overtaken by a demon." Cf. Preuss, *Bib.-talmud. Medizin*, p. 342: Epilepsy is described as a "seizure"; Zimmels, p. 34, that epilepsy is of "demoniac origin."

[197] *'Emunat Shemu'el*, no. 6, fol. 7a: *ḥoli nikhpeh*. Cf. fol. 9a, that epilepsy is intensified by sexual relations. Cf. "Medicine," *RCC*, cit.

[198] *B. D.*, fol. 35a: *ayer-klor, ay-vays* (Yid.); cf. *eiweiss*, "the white of an egg."

[199] *Ibid.*, 35b. See "argol," above n. 75 to p. 125. See in Grunwald, *MGJV*, V, 68, #242, a popular way of cleaning garments.

[200] See, for example, "tangled hair" in *Ma'aseh Ṭobiyah*, Pt. 2, fol. 109b-110a; Zimmels, pp. 98-99, n. 33.

[201] *B. D.*, 39b: Prob. *shtinkendig otem* (Yid.) = "bad breath." גארפיליי(?);

perhaps related to *graptolith* = "graptolite."גליאנינא(?); may be related to *gallenkraut* = "hedge-hyssop." Prob. *eluli*; cf. *elymus* = "elymus, lyme grass." Cf. "bad breath": *Dimyon ha-Refu'ot*, p. 17.

[202] See p. 128 for Abraham Lissa.

[203] *M. H.*, fol. 34a. See remedy for insomnia in Bernstein, *Davke*, XVII, 349. No one cause accounts for insomnia.

[204] *Ibid.*, fol. 33b-34a. Cf. *B. D.*, fol. 43b, toothache remedies include absinthe (above, n. 160) and alum. For popular toothache remedies, cf. Lefin, *Refu'ot ha-'Am*, sec. 8; *Ṭa'ame ha-Minhagim*, II, 47a-b; Grunwald in *MGJV*, V, 47, #123; V, 48-49, #125; Bernstein in *Davke*, XVII, 354. See Höfler, p. 29, that a cookie would be made of the elderberry *(hollerküchel)* to ease the toothache. Cf. the examples of foods used as amulets, herein, p. 102, n. 53; nn. 93, 94 to p. 127.

[205] *Ibid.*, fol. 34a-b. See again the examples of "transferring sickness" and "sympathetic magic" on p. 119, n. 36; p. 128; p. 135, n. 164. See Bernstein in *Davke*, XVII, 344, a nosebleed is checked by using a "sympathetic" remedy: "Write on the forehead with the third finger the words, *'agf, ngf, sgf*, using some of the blood [of the nose]." Also, Sosnovik in *Yid. Filolog.*, I, 167, #38, that a "red thread" wound around the neck or head checks a nosebleed. Likewise, Archer Taylor, "Germanic Folklore," *Stand. Dict. Folklore* (Funk and Wagnalls), I, 447, states that a red string tied about a wound will have the sympathetic effect of checking the flow of blood. Furthermore, Hovorka-Kronfeld, II, 893; Lilienthal in *Yid. Filolog.*, I, 251-52: The color red is used to frighten away the evil spirit. And, Black, *Folk-Medicine*, p. 111: "Red cords and red bands play an important part in folk-medicine." Hence, a red cloth is worn for scarlet fever, whooping cough, sore throats, and nosebleeds.

[206] *M. H., velshe nus* (Yid.); cf. *welsche nuss*, "large walnut." See Wittstein, *Handwörterbuch*, 885-86, the root of the walnut *(welsche nuss, wallnuss)* is used as a folk remedy for fever, gout, and inflammation.

Cf. in *Ma'aseh Ṭobiyah*, II, fol. 123b, #50, the injuries that occurred in the home. See Fried in *MGJV*, XXXVI, 168, #2, that dew is a remedy for a wound. See Wuttke, *Deut. Volksaberglaube*, pp. 324, 516, for folk practices to heal wounds and check bleeding.

[207] *B. D.*, fol. 35b. See "nettle plant," above p. 128, n. 101. Cf. *Sefer Refu'ot*, fol. 4a, "the bite of a mad dog." Cf. Lefin, *Refu'ot ha-'Am*, #195: Salt is used to treat the bite of a "mad dog"; *Toledot 'Adam*, Pt. 2, fol. 9a, #50: "If anyone is bitten by a mad dog, place olive oil and salt on the wound immediately." The tooth of a mad dog can have a "sympathetic" function: Bernstein in *Davke*, XVII, 342. The tooth is used as: (a) a remedy for a mad dog bite; (b) a safeguard against an attack by a dog; (c) an amulet to be worn by a child to ease the growth of his teeth. In general folklore the head of a mad dog is considered effective as a cure: Black, *Folk-Medicine*, p. 149.

208 *B. D.*, fol. 39a.

Cf. *Refu'ot ha-'Am,* chap. 12, sec. 188 ff. (no fol. mark), for a vivid portrayal of a mad dog. See also in Walsh, *Medieval Medicine,* p. 80, description of the behavior of a mad dog, based on the account of Lanfranc, a French surgeon: "His description of how one may recognize a rabid animal is rather striking in the light of our present knowledge, for he seems to have realized that the main diagnostic element is a change in the disposition of the animal, but above all a definite tendency to lack playfulness." (*Biographie Universelle,* XXIII, 160: Lafranc was born in Milan, middle of the 13th cent., and settled in Paris in 1295.) Note the similarity of Lefin, *Refu'ot ha-'Am,* #189: "And the mad dog constantly refuses food, and especially water. It does not recognize its master; its voice changes, and it will let no animal come near it." The medical source that Lefin used must have been considered scientifically accurate.

209 *B. D.,* fol. 39b. See the use of urine in folk medicine, above p. 125, n. 73, Cf. an antidote to poison in *Toledot 'Adam,* fol. 9a, #50.

210 See pp. 124-25; p. 126, n. 81; p. 128, n. 98.

211 Cf. Kaufmann (ed.), *Glikl,* p. 318; *Shebut Ya'akob,* III, no. 75, fol. 12b.

212 Kaufmann (ed.), *Glikl,* p. 198:

... דאר נאך זענין יותר דאקטורים אונ׳ ברויך שניידירש גיקומין. ...

Prob. *broykh-shnayder,* cf. Feilchenfeld, p. 176; Lowenthal, p. 150: *bruchschneider* (Ger.), "rupture-cutter, chirurgeon, surgeon." See the practice of surgery in Lewin in *JJLG,* XV, 88; also in Riesman, *Med. in Middle Ages,* p. 204; E. Nicaise, *La grande chirurgie de Guy de Chauliac,* p. 7.

213 Kaufmann, pp. 198-99; Feilchenfeld, p. 176; Lowenthal, p. 150; B. Z. Abrahams, p. 107.

214 *Shebut Ya'akob,* III, no. 75, fol. 12b.

215 *'Emunat Shemu'el,* no. 1, fol. 3b.

216 *Shebut Ya'akob, op. cit.* See above, p. 114, n. 7.

217 Christopher Marlowe (d. 1593, England), "From the Tragical History of Doctor Faustus," Newcomer-Andrews (eds.), *Twelve Centuries of English Poetry and Prose* (Chicago, 1910), pp. 151-52.

218 *Shebut Ya'akob,* III, no. 51, fol. 9a. The precedent for this practice is based on the *sugya',* "usage," in *Sukkah,* fol. 26a: "R. Simeon ben Gamliel said, On one occasion I was suffering with my eyes in Caesarea and R. Jose Berebi permitted me and my attendants to sleep outside the *Sukkah."* That "sick persons and their attendants are exempt from fulfilling the obligation of the Sukkah," cf. *Sukkah* 2:4; also, *M. T.,* "Hil. Sukkah," 6:2; *'O. Ḥ.* 640:3 ("Hil. Sukkah").

219 With regard to the ancient tradition and established communal practice of visiting and caring for the sick, see n. 150 to p. 41; and in addition, among others, *Y. D.,* sec. 335; Weisel in *BSV,* XVII, 209.

220 *Shebut Ya'akob,* III, no. 104, fol. 17a:

... במיני קטניו׳ שהם יפות מבחוץ . . . וכשנוטלין הקליפה העליונה יש בו תולעים וזבובים חיים ויש מי שקורין אותם בלע״ז ויקין . . . וכן אותן מיני קטניו׳ שקורין אותן חזיר בונין . . . ובאיזה מדינו׳ נצטוו אפי׳ מהשררה שלא לאכול מיני קטניו׳ אלו לפי שרופאי׳ אומרים שיש בהם נחש וארס. . . .
Cf. "Health Standards," *RCC,* cit. Note: the region to which the regulation refers is not specified; it may have been Bohemia.
vikin; prob. related to *wiecken* (Ger.) = "leguminous plant, tendril vine (e. g., bean)." *ḥazir bonin;* cf. *bohnen* (Ger.) = "bean," "hog bean." See herein, p. 99, n. 30; "bean blossom" in *Dimyon ha-Refu'ot*, p. 75. *naḥash ve-'eres* (Heb.) = "serpent's poison, disease carrier." Cf. the poison-pocket in leguminous plants: Blondheim, *Gloses françaises,* p. 170, #1046, cit. of Steinschneider, *Gifte von Maimon.,* p. 104, n. 67; Moshe b. Maimon, *Same ha-Mavet* (*Poisons and their Antidotes,* ed. Muntner), p. 106, n. 26; p. 107, n. 27.

See above, p. 114, n. 7, regarding the interest shown in the health of the public; also, p. 111 as to the concern in alerting everyone not to eat contaminated foods.

221 *Shebut Ya'akob,* II, no. 57, fol. 9a: ". . . A disease was found in cattle that is called *shvindzukht*. . . ." Cf. *schwindsucht* (Ger.), "consumption, tuberculosis." Cf. "Health Standards," *RCC,* cit. For another communal health problem, see Zimmels, p. 75: The question had been raised whether the milk of a mother could have poisoned her child, thereby causing its death.

222 *Dimyon ha-Refu'ot,* p. 31: *Embser bod* = Emser bath. (Ems [Bad Ems], known for its mineral springs; loc. in West Germany.)

Aron Freimann in *Ḳobeẓ 'al Yad,* VIII (1898), 41: *zoyer-brunen.* Cf. *(ibid.),* n. 1: *sauerbrunnen* (Ger.) = "mineral water." See "the 'cure' at Karlsbad" in Marcus, *Communal Sick-Care,* p. 150 (Karlsbad is northeast of Eger, a distance of about twenty miles).

223 Haggard, *Mystery, Magic, and Medicine,* p. 14. This statement does not apply to plant remedies that proved to be beneficial. The same criticism might be made of the success of medicine at various times.

Notes to Chapter VII

Shelah, I, fol. 214b (sec. "Rosh ha–Shanah"):
...ומזה רבו המנהגים כל מקום ומקום לפי מנהגו כמו באשכנז....

2 *J. M.,* II (chap. 6), 84; the "Klaglied": III (No. 3), 65; Kracauer, *Judengasse in Frankfurt a. M.,* p. 124; Kaufmann, *Urkund. aus dem Leben Samson Wertheimers,* p. 71; Ocksman in *Reshumot,* III, 100; Steinschneider, *Geschichtsliteratur der Juden,* I, 138, #217.

3 See in S. H. Lieben, "Die Prager Brandkatastrophen," *JJLG,* XVIII (1926),

190-92 (suppl. 1-2), the memorial prayer and dirge *(ḳinah)* recited in Prague in observance of the tragedy resulting from the fires of 1689 and 1754. Also in D. Kaufmann, "*Seliḥot* of Lundenburg" (Hebrew), *'Oẓar ha-Safrut,* II (1888), 112, the penitential prayer recited annually in remembrance of the fire that broke out in the synagogue in 1698.

[4] See pp. 22–23; p. 37, n. 23; pp. 44, 46–47, 60, 82. Cf. Mayer, *Wiener Juden,* p. 154.

[5] *M. F.,* fol. 2b, #4; fol. 4b, #21; *Y. 'O.,* #487. Cf. *Shelah,* I, 228b (sec. "'Amud ha-'Abodah"). Also, in *N. K. Y.,* fol. 1b, #10, the *shammash* called the members of the community to attend services. Cf. *J. M.,* I (Bk. 4, chap. 14), 218, #3: The *schulklopfer* (*shulklaper,* Yid.) of Prague summoned everyone to the synagogue; a bell was used to assemble communal meetings. Note the *schulklopfer* in Abrahams, *Jewish Life,* p. 70, n. 3. See also Barbeck, *Juden in Nürnberg und Fürth,* p. 56, concerning the *Taḳḳanah* of March 2, 1719, which designates the *schulklopfer* as one of the four persons (viz., rabbi, cantor, gravedigger) whose services are to be remunerated by the community. For the role of the *shammash* as a communal functionary, see *Derushe ha-Ẓelaḥ,* no. 3, fol. 7a, #14; *Ẓemaḥ Ẓedeḳ,* nos. 1-2, fol. 1a-b; H. Flesch, "Juden in Mähren," *JJLG,* XVIII (1926), 43–45; also in this volume, n. 154 to p. 42; p. 66; pp. 143–44, n. 218.

[6] *M. F.,* fol. 2b, #7.

[7] Cf. Isserles on *'O. Ḥ.* 338:1.

[8] *N. K. Y.,* fol. 40b, #28, sec. 300 ("Hil. Shab.").

[9] Eckstein, "Bamberg Taḳḳanot von Jahr 1678," *JL,* XXII (1893), no. 22, 75, #2; *idem, Juden . . . Bamberg,* p. 67, #2; Kaufmann, "The Minute Books of the Province of Düsseldorf," 1698-1776 (Hebrew), *'Oẓar ha-Safrut,* III, 7, #1; Assaf, I, 137, #17.

[10] Eckstein in *JL,* XXII (no. 22), 75.

[11] Kaufmann in *'Oẓar ha-Safrut,* III, 7, #1. If the number of residents in a town is too small for a *minyan,* then joint services are to be held with a nearby community.

[12] Wachstein, "Pinkas Runkel," *ZGJD,* IV, 135, #33.

[13] The authority of the community was maintained by resorting to a fine, corporal punishment, or excommunication. Cf. Kaufmann, "Communauté de Metz," *REJ,* XIX (1889), 127 (Hebrew text); S. Haenle, *Juden . . . Ansbach,* p. 38, #5-6; Munk in *Jubelschrift . . . Hildesheimer,* p. 73. Likewise, *Shebut Ya'aḳob,* I, no. 11, fol. 3a: ". . . Thus they established authority by [threatening to resort to] the force of excommunication. [It was emphasized] that no one should raise his voice in the synagogue, and whoever did so would be fined fifty *zehubim* [= *gulden,* Ger. = guilders] and be excommunicated. . . ." Cf. "Communal Standards," *RCC,* cit. See p. 41, n. 151; also, p. 72, n. 148.

[14] *Derekh Ṭobim,* fol. 20, #20.

[15] *Derushe ha-Ẓelaḥ,* no. 3, fol. 7a, #14; cf. no. 4, fol. 9a, #18; fol. 9b, #20. That Landau was dissatisfied with Prague, see B. Z. Katz, *Rabbanut,* I, Pt. 2, 197.

See the practice in small towns of setting aside a single room in a home to hold daily *minyan* services: *Noda‘ bi-Yehuda* (Prague, 1811), I, no. 17, fol. 5b (sec. "'O. Ḥ."); cf. Wind in *Ḥoreb,* X, 72, n. 64.

[16] Kaufmann (ed.), *Glikl,* p. 332:

...אונ׳ עשרה למדני׳ גידונגין די אלי יום למחרות אום ט׳ אוהר זולין לב״ה גין....

Cf. "the ten *baṭlanim* (men of leisure) of the synagogue": *San.,* fol. 17b; *Sanhedrin,* I (*Neziḳin,* V, Son. edit.), 89, n. 8; also, *Meg.,* 3b.

[17] See p. 41. See Mayer, *Wiener Juden,* p. 154: The synagogue was attended twice daily, in the morning and evening.

[18] *Sefer Zekhirah,* fol. 9b:

יזהר שלא יעכב זמן תפלה ויראה שיהא גוף נקי ולא שום צואה או טיפת מי רגלים או שכבת זרע על הכתונת....

See pp. 1, 23; also below, n. 139 to 172, that facilities were lacking to maintain sanitary living conditions and cleanliness.

[19] *N. K. Y.,* fol. 1b, #8, cit. Cf. *'Orḥot Ḥayyim,* fol. 15a-b, #49b: "Do not delay in rushing to the synagogue *(bet ha-tefillah)* and be careful that your feet are not soiled. . . ." Cf. Sabbatai (Sheftel) Horowitz, "Ethical Will" in *Ẓavva'ot . . . Dibre Ḳedoshim,* p. 5, #8: Out of doors, people invariably had to walk in filth.

[20] Güdemann, *Gesch.,* III, 98. Note the "desire to protect the synagogue from the dirt and refuse of unpaved streets": Baron, *Community,* II, 129.

[21] *Shelah,* I. fol. 228b (sec. "'Amud ha-'Abodah"). Cf. *Maharil* (Warsaw, 1874), fol. 45a: ". . . When anyone wishes to go to the synagogue *(bet ha-keneset)* on *Kol Nidre* evening he should remove his shoes, leave them in his house and not wear them to the synagogue because of [the] filth."

[22] *Shelah,* I, fol. 228b. It is the tradition not to wear shoes on the Ninth of *'Ab* as a sign of mourning to commemorate the destruction of the Temple of Jerusalem.

[23] *Y. 'O.,* #4. Cf. *Sefer Zekhirah,* fol. 9b, that each individual should provide himself with a pair of shoes to be worn only to the synagogue.

[24] *N. K. Y.,* fol. 1a-b, #18:

לכן המנהג בקהלות קדושות שיש להם ברזל לפני פתח בה״כ שמנקין בו את המנעלים.

[25] *S. H.,* II (ed. Shatzky), fol. 17a. His observations were based on travel. Cf. *S. H.,* II, Intro., pp. 19, 33, with regard to the travels of Kirchan and his association with "isolated, scattered towns in his vicinity." Erik (pp. 302-303) suggests that Kirchan may have been an itinerant *maggid,* preacher. (As the *maggid* traveled from town to town, he would follow a set pattern of discourse in which he excoriated the people for their conduct and manners. It was not unusual for the *maggid* to condemn simple folk in small towns for extravagance and luxurious living.)

[26] *S. H.,* II, 17b.

[27] Kaufmann in *'Oẓar ha-Safrut,* III, 7, #1.

[28] *Derushe ha-Ẓelaḥ,* no. 4, fol. 9b, #19.

[29] Barbeck, *Juden in Nürnberg und Fürth,* p. 56. The content of the *taḳḳanah,* not the text, is cited.

[30] *Sefer Zekhirah,* fol. 9b.

[31] *Y. 'O.,* #62. Cf. Levesohn, *Meḳore Minhagim,* p. 19, sec. 15.

[32] *Y. 'O.,* #63. Cf. Güdemann, *Quellen.,* p. 111; Abrahams, *Jewish Life,* p. 39, n. 1; Löw, *Lebensalter,* p. 134, as to the disorderly behavior of children in the synagogue. See also Abrahams, "Ethical Wills," *JQR,* III (1891), 479, for the way in which the Sephardim made the children behave. The children were kept in one place and "an overseer stood over them . . . with a stick."

[33] *Vave ha-'Amudim,* fol. 9b.

[34] *Derekh Ṭobim,* fol. 5a, #3.

[35] *N. K. Y.,* fol. 1b, #11:
...דוקא מותר לו לאדם זקן או חלש שאינם יכולים לעמוד על נפשם עד עת יציאת הצבור מבה״כ...לשתות מים וצוק״ר כמו הקאפ״ע ט״ע או שאקלא״ד.

[36] See below, p. 196.

[37] Flesch in *JJLG,* XVIII, 26, 28-30, 31, sec. 4; 32-33, sec. 28 (Hebrew and Yiddish texts).

[38] Flesch, *op. cit.,* 26-27.

[39] *Ẓemaḥ Ẓedeḳ,* no. 94, fol. 114b-115a.
(fol. 114b) וגם להעמיד העמוד שלפניהם שעליו מניחים הספרים מה שאנו קורין שטענדי״ר....

Prob. *stendir* (Yid.) = "bookholder" (i. e., lectern); cf. *stender* (mod. Yid.); *ständer* (Ger.), same meaning.

Cf. *Naḥalat Shib'ah,* II, no. 3, fol. 4b, in which an old principle is restated that "the community *(kehal)* should collect from the wealthy according to his wealth and from the poor according to his means [lit., poverty]. . . ."

In her study of "Mutual Influences between Eastern and Western Europe in Synagogue Architecture, 12-18th Centuries" (Yiddish), *Yivo Bleter,* XXIX (1947), 3-4, 6-7, Rachel Wischnitzer points out that the *balemer* (reading table) was in the center of the synagogue. Also, note the location of the *balemer* in pictures of the interior of synagogues in Metz, Worms, Kirchheim (Kircheim, Württemberg), Bechhofen (Bavaria), and Prague (the *Alt-Neu*) : *ibid.,* no. 2, p. 6; nos. 31-32, p. 44; no. 33, p. 45; no. 36, p. 46. That a change in the design of the synagogue would not be permitted if it meant altering the location of the *bimah* in the center, cf. *Noda' bi-Yehudah* (Prague, 1811), I, no. 18, fol. 6a (sec. "'O. Ḥ."); and Wind in *Ḥoreb,* X, 74, n. 75.

[40] *Y. 'O.,* #589. Cf. *ibid.* (1928 edit.), "Biographical Sketch," p. vi. The original text reads: לקראת שבת לכו ונלכה; the verse by Hahn: לבבתני שבת מלכה.

Cf. *Shab.,* fol. 119a: "R. Ḥanina robed himself and stood at sunset of

Sabbath eve [and] exclaimed, 'Come and let us go forth to welcome the queen Sabbath.' R. Jannai donned his robes on Sabbath eve and exclaimed, 'Come, O bride, Come, O bride!'"

[41] *J. M.*, I (Bk. 4, chap. 14), 218, #3.

[42] *Ibid.*, II (Bk. 6, chap. 34), pp. 284-85, #22.

[43] Lieberman, *'Or Nogah* (published with *Nogah ha-Ẓedeḳ*, Responsa, 1818), I, no. 4, p. 17, #3:

גם לא נשכח מני אשר ספרו לי כמה זקנים בעת היותי בפראג שזוכרים האורגל אשר הי׳ שם בב״הכנ על תנאי, והיו מנגנים בה בכל ליל שבת, בר״ח וי״ט. ועוד היום מקבלים שבת בב״הכנ הישנה בכלי זמר, ונמשך המוזיקא עד חצי שעה בלילה, והמנגנים יהודים המה.

See the controversy over the introduction of the organ in Krauss, *Zur Orgelfrage*, p. 27; Max Joseph and Caesar Seligmann, "Orgelstreit," *JLex*, IV (1930), 601; Seligmann, "Organ," *UJE*, VIII (1942), 321. Also, Abrahams, *Jewish Life*, p. 149, n. 1: Before the Sabbath began, hymns would be accompanied by musical instruments.

[44] Krauss, *Zur Orgelfrage*, p. 27, n. 1, cit. See Kaufmann, "Synagogue Meisel," *REJ*, XXI (1890), 143: "Elle [la synagogue de Meisel] contenait, comme la 'Altneuschule', un orgue pour célébrer l'entrée du sabbat aux sons de la musique." (The cornerstone of the Meisel synagogue was dedicated in 1590.) Cf. Kaufmann in *REJ*, XI, 143, n. 5; Steinschneider, *Catalog. Bodl.*, II, 2391, n. 1: *zemer na'eh* (a beautiful hymn) "that was sung before *Lekhah Dodi* in the Meisel Synagogue of Prague, accompanied by the organ: *(be-uggab u-bi-nebalim)*. . . ."

[45] Kaufmann, "Jair Chayim Bacharach," *JQR*, III (1891), 298, n. 4. (At the time, the parents of Bacharach were living in Goding, Moravia.) The writer did not locate the *responsum* cited from *Ḥavvot Ya'ir*.

[46] *N. K. Y.*, fol. 39a, #15, sec. 300 ("Hil. Shab."). The translation of *nebalim* and *kinnorim* as "bass fiddle and violin" has been suggested by portraits of musical instruments played by the *klezmorim;* see n. 126 to p. 37. See also Joachim Stutschewsky, *Ha-Klezmorim* (Jewish Folk Musicians), plates 4-5 (pp. 229-30), for similar portraits of Jewish musicians in Germany during the 17th and 18th centuries.

[47] *Y. 'O.*, #889. Cf. *'Eleh Dibre ha-Berit*, p. 61: "But on all occasions instrumental music is forbidden and is only permitted at a wedding celebration. . . ." The popularity of instrumental music at festivities is discussed above, p. 37. See also Isaac Rivkind, "The Cantor and Marriage Jester (Minstrel) . . . prior to the 17th Century" (Hebrew), *Minḥah li-Yehudah . . . Zlotnik*, p. 242. Cf. Löw, *Lebensalter*, pp. 311-12, that Jewish orchestras entertained in Christian homes during celebrations. For other instances of Jewish and non-Jewish social relations, see herein, pp. 10, 12–13; pp. 164–65, n. 99; pp. 165–66, n. 103; p. 173.

[48] After the Chmielnicki pogroms, communal regulations of 1649 and 1654 in Eastern Europe restricted the use of music at public gatherings. During the

wedding festivity, the customary procession was not permitted on the street. Instrumental music could only be played when the bride appeared in her veil, and after the wedding ceremony the jester could perform in the yard of the synagogue or *tants-hoyz*. Cf. A. L. Feinstein, "Taḳḳanot," *Ha-'Asif*, VI (1893), 172.

[49] *Y. 'O.*, #889. Cf. Boaz Cohen, "Responsum of Maimonides Concerning Music," in *idem, Law and Tradition in Judaism*, p. 181, n. 53. The rabbinic attitude toward instrumental music is traced in this essay; there is evidence that "the law prohibiting music was never fully observed, because it ran counter to human nature."

[50] *Y. 'O.*, Pt. 2, p. 281:

... ״תינוקות ״של ״בית ״רבן ״גזירות ״רעות ״מבטלין.

The first letters of these seven words spell *tashber gorem*, which means "causing to shatter to bits," i.e., the devices of the "evil one." Cf. *Shab.*, fol. 119b, as an example of the efficacious effect schoolchildren can have on the adult community.

Description of the custom of a father blessing his children on Friday evening when he returns home from the synagogue is in *N. K. Y.*, fol. 39b, #22, sec. 300 ("Hil. Shab.").

[51] Mayer, *Wiener Juden*, p. 122; Salfeld, "Welt und Haus," *JJGL*, XXXIII (1920), 74. See chap. II, p. 20, n. 43.

[52] *Brandshpigl*, sec. 5, fol. 2b (fols. not numbered). See pp. 89–90, n. 38, the instance of a husband who lost his life while he was away from home selling goods.

[53] *N. K. Y.*, fol. 37b, #1, sec. 300 ("Hil. Shab."); cf. *Sefer Ḥasidim*, #149. For the individual's obligation to arrange for the Sabbath, see Isserles on *'O. Ḥ.* 260:1, 262:2. Cf. also *Sefer Ḥasidim* (ed. Reuben Margulies) #150, p. 152, nn. 2, 5, cits.: *'Ab. Zar.*, 3a; *Shab.*, 117b.

Cf. *Derushe ha-Ẓelaḥ*, no. 3, fol. 8b, #9, in which Landau censures the Jews of Prague for shirking their responsibility by having a non-Jew purchase and prepare food for the Sabbath.

[54] *Brandshpigl*, sec. 8, fol. 1b.

[55] *Yesh Noḥalin*, fol. 26b (sec. "'Inyan Shab.").

[56] *Brandshpigl*, *op. cit.*

[57] *N. K. Y.*, fol. 28b, #7, sec. 59 ("Hil. Neṭilat Yadayim"). Cf. *'O. Ḥ.* 260:1.

[58] *N. K. Y.*, fol. 38b. Cf. *Brandshpigl*, sec. 13, fol. 13a, for a description of the religious duties of a woman, based on ancient rabbinic instruction: ". . . She should take the *khaleh* [i. e., follow the law of *ḥallah* by separating the priest's share from the dough: Num. 15:19-20; *Ket.* 7:6] and light the candles for the Sabbath [cf. *'O. Ḥ.* 263:2]. . . ."The obligations of a woman are derived from *Ḳid.* 1:7; fol. 35a; *Rosh ha-Shanah*, 30a; see also *Nashim* (*Mishnayot*, ed. Blackman), III, 455, n. 6; *Rosh ha-Shanah* (*Mo'ed*, VII, Son. edit.), 140, n. 4.

[59] *Yesh Noḥalin*, fol. 41b (sec. "'Inyan Shabbat"); *Ḳ. Shelah*, 49b. Cf.

Is. 58:13, "And call the Sabbath a delight"; *Shab.*, fol. 118b, ". . . *'oneg* (delight) means the enjoyment of the Sabbath." Cf. also *Brandshpigl*, Pref.: "Furthermore, the sages called the Sabbath 'the world to come' (*olom ha-bo*); this is the sublime [lit., great] rest and delight about which the prophet spoke. . . ." Cf. *Ber.*, fol. 57b, that "the Sabbath is similar to the *'olam ha-ba'*."

[60] *Ḥavvot Ya'ir*, no. 11, fol. 18a.

[61] *Y. 'O.*, p. 266. Cf. *Shab.*, fol. 118b: "Even a trifle, if it is prepared in honor of the Sabbath, is delight." Also, *Shab.*, fol. 119b: "One should always set his table on the eve of the Sabbath, even if he needs only the size of an olive."

[62] Cf. *Shab.*, 118b: "Wherewith does one show his delight therein? . . . With a dish of beets, large fish, and cloves of garlic." See chap. V, p. 100, fish as a popular food on the Sabbath. Cf. also *Leḳeṭ Yosher*, I, p. 52.

[63] Procreation on the Sabbath fulfilled the commandment, "Be fruitful and multiply": Gen. 1:28; *'E. H.* 1:1.

Cf. Eisenstein, "Fish" (Hebrew), *'Oẓar Yisra'el*, IV (1906), 13; Grunwald, "Aus Hausapotheke," *MGJV*, V (1900), 56, n. 173. That fish symbolizes fertility, see herein, p. 102, nn. 50–51.

[64] *N. K. Y.*, fol. 37b, #1, sec. 300 ("Hil. Shab."). Cf. *Ẓemaḥ Ẓedeḳ*, no. 28.

[65] *Ẓemaḥ Ẓedeḳ*, no. 28, fol. 24b-25a. Cf. *Keritot* 1:7, the example given by Krochmal of R. Simeon ben Gamliel being instrumental in lowering the price of a pair of pigeons. In his support of the position taken by the community, Krochmal cites as evidence the Biblical verse (Ps. 119:126), "It is time to work for the Lord; They have made void Thy law," and the Talmudic teaching (*Shab.*, 151b): Desecrate one Sabbath so that you may keep many Sabbaths.

[66] Cf. *Pes.*, fol. 112a; ". . . yet one must prepare something trifling at home [i. e., in honor of the Sabbath]. What is it? Fish hash." Cf. also *Shab.*, 118b, "a pie of fish hash." See *Pesaḥim* (*Mo'ed*, IV, Son. edit.), 576, n. 5: "Thus even the poorest must make an effort to honour the Sabbath."

[67] *Y. 'O.*, #588.

[68] *Ibid.*, #590. As to the custom of studying before and after the meal, see p. 68, p. 108; *Yesh Noḥalin* (Ethical Will), chap. 1, cit. in Abrahams, *Hebrew Ethical Wills*, II, 253. See also Abrahams, *Jewish Life*, p. 149, how, during the winter, on Friday evenings, the family spent "hours round the table, singing . . . hymns." See above, p. 108, nn. 98-99, for some examples of table songs.

[69] *Sefer Ḥasidim*, #1147; *N. K. Y.*, fol. 40a, #25, sec. 300, also cit.

[70] Shiper, *Yid. teater*, I, 59.

[71] *Derushe ha-Ẓelaḥ*, no. 4, fol. 8b, #9. Cf. *ibid.*, no. 23, fol. 35b, #20: "And on the Sabbath they do whatever they wish; they go outside on the street, and men and women congregate in groups and act disgracefully, engaging in gossip, slanderous and idle talk. All of this takes place on the holy day of the Sabbath."

[72] *N. K. Y.*, fol. 41a-b, #35, sec. 300. Cf. *Derushe ha-Ẓelaḥ*, no. 4, fol. 8b, #9: The suggestion is made that "something new should be studied each Sabbath, according to one's ability."

[73] See pp. 68, 70, 73 ff.

[74] Berliner, "Jüd. Speisetafel," *JJGL*, XIII (1910), 205. See above, p. 177, n. 40, *tsholnt*. In the opinion of the writer, the hour for the meal could have developed in the Jewish community independent of external influence.

[75] Berliner, *op. cit.*, 206.

[76] *Shelah*, I, fol. 133b; cf. the third meal on the Sabbath *(shalosh se'udot, se'udah shelishit)* in *B. Bat.*, fol. 9a; *Shab.*, 117b-118a; *'O. Ḥ.*, sec. 291; *Y. 'O.*, #677. See also *Leḳeṭ Yosher*, I, pp. 51, 56.

[77] Isaac Ze'ev Cahana (ed.), *Rabbi Me'ir . . . me-Rothenburg, Teshubot . . . u-Minhagim*, p. 220, #256. See *Maharil* (Warsaw, 1874), fol. 28b ("Hil. Shab."). During the summer the Maharil (fol. 28a) ate the third meal before the *minḥah* service. He would not permit his students to eat between *minḥah* and *ma'arib*.

Cf. comment of Isserles on *'O. Ḥ.* 291:2. There are those who do not favor the custom of eating the third meal between *minḥah* and *ma'arib*. This is not the time to be joyous; between *minḥah* and *ma'arib* the souls return to *gehinnom* after having been released for the *Shabbat*. That "the dead are conscious of the Sabbath," cf. *Mid. Tanḥuma'*, Sid. "Ki Tissa," sec. 36.

[78] See pp. 89, 91, 93, n. 58. Cf. *M. F.*, fol. 16b, #99: ". . . The Sabbath mantle [decorated] with the *kragen* (collar)." The mantle and cape were also worn on festivals and celebrations. Cf. n. 53 to p. 92.

It was an ancient tradition to set aside special garments for the Sabbath. Cf. *Shab.*, 113a: ". . . that thy Sabbath garments should not be like thy weekday garments." And *Yer. Pe'ah*, VIII, 7, 21b: "Each person should have two wraps, one for weekdays and one for the Sabbath." Cf. also E. G. Hirsch, "Sabbath," *JE*, X (1905), 590, cits.

[79] *Y. 'O.*, #3:

. . . שהיה לרוב בעלי בתים סרבל מיוחד לב״ה העשויה בקמטים . . . וכן עטיפת המטרון שקורין קאפא שהנהיגו קדמונים.

See *kape* (Yid.) = "hood." Prob. *mitron* (Yid.); cf. *mitra* (mod. Yid.) = "miter, headgear."

Cf. *S. H.*, I, fol. 50a, that the Sabbath dress should be better than the clothing worn on weekdays.

[80] See p. 93, n. 62.

[81] *Y. 'O.*, #591:

אכתוב לפרש טעם המנהג הנהוג בינינו בשינוי סרבל המיוחד לשבת ויום טוב על פי קבלתי כי כל מנהג אבותינו תורה ומה שלא ידענו הוא לקוצר דעתנו ואבדת ספרים הקדומים בגזירות שעברו על ראשי קדמונינו ז״ל. . . .

Cf. Tsinberg, *Gesh. fun der lit.*, V, 90.

Cf. *Y. 'O.*, #98: *hendshukh* (*hentshukh,* Yid.) = "glove": i. e., a "closed sleeve" worn over the hand at night "to keep the person from touching his body"; cf. *handschuh* (Ger.). See n. 41 to p. 91.

[82] Barbeck, *Juden in Nürnberg und Fürth,* p. 56; also pp. 84-85. Landau, for instance, finds fault with "the ostentatious dress" of the day *(malbushe ga'avah): Derushe ha-Ẓelaḥ,* no. 23, fol. 36a, #21.

See antiluxury laws herein, p. 22, n. 48; p. 86, n. 8. For further examples of sumptuary legislation, cf. *S. H.*, II, fol. 13b; Kracauer, *Judengasse in Frankfurt,* p. 337, n. 7; Abrahams, *Jewish Life,* pp. 160-61; Horovitz, *Frank. Rabbin.*, II, 52; Ocksman in *Reshumot,* III, 103-5; J. Meisl, "Communal Legislation for the Circumcision Ceremony . . . Halberstadt Community" (Hebrew), *Reshumot,* I, (1945), 142-43; 145, #9; 146-47, #11-12, #14; Haarbleicher, *Gemeinde in Hamburg,* p. 15, #9.

[83] This does not imply that in other periods prayers were not recited in Yiddish. See Zunz, *Ritus des synagogalen Gottesdienstes,* pp. 154-55: "The translation of prayers into the vernacular existed earlier than it may seem. . . ." See also Freehof, *Reform Jewish Practice,* I, 35-37; 38, cit.; *idem,* "Devotional Literature in the Vernacular," *CCARY,* XXXIII (1923), 380-84.

[84] Elzet, "Customs in Jewish Life" (Hebrew), *Reshumot,* I (1918), 345. The cit. of *Ṭa'ame ha-Minhagim,* III, 84, could not be confirmed.

[85] *Derushe ha-Ẓelaḥ,* no. 4, fol. 8b, #9; *Derekh Ṭobim,* fol. 4b, #2. That Yiddish was the vernacular, see in this volume, n. 51 to p. 58, p. 63, n. 89; p. 69, n. 135; p. 159, n. 70.

[86] *N. K. Y.*, fol. 7a.

[87] Max Grunwald, "Altjüd. Gemeindeleben," *MGJV,* XLIII (1912), 80, #10. See in Baron, *Community,* II, 134, the "offering of candles for the illumination of synagogues." Also, chap. III, p. 61, n. 71, that the *bar miẓvah* youth presented a gift of tallow to the synagogue.

[88] *Ẓemaḥ Ẓedeḳ,* no. 72, fol. 87a. See also this custom in Scholem Ochser, "Pinkas . . . Gemeinde Kuttenplan," *MGJV,* XXXIII (1910), 74, #114-15; Wachstein in *ZGJD,* IV, 138, #33.

[89] Ocksman in *Reshumot,* III, 103. In the administration of charity, the aim was to fulfill an ideal whereby "the donor and the recipient remained anonymous to each other," *matan ba-seter*. Cf. *ḳuppah,* the communal fund that provided weekly allowances to the poor on Friday, as described in *B. Bat.*, fol. 8b; *Pe'ah* 8:7; Cronbach, "Philanthropy in Rabbinics," in *idem, Religion and Its Social Setting,* pp. 114-15, cit.; Frisch, *An Historical Survey of Jewish Philanthropy,* pp. 49-50, cit. See also in Haarbleicher, *Gemeinde in Hamburg,* pp. 16-17, the provision in the Hamburg communal legislation of April, 1752, to care for the poor.

[90] *Shelah,* I, 133a. Cf. *Y. 'O.*, #130; Pt. 2, p. 321, for the tradition of befriend-

ing a stranger and inviting the poor to eat at one's table. Cf. also *Sefer Ḥasidim* (ed. Wistinetzki), p. 214, #850. Cf. *Shab.*, 118a, that the needy transient has to be provided with three meals on the Sabbath. As examples of the influence of ancient rabbinic teaching in befriending strangers, see *Ṭa'ame ha-Minhagim*, III, fol. 84b, n.; *Zikhron Berit la-Rishonim*, p. 5, n. 1. Cf. in *Ḳ. H.* 10:1, 14; 87:1, 4, 14, the popular view, based on Cabala, that it is a good omen to befriend and give charity to the poor. In this regard, see herein, n. 31 to p. 55; also, p. 48, n. 194.

For other instances of extending hospitality to a stranger, see Wachstein, *Juden in Eisenstadt*, p. 152, #34; Brauer, *Yehude Kurdistan*, p. 135; Cronbach, "Jewish Philanthropic Institutions . . . Middle Ages," in *idem*, *Religion and Its Social Setting*, pp. 130-32; Frisch, *op. cit.*, pp. 95-98.

That communal philanthropy was popularly interpreted as "an ethical responsibility," cf. *Y. 'O.*, #336: "Furthermore, no one should specify exactly the amount given to aid the poor as he does when he pays the price for meat . . . or determines what he should receive for his work. . . ."

[91] See *marshelik*, p. 37.

[92] Wolf-Grunwald, "Fahrende Leute bei den Juden," *MGJV*, XXIX (1909), 4 f.; XXX (1909), 41 f. See the account of Jewish migrants in German lands in Shiper, *Yid. teater*, II, 67-68. See also Max Köhler, *Juden in Halberstadt und Umgebung*, p. 79; I. Eisenstadt-Barzilay, "Background of the Berlin Haskalah," in *Essays . . . in Honor of S. W. Baron* (ed. Blau, Friedman, *et al.*), p. 193, n. 39.

[93] Haarbleicher, *Gemeinde in Hamburg*, p. 49, based on the Altona *Taḳḳanah* of 1782; Güdemann, *Gesch.*, III, 102, n. 8; Munk in *Jubelschrift . . . Hildesheimer*, p. 80, #24; Eckstein, *Juden . . . Bamberg*, p. 67, #3 (*Taḳḳanah* of August, 1678), also p. 94; Abrahams, *Jewish Life*, p. 158, n. 1; p. 335; Grunwald, "Altjüd. Gemeindeleben," *MGJV*, XLIII (1912), 80, #11; Kaufmann, "Minute Book of Bamberg," 1698 (Hebrew), *Ḳobeẓ 'al Yad*, VII (1896-97), 3, #2; Wachstein in *ZGJD*, IV, 134, #5; 136, #21; 138, #33; 140, #38; *idem*, "Pinḳas Runkel," *Yivo Bleter*, VI (1934), 91, #5; *idem*, *Juden in Eisenstadt*, p. 152, #34; Flesch in *JJLG*, XVIII, 45, n. 1. The *pletn (billette)* were distributed among the poor, the sick, and transients. Cf. *'Eben ha-Shoham*, no. 32, fol. 15b: In Hildesheim "tickets were provided to the poor": . . . *ve-gam pletin (pletn) liten parnasah la-'aniyim*. . . . Cf. "Charity," *RCC*, cit. Note the use of *pletn*: Güdemann, *loc. cit.* (ref. to *Ḥavvot Ya'ir*, 53b, could not be confirmed); "billeting students": Fishman, *Jewish Education*, p. 33; caring for itinerant sick: Marcus, *Communal Sick-Care*, p. 177, and Köhler, *Juden in Halberstadt*, p. 81.

Plet (Yid.) = "ticket." Cf. Harkavy, *Verterbukh* (New York, 1925), p. 373: A ticket was assigned to a poor man to secure a Sabbath meal. Cf. *billet* (Ger.) = "ticket": Wachstein in *ZGJD*, IV, 134, #5, n. 14; *idem*, *Yivo Bleter*, VI, 91, #5, n. 17.

[94] *S. H.* (ed. Shatzky), II, fol. 17b; also Intro., p. 36.

[95] Aron Freimann, "A Song of Complaint against a Communal Worker of Frankfort" (publ. in 1708, prob. Hanau, Yiddish), *Filolog. Shrift.*, II (1928, Vilna), 170-171.

[96] *Ḥavvot Ya'ir,* no. 169, fol. 159a-b.

[97] M. Bernstein, "Jewish Gangs of Thieves and Robbers" (Yiddish), in *idem, Nisht derbrente shaytn,* p. 43.

[98] Haenle, *Juden . . . Ansbach,* p. 136. For a realistic portrayal of the activities of Jewish thieves in Germany in the 17th and 18th centuries, and the steps taken by rabbinic and communal authorities to cope with them and isolate them by having them excommunicated, see Shohet, *'Im Ḥillufe Teḳufot,* pp. 153 ff. The *plet* would be distributed among transients in order to be able to check each person before he was admitted to a home (*ibid.*, p. 154). Evidently there were those rabbis, such as Ya'ir Hayyim Bacharach, who did not deal harshly with the Jewish thief but regarded him to be the victim of poverty (*ibid.*, p. 155, n. 106). Communal concern for the homeless person who might have been inclined to thievery was nevertheless expressed (*ibid.*, pp. 157-58).

[99] See Y. Triwaks, "Yiddish 'Argots': Languages of Thieves, Musicians, and Wagon-Drivers" (Yiddish), *Bay uns yidn* (ed. M. Wanwild), Pt. 2, p. 159; M. Bernstein in *op. cit.*, pp. 45-46. R. Glanz, "The Investigation of 'Jewish Cant' in the Speech of Thieves" (Yiddish), *Filolog. Shrift.*, II (1928), 358 ff., presents a critical analysis of the studies of Avé-Lallemant and others with regard to the Jewish influence on the language of thieves.

Jewish transients who committed crimes were the cause for strained relations between non-Jews and the Jewish community. In Moravia severe measures were taken against the Jewish migrant who commits an offense against a non-Jew. Cf. Halpern, *Taḳḳanot Mähren,* p. 88, #265; J. Katz, *Ben Yehudim la-Goyim,* pp. 161-62, n. 15; Eng. trans., *Exclusiveness and Tolerance,* pp. 160-61, n. 2.

[100] Note the trial and execution of Samuel Lev in Wildenberg, Bavaria, in 1760, as described by M. Bernstein in *op. cit.*, pp. 46-55.

[101] *S. H.*, II, fol. 18b, 19a; *Ḳ. Shelah,* 47a.

[102] *S. H.*, II, 19a. Cf. the criticism made by Ezekiel Landau, in *Derushe ha-Ẓelaḥ,* no. 3, fol. 8b, #9, that the *teḥum* was violated on the Sabbath; people went beyond the distance of the *teḥum*. See also the violation of the *teḥum* in Shohet, *'Im Ḥillufe Teḳufot,* p. 142.

[103] *Panim Me'irot,* III, no. 1, fol. 1a:

...שמתקבצים פעמים בשנה קיבוץ גדול ליהודים בעיר קרעמז ושוכרים מנכרים הכיפות ובתים שמניחים שם סחורתם והיהודים מפוזרים בכל עיר זה בכה וזה בכה והבתים והכיפות מיוחדים לסחורות שלהם מה משפט העיר ההוא לענין טילטול בכל העיר בשבת....

Cf. p. 10, n. 66; below, p. 173, n. 147.

[104] *S. H.*, I, 54a. (Samuel Kaidanover was the father of Ẓebi Hirsh Kaidanover; Kirchan was married to the daughter of Ẓebi Kaidanover. See below,

Bibliography, p. 352.) Cf. *'Erub.* 7:11, with regard to the legal use of the *'erub.* Cf. also in *Ma'aseh ha-Geonim,* p. 13, #23, the summary of the rules to make an *'erub.* For a popular description of establishing the *'erub,* cf. *S. H.,* I, 56b. Cf. the illustration of the use of an *'erub* in Munk, *Jubelschrift . . . Hildesheimer,* p. 81, #29, and the comment of Shatzky, *S. H.,* II, Intro., p. 16, on the controversy between the towns of Kirchan, Umelberg (? probably Homberg), and Mardorf over the legality of an *'erub.*

105 *S. H.,* II, 17b. Cf. Erik, p. 308. Kirchan also relates: "On Friday evening, in various localities I saw them place food in the oven, apples . . . to be roasted. . . . They would build a fire on the ashes to prepare tasty food." Cf. *N. K. Y.,* fol. 28a, #8, sec. 300 ("Hil. Shab."): On the Sabbath, food was heated on ashes, not on a stove.

106 *S. H.,* II, 17b. Cf. *Derushe ha-Ẓelaḥ,* no. 15, fol. 15b, #13. Since they would wait until it became dark, the Sabbath was not ushered in on time. Cf. also Wind in *Ḥoreb,* X, 61, n. 24.

107 *S. H.,* I, 60a. The passage concludes: "It is forbidden to eat the meat of the animals that they slaughtered." Cf. the critical statement about *shoḥaṭim* on p. 283, n. 111, cits. See further Jacob Emden's comments in *She'elat Ya'abeẓ,* I, no. 56, fol. 83a: "They [the *shoḥaṭim*] do not examine the animal thoroughly from head to foot after it is slaughtered. Among them, there are no judges [i. e., those who are competent to check on them]. . . . There is no one who prevents them from engaging in such practices and the situation will never improve."

108 *Derushe ha-Ẓelaḥ,* no. 15, fol. 25b, #13.

109 *S. H.,* II, fol. 18a.

110 *Derushe ha-Ẓelaḥ,* no. 4, fol. 8b, #9. Cf. examples of the neglect of the Sabbath by Jews of Germany as cited by Shohet, *op. cit.,* pp. 141-43.

111 *S. H.,* I, 54a. Cf. *Derushe ha-Ẓelaḥ,* no. 4, fol. 9a, #13, a sermon on the care of animals. Cf. *Y. 'O.,* #335, that animals must be treated with kindness; they must be fed before one partakes a meal, and even chickens should not have to become scavengers, roaming around in search of food. For laws relating to the treatment of animals on the Sabbath, cf., for example, *M. T.,* "Hil. Shab." 10:1; *'O. Ḥ.* 305:10: "You do not hang a basket [with fodder] around the neck of an animal in order to feed it. . . ."

112 *Ẓemaḥ Ẓedeḳ,* no. 35, fol. 31b.

113 Cf. Wind in *Ḥoreb,* X, 60.

114 Cf. *'O. Ḥ.,* sec. 308.

115 *Panim Me'irot,* II, no. 123, fol. 61b:

. . . שהוא רק ע״פ המנהג ובזה לא קיבלו עליהם היהודים מתחילה לאיסור כמו שראיתי בכמה קהלות שאפילו לומדים כשדורשים ברבים לוקחים מכיסם האוה״ר. . . .

See *uhr,* "watch" (Yid.); also Ger.

Cf. "Sabbath: Sabbath Laws," *RCC,* cit. See p. 87.

[115a] Cf. Maharil, *She'elot u-Teshubot,* no. 200, fol. 82a.

[116] *Shebut Ya'aḳob,* III, no. 23, fol. 4a:

... במדינה זו רבי׳ וגם שלמים שקורין בשבת בכתביהם שנדפסו חדושיהם מסיפורי מלחמו׳
וכיוצא בהם שקורין בל״א נייא צייטונג. ...

Cf. "Sabbath," *RCC,* cit.

Cf. "Neue Zeitungen," *Der Grosse Brockhaus,* XIII (1932), 298. First published in the 16th century, the *zeitungen* in Germany, sold at markets and fairs, were bulletins containing current events and local news. The *zeitung* was "a broadside," as the forerunner of the extra edition of a newspaper. According to Erik (p. 18), the first Yiddish *tsaytung* ("broadside") appeared in Amsterdam (1686-87). Subsequently, *tsaytungen* were published in Amsterdam during 1743 and 1776. See the facsimile of the Amsterdam *tsaytung* of 1686 in Erik, p. 19; the broadside covered news about the Crimean War.

[117] *She'elat Ya'abeẓ,* I, no. 162, fol. 141a:

ולענין לקרות בקורנטין הנדפסים בכרכים ועיירות גדולות מדי שבוע בשבוע במדינה זו,
להודיע בקרב הארץ חדשות וקורות מתרגשות מעניני מלחמה ושאר מאורעות זולתיות ההווים
בעולם יום יום. ...

See *kurantn* (Yid.) = "currents," i. e., the news. Cf. *kurant* (Ger.), same meaning. For its origin (*courant,* Fr.), cf. Max Weinreich, *Bilder . . . yid. literaturgeshikhte,* p. 265, n. 2. *Ibid.,* p. 265: The first Yiddish broadside, in Amsterdam, was issued twice weekly, on Tuesday and Friday. See *ibid.,* p. 266, for a reproduction of a page from a Friday *kurantn.* Cf. marginal caption to the *responsum: ḳeri'at ha-gazetin (gazetn) be-Shabbat. . . .* Cf. B. Z. Katz, *Rabbanut,* I, Pt. 1, 157, n. 53.

[118] *She'elat Ya'abeẓ,* I, no. 41, fol. 66a. Cf. Katz, *op. cit.,* n. 54.

[119] See p. 73, n. 154.

[120] See pp. 79–81.

[121] *N. K. Y.,* fol. 69b, #7 ("Hil. Yeme ha-Seliḥot").

[122] Cf. *Ta'anit* 2:2.

[123] See comment on fol. 16a in *Ta'anit* (ed. Malter), p. 113, n. 247.

[124] *M. F.,* fol. 13b, #79:

ותוקעין כל חודש אלול ערבית ושחרית אחר התפילה. ...

According to the *Maharil* (Warsaw, 1874), fol. 35b, gloss, (sec. "Hil. Yamim Nora'im") and the *Shulḥan 'Arukh* (*'O. Ḥ.* 588:1), the *shofar* is blown during the daytime. However, as Isserles points out (gloss on *'O. Ḥ.* 581:1), during the month of *'Elul* "there are places where the *shofar* is also blown in the evening. . . ." This would imply another variation in the observance of a custom.

[125] *S. H.,* I, 42a: *. . . men shloft nit an Rosh ha-Shanah, men lernt. . . .* That study was combined with the observance of festivals, see p. 191.

[126] *Ibid.,* II, 17a. Cf. Erik, p. 308; *S. H.,* II (ed. Shatzky), Intro., p. 36.

The role of the cantor, as well as of all other religious professionals of the period, deserves special study. A critical appraisal of the cantor as a professional will be found in Emden, *She'elat Ya'abeẓ*, I, no. 161, fol. 140b. In this *responsum* Emden reprimands the conduct of cantors for currying the favor of persons who offer them remuneration for personal services rendered. At the same time Emden shows sympathetic awareness of the economic hardships that cantors were facing. Due to economic conditions, not all communities could guarantee the cantor a fixed annual stipend. See the evaluation of cantors of the 17th century in Shiper, *Yid. teater*, I, 153-54, inc. cits. From the 18th century on they were becoming more secularized and worldly: *ibid.*, 187.

127 *N. K. Y.*, fol. 70b, #2 ("Hil. 'Ereb Rosh ha-Shanah ve-Rosh ha-Shanah").

128 See *Rosh ha-Shanah*, fol. 16b-17a.

129 Cf. *ibid.*, fol. 16b.

130 *Y. 'O.*, #975:

...וכן היה המנהג פשוט פה כל הימים עד איזה השנים ששומרי שער נהר מיין המה בעלי מלחמות שכמעט נשכח המנהג דרובא דעלמא ואפי׳ המדקדקי׳ אינם הולכים רק אל המלוא שקורין וואל במקום שמוצאין למטה בחריץ שקורין גראבין צינור קטן עם מים והנה מלבד שאינם יוצאים... גם נכשלין שאומרים פסוקי׳ במקום הטנופות שיש במלוא....

Prob. *val* (Yid.). Cf. *val* (mod. Yid.) = "rampart, bulwark"; *wall* (Ger.) = "dam." Cf. *millo'* (Heb.) = "dam."

Prob. *grabin* (Yid.). Cf. *grobn* (mod. Yid.) = "ditch"; *graben* (Ger.), the same meaning. See *wollgraben*, below, p. 195, n. 260. Cf. Tsinberg, *Gesh. fun der lit.*, V, 88, cit. Cf. the *tashlikh* ceremony as described in *Shelah*, I, fol. 214b (sec. "Rosh ha-Shanah"). See the popular explanation and description of *tashlikh* in *S. H.*, I, fol. 42a; *Ḳ. Shelah*, 60b; also *Ṭa'ame ha-Minhagim*, I, #724. Note folk beliefs related to *tashlikh* in Lauterbach, *Rabbinic Essays*, pp. 337, 340, 367.

131 *Y. 'O.*, #975.

132 *Shelah*, I, fol. 228b. For the antecedents of this practice, cf. *Maharil*, fol. 45a (sec. "Hil. Lel Yom Kippur"); Isserles on *'O. Ḥ.* 131:8. See also Abrahams, *Jewish Life*, p. 44, n. 1.

133 Cf. Abrahams, *op. cit.*, pp. 43-44; Baron, *Community*, II, 138; III, n. 16 to p. 146.

134 *Shelah*, I, fol. 229a; *Ḳ. Shelah*, fol. 63b. The recitation of verses from the Psalms is "a protection against a seminal emission" on the eve of *Yom Kippur*, since the Psalms "have 306 letters and 4 verses, which total 310, the numerical value of the word *ḳeri* (emission)." Cf. *Maharil*, fol. 45b; also *'O. Ḥ.* 315:2 and comment by "Ba'er Heṭeb," n. 2.

135 See n. 121 to p. 68.

136 See below, pp. 173, 191. See the custom of staying up to study on the nights of major holidays and festivals in M. D. Gaon. "Festivals and the Order of Studies" (Hebrew), *Yeda'-'Am*, III (Nos. 2-3, 1955), 112.

137 *Shelah*, I, 229a; *Ḳ. Shelah*, 63b.

138 *N. K. Y.*, fol. 75a, #10 ("Hil. 'Ereb Yom Kippur"). With regard to

the importance of avoiding a "nocturnal emission" on *Yom Kippur,* see *Yoma* 1:1; fol. 88a.

139 *Derushe ha-Ẓelaḥ,* no. 4, fol. 9b, #11:

וגם סביבות הסוכה יהיה נקי ומה מאד צריך ליזהר בסוכה מן היתושים והזבובים דשכחי ... מאד בסוכה. ...

See the *sukkah* (booth) built in the yard of the home, in Flesch, *JJLG,* XVIII, 61 (Hebrew text).

Cf. the unsanitary conditions that prevailed in German towns and the unhealthy physical surroundings that affected the life of the peasants, as described by Schultz, *Deut. Leben,* I, 167, 171. The main characteristics of the physical environment of the *gas* has already been suggested on pp. 1–2, 23; p. 149, n. 19.

140 *Shebut Ya'aḳob,* II, no. 45, fol. 7b: . . . *le-ha'amid sam ha-mavet la-zebubim. . . .* Cf. "Sabbath: Sabbath Laws, Insecticide," *RCC.* cit.

141 *N. K. Y.,* fol. 81a, #19 (sec. "Hil. Sukkot").

142 Cf. *Sefer Ṭa'ame ha-Minhagim,* I, fol. 95a, #811.

143 *N. K. Y., op. cit.*

144 *Ibid.* As to the cabalistic origin of the *Tiḳḳun,* see Gaon in *Yeda'-'Am,* III, 112.

145 *Mo'ed Ḳaṭan* 3:1.

146 Cf. *'O. Ḥ.* 542:2.

147 *Noda' bi-Yehudah,* I, no. 13, fol. 4a. Cf. Wind, *R. Yeḥezḳe'l Landau,* pp. 27-29, 71-72, that Landau was sensitive to the social and economic needs of his time, the period preceding Emancipation.

148 *S. H.,* II (ed. Shatzky), fol. 6a:

דארפֿשט קיין פֿייער מאכֿין אונ׳ דריבר שפרינגן מיט פֿישן. אונ׳ דארפֿשט אך ניט מיט בולפֿר שיסן.

בולפֿר = prob. *bulfer* (Yid.); cf. *pulver* (mod. Yid.), "powder"; also *pulver* (Ger.), same meaning.

149 Cf. "Ba'er Heṭeb," n. 1, on *'O. Ḥ.* 669:1:

וכ״ש דאסור להבעיר פולווי״ר להשמיע קול לשמחה וכן ראיתי שמיחו הגדולים אשר בארץ מ״א [מגן אברהם]. ומ״מ מותר לקבוע פולווי״ר בנר אעפ״י שגורם שהנר יכבה מחמת זה. ...

Cf. "Magen 'Abraham" in *Meginne 'Ereẓ* (Nuremberg, 1924), III, fol. 248a, comment on *'O. Ḥ., loc. cit.* (Note: Judah Ashkenazi, the author of the commentary, "Ba'er Heṭeb," lived in Tikotzin [Tiktin], Poland, in the middle of the 18th century.) Cf. also Ochser, "Simḥat Torah," *JE,* XI (1905), 365, cit. This practice is also referred to in Robert Gordis, "Simḥath Torah—Triumph of the Democratic Spirit," in *idem, Judaism for the Modern Age,* p. 198.

150 A. Epstein in *Gedenkbuch . . . David Kaufmann,* p. 313.

Cf. in Landsofer, "Ethical Will," *Derekh Tobim,* fol. 5b, #5; Grunwald in *MGJV,* XXXIV, 78, #151, the traditional customs, observed at that time, on *Simḥat Torah.*

[151] Erik, *Gesh. fun yid. lit.*, p. 308: . . . *minhag fun Yohanis-Fayer*. . . . The contention may be made that Erik's explanation of the origin of the *Johannes Feuer* is based on a forced parallel.

[152] See p. 119, n. 39; p. 127, n. 93; p. 128, nn. 97–98.

[153] Cf. Sartori, *Sitte und Brauch*, II, 111: "Sehr zauberkräftig ist das Springen über das Johannisfeuer"; also, Grimm, *Deut. Myth.*, I, 512; III, 177; 468, n. 918; Wuttke, *Deut. Volksaberglaube*, p. 67; Wilhelm Mannhardt, *Wald und Feldkultur*, I, 186; Höfler, *Deut. Krankheitsnamen-Buch*, p. 136; Mogk, *Deut. Sitten und Bräuche* (ed. Fossler), p. 62; Meier, *Deut. Volkskunde*, p. 57; *Der Grosse Brockhaus*, IX (1931), 444. Cf. further *Johannisnacht* in Seligmann, *Böse Blick*, II, 70; *Johannisfest* in Josef Hanika, "Kultische Vorstufen des Pflanzenanbaues," *ZVV*, L (N. S., 1953), 57.

[154] Cf. Epstein in *Gedenkbuch . . . David Kaufmann*, p. 313, n. 1, the comment of Rashi on *ke-mashuvarta' de-Purayya', San.*, fol. 64b, which is translated (*Sanhedrin*, I [*Neziḳin*, V, Son. edit.], 440, n. 4): "It was like the children's leaping about on Purim." Cf. Shiper, *Yid. teater*, III, 7-9, cits.; 21, who has traced the course of this custom from Byzantium to Italy (ca. 12th century), then to Germany and Eastern Europe.

[155] Shiper, *op. cit.*, III, 8-11, 15-16.

[156] For other examples of the dominant influence that popular practice had, even over legal, scholarly opinion, cf. Assaf, *Teḳufot ha-Ge'onim*, n. 12 to p. 60; chap. VI on "Folk Medicine," esp. pp. 114–116; 125, n. 76; 127–28. See also the effect that popular *Simḥat Torah* customs had on religious life, in Gordis, *op. cit.*, pp. 197-99.

[157] Cf. Wind in *Ḥoreb*, X, 74, n. 73: Wealthy Jewish persons who owned property could enjoy outdoor life.

[158] *Ḳ. Shelah*, 48a.

[159] Cf. *Ex. R.* 20:6; *Levit. R.* 11:8.

[160] *'Or Pene Mosheh*, fol. 75b ("Par. *Be-Shallaḥ*"). Cf. the accounts of *Shabbat Shirah* in Eisenstein, *'Oẓar Dinim u-Minhagim*, p. 402, cits.; *Sefer Ṭa'ame ha-Minhagim*, II, fols. 21b-22a, #97, cit.

[161] Cf. *Ex. R.* 25:14.

[162] *'Oẓar Kol Minhage Yeshurun*, p. 288, #37.

[163] See pp. 91–93.

[164] *M. F.*, fol. 10a, #55; also, fol. 7b, #40. For the Sabbath mantle and cape, see above, p. 160.

[165] *Ibid.*, fol. 9a-b, #48-50.

[166] Wolf, *Mähren Statuten*, p. 1, #4.

[167] *Y. 'O.*, #1062.

[168] Cf. *ma'ot shel ẓedaḳah*, charity fund collected on *Purim: 'Ab. Zar.* 17b. Cf. also *Purim* charity in *Maharil*, 59b (sec. "Hil. Purim"); Levesohn, *Meḳore*

Minhagim, p. 88, sec. 61. For the social uses of *Purim-gelt* through the ages, see I. Rivkind, *Yid. gelt,* pp. 188-90.

169 *S. H.,* I, 59b; *Y. 'O.,* #1087; *M. F.,* fol. 9b, #53; Ocksman in *Reshumot,* III, 102.

170 *Y. 'O.,* #1087; Ocksman in *Reshumot,* III, 102.

Cf. Lewin in *JJGL,* XXX, 185: In Cracow, *'etrogim* were sold and the proceeds therefrom went to the community chest to aid the poor.

171 Cf. *Maharil,* 76b.

172 Cf. *Y. 'O.,* #1087; Ocksman in *Reshumot,* III, 102.

173 *S. H.,* I, 59b; *Y. 'O.,* #1087. The "sending of portions to one another" originated with the Book of Esther (9:22) and continued thereafter: see *Meg.,* 7a; *Maharil,* 77b (sec. "Hil. Purim"); *'O. Ḥ.* 694:1, 695:4; Jacob Reifmann, *Mishloaḥ Manot,* pp. 12-14.

174 *N. K. Y.,* fol. 53a (sec. "Hil. Purim").

175 *S. H.,* II, 17a.

176 *N. K. Y.,* fol. 53a, #14 (sec. "Hil. Purim"). Cf. *Meg.* 16b; *Megillah* (*Mo'ed,* VIII, Son. edit.) 99, nn. 4-5.

Cf. the gloss of Isserles on *'O. Ḥ.,* 695:2; this earlier statement is reiterated by Kosman in this passage.

177 *N. K. Y.,* fol. 53a, #14. Cf. *Terumat ha-Deshen,* no. 111, fol. 19a; *Shelah* I, fol. 261a.

Cf. *Maharil,* 77b: The *Purim se'udah* started in the middle of the day; *minḥah* was recited and the meal continued until the middle of the night. After the meal *ma'arib* services were said.

178 *N. K. Y.,* fol. 53b, #16. Cf. Isserles, gloss on *'O. Ḥ.* 695:1.

179 *Terumat ha-Deshen,* fol. 19a.

180 *Shelah,* I, 261a.

181 *N. K. Y.,* fol. 53b, #16.

182 That restrictions were relaxed on the festivals of *Ḥanukkah* and *Purim* to allow gambling, see Horovitz, *Frankfurt. Rabbin.,* II, 52. The practice of gambling on *Ḥanukkah* is described by Rivkind, *Kamf kegn azartshpiln,* pp. 29, 101. When a child was born, relatives could gamble as part of their celebration.

See Wachstein, *ZGJD,* IV, 139, #37; also 137-38, #28, the legislation of Runkel, January 11, 1757, that permits cardplaying once a week for six hours, during the day or evening. Cardplaying, however, is prohibited on fast days and those occasions when the *Taḥanun* prayer (2 Sam. 24; Ps. 6) is not recited. (*Taḥanun* is omitted on *Rosh Ḥodesh,* the new moon or month; on holidays, festivals, throughout the month of *Nisan,* and the period from the first of *Sivan* through *Shabu'ot.*)

The prohibition of cardplaying and gambling in the German community (Schultz, *Deut. Leben,* I, 175) could have had an influence on the Jewish society; in this regard, see below, p. 183, n. 188.

183 *Ḥavvot Ya'ir,* no. 61, fol. 63a:

... בימי פורים הטילו גורל על כוס כסף גדול מזהב....

Cf. "Manners and Customs," *RCC,* cit. Jews in the 17th century also took part in the lotteries in the German community; see Simon Cohen, "Gambling," *UJE,* IV (1941), 508.

184 *N. K. Y.*, fol. 48b, #12 ("Hil. Ḥanukkah").

...(והיינו שקורין בל״א טיקטא״ק או פר קעהר״ניס) ששחקין בהן כגון צחקת השקאקי ודומיהן (היינו שקורין בל״א שא״ך שאוו״ל)....

See *ticktack* (Ger.), the same in English. Prob. *farkehrnis* (Yid.); cf. *verkehren* (Ger.) = "to turn topsy-turvy." *ha-shekaki:* cf. *ha-shkaki* in *Sefer Ḥasidim* (ed. R. Margulies), #400, p. 288 (Kosman cites part of the passage from *Sefer Ḥasidim*); probably related to *schak,* "chess," as in Lübben, *Mittelniederdeut. Handwörterbuch,* p. 318. Prob. *shakh-tsavil* (Yid.) = "chessboard." Cf. *shakh-tsafil shpil, shakh-tsavil shpil* (Yid.) in Rivkind, *op. cit.,* p. 199; also n. 93. Cf. *zabel* (Ger.), "chessboard." Cf. also Kluge, *Wörterbuch,* p. 619: *schachzabel* (Ger.), "chessboard." Cf. "chess game" in *J. M.*, II, Bk. 6, chap. 35, 317; Steinschneider, *Schach bei den Juden,* p. 191, cit.; Grunwald, "Aus unseren Sammlungen" (Pt. 1), *MGJV,* I (1898), 68, sec. 7.

185 *J. M.*, II, 317, #21. Card games, according to Schudt (*J. M.*, II, Bk. 6, chap. 35, 317, #21) were: *klaufflabethe, trischaken, à lombre.* Cf. these games in Rivkind, *op. cit.,* p. 194, n. 22. See similar card games in Löw, *Lebensalter,* p. 330; Rivkind, *op. cit.,* p. 195, n. 29. As Abrahams states (*Jewish Life,* p. 415; p. 418, n. 1; pp. 420-21), card games made inroads after the 15th century.

The better-known games of the Middle Ages are described in Güdemann, *Gesch.*, II, 210; *idem,* "Games and Sports," *JE,* V (1903), 564-65; Löw, *Lebensalter,* pp. 328-31, 334; Abrahams, *Jewish Life,* pp. 412-16, 421-22; Steinschneider, *Schach bei den Juden,* pp. 159 ff., 185 ff.; Rivkind, *op. cit.,* pp. 28 ff.; *idem,* "A Responsum of Rabbi Moses [ben Abraham] Provençal on Ball Games" (Hebrew), *Tarbiẓ,* IV (1933), 368-70; S. Rappaport, "Spiele," *JLex,* IV^2 (1930), 550-53, cits.

186 Contempt for the diceplayer, also known as "a dissolute scoundrel" (*J. M.*, II, 317), has its basis in San. 3:3, fol. 24b; *R. H.* 1:8; *Shab.* 23:2. Cf. *Mo'ed* (*M.*, ed. Blackman), I, 90, n. 4; 386-87, nn. 1-2, 4. Cf. also *Sanhedrin,* I (*Neziḳin,* V, Son. edit.), 143, n. 4: Dice players "do not contribute to the stability of civilized society." That this attitude was voiced in later times, see *'O. Ḥ.* 322:5; Rivkind in *Tarbiẓ,* IV, 373, n. 31. Cf. *Shelah,* I, 108b (sec. *Sha'ar ha-'Otyot*), in which the advice is given not to be in the company of the diceplayer or any other gambler.

187 *N. K. Y.*, fol. 48b. Cf. *Sefer Ḥasidim,* #400; cits. are from *Ber.*, 5b; *B. Ḳ.*, 27b. The statement of Judah he-Ḥasid is among the principal opinions quoted whenever gambling is opposed. Rivkind, "Laws concerning Gamblers," *Ḥoreb,* II^1 (1935), 61, n. 5, suggests that the above passage from *Sefer Ḥasidim* was considered cogent because its ethical approach had a legal basis.

[188] For a summary of the literature dealing with the communal ban on gambling, see Wolf, *Mähren Statuten*, p. 73, #280; Baron, *Community*, II, 316; III, 207-208; n. 30; Wachstein (ed.), *Grabschriften . . . in Eisenstadt*, p. 69, n. 1. The traditional reasons for opposing all forms of gambling are in *Shab.*, 149a-b.

As examples of legislation to curb gambling, popular games of chance, cardplaying and lottery, in the Germanic-Jewish community in the 17th and 18th centuries, see H. Flesch, "Mässigkeitsverordnungen," *ZGJT*, I^3 (1931), 280 (sumptuary legislation, 1728); I. Rivkind, *Azartshpiln*, pp. 22-23, 106-107, 124. The opposition to gambling was voiced in folk literature as well as in communal legislation: Rivkind, *op. cit.*, pp. 8, 36-37, 190.

Suggested by Baron, *Community*, II, 312-13, 315-17; III, 207, n. 29; Rivkind in *Ḥoreb*, II^1, 62; *idem* in *Tarbiẓ*, IV, 639.

[189] In *San.* 24b, a distinction is made between the professional gambler who plays for money and has no other occupation, and the person who does not have to rely on the game as his means of livelihood, for he has another occupation. For the latter, the game would be considered a form of recreation, since he plays only for pastime.

Note the gloss of Isserles on *'O. Ḥ.* 338:5, in which women and children are allowed to play games on Sabbath. One of the games was described as playing with "bones *('aẓmot)* that are called chess"; the other with a ball *(kadur)*. Cf. J. H. Greenstone, "Gambling," *JE*, V (1903), 563, cit. That games were permitted on the Sabbath for amusement only, not for gambling, see Rivkind, *Azartshpiln*, n. 54 to p. 199. See also in Rivkind, *Tarbiẓ*, IV, 369–70, 372–73, the differentiation made between the game for sport, relaxation, or friendship, and the one played for stakes.

[190] *J. M.*, II, 317; Kracauer, *Juden in Frankfurt a. M.*, II, 123-24. Cf. also Kracauer, *Judengasse in Frankfurt a. M.*, pp. 336-37; Freimann-Kracauer, *Frankfort* (trans. by Levin), pp. 133-34, in which there is a similar account of the effect that the Frankfort fire had on the mood of the time.

[191] Shiper, *Yid. teater*, II, 82; also Steinschneider, "Purim und Parodie," *MGWJ*, XLVI (1902), 177-81; Berliner, *Deut. Juden im Mittelalter*, p. 32; Davidson, *Parody in Jewish Lit.*, Intro., pp. xiii-xiv; N. M. Nathan, "Aus den Jugenderinnerungen Karl Friedrichs von Klöden," *JJGL*, XX (1917), 142-43.

[192] Gloss of Isserles on *'O. Ḥ.* 696:8:

...מה שנהגו ללבוש פרצופים בפורים וגבר לובש שמלת אשה ואשה כלי גבר אין איסור בדבר....

Cf. Davidson, *Parody*, Intro., p. xiv, n. 5; Steinschneider in *MGWJ*, XLVI, 181-82.

See the Prologue to the *Purim* play, *Ashmeday-shpil*, in Shiper, *op. cit.*: "Today is *Purim*; in all lands there is great joy among the Jews. . . . On *Purim* there is the custom all over the world for poor people to wear masks."

[193] Isserles' gloss, *op. cit.; N. K. Y.*, fol. 53b, #17 (sec. "Hil. Purim"), also cit.

[194] *N. K. Y.*, fol. 53b; *Y. 'O.*, #1105. Cf. *Ṭur Y. D.*, sec. 182; comment of "Ba'er Heṭeb," no. 13 on *'O. Ḥ.* 696:8. Cf. also Y. Lifshitz in *Arkhiv far der gesh. fun yid. teater,* I (ed. J. Shatzky), 452, #2; Fecht, *Gesch. . . . Karlsruhe,* p. 247, #3b (has the document cited by Lifshitz, *loc. cit.*); Löwenstein, *Nathanael Weil* (*Beiträge zur Gesch. der Juden in Deut.;* 2 vols. in one), II, no. 9, 56, #b (includes the document in Fecht). In opposing the masquerade, Weil argues that the dress is *sha'aṭnez.*

In Sugenheim, Franconia, the *Takḳanah* of 1756 includes a prohibition against the masquerade. Cf. Marcus, *Med. World,* p. 220: "No one shall dare mask himself or run around in clown's garb or with candles and torches on Purim. . . ." Cf. also Baron, *Community,* II, 207, n. 30.

[195] Steinschneider, "Purim und Parodie," *MGWJ,* XLVII (1903), 87, #2. Cf. Shiper, I, 190-91; 192, n. 3.

[196] *J. M.*, II, Bk. 6, chap. 35, 314-15, #19.

It was not only for diversion but as a source of income that students joined groups of traveling actors. Cf. I. Tsinberg, "The *Purim-shpil* in Different Periods" (Yiddish), in *idem, Kultur-Historishe Shtudies,* pp. 278-79.

[197] See *J. M.*, II, 314; Shiper, I, 207.

[198] In the transliteration of the titles of the *Purim-shpiln* the Yiddish pronunciation is used to correspond to the language in which the plays are written.

The texts of both plays are in *J. M.*, III (No. 9), 202-25, "Dos Akhashveyros-shpil fun Homen, Mordekhai un Ester" (Frankfort, 1708 pub.); III (No. 10), 226-327, "Mekhires-Yosef" (pub. 1712, Frankfort). Cf. Kracauer, *Juden in Frankfurt,* II, 123-24, n. 1; *idem, Judengasse in Frankfurt,* p. 337, n. 5.

For other versions of the *Purim* play, see S. Weissenberg, "Das Purimspiel von Ahasverus und Esther," *MGJV*, XIII (1904), 4-28; Noah Prilucki, *Yid. folklor,* II, 57-143: "*Purim*-shpilen"; Shiper, II, 256-61: "Mekhires-Yosef-shpil"; Jacob Shatzky, "An 'Akhashveyros-shpil' in Prague a Hundred Years Ago" (Yiddish) in *idem* (ed.), *Arkhiv far der gesh. fun yid. teater,* I, 159-74. Cf. also M. Weinreich, "Tsu der gesh. fun der elterer 'Akhashveyros-shpil'" (Yiddish), *Filolog. Shrift.*, II (1928, Vilna), 425-52.

[199] Cf. *J. M.*, II, Bk. 6, 314; Shiper, I, 87; 95-96; 191, n. 1; 194-95; II, 58, 61-62, 78-79.

[200] See Steinschneider in *MGWJ,* XLVII, 86, #1; 87, #2-3; 88, #10; A. Landau, "Anmerkungen," *MGJV,* XIII (1904), 29; Shiper, I, 193, n. 1. Cf. also J. Shatzky, "Di ershte gesh. fun yid. teater," *Filolog. Shrift.*, II, 241-42; M. Weinreich in *op. cit.*, 425.

[201] *J. M.*, III (No. 9), 202.

Cf. Steinschneider in *MGWJ,* XLVI, 176: "Only a step divides the sublime from the ridiculous." Parody and jest were therefore no sacrilege, for those who "mocked" on *Purim* felt at ease because of deep roots in devotion and respect.

[202] *J. M., loc. cit.* Cf. Kracauer, *Juden in Frankfurt,* II, 123. See the description of the *Purim* play being presented in a home: Shiper, I, 110-11; II, 81.

[203] Cf. Tsinberg in *Kultur-Hist. Shtudies,* p. 279; Erik, *Yid. lit.,* p. 140; Davidson, *Parody,* p. 50.

[204] *J. M.,* III, 203.

See Shiper, I, 205. Cleavages between the communal leaders and the people were indicated in the *Purim-shpil.* Wealthy individuals were made the subject for ridicule. Cf. chap. III, pp. 74–75, n. 158; p. 75, n. 161.

[205] *J. M.,* III, 213: ". . . We shall plan to drive out and starve the roguish *(shelmishn)* Jews; thereby I shall receive 10,000, 30,000 'coins' [from them] to buy [i. e., save, ransom] the roguish Jew Mordecai—not only Mordecai but especially the entire roguish Jewish community."

צענטנר = prob. *tsentnr* (Yid.). Cf. *cent* (Ger.), related to *centum* (Lat.) = "a coin," having the value of 1/100 of a guilder: G. J. Adler, *Dict. of Ger. and Eng. Langs.* (New York, 1883), p. 121.

Cf. Shiper, II, 174-75, who has detected in an 18th century *Akhashveyros-shpil* of Leipzig that, through the character of Haman, the Jew expressed a new tone of *musar* and a new conception of himself: "Let every person learn the lesson from me, Mr. Haman, that no Christian should try to harm a Jew." It could have meant that the Jew was now seeking a change in his political status—that it was another sign of developments within the Jewish community heralding Emancipation.

[206] *J. M.,* III, 215.

Concerning the comic role given to Mordecai in *Purim-shpiln,* see in Weissenberg, *MGJV,* XIII, 5, 13-14: "Dus Pirimspiel. Du spielt die Rolle Humen in Mordche"; Landau in *MGJV,* XIII, 31; Shatzky in *Arkhiv . . . fun yid. teater,* 1, 169, n. 1; Shiper, I, 205. Cf. Mordecai as a *shadkhan,* "matchmaker," for the king, in Weissenberg, *op. cit.,* 12-14; Davidson, *op. cit.,* p. 50, n. 37; Shatzky in *op. cit.,* 167-68.

[207] *J. M., op. cit.* Cf. the *Purim-ḳiddush* in Weissenberg, *MGJV,* XIII, 28 (text). See the description of the *Purim-ḳiddush* in Davidson, pp. 50-51, n. 40.

[208] *J. M.,* II (Bk. 6, chap. 35), 316, #20. Schudt states that he learned of the incident from a Jewish person. Shiper, I, 206, n. 1, was inclined to accept Schudt's report as factual. Cf. Meyer Waxman, *Hist. Jewish Lit.* (rev. edit.), II, 659, that the *Purim* play "was condemned to be burned by the elders of the Frankfurt community, yet it continued to be played."

[209] *Ya'arot Debash,* II, fol. 47a:

. . . ומכ״ש למקום שקורין שויא שפיל קאמדיע אופרייא המשחקי׳ שם על טיאטרוס שזה אמרו חז״ל במושב לצים לא ישב אלו בתי טיאטרות. . . .

Cf. Löw, *Lebensalter,* p. 298, n. 71; Shiper, I, 207, cit.

[210] *J. M.,* III, 215. Cf. Davidson, p. 50, n. 37; p. 203, sec. C (text). Cf. a variant of the text in Shatzky, *Arkhiv . . . yid. teater,* I, 169, #10.

See the parody of a *teḥinnah,* a "prayer of supplication," in Weissenberg, *MGJV,* XIII, 9-10 (text). Cf. Davidson, pp. 199-200, sec. A (text).

[211] See Shiper, II, 247, concerning the place of the *klag-lid* in the *Mekhires-Yosef-shpil.*

[212] *J. M.,* III (No. 10), 255. See Shiper, II, 245, cit. from *Mekhires-Yosef-shpil* of Rachel replying to Joseph from her grave. In rabbinic lore it is the appeal of mother Rachel that is heard on high when the Temple of Jerusalem was destroyed. Cf. for example, *Mid. 'Ekhah Rabbati,* "Petiḥta," sec. 24; trans. *Lament., Mid. R.* (Son. edit.), VII, "Proems," sec. 24, p. 49: "Immediately the mercy of the Holy One, blessed be He, was stirred, and He said, 'For thy sake, Rachel, I will restore Israel to their place.'"

[213] This custom is discussed on pp. 47–48 and p. 193, n. 254.

[214] *J. M.,* II (Bk. 6, chap. 35), 314, #19. Cf. "Pickelhering" ("Pickelhäring") of the *Mekhires-Yosef-shpil* in Kracauer, *Juden in Frankfurt a. M.,* II, 124; *idem, Judengasse in Frankfurt a. M.,* p. 337; also, Piklhering in Shiper, I, 206.

See the description of the *Purim* clown dressed in comical attire, in N. Prilucki, *Zamelbikher,* II, no. 12, 109. Cf. Shiper, II, 56, n. 1; 106.

[215] *J. M.,* III, 275.

[216] Cf. Shiper, II, 117-19, 210; Erik, pp. 137-39. See portraits of the *Purim* clown in *Minhagim* (Amsterdam, 1723), fol. 56b; Shiper, II, 211–13; also in Erik, p. 138, the portrait in *Minhagim, loc. cit.,* and Fig. 15 of this volume.

[217] W. Creizenach (ed.), *Die Schauspiele der engl. Komödianten,* Intro., pp. xciii-xcv (reprint from Joseph Kürschner, ed., *Deut. National-Lit.,* XXIII); Meyers, *Lexikon,* IX (1928, 7th edit.), 860, cit.; Shiper, II, 248, n. 165.

Cf. also in Creizenach, pp. ciii-cv, a description of Pickelhäring, the clown. As an example of the incongruous dialogue spoken by Pickelhäring on the stage, see his part in the comedy, *Tugend- und Liebes-Streit (A Conflict between Virtue and Love),* in Creizenach, pp. 75-84, 94-106, 121-22. (Spelling of Pickelhäring corresponds to usage in sources.)

[218] Cf. Löw, *Lebensalter,* p. 297; Davidson, Intro., p. xiii; pp. 26-27, n. 61; Shiper, III, 89, n. 1. Cf. the influence on the *Purim* play via the *Fastnachtsspiel,* the carnival and dramatic farce held on Shrove Tuesday. The *Fastnachtsspiel* is regarded as the possible source of origin for the *Purim-shpiln.* The morality plays presented on Shrove Tuesday were adapted to the Jewish stage for merrymaking. See Shiper, II, 81; III, 19; Shatzky in *Arkhiv . . . yid. teater,* I, 161.

[219] M. Grunwald, "Aus unseren Sammlungen," *MGJV,* I (1898), 69, #6 (sec. VII, "Spiele").

The pantomime *barbiertanz,* "barber dance," was staged in Germany in the 18th century. See Böhme, *Gesch. des Tanzes,* I, 209.

[220] See Shiper, II, 61–62. See chap. VI, p. 118, nn. 32–33.

[221] Cf. *Shelah,* I, fol. 329a (sec. "Torah she-bi-Khetab"); *Y. 'O.,* #1100; *N. K. Y.,* fol. 53a, #14 (sec. "Hil. Purim").

[222] See n. 47 to p. 91. Cf. Y. Lifshitz in *Arkhiv . . . yid. teater,* I, 452–53; Fecht, *Gesch. . . . Karlsruhe,* p. 247; Löwenstein, *Nathanael Weil,* II, no. 9, 55–58: R. Yedidiah Weil (d. 1805) sent a written appeal to the chief bailiff *(oberamt)* of Karlsruhe, asking for his support in checking the unruly conduct and "corrupt morals" in the Jewish community, especially during *Purim.* It was not a usual procedure to contact government officials to regulate any part of Jewish communal life.

[223] Yuspa Shammash, *Minhagim* MS, fol. 67b; cit. by Epstein in *Gedenkbuch . . . David Kaufmann,* pp. 314-15; Holzer in *ZGJD,* V, 174-75, "Bachurimsabbat"; Assaf, *Meḳorot,* I, 121-22, #6; IV, 84, n. 3; Tsinberg, *Gesh. fun der lit.,* V, pp. 89–91, nn. 6, 9; Shiper, III, 90–92. Cf. herein, p. 94, n. 64; p. 160, n. 78; p. 161, n. 79.

קנע"ל = prob. from *kneln* (Yid.), "to teach children, argue, inculcate"; cf. Harkavy, *Verterbukh* (New York, 1925), p. 463. קנע"ל גבא"י = *knel-gabay* (Yid.), "an attendant to supervise school children." Cf. Assaf, *Meḳorot,* IV, sec. 76, p. 85, #25 (*Taḳḳanot* of the *Kloyz* in Mannheim, established in 1708): The *knel-gabay* was responsible for maintaining decorum in the school and meting out punishment when a child misbehaved.

[224] Yuspa Shammash, *Minhagim,* in Epstein, *op. cit.,* p. 315.

A lilac wreath was worn on the Feast of Fools: cf. Shiper, III, 94. Cf. H. Boos, *Gesch. der rheinisch. Städtekultur,* III, 340: On the Feast of St. Nicholas, in Germany, children carried saplings.

There is a possible relationship between the Feast of Fools and *Shabbat ha-Baḥurim,* as suggested in Epstein, *op. cit.,* p. 314, cit.; Boos, *op. cit.,* III, 340; Shiper, III, 92-93; Davidson, pp. 26-27. These are some of the characteristics of the Feast of Fools: The students held a mock ceremony, elected "a bishop" from their ranks, took possession of the cathedral, and served as the clergy. In their celebration they would burlesque the sacred.

[225] Cf. Steinschneider in *MGWJ,* XLVI, 177: For *Purim,* the students of R. David Oppenheim presented "a caricature" of their teacher in a language that was "more colloquial than Biblical."

[226] See p. 53, n. 15; p. 59, n. 57.

[227] Cf. children's customs on *Simḥat Torah* in Assaf, "Erziehung: II. Im

Mittelalter," *EJ,* VI (1930), 751; Grunwald in *MGJV,* XI, 11-12, #28-29; Gaster, *Holy and Profane,* pp. 132-33.

228 Bamberger, "Minhagimsammelmappe," *JJV,* I (1923), 330, #9 ("Das Beschütten des Kindes").

229 Epstein in *Gedenkbuch . . . David Kaufmann,* p. 312.

230 *Ibid.,* pp. 312-13.

231 Grunwald, "Jüd. Volkskunde auf der 'Pressa,'" *Menorah,* VI (1928, Vienna), 356-57.

232 *'Oẓar Minhage Yeshurun,* p. 132, #14.

233 *Zikhron Yosef,* no. 5, fol. 5b:

בכל מדינות וגלילות אשכנז. . . . שהי׳ בימים ההם להעמיד שני נערים קטנים אצל הש״ץ אחד מימינו ואחד משמאלו ובהגיע החזן . . . מתחיל אחד מן הקטנים לשורר פסוק אחד והשני אחריו פסוק השני עד גמירא.

234 *'Eben ha-Shoham,* I, no. 50, fol. 27a:

נשאלתי אם מותר לנגן בכלי שיר כגון נבל וכנור בחה״מ או לא. . . .
תשובה מנהג שישראל תורה היא . . . ראיתי שהבחורים עושך מחולות בחה״מ ויהודים מנגנים בכלי שיר ואין מוחין בידם. . . .

Cf. Baron, *Community,* III, 206, n. 29.

235 See above, n. 189 to p. 183; cf. p. 174, n. 149.

236 *Shelah,* I, fol. 179b ("Mas. Shabu'ot"). Cf. this practice in *S. H.,* I, fol. 56a; *N. K. Y.,* fol. 63a, # 2 ("Hil. Shab."), and above, pp. 172, 173, for a similar observance on other holidays.

237 *Ḳ. Shelah,* 55b.

238 *Pirḳe Rabbi 'Eli'ezer* (Warsaw, 1885), sec. 41, p. 81.

239 "Magen 'Abraham" comment on *'O. Ḥ.,* sec. 604. Cf. *Ṭa'ame ha-Minhagim,* I, fol. 74a, #618; Zevin, *Ha-Mo'adim be-Halakhah,* p. 310, n. 36.

240 Cf. suggestion in Eisenstein, "Shabu'ot," *'Oẓar Yisra'el,* X (1913), 30; *idem,* "Pentecost," *JE,* IX (1905), 593.

241 *Zohar,* fol. 97b-98a (Sid. "'Emor": *Va–Yiḳra');* trans. from *Zohar* (Son. edit.), V, 123. Cf. Zevin, pp. 310-11, n. 37; Eisenstein in *'Oẓar Yisra'el,* X, 30.

242 *Shelah,* I, 179b.

243 Cf. Scholem, *Trends in Jewish Mysticism,* pp. 226-27, for "sexual imagery" in Cabala.

244 *Pirḳe Rabbi 'Eli'ezer,* sec. 41, p. 81.

245 Above, n. 241.

246 *Zohar,* fol. 98a; trans. from Son. edit., *op. cit.*

247 *Shelah,* I, 179b-180a. See also cit. of *Shelah* in Gaon, *Yeda'-'Am,* III, 113. Cf. the list of readings for *Shabu'ot* night as enumerated in Eisenstein, *JE,* IX, 593.

[248] As an example, cf. the *Tiḳḳun Lel Shabu'ot* (Sulzbach, 1827); the title page states that the book was published "according to the plan outlined in the *Shelah*." Cf. above, p. 173, n. 144.

[249] See above, p. 173.

[250] *N. K. Y.,* fol. 66b, #1 (sec. "Hil. 'Ereb Tish'ah be-'Ab"). Cf. *Sefer ha-Manhig,* fol. 49b, #18; *'O. Ḥ.* 549:1-2. Cf. also the "mourning for Jerusalem" in B. Bat., 60b.

[251] *N. K. Y., op. cit.* Cf. *Sefer ha-Manhig,* fol. 50b, #24; *'O. Ḥ.* 552:1, 4. Cf. also gloss of Isserles on *ibid.,* #4, that hard-boiled eggs are "the food of mourners." See food for the Ninth of *'Ab,* herein, p. 102, n. 58.

[252] *N. K. Y., op. cit.*

[253] Since intercourse is forbidden on the Ninth of *'Ab,* cold foods are eaten to reduce sexual desire. Cf. *N. K. Y., op. cit.; 'O. Ḥ.* 557:1.

[254] *N. K. Y.,* fol. 67a, #9, cit. (sec. "Hil. Tish'ah be-'Ab"); *Ta'anit,* fol. 16a. Cf. *Ḥag.,* fol. 22b: "At once, Rabbi Joshua went and prostrated himself upon the graves of Bet Shammai." Cf. also related practices on pp. 47, 188.

[255] Comment by Rashi on *yoẓ'in le-bet- ha-ḳebarot, Ta'anit,* 16a; cf. *N. K. Y., op. cit.*

Cf. *N. K. Y., loc. cit.,* that *ẓaddiḳim,* "righteous men," would visit cemeteries "to mourn the destruction of the Temple of Jerusalem."

[256] *N. K. Y.,* fol. 67a, #9.

[257] Cf. the *Stättigkeit,* December 7, 1705, #29, in *J. M.,* III (No. 6), 166. If there is a violation, the government will impose a fine of half a guilder. Cf. also Kracauer, *Gesch. Frankfurt. Juden,* II, 119, n. 2. (Note the definition of *Stättigkeit* in Toni Oelsner, "Jewish Ghetto of the Past," *Yivo Annual Jew. Soc. Sc.,* I, 29, n. 10.)

This *Stättigkeit* was issued by Emperor Joseph I, ruler of the Holy Roman Empire, who succeeded his father, Leopold I, in 1705. Cf. *J. M., op. cit.,* 156; Kracauer, *op. cit.,* 114; Freimann-Levin, *Frankfort,* p. 129.

[258] Kracauer, *op. cit.,* 119; Freimann-Levin, *op. cit.,* p. 130. The above *Stättigkeit* (*J. M., op. cit.,* 166, sec. 29) specifies: "Es sollen der Juden nicht mehr als zween mit einander gehen. , . ."

[259] Kracauer, *op. cit.,* I, 200; Freimann-Levin, p. 41; Oelsner in *op. cit.,* I, 29; "Frankfort-on-Main," *Ency. Brit.,* XI (11th edit., 1910), 17, 21 cits.; Horne, *Gesch. von Frankfurt am Main,* p. 35; bet. pp. 16-17, the map, "Hist. Erweiterungs-Plan von Frankfurt a/Main" (n. d.), showing the location of the *Fischerfeld.*

[260] Oelsner in *op. cit.;* Horne, pp. 16-17, 24-25, 32. Cf. the map of Frankfort with the three "city fortifications" in Horne, bet. pp. 16-17. Cf. the location of the *gas* on the map, "Plan of Frankfort-on-the-Main in 1552" (taken from the *Archive für Frankfurt. Gesch. und Kunst*), JE, V (1903), 485. Cf. also the location of the *gas* in Frankfort, herein, p. 1, n. 8; p. 171.

[261] Oelsner in *op. cit.;* map in Horne, *op. cit.,* bet. pp. 16-17.

[262] *'O. Ḥ.* 551:2. Removal of the shoes was a sign of mourning, as in Ezek. 24:17.

[263] *N. K. Y.*, fol. 67a-b, # Cf. p. 94, n. 70; p. 173, n. 147, for instances when feelings of non-Jews are considered in determining Jewish religious practice. Cf. the relation of Jews and non-Jews in Germany during the 17th and 18th centuries in J. Katz, *Ben Yehudim la-Goyim,* chap. xi; also, chaps. i-ii for the early Middle Ages. Cf. also Baron, *Soc. and Relig. Hist.*, II, 87-88, 91, for the social position of the Jew in medieval times.

[264] *N. K. Y., op. cit.* See p. 149, nn. 20, 22.

[265] *Y. 'O.,* #877. (The author did not locate Isserlein's statement in either *Terumat ha-Deshen* or *Leḳeṭ Yosher.*)

[266] *S. H.,* II (ed. Shatzky), fol. 17a; cf. Intro., p. 36.

[267] J. C (assuto), "Protokollbuch der Portug.-Jüd. Gemeinde in Hamburg," *JJLG,* XI (1916), 25.

[268] *Y. 'O.,* #886.

[269] *Ibid.* Cf. the complaint of Jonah Landsofer, pp. 74–75, n. 158.

Abbreviations

B. D.	—*Bet David,* by David Tevle Ashkenazi
BSV	—Beiträge zur sudetendeutschen Volkskunde
BDBV	—Beiträge zur deutsch-böhmischen Volkskunde
CCARY	—Central Conference of American Rabbis Yearbook
'E. H.	—*'Eben ha-'Ezer* (a section of the *Ṭurim,* by Jacob b. Asher, and the *Shulḥan 'Arukh,* by Joseph Karo)
EJ	—Encyclopædia Judaica
H. 'A.	—*Hanhagot 'Adam*, by David Oppenheim
HB	—Hebräische Bibliographie
HDA	—Handwörterbuch des deutschen Aberglaubens
HJ	—Historia Judaica, ed. Guido Kisch
HUCA	—Hebrew Union College Annual
JE	—Jewish Encyclopedia
JJGL	—Jahrbuch für Jüdische Geschichte und Literatur
JJLG	—Jahrbuch der Jüdisch-Literarischen Gesellschaft
JJV	—Jahrbuch für Jüdische Volkskunde
JL	—Jüdisches Literaturblatt, ed. Moritz Rahmer
JLex	—Jüdisches Lexikon
J. M.	—*Jüdische Merckwürdigkeiten,* by Johann Jacob Schudt
JQR	—Jewish Quarterly Review (Old and New Series)
JSS	—Jewish Social Studies
Ḳ. H.	—*Ḳab ha-Yashar,* by Ẓebi Hirsh Kaidanover
Ḳ. Shelah	—*Ḳiẓur Shene Luḥot ha-Berit,* by Yeḥiel Mikhel Epstein
M. H.	—*Mafteaḥ ha-Yam,* by Jacob Meir Coblenz
M. F.	—*Minhag Ḳ. Ḳ. Fürth,* by Israel and Dov Jacob Gumpiel
M.	—Mishnah
M. T.	—*Mishneh Torah,* by Maimonides
MGJV	—Mitteilungen der Gesellschaft für jüdische Volkskunde

MGWJ	—Monatsschrift für Geschichte und Wissenschaft des Judentums
N. K. Y.	—*Noheg ka-Ẓo'n Yosef,* by Joseph Kosman
'O. Ḥ.	—*'Oraḥ Ḥayyim* (a section of the *Ṭurim,* by Jacob b. Asher, and the *Shulḥan 'Arukh,* by Joseph Karo)
RCC	—*Responsa* Card Catalogue, Jewish Division, New York Public Library
REJ	—Revue des études juives
Shelah	—*Shene Luḥot ha-Berit,* by Isaiah ben Abraham Horowitz
S. H.	—*Simḥat ha-Nefesh,* by 'Elḥanan Haenle Kirchhan (Vol. II, ed. Jacob Shatzky)
Tos.	—Tosafot
Tosef.	—Tosefta
UJE	—Universal Jewish Encyclopedia
Y. D.	—*Yoreh De'ah* (a section of the *Ṭurim,* by Jacob b. Asher, and the *Shulḥan 'Arukh,* by Joseph Karo)
Y. 'O.	—*Yosif 'Omeẓ,* by Joseph Yuspa Hahn
ZGJD	—Zeitschrift für die Geschichte der Juden in Deutschland (Old and New Series)
ZGJT	—Zeitschrift für die Geschichte der Juden in der Tschechoslovakei
ZHB	—Zeitschrift für hebraeische Bibliographie
ZVV	—Zeitschrift des Vereins für Volkskunde

Bibliography

Comment on Sources

The Bibliography is divided into four parts: (1) bibliographical and bio-bibliographical sources; (2) manuscripts; (3) other primary sources; (4) secondary sources pertaining to (a) German-Jewish communal, social and cultural life, folk attitudes and practices; (b) German, general European and non-European social and cultural life; German folklore.

Primary sources are a sample of literary works from German-Jewish society, including popular, informal books intended for wide distribution. The literature consists of local collected customs (the book of *minhagim),* ethical treatise *(musar)*, ethical wills *(ẓavva'ot)*, homily *(derush)*, and the popularized code of law *(Shulḥan 'Arukh). Responsa (she'elot u-teshubot)* provide a realistic account of daily events, and the communal legislation *(taḳḳanot)* and minute book *(pinḳasim)* contain the practices and institutional procedures of a local area. Aspects of folk life are recounted and described in the autobiography and the *memor*-book. The Bibliography includes the sources cited, as well as those references that were consulted or checked.

In selecting sources, dates and geographical boundary lines could not always be adhered to; flexibility had to be allowed as there were authors who had resided in Eastern Europe as well as in Germanic lands. Some sources published before 1648 were relevant for a later period. As we have already stated, Jewish practices were not limited to specific geographical areas; hence, a source dealing with a custom in Eastern Europe might be referred to if it seemed related to German-Jewish folk life. Collected customs of an earlier period were also consulted in order to consider the continuity and development of a folk tradition. In revising the final copy for publication, the author has endeavored to incorporate more recent sources, such as the new translation of Glikl of Hameln's autobiography, by Mrs. Beth-Zion Abrahams, and *'Im Ḥillufe Teḳufot (Beginnings of the Haskalah among German Jewry),* by Azriel Shohet. As yet, *Bericht an einige Christliche Freunde . . . ,* by J. H. Callenberg, and related missionary sources have not been examined. Hopefully, this is to be undertaken when the present area of study will be pursued further.

Standard texts, Talmud, Midrash, *Mishneh Torah, Shulḥan 'Arukh, Zohar,* are not in the Bibliography. Dictionaries and lexicons that are in common use are not listed.

Bibliography

SECTION 1

Abrahams, Israels, *Jewish Life in the Middle Ages*. New edition, enlarged and revised on the basis of the author's material by Cecil Roth. London: E. Goldston, 1932.

"'Ish Shub," *Sefer Ṭa'ame ha-Minhagim*. 2d edit. reprint. 4 vols. in one. Lemberg, [n. d.] ("'Ish Shub" is identified as Abraham Yiẓḥaḳ Danzig by Friedberg, *Bet 'Eḳed Sefarim*, p. 250, #117. Prefatory comment in *Ṭa'ame ha-Minhagim* refers to שו״ב דק״ק לבוב, שוחט בודק, an examiner of ritual slaughtering in the community of Lwów.)

Assaf, Simḥa, *Meḳorot le-Toledot ha-Ḥinnukh be-Yisra'el* (Sources for the history of Jewish education; from the beginning of the Middle Ages to the Haskalah period). 4 vols. Tel-Aviv–Jerusalem, 1925-42.

Azulai, Ḥayyim Yosef David, *Sifre Shem ha-Gedolim . . . 'im Va'ad la-Ḥakhamim* (Bio-bibliographical source). 2 vols. in one. Vilna: Rom (Romm), 1852.

Baron, Salo W., *A Social and Religious History of the Jews*. Vol. III. New York: Columbia University Press, 1937.

———, *The Jewish Community*. Vol. III. Philadelphia: Jewish Publication Society, 1945.

Berger, Abraham, *The Literature of Jewish Folklore: A Survey, with special Reference to Recent Publications*. Reprint of *Journal of Jewish Bibliography*, Vol. I, Nos. 1-2, October 1938-January 1939.

Bibliography of Anthropology and Folklore. Edited by N. W. Thomas. 3 vols. London: Royal Anthropological Institute, 1906-8.

Cohen, Boas, *Ḳunṭres ha-Teshubot* (A bibliography of *responsa* literature). Budapest, 1930.

Cowley, A. E., *Catalogue of Hebrew Printed Books in the Bodleian Library*. Oxford: Clarendon Press, 1929.

Dahlmann-Waitz, *Quellenkunde der deutschen Geschichte*. Edited by Hermann Haering. 9th edit. 2 vols. Leipzig: Koehler, 1931-32. (Gesellschaft "Jahresberichte für deutsche Geschichte.")

Dubnow, Simon, *Dibre Yeme 'Am 'Olam* (Hebrew edition of *Weltgeschichte des jüdischen Volkes*). Edited by Barukh Krupnick. Vols. VI-VII. Tel-Aviv, 1945-46. (See bibliography, vol. VI, pp. 274-77; vol. VII, pp. 313-16.)

Eisenstein, J. D., *'Oẓar Dinim u-Minhagim* (A collection of laws and customs in Jewish life). New York, 1917.

Elfenbein, Israel S. (ed.), *Minhagim Yeshenim mi-Dura* (Customs derived from Isaac of Düren, a Talmudic authority of the 13th century; the author of *Sha'are Dura,* a halakhic work). New York, 1948.

Erik, Max (Zalman Merkin), *Di geshikhte fun der yidisher literatur* (The history of Jewish literature). Warsaw: Kultur League, 1928.

Fishman, Isidore, *The History of Jewish Education in Central Europe: From the End of the Sixteenth to the End of the Eighteenth Century.* London: Goldston, 1944.

Frank, Moses, *Ḳehillot 'Ashkenaz u-Bate Dinehen* (A study of the legal system of German-Jewish communities). Tel-Aviv, 1938.

Friedberg, B., *Bet 'Eḳed Sefarim* (A bibliographical collection of Jewish literature). 8 vols. in one. Antwerp, 1928-31.

Grünbaum, Max, *Jüdischdeutsche Chrestomathie.* Leipzig: Brockhaus, 1882.

———, *Die jüdisch-deutsche Litteratur in Deutschland, Polen und America.* Trier: S. Mayer, 1894. (Reprint of Winter-Wünsche, *Die jüdische Litteratur seit Abschluss des Kanons,* III [1894], 531-623.)

Güdemann, Moritz, *Quellenschriften zur Geschichte des Unterrichts und der Erziehung bei den deutschen Juden.* Berlin: Hofmann, 1891.

Haskell, Daniel C., "Jewish Customs: A List of Works Compiled by A. S. Freidus," in *Studies in Jewish Bibliography and Related Subjects: In Memory of Abraham Solomon Freidus,* pp. lxxviii-cxxx. New York, 1929.

Hebräische Bibliographie. Edited by Moritz Steinschneider. 18 vols. Berlin, 1858-78.

Hirschowitz, Abraham Eliezer, *'Oẓar Kol Minhage Yeshurun* (A collection of customs in Jewish Life). Lwów, 1930.

Horovitz, Marcus, *Frankfurter Rabbinen. Ein Beitrag zur Geschichte der israelitischen Gemeinde in Frankfurt a. M.* 3 vols. in one. Frankfort: Jaeger, 1882-84. (See vols. II-III.)

Karpeles, Gustav, *Geschichte der jüdischen Literatur.* Vol. II. Berlin: Oppenheim, 1886.

———, *Histoire de la littérature juive.* Edited by Isaac Bloch and Emile Levy. Paris: Leroux, 1901.

———, *Jewish Literature and Other Essays.* Philadelphia: Jewish Publication Society, 1895.

Kohut, George Alexander, "Bibliography of the Writings of Professor Dr. Moritz Steinschneider," in *Festschrift . . . Steinschneider's,* pp. v-xxxix. Leipzig: Harrassowitz, 1896.

Landshut, Eliezer, *Toledot 'Anshe ha-Shem u-Pe'ullatam be-'Adat Berlin,* 1671–1871 (A history of Jewish personalities in Berlin). Vol. I. Berlin: Poppelauer, 1880.

Section 1

Marcus, Jacob R., *Communal Sick -Care in the German Ghetto.* Cincinnati: Hebrew Union College Press, 1947.

———, and Albert J. Bilgray, *An Index to Jewish Festschriften.* Cincinnati: Hebrew Union College, 1937.

Marx, Alexander, and Hermann Meyer (eds.), *Festschrift für Aron Freimann zum 60. Geburtstag.* Berlin: Soncino, 1935. (See bibliography, pp. 5-10.)

Mitteilungen der Gesellschaft für jüdische Volkskunde. Edited by Max Grunwald. 23 vols. Hamburg-Vienna, 1898-1922.

Patai, Raphael, "On Culture Contact and Its Working in Modern Palestine," *American Anthropologist,* XLIX (N. S., 1947), Pt. 2, 47-48 (bibliography).

Pines, Max, *Histoire de la littérature judéo-allemande.* Paris: Jouve, 1911.

———, *Die Geschichte der jüdischdeutschen Literatur. Nach dem französischen Original bearbeitet.* Edited by Georg Hecht. Leipzig: Engel, 1913.

Quellen und Forschungen zur deutschen Volkskunde. Edited by E. K. Blümml. 3 vols. Vienna: Ludwig, 1908-12. (See vol. III in particular.)

Quellen zur deutschen Volkskunde. Edited by V. Geramb and L. Mackensen. 6 vols. Berlin: Walter de Gruyter. 1927–35. (Vols. I-II are more relevant.)

Rivkind, Isaac, *Le-'Ot u-le-Zikkaron, Toledot Bar-Miẓvah ve-Hitpatḥuto be-Ḥayye ha-'Am ve-Tarbuto: Bar Mitzvah, a Study in Jewish Cultural History.* New York: Shulsinger, 1942.

Sassoon, David S., *'Ohel David: Descriptive Catalogue of the Hebrew and Samaritan Manuscripts in the Sassoon Library, London.* 2 vols. London: Oxford University Press, 1932.

Shulman, Eleazar, *Sefat Yehudit-'Ashkenazit ve-Safrutah* (The Yiddish language and its literature). Riga: Eli Levin, 1913.

Simḥath Hanefesh (Delight of the Soul). A Book of Yiddish Poems, by Elḥanan Kirchhan. An Exact Facsimile Reproduction of the First and Only Edition Published in Fürth, in the Year 1727. Edited by Jacob Shatzky. New York: Maisel, 1926. (See Intro., pp. 11-50.)

Steinschneider, Moritz, *Allgemeine Einleitung in die jüdische Literatur des Mittelalters.* Jerusalem: Bamberger-Wahrmann, 1938. (Cf. *JQR,* XV [O. S., 1903], 302-29; XVI [O. S., 1904], 373-95, 734-64; XVII, 148-62, 354-69, 545-82.

———, *Catalogus Librorum Hebraeorum in Bibliotheca Bodleiana.* 2 vols. Berlin: Friedländer, 1852-60.

———, *Die Geschichtsliteratur der Juden.* Vol. I. Frankfort: Kauffmann, 1905. (Nothing further appeared.)

———, "Jüdische Literatur," *Allgemeine Encyklopädie der Wissenschaften und Künste,* XXVII (1850), sec. 2, 357-471. English translation: *Jewish Literature from the Eighth to the Eighteenth Century,* London: Longman-Roberts, 1857.

———, *Safrut Yisra'el* (A history of Jewish literature). Translated by Zevi Malter. Warsaw: 'Aḥi'asaf, 1923.

———, "Ueber die Volkslitteratur der Juden," *Archiv für Litteraturgeschichte,* II (1871), 1-21.

The Standard Dictionary of Folklore, Mythology and Legend. Edited by Marcia Leach. 2 vols. New York: Funk and Wagnalls, 1949-50.

Trachtenberg, Joshua, *Jewish Magic and Superstition. A Study in Folk Religion.* New York: Behrman, 1939.

Tsinberg (Zinberg), Israel, *Di geshikhte fun der literatur bay yidn* (A history of Jewish literature). Vol. V-VI. Vilna: Tomor, 1935. Cf. *idem, Toledot Safrut Yisra'el.* Vol. IV. Tel-Aviv: Sifriat Po'alim, 1958.

Volkskundliche Bibliographie. Edited by Edward Hoffman-Krayer and Paul Geiger. Strassburg-Berlin-Leipzig, 1917-41. (Vol. no. not indicated. Years 1917-33 were checked; later vols. not available.)

Wachstein, Bernhard, *Katalog der Salo Cohn'schen Schenkungen* (Bibliothek der Israelitischen Kultusgemeinde Wien). Vienna: Gilhofer-Ranschburg, 1911.

Waxman, Meyer, *A History of Jewish Literature, from the Close of the Bible to Our Own Day.* rev. edit. Vol. II. New York: 1960, T. Yoseloff. (See chaps. iv, xii, and "Additions" to chap. iv.)

Weinreich, Uriel and Beatrice, *Yiddish Language and Folklore: A Selective Bibliography for Research.* The Hague: Mouton, 1959.

Wiener, Leo, *History of Yiddish Literature.* New York: Scribner's Sons, 1899. (See pp. 25-52.)

Zedner, Joseph, *Catalogue of the Hebrew Books in the Library of the British Museum.* London-Berlin, 1867.

Zeitschrift für die Geschichte der Juden in Deutschland, O. S. Edited by Ludwig Geiger. 5 vols. Braunschweig, 1886-92.

Zeitschrift für die Geschichte der Juden in Deutschland, N. S. Edited by Ismar Elbogen, Aron Freiman, Max Freudenthal. 7 vols. Berlin, 1929-37.

Zeitschrift für hebraeische Bibliographie. Edited by Heinrich Brody and Aron Freimann. 20 vols. Frankfort, 1896-1920. (*ZHB* was the sequel to *HB.*)

Zimmels, Hirsch Jacob, *Magicians, Theologians and Doctors. Studies in Folk-Medicine and Folk-Lore as Reflected in the Rabbinical Responsa (12th-19th Centuries).* London: Goldston, 1952.

Zunz, Leopold, *Zur Geschichte und Literatur.* Vol. I. Berlin: Veit, 1845. (No further volumes published.)

SECTION 2

Actum Homburg . . . 1771 (Documents). Microfilm, Archives of the YIVO Institute for Jewish Research, New York City.

Minhagim de-Ḳ. Ḳ. Worms (Customs of the community of Worms), by Yuspa Shammash (d. 1678). Microfilm, MS OPP. 751, Oxford, Bodleian. This source cited in:

Section 3

(a) Güdemann, *Quellenschriften,* p. 218, n. 1: Neubauer, *Oxford Catal.,* No. 909, fol. 79 f. (Note: Neubauer, *Catalogue of Hebrew Manuscripts,* No. 909, p. 196: *Minhagim of Worms,* 107 ff., no title.)

(b) Tsinberg, *Gesh. fun der lit.,* V, 89, n. 8, cit., who refers to Güdemann and Epstein, *Minhagim de-Ḳ. Ḳ. Worms* (Customs of Worms).

(c) Assaf, *Meḳorot,* I, 117-19, select. from *Minhagim Worms* in Güdemann and Epstein.

Pinḳas fun ha-Kneset 'Orḥim in Nordstett (Minute Book of the Society to Befriend Strangers, April, 1801). Microfilm, Archives of the YIVO Institute for Jewish Research, New York City.

Pinḳas Fürth, 1785 (Minute Book of the congregation; recorded by various individuals). Microfilm, Archives of the YIVO Institute for Jewish Research, New York City.

Pinḳas Ẓavva'ot (Copies of Wills), Fürth VII, 1787-1819. Hebrew Union College-Jewish Institute of Religion Library, Cincinnati, Ohio.

Toḳef me-ha-Ḥebrah Kaddisha' de-Biḳur Ḥolim she-Nityased bi-Shenat Tas"a. . . . (The *Ḥebrah Ḳaddisha'* of Altona, 1701). Microfilm, Archives of the YIVO Institute for Jewish Research, New York City.

Note: MSS appended to secondary sources are not listed separately but will be cited as used.

SECTION 3

Abraham b. Nathan (Ibn ha-Yarḥi; 12th cent., France and Spain), *Sefer ha-Manhig* (Collected *responsa* with material on European customs and observances). Berlin, 1899.

Abrahams, Israel (ed.), *Hebrew Ethical Wills* (Hebrew text and English trans.). Vol. II. Philadelphia: Jewish Publication Society, 1926.

Abravanel (Abrabanel), Isaac (d. 1509, Naples), *Naḥalat 'Abot* (commentary on *Pirḳe 'Abot*). Constantinople, 1505.

Abudarham, David b. Joseph (ca. 1340, Seville), *Sefer Abudarham* (A guide to liturgy and ritual). Lemberg, 1857.

Alexander Suslin ha-Kohen (d. 1349, Frankfort), *Sefer ha-'Aguddah* (Collection of legal decisions based on the Talmud). Facsimile of Cracow edit., 1571. New York: Noble [n. d.].

Altshuler (Altschuler, Altschul) Moses ben Ḥanokh (Moses Ḥanokh, Moses Ḥanokhs; Prague, d. 1633), *Brandshpigl* (A popular religio-ethical guide, directed especially to women). Frankfort, 1676. (Cf. Tsinberg, *Gesh. fun lit.,* VI, 179-80; Minkoff in *Jewish People,* III, 160. Note the influence of *Brandshpigl* on *Simḥat ha-Nefesh;* like *Brandshpigl, Simḥat ha-Nefesh* has an optimistic outlook.)

Asher b. Yeḥi'el (Rash; d. 1328, Toledo), *'Orḥot Ḥayyim* (A guide for daily conduct). Edited by Yom Tob Lippman Heller. Metz, 1767.

Ashkenazi, David Tevle (d. 1734, Moravia), *Sefer bet David* (A Talmudic discourse with folk-medicine remedies). Wilhelmsdorf, 1734.

Ashkenazi, Gershon (d. 1693, Metz), *'Abodat ha-Gershuni* (Responsa). Lemberg, 1861.

Ashkenazi, Ẓebi Hirsh (d. 1718, Altona; father of Jacob Emden), *Ḥakham Ẓebi* (Responsa). Vol. I. Amsterdam, 1712.

A Treatise on the Canon of Medicine of Avicenna, Incorporating a Translation of the First Book. Edited by O. Cameron Gruner. London: Luzac, 1930.

Bacharach, Ya'ir Ḥayyim (Jair Chajim; d. 1702, Worms), *Ḥavvot Ya'ir* (Responsa). Frankfort, 1699. (Cf. Assaf, *Meḳorot,* I, 128, #58.)

Bass, Sabbatai (d. 1718, Prague), *Sifte Yeshenim lifne Na'arim u-Zeḳenim* (Bibliographical Manual). Vol. I (2 vols. in one). Amsterdam, 1680. (Cf. Erik, *Gesh. fun yid. lit.,* p. 233.)

Berechiah, Aaron (d. 1639, Modena), *Ma'abar Yabboḳ*. (Discourses on illness and death, with prayers for the sick and burial customs). Mantua, 1626. (Cf. Gen. 32:23 for the origin of the title.)

Breslau, 'Aryeh Löb (Leyb) b. Ḥayyim, *Pene 'Aryeh* (Responsa). Amsterdam, 1790. (b. 1741, Breslau; d. 1809, Rotterdam. A noted Talmudic authority who lived in Berlin and Emden.)

Coblenz, Jacob Meir (d. ca. mid. 18th cent., Offenbach), *Mafteaḥ ha-Yam* (Popularized *Shulḥan 'Arukh,* with folk-medicine remedies). Offenbach, 1788.

Cohen (ha-Kohen), Naphtali (d. 1718), *Semikhat Ḥakhamim* (A cabalistic, ethical discourse). Reprint of Frankfort edit., 1704. New York, 1945.

———, *Sefer Ẓavva'ah* (Ethical Will), Amsterdam [n. d.].

———, *Sha'ar Naftali* (Prayer Book). Brunn, 1757.

(Naphtali Cohen came to Frankfort in 1704. The Frankfort fire started in his home, January 15, 1711. Cf. Horovitz, *Frankfurt. Rabbin.,* II, 60-66; Kaufmann, *Urkund. . . . Samson Wertheimers,* pp. 67-71; Kracauer, *Judengasse in Frankfurt,* pp. 334, 338; *idem, Juden in Frankfurt,* II, 123; *J. M.,* II [chap. 6], 68, 70-71; Brann, "Landrabbinat in Schlesien," *Graetz . . . Jubelschrift,* pp. 232-33.)

Cohn (Cohen), Tobias (d. 1729; a physician in Poland and Turkey), *Ma'aseh Ṭobiyah* (A treatise on natural science and medicine). 3 Pts. in one vol. Venice, 1707-8.

Danzig, Abraham b. Yeḥiel (d. 1820, Vilna), *Ḥayye 'Adam* (A popular rendition of the *Shulḥan 'Arukh,* with later laws and customs). Published with *Tosafot Ḥayyim.* Warsaw, 1893. (Danzig studied in Prague and Vilna; Ezekiel Landau of Prague was his teacher. He showed the influences of both German and East European Jewish cultural life. Cf. Bernstein in *Argentin. IWO Shrift.,* VI, 123-24.)

Section 3

Dubnow, Simon (ed.), *Pinḳas ha-Medinah 'o Pinḳas Va'ad ha-Ḳehillot ha-Ro'shiyot be-Medinat Lita'* (A collection of communal minute books; the legislation of the main communities of Lithuania, 1623-1761). Berlin: "Ajanoth," 1925.

Edelstein, Jacob Eliezer (ed.), *Ẓavva'ot ve-gam Dibre Ḳedoshim* (A collection of Ethical Wills, which include the testaments of Sheftel [Sabbatai] Horowitz and Naphtali Cohen). Warsaw, 1878.

Eibeschütz, Jonathan (d. 1799, Altona), *Ya'arot Debash* (A collection of homilies delivered in Metz). 2 vols. Sulzbach, 1799.

Eliasberg, Judah, *Marpe' le-'Am* (A "handbook" of medicine). 2 vols. Vilna-Grodno, 1834-42.

Eisenmenger, Johann Andreas, *Entdecktes Judenthum.* 2 vols. Königsberg, Prussia, 1711.

———, *The Traditions of the Jews.* Vol. I. Trans. by Johann Peter Stehelin. London: G. Smith, 1742.

Eisenstadt, Meir b. Isaac (d. 1744; Eisenstadt, Hungary), *Panim Me'irot* (Responsa). 4 vols. in one. Lemberg, 1899. (Eisenstadt was the teacher of Jonathan Eibeschütz, in Prossnitz, Moravia.)

'Eleh Dibre ha-Berit (Legal opinions of Hamburg rabbis in opposition to religious reforms). Altona, 1811.

Eliezer b. Yehudah (Jehudah) of Worms (d. 1238), *Sefer ha-Roḳeaḥ* (A cabalistic treatise on the *Shulḥan 'Arukh).* Warsaw, 1880.

Elijah b. Solomon Abraham (d. 1729, Smyrna), *Shebeṭ Musar* (A popular ethical treatise). Fürth, 1781.

Emden, Jacob (d. 1776, Altona), *Yaẓẓib Pitgam* (Eulogy for his father, Zebi Ashkenazi); *Megillat Sefer* (Autobiography). Both works in one vol. Kolomea, Galicia, 1886.

———, *Leḥem Shamayim: 'Al Seder Zera'im-Mo'ed* (A commentary on *M. Zera'im.*) Jerusalem, 1958.

———, *Megillat Sefer.* Edited by David Kahana. Warsaw, 1897.

———, *Migdal 'Oz* (A liturgical guide with ethical discourses). Zhitomir, 1873.

———, *She'elat Ya'abeẓ* (Responsa). Vol. I. Altona, 1739.

———, *She'elat Ya'abeẓ* (Responsa). 2 vols. in one. Lemberg, 1884.

Ephraim ha-Kohen (d. 1678, Ofen, Hungary), *Sha'ar 'Efrayim* (Responsa). Sulzbach, 1688.

Epstein, Abraham, and Jacob Freimann (eds.), *Sefer Ma'aseh ha-Ge'onim* (*Responsa* of early medieval period, for Speyer, Worms, and Mainz). (Publication of *Mekiẓe Nirdamim,* vol. III, No. 2.) Berlin, 1909.

Epstein, Yeḥiel Mikhel, *Ḳiẓur Shene Luḥot ha-Berit* (A popular guide for conduct; supplement to the *Shelah*). Dyhernfurth, 1770. (Cf. Steinschneider, *Safrut Yisra'el,* p. 366; *idem, Jewish Literature,* p. 230, that Epstein wrote this work in Prossnitz, Moravia, 1683. Cf. Noble, "Yehiel Mikhel Epstein," *Yivo Annual*

Jewish Social Science, VI [1951], 317, that it is not possible to confirm where Epstein lived; he cites "customs current in . . . Moravia, Frankfurt-am-Main, Fürth and other places.")

———, *Derekh ha-Yashar le-'Olam ha-Ba'* (Laws, ritual, and customs in Yiddish). Vilna, 1874.

———, *Seder Tefillah Derekh Yesharah* (Liturgy of daily prayers, with a summary of laws and customs in Yiddish). Offenbach, 1791 (?). Also, Fürth, 1768.

Gans (Ganz), David (d. 1613, Prague), *Ẓemaḥ David* (A historical chronicle). Frankfort, 1692.

Gaster, Moses (ed.), *Exempla of the Rabbis*. 2 Pts., with Hebrew text and English translation. (Oriental series, ed. Bruno Schindler.) Leipzig-London: Asia Publishing Co., 1924.

———, *Ma'aseh Book* (Yiddish household folktales of the Middle Ages translated into English). 2 vols. Philadelphia: Jewish Publication Society, 1934.

Gerondi, Jonah (d. 1263, Gerona), *Sefer ha-Yir'ah* (An ethical discourse). Published with *Ḳab ha-Yashar*. Lemberg, 1862.

Geyer, Rudolf, and Leopold Sailer, *Urkunden aus Wiener Grundbüchern zur Geschichte der Wiener Juden im Mittelalter*. Vienna, 1931.

Glikl of Hameln:

Abrahams, Beth-Zion (ed.), *The Life of Glückel of Hameln, 1646-1724*. Written by Herself (English trans.). New York: Yoseloff, 1963.

Feilchenfeld, Alfred (ed.), *Denkwürdigkeiten der Glückel von Hameln* (German trans.). Berlin: Jüdischer Verlag, 1923.

Kaufmann, David (ed.), *Zikhronos Moras (M''rs) Glikl Hamil* [*fun Hamil*]; *mi-shenas t''z 'ad t''eṭ* [*1647–1719*]. (The memoirs of Glikl in Yiddish). Frankfort: Kaufmann, 1896.

Lowenthal, Marvin (ed.), *The Memoirs of Glückel of Hameln* (English trans.). New York-London: Harper, 1932.

Rabinowitz, A. S. (ed.), *Zikhronot Glikl* (Hebrew trans.). Tel-Aviv: Dvir, 1929.

Götz, Elyakim b. Meir (d. 18th cent., Posen), *'Eben ha-Shoham u-Me'irat 'Enayim* (Responsa). Vol. I. Dyhernfurth, 1733.

Gumpiel, Israel, and Dov Jacob, *Minhag Ḳ. Ḳ. Fürth* (The customs of the community of Fürth). Fürth, 1767.

Hahn, Joseph Yuspa (Juzpa) (d. 1637, Frankfort), *Yosif 'Omeẓ* (A collection of the customs of Frankfort). Frankfort, 1723.

———, *Yosif 'Omeẓ*. Frankfort: Hermon, 1928. (Cf. Brisch, *Juden in Cöln*, II, 112, 115: At the time of the Thirty Years' War, Joseph Hahn was living in Bonn, where his father-in-law, Abraham Breitingen, was a *shtadlan*, an intermediary with civil authorities in behalf of the Jewish community. Cf. Brisch, II, 112; Marcus, *Communal Sick-Care*, p. 228, n. 227, that *Y. 'O.* "incorporated the ritual tradition of Frankfort." For the life and work of Joseph Hahn, see also Saul Esh in *'Ḳobeẓ' in Memory of Eliezer Shamir*, pp. 155-58.)

Halpern (Halperin), Israel (ed.), *Pinkas Va'ad 'Arba' 'Arazot, 1580-1764* (Minutes of the Council of Four Lands in Poland). Jerusalem: Mosad Bialik, 1945.

———, *Takkanot Medinat Mähren, 1650-1748* (Communal legislation of Moravia). Jerusalem: Merkhaz (Meḳiẓe Nirdamim with Mosad Harav Kook), 1952.

Ḥayyim 'Aryeh Leyb (Löb) b. Yosef ([n. d.], Jedwabno, Poland), *Sha'ar Bat Rabbim* (Commentary on the Bible). Vol. II, Exodus. Warsaw, 1903.

Heilprin, Joel, *Mif'alot 'Eloḳim* (A folk-medicine book containing the cabalistic writings of Naphtali Cohen when he was in Posen, 1690-1704.) Lwów, 1805.

Heilprin, Elijah and Joel, *Toledot 'Adam* (A cabalistic folk-medicine treatise). Wilhelmsdorf, 1734. (A Polish Ḥasidic rabbi, Joel Heilprin was known as the *Ba'al Shem* in his community; d. ca. mid. 17th cent., Ostrog.)

Higger, Michael (ed.), *Masekhet Semaḥot* (Minor Talmudic treatises). New York: Bloch, 1931.

Hohberg, W. H. (d. 1688), *Georgica Curiosa Aucta; Adelichen Land- und Feld-Lebens*. 3 vols. Nuremberg: Martin Endters, 1716-49. (See *Koch-Buch* in vol. iii).

Horowitz, Abraham Sheftel, *Yesh Noḥalin* (An Ethical Will; published with the Ethical Will of his grandson, Sheftel). Amsterdam, 1701.

———, *'Emeḳ Berakhah* (A popular guide to prayers and observances, with prefatory comments by his son Isaiah, the author of *Shelah*). Amsterdam, 1729.

Horowitz, Isaiah b. Abraham (d. 1628), *Shene Luḥot ha-Berit* (Intended as an Ethical Will, a popular cabalistic, legal, moral writing, containing folk views and practices). 2 vols. Facsimile of Amsterdam edit., 1698. New York: Goldwarm, 1946. (For the cultural influence of *Shelah,* cf. Güdemann, *Quellen.,* pp. 104, 106; L. Löwenstein, "Zur Gesch. der Juden in Fürth," *JJLG,* VI (1908), 154, 215; Tsinberg, *Gesh. fun der lit.,* VI, 139, 141-43, 181, 186. Isaiah Horowitz served as chief rabbi of Frankfort and Prague. Cf. also the account of Isaiah Horowitz in B. Z. Katz, *Rabbanut,* I, 48-52.)

Horovitz, Markus (ed.), *Die Inschriften des alten Friedhofs der israelitischen Gemeinde zu Frankfurt a. M.* Frankfort: Kauffmann, 1901.

———, Mordecai Halevi (Markus) (ed.), *Sefer 'Abne Zikkaron, ha-Ketab ve-ha-Mikhtab mi-Bet ha-Ḳebarot ha-Yashan de-Ḳ. Ḳ. Frankfurt a. M.: Die Inschriften des alten Friedhofs der israelitischen Gemeinde zu Frankfurt a. M.* Frankfort: Kauffmann, 1901.

Horowitz, Sabbatai (Sheftel; d. 1660, Vienna), *Vave ha-'Amudim* (An ethical discourse). Published with *Shelah,* Vol. II. (Sabbatai Horowitz also served as rabbi in Fürth. Cf. Löwenstein in *JJLG,* VI, 215, Supplement.)

Isaac b. Eliakim of Posen (16th cent.), *Sefer Leb Tob* (A popular code and ethical guide in Yiddish). Amsterdam, 1723.

Isserlein, Israel (d. 1460, Neustadt), *Terumat ha-Deshen* (Responsa on laws and customs). Sudilkov, 1835.

Isserlein, Israel, *Leḳeṭ Yosher* (Includes customs, legal decisions, and responsa.) Facsimile of Berlin edit., by Jacob Freimann, 1903–1904. 2 vols. in one. Jerusalem, 1964.

Jaffe, Mordecai (b. Prague, ca. 1530; d. Posen, 1612). *Lebush ha-Tekhelet: 'Oraḥ Ḥayyim.* Vol. I. Prague, 1646. *Lebush 'Aṭeret Zahab: Yoreh De'ah.* Vol. III. Berdiczew, 1819. (The *Lebush* is a legal and ritual code in the order of the *Ṭurim* and the *Shulḥan 'Arukh.)*

Joseph b. Moses of Münster (15th century), *Leḳeṭ Yosher,* based on the collection of laws and customs in *Terumat ha-Deshen,* by Israel Isserlein. Edited by Jacob Freimann. 2 vols. Berlin: Itzkavsky, 1903-1904. (Vol. I was consulted.)

Joshua Hoeschel b. Joseph (d. 1648, Cracow), *Pene Yehoshua'* (Responsa). Vol. I. Amsterdam, 1715. Vol. II. Lemberg, 1800.

Judah b. Enoch (d. ca. begin. 18th cent.; Pfersee, loc.: near Augsburg), *Ḥinnukh bet Yehudah* (Responsa). Frankfort, 1708.

Judah Löw b. Bezalel (the Maharal of Prague, chief rabbi; d. 1609), *Neẓaḥ Yisra'el* (Homilies). Warsaw, 1889.

Judah he-Ḥasid (d. 1217, Regensburg), *Sefer Ḥasidim* (a mystical, ethical writing of wide influence portraying folk beliefs). Basel, 1581.

———, *Sefer Ḥasidim.* Edited by Jehuda Wistinetzki. (Mekiẓe Nirdamim Publication, vol. vii.) Berlin, 1891-92.

———. Edited by Reuben Margulies. Jerusalem: Mosad Harav Kook, 1957.

Kaidanover, Aaron Samuel (d. 1676, Cracow), *'Emunat Shemu'el* (Responsa). Lemberg, 1884. (The father of Ẓebi Hirsh, he served as rabbi in several communities, including Nikolsburg, Fürth, Frankfort.)

Kaidanover, Ẓebi Hirsh (d. 1712, Frankfort), *Ḳab ha-Yashar* (A popular cabalistic, ethical work, with folk attitudes and practices). Vilna: Rom (Romm), 1925. (In contrast with *Simḥat ha-Nefesh, Ḳab ha-Yashar* is gloomy, pessimistic, and fearful of demons. Cf. *S. H.,* II [ed. Shatzky], Intro., p. 40; Waxman, *Jewish Lit.,* II (rev. edit.), 647-48; Tsinberg, *Der lit.,* V, 190; Minkoff in *Jewish People,* III, 162.)

Karo, Joseph, *Shulḥan 'Arukh: Yoreh De'ah* (Code of law covering the standards for ritual cleanliness), with the commentary of Shak ("Sifte Kohen"). Vienna: Menorah, 1926. (Shabbetai Kohen [1621-62], a famous legalist of Vilna, settled in Holeschau, Moravia, following the Chmielnicki pogrom. He was the author of "Sifte Kohen," a commentary on *Yoreh De'ah.* Cf. Azulai, *Shem ha-Gedolim,* I, 160, n. 10; B. Friedberg, "Shabbethai b. Meir Ha-Kohen [SHaK]," *JE,* XI [1905], 217-18.)

Katzenellenbogen, Ezekiel (d. 1749, Altona), *Keneset Yeḥezḳe'l* (Responsa). Altona, 1730.

———, *Sefer Mayim Yeḥezḳe'l* (Homilies). Poritzk, 1786.

———, *Ẓavva'ah* (Ethical Will). Vilna, 1871.

Kirchan (Kirchhan), 'Elḥanan Haenle, *Simḥat ha-Nefesh,* I (A popular folk work that served as a daily guide). Sulzbach, 1798. (Kirchan lived at the end of the 17th cent.; born in Kirchan, near Marburg, his work had bearing on small towns in the Frankfort area. Cf. *S. H.*, II, [ed. Shatzky], Intro., 16-30; Karpeles, *Gesch. jüd. Lit.*, II, 1017: "His [Kirchan's] book was a true household friend to Jewish families"; Erik, p. 307: "Therefore, the cultural value of the book is great in that it portrays many significant aspects of life in the small, isolated German communities. A series of noteworthy observations about customs are scattered throughout the book." Cf. also Steinschneider, *Safrut Yisra'el,* p. 358.)

Kirchner, Paul Christian, *Jüdisches Ceremoniel, das ist: Allerhand Jüdische Gebräuche*. Frankfort, 1720. (Published with Johannes Meelführer, *Synopsis Institutionum Hebraicarum.)* (Kirchner was a convert to Christianity.)

Kohen, Benjamin Benisch (Benash, Benush) b. Judah Löb (Leyb), "the *Ba'al Shem Tob* of Krotoszyn" (Krotoschin, Prussia; d. begin. 18th cent.), *'Amtaḥat Binyamin* ("Benjamin's Bag," a handbook consisting of a collection of folk remedies based on cabalistic sources). Wilhelmsdorf, 1716. (Cf. account of "Benjamin Benash," by Philip Block, *JE,* II [1902], 685.)

Kol Bo (An "all-inclusive" collection of laws, customs, and daily practices). Venice, 1547.

Kosman (Kossmann), Joseph b. Moses (d. 1758), *Noheg ka-Ẓo'n Yosef* (A book of *Minhagim;* special customs and ritual observances of Frankfort). Hanau, 1718. (Kosman was the grandson of Joseph Hahn: cf. Horovitz, *Frankfurt. Rabbin.,* II, 75, n. 3. Cf. Samuel, *Juden in Essen,* p. 48, for Kosman's family background and his rabbinical position in Deutz.)

Krochmal, Menaḥem Mendel b. Abraham (d. 1661, Nikolsburg), *Ẓemaḥ Ẓedeḳ* (Responsa). Fürth, 1766. (He was the teacher of Gershon Ashkenazi.)

Landau, Alfred, and Bernhard Wachstein (eds.), *Jüdische Privatbriefe aus dem Jahre 1619.* Vienna-Leipzig: Braumüller, 1909. (Historische Komission der Israelitischen Kultusgemeinde in Wien. Quellen und Forschungen zur Geschichte der Juden in Deutsch-Österreich, vol. iii.) (Note: this source comprises 46 letters, mainly written in Yiddish, that were sent from families in Prague to Vienna.)

Landau, Ezekiel (d. 1793, Prague), *'Ahabat Ẓiyon* (Homilies). Published with *Doresh le-Ẓiyon,* I (Talmudic discourse). Prague, 1827.

———, *Derushe ha-Ẓelaḥ* (Homilies). Warsaw, 1886.

———, *Derush Hesped* (Eulogy for Maria Theresa). Prague, 1781.

———, *Noda' bi-Yehudah* (Responsa; considered "a classic" of the period). Vol. I. Berdiczew, 1812.

———, *Noda' bi-Yehudah.* 2 vols. Facsimile of Prague edit., 1811. New York: M. P. Press, 1958.

Landsofer, Jonah (d. 1712, Prague), *Kanfe Yonah* (Novellae on legal codes). Prague, 1812.

Landsofer, Jonah, *Me'il Ẓedaḳah* (Responsa). Prague, 1757.

Lefin (Levin), Menahem Mendel, *Refu'ot ha-'Am* (Medical handbook, a translation of the work of Andre David Tissot of Switzerland). Żólkiew, 1794. (Lefin [1741-1819] was a Polish scholar.)

Lentshits, Solomon (d. 1618, Prague; a famous preacher), *'Olelot 'Efrayim* (Homilies). Amsterdam, 1710.

———, *'Amude Shesh* (Homilies). Amsterdam, 1772.

Lieberman (Liebermann), Eliezer, *'Or Nogah* (Responsa). 2 vols. in one. Published with *Nogah ha-Ẓedeḳ* (Responsa). Dessau, 1818. (Eliezer Lieberman was the son of Yuspa Shammash: cf. Erik, p. 51; Minkoff in *Jewish People,* III, 158.)

Lipschütz, Schabsza (Sabbatai), *Segullot Yisra'el* (A collection of folk remedies). Munkacs, 1905.

Me'ir (b. Barukh) of Rothenburg (Maharam; d. 1293), *She'elot u-Teshubot* (Responsa). Lwów, 1860.

Me'ir of Rothenburg (Maharam), *Teshubot, Posḳim, u-Minhagim: Responsa, Rulings, and Customs.* Vol. I. Edited by I. Z. Cahana. Mosad Harav Kook: Jerusalem, 1957.

Minhagim (A book of customs with illustrated pictures, consisting of the practices followed in various countries, including "Germany, Poland, Moravia, Italy"). Amsterdam, 1723.

Minz, Moses (German rabbi, 15th cent.), *Maharam Minz* (Responsa). Published with *Besamim Ro'sh.* Cracow, 1881. (Minz was rabbi in Mainz, Landau, Bamberg; a contemporary of Isserlein.)

Molin (Mölln), Jacob Levi (d. 1427, Worms), *Sefer Maharil* (*Minhagim* observed in Ashkenazic communities; especially relevant to western Germany). Sabionetta, 1556.

———, *Sefer Maharil.* Warsaw, 1874.

———, *She'elot u-Teshubot* (Responsa). Cracow, 1881.

Moses Isaac ha-Levi ([n. d.], Złótowó), *Ẓavva'ot* (Ethical Will). Published with *Naḥalat 'Abot* (*Memor*-book honoring Raphael J. Karger). Frankfort, 1898.

Oppenheim, David (d. 1736, Prague), *Hanhagot 'Adam* (A guidebook for daily behavior). [n. p.], 1837. (Cf. title page: Oppenheim served as the *'Ab Bet-Din* of Nikolsburg, Moravia, and Prague. Also, Wolf, *Mähren Statuten,* Pref., vii, cit.; p. 119, #2-3, that he served as *Landesrabbiner.* Cf. Eisek Metz, *Kehillat David, Collectio Davidis* [Hamburg, 1826], for a catalogue of the books in his famous library. An account of the library is to be found in Graetz, *Gesch.,* X, 319; Wolf, *op. cit.,* Pref., vii; C. Duschinsky, "Rabbi David Oppenheim," *JQR,* XX [1930] [who calls Oppenheim "the first great collector of a Hebrew library"]; Marx, *Studies in Jewish Hist. and Booklore,* pp. 238 ff.)

'Orḥot Ẓaddiḳim (Ethical work, 15th cent., Germany). Author Anonymous, Prague, 1581.

Picart, Bernard (1673-1733, illustrator), *Cérémonies et coutumes religieuses de tous les peuples du monde*. [n. p.], 1807-10.

———, *The Ceremonies and Religious Customs of the Various Nations of the Known World, with Historical Annotations, and Curious Discourses*. [n. p.], 1733-37.

Plungian, Zechariah (d. 1715, Zamość), *Sefer Zekhirah* (A cabalistic folklore work counseling the individual how to conduct himself). Wilhelmsdorf, 1729.

Poppers, Meir (b. Prague; d. 1662, Jerusalem), *Sefer Musar* (An ethical guide based on Lurianic Cabala). Appended to his *'Or Ẓaddiḳim ve-Derekh Se'udah*. Warsaw, 1889.

Pribram, Alfred F. (ed.), *Urkunden und Akten zur Geschichte der Juden in Wien. 1526-1847 (1849)*. 2 vols. Vienna-Leipzig: Braumüller, 1918. (Historische Kommission der Israelitischen Kultusgemeinde in Wien, viii.)

Rabbenu Moshe b. Maimon, *Same ha-Mavet ve-ha-Refu'ot Kenegdam:* Maimonides, *Poisons and their Antidotes*. Edited by Suessman Muntner. Jerusalem: Rubin Mass, 1942. (Maimonides, *Medical Works,* ed. Suessman Muntner, vol. ii.)

———, *Sefer ha-Kaẓẓeret:* Maimonides, *The Book on Asthma*. Edited by Suessman Muntner. Jerusalem: Rubin Mass, 1940. (Maimonides, Medical Works, ed. Suessman Muntner, vol. i.)

Rabbenu Gershom (Me'or ha-Golah), *Teshubot* (Responsa). Edited by Shlomo Eidelberg. Yeshiva University: New York, 1955.

Rabbi Shabetai [Shabbetai] Donnolo, *Kitbe ha-Refu'ah, ha-Ri'shonim she-Nikhtabu be-'Ivrit be-'Eropah: Medical Works, on the Occasion of the Millenium of the Earliest Hebrew Book in Christian Europe*. Edited by Suessman Muntner. 2 vols. in one. Jerusalem: Mosad Harav Kook, 1949. (See vol. i.)

Reifmann, Jacob, *Mishloaḥ Manot* (A handbook for *Purim* that includes explanations, sources, *piyutim,* and selected readings). Prague, 1860.

Reischer, Ephraim [n. d.], *Sha'ar 'Efrayim* (Homiletical, ethical discourses, with material on folk medicine). Fürth, 1728. (The subject of folk medicine has not been included in the text.) ...

Reischer, Jacob (d. 1733, Prague), *Shebut Ya'aḳob* (Responsa). 3 vols. in one. Lemberg, 1897.

Responsa Card Catalogue, Jewish Division, New York Public Library.

Salfeld, Siegmund (ed.), *Das Martyrologium Nürnberger Memorbuches*. Berlin: L. Simon, 1898. (Quellen zur Geschichte der Juden in Deutschland. Published by the Historische Commission für Geschichte der Juden in Deutschland, vol. iii.)

Samuel b. David Moses ha-Levi of Meseritz (d. 1681, Kleinsteinach, Bavaria), *Naḥalat Shib'ah* (Responsa). Vol. I. Amsterdam, 1667. Vol. II. Fürth, 1692. (Before coming to Bavaria, he was a rabbi in Halberstadt and Bamberg [1660-65].)

Schuck, Salamon, *Taḳḳanot u-Tefillot . . . Die kirchlichen und bügerlichen Gesetze des Judenthums . . . bis 5631 (1870).* Munkacs, 1890.

Schudt, Johann Jacob, *Jüdische Merckwürdigkeiten.* 4 vols. in two. Frankfort-Leipzig, 1714-17. (While a primary source for the social life of German Jews in the 18th century, Schudt must be read critically because of his religious bias.)

Seder ha–Tiḳḳun (Readings for *Hosha'ana' Rabbah).* Edited by Judah Leon Templo. Amsterdam, 1727.

Sefer Derekh Ṭobim, containing the Ethical Wills of Jonah Landsofer and Moses Ḥasid (d. 18th cent., Prague). Frankfort, 1717.

Sefer Minhagim (A book of customs). Offenbach, [n. d.]. Probably published at the end of the 18th cent., according to Isaac Rivkind.

Sefer Refu'ot (A book of remedies, including drugs). Edited by David Solomon Eibenschütz (d. 1812, Russian rabbi), based on MS *'Eben Yeḳarah.* Appended to *Ẓavva'ot ve-gam Dibre Ḳedoshim.* Lemberg, 1884. Also edited by Joseph Freedman. Galicia: Kolomea, 1881.

Sefer Refu'ot ha-Nefesh (Selections from *Shelah,* to be used when a person is ill or on his deathbed). Author anonymous. Altona, 1765.

Simḥah of Vitry, *Maḥzor Vitry* (Liturgy; ritual and customs of the early medieval period, based on a MS in the British Museum). Edited by S. Hurwitz. Nuremberg: J. Bulka, 1923.

Sirkes, Joel ben Samuel (d. 1640, Cracow), *Bet Ḥadash* (Responsa). Frankfort, 1697.

Slonik, Benjamin Aaron (ben Abraham) (d. ca. 1619, Poland), *Mas'at Binyamin* (Responsa). Vilna, 1894.

Sofer (Schreiber), Moses (b. 1763, Frankfort; d. 1839, Pressburg), *Ḥatam Sofer: 'Oraḥ Ḥayyim,* Pressburg, 1855; *'Eben ha-'Ezer,* Pressburg, 1865; *Yoreh De'ah* Vienna (printed in Pressburg), 1871.

———, *'Or Pene Mosheh* (Commentary on the Pentateuch and the Five Megillot). Lemberg, 1851.

Steinhardt, Joseph (Joseph of Steinhardt; d. 1776, Fürth), *Zikhron Yosef* (Responsa). Fürth, 1773.

Taḳḳanot Ḥebrat Baḥurim de-Ḳ. Ḳ. Eisenstadt (The Constitution of the Society of Young Men in the community of Eisenstadt). Halberstadt, 1867.

Täubler, Eugen, and Jacob Jacobson (eds.), *Mitteilungen des Gesamtarchivs der deutschen Juden.* 5 vols. Leipzig: G. Fock, 1909-15.

Thiemen, Johann Christoph, *Haus- Feld- Artzney- Koch- Kunst- und Wunder-Buch.* Nuremberg: John Hofmann, 1694.

Tiḳḳun Lel Shabu'ot (Selections for reading during the night of *Shabu'ot*). Sulzbach, 1827.

Tyrnau, Isaac, (d. ca. 1460, Hungary) *Minhagim shel kol ha-Medinot* (Ashkenazic customs of different lands). Amsterdam, 1708. (Tyrnau was a fellow-student of Molin. His *Minhagim* was translated into Yiddish by Simon L. Ginzburg.)

Wachstein, Dober (Bernhard) (ed.), *Die Grabschriften des alten Judenfriedhofes in Eisenstadt.* Vienna: R. Löwit, 1922. (Eisenstädter Forschungen, ed. Sandor Wolf, vol. i.)

———, Bernhard (ed.), *Die Inschriften des alten Judenfriedhofes in Wien (1540-1670).* 2 vols. Vienna-Leipzig: Braumüller, 1912-17. (Historische Kommission der Israelitischen Kultusgemeinde in Wien, vol. iv.)

———, *Urkunden und Akten zur Geschichte der Juden in Eisenstadt und den Siebengemeinden.* Vienna: Braumüller, 1926. (Eisenstädter Forschungen, ed. Sandor Wolf.)

Wallich, Abraham (d. 1699, Frankfort), *Sefer Dimyon ha-Refu'ot: Harmonia Wallichia Medica* (Medical book with a moral emphasis). Frankfort, 1700. (In 1657, Wallich settled in Frankfort as a physician.)

Weil, Jacob (d. ca. 1450, Erfurt), *She'elot u-Teshubot* (Responsa). Hanau, 1610. (He was a pupil of the "Maharil.")

Weiss, Isaac, *'Abne Bet ha-Yoẓer* (A history of scholars and rabbis of Pressburg, based on tombstone inscriptions). Paks, Hungary, 1900.

Wiener, Max (ed.), *Regesten zur Geschichte der Juden in Deutschland während des Mittelalters.* Vol. I. Hannover, 1862. (No further publication.)

Wolf, Benjamin Ze'eb ([n. d.], 17th cent., Bjełozierka), *Sefer Ṭaharot ha-Ḳodesh* (Customs relating to personal conduct, the home, synagogue, Sabbath, and festivals). Amsterdam, 1733.

Wolf, Gerson (ed.), *Die alten Statuten der jüdischen Gemeinden in Mähren samt den nachfolgenden Synodalbeschlüssen.* Vienna: Holder, 1880.

Würfel, Andreas (ed.), *Historische Nachricht von der Judengemeinde in dem Hofmarkt Fürth unterhalb Nürnberg. In das Teutsche übersetzt und mit Anmerkungen erläutert.* 2 Pts. Frankfort, 1754. (See Pt. 2, *Taḳḳanot.*) (b. 1718, Würfel was a pastor in Obergumbach [?] = prob. Obergrombach, No. Baden.)

Yellinek, Aaron (ed.), *Ḳunṭres Worms u-Ḳehal Wien* (*Memor*-book of Worms and Vienna, which includes the martyrs of Worms in 1696). Vienna: J. Schlossberg, 1880.

Yuspa Shammash, *Ma'aseh Nissim* (Collection of tales about miraculous workers, gleaned from *Sefer Sha'are Yerushalayim*). Edited by Eliezer Lieberman. [n. p.], 1901. (Cf. Erik, pp. 51, 57: These tales became part of the *Mayse-bukh.*)

SECTION 4A

Abrahams, Israel, "Ethical Wills," *JQR,* III (O. S., 1891), 436-81.

Adler, Salomon, "Die Entwicklung des Schulwesens der Juden zu Frankfurt am Main bis zur Emanzipation," *JJLG,* XVIII (1926), 143-73.

BIBLIOGRAPHY

Altman, Adolf, *Geschichte der Juden in Stadt und Land Salzburg von den frühesten Zeiten bis auf die Gegenwart. Nach handschriftlichen und gedruckten Quellen.* Berlin: Lamm, 1913.

Altman, Berthold, "The Autonomous Federation of Jewish Communities in Paderborn," *JSS,* III (1941), 159-88.

———, "Geschichte der Juden in Stadt und Land Salzburg," *JJLG,* XV (1923), 156-216; XVII (1925), 1-56. (See pp. 1-10.)

Aronstein, R. P., "Notes on the History of the Jews of Germany in the 17th and 18th Centuries" (Hebrew), *Tarbiẓ,* XVII (1946), 105-9.

Assaf, Simḥa, "Erziehung: II. Im Mittelalter," *EJ,* VI (1930), 147-53.

———, "Events of the Rabbinate in Germany, Poland, Lithuania" (Hebrew), *Reshumot,* II (1927), 259-300.

Auerbach, Benjamin H., *Geschichte der israelitischen Gemeinde Halberstadt.* Halberstadt: H. Meyer, 1866.

Bacher, W., "Ein Lied zu Simchath-Torah," *MGJV,* XXII (1907), 37.

Baer, Fritz, *Das Protokollbuch der Landjudenschaft des Herzogtums Kleve.* Vol. I. Berlin: Schwetschke, 1922. (Nothing further published.)

Bamberger, Herz, *Geschichte der Rabbiner der Stadt und des Bezirkes Würzburg.* Wandsbek, 1905. (Published posthumously by his brother, S. Bamberger.)

Bamberger, M. L., *Ein Blick auf die Geschichte der Juden in Würzburg.* Würzburg: J. Frank, 1905.

———, "Aus meiner Minhagimsammelmappe," *JJV,* I (1923), 320-32.

Bamberger, Salomon, *Historische Berichte über die Juden der Stadt und des ehemaligen Fürstentums Aschaffenburg.* Strassburg: Singer, 1900.

Barbeck, Hugo, *Geschichte der Juden in Nürnberg und Fürth.* Nuremberg: Heerdegen, 1878.

Baron, Salo W., *A Social and Religious History of the Jews.* rev. edit. Vols. II, V. New York: Columbia University Press, 1952, 1957.

Barzilay-Eisenstein, Isaac, "The Background of the Berlin Haskalah," in *Essays on Jewish Life and Thought . . . in honor of Salo Wittmayer Baron* (eds. Joseph L. Blau, Philip Friedman, *et al.*), pp. 183-97.

Basse, W., "Die Juden und die Spaziergänge in Frankfurt a. M. im Jahre 1769," *Zeitschrift für deutsche Kulturgeschichte,* IV (1859), 564-72. (Reprinted in *Jeschurun,* VI.)

Bato, Ludwig, *Die Juden im alten Wien.* Vienna: Phaidon, 1928.

Bauer, Moritz, "Gaya," *JE,* V (1903), 576-77.

Bender, A. P., "Beliefs, Rites, and Customs of the Jews, connected with Death, Burial, and Mourning," *JQR,* VI (O. S., 1894), 317-47, 664-71; VII (O. S., 1894-95), 101-18, 259-69.

Bergman (Bergmann), Jehuda, "Folk-Medicine" (Hebrew), *Edoth,* I (No. 4, 1946), 199-212.

Bergman (Bergmann), Jehuda, "Schebua ha-ben," *MGWJ,* LXXVI (1932), 467–70.

Berliner, Abraham (Adolph), *Aus dem inneren Leben der deutschen Juden im Mittelalter.* Berlin: Poppelhauer, 1900.

———, "Die jüdische Speisetafel," *JJGL,* XIII (1910), 201-11.

———, *Ḥayye ha-Yehudim be-'Ashkenaz bi-Yeme ha-Benayim* (Hebrew edit. of *Aus dem inneren Leben*). Warsaw: 'Aḥi'asaf, 1900.

——— (ed.), "*Memor*-book of the Community of Worms, 1698" (Hebrew), *Ḳobeẓ 'al Yad,* III (1887), 1-62.

Berman, Aaron, *Toledot ha-Ḥinnukh be-Yisra'el u-be-'Amim* (A history of Jewish and general education). Tel-Aviv: Chachik, 1945-46.

Bernstein, Mordecai, *Nisht derbrente shaytn (Unconsumed Logs).* (A series of studies of manuscripts extant in German archives after World War II.) Buenos Aires: Yiddish Scientific Institute, 1956.

———, *Takones bay yidn kegn lukses un oysbrengeray* (Jewish sumptuary legislation). Buenos Aires, 1955 (Reprint from the *Yorbukh* of the Jewish community of Buenos Aires, 1955.)

———, "The Yiddish Glossary in the Work of *Ḥayye 'Adam*" (Yiddish), *Argentin. IWO Shrift.,* VI (Buenos Aires, 1955), 123-57.

———, "Two *Retsepten-Bikher* (Folk Remedy Books) in Old Yiddish, 1474 and 1509" (Yiddish), *Davke,* XVII (Buenos Aires, 1953), 330-61.

Bettan, Israel, "The Sermons of Ephraim Luntshitz," *HUCA,* VIII-IX (1931-32), 443-80.

Black, Samuel, "Aus dem ehemaligen Kurhessen," *Menorah,* IV (Vienna, 1926), 583-90.

Blau, Ludwig, "Dreams," *JE,* IV (1903), 654-57.

———, "Magic," *JE,* VIII (1904), 255-57.

Blondheim, David S., *Les gloses françaises dans les commentaries talmudiques de Raschi.* Baltimore: Johns Hopkins University Press, 1937. (The Johns Hopkins Studies in Romance Literatures and Languages, Extra vol. xi.)

Bodenheimer, Rosy "Beitrag zur Geschichte der Juden in Oberhessen von ihrer frühesten Erwähnung bis zur Emanzipation," *ZGJD,* III (1931), 251-62; IV (1932), 11-30.

Bondy, Gottlieb, and Franz Dworský (eds.), *Zur Geschichte der Juden in Böhmen, Mähren, und Schlesien von 906 bis 1620.* 2 vols. Prague, 1906. (See vol. ii.)

Bornstein, D. J., "Bar Mizwa," *EJ,* III (1929), 1035-38.

Boos, Heinrich, *Geschichte der rheinischen Städtekultur.* Vol. III. 2d edit. Berlin: Stargardt, 1889. (See pp. 159-177, "Die Juden.")

Brann, Marcus, "Die Grabschriften der Familie Frankel-Spira in Prag," *MGWJ,* XLVI (1902), 450-73, 556-60.

———, "Etwas von der schlesischen Landgemeinde," *Festschrift . . . Jakob Guttmann* (Leipzig, 1915), pp. 225-255.

Brann, Marcus, "Geschichte des Landrabbinats in Schlesien," *Jubelschrift . . .H. Graetz* (Breslau, 1887), pp. 218–78.

———, *Geschichte der Juden in Schlesien.* 6 vols. in one. Breslau: Schatzky, 1896-1917. (Jahresbericht des Jüdisch-theologischen Seminars.) (See vols. iv-v.)

Brauer, A. (Erich), *Yehude Kurdistan. Meḥḳar 'Etnologi.* (An ethnographic study of the Jews of Kurdistan). Jerusalem, 1947. (Publication of the Institute of Folklore and Ethnology, Jerusalem, ed. Raphael Patai, vol. ii.)

———, Erich, "Birth Customs of the Jews of Kurdistan" (Hebrew), *Edoth,* I (No. 2, 1946), 65-72.

———, "Circumcision and Childhood among the Jews of Kurdistan" (Hebrew), *Edoth,* I (No. 3, 1946), 129-38.

Breuer, Mordecai, "The 'Ashkenazi Semikha'" (Hebrew), *Zion,* XXXIII (N. S., 1968), 13-46.

Brilling, Bernhard (Dob), "Der Prager 'Schammes' in Breslau," *ZGJT,* I^3 (1931), 139-59.

———, "First-Born Domestic Animals in Frankfort on the Main," *Yeda'-'Am* (Journal of the Israel Folklore Society), III (No. 1, 1955), 15-17.

Brisch, Carl, *Geschichte der Juden in Cöln und Umgebung aus ältester Zeit bis auf die Gegenwart; nach handschriftlichen und gedruckten Quellen bearbeitet.* 2 vols. in one. Mülheim: Carl Meyer, 1879–82.

Bronner, Jakob, "Die mährischen Juden im Goldschmiedwerk," *ZGJT,* I^3 (1931), 243-52.

Brück, Moses, *Rabinische Ceremonialgebräuche in ihrer Entstehung und geschichtlichen Entwickelung.* Breslau: A. Schulz, 1837.

Burckhardt, G. A. H., and Moritz Stern, "Aus der Zeitschriften-Literatur zur Geschichte der Juden in Deutschland," *ZGJD,* II (O. S., 1888), 1-46; 109-49.

Brüll, Adolf, *Trachten der Juden im nachbiblischen Alterthume. Ein Beitrag zur allgemeinen Kostümkunde.* Vol. I. Frankfort: Isaac St. Goar, 1873. (No further publication.)

Cahan, Y. L., *Shtudies vegn yidisher folksshafung* (Studies in Jewish folklore). Edited by Max Weinreich. New York: Yiddish Scientific Institute–Yivo, 1952.

——— (ed.), *Yidisher folklor.* (Publications of the Yiddish Scientific Institute–Yivo, vol. ix; Philological Series, vol. v). Vilna, 1938.

———, *Yidishe folkslider mit melodyes* (Jewish Folk Songs with Melodies). Edited by Max Weinreich. New York: Yivo Institute for Jewish Research, 1957.

Cahen, Abraham, "Le rabbinat de Metz pendant la période française (1567-1871)," *REJ,* VII (1883), 103-16; VIII (1884), 255-74; XII (1886), 283-97; XIII (1885), 106-26.

C(assuto), J., "Aus dem ältesten Protokollbuch der Portugiesisch-Jüdischen Gemeinde in Hamburg," *JJLG,* VI (1909), 1-54; VII (1910), 159-210; VIII

(1911), 227-90; IX (1912), 318-66; X (1913), 225-95; XI (1916), 1-76; XIII (1920), 55-118.

Chajes, Ẓebi Hirsch, *'Aṭeret Ẓebi* (Essays on theological, philosophical, and legal subjects). Żólkiew: S. Meyerhoffer, 1841.

Chayes, Ch., "Beliefs and Customs Associated with Death" (Yiddish), *Filolog. Shrift.*, II (1928, Vilna), 281-328.

Chone, Heymann, "Zur Geschichte der Juden in Konstanz," *ZGJD,* VI (1935), 3-16. (Konstanz [Constance]: loc. in So. Baden.)

Cohen, Arthur, "Die Münchener Judenschaft 1750-1861. Eine bevölkerungs- und wirtschaftsgeschichtliche Studie," *ZGJD,* II (1930), 262-83.

Cohen, Boaz, "Responsum of Maimonides Concerning Music," in *idem, Law and Tradition in Judaism,* pp. 167-81 (New York: Jewish Theological Seminary, 1959).

Cohen, Mortimer J., *Jacob Emden, A Man of Controversy.* Philadelphia: Dropsie College, 1937.

Cohn, Jacob, *Ehrenrettung des R. Jonathan Eibeschütz, ein Beitrag zur Kritik des Grätz'schen Geschichtwerkes.* Hanover: Brandes, 1870. (Blätter aus der Michael-David'schen Stiftung in Hannover.)

Cohn, Josef, *Das Eschweger Memorbuch; ein Beitrag zur Geschichte der jüdischen Stadt . . . im Kreise Eschwege.* Hamburg: Ackermann-Wulff, 1930.

Cronbach, Abraham, *Religion and Its Social Setting, together with Other Essays.* Cincinnati, 1933.

———, Social Thinking in the 'Sefer Hasidim.' Cincinnati, 1949. (Reprint of *HUCA,* Vol. XXII.)

Dembitzer, Ḥayyim Nathan. *Kelilat Yofi* (The rabbinate of Lwów). Cracow: Fischer, 1888. (See pp. 520 ff.)

Deutsch, Gotthard, "Ḥebra Ḳaddisha," *JE,* VI (1904), 298-300.

———, "Klaus," *JE,* VII (1904), 518-19.

Diamont, P. J., "The Origin of the Shield of David as a Symbol of Jewry" (Hebrew), *Reshumot,* V (N. S., 1953), 93-103.

Die Juden in Prag. Bilder aus ihrer tausendjährigen Geschichte. Festgabe der Loge Praga des Ordens B'nai B'rith. . . . Edited by Samuel Steinherz. Prague: P. Steindler and J. Bunzl-Federn, 1927.

Dinburg, Ben-Zion, *Toledot Yisra'el ba-Golah* (Jewish history from ancient times to the present). Vol. I, Pts. 1-2. Tel-Aviv: Dvir, 1926.

Donath, L., *Geschichte der Juden in Mecklenburg von ältesten Zeiten (1266) bis auf die Gegenwart (1874); auch ein Beitrag zur Kulturgeschichte Mecklenburgs.* Leipzig: O. Leiner, 1874.

Dubnow, Simon, *Weltgeschichte des jüdischen Volkes von seinen Uranfängen bis zur Gegenwart.* Edited by A. Steinberg. Vols. VI-VII. Berlin: Jüdischer Verlag, 1927–28. (See Hebrew edit., above, p. 343.)

Duckesz (Dukesz), Eduard, "Das Testament Wolf Wertheimers," *MGJV,* LII (1914), 109-24.

———, *Ḥakhme AHU* (A biographical history of Altona, Hamburg, Wandsbek). Hamburg: Goldschmidt, 1908.

———, *IWoH le-Moshab* (A communal history of Altona, Hamburg, Wandsbek). Cracow: Fischer, 1903.

Duschinsky, Charles (J. K.), "The Book *Ma'aseh Bet Din* of the Frankfort Community . . . 1769-99" (Hebrew), *Ha-Zofeh,* X (1926), 106-15.

———, "Rabbi David Oppenheimer, Glimpses of his Life and Activity, derived from his Manuscripts in the Bodleian Library," *JQR,* XX (1930), 217-47.

Eckstein, Adolf, "Bamberg Tekanoth . . . 1678," *JL,* XXII (1893), no. 20-22; 75-76, 79-80, 83-84, 86-87.

———, *Geschichte der Juden im ehemaligen Fürstbistum Bamberg.* Hamburg: Handels, 1898.

———, *Geschichte der Juden im Markgrafentum Bayreuth.* Bayreuth: B. Seligsberg, 1907.

Ehrentreu, H., "Sprachliches und Sachliches aus dem Talmud," *JJLG,* IX (1911), 1-44.

———, "Ueber den 'Pilpul' in den alten Jeschiboth," *JJLG,* III (1905), 206-19.

Eisenstein, J. D., "Birth" (Hebrew), *'Oẓar Yisra'el,* V (1911), 108-109.

———, "Burial," *ibid.,* IX (1913), 90-94.

———, "Death, Views and Customs Concerning," *JE,* IV (1903), 483-86.

———, "Dreams," *ibid.,* IV (1910), 283-84.

———, "Fish," *ibid.,* IV (1910), 12-14.

———, "Magic," *ibid.,* V (1911), 298-99.

———, "Sandeḳ," *ibid.,* VII (1912), 224.

———, "Skin, Skins," *ibid.,* VIII (1912), 36-37.

Eliav, Mordechai, *Ha-Ḥinnukh ha-Yehudi be-Germanniyah bi-Yeme ha-Haskalah ve-ha-'Emanẓipaẓyah* (Jewish Education in Germany in the Period of the Enlightenment and Emancipation). Jerusalem: Sivan Press, 1960.

Elsass, B., "Der Haushalt eines Rabbiners im 18. Jahrhundert," *MGJV,* XVI (1905), 95-103.

Elzet (Zlotnik), Jehuda (Judah Leyb), "Some Customs in Jewish Life" (Hebrew), *Reshumot,* I (1918), 335-77.

———, *Yidishe maykholim* (A folk book on Jewish foods). 2 Pts. in one vol. Warsaw, 1920. (Der vunder-oytser fun der yidisher shprakh, vol. iv.)

Epstein, Abraham, "Die Wormser Minhagbücher, Literarisches und Culturhistorisches aus denselben," *Gedenkbuch . . . David Kaufmann* (Breslau, 1900), pp. 300-17.

Erik, Max, *Di geshikhte fun der yidisher literatur. Fun die eltste tsaytn biz der haskaleh-tekufeh, 1400-1800* (The History of Yiddish Literature, from the Earliest Times until the Haskalah Period). Warsaw: "Kultur-Lige," 1928.

Esh, Saul, "Changes in the Book *Yosif 'Omeẓ* and the Historical Background" (Hebrew), *'Ḳobeẓ' in Memory of Eliezer Shamir* (Sedeh-'Eliyahu, Israel, 1957), pp. 155-62.

Feilchenfeld, Alfred, *Aus der älteren Geschichte der portugiesisch-israelitischen Gemeinde in Hamburg*. Hamburg: Lessman, 1898. (Reprint from *MGWJ*, XLIII.)

———, "Die älteste Geschichte der deutschen Juden in Hamburg," *MGWJ*, XLIII (1899), 271-82, 322-28, 370-81.

Feinstein, A. L., "Communal *Taḳḳanot* of Lithuania and Poland (1623-1761)" (Hebrew), *Ha-'Asif*, VI (1893), 164-78. (Bearing on education, clothing, and food practices.)

Finesinger, Sol, "The Custom of Looking at the Fingernails at the Outgoing of the Sabbath," *HUCA*, XII-XIII (1937-38), 347-65.

———, "The Shofar," *HUCA*, VIII-IX (1931-32), 193-228.

Festschrift zum 200-jährigen Bestehen des israelitischen Vereins für Krankenpflege- und Beerdigung-Chevra Kaddischa zu Königsberg (1704-1904). Königsberg: Hartung, 1904.

Flesch, Heinrich, "Beiträge zur Geschichte der Juden in Mähren," *JJLG*, XVII (1925), 57-84; XVIII (1926), 23-64.

———, "Der Pinax von Austerlitz." *JJV*, II (1925), 564-616. (Austerlitz: loc. in Bohemia.)

———, "Die Statuten der Chewra Kadischa Neu-Raussnitz," *MGWJ*, LXX (1926), 166-80. (Neu-Raussnitz: loc. in Moravia.)

———, "Mässigkeitsverordnungen," *ZGJT*, I^3 (1931), 279-95.

———, "Sympathetische Mittel und Rezepte aus dem Buche *Mif'alot 'Eloḳim* des Rabbi Naftali Kohen und Rabbi Joel Ba'al Schem," *MGJV*, XLII (1912), 41-48.

———, "Zur Geschichte der mähr. 'heiligen Vereine' (Chewra Kadischa)," *JJLG*, XXI (1930), 217-58.

Frankel, Zechariah, "Ezechiel Landau's Gesuch an Maria Theresia gegen Jonathan Eibeschütz. Ein Aktenstück," *MGWJ*, XXVI (1877), 17-25.

Freehof, Solomon B., "Devotional Literature in the Vernacular (Judeo-German, prior to the Reform Movement)," *CCAR*, XXXIII (1923), 375-415.

———, *Reform Jewish Practice*. 2 vols. Cincinnati: Hebrew Union College Press, 1944-52.

Freiher, Max, "Jüdisch-Deutsche Lieder aus dem 17. Jahrhundert," *ZGJD*, III (1889), 78-83.

Freimann, Aron, and Isidore Kracauer, *Frankfort*. Edited by Bertha Szold Levin. Philadelphia: Jewish Publication Society, 1929. (Jewish Community Series.)

Freimann, Aron, "A New Song of Complaint against a Communal Worker of Frankfort" (pub. in 1708, prob. Hanau: Yiddish), *Filolog. Shrift.*, II (Vilna, 1928), 169-74.

Freimann, Aron, "Biographical Account: Samuel Tausig (Taussig), the 'First Citizen'; Events in the Jewish Community of Prague 1704" (Hebrew), *Ḳobeẓ 'al Yad,* IX (1899), 1-29.

———, *"Sefer 'Iggeret Maḥalot,"* (A document on community ills: Hebrew): "Beiträge zur Geschichte der Juden in Prag, in den Jahren 1742-1757," *Ḳobeẓ 'al Yad,* VIII (1898), 1-74.

———, "Zur Geschichte der Juden in Prague," *ZHB,* XVI (1913), 97-100, 143-53. (A Yiddish text presented as a supplement to *ibid.,* dealing with the "suffering of the Jews in Prague during the War of the Austrian Succession," 1740-48.)

Freimann, J., "Geschichte der Juden in Prossnitz," *JJLG,* XV (1923), 26-58.

Freudenthal, Max, "David Oppenheim als Mährischer Landrabbiner," *MGWJ,* XLVI (1902), 262-74.

———, "Die Eigenart der Wormser Gemeinde in ihrer geschichtlichen Wiederkehr," *ZGJD,* V (1935), 107-14.

Fried, M., "Volksmedizinisches und Diätetisches aus Ostgalizien," *MGJV,* XXXVI (1910), 167-68.

Friedberg, Bernhard, "Shabbethai b. Meir Ha-Kohen (SHaK)," *JE,* XI (1905), 217-18.

Friedman, Philip, "The Jewish Badge and the Yellow Star in the Nazi Era," *HJ,* XVII (1955), 41-70.

Friedländer, Max Hermann, *Tiferet Jisrael. Schilderungen aus dem inneren Leben der Juden in Mähren in vormärzlichen Zeiten. Ein Beitrag zur Cultur- und Sitten-Geschichte.* Brunn: R. M. Rohrer, 1878.

Frisch, Ephraim, *An Historical Survey of Jewish Philanthropy, from the Earliest Times to the Nineteenth Century.* New York: Macmillan, 1924.

Gaon, M. D., "Festivals and the Order of Studies" (Hebrew), *Yeda'-'Am,* III (Nos. 2-3, 1955), 112-15.

———, "Folk Beliefs and Remedies among Oriental Jews" (Hebrew), *Yeda'-'Am,* IV (Nos. 1-2, 1956), 31-37.

Gaster, Moses, "The Maasehbuch and the Brantspiegel," *Studies in Memory of George A. Kohut* (New York, 1935), pp. 270-78.

———, *Studies and Texts in Folklore, Magic, Medieval Romance. . . .* Vol. II. London: Maggs, 1925-28.

Gaster, Theodor H., *The Holy and the Profane.* New York: William Sloane, 1955.

Geiger, Ludwig, "Vor hundert Jahren. Mitteilungen aus der Geschichte der Juden Berlins," *ZGJD,* III (O. S., 1889), 185-233.

———, "Kleine Beiträge zur Geschichte der Juden in Berlin (1700-1817)," *ZGJD,* IV (O. S., 1890), 29-65.

Ginsburger, M., "Jüdische Volksmedizin in Elsass," *MGJV, XXI* (1907), 1-10.

Ginzberg, Louis, *Jewish Folklore, East and West.* Cambridge: Harvard University Press, 1937. (Reprint of Harvard Tercentary Publications.) (Pub. as chap. iii in *idem, On Jewish Law and Lore,* Jewish Publication Society: Philadelphia, 1955.)

———, "Shabbethai b. Joseph Bass," *JE,* II (1902), 583-84.

———, *Students, Scholars and Saints.* Philadelphia: Jewish Publication Society, 1928.

———, *The Legends of the Jews.* 7 vols. Philadelphia: Jewish Publication Society, 1909-38.

Glanz, Rudolph, "The Investigation of 'Jewish Cant' in the Speech of Thieves," *Filolog. Shrift.,* II (Vilna, 1928), 353-68.

Glasberg, Jacob, *Zikhron Berit la-Ri'shonim* (Talmudic and early medieval sources pertaining to circumcision). Cracow: Joseph Fischer, 1892.

Gold, Hugo, "Zur Geschichte der Juden in Pirnitz," *ZGJT,* I^1 (1930), 51-53.

Goldmann, Arthur, "The *Vakhnakht* among the Jews of Vienna at the Beginning of the 15th Century" (Yiddish), *Filolog. Shrift.,* I (Vilna, 1926), 91-94.

Goldschmidt, Daniel (E. D.), "The Worms *Maḥzor*" (Hebrew), *Kirjath Sefer,* XXXIV (Nos. 3-4, 1959), 388-96; 513-22.

Graetz, Heinrich, *Geschichte der Juden von den ältesten Zeiten bis auf die Gegenwart.* Vol. X. Leipzig: Leiner, 1868.

———, *Geschichte der Juden von der dauerenden Ansiedlung der Marranen in Holland (1618) bis zum Beginne der Mendelsohn'schen Zeit (1750).* Vol. X. 3d edit. Edited by Marcus Brann. Leipzig: Leiner, 1897.

Gronemann, S., *Familienblätter zur Erinnerung an unseren verewigten Vater Raphael J. Karger.* Frankfort: Hoffman, 1898. (Genealogische Studien über die alten jüdischen Familien Hannovers.)

Grotte, Alfred, "Beschneidungsbänke in Ostdeutschland," *Menorah* (Vienna), VI (1928), 259-60.

Grunwald, Max, "Altjüdisches Gemeindeleben," *MGJV,* XLIII (1912), 73-88; XLVI (1913), 27-31; LIX-LX (1918), 55-64.

———, "Altjüdisches Gemeindeleben. Bestimmungen der Chebra Kaddischa Horn 1784 u. a.," *Menorah* (Vienna-Leipzig), IV (1926), 599-604. (Reprinted in *MGJV,* XXIX [N. S., 1926], 599-604.)

———, "Aus dem jüdischen Kochbuch," *Menorah* (Vienna), VI (1928), 518-20. (Reprinted in *MGJV,* XXXI-XXXII [N. S., 1929], 40-49.)

———, "Aus Hausapotheke und Hexenküche," *MGJV,* V (1900), 1-73; XXX (N. S., 1927-28), 27-29, 178-226.

———, "Aus unseren Sammlungen," *MGJV,* I (1898), 1-116.

———, "Beiträge zu den Memoiren der Glückel von Hameln," *MGJV,* LIV (1915), 63-70.

———, "Beiträge zur Volkskunde und Kunstgeschichte," in *Occident and Orient* (Gaster Anniversary Volume, 1936), pp. 184-204.

———, "Bibliomantie und Gesundbeten," *MGJV,* X (1902), 81-98.

Grunwald, Max, "Das Josefspiel," *MGJV,* XXXV (1910), 93-97.

———, "Das Testament Wolf Wertheimers," *MGJV,* XLIX (1914), 13-29, 55-61.

——— (ed.), *Die Hygiene der Juden; im Anschluss an die Internationale Hygiene-Ausstellung Dresden 1911.* Dresden, 1911.

——— "Die jüdische Volkskunde auf der 'Pressa,'" *Menorah* (Vienna), VI (1928), 356-64.

———, "Die Statuten der 'Hamburg-Altonaer Gemeinde' von 1726," *MGJV,* XI (1903), 1-64.

———, "Fünfundzwanzig Jahre jüdische Volkskunde," *JJV,* I (1923), 1-22.

———, "Gemeinde Proklamationen der Dreigemeinden (Hamburg, Altona u. Wandsbek), von 1724-34," *MGJV,* XXXIX (1911), 121-27.

———, *Geschichte der Wiener Juden bis 1914.* Vienna: Israelitische Kultusgemeinde, 1926.

———, *Hamburgs deutsche Juden bis zur Auflösung der Dreigemeinden 1811.* Hamburg: Janssen, 1904. (Based on *MGJV,* XII, XIII, XIV, XVI.)

———, "Jüdische Amulete: Anhang 1," *MGJV,* V (1900), 74-79.

———, "Jüdische Waisenfürsorge in alter und neuer Zeit," *MGJV,* LXVI (1922), 3-29.

———, "Kleine Beiträge zur jüdischen Kulturgeschichte," *MGJV,* XVI (1905), 144-75; XVII (1906), 14-38 (excerpts from the *Memoirs* of Glückel of Hameln); XIX (1906), 96-120; XXIV (1907), 118-45.

———, "Luxusverbot der Dreigemeinden (Hamburg-Altona-Wandsbek) aus dem Jahre 1715," *JJV,* I (1923), 227-34.

———, "Mattersdorf," *JJV,* II (1925), 402-563. (Mattersdorf: loc. in west. Hungary.)

———, "Memoiren eines böhmischen Juden. Josef Kraus und seine Erlebnisse in den napoleonischen Feldzügen," *MGJV,* LI (1914), 67-92.

———, *Samuel Oppenheimer und sein Kreis (Ein Kapitel aus der Finanzgeschichte Österreichs).* Vienna, 1913. (Historische Kommission der Israelitischen Kultusgemeinde in Wien. Quellen und Forschungen zur Geschichte der Juden in Deutsch-Österreich, vol. v.)

———, "V. Spiele," *MGJV,* III (1898), 34-40.

———, "Trachten der Juden," *JLex,* IV² (V, 1930), 1009-27.

———, "IV. Trachten und Sitten. Aus den Gemeindeverordnungen der Dreigemeinden Hamburg, Altona, Wandsbek vom Jahre 1726," *MGJV,* III (1898), 29-33.

———, "Various Charms and Magical Recipes" (Hebrew), *Edoth,* I (No. 4, 1946), 241-48.

———, *Vienna.* Philadelphia: Jewish Publication Society, 1936. (Jewish Community Series.)

———, "II. Zur Bibliothek," *MGJV,* II (1898), 54-55.

Güdemann, Moritz, "Education," *JE,* V (1903), 44-48.

Section 4A

Güdemann, Moritz, *Geschichte des Erziehungswesens und der Cultur der abendländischen Juden während des Mittelalters und der neueren Zeit.* 3 vols. Vienna: A. Holder, 1880-82.

———, *Yidishe kultur-geshikhte in mitlalter. Yidn in Daytshland dos XIV und XV yorhundert.* A Yiddish edition of the *Geschichte des Erziehungswesens.* Edited by Naḥum Shtif. Berlin: Klal, 1922.

Günzig, Azriel (Israel), "Rabbi Isaiah Horowitz, the Author of Shelah" (Hebrew), *'Oẓar ha-Safrut,* VI (1902), 36-42.

Haarbleicher, Mose M., *Aus der Geschichte der deutsch-israelitischen Gemeinde in Hamburg.* 2d edit. Hamburg: Meissner, 1886.

Habermann, A. M., "Practices Pertaining to the Month of *'Adar* in the 'Customs of Worms' by Joseph Yuzpa Shammash" (Hebrew), *Sinai: Sefer Yobel.* Jerusalem: Mosad Harav Kook, 1958.

Haenle, S., *Geschichte der Juden im ehemaligen Fürstenthum Ansbach.* Frankfort: Hofmann, 1867.

Hallo, Rudolf, *Jüdische Volkskunst in Hessen. Festschrift der Sinai-Loge zu Kassel.* Kassel, 1928.

Halpern (Halperin), Israel, "The 'Rush' into Early Marriages among Eastern European Jews." *Zion.* XVII (N. S., 1962), 36-58. Of value in comparing different regions.

———, *Bet Yisra'el be-Polin.* 2 vols. Jerusalem: Merkhaz, 1948-53.

Hamm, Julius W., *Geschichte der Juden in der Reichsstadt Augsburg.* Augsburg: J. W. Hamm, 1803.

Haneman, Frederick T., "Medicine: In Post-Talmudic Times," *JE,* VIII (1904), 414-20.

Hecht, E., "Ein jüdisches Gemeinde-Tanzhaus" (Augsburg, 1290), *MGWJ,* X (1861), 280, sec. "Notes."

———, "Zur Geschichte der Juden in Mecklenburg," *MGWJ,* VIII (1859), 45-66.

Heilig, O., "Jüdische Namen aus Schwaben," *MGJV,* XXXVII (1911), 25-28.

Hintze, Erwin (ed.), *Katalog der vom Verein 'Jüdisches Museum Breslau' in den Räumen des Schlesischen Museums für Kunstgewerbe und Altertümer veranstalteten Ausstellung 'Das Judentum in der Geschichte Schlesiens.'* Breslau: Grass-Barth, 1929 [?].

Holub, David, *Pardes David, 'o Toledot Rofe' Yisra'el* (A history of Jewish physicians from the earliest times to the present). Vienna: Brog, 1884. (Reprint of *Ha-Shaḥar,* vols. XI-XII.)

Holzer, Isaak, "Aus dem Leben der alten Judengemeinde zu Worms, nach dem 'Minhagbuch' des Juspa Schammes," *ZGJD,* V (N. S., 1935), 169-86.

Horodetzky, S. A., *Le-Ḳorot ha-Rabbanut* (Some aspects of the history of the rabbinate). Warsaw: Toshya, 1911.

Horowitz, H., "Die Rabbiner und jüdischen Gelehrten Prags im 15. Jahrhundert," *ZGJT,* I^4 (1931), 229-42.

Horwitz, L[udwig], *Die Israeliten unter dem Königreich Westfalen.* Berlin: Calvary, 1900.

Hülsen, Julius, *Der alte Judenfriedhof in Frankfurt a. M.* 2d edit. Frankfort: Braun, 1932.

Idelsohn, A. Z., "Cantors in Jewish Communities" (Hebrew) *Reshumot,* V (1927), 351-61; VI (1930), 411-22.

———, *The Ceremonies of Judaism.* Cincinnati, 1930.

Jakobovits, Immanuel, *Jewish Medical Ethics. A Comparative and Historical Study of the Jewish Religious Attitude to Medicine and Its Practice.* New York: Philosophical Library, 1959.

Jacobs, Joseph, "Costume," *JE,* IV (1903), 294-301.

———, "Folk-Medicine," *JE,* V (1903), 426-27.

Joel, D., *Der Aberglaube und die Stellung des Judenthums zu demselben.* Vol. II. Breslau: Koebner, 1883.

Joffe, Judah A., "Mutual Borrowings Between Yiddish and Slavic Languages," in *Harry A. Wolfson Jubilee Volume* (eds. Saul Lieberman, Shalom Spiegel, *et al.),* I, 423-46.

Joseph, Max, and Caesar Seligmann, "Orgelstreit," *JLex,* IV[1] (1930), 601-3.

Katz, Ben-Zion, *Rabbanut, Ḥasidut, Haskalah. Le-Toledot ha-Tarbut ha-Yisra'elit mi-Sof ha-Me'ah ha-Sheba' 'Esreh 'ad Reshit ha-Me'ah ha-Tesha' 'Esreh.* (The Rabbinate, Ḥasidism, and the Enlightenment. A History of Jewish Culture from the End of the Seventeenth Century to the Beginning of the Nineteenth Century.) 2 vols. Tel-Aviv: Association of Hebrew Writers and Dvir, 1956-58.

Katz, Jacob, *Ben Yehudim la-Goyim. Yaḥas ha-Yehudim li-Shekhenehem bi-Yeme ha-Benayim u-bi-Teḥillat ha-Zeman he-Ḥadash.* Jerusalem: Mosad Bialik, 1960. English translation: *Exclusiveness and Tolerance: Studies in Jewish-Gentile Relations. . . .* Oxford University Press, 1961.

———, "Marriage and Sexual Life among the Jews at the Close of the Middle Ages" (Hebrew), *Zion,* X (N. S., 1946), 21-54.

———, *Massoret u-Mashber. Ha-Ḥebrah ha-Yehudit be-Moẓ'e Yeme ha-Benayim.* Jerusalem: Mosad Bialik, 1958. English translation: *Tradition and Crisis: Jewish Society at the End of the Middle Ages.* New York: Free Press, 1961.

Katzenelsohn, I. L., *Ha-Talmud ve-Ḥokhmat ha-Refu'ah* (The Talmud and medicine). Berlin: "Ḥayyim," 1928.

Kaufmann, David, and Max Freudenthal, *Die Familie Gomperz.* Frankfort: Kauffmann, 1907. (Zur Geschichte jüdischer Familien, vol. iii.)

Kaufmann, David, *Aus Heinrich Heine's Ahnensaal.* Breslau: S. Schottlaender, 1896.

——— (ed.), "Communal Minute Book of Bamberg, 1696" (Hebrew), *Ḳobeẓ 'al Yad,* VII (1896-97), 1-46.

———, *Die letzte Vertreibung der Juden aus Wien und Niederösterreich, ihre Vorgeschichte (1625-1670) und ihre Opfer.* Vienna: *Konegen,* 1889.

Kaufmann, David, "Die Memoiren der Glückel von Hameln" in M. Brann (ed.), *Gesammelte Schriften von David Kaufmann*, I (Frankfort, 1908), 174-93.

———, "Extraits de l'ancien livre de la communauté de Metz," *REJ* (1889), XIX, 115-30. (Fragments of the Communal Minute Book of 1645, 1699-1702, 1709.)

———, "Jair Chayim Bacharach: A Biographical Sketch," *JQR*, III (O. S., 1891), 292-313; 485-536.

———, "La lutte de R. Naftali Cohen contre Hayyoun," *REJ*, XXXVI (1898), 256-71.

———, "Notes et mélanges. La synagogue de Mardochée Meisel et Jacob Segré," *REJ*, XXI (1890), 143-45.

———, "R. Naftali Cohen im Kampfe gegen Chajjun," *JJGL*, II (1899), 123-47.

———, *Samson Wertheimer der Oberhoffaktor und Landesrabbiner (1658-1724) und seine Kinder*. Vienna: F. Beck, 1888.

——— (ed.), *Sefer ha-Millu'im* (MS text: supplement to Worms *Memor*-Book, 1573-1866, ed. Abraham Berliner). Cracow: Fischer, 1894. (Reprint of *Mekiẓe Nirdamim*, ix.)

———, "*Seliḥot* of Lundenburg: Communal Sources, II" (Hebrew), *'Oẓar ha-Safrut*, II (1888), 112-13.

———, "Sources of Jewish History: Communal Minute Books of Metz (1691), Düsseldorf (1752), Prossnitz (1774, 1793: Hebrew)," *'Oẓar ha-Safrut*, II (1888), 88-111; III (1888), 1-17.

———, *Urkundliches aus dem Leben Samson Wertheimers*. Vienna: Konegen, 1892.

———, "Zu den jüdischen Namen," *MGJV* (1898), I, 116-18.

———, "Zu R. Jakob Emden's Selbstbiographie," *Archiv für Geschichte der Philosophie*, XI ([n. d.], No. 3), 426-29. (Reprint.)

Kayserling, M., "Luxusverbote," *MGJV* (1904), XIII, 40-43.

———, "Zur Geschichte der Juden in Hamburg," *MGWJ*, VII (1858), 408-18.

Kessler, Gerhard, *Die Familiennamen der Juden in Deutschland*. Leipzig, 1935. (Mitteilungen der Zentralstelle für deutsche Personen- und Familiengeschichte.)

Kisch, Alexander, "Samuel Oppenheimer," *JE*, IX (1905), 419.

Kisch, Guido, "Privatbriefe als Quellen der jüdischen Familienforschung," *Jüdische Familien-Forschung*, XII (1936), 702-23. (Mitteilungen der Gesellschaft für jüdische Familien-Forschung.)

———, *The Jews in Medieval Germany, A Study of their Legal and Social Status*. Chicago: University of Chicago Press, 1949.

———, "The Yellow Badge in History," *HJ*, IV (1942), 95-144.

Kober, Adolf, *Cologne*. Translated by Solomon Grayzel. Philadelphia: Jewish Publication Society, 1940. (Jewish Community Series.) (See chap. ii.)

———, "Die Reichsstadt Köln und die Juden in den Jahren 1685-1715," *MGWJ*, LXXV (1931), 412-28. (See p. 422 f., list of Jewish names from the *Ratsprotokollen*, bet. 1685-1715.)

Kober, Adolf, "Jüdische Studenten und Doktoranden der Universität Duisburg im 18. Jahrhundert," *MGWJ*, LXXV (1931), 118-27. (Duisburg: loc. on the Rhine.)

———, "Köln," *EJ*, X (1934), 219-30.

Kobler, Franz (ed.), *Jüdische Geschichte in Briefen aus Ost und West. Das Zeitalter der Emanzipation*. Vienna: Saturn, 1938. (See pp. 148-49: "Zwi Hirsch Katzenelenbogen an seinen Sohn Gerson Gabriel.")

——— (ed.), *Letters of Jews through the Ages; from Biblical Times to the Middle of the Eighteenth Century*. Vol. II. London: Ararat and East West Library, 1952. (See no. 11, pp. 473-74.)

Köhler, Max, *Beiträge zur neueren jüdischen Wirtschaftsgeschichte. Die Juden in Halberstadt und Umgebung bis zur Emanzipation*. Berlin: K. Curtius, 1927. (Studien zur Geschichte der Wirtschaft . . . , ed. Rudolf Häpke, vol. iii.)

Kohlbach, Berthold, "Feuer und Licht im Judenthum," *ZVV*, XXIII (1913), 225-49.

Kohler, Kaufmann, "Apple," *JE*, II (1902), 23-24.

———, "Bar Miẓwah," *JE*, II (1902), 509-10.

Kohut, Adolph, *Geschichte der deutschen Juden*. Berlin, 1898-99. (See Pt. 3.)

Kosover, Mordecai, "Jewish Foods: A Study in the History of Culture and Linguistics" (Yiddish) in *Yuda A. Yofe-bukh* (ed. Yudel Mark), pp. 1-145.

Kracauer, Isidor, "Beiträge zur Geschichte der Frankfurter Juden im dreissigjährigen Kriege," *ZGJD*, III (O. S., 1889), 130-56, 337-72; IV (O. S., 1890), 18-28.

———, *Die Geschichte der Judengasse in Frankfurt am Main*. Reprint of *Festschrift zur Jahrhundertfeier der Realschule der israelitischen Gemeinde (Philanthropin) zu Frankfurt am Main (1904)*, pp. 307-453.

———, "Die Juden Frankfurts im Fettmilch'schen Aufstand 1612-1618," *ZGJD*, IV (O. S., 1890), 127-69, 319-65.

———, *Die politische Geschichte der Frankfurter Juden bis zum Jahre 1349*. Reprint of *Beilage zum Programm des Philanthropins (1911)*, pp. 1-46.

———, *Geschichte der Juden in Frankfurt a. M. (1150-1824)*. 2 vols. Frankfort: Kauffmann, 1925-27.

Krauss, Samuel, "Aus der jüdischen Volksküche," *MGJV*, LIII (1915), 1-40.

———, "Jewish Foods and Dishes" (Hebrew) in *Festschrift, Sefer ha-Yobel li-Khebod Naḥum Sokolow* (Warsaw, 1904), pp. 488-99.

———, "Kleidung," *EJ*, X (1934), 78-110.

———, "The Jewish Rite of Covering the Head," *HUCA*, XIX (1945-46), 121-68.

———, "Wiener Synagogen in der Vergangenheit," *Menorah* (Vienna), IV (1926), 9-19.

———, *Zur Orgelfrage*. Vienna, 1919.

Krengel, Johann, *Das Hausgerät in der Mischnah*. Frankfort, 1899.

Kurrein, V., "Die Symbolik des Körpers in den rituellen Bräuchen," *MGWJ*, LX (1926), 41-50.

Kwasnick-Rabinowicz, Oskar, "Wolf Eibenschitz," *ZGJT*, I[4] (1931), 267-68. (He was the son of Jonathan Eibeschütz.)

Lamm, Louis, "Das Memorbuch von Oettingen," *JJLG*, XXII (1931-32), 147-59.

Landau, Alfred, "Anmerkungen," *MGJV*, XII (1904), 29-37. (Comments on the *Purim* play.)

———, "Die Sprache der Memoiren Glückel von Hameln," *MGJV*, VII (1901), 20-68.

———, "Fragekasten. Holekreisch," *MGJV*, IV (1899), 146-47.

———, "Holekreisch," *ZVV*, IX (1899), 72-77.

Lauterbach, Jacob Z., "Should One Cover the Head when Participating in Divine Worship?" *CCARY*, XXXVIII (1928), 589-603.

———, "*Tashlik*, a Study in Jewish Ceremonies," *HUCA*, XI (1936), 207-340. (Reprinted in *idem*, *Rabbinic Essays*. Cincinnati: Hebrew Union College Press, 1951, pp. 299-433.)

———, "The Belief in the Power of the Word," *HUCA*, XIV (1939), 289-302.

———, "The Ceremony of Breaking a Glass at Weddings," *HUCA*, II (1925), 351-80.

———, "The Naming of Children," *CCARY*, XLII (1932), 316-60.

———, "The Ritual for the Kapparot-Ceremony," in *Jewish Studies in Memory of George A. Kohut* (New York, 1935), pp. 413-22.

Lebermann, J., "Jüdische Schul- und Lehrerverhältnisse in Hessen," *JJLG*, XVIII (1926), 65-142.

Leksikon ha-Folklor ha-'Ibri (Lexicon of Jewish folklore). Edited by Akiba Golenpol. Vol. I. New York, Kaunas, 1940.

Levesohn, Abraham, *Meḳore Minhagim* (Sources of Jewish customs). Berlin: Kornegg, 1846.

Lévi, Israel, "Contes juifs," *REJ*, XI (1885), 209-34.

Levias, Caspar, "Father," *JE*, V (1903), 351-52.

Levy, Alphonse, *Die Geschichte der Juden in Sachsen*. Berlin: S. Calvary, 1900.

Levy, Benas, *Die Juden in Worms: ein Vortrag, im Verein für jüdische Geschichte und Literatur*. Berlin: M. Poppelauer, 1914.

Levy, Ernest, "Hokuspokus," in *Mélanges . . . Israel Lévi . . .*, *REJ*, LXXII (1926), 401-10.

Levy, Ludwig, "Die Schuhsymbolik im jüdischen Ritus," *MGWJ*, LXII (1918), 178-85.

Lewin, Adolf, *Geschichte der badischen Juden seit der Regierung Karl Friedrichs, 1738-1809*. Karlsruhe: G. Braun, 1909.

———, "Das Coblenzer Memorbuch," *JL*, X (1881), no. 22, 86-87.

Lewin, Louis, "Die jüdischen Studenten an der Universität Frankfurt an der Oder," *JJLG*, XIV (1921), 217-38; XV (1923), 59-96; XVI (1924), 43-85.

———, "Jüdische Briefe aus dem Jahre 1588," *JJGL*, XXX (1937), 173-86.

Lewin, [n. n.], "Purim Lied aus Pinne," *MGJV*, XVIII (1906), 86, sec. B.

Lewinski, Yom-Tow (Yom-Tov), "A Child's Foreskin and the Protuberance of an Ethrog" (Hebrew), *Yeda'-'Am,* I, (Nos. 5-6, 1950), 2-3.

———, "'Stagnant Water' as a Folk Remedy," *Yeda'-'Am,* I, (Nos. 3-4, 1949), 3-5.

Lewinsky, A., "Zur Geschichte der Juden in Deutschland im 18. Jahrhundert nach Hildesheimer Zeitungsstimmen," in *Festschrift . . . Jakob Guttmanns* (Leipzig, 1915), pp. 256-72.

Lewy, Heinrich, "Beiträge zur jüdischen Volkskunde," *ZVV,* XXXVII (1927), 81-89.

———, "Kleine Beiträge zu Bibel und Volkskunde," *MGWJ,* LXXV (1931), 19-29.

Liebe, Georg, *Das Judentum in der deutschen Vergangenheit. Mit 106 Abbildungen und Beilagen nach Originalen, grösstenteils aus dem fünfzehnten bis achtzehnten Jahrhundert.* Leipzig: Diederich, 1903. (Monographien zur deutschen Kulturgeschichte, ed. George Steinhausen, vol. xi.)

Lieben, Salomon Hugo, "David Oppenheim," *JJLG.* XIX (1928), 1-38.

———, "Handschriftliches zur Geschichte der Juden in Prag in den Jahren 1744-1754," *JJLG,* II (1904), 267-330 (with Hebrew texts; see Supplement, 302 ff.); III (1905), 241-92.

———, "Die Prager Brandkatastrophen . . . 1689 und 1754," *JJLG,* XVIII (1926), 175-93.

Lilienthal, Regina, "Das Kind bei den Juden," *MGJV,* XXV (1908), 1-18; XXVI (1908), 1-55.

———, "Evil Eye" (Yiddish), *Yidishe Filologye,* I (1924), 245-71.

Löb, Abraham, *Die Rechtsverhältnisse der Juden im ehemaligen Königreiche und der jetzigen Provinz Hannover.* Frankfort: Kauffmann, 1908.

Loeb, Isidore, "Le folk-lore juif dans la chronique du Schébet Iehuda d'Ibn Verga," *REJ,* XXIV (1892), 1-29. (While not directly related to the subject of this study, the article—as well as others in the field of folklore—was consulted to consider (a) method and (b) relationship of folklore to Jewish social and cultural history.)

Löw, Immanuel, "Das Salz. Ein Kapitel aus meinen Mineralien der Juden," in *Jewish Studies in Memory of George A. Kohut* (New York, 1935), pp. 429-62.

———, "Die Finger in Litteratur und Folklore der Juden," in *Gedenkbuch . . . David Kaufmann* (Breslau, 1900), pp. 61-85.

———, *Die Flora der Juden.* 4 vols. in one. Vienna-Leipzig: R. Löwit, 1924-34. (Veröffentlichungen der Alexander Kohut Memorial Foundation, vol. ii-iv, vi).

Löw, Leopold, *Die Lebensalter in der jüdischen Literatur.* Szegedin, 1875. (Beiträge zur jüdischen Alterthumskunde, vol. ii.)

Loewe, Heinrich, "Die Juden in Deutschland. Bibliographische Notizen," *ZGJD,* IV (1932), 223-41.

Loewe, Heinrich, "Bass. Sabbatai ben Josef," *JLex*, I (1927), 1154-57.

Löwenstein (Levenstein), Leopold, (Judah Loeb), "Das Wiener Memorbuch in der Klaussynagoge von Fürth," *MGWJ*, XLII (1898), 272-78.

———, "David Oppenheim," in *Gedenkbuch . . . an David Kaufmann* (Breslau, 1900), pp. 538-59.

———, *Geschichte der Juden in der Kurpfalz*. Frankfort: Kauffmann, 1895. 2 vols. in one. Vol. II: *Nathanael Weil: Oberlandrabbiner in Karlsruhe und seine Familie*. Frankfort: Kauffmann, 1895-98. (Beiträge zur Geschichte der Juden in Deutschland, vol. i.)

———, "Jüdische und jüdisch-deutsche Lieder," in *Jubelschrift . . . Hildesheimer* (Berlin, 1890), pp. 126-44.

———, "Memorbücher," *ZGJD*, II (O. S., 1887), 389-91.

———, "The Hardships Experienced in Worms during 1636" (Hebrew), *Ḳobeẓ 'al Yad*, VIII (1898), 1-12.

———, "Zur Geschichte der Juden in Fürth," *JJLG*, VI (1908), 153-233; VIII (1910), 65-213; X (1912), 49-192.

Lowenthal, Marvin, *The Jews of Germany, a Story of Sixteen Centuries*. New York-Toronto: Longmans, Green, 1936.

Löwinger, Adolf, "Der böse Blick," *Menorah*, X (Vienna-Leipzig, 1926), 551-69. (Reprinted in *MGJV*, XIX.)

———, "Der Traum in der jüdischen Literatur," *MGJV*, XXV (1908), 25-34; XXVI (1908), 56-78.

Mainzer, Moritz, *Gedenkblätter zur Erinnerung an das 175 jährige Jubiläum des Wohltätigkeitsvereins im ehemaligen Amt Starkenburg, 1739-1914: Ḥebra' Ḳaddisha' de-Gomle Ḥasadim be-Medinot Mainz be-Amt Starkenburg*. Frankfort: Droller, 1914. (See *Pinḳas*, Pt. 2, p. 28 ff.)

Mandl, Bernhard, "Zur Geschichte der jüdischen Gemeinde in Holitsch," *ZGJT*, I^3 (1931), 180-95.

Mannheim, Moses, *Die Juden in Worms, ein Beitrag zur Geschichte der Juden in den Rheingegenden*. Mit einem Vorwort von J. M. Jost. Frankfort: J. S. Adler, 1842.

Mannheimer, S., "Joseph Juspa Nördlinger Hahn," *JE*, VI (1904), 152.

Marcus, Jacob R., "The Triesch *Ḥebra Ḳaddisha*, 1687-1828," *HUCA*, XIX (1945-46), 168-204. (Triesch: loc. in Moravia.)

Markgraf, Richard, *Zur Geschichte der Juden auf den Messen in Leipzig von 1644-1839*. Bischofswerda: Friedrich May, 1894. (Doctoral dissertation.)

Markon, Isaak, "Sabbatai ben Josef Bass," *EJ*, III (1929), 1154-57.

Marmorstein, Arthur (Abraham), "Beiträge zur Religionsgeschichte und Volkskunde," *JJV*, I (1923), 280-319.

———, "The Place of Popular Traditions in the History of Religion" (Hebrew), *Edoth*, I (No. 3, 1946), 75-89, 138-50.

Marx, Alexander, "A Seventeenth Century Autobiography. A Picture of Jewish

Life in Bohemia and Moravia. From a Manuscript in the Jewish Theological Seminary," *JQR,* VIII (1917-18), 269-304. (Reprinted in *idem, Studies in Jewish History and Booklore.)* (The study deals with the community of Lichtenstadt, a day's journey from Prague.)

———, "Some Notes on the History of David Oppenheimer's Library," in *Mélanges . . . Israel Lévi . . ., REJ,* LXXXII (1926), 451-60.

———, "Some Notes on the Life of R. Yair Hayyim Bacharach," *Essays Presented to J. H. Hertz,* (London, [n. d.]), pp. 307-11. (The article is based on a MS.)

———, "The History of David Oppenheimer's Library," in *idem, Studies in Jewish History and Booklore* (New York, 1944), pp. 238-55.

Maser, Karl, *Die Juden der Frei- und Reichsstadt Dortmund und der Grafschaft Mark.* Witten-Ruhr: Pott, 1912. (Dissertation.)

Mayer, Sigmund, *Die Wiener Juden, Kommerz, Kultur, Politik (1700-1900).* 2d edit. Vienna-Berlin: R. Lowit, 1918.

Meisl, Joseph, "The Communal Legislation of Halberstadt Bearing on the Regulation of Circumcision Festivities, 1776" (Hebrew), *Reshumot,* I (1945), 142-50.

———, "The *Memor*-Book of the Halberstadt *Kloyz,* 1695" (Hebrew), *Reshumot* III (1947), 181-205.

Meitlis, Jakob, *Das Ma'assebuch. Seine Entstehung und Quellengeschichte; zugleich ein Beitrag zur Einführung in die altjiddische Agada.* Berlin: Mass, 1933.

———, "The Bodleian Manuscript, 'Libes Brif'—a Pre-Haskalah Reform Writing" (Yiddish), *Yivo Bleter,* II (1931), 308-33.

Michaelis, Alfred, *Die Rechtsverhältnisse der Juden in Preussen. . . .* Berlin: Lamm, 1910.

Minkoff, N. B. (in collaboration with Judah A. Joffe), "Old-Yiddish Literature," *The Jewish People: Past and Present,* III (1952), 145-64.

Müller, Willibald, *Urkundliche Beiträge zur Geschichte der mährischen Judenschaft im 17. und 18. Jahrhundert.* Olmutz: L. Kullil, 1903.

Munk, Judah (Leon), "Die Constituten der sämmtlichen hessischen Judenschaft im Jahre 1690," in *Jubelschrift . . . Hildesheimer,* (Berlin, 1890), pp. 69-82, German sec.; pp. 77-85, Hebrew sec. (The Hebrew article is based on the German.)

Munz, P., "Die hygienische Bedeutung der jüdischen Speisegesetze," *MGJV,* XL (1911), 144-52.

Nacht, Jacob, "Bar-Mitsvah Customs in the Synagogue" (Hebrew), *Yeda'-'Am,* III (Nos. 2-3, 1955), 106-111.

Nathan, N. M., "Aus den Jugenderinnerungen Karl Friedrichs von Klöden. Ein Beitrag zur jüdischen Volkskunde," *JJGL,* XX (1917), 138-48. (For the period of 1796-1801, when Karl Friedrich von Klöden lived in Mark-Friedland; has particular bearing on chap. III.)

Neher, André, "The Humanism of the Maharal of Prague," *Judaism,* XIV (No. 3, 1965), 290-304.

Neubauer, Adolf, "Le memorbuch de Mayence, essai sur la littérature des complaintes," *REJ,* IV (1882), 1-30.

Neustadt, L., "Die Bedeutung der jüdischen Gemeinde in Frankfurt a. M.," *ZGJD,* I (O. S., 1887), 190-93.

———, *Die letzte Vertreibung der Juden in Schlessien.* Breslau: Schatzky, 1893.

———, "Zur Geschichte der deutschen Juden im sechzehnten Jahrhundert," *MGWJ,* XXXIII (1884), 188-92, sec. "Notes."

Noble, Shlomo, "Rabbi Yeḥiel Mikhel Epstein," *Yivo Annual of Jewish Social Science,* VI (1951), 302-319.

"Notizen: Ein jüdisches Gemeinde-Tanzhaus," *MGWJ,* X (1861), 280.

Nowack, Wilhelm, *Lehrbuch der hebräischen Archäologie.* 2 vols. in one. Freiburg-Leipzig: J. Mohr, 1894. (Sammlung Theologische Lehrbücher.) (See Pt. 2, pp. 109 ff., secs. on food, clothing, and shelter.)

Ochser, Sch. (Scholem), "Der Pinkas der Gemeinde Kuttenplan," *MGJV,* XXXIII (1910), 32-39; XXXIV (1910), 57-89. (Kuttenplan: loc. in Bohemia.)

Ocksman, Jacob, "Some Customs of Frankfort" (Hebrew), *Reshumot,* III (1947), 100-105.

Oelsner, Toni, "The Jewish Ghetto of the Past," *Yivo Annual of Jewish Social Science,* I (1946), 24-43.

Patai, Raphael, "Jewish Folklore and Ethnology: Problems and Tasks" (Hebrew), *Edoth,* I (No. 1, 1945), 1-12.

Peller, Sigismund, "Ueber die böhmischen und österreichischen Juden zur Zeit Maria Theresias," *MGWJ,* LXII (1926), 284-88.

Perles, Joseph, "Das Memorbuch der Gemeinde Pfersee," *MGWJ,* XXII (1873), 508-15.

———, "Die Berner Handschrift des kleinen Aruch," in *Jubelschrift . . . Graetz* (Breslau, 1887), pp. 1-38.

———, "Die jüdische Hochzeit in nachbiblischer Zeit," *MGWJ,* IX (1860), 339-60.

———, "Die Leichenfeierlichkeiten im nachbibl. Judenthume," *MGWJ,* X (1861), 345-55, 376-94.

Perlmuter, Moshe Arie, *Rabbi Yehonatan Eibeschütz vi-Yaḥaso el ha-Shabta'ot: Rabbi Jonathan Eibeschütz and His Attitude towards Sabbatianism. New Researches Based on the Manuscript of the Book, "Va-'Avo ha-Yom el ha-'Ayin."* Jerusalem-Tel-Aviv: Shocken, 1947. (Studies and Texts in Jewish Mysticism, ed. Gershom Scholem, vol. iii.)

Philipson, David, "Old Age," *JE,* I (1901), 230-31.

Pinthus, Alexander, "Studien über die bauliche Entwicklung der Judengassen in den deutschen Städten," *ZGJD,* II (1930), 101-30.

Plaut, W. Gunther, "The Origin of the Word 'Yarmulke'," *HUCA,* XXVI (1955), 567-70.

Popper, Moriz, "Aus Inschriften des alten Prager Judenfriedhofes. Culturhistorisches und Historisches," *ZGJD,* V (O. S., 1892), 348-75.

Posen, Ida, "Judentrachten," *Menorah* (Vienna), VI (1928), 681-84.

Press, Jesajas, "Zu Schebua ha-ben," *MGWJ*, LXXVI (1932), 575-77.

Preuss, Julius, *Biblisch-talmudische Medizin: Beiträge zur Geschichte der Heilkunde und der Kultur überhaupt*. Berlin: S. Karger, 1911.

Prilucki, Noah, *Der yidisher konsonantizm*. 2 vols. Warsaw: Nayer Ferlag, 1917.

———, *Dos gevet: dialogen vegn shprakh und kultur* (The Wager: Dialogues on Language and Culture). Warsaw: "Kultur-Lige," 1923.

———, *Yidishe folkslider*. 2 vols. Warsaw: Bikher-far-Alle and Nayer Ferlag, 1911-13.

——— and S. Lehman (eds.), *Noah Prilucki's Zamelbikher far yidishen folklor, filologie un kulturgeshikhte*. 2 vols. Warsaw: Nayer Ferlag, 1912-17.

Pritsker, Asher, "Burial and Mourning Customs" (Hebrew), *Yeda'-'Am*, III (No. 1, 1955), 20-21; (No. 2-3, 1955), 115-17; IV (Nos. 1-2, 1956), 38-40.

Rabinowicz, J., *Der Todtenkultus bei den Juden*. Frankfort: Kauffmann, 1889.

Rappaport, Samuel, "Chanukahspiele der Jugend," *Menorah*, IV (Vienna-Leipzig), 671-78.

Rappoport, Angelo S., "Flora in Jewish Folklore" (Hebrew) *Yeda'-'Am*, IV (Nos. 1-2, 1956), 29-30. (Cf. *idem, Folklore of the Jews*, chap. iv.)

———, *The Folklore of the Jews*. London: Soncino, 1937.

Ratzhabi, Jehuda, "A Yemenite Book of Dreams" (Hebrew), *Edoth*, II (Nos. 1-2, 1946-47), 121-25.

Richter, E., and A. Schmidt, "Die Hotzenplotzer Judengemeinde 1334-1848," *MGJV*, XXXVII (1911), 29-36. (Hotzenplotz: loc. in Moravia.)

Ritter, Bernhard, "Aus dem Frankfurter Gemeindebuche," *MGWJ*, XXVIII (1879), 36-38. (For the period of 1583 and 1688.)

Rivkind, Isaac, "A Codex of Prague Ordinances" (Hebrew), *Reshumot*, IV (1925), 345-52.

———, "A *Responsum* of Leon da Modena on Uncovering the Head" (Hebrew), in *Louis Ginzberg Jubilee Volume* (New York, 1946), pp. 401-23.

———, "A *Responsum* of Rabbi Moses Provençal on Ball Games" (Hebrew), *Tarbiẓ*, IV (1933), 366-76. (Moses ben Abraham Provençal, d. 1576, Mantua, Italy; see *ibid.*, 370.)

———, "The Artisan *(bal-melokheh)* in the Old-Yiddish Folk Song," *Filolog. Shrift.*, I (1926, Vilna), 42-50.

———, *Der kamf kegn azartshpiln bay yidn. A shtudie in finf hundert yor yidishe poezye un kultur-geshikhte*. (The Fight against Gambling among Jews. A Study of Five Centuries of Jewish Poetry and Cultural History.) New York: Yiddish Scientific Institute–Yivo, 1946.

———, "Pedigreed Words: from My Lexicon," *Yid. Shprakh*, XIII (1953), 15-17; 84-88; XIV (1954), 21-29, 46-59, 110-20; XV (1955), 20-30, 48-58.

———, "Sources Pertaining to the Cantor and Marriage Jester (Minstrel) for the Period prior to the 17th Century" (Hebrew), in the *Festschrift, Minḥah li-Yehudah . . . Zlotnik* (Jerusalem, 1950), pp. 238-57.

Rivkind, Isaac, "The Laws Concerning Gamblers" (Hebrew), *Ḥoreb*, II[1] (1935), 60-66.

———, *Yidishe gelt, in lebensshteyger kultur-geshikhte un folklor. A leksikologishe shtudie. (Jewish Money: In Folkways, Cultural History, and Folklore. A Lexicological Study.)* New York: American Academy for Jewish Research, 1959.

Rixen, Carl, *Geschichte und Organisation der Juden im ehemaligen Stifte Münster.* Münster: Westfälische Vereinsdruckerei, 1906. (Dissertation.)

Rodkinson, Michael L., *History of Amulets, Charms, and Talismans. A Historical Investigation into their Nature and Origin.* New York, 1893.

Rokycana, Jaroslav, "Die Häuser des Jakob Bassevi von Treuenberg," *ZGJT,* I[3] (1931), 253-66.

Rosenfeld, Moritz, "Klaus," *JLex,* (1929), 731-32.

Rosenthal, Berthold, "Aus den Jugendjahren der jüdischen Gemeinde Karlsruhe," *MGWJ,* LXXI (1927), 207-28.

———, "Briefe von Mannheimer Juden aus den Jahren 1695 bis 1697," *ZGJD,* VII (N. S., 1937), 98-107.

Roth, A. Z. N., "*Memento Moris* [Memorial of the Dead] in the Customs of the *Chevra Kadisha*" (Hebrew), *Yeda'-'Am,* III (No. 1, 1955), 17-20.

Rotter, Hans, and Adolf Schmieger, *Das Ghetto in der Wiener Leopoldstadt.* Vienna: Burg, 1926.

Rubin, Shlomo, "The Dance of Death, *Danse macabre*" (Hebrew), *Ha-Shaḥar,* VIII (1873), 3-24.

———, *Segullot ha-Ẓemaḥim ve-'Ototam, be-Haggadot u-be-Datot kol ha-'Amim* (Plant remedies and their symbolic meaning in the lore and tradition of nations). Cracow: J. Fischer, 1898.

———, *Segullot Ba'ale Ḥayyim ve-'Ototam, be-Haggadot u-be-Datot Kol ha-'Amim* (Animal remedies and their symbolic meaning in the lore and tradition of nations). Cracow: J. Fischer, 1900.

Sadan (Stock), Dov, *Yerid ha-Sha'ashu'im (A Market of Pleasure).* (History and literary analysis of riddles and aphorisms.) Tel-Aviv: Massadah, 1964.

Salfeld, Siegmund (ed.), *Das Martyrologium des Nürnberger Memorbuches.* Berlin: Leonhard Simon, 1898. (Quellen zur Geschichte der Juden in Deutschland, vol. iii.)

———, "Welt und Haus des deutschen Juden im Mittelalter," *JJGL,* XXIII (1920), 61-85.

Samuel, Salomon, *Geschichte der Juden in Stadt und Stift Essen bis zur Säkularisation des Stifts, von 1291-1802.* Berlin: Poppelauer, 1905.

Schaab, Carl (Karl) A., *Diplomatsche Geschichte der Juden zu Mainz und dessen Umgebung, mit Berücksichtigung ihres Rechtzustandes in den verschiedenen Epochen.* Mainz: V. Zabern, 1855.

Schauss, Hayyim, *The Jewish Festivals, from their Beginnings to Our Own Day.* Translated by Samuel Jaffe. Cincinnati: Union of American Hebrew Congregations, 1938.

———, *The Lifetime of a Jew, throughout the Ages of Jewish History.* Cincinnati: Union of American Hebrew Congregations, 1950.

Schay, Max, "Die Protokolle der 'Chewra-Kadischa' der jüdischen Gemeinde in Pressburg," *ZGJT,* III[2] (1933), 71-88.

Schechter, Solomon, "The Child in Jewish Literature," in *idem, Studies in Judaism,* First Series (Philadelphia, 1911), pp. 282-312.

———, "The Memoirs of a Jewess of the Seventeenth Century," in *idem, Studies in Judaism,* Second Series (Philadelphia, 1908), pp. 126-47.

Scheftelowitz, Isidor, "Tierorakel im altjüdischen Volksglauben," *ZVV,* XXIII (1913), 383-90.

Schnapper-Arndt, Gottlieb, "Mittheilungen über jüdische Interieurs zu Ende des siebzehnten Jahrhunderts," *ZGJD,* II (O. S., 1888), 182-93.

Schochat (Shohet), Azriel, "The German Jews Integration within their Non-Jewish Environment in the First Half of the 18th Century" (Hebrew), *Zion,* XXI (N.S., 1956), 207-35.

———, *'Im Ḥillufe Teḳufot; Reshit ha-Haskalah be-Yahadut Germanniyah (Beginnings of the Haskalah among German Jewry).* Jerusalem: Mosad Bialik, 1960.

Schüler, Meier, "Beiträge zur Kenntnis der alten jüdisch-deutschen Profanliteratur," in *Festschrift . . . Realschule mit Lyzeum . . . Frankfurt a. M.* (Frankfort, 1928), pp. 79-132.

Schwarz, Ignaz, *Das Wiener Ghetto, Seine Häuser und seine Bewohner.* Vienna-Leipzig: M. Braumüller, 1909. (Quellen und Forschungen zur Geschichte der Juden in Deutsch-Österreich. Herausgegeben von der Historischen Kommission der Israelitischen Kultusgemeinde in Wien, vol. ii.)

Schwenger, Heinrich, "Die Namensbeilegung der Juden in Kostel im Jahre 1787," *ZGJT,* I[2] (1930), 116-28.

———, "Über die zweite Ansiedlung der Juden in Lundenburg," *ZGJT,* I[1] (1930), 37-40.

Seeligmann, Sigmund, "Purimlied," *MGJV,* XXX (1909), 33-36.

Sefer ha-Munnaḥim li-Refu'ah u-le-Madda'e ha-Ṭeba': Dictionary of Medicine and Allied Sciences. Latin, English, Hebrew. Edited by Aaron H. Masie. Jerusalem, 1934.

Seligmann, Caesar, "Organ," *UJE* (1942), VIII, 321-22.

Seligsohn, Max, "Wallich," *JE,* XII (1905), 460-61.

Shatzky, Jacob (ed.), *Arkhiv far der geshikhte fun yidishn teater un drame,* I. Vilna-New York: Yiddish Scientific Institute–Yivo, 1930.

———, "*Sefer ha-Ḥesheḳ* and Its Author—a Lost 'Medicine Book' Written in Yiddish in the 18th Century," *Yivo Bleter,* IV (1932), 223-35.

Shatzky, Jacob, "The First History of the Jewish Theater: A Review of Isaac Shiper, *Geshikhte fun yidisher teater-kunst un drame, Filolog. Shrift.*, II (Vilna, 1928), 215-64.

Shiper (Shipper), Isaac, *Geshikhte fun yidisher teater-kunst un drame. Fun die eltste tsaytn biz 1750* (History of Jewish Theater and Drama, from Earliest Times until 1750). 3 vols. in 2. Warsaw: "Kultur-Lige," 1927-28.

Shmueli, Ephraim, *Toledot 'Amenu bi-Zeman he-Ḥadash* (History of the Jews in Modern Times, 1492-1782). 2 vols. Tel-Aviv: Javneh, 1945.

Shwartz, Yeḥiel, "The Dream and the Interpretation" (Hebrew), *Yeda'-'Am*, I (Nos. 5-6, 1950), 14.

Simon, I., "Medieval Jewish Science," in *Ancient and Medieval Science: From Prehistory to* A.D. 1450 (ed. René Taton), I, 453-66.

Singer, Leopold, "Aus der Geschichte der jüdischen Gemeinde in Palota (Ungarn)," *JJLG*, XVIII (1926), 195-202.

Sosis, I., "Counter-Social Legislation in Jewish Communities during the 16th and 17th Centuries, based on Rabbinic Responsa" (Yiddish), *Zeitschrift*, I (Minsk, 1926), 225-35.

Sosnovik, E., "Jewish Popular Medicine in White Russia," *Yidishe Filologye*, I (1924), 160-68.

Stahl, Rudolf, *Geschichte der Nauheimer Juden*. Bad Nauheim: L. Wagner, 1929. (Nauheim: loc. in Hesse.)

Stein, Salomon, *Geschichte der Juden in Schweinfurt. Zwei Vorträge, gehalten im Verein für jüdische Geschichte und Literatur zu Schweinfurt*. Frankfort: Kauffmann, 1899. (Schweinfurt: loc. in Bavaria.)

Steinschneider, Moritz, *Die hebräischen Übersetzungen des Mittelalters und die Juden als Dolmetscher*. Berlin, 1893.

———, "Der Aberglaube. Vortrag im Verein junger Kaufleute zu Berlin (1863)," *Sammlung gemeinverständlich wissenschaftlicher Vorträge*, XV (N. S., 1900), 343-76.

———, "Hebräische Drucke in Deutschland. 5. Altona," *ZGJD*, I (O. S., 1887), 281-82.

———, "Literarische Beilage: Lapidarien," *HB*, XVI (1877), 104-6.

———, "Purim und Parodie," *MGWJ*, XLVI (1902), 176-87, 473-78; XLVII (1903), 84-89.

———, *Schach bei den Juden. Ein Beitrag zur Cultur- und Litteratur-Geschichte*. Berlin: Julius Springer, 1873. (Reprint from *Geschichte und Bibliografie des Schachspiels*, by Antonius van der Linde, pp. 155-201.)

Stern, Moritz (Mosheh), *Beiträge zur Geschichte der Juden in Berlin*. Berlin: "Hausfreund," 1909.

———, "Jugendunterricht in der Berliner jüdischen Gemeinde während des 18. Jahrhunderts," *JJLG*, XIX (1928), 39-68.

———, "The Old *Memor*-Book of the Community of Vienna before the Expulsion"

(Hebrew), in *Festschrift . . . Berliner's* (Frankfort, 1903), pp. 113-30. (The *memor*-book was compiled in 1670, a year before the expulsion.)

Stern, Selma, *Josel von Rosheim: Befehlshaber der Judenschaft im Heiligen Römischen Reich Deutscher Nation.* Stuttgart: Anstalt, 1959.

———, *Josel of Rosheim: Commander of Jewry in the Holy Roman Empire of the German Nation.* Translated from the German by Gertrude Hirschler. Philadelphia: Jewish Publication Society, 1965.

———, *The Court Jew: a Contribution to the History of the Period of Absolutism in Central Europe.* Translated from a German manuscript by Ralph Weiman. Philadelphia: Jewish Publication Society, 1950.

Stobbe, Johann Ernst Otto, *Die Juden in Deutschland während des Mittelalters in politischer, socialer und rechtlicher Beziehung.* Braunschweig: Schwetschke, 1866.

Strassburger, B., *Geschichte der Erziehung und des Unterrichts bei den Israeliten. Von der vortalmudischen Zeit bis auf die Gegenwart.* Mit einem Anhang: Bibliographie der jüdischen Pädagogie. Stuttgart: Levy-Müller, 1885.

Straus, Raphael, *Die Judengemeinde Regensburg im ausgehenden Mittelalter. Auf Grund der Quellen kritisch untersucht und neu dargestellt.* Heidelberg: Carl Winter, 1932. (Heidelberger Abhandlungen zur mittleren und neueren Geschichte, eds. Karl Hampe and Willy Andreas, vol. lxi.)

———, "The 'Jewish Hat' as an Aspect of Social History," *JSS,* IV (1942), 59-72.

Stutschewsky, Joachim, *Ha-Klezmorim: Toledotehem, 'Orah Ḥayyehem vi-Yeẓirutehem* (Jewish Folk Musicians: History, Folklore, and Compositions). Jerusalem: Mosad Bialik, 1959.

Sulzbach, A., "Ein alter Frankfurter Wohltätigkeitsverein," *JJLG,* II (1904), 241-48.

Taglicht, J. (ed.), *Nachlässe der Wiener Juden im 17. und 18. Jahrhundert. Ein Beitrag zur Finanz-, Wirtschafts- und Familiengeschichte des 17. und 18. Jahrhunderts.* Vienna-Leipzig: W. Braumüller, 1917. (Quellen und Forschungen zur Geschichte der Juden in Deutsch-Österreich. Herausgegeben von der Historischen Kommission der Israelitischen Kultusgemeinde in Wien, vol. vii.)

Täubler, Selma Stern, *Der preussische Staat und die Juden.* Berlin: Schwetschke, 1925.

———, "Die geistigen Strömungen des 18. Jahrhunderts und das Judenproblem," *ZGJD,* VII (1937), 71-76.

Thieberger, Friedrich (ed.), *Jüdisches Fest, jüdischer Brauch.* Berlin, 1936.

Tietze, Hans. *Die Juden Wiens.* Leipzig-Vienna: Tal, 1933.

Tsinberg (Zinberg), Israel, *Kultur-Historishe Shtudies* (Studies in Jewish Culture and History). New York: Sklarsky, 1949.

Twersky, Isadore, *Rabad of Posquières: A Twelfth-Century Talmudist.* Cambridge, Mass.: Harvard University Press, 1962. (Harvard Semitic Series, vol. xviii.)

Unna, Isak, "Die Verordnungen für die Lemle Moses Klausstiftung in Mannheim," *JJLG,* XVII (1925), 133-45.

Wachstein, Bernhard (Dober), "A Jewish Community in the Eighteenth Century: Pinḳas Runkel" (Yiddish), *Yivo Bleter,* VI (1934), 84-116. (Runkel: loc. in Hesse-Cassel.)

———, "An Index of Ethical Wills" (Hebrew), *Kirjat Sefer,* XI (1934-35), 235-44; XII (1935-36), 98-104.

———, "Bibliographie der Schriften Gerson Wolfs," *ZGJT,* X[1] (1930), 17-35.

———, "Das Statut der jüdischen Bevölkerung der Grafschaft Wied-Runkel (Pinkas Runkel)," *ZGJD,* IV (1932), 129-49.

———, "Der Bücherbesitz von Samuel Oppenheimer dem Jüngeren und Marx Lion Gomperz," *MGJV,* XXX (1909), 36-39.

———, "Die Gründung der Wiener Chewra-Kadischa im Jahre 1763," *MGJV,* XXXII (1909), 97-102; XXXIII (1910), 6-28. (The basis for his book on the same subject: Leipzig, 1910.)

———, "Notizen zur Geschichte der Juden in Prossnitz," *JJLG,* XVI (1924), 163-76.

———, "The Prague Sumptuary Legislation of 1767" (Yiddish), *Yivo Bleter,* I (1931), 335-54.

——— (ed.), *Urkunden und Akten zur Geschichte der Juden in Eisenstadt und den Siebengemeinden.* Vienna-Leipzig: Braumüller, 1926. (Eisenstädter Forschungen, ed. Sandor Wolf.)

Wanie, Paul, *Geschichte der Juden von Teplitz.* Kaaden: V. Uhl, 1925. (Teplitz: loc. in Bohemia.)

Wanwild, M. (ed.), *Bay uns yidn* (An anthology of folklore and philology). Warsaw: P. Grubard, 1923.

Wehrhan, Karl, "Brautstand und Hochzeit im Lippischen," *ZVV,* VI (N. S., 1934), 50-61; VII (N. S., 1935), 133-42. (Lippe: a principality in northwest Germany in the 17th cent.)

Weihs, Friedrich, *Aus Geschichte und Leben der Teplitzer Judengemeinde (1782-1932).* Brünn-Prague: Jüdischer Buch- und Kunstverlag, 1932.

Weill, Emmanuel, "Le Yidisch Alsacien-Lorrain," *REJ,* LXX (1920), 180-94; LXXI (1920), 66-88, 165-89; LXXII (1921), 65-88.

Weinberg, Magnus, "Das Memorbuch von Hagenbach," *JJLG,* XVIII (1926), 203-16. (Hagenbach: loc. in Bavaria.)

———, "Memorbücher," *Menorah* (Vienna), VI (1928), 697-708.

———, "Untersuchungen über das Wesen des Memorbuches," *JJLG,* XVI (1924), 253-320.

Weinreich, Max, *Bilder fun der yidisher literaturgeshikhte fun di onheybn biz Mendele Moykher Sforim* (Studies in the History of Yiddish Literature, from its Beginning to the Time of Mendele). Vilna: Y. Kamermachera, 1928.

Weinreich, Max, "Concerning the History of the Older *Akhashveyros-shpil," Filolog. Shrift.*, II (Vilna, 1928), 425-52.

———, "Fundamentals in the History of Yiddish," *Yid. Shprakh,* XIV (1954), 97-110; XV (1955), 12-19.

———, "Yiddish," part of a series on "Languages of the Jews," *Algemayne Entsiklopedye,* II (1940), 25-90.

Weinreich, Uriel (ed.), *The Field of Yiddish. Studies in Yiddish Language, Folklore, and Literature.* New York, 1954. (Publications of the Linguistic Circle of New York—No. 3. Edited by Uriel Weinreich. Published on the Occasion of the Bicentennial of Columbia University.)

———, "Mapping a Culture," Columbia University *Forum,* VI (No. 3, 1963), 17-21.

Weinryb, Bernhard (Dob Ber), "Musar Movement," *UJE,* VIII (1942), 43-44.

——, "Problems in the Economic and Social History of German Jews" (Hebrew), *Zion,* I (1936), 284-315.

Weisel, Leopold, "Die Prager Juden, wie sie leben," *BSV,* XVII (1926), 192-212.

———, "Die Jeschiboth oder jüdischen Hochschulen." *BSV,* XVII (1926), 180-86.

Weissenberg, S., "Das Feld- und das Kejwermessen," *MGJV,* XVII (1906), 39-45. Relating to customs observed in the cemetery.

———, "Das Purimspiel von Ahasverus und Esther," *MGJV,* XIII (1904), 1-27.

———, "Eine jüdische Beschwörungsformel gegen den bösen Blick," *MGJV,* XXXVI (1910), 166-67.

———, "Eine jüdische Hochzeit in Südrussland," *MGJV,* XV (1905), 59-74.

———, and Max Grunwald, "Josef und Seine Brüder," *MGJV,* XXXV (1910), 97-117.

Wellesz, J., "Kabbalistische Rezepte, Wundermittel und Amulette," *MGJV,* XXXIX (1911), 127-30.

———, "Volksmedizinisches aus dem jüdischen Mittelalter," *MGJV,* XXXV (1910), 117-20.

Wenisch, Rudolf, "Juden als Hausbesitzer in Komotau vor der Ausweisung (1468-1526)," *ZGJT,* I^2 (1930), 91-98.

Wettstein, F. H., "The Past History of the Jews of Cracow and Poland Based on Early Communal Minutes" (Hebrew), *'Oẓar ha-Safrut,* IV (1892), 577-642. (For the period of the 16th and 18th centuries.)

Weyden, Ernst, *Geschichte der Juden in Köln am Rhein von den Römerzeiten bis auf die Gegenwart. Nebst Noten und Urkunden.* Cologne: Du Mont-Schauberg, 1867.

Weynart, Herman, "Nachlese zur Geschichte der Juden in Österreich," *Jahrbuch für die Gesch. der Juden und des Judenthums,* II (1861), 380-99.

Wiener, Adolph, *Die jüdischen Speisegesetze nach ihren verschiedenen Gesichtspunkten; zum ersten Male wissenschaftlich geordnet und kritisch beleuchtet.* Breslau: Schottlaender, 1895.

Wiener, M., "Geschichte der Juden in der Residenzstadt Hannover," *MGWJ,* X (1861), 241-58.

Wiernik, Peter, "Mendel Levin," *JE,* VIII (1905), 41.

Wind, Solomon, *Rabbi Yeḥezḳe'l Landau, Toledot Ḥayyav u-Pe'ullotav* (Ezekiel Landau: The History of His Life and Work). Jerusalem: Da'at Torah and Mosad Harav Kook, 1961.

———, "The *Responsum Noda' bi-Yehudah* as a Source for Jewish History" (Hebrew), *Ḥoreb,* X (1948), 57-76.

Wirth, Louis, *The Ghetto.* University of Chicago Press, Phoenix Book, 1956. Reprint 4th edit.

Wischnitzer, Rachel, "Mutual Influences between eastern and western Europe in the Synagogue Architecture from the 12th to the 18th Century" (Yiddish), *Yivo Bleter,* XXIX (1947), 3-50.

Wolf, Albert, and Max Grunwald, "Fahrende Leute bei den Juden," *MGJV,* XXVII (1908), 89-96; XXVIII (1908), 150-56; XXIX (1909), 4-29; XXX (1909), 40-62; XXXI (1909), 90-94.

Wolf, Gerson, *Die Juden.* Mit einer Schlussbetrachtung von Wilhelm Goldbaum. Vienna-Teschen: K. Prochaska, 1883. (Die Völker Oesterreich-Ungarns; Ethnographische und culturhistorische Schilderungen, vol. vii.)

———, *Die jüdischen Friedhöfe und die 'Chewra Kadischa' (fromme Bruderschaft). . . .* Vienna: A. Hölder, 1879. (Veröffentlicht vom Vorstande der 'Chewra Kadischa' in Wien . . . . A pamphlet.)

———, *Die Juden in der Leopoldstadt ("unterer Werd") im 17. Jahrhundert in Wien.* Vienna: Herzfeld-Bauer, 1864.

———, *Ferdinand II. und die Juden. Nach Aktenstücken in den Archiven der k. k. Ministerien des Innern und des Aeussern.* Vienna: W. Braumüller, 1859.

———, *Geschichte der Juden in Wien (1156-1876).* Vienna: A. Hölder, 1876.

———, "Verzeichnis der Prager Juden, ihrer Frauen, Kinder und Dienstboten im Jahre 1546," *ZGJD,* I (O. S., 1887), 177-89.

———, "Zur Geschichte der Juden in Deutschland," *ZGJD,* III (O. S., 1889), 159-84.

———, "Zur Geschichte der Juden in Worms und des deutschen Städtewesens," *MGWJ,* X (1861), 361-76, 410-30, 453-63.

———, *Zur Geschichte der Juden in Worms und des deutschen Städtewesens. Nach archivalischen Urkunden des k. k. Ministeriums des Aeussern in Wien.* Breslau: Schletter, 1862.

Yellenik, Aaron, "The *Memor*-Book of Worms, 1696" (Hebrew), *Ḳobeẓ 'al Yad,* III (1887), 5-62.

Ysaye, L., and A. Landau, "Einiges aus den Memoiren der Glückel von Hameln," *MGJV,* VII (1901), 1-68.

Zeitlin, William, "Zur Geschichte des Totenaberglauben," *MGJV,* XLIV (1912), 134-35.

Zevin, Solomon Joseph, *Ha-Mo'adim be-Halakhah* (The relation of festivals to Jewish law). Tel-Aviv: A. Zioni, 1953.

Ziegler, Ignaz, *Dokumente zur Geschichte der Juden in Karlsbad (1791-1869).* Karlsbad: R. Hengstenberg, 1913. (See pp. 7-39, covering from the Middle Ages through 1806.)

Zimmels, H. J., *Ashkenazim and Sephardim: Their Relations, Differences and Problems as Reflected in the Rabbinical Responsa.* London: Oxford University Press, 1958. (Jews' College Publications, New Series, No. 2.)

Zuckerman, M., *Dokumente zur Geschichte der Juden in Hannover.* Hanover, 1908.

Zum 900-jährigen Bestehen der Synagoge zu Worms. Eine Erinnerungsgabe des Vorstands der Israelitischen Religionsgemeinde Worms. Edited by Alfred Hirschberg. Berlin: Philo, 1934.

Zunz, Leopold, *Die gottesdienstlichen Vorträge der Juden, historisch entwickelt.* Frankfort: Kauffmann, 1892.

———, Yom-Ṭob Lippmann (Leopold), *Ha-Derashot be-Yisra'el ve-Hishtalshelutan ha-Hisṭorit.* Hebrew edition of *Die Gottesdienstlichen Vorträge.* Edited by Chanoch Albeck. Jerusalem: Mosad Bialik, 1947. (Sifre Mofet be-Ḥokhmat Yisra'el: Significant Books in the Scientific Study of Judaism, ed. J. P. Lachover, vol. i.)

———, *Die Ritus des synagogalen Gottesdienstes, geschichtlich entwickelt.* Berlin: Springer, 1859. (*Die Synagogale Poesie des Mittelalters,* vol. ii.)

SECTION 4B

Albers, Johann Heinrich, *Das Jahr und seine Feste. Die Feste und Feiertage des Jahres, ihre Entstehung, Entwicklung und Bedeutung in Geschichte, Sage, Sitte und Gebrauch.* Stuttgart: J. Wegner, 1917.

Aus Hamburgs Vergangenheit. Edited by Karl Koppmann. 2 vols. Hamburg-Leipzig: Voss, 1886.

Avé-Lallemant, Friedrich Christian Benedict, *Das deutsche Gaunerthum in seiner sozial-politischen, literarischen und linguistischen Ausbildung zu seinem heutigen Bestande.* 4 vols. in 2. Leipzig: F. A. Brockhaus, 1858-62. (Due to his bias, he has to be read critically as one does Schudt, p. 356.)

Bauer, Max, *Das Geschlechtsleben in der deutschen Vergangenheit.* Leipzig: H. Seemann, 1902.

Bach, Adolph, *Deutsche Volkskunde, ihre Wege, Ergebnisse und Aufgaben.* Leipzig: S. Hirzel, 1907.

Bax, Ernest B., *German Culture, Past and Present.* New York: McBride-Nast, 1915.

Before Philosophy; the Intellectual Adventure of Ancient Man. An Essay on Specu-

lative Thought in the Ancient Near East. Edited by Henri Frankfort, *et al.* Aylesbury-London: Penguin Books, 1949. (Original edition, *The Intellectual Adventure of Ancient Man.* University of Chicago Press, 1946.)

Benedict, Ruth, "Folklore," *Encyclopaedia of the Social Sciences,* VI (1931), 288-93.

Bielenstein, Martha, "Bast und Rinde an der Kleidung der alten Letten," *ZVV,* III (1931), 147-56.

Black, G. W., *Folk-Medicine; a Chapter in the History of Culture.* London: Stock, 1883. (Publications of the Folklore Society, vol. xii.)

Blau, Joseph, *Böhmerwälder, Hausindustrie und Volkskunst.* Vol. II. Prague: J. G. Calve, 1918. (*BDBV,* xiv².)

Bode, Wilhelm, *Kurze Geschichte der Trinksitten und Mässigkeitsbestrebungen in Deutschland.* Munich: J. F. Lehmann, 1896.

Bodemeyer, Hildebrand, *Hannoversche Rechtsalterthümer. Die Luxus- und Sitten-Gesetze.* Göttingen: Dieterich, 1857. (See "Kleiderordnungen," sec. 1.)

Boehn, Max, *Deutschland im XVIII. Jahrhundert.* 2 vols. Berlin: Askan, 1922.

———, *Die Mode; Menschen und Moden im siebzehnten Jahrhundert nach Bildern und Stichen der Zeit.* Edited by Oskar Fischel. Munich: Bruckmann, 1913.

———, *Die Mode; Menschen und Moden im achtzehnten Jahrhundert. nach Bildern und Stichen der Zeit.* Edited by Oskar Fischel. 3d edit. Munich: Bruckmann, 1923.

Böhme, Franz Magnus, *Geschichte des Tanzes in Deutschland. Beitrag zur deutschen Sitten-, Literatur-, und Musikgeschichte. Nach den Quellen zum erstenmal bearbeitet und mit alten Tanzliedern und Musikproben.* 2 vols. in one. Leipzig: Breitkopf-Härtel, 1886.

Bonser, Wilfred, "General Medical Practice in Anglo-Saxon England," *Science, Medicine and History: Essays . . . in Honour of Charles Singer* (Oxford University Press, 1953), I, 154-63.

Boos, Heinrich, *Geschichte der rheinischen Städtekultur von ihren Anfängen bis zur Gegenwart mit besonderer Berücksichtigung der Stadt Worms.* 2d edit. Vol. III. Berlin: Stargardt, 1889.

Bothe, Friedrich, *Geschichte der Stadt Frankfurt am Main.* Frankfort: Diesterweg, 1913.

Brand, John, *Popular Antiquities of Great Britain; Faiths and Folklore; a Dictionary of . . . Popular Customs, Past and Current.* Edited by W. Carew Hazlitt. 2 vols. London: Reeves-Turner, 1905.

Byloff, Fritz, "Volkskundliches aus Strafprozessen der Österreichischen Alpenländer, mit besonderer Berücksichtigung der Zauberei- und Hexenprozesse 1455 bis 1850," *Quellen zur deutschen Volkskunde,* III (1929), 1-68.

Cassirer, Ernst, *An Essay on Man. An Introduction to a Philosophy of Human Culture.* New York: Doubleday, 1953. (A Doubleday Anchor Book.)

Chambers, R., *The Book of Days, a Miscellany of Popular Antiquities in connection with the Calendar*. 2 vols. Philadelphia: J. B. Lippincott, 1891.

Creizenach, Wilhelm (ed.), *Die Schauspiele der englischen Komödianten*. Berlin-Stuttgart: W. Spemann, 1889. (Deutsche National-Literatur, ed. Joseph Kürschner, vol. xxiii.)

Darmstaedter, Paul, *Das Grossherzogtum Frankfurt*. Frankfort: J. Baer, 1901.

Das deutsche Volkstum. Edited by Hans Meyer. rev. edit. Leipzig-Vienna: Bibliographisches Institut, 1899.

Dieffenbacher, Julius, *Deutsches Leben im 12. und 13. Jahrhundert*. 2 vols. Berlin-Leipzig: G. J. Goschen, 1918-19. (See vol. II, secs. on furniture, clothing, the chase.)

Deutsche Volkskunde, inbesondere zum Gebrauch der Volkschullehrer. Edited by John Meier. Berlin-Leipzig: W. de Gruyter, 1926. (Im Auftrage des Verbandes Deutscher Vereine für Volkskunde.)

Deutsches Krankeitsnamen-Buch. Edited by Max Höfler. Munich: Piloty-Loehle, 1899.

Diepgen, Paul, *Geschichte der Medizin; die historische Entwicklung der Heilkunde und des ärztlichen Lebens*. 2 vols. Berlin-Leipzig: J. Goschen, 1913-14.

Duller, Eduard, *Das deutsche Volk in seinen Mundarten, Sitten, Gebräuchen, Festen und Trachten. Mit 50 kolorirten Bildern*. Leipzig: Wigand, 1847.

Englisch-deutsche botanische Terminologie. Edited by Helen and Eric Ashby, Harald Richter, and Johannes Bärner. London: T. Murby, 1938.

Ennemoser, Joseph, *The History of Magic*. Translated by William Howitt. 2 vols. London: H. G. Bohn, 1894.

Falke, Jakob, *Die deutsche Trachten- und Modenwelt; ein Beitrag zur deutschen Culturgeschichte*. 2 vols. Leipzig: G. Mayer, 1858. (Deutsches Leben. Eine Sammlung abgeschlossener Schilderungen aus der deutschen Geschichte, vol. i.)

Fecht, Karl G., *Geschichte der Haupt- und Residenzstadt Karlsruhe*. Karlsruhe: Macklot, 1887.

Freybe, Albert, *Der deutsche Volksaberglaube in seinem Verhältnis zum Christentum und im Unterschiede von der Zauberei*. Gotha: F. A. Perthes, 1910.

Friedländer, Ludwig Hermann, *Vorlesungen über die Geschichte der Heilkunde*. Leipzig: Voss, 1839.

Fuhse, Franz, *Sitten und Gebräuche der Deutschen beim Essen und Trinken von den ältesten Zeiten bis zum Schlusse des XI. Jahrhunderts*. Wolfenbüttel: O. Wollermann, 1891. (Dissertation.)

Geramb, Viktor, "Die Knaffl-Handschrift, eine obersteirische Volkskunde aus dem Jahre 1813," *Quellen zur deutschen Volkskunde*, II (1928), 7-172. (See bibliography and secs. on folk medicine, marriage, burial customs, and dress.)

Section 4B

Gleichen-Russwurm, Alexander, *Die gotische Welt: Sitten und Gebräuche im späten Mittelalter.* Stuttgart: J. Hoffmann, 1919.

Goetz, Wilhelm, "Speise und Trank vergangener Zeiten in deutschen Landen," *Oeffentliche Vorträge gehalten in der Schweiz,* VI (1882), 3-24.

Gomme, George Lawrence, *Folklore as an Historical Science.* London: Methuen, 1908.

Grimm, Jakob, *Deutsche Mythologie.* Edited by Elard Hugo Meyer. 4th edit. 3 vols. Berlin: Ferd. Dümmler, 1876-78.

Gubernatis, Angelo de, *La mythologie des plantes; ou, Les légendes du règne végétal.* 2 vols. Paris: Reinwald, 1878-82.

Haas, William S., *The Destiny of the Mind, East and West.* New York: Macmillan, 1956.

Häberlin, Karb, "Trauertrachten und Trauergebräuche auf der Insel Föhr," *ZVV,* XIX (1909), 261-81. (Föhr: North Frisian Island.)

Haendcke, Berthold, *Deutsche Kultur im Zeitalter des 30jährigen Krieges.* Leipzig: E. A. Seemann, 1906.

Haggard, Howard W., *Mystery, Magic, and Medicine; the Rise of Medicine from Superstition to Science.* Garden City, N. Y.: Doubleday-Doran, 1933.

Hampe, Theodor, *Die fahrenden Leute in der deutschen Vergangenheit.* Leipzig: E. Diederich, 1902. (Monographien zur deutschen Kulturgeschichte, vol. x.)

Handbook of Plants. Edited by Peter Henderson. New York, 1881.

Handwörterbuch der Pharmakognosie des Pflanzenreichs. Edited by Georg C. Wittstein. Breslau: Trewendt, 1882.

Hanika, Josef, "Kultische Vorstufen des Pflanzenanbaues," *ZVV,* L (N. S., 1953), 49-65.

Heintze, Albert, *Die deutschen Familiennamen geschichtlich, geographisch, sprachlich.* Edited by Paul Cascorbi. 6th edit. Halle a. d. Saale: Buchhandlung des Waisenhauses, 1925.

Henne am Rhyn, Otto, *Kulturgeschichte des deutschen Volkes.* 2 vols. Berlin: Grote, 1886.

Heyne, Moriz, *Körperpflege und Kleidung bei den Deutschen von den ältesten geschichtlichen Zeiten bis zum 16. Jahrhundert.* Leipzig, 1903.

Höfler, Max, *Volksmedizinische Botanik der Germanen.* Vienna: R. Ludwig, 1908. (Quellen und Forschungen zur deutschen Volkskunde, ed. E. K. Blümml, vol. v.)

Horne, Anton, *Geschichte von Frankfurt am Main.* Edited by H. Grotefend. 2d edit. Frankfort: Carl Jügel, 1882.

Hottenroth, Friedrich, *Deutsche Volkstrachten vom XVI. bis zum XIX. Jahrhundert.* 2d edit. 3 vols. in one. Frankfort: H. Keller, 1923.

Hovorka, Oskar, and Adolf Kronfeld, *Vergleichende Volksmedizin. Eine Darstellung volksmedizinischer Sitten und Gebräuche, Anschauungen und Heilfaktoren des*

Aberglaubens und der Zaubermedizin. 2 vols. Stuttgart: Strecker-Schröder, 1908-1909.

Huss, Karl, *Die Schrift 'Vom Aberglauben.' Nach dem in der fürstlich Metternichschen Bibliothek zu Königswart befindlichen Manuskripte.* Edited by Alois John. Prague: J. Calve, 1910. (*BDBV,* vol. ix, Pt. 2.)

Kirchner, Anton, *Ansichten von Frankfurt am Main und seiner Umgegend.* 2 vols. Frankfort: Wilman, 1818.

Krappe, Alexander H., *The Science of Folk-Lore.* New York: Macveagh, 1930.

Kretschmer, Albert, *Deutsche Volkstrachten. Original-Zeichnungen mit erklärendem Text.* 2d edit. Leipzig: J. G. Bach's Verlag (F. E. Köhler), 1887-89.

Kriegk, George Ludwig, *Frankfurter Bürgerzwiste und Zustände im Mittelalter. Beitrag zur Geschichte des deutschen Bürgerthums.* Frankfort: Sauerländer, 1862. (See chap. ix, "Das Innere der Stadt Frankfurt im Mittelalter.")

Kück, Eduard, and Heinrich Sohnrey (eds.), *Feste und Spiele des deutschen Landvolks.* 2d edit. Berlin, 1911. (Im Auftrage des deutschen Vereins für Ländliche Wohlfahrts- und Heimatspflege.)

Laufer, Otto, "Jungfernkranz und Brautkrone," *ZVV,* II (N. F., 1930), 25-29.

Lehmann, Alfred, *Aberglaube und Zauberei.* Edited by D. Peterson. 3d edit. Stuttgart: Enke, 1925.

Leithaeuser, Julius, *Bergische Pflanzennamen.* Elberfeld: Martini-Grutefien, 1912.

Lippert, Julius, *Deutsche Sittengeschichte.* 3 vols. Leipzig-Prague: Freytag-Tempsky, 1889. (Das Wissen der Gegenwart: Deutsche Universal-Bibliothek für Gebildete, vol. lxviii-lxx.)

Loewe, Richard, *Germanische Pflanzennamen.* Heidelberg: Carl Winter, 1913.

Magnus, Hugo, *Der Aberglaube in der Medizin.* Breslau: Kern, 1903. (Abhandlungen zur Geschichte der Medizin, vol. vi.)

———, *Die Volksmedizin, ihre geschichtliche Entwicklung und ihre Beziehungen zur Kultur.* Breslau: Kern, 1905. (Abhandlungen zur Geschichte der Medizin, vol. xv.)

Malinowski, Bronislaw, *Magic, Science and Religion, and Other Essays.* With an introduction by Robert Redfield. New York: Doubleday (Doubleday Anchor Book), 1954.

Mannhardt, Wilhelm, *Wald- und Feldkulte.* 2 vols. 2d edit. Berlin: Borntraeger, 1904-1905.

Martin, Alfred, "Deutsche Volksmedizin," in *Handbuch der deutschen Volkskunde* (ed. Wilhelm Pessler), I (Leipzig, 1934), 271-85.

———, "Geschichte der Tanzkrankheit in Deutschland," *ZVV,* XXIV (1914), 113-34, 225-39.

Medical Dictionary. Edited by Emmanuel Veillon. New York: Grune-Stratton, 1950.

Meigen, Wilhelm, *Die deutschen Pflanzennamen.* Berlin: Allgemeiner deutscher Sprachverein (F. Berggold), 1898.

Section 4B

Michelet, Jules, *Satanism and Witchcraft. A Study in Medieval Superstition.* Translated by A. R. Allinson. New York: Citadel, 1926.

Mogk, Eugen, *Deutsche Sitten und Bräuche.* Edited by Laurence Fossler. New York: Henry Holt, 1912.

Montanus, pseud. (Zuccalmaglio, Vincenz), *Die deutschen Volksfeste, Volksbräuche und deutscher Volksglaube in Sagen, Märlein und Volksliedern. Ein Beitrag zur vaterländischen Sittengeschichte.* 2 vols. in one. Iserlohn-Elberfeld: J. Bädeker, 1854-58. (See pp. 79-90.)

Neuburger, Max, *Geschichte der Medizin.* Vol. II, Pt. 1. Stuttgart: Enke, 1911.

Nicaise, E., *La grande chirurgie de Guy de Chauliac, composée en l'an 1363.* Paris: F. Alcan, 1890.

Opitz, Karl, "Avicenna, das Lehrgedicht über die Heilkunde (Canticum de Medicina). Aus dem Arabischen übersetzt," *Quellen und Studien zur Geschichte der Naturwissenschaften und der Medizin,* VII (1940), 150-220.

Paul, Hermann, "Das volkskundliche Material," in *idem, Grundriss der germanischen Philologie,* XII (1935), 277-307, 315-17.

Pessler, Wilhelm (ed.), *Handbuch der deutschen Volkskunde.* Vol. I. Potsdam, 1934.

Peuckert, Will-Erich, and Otto Laufer, *Volkskunde; Quellen und Forschungen seit 1930.* Bern: A. Francke, 1951. (Wissenschaftliche Forschungsberichte. Geisteswissenschaftliche Reihe, vol. xiv.)

Pritzel, Georg, and Karl Jessen, *Die deutschen Volksnamen der Pflanzen. Neuer Beitrag zum deutschen Sprachschatze. Aus allen Mundarten und Zeiten zusammengestellt.* Hanover: P. Cohen, 1882.

Radford, Edwin and M. A., *Encyclopædia of Superstitions.* New York: Philosophical Library, 1949.

Randall, John Herman, Jr., *The Making of the Modern Mind. A Survey of the Intellectual Background of the Present Age.* Boston-New York: Houghton Mifflin, 1926.

Renner, H. D., *The Origin of Food Habits.* London: Faber-Faber, 1944.

Richter, Albert, *Bilder aus der deutschen Kulturgeschichte.* Vol. 2. Leipzig: Brandstetter, 1882.

Riesman, David, *The Story of Medicine in the Middle Ages.* New York: Hoeber, 1935.

Ritter, Moriz, *Deutsche Geschichte im Zeitalter der Gegenreformation und des Dreissigjährigen Krieges (1555-1648).* 3 vols. Stuttgart-Berlin: I. G. Cotta, 1889-1908. (See vols. II-III.)

Rochholz, Ernst Ludwig, *Deutscher Glaube und Brauch im Spiegel der heidnischen Vorzeit.* 2 vols. in one. Berlin: Dümmler, 1867.

Sach, August, *Deutsches Leben in der Vergangenheit.* 2 vols. Halle a. d. Saale: Waisenhaus, 1890-91. (See vol. ii, chaps. 19, 30.)

Sachs, Curt, *World History of the Dance.* Translated by Bessie Schönberg. New York: W. W. Norton, 1937.

Sächsische Volkskunde. Edited by Robert Wuttke. 2d edit. Dresden: Schonfeld, 1901.

Sachwörterbuch der Deutschkunde. Vol. II. Edited by Walther Hofstätter and Ulrich Peters. Leipzig-Berlin: Teubner, 1930.

Saldanha, J. A., "The Province of Folklore in Religion, Law and Science," *The Journal of Anthropological Society*, XII (Bombay, 1922), 277-90.

Sarton, George, *Introduction to the History of Science*. Vol. II, Pt. 1, "From Ben Ezra to Roger Bacon." Vol. II, Pt. 2, "From Robert Grosseteste to Roger Bacon." Baltimore: Williams-Wilkins (Pub. for the Carnegie Institution of Washington), 1931. (See Pt. 1, chaps. x, xxiv, "Medicine"; Pt. 2, chaps. xi, xxxviii, "Medicine.")

Sartori, Paul, *Sitte und Brauch*. 3 vols. Leipzig: Heims, 1910-14.

Schairer, I., *Das religiöse Volksleben am Ausgang des Mittelalters, nach Augsburger Quellen*. Leipzig-Berlin: B. G. Teubner, 1914. (Beiträge zur Kulturgeschichte des Mittelalters und der Renaissance, ed. Walter Goetz, vol. xiii.) (Doctoral dissertation.)

Schmidt, Georg (ed.), *Mieser Kräuter- und Arzneienbuch*. Prague: J. G. Calve, 1905. (*BDBV*, vol. v, Pt. 3.)

Schnapper-Arndt, Gottlieb, *Studien zur Geschichte der Lebenshaltung in Frankfurt a. M. während des 17. und 18. Jahrhunderts*. Auf Grund des Nachlasses von Gottlieb Schnapper-Arndt. Herausgegeben von Karl Bräuer. 2 vols. Frankfort: J. Baer, 1915. (Historische Kommission der Stadt Frankfurt a. M.)

Schramek, Josef, *Das Böhmerwaldbauernhaus*. Prague: Calve, 1908. (Beiträge zur deutsch-böhmischen Volkskunde, vol. ix, Pt. 1.)

Schultz, Alwin, *Das häusliche Leben der europäischen Kulturvölker vom Mittelalter bis zur zweiten Hälfte des XVIII. Jahrhunderts*. Munich-Berlin: R. Oldenbourg, 1903. (Handbuch der Mittelalterlichen und Neueren Geschichte, eds. G. Below and F. Meinecke, vol. iv.)

———, *Deutsches Leben im XIV. und XV. Jahrhundert*. 2 vols. Vienna: Tempsky, 1892.

Seligmann, Siegfried, *Der böse Blick und Verwandtes. Ein Beitrag zur Geschichte des Aberglaubens aller Zeiten und Völker*. 2 vols. Berlin: Barsdorf, 1910.

Sidgwick, Alfred (Mrs.), *Home Life in Germany*. London: Methuen, 1908.

Singer, Charles, *A Short History of Medicine. Introducing Medical Principles to Students and Non-Medical Readers*. New York: Oxford University Press, American Branch, 1928.

Specht, Franz Anton, *Gastmähler und Trinkgelage bei den Deutschen, von den ältesten Zeiten bis ins neunzehnte Jahrhundert. Ein Beitrag zur deutschen Kulturgeschichte*. Stuttgart: J. C. Cotta, 1887.

Steinhausen, Georg, *Geschichte des deutschen Briefes. Zur Kulturgeschichte des deutschen Volkes*. Berlin: R. Gaertner, 1889. (See chap. 3, "Wie man mit einander verkehrte.")

Section 4B

Steinhausen, Georg, *Häusliches und gesellschaftliches Leben im neunzehnten Jahrhundert.* Berlin: S. Cronbach, 1898.

Sudhoff, Karl, *The Earliest Printed Literature on Syphilis, being Ten Tracts from the Years 1495-1498. In Complete Facsimile with an Introduction and other Accessory Material.* Edited by Charles Singer. Florence: R. Lier, 1925.

Taylor, Archer, "Germanic Folklore," *Standard Dictionary of Folklore* (Funk and Wagnalls), I, 445-51.

Thompson, Stith, "Folklore and Literature," *PMLA* (Publications of the Modern Language Association), LV (1940), 866-74.

———, "Folklore at Midcentury," *Midwest Folklore,* I (No. 1., 1951), 5-12.

———, *The Folktale.* New York: Dryden Press, 1946. (See esp., pp. 17, 234-43, 378.)

———, "The Importance of Folklore Study in the Near East and in Israel" (Hebrew), *Yeda'-'Am,* III (No. 1, 1955), 3-4.

Thorndike, Lynn, *A History of Magic and Experimental Science during the First Sixteen Centuries of Our Era.* 6 vols. New York: Macmillan and Columbia University Press, 1929-41. (See vol. iv.)

Vaillat, Léandre, *Histoire de la danse.* Paris: Plon, 1947. (Collection *ars et historia,* ed. J. and R. Wittmann.)

Walsh, James J., *Medieval Medicine.* London: Black, 1920.

Walsh, William S., *Curiosities of Popular Customs and of Rites, Ceremonies, Observances, and Miscellaneous Antiquities.* Philadelphia: J. B. Lippincott, 1900.

Weiss, Hermann, *Kostümkunde. Geschichte der Tracht und des Geräthes vom 14ten Jahrhundert bis auf die Gegenwart.* 2 vols. Stuttgart: Ebner-Seubert, 1872.

Wuttke, Adolf, *Der deutsche Volksaberglaube der Gegenwart.* 2d edit. Berlin: Wiegand-Grieben, 1869.

NAME INDEX

Name Index

Mordecai, 184, 187, 188
Moritz, Prince of Nassau, 13

Naḥmanides, Moses, 8

Oppenheim, David, of Prague, 8, 94, 95, 98, 99, 101, 107, 184
Oppenheimer, Samuel b. Emanuel, 7

Poppers, Meir, of Posen, 108
Plungian, Zechariah, 17, 105, 107, 149
Prager, Samuel, 152

Rachel, 188, 334 n. 212
Rashi, 76, 77
Reischer, Jacob, 123, 125, 128, 130, 131, 138, 142, 143, 168, 169
Rivkind, Isaac, 59–60
Rosanes, Judah, 8
Rubin, Shlomo, 38

Sabbatai (Shabbetai) Ẓebi of Smyrna, 93, 243 n. 91
Sammael, 117
Samson of Kamenetz, 133
Schechter, Solomon, 59, 63
Schudt, Johann Jacob, 17, 86, 89, 120, 154, 256 n. 3, 264 n. 54
Seligmann zur goldnen Crone (Kronė), 4, 5, 6
Shabbetai Kohen (Shakh), 41, 110
Sirkes, Joel, 34
Sofer, Moses ("Ḥatam Sofer"), 178
Solomon ibn Adret (Rashba), 8, 79

Uceda, Samuel de, 8

Wallich, Abraham, 128, 138
Wolf, Christoph, 8

Yeḳutiel b. Abigdor, 8
Yuspa Shammash (Shammes), xvi, 18, 22, 24, 33, 60, 154, 174–75, 189, 190

Ẓipporah, daughter of Glikl of Hameln, 13, 38, 131
Zisel, wife of Samuel Prager, 152

SUBJECT INDEX

Subject Index

Incense box, 5
Individual, freedom of, 32
Individual responsibilities, 67–68, 148, 227 n. 150, 228 n. 156, 246 n. 116
Individualism, rise of, 218 n. 80
Insomnia, remedy for, 141
Instrumental music, 35, 80–81, 154–55, 191, 254 n. 190, 317 nn. 43–44, 46–47, 317–18 n. 48, 336 n. 234
Iron object, as protection for mother in delivery, 16
Isserles: glosses, 101, 325 n. 124, 329 n. 176, 332 n. 193, 337 n. 251

Jahrzeit. See Yortsayt
Jerusalem, fall of, 29, 106, 155, 193, 223 n. 122, 337 n. 250. *See also* Ninth of *'Ab*
Jester, 33, 35, 184, 224 n. 126. *See also Badḥan*; *Marshelik*
Jews and non-Jews, 80, 121, 155, 216 n. 63, 239 n. 50, 263 n. 49
  relationships between, 10–14, 96, 159, 190, 195, 209 n. 70, 296 n. 81, 299 n. 99, 338 n. 263
Johannes Feuer, 175, 177, 328 n. 151
Judengasse, 63, 202 n. 6. *See also Gas*

Ḳaddish, 44, 148, 229 n. 159, 231 n. 172
Ḳaddish de-Rabbanan, 72
Kameoth, 115. *See also* Amulets
Kapelushin, 266 n. 69
Kashe, 97, 112, 268–69 n. 13
Kehillah, 50
Ḳiddush cup, 219 n. 92
Kikhelekh, 106, 112, 280 n. 84
Ḳinot, 196
Kirchheim, synagogue of, 316 n. 39
Kitl, 45
Klaffzimmer, 80, 254 n. 190
Klag-lider, 188
Kleinsteinach, 27
Klezmer. See Musicians
Kloyz, frontispiece, 72–73, 335 n. 223
Ḳnas-mol (*ḳnas*–meal), 29–30, 36, 219 n. 84, 309 n. 186
Kneydlekh, 97, 112, 268 n. 12
Kohanim, 93
Kota, 85, 89, 91, 94, 260–61 n. 35
Kotsn (*ḳaẓin*), 47, 233 n. 187, 246 n. 113
Kragn, 46, 90, 91, 92 (Fig. 8), 93, 94, 262 n. 39
Krems, 165–66, 209 n. 70, 323 n. 103
  legislation, communal in, 219 n. 85
Kugl, 112, 275 n. 39
Kurdistan, Jews of, 22, 212 n. 17. *See also* Night of Sheshah
Kvater, 23–24, 215 n. 52. *See also Sandeḳ*
Kvaterin, 24. *See also Sandeket*

Lag ba-'Omer, 36
Laḥash. See Incantations
Lamentations, 196
Latwerge, 271 n. 28, 272 n. 29
Layman, 32, 47, 233 n. 187
Leb Tob, 8, 69
Legislations
  communal, 6
    Altona, Hamburg, and Wandsbek, 20, 31, 32, 60, 65, 259 n. 20
    Austerlitz, Moravia, 220 n. 96
    Bamberg, 148, 219 n. 92
    Budapest, 270 n. 23
    Düsseldorf, 148
    Frankfort, 86, 258 n. 19
    Gaya, 36, 219 n. 93, 220 n. 97, 238 n. 37
    Hesse, province of, 35
    Karlsruhe, 221 n. 103
    Krems, 219 n. 85
    Nikolsburg, 63
    Nuremberg and Fürth, 86, 161
    Prague, 246 n. 16, 304 n. 127
    Runkel, 39, 148, 329 n. 182
  governmental, 85–86, 131, 144, 209 n. 71, 261 n. 35
    Stättigkeiten, 9, 89, 195, 256 n. 2, 337 nn. 257–58
Lehrschule. See Bet ha-midrash
Lekhah Dodi, 153, 154

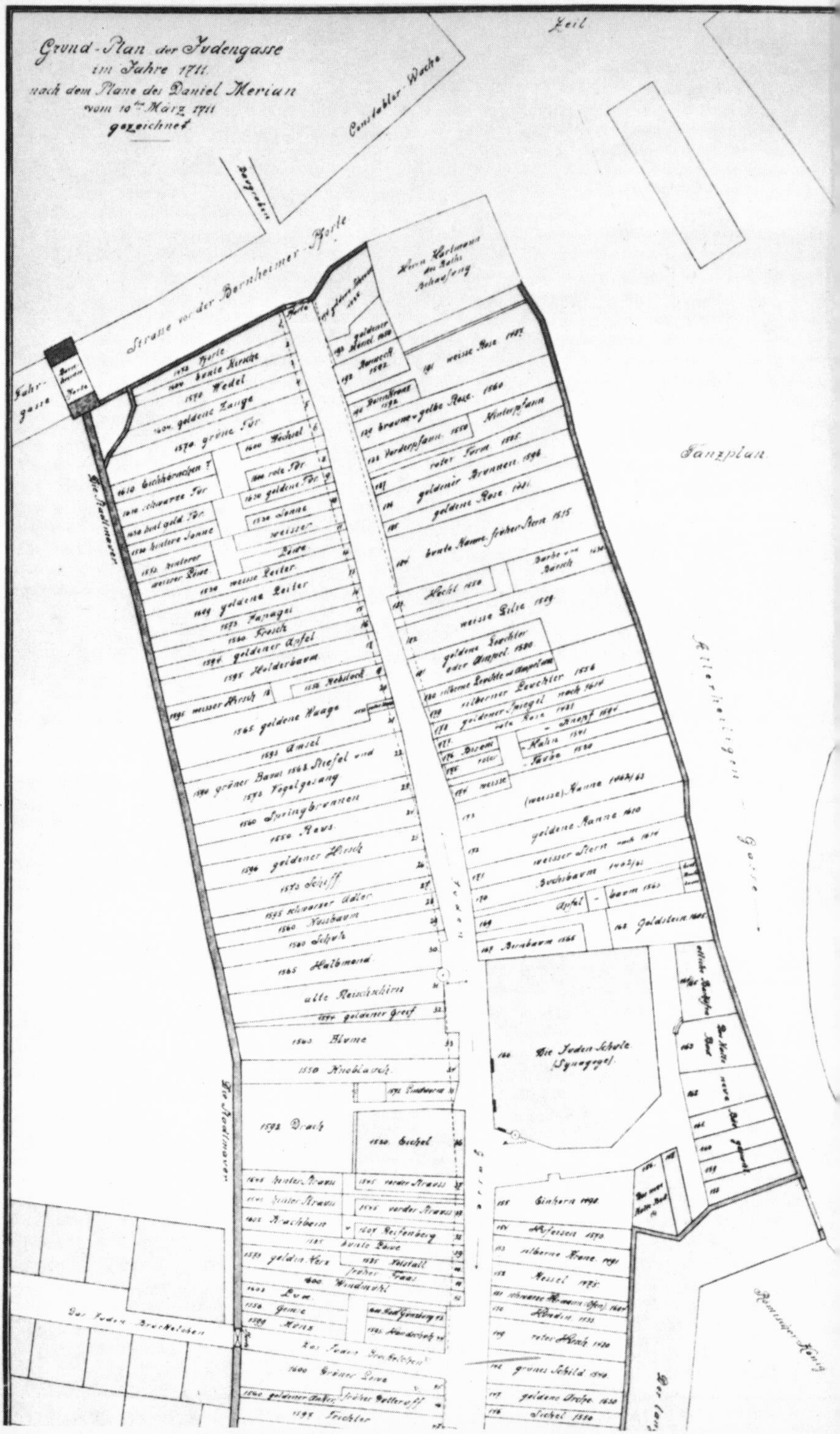
Grund-Plan der Judengasse
im Jahre 1711
nach dem Plane des Daniel Merian
vom 10ten März 1711
gezeichnet
Zeil
Constabler-Wache
Strasse vor der Bornheimer-Porte
Fahrgasse
Tanzplan
Allerheiligen Gasse
Die Stadtmauer
Die Juden-Schule (Synagoge)
Das Juden Brückelchen

1565 fröhlicher Mann
1570 roter Apfel
1560 Paradies
Pelikan oder Hochzeitshaus
1540 Büchse
1506 goldener Schwan
Vorder-
1515 Schlüssel
1565 Schloss und
1590 weisse Gans
1585 goldener Helm
1550 hinterer Falke
1570 hinterer Kranich
1590 Kranich
1585 enge Tür
1575 hinterer Pflug
1575 Pflug
nach 1614
Ampel
1565 Salmen
1586 weisses Lamm
1585 goldene Stelz
1530 Maus
1585 goldene Geiss
1590 goldenes Schaf
1596 schwarzer Kappe
1599 goldener Hut
1590 goldener Hahn
1585 weisser Turm
1585 schwarzer Hirsch
1550 (rotes) Schwert
1590 goldenes od. weisses Schwert
1600 Kastenbaum
1600 Feigenbaum
1550 goldene Kette
1589 goldener Adler
1580 schwarzer Schild
roter Hut
1560 Steeg
1560 Stuhl
1595 goldener Knopf
1575 Eule
goldene Ente
Bad und Schlachthaus
roter Löwe
goldener Rautenkranz
Weintass
schwarzer Bär
wilder Mann
weisser Bär
schwarzer Bär
goldener Engel
Wetterhahn
goldene Krone
goldener Bär
Horn
Kante
Mohr
weisser Spiegel
Hirschhorn
weisses Schild
grüne Traube
rote Traube
goldenes Fass
weisser Schwan und Riese
grüner Hut
schwarzer Ring
Rost und gelber Ring
weisser Ring
Krone
Storch
weisser Hirsch
grüner Wald
Kamel
Tanzhaus
Sperber
roter Widder
weisser Widder
roter Krebs
Elefant
Fremdenhospital auch Holzhaus und Metzlerhaus
goldener Pfau
Pfau
Die Stadtmauer
Der Wallgraben
Der lange Gang
Dietzischer Bleichgarten
goldene Luft
Eysen-Brauhaus
Judenmauer
Jüdischer Begräbnisplatz
Jüdisches Hospital
Hinter
Völkerische Bleichgarten
Juden Gasse